J. Simms
(408) 483-0425

Experiencing Music Technology

Experiencing Music Technology

Software, Data, and Hardware

SECOND EDITION

David Brian Williams
Illinois State University

Peter Richard Webster
Northwestern University

SCHIRMER

THOMSON LEARNING

Australia • Canada • Mexico • Singapore • Spain • United Kingdom • United States

Wadsworth Group/Thomson Learning
10 Davis Drive
Belmont CA 94002-3098
USA

For information about our products, contact us:
Thomson Learning Academic Resource Center
1-800-423-0563
http://www.wadsworth.com

For permission to use material from this text, contact us by
Web: http://www.thomsonrights.com
Fax: 1-800-730-2215
Phone: 1-800-730-2214

Printed in the United States of America
10 9 8 7 6 5 4 3

Library of Congress Cataloging-in-Publication Data

Williams, David Brian.
    Experiencing music technology : software, data, and hardware /
David Brian Williams and Peter Richard Webster. — 2nd ed.
        p.   cm.
    Includes bibliographical references (p.   ) and index.
    ISBN 0-02-865324-6 (pbk.)
        1. Music—Data processing.   I. Webster, Peter Richard, 1947- .
II. Title.
ML74.W55 1999
780.285—dc21   98-54076
                                                                                    CIP
                                                                                    MN

This paper meets the requirements of ANSI/NISO Z.39.49–19-1992 Permanence of Paper).

Trademark Acknowledgments

All terms mentioned in this book that are known to be trademarks or service marks have been appropriately capitalized. Schirmer Books and the authors cannot attest to the accuracy of this information. Use of a term in this book should not be regarded as affecting the validity of any trademark or service mark.

Windows, Windows 95, Windows 98, and MS-DOS are registered trademarks of Microsoft Corporation.
Apple, Macintosh, OS 8, the Apple and QuickTime logo, QuickTime, and HyperCard are registered trademarks of Apple Computer, Inc. All rights reserved.
IBM is a registered trademark of the IBM Corporation.
PostScript is a registered trademark of Adobe Systems, Inc.
Buz, Jaz, and Zip are registered trademarks of Iomega Corporation.
Fatar is a registered trademark of Music Industries Corporation.

To Kay and Connie

About the Authors

David Williams and Peter Webster have worked together on music technology projects for over a decade. Their popular sessions on all aspects of music technology, from HyperCard to multimedia to curriculum to web design and the Internet, have appeared on programs for MENC, CMS, ATMI, and NASM. Workshops they have hosted in their music computer labs at Illinois State and Northwestern have offered educators and musicians across the country training in the design and application of software for music instruction and multimedia. This textbook is the result of eight years of research, field testing, and writing.

David Williams is Associate Dean for Research and Technology in the College of Fine Arts, Director of the Office of Research in Arts Technology, and Professor of Music at Illinois State University. He holds a Ph.D. in Systematic Musicology from the University of Washington. Williams has been involved with educational technology and music technology for over 35 years and is best known for his work with computer-based music instruction and arts technology. In the late 1970s he co-founded Micro Music, Inc., which produced the first digital sound card, music software for the Apple II computer, and one of the most extensive libraries of CAI software for music education. In the 1980s he established the Office of Research in Arts Technology (ORAT) at Illinois State to help promote the use of computer-based technology in the arts and arts education. Currently, he is developing a graduate and undergraduate program in arts technology to train students to work in multimedia fields. He has served as consultant and clinician to many major school districts and universities nationally, and frequently gives presentations and lectures on technology and its application to the arts. He co-authored *Designing Computer-Based Instruction for Music and the Arts* with Dennis Bowers and has published in many professional journals including *Music Educators Journal, CRME Bulletin, Journal of Research in Music Education, Design for Arts Education,* and *Psychomusicology.* His software programs include Melodious Dictator, Interval and Chord Mania, Toney Music Games, HyperCard Etudes, and the ORAT Review Shell. His current interests include authoring multimedia software, distance learning, and Internet delivery of instruction, Web design and writing. He teaches a two-semester course at Illinois State: Software Design in the Arts I and II.

Peter Webster is the John Beattie Professor of Music Education and Director of the Center for Music Technology at Northwestern University's School of Music. He holds master's and doctoral degrees from the University of Rochester's Eastman School of Music in the field of music education. Since his work at Eastman, his research has centered on the study of creative thinking in music as part of the developmental patterns of children. He is the author of Measure of Creative Thinking in Music, an assessment tool designed for children aged 6–10. A new computer-based version is now being developed and tested. He has published in numerous professional publications (*Music Educators Journal, Journal of Research in Music Education, CRME Bulletin, Contributions to Music Education, Design for Arts in Education, Psychomusicology*). He has authored chapters in several books, including *Handbook of Research on Music Teaching and Learning, Music and Child Development*, and *Applications of Research in Music Behavior*. Webster taught public school in Maine, Massachusetts, and New York. He has more than 25 years of college teaching experience, including course responsibilities in music history, music theory, music listening, instrumental methods, conducting, brass pedagogy, philosophy of music education, psychology of music, research techniques, assessment, creative thinking in music, and computer technology. His current teaching responsibilities at Northwestern include three music technology courses (including a university-wide course in multimedia), developmental psychology of music, qualitative and quantitative research methods, and creative thinking in music. He is currently coordinating the Music Education Program at Northwestern and is finishing a new book for teachers dealing with music composition in the schools.

Contents

**Viewport IV:
Desktop
Publishing for
Musicians**

Preface

"Where shall I begin, please your Majesty?" he asked. "Begin at the beginning," the King said . . . "and go on till you come to the end: then stop."

—Lewis Carroll, *Alice in Wonderland* (1865)

For many composers, the [computer] has replaced pencil and paper; for other musicians, it has replaced the orchestra; for some, it is replacing the tape-recorders; and for educators, the [computer] is opening up new pedagogical strategies that have no corollary in traditional teaching methods.

—Christopher Yavelow, *MacWorld Music & Sound Bible* (1992)

*E*xperiencing *Music Technology, Second Edition,* covers the essential topics a musician should consider when exploring the use of computers and technology in the many aspects of the music experience: listening, performing, composing, teaching, and managing.

Should I Read This Book?

This book is designed as an introductory resource for a wide audience both inside and outside the academic setting. The primary impetus in its creation, however, was an objective proposed by the National Association of Schools of Music: "Through study and laboratory experience, students should be made familiar with the capabilities of technology as they relate to composition, performance, analysis, teaching, and research."

The book is modular in design, and its resources can be used in many ways. Although intended as the text for a complete undergraduate or graduate course of study devoted to music technology, it can also serve as a supplemental resource for other courses in the curriculum: general musicianship, piano pedagogy, theory and aural skills, arranging and orchestration, music composition and improvisation, instructional design, and other contemporary topics.

In addition, the book can be easily read and used for self-study by people who are simply curious about and intrigued by the use of computers for music making. Professional musicians, parents, children, computer aficionados, and lay musicians of all kinds may find the book helpful in increasing their understanding of music technology.

Objectives

Experiencing Music Technology is designed to meet the following objectives:

▶ Provide a conceptual overview of music and technology, by combining tutorial material with essential reference material

▶ Give a broad perspective to the many ways people can use technology in music applications

▶ Offer modular organization of the material to provide flexibility for the reader and the instructor

▶ Chronicle the historic milestones in music computing and technology

▶ Promote a systems approach to computer understanding, planning, and implementation by stressing five components: people, procedures, data, software, and hardware

▶ Emphasize hardware and software unique to music applications

▶ Focus on the conceptual and generic issues and concepts that underlie current commercial hardware and software

▶ Minimize references to commercial or industry-specific applications that are quickly outdated

Contents

Experiencing Music Technology, Second Edition, provides a comprehensive systems approach to using and understanding computers and music. Rather than placing the main focus on current commercial hardware and software concerns, we consider broader themes of people, procedures, data structures, software applications, hardware, software development, and environment. You will find these themes appearing throughout the textbook.

Among these themes, *people* and *procedures* take precedence. We have coined a term to describe our people-procedures perspective of computing: the term is *viewport*. Much as Alice in Wonderland used her looking glass for creative views of the world behind her mirror, we provide technology ports for viewing the ways in which musicians can apply computers and technology to their daily music experiences. The eight viewports are perspectives on using computers and technology in music, each providing an in-depth study of these various themes as follows:

People and Procedures

The text illustrates the many ways musicians can use technology in music applications and provides a historical perspective on computers in music. Viewport I is devoted to these people issues, and the introduction to every viewport in the text provides historical timelines and interviews with a variety of music personalities who demonstrate technology in action.

Software and Hardware

The text stresses an understanding of the technical aspects of computers and technology as they are applied to music activities. In each viewport separate modules are devoted to specific music software applications and to the hardware required for fully using these applications:

Music Computer-Assisted Instruction (Viewport III)

Desktop Publishing for Musicians (Viewport IV)

Music Notation (Viewport V)

Music Sequencing and MIDI (Viewport VI)

Creating Sounds and Music with Digital Audio (Viewport VII)

Data Structures

The text provides an overview of the substance of music technology by demystifying music information as it is represented in and transformed by computer. The fundamental data structures for computer operating systems and networking are first introduced in Viewport II. Subsequent viewports address details of music and computer data structures as they apply to such topics as notation, computer graphics, digital and MIDI sound, and computer languages.

Software Development

The text suggests ways to develop custom software using authoring systems and Internet resources, hypermedia languages, and multimedia equipment. Viewport VIII features extensive coverage of slide-based, card-based, time-based, and Web-based authoring environments for developing multimedia experiences for music.

Environments

The text focuses on guidelines for helping people implement computer applications in home, studio, and school settings. Each viewport ends with a summary that brings together the concepts addressed in that viewport and makes practical recommendations.

Timelines for Your "Think-Time"

In each viewport, you will encounter *timelines* that chronicle some of the most important people and historical achievements in music technology. They provide a marvelous overview of why music technology is as it is today. Recommendations for supplemental readings, for those wanting to investigate further topics of interest or just looking for fascinating reading, end each viewport.

Modular Design

Experiencing Music Technology, Second Edition, is designed with a flexible modular format. The term *modules* is used to represent chapters or sections for this reason. Students or instructors can fine-tune their use of the book's resources to fit their particular objectives for a course of study. Some may prefer to emphasize such music experiences as computer-assisted instruction, desktop publishing, and multimedia development. Others may wish to concentrate on digital audio, sequencing, and notation. A hands-on approach may emphasize the software application modules, using the data and hardware modules as reference tools. A course of study with a strong emphasis on sound techniques could use all the modules—software, data, and hardware—that deal with MIDI, digital audio, music coding and notation, and laser audio and video. We do recommend that everyone study Viewports I and II; they provide an introduction to the text and to computer operating systems and the Internet.

Do not feel compelled to use *all* the materials in the book; treat them as resources to use in designing your own course of study. Each viewport contains a convenient overview and list of objectives at the beginning, and a summary section at the end. Use these as an easy way to determine the content and focus of each viewport.

So What's New in the Second Edition?

We have been gratified by the many positive reactions to our first edition. Following the results of a survey of users and our own continued study of the field, we decided on the following changes:

▶ A greater emphasis on the Internet and Web-based material. We feel that Internet software is now closely associated with the design of computer operating systems. Viewport II now contains an additional emphasis on using the computer in both stand-alone and networking environments including the Internet. Material from the old Viewport VIII on communications is now part of the new Viewport II.

▶ Viewport III on computer-assisted instruction has expanded categories to include a broader range and definition of this important part of music technology.

▶ Viewport IV has been reworked to focus on desktop publishing and graphics.

▶ Viewport V includes a new opening section that stresses the merger of music notation, sequencing, and digital audio.

▶ Viewport VI on sequencing has been recast with more emphasis on the integration of digital audio tracks to MIDI. More attention has been given to the use of interactive MIDI in performance, both in the software and hardware modules.

▶ Viewport VII has received a major facelift, with more emphasis on digital audio editing, multitrack digital audio, and hard disk recording. A total digital solution is offered in the hardware module for a digital audio editing workstation.

▶ We have completely rewritten the multimedia and authoring section (now Viewport VIII) to include four sample projects, including one on Web authoring. The data structures module includes new material on Java, JavaScript, and HTML. The laser disc module has been moved to this viewport with new information on DVD technology, as well as writeable and rewriteable laser technologies.

▶ The data and hardware modules have all been updated with the newest information on file formats and hardware developments. The laser disc sections have been expanded to include information on DVD and other new hardware developments.

▶ Information related to the Internet, universal file formats used over the Internet, and technologies for presenting music and graphics over the Internet have been incorporated throughout the book.

▶ The book has many new screen shots and pictures. The historical timelines have all been expanded and updated, as have the references at the end of each viewport.

▶ The book has more examples of Windows programs, while continuing to offer ample examples drawn from the Macintosh environment.

▶ Finally, we welcome three new featured musicians, joining our first group of artists and scholars: Henry Panion, Dale Olsen, and Tim Smith. Each is doing extraordinary work with music technology in teaching, composition, and performance. Fictional characters have been removed.

How Long Will This Book Play?

*E*xperiencing *Music Technology, Second Edition,* is designed to emphasize broad, overarching concepts in computer and music technology, concepts that should endure in the face of rapid change and evolution.

This book *is not* designed as a how-to book for learning specific music software or a construction kit for building your own music workstation. Materials of this nature are quickly dated; other books are more appropriate for such hands-on tutorials. Many of these are noted at the conclusion of each viewport.

This book *is* designed to help you grasp the more general skills and knowledge you will need in order to evaluate, adapt, and implement new technologies as they emerge. The software modules, for example, explore the common features that are found across a variety of applications for operating systems and communications, computer-assisted instruction, desktop publishing, notation, sequencing, digital audio, and authoring. Current commercial software serves only as illustrations. The graphical user interface (GUI) is also stressed throughout the book. Though the look and feel of the GUI operating system may evolve, the basic concepts of how it operates will not. The same applies to the study of such topics as MIDI, MIDI instruments and interfaces, digital sound production, and bitmapped and object-oriented graphics.

Definitions

In addition to the term *viewport*, there are a few other terms that are critical in this book. We need to be sure that we share a common understanding of what terms like *computer, technology, music experience,* and *musician* mean for us.

Computer

The term *computer,* as used in this book, refers to small computer systems, personal computers (PCs), or microcomputers. When we use the acronym *PC,* we are referring to all personal computers generically, not just IBM PCs and their compatibles. We have chosen not to recommend specific brands of commercial hardware or software. However, hardware and software that were predominately in use at the time of this writing are used throughout the book to illustrate major points.

In creating our illustrations, we have chosen to focus on the two primary icon-based computing environments used today by musicians: Macintosh and IBM PCs and their compatibles using the Windows operating system. Throughout the book we refer to these as either "Macintosh" or "Wintel" machines, and "Macintosh" or "Windows" operating systems, regardless of whether the versions are OS 8, Windows 95 or 98, or any future versions of these. By *icon-based,* we mean operating systems that use graphic images or *icons* for common operations with the computer. Similar operating systems can be found on other computers like the SGI and Sun workstations.

Technology

The term *technology* refers to computers and all of the music and nonmusic peripherals that are needed to perform music tasks with computers. These peripheral devices include such hardware as electronic music keyboards, MIDI controllers, printers, scanners, CD players, and so on.

Music Experience

Music experience refers to the fundamental ways we interact with music cognitively, emotionally, and aesthetically as humans. Included in this are the processes of listening, performing, and composing music that are the hallmarks of music as art. Throughout this book, we are interested in ways that technology can enhance these fundamental aspects of experiencing music. In addition, we are concerned with how technology can aid the teaching and studying of music and the management of music activities. Although not primary music experiences, these activities are vital to music as practiced in our society.

Musician

The term *musician* refers to anyone, at any level of sophistication, engaged in music experiences. This definition of musician includes the parent, child, student, teacher, administrator, performer, and composer. We realize that the usual use of this term refers to individuals with advanced skills in music. However, in the interest of promoting a view of music computing that is accessible to the widest possible audience, we have chosen this more relaxed definition.

Book Format

Most viewport sections in the textbook use the following organizational scheme:

Introduction
► Philosophical Quotations
► Overview and Learning Objectives
► Historical Timeline
► The People: presentations of musicians who are successfully using music technology

Main Content
► Introduction
► Modules on Software, Data, and Hardware

Viewport Summary
► Summary
► Supplementary Readings

Experiencing Music Technology **Companion CD-ROM**

Acompanion CD-ROM disc is included with this text and is designed to run on both Macintosh and Windows computers. While the textbook illustrates concepts of music technology with a broad range of software examples, the CD-ROM provides hands-on activities focused on specific commercial software to parallel the major topics in the book. All of the materials on the CD-ROM have been designed as Web pages that can be easily viewed through a Web browser like Netscape Navigator or Microsoft Internet Explorer.

Each CD-ROM software activity is a tutorial that features step-by-step directions in using a specific software application. A generous number of screen shots are provided to illustrate the steps in the tutorials. Links are included to related materials, including worksheets that students can use to track their progress and for teacher evaluation of work completed. These worksheets can be viewed and printed right from the Web browser or from any standard word processor.

The CD-ROM includes much additional information, including Internet links to major software vendors for music technology and to a support site for the textbook and the CD-ROM. Watch for the CD-ROM icon in the left margin of the textbook. This is a visual cue to remind you that a hands-on software activity is available on the CD-ROM to accompany the current discussion in the textbook.

Below is a listing of the software used on the CD-ROM and organized by the textbook's viewports. Web links on the CD-ROM will lead you to demonstration copies of software for many of the activities if a full working version is not available for your use.

Viewport II

VirusScan for Windows

Virex for Mac

Acrobat Reader for Mac or Windows

Eudora Lite for Mac or Windows

Netscape Navigator for Mac and Windows

NewsXpress for Windows

NewsWatcher for Mac

Viewport III

Practica Musica for Mac

MiBAC Music Lessons for Mac and Windows

Band-in-a-Box for Mac or Windows

Viewport IV

AppleWorks for Mac and Windows

Viewport V

Encore for Mac and Windows

Finale for Mac and Windows

Viewport VI

OMS (Opcode Music System) for Mac

MusicShop for Mac and Windows

MasterTracks Pro for Mac and Windows

Cakewalk Home Studio for Windows

VisionDSP for Mac

Viewport VII	Viewport VIII
Peak LE for Mac	QuickTime for Mac and Windows
SoundEdit 16 for Mac	Photoshop for Mac and Windows
SoundForge XP for Windows	PowerPoint for Mac and Windows
	HyperStudio for Mac and Windows
	Netscape Composer for Mac and Windows

Acknowledgments

▶ Our students at Northwestern and Illinois State University who have used our first edition and have offered so many excellent suggestions.

▶ Illinois State University staff and faculty who provided ongoing help for Dave: Georgia Bennett, Joe Bernert, Connie Brown, Bill Cummins, Jody DeCremer, Teri Derango, Jeff Imig, Dave Kuntz, Rhondal McKinney, Jonathan Monhardt, Roar Schaad, Charles Stokes, Stephen Taylor, and others.

▶ The Northwestern University School of Music staff and faculty who provided ongoing help for Peter: Gary Kendall, Richard Ashley, Stephen Syverud, Amnon Wolman, and Maud Hickey.

▶ Our graduate students for their valuable assistance with research, proofreading, and CD-ROM materials: Marian Dura, Ken Fansler, Milner Siefert, Robin Heller, Katy Strand, Emily Luxton, and Ken Heulhorst.

▶ Our Deans, Alvin Goldfarb, Ronald Mottram, and Bernard Dobroski, for providing time for us to work on the book away from teaching and administrative duties.

▶ The ten distinguished musicians who agreed to be interviewed: Edward Asmus, Pierre Boulez, David Cope, Christine Hermanson, Fred Hofstetter, Libby Larsen, Max Mathews, Dale Olsen, Henry Panion, and Tim Smith.

▶ The many experts who read and offered comments on the book content, including Ken Pohlmann for his excellent edits on the digital audio and CD sections; Charlie Stokes for his helpful suggestions on MIDI; Donald Byrd for his comments on the notation section; John Norstad for his networking, communications, and virus protection expertise; Gary Wittlich; and Scott Wilkinson.

▶ Our many colleagues who responded to the survey, and the seven experts who did technical critiques of the viewports for the second edition: John Norstad, Sam Reese, Peter Bushell, Steve Taylor, Doug Smith, Ken Pohlmann, and Frank Clark.

▶ The Internet for keeping us connected and those many Cybernauts who generously offered help and information through news groups, listservs, and e-mail: Jon Appleton, James Beauchamp, Kenneth Beesley, Don Byrd, Joel Chadabe and the Electronic Music Foundation, Paul Copeland, Kirk Corey, Steve Day, Stephen Fisse, Robby Gunstream, Lippold Haken, Jose Tomas Henriques, Fred Hofstetter, Ken Johnson, Josef Jurek, Billee Kraut, Jim Lee, Mark Lochstampfor, Will McCauley, Sam Reese, Carter Schuld, Dan Slater, Jack Taylor, Ryan Thomas, Nick Trio, the Whitmores, James Williams, Christopher Yavelow, Dee Young, and Rod at cumulus.csd.unsw.oz.au.

▶ The World Wide Web (and Tim Berners-Lee for inventing it).

▶ Those librarians who, true to their cause, offered essential assistance, including Debbie Stannard at the Northport Library (Michigan), Paul Gehl and Mary Wyly at the Newberry Library (Chicago), Lisa Williams (Moline Public Library), Chad Buckley (Illinois State University Library), D. W. Krummel (University of Illinois), and Don Roberts (Northwestern University Music Library).

▶ For their kind willingness to help us with the monumental task of finding photos and permissions: Charles Ames and Joan Truckenbrod for their computer-generated art; Bruce Bruemmer at the Charles Babbage Institute; Don Buchla; Chris deHaas, Jon Sievert, and Gina Boger-Haney, all Roy "Future Man" Wooten fans; Corrine Effinger; Paul Gehl, Mary Wyly, and Jack Scott at the Newberry Library in Chicago; Marlene Mallicoat, our connection to Ted Nelson; Bob Moog and Big Briar, Inc.; Reynold Weidenaar; Tom Hershenson at General Magic; James Moorer at Sonic Solutions; Phyllis Smith at the David Sarnoff Research Center, a fan of the work of Harry Olson and Herbert Belar; Nancy Strader at Digital Equipment Corporation; Jim Wallace, Elizabeth McCullough, and Lisette at the Smithsonian Institution; Jerry Welch at the Organ Service Company; Brian Williams for his cartoon sketches; and Michael Yeates at the MIT Museum.

▶ All the software vendors and their representatives who kindly loaned and donated software to be used.

▶ All the hardware vendors that provided photographs and information about their products.

▶ The person who got us started on this project: Maribeth Anderson Payne.

▶ The Schirmer Books staff for the finished product that you see before you: Richard Carlin, Ira Brodsky, and their many colleagues.

▶ Those things that kept us sane through the three-year adventure of putting this book together and the months and months of work for the second revision: The *Joy of Cooking* for fruit pie recipes, Trek for making great bikes, Interstate 55 between Winnetka and Normal, Northern Michigan and the Leelanau Peninsula for being what it is, the Beaudrys and the Vanderschies of Cherry Homes, and the Waldenesque solitude of the mountains of southwest Pennsylvania thanks to the Chizmar family.

▶ And, to all of you, and to those we may have overlooked: Thank You!

Introduction

If you go through life convinced that your way is always best, all the new ideas in the world will pass you by.

—Akio Morita, cofounder of Sony Corporation, *Made in Japan* (1986)

Computers and technology have quietly crept into the daily affairs of music making. Typewriters have given way to word processors. Musicians can achieve publication quality calligraphy through computer desktop notation. Music teachers have the aid of increasingly sophisticated surrogates through computer-based music instruction. Diverse electronic keyboards, drum machines, wind controllers, guitars, and the like easily communicate through the Music Instrument Digital Interface (MIDI). Desktop composing offers the palettes of musical elements and form to anyone from child to professional through computer sequencers and improvisers.

The sonic basis of music—even beyond the range of the human ear—can be captured in minute time slices by the computer and preserved as optically reflective particles on discs with a life span of many years. And words and acronyms like digital, DAT, DSP, MIDI, memory, and gigabytes are joining the musicians' common lexicon, along with sampling and oversampling audio, SMPTE, sequencing and quantizing, and the laser optical family of terms including CD-ROM, compact disc, and DVD.

Technology as a Music Tool

It's difficult to imagine any aspect of music today that is not touched by technology. As listeners, we hear recorded music that has been produced by advanced digital techniques. As performers, we use instruments and perform in spaces that have benefited from countless technological advances in materials and design. As composers and arrangers, we no longer rely on pencil and paper alone to help represent our music visually; powerful computers, printers, and electronic sound devices provide additional resources for our creative thinking. As educators and scholars engaged in thinking, writing, and talking about music, we use many advanced tools to support our analyses and illustrations. Certainly, the way we experience music today is far different from the way our parents did when they were young. This book helps to explain why this is so.

Some argue that technology of this sort fundamentally changes the nature of music, often for the worse. We disagree! While it is true that technological developments often change the *way* in which we experience music, it remains debatable whether such developments really change the *essence of music itself*. To us, technology remains secondary to music as art. Technology is only a *tool*, like valve oil, bow rosin, or music stands. It is a very powerful tool, to be sure, but not the main point of the music experience.

For example, the kind of digital production that allows Beethoven string quartets to be recorded on a compact disc doesn't change the music; it enhances the recorded sound and makes it more convenient to experience. The wind controller that a performer uses to play a work by a new composer is not what we should care about; we should care about the music itself. That the wind controller is sending messages to five different MIDI devices during the course of the performance is trivial. If the music is good and performed musically, we are impressed. If it is bad music or played inaccurately or insensitively, no amount of technology can make it better. Likewise, if a teacher uses the slickest of multimedia devices to illustrate a class presentation but the information is unfocused, boring, and nonmusical, the technology will not save the lesson. Technology is a powerful tool but only if it is used musically. Think of technological advancements not as competitors or as threats to music as art, but rather as aids to its evolution.

Historical Perspective

Just a little history will give you a sense of the evolution of music technology and help to set the stage for what's to come. Experimentation with technology applied to music is hardly a phenomenon of this century alone. The history of technology in music is a wonderfully rich and fascinating account as old as music itself. It covers not only music, but also the history of computing and calculating machines for processing and transforming information.

Development in music technology didn't occur without the help of physicists, engineers, inventors, and mathematicians interested in music. As these people have collaborated, an avenue of technological development has been built. Often, these inventive minds kept coming back to the same problems, each time with a new level of sophistication. You will see that the pursuit of both better music and better number machines aided in the improvement of both technologies. Throughout the book you will find references to both music and computer technology from five historical periods.

Swiss music box with music coded as pins on
a cylinder
(Courtesy of the Smithsonian Institution)

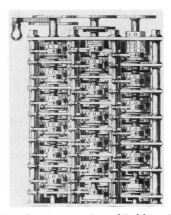

Woodcut impression of Babbage's
Difference Engine No. 1
(Courtesy of the Charles Babbage
Institute, University of Minnesota,
Minneapolis)

Phase 1 (1600s–Mid-1800s). In this period, number and music machines depended upon imaginative applications of mechanical gears, cogs, cams, and levels. Here we see music machines such as music boxes, calliopes, mechanical organs, player pianos, and mechanical phonograph recorders and jukeboxes—machines that you have to wind up and crank! Number machines include the Calculating Clock, the Pascaline, and the Babbage Difference Engine.

Hammond Model A organ with
sound produced with motorized
spinning disks
(Courtesy of the Organ Service
Company, La Grange, Illinois)

One of the dynamos from
Cahill's Telharmonium
(From "New Music for an Old
World" by R. Baker, *McClure's
Magazine*, 1906)

Phase 2 (Mid-1800s–Early 1900s). In this period, number and music machines took advantage of the invention of electricity and electric motors to automate the mechanical solutions of Phase 1, thanks to Thomas Edison and others. Here we see music machines such as the Singing Arc, the Telharmonium, and the Hammond Organ. For number machines, we have the Arithmometer, the early calculators of Moore and Burroughs, and the early analog computers of Bush and Zuse.

Phase 3 (Early 1900s–Mid-1900s). In this period, number and music machines benefited from the unique technology that vacuum tubes and electromagnetic relay switches provided. Lee de Forest's invention of oscillators and amplifiers from vacuum tubes had a revolutionary impact on music and computer technology.

Migration from tubes to transistors to integrated circuits
(Photos by Rhondal McKinney)

The vacuum-tube oscillator was an incredible boon to music machines. Not only did it lead to the design of amplifiers, phonographs, tape recorders, jukeboxes, and even early electric guitars, but it provided the earliest attempts at electronic performing instruments. Products of this generation include the Theremin, Trautonium, Ondes Martenot, and the early synthesizers of Givelet and Coupleux. Even today, some musicians prefer the soft and smooth sound of tube technology. For number machines, vacuum tubes led to the construction of "tube-monster" computers like the ENIAC, EDVAC, UNIVAC, and ABC, and for music, the Columbia-Princeton Mark I Music Synthesizer. Many covered city blocks in size.

Harry Olson with the 1955 Columbia-Princeton Mark I Music Synthesizer
(Courtesy of the David Sarnoff Research Center)

Modern-day rendition of the original vacuum tube Theremin
(Big Briar 91A, photo courtesy of Robert Moog)

ENIAC computer, a city block of vacuum tubes
(Courtesy of the Charles Babbage Institute, University of Minnesota, Minneapolis)

Phase 4 (Mid-1900s–1970s). In the fourth phase, number and music machines were completely transformed by the transistor and semiconductors. With the invention of the transistor—thanks to the engineers at Bell Labs—came modularity, smallness, and electronic flexibility. Robert Moog's design of voltage-controlled circuits and Donald Buchla's electronic sequencers led to the first portable commercial music synthesizers. Almost any school or musician could purchase an ARP or a Putney and begin exploring electronic music and the world of sound and acoustics. The same trend transformed number machines. Not only did the "big iron" get bigger (computers like the IBM 360 series and the CDC 6000s and Cybers), but computers became portable, commercial, and common. The DEC PDP-8 ushered in the era of minicomputers.

ARP 2600 transistor-based synthesizer
(Photo courtesy of Rhondal McKinney)

Popular transistor-based portable Buchla music synthesizer
(Reproduced by permission of Don Buchla)

DEC transistor-based PDP-8 mini-computer
(Courtesy of Corporate Photo Library, Digital Equipment Corporation)

Phase 5 (1970s–Present). In the current phase of technology, number and music machines became exponentially smaller and more powerful, thanks to the inventions of Jack Kilby and Robert Noyce that led to the mass production of integrated circuits (ICs). The transistor was soon followed by the first Intel microprocessor chip. With ICs and chips, music and number

Roland Super Sound Canvas using integrated circuits
(Courtesy of Roland Corporation)

The first Macintosh Powerbook 100
(Courtesy of Apple Computer, Inc.)

machines became ever smaller and cheaper. Music and number machines joined forces and out came music synthesizers with computing power rivaling that of the minicomputers of the last decade. MIDI and FM, digital, and physical modeling synthesis all emerged in small portable boxes: keyboards, controllers, drum machines, sound modules, and more. For the number machines, the personal computer or PC put more CPU power and memory into every home and on every desktop than the designers of the city-block-wide ENIAC ever dreamed of. The Apple, IBM PC, Macintosh, and many other microcomputers were born.

Systems Perspective

"What kind of computer should I use or buy?" is usually the *first* question musicians ask when they become interested in computers. As you will see, the type of computer hardware should be the *last* question to ask. Let's expand upon this important point.

It is important to think of a computer not simply as a piece of hardware ready to plug in, like a television, but as a complete, integrated system. Consider that there are five essential ingredients to any computer system:

▶ People

▶ Procedures

▶ Data

▶ Software

▶ Hardware

Before deciding what computer to use, for each of the five ingredients you would ask the following questions:

▶ Who will use the computer?

▶ What tasks will you want to perform?

▶ What kind of information or data will you use?

▶ What do you want the computer to do with these data?

▶ What computer machine will you use?

You can see that there are several things to think about before selecting the computer hardware.

First, consider *people* and the computer system. This refers to *who* is going to use the computer individually, in groups, or in combination: music students, children, teachers, performers, composers, conductors, or administrators. The *people* or musicians who use computers are the most important ingredient in building a computer system and, for that reason, a very important focus in this book.

Second, you should consider the *procedure* ingredient of the computer system. Now you need to think about *how* musicians are going to use the computer. Consider the array of tasks they would like the computer to do for them: teaching, performing, composing and arranging; marching-band charting; designing newsletters, programs, and sheet music; maintaining records, inventories, and mailing lists; writing, budgeting, and scheduling.

Third, consider the *data* ingredient. What kind of information is going to be processed or transformed by your computer? That's what a computer is after all: an electronic blender that transforms information. For musicians the data can be numbers, text, music notation, graphics images, music sounds, and music performance information from a keyboard, instrument controller, or drum machine.

Fourth, consider the *software*. The software ingredient comprises the instructions that give the computer machine its ability to perform a task. You need to investigate what computer programs are available to perform the procedure you need on the type of data you want to work with.

Finally, we arrive at the last ingredient of a computer system, the *hardware*. Given the decisions you have made about the people, procedures, data, and software ingredients, only now are you ready to select the best hardware for the task at hand.

If all this sounds overwhelming, we understand. We designed this book to guide musicians through the process of becoming informed, discriminating computer users. We will visit *people, data, software,* and *hardware* many times, and *procedures* will be our main organizing theme.

Lifeguard Icons in This Book

Your first line of lifeguard help should be this book. To help you as you progress through each chapter, we have created several icons that will alert you to different levels of help. Watch for these icons:

▶ LINKS to helpful information related to this topic elsewhere in the book

▶ TIPS that are especially helpful to those just starting to use computers and music technology

▶ ASIDES that are interesting notes for reading enjoyment and mind expansion

▶ DEEP WATER cautionary warning: information that is appropriate for the "high divers"—this material may be a little more detailed but it's well worth the time!

 ▶ CD-ROM tutorial materials: training on the CD-ROM that accompanies this textbook and provides hands-on experiences with software noted in the textbook.

Viewport I
People and Procedures

Computing is not about computers anymore. It is about living.
> —Nicholas Negroponte, *Being Digital* (1995)

Technology is easy; people are hard.
> —John Gage of Sun Microsystems, *CAUSE Computer Conference,*
> Orlando (1997)

Whether or not you like a piece of music is a reflection on the musician who made the music, not the instruments or tools used to produce the music.
> —Bob Moog, *MENC Conference*, Phoenix (1998)

Overview

Our first viewport focuses on the most important components of a computer music system: the *people* or musicians who use computers and music technology, and the *procedures* they choose to employ. We are also interested in correcting certain commonly held misconceptions about music technology in hopes of improving general attitudes that surround this subject. We shall:

▶ Emphasize people as the primary decision makers in using computer music systems

▶ Present profiles of the guest musicians whose work will be featured in upcoming viewports

▶ Reflect on misconceptions and attitudes surrounding music technology

▶ Define categories of computer procedures in music technology, organized by difficulty level and related to real music tasks in the coming viewports

▶ Describe sources of help for using computers and music technology

HISTORICAL TIMELINE
The People in Music Technology and Computing

1646–1716	Leibniz, Wilhelm	Studied binary system of numbers and proposed the binary calculator
1653–1716	Sauveau, Joseph	Discovered overtone series
1768–1830	Fourier, Jean	Developed Fourier synthesis, the basis for systems of music synthesis
1791–1871	Babbage, Charles	Designed the earliest calculating machines that would automate computing of navigation tables and solve mathematical problems
1815–1864	Boole, George	Founder of Boolean algebra or logic; pivotal concept in internal logic operations of computers
1821–1894	von Helmholtz, Hermann	Pioneering work on physics and acoustics of sound, *On the Sensations of Tone*
1847–1931	Edison, Thomas	Founder of phonograph and many other inventions that figured critically in development of music technology
1860–1929	Hollerith, Herman	Filed first set of patents for electromechanical system that counted and punched cards; his Tabulating Machine Company became IBM in 1924
1867–1934	Cahill, Thaddeus	Inventor of Telharmonium; explored synthesis of complex tones
1873–1961	de Forest, Lee	Credited with designing first electrical oscillator and first valve amplifier with vacuum tubes
1882–1961	Grainger, Percy	With Burnett Cross, built early music synthesizer with eight oscillators that could be synchronized
1883–1965	Varèse, Edgard	Wide use of various electronic composition techniques; *Equatorial* used Theremins, *Déserts* used tape techniques
1889–1963	Givelet, Armand	With Coupleux, developed one of first analog synthesizers, with four oscillators controlled by punched paper rolls
1895–1973	Hammond, Laurens	Designed and produced Hammond Organ in 1928
1896–1980	Dudley, Homer	Invented Vocoder, a device that digitally synthesized speech, at Bell Labs
1896–1993	Theremin, Leon	Inventor of early popular electronic performing instrument called the Theremin
1900–1996	Luening, Otto	Produced some of the first taped compositions in U.S.; cofounded Columbia-Princeton Electronic Music Center with Ussachevsky
1901–1982	Olson, Harry	With Herbert Belar, constructed RCA Mark I and II music synthesizers used at Columbia-Princeton
1903–1995	Atanasoff, John V.	With Clifford Berry, invented first computer, the ABC
1903–1957	von Neumann, John	Designed the first electronic computer, the EDVAC, with a stored computer program
1907–1980	Mauchly, John W.	With Brainerd and Eckert, built one of first general-purpose electronic digital computers, the ENIAC (used 17,468 vacuum tubes!)
1910–1989	Shockley, William	One of the inventors of the transistor at Bell Labs; his California company started Silicon Valley
1911–1990	Ussachevsky, Vladimir	Produced some of the first taped composition in U.S.; collaborated with Luening

1914–	Kuhn, Wolfgang	With Reynold Allvin, developed early computer-based instruction with mainframe computer connected to electronic organ
1916–	Babbitt, Milton	Composed *Ensembles for Synthesizer and Philomel* on RCA Mark II Synthesizer; worked with Luening and Ussachevsky
1916–	Shannon, Claude E.	Applied symbolic logic to relay circuits; information can be quantified and manipulated by machine
1918–	Forrester, Jay W.	Developed magnetic-core memory as alternative to vacuum-tube technology; used in MIT Whirlwind computer system
1923–	Kilby, Jack	Invented first working integrated circuit
1923–	Eichelberger Ivey, Jean	Her methods for teaching had great impact on electronic music curriculum; composer and founder of the Peabody Conservatory Electronic Music Studios in 1967
1924–1994	Hiller, Lejaren	With Isaacson at University of Illinois, created first computer-composed composition, *Illiac Suite* (1957)
1925–	Boulez, Pierre	Promenant contemporary electronic composer and founder of Institut de Recherche et Coordination Acousticque/Musique (IRCAM)
1925–	Smith, Leland	Wrote SCORE notation program; among first powerful notation programs for minicomputer, later translated to the IBM PC
1926–	Mathews, Max	Considered the father of digital sound synthesis; created first software at Bell Labs to control the parameters of music through a computer
1927–	Carlsen, James C.	Created one of the first commercially successful programmed instruction tape series for melodic dictation published by McGraw-Hill
1927–1990	Noyce, Robert	Led the team at Fairchild Semiconductor that invented the planar integrated circuit, paving the way for mass manufacturing of reliable computer chips
1928–	Stockhausen, Karlheinz	First to explore additive synthesis and to carefully score his electronic works; composed *Studies I and II* in 1953
1931–	Deihl, Ned C.	Developed one of earliest music CAI programs with IBM 1500 and prerecorded tapes
1932–	Oliveros, Pauline	First woman to be known primarily for her electronic music work and helped to found the San Francisco Tape Center in 1961
1934–	Bitzer, Don	Inventor of Control Data PLATO computer-assisted instruction system at University of Illinois
1934–	Chowning, John	Inventor of FM synthesis; established Center for Computer Research in Music and Acoustics (CCRMA)
1934–	Moog, Robert	Name synonymous with synthesizers due to popularity of his instruments; built first synthesizer using voltage-controlled oscillators, amplifiers, and semiconductors
1937–	Beauchamp, James	Developed early techniques for using tone generators in music composition; edited *Music by Computers* with von Forester
1937–	Buchla, Donald F.	Designed popular voltage-controlled modular synthesizer installations of the 1970s; collaborated with composer Morton Subotnick
1937–	Hoff, Marcian E., Jr.	Invented first microprocessor chip, Intel 4004/8008
1937–	Nelson, Theodor (Ted)	Coined the terms *hypertext* and *hypermedia* and implemented the concepts through his Xanadu software

1938–	Risset, Jean-Claude	Bell Labs; worked with Mathews; pioneering work with analysis of complex tones and waveshapping synthesis
1939–	Appleton, John	Composer and collaborator in the development of Synclavier synthesizer and ABEL computer
1942–	Peters, G. David	Developed early CAI applications for PLATO system and founded Electronic Courseware Systems
1943–	Williams, David B.	With David Shrader, founded Micro Music, Inc., and developed some of the first commercial CAI music programs for personal computers
1945–	Moorer, James	Produced some of the first 3-D analyses of music waveforms at Stanford
1945–	Winter, Robert	Authored first commercial music HyperCard stack to use interactive audio CD
1946–	Speigel, Laurie	Composer and codeveloper of GROOVE music system at Bell Labs, designer of music software and hardware devices, like Music Mouse
1947–	Anderson, Laurie	A multitalented, eccentric, and controversial performance artist whose live performances and recordings span a variety of media including film, acoustic music, unusual electronic instruments and effects, slides, costumes, and dance; her book *Stories from the Nerve Bible* (1994) provides a 20-year perspective of her work
1948–	Turkle, Sherry	MIT professor and author of *Life on the Screen: Identity in the Age of the Internet* (1995) and *The Second Self: Computers and the Human Spirit* (1985), she has made a unique contribution in her study of the psychological and cultural impact of technology, computers, and the Internet
1948–	Kurzweil, Ray	With Robert Moog, created Kurzweil Music System that produced authentic grand piano sound for portable music keyboard
1948–	Rundgren, Todd	Versatile recording artist, songwriter, software developer, and interactive multimedia artist who produced the first digital painting program for PCs, first music video with live action and computer graphics, the "Individualist" multimedia CD album, and an Internet service, PatroNet, to underwrite music recordings with Web audio delivery.
1949–	Hofstetter, Fred	Author of GUIDO music curriculum developed initially for Plato system, and producer of the Delaware Videodisc Music Series
1950–	Wozniak, Steve ("Woz")	With Steve Jobs, built 6502-based microcomputer with BASIC in 1975, Apple I, and founded Apple Computer, Inc. in 1975
1951–	Atkinson, Bill	Created MacPaint and HyperCard (1987)
1953–	Machover, Tod	Composer of numerous contemporary works and designer of new technology for music; his *Brain Opera* invites the audience to use his "hyperinstruments" to participate in the music live or over the Internet
1955–	Gates, William (Bill)	With Paul Allen, wrote BASIC interpreter for Altair 8800 microcomputer and founded Microsoft Corporation
1955–	Berners-Lee, Tim	Created the concept of the Web, the first Web client and server, and he defined URL, HTTP, and HTML in 1990 at CERN, the European Particle Physics Laboratory

1958–	Gannon, Peter	A Canadian physician and amateur musician who created the first computer-aided accompaniment software, Band-in-a-Box, and founded PG Music Inc. in 1988
1962–	May, Joel	Founded Harmonic Vision, Inc., and created MusicAce I and II, popular CAI software that uses guided instruction, game, and creative techniques to teach the basics of music to young children
1963–	Glaser, Rob	Founded RealNetworks, the company that pioneered the RealAudio digital compression scheme enabling high-quality, streaming audio delivery over the Internet
1971–	Andreesen, Marc	Designed the first graphical browser for the World Wide Web, NCSA Mosaic, and cofounded Netscape Communications with James Clark, founder of Silicon Graphics

The Importance of People

The Unexpected Turn

Watch for the the CD-ROM icon throughout the book for hands-on software experiences on the CD-ROM enclosed with this textbook!

Software activities: "Interviewing Professionals Who Use Technology" and "Building a Database of Classmates' Computer Experiences."

Before we go further in our study of computers and music technology, it's important that something be clearly understood: a person using technology is *the* most important component of a computer music system. Whatever great achievements flow from the process of using technology in music making, it is not the machines that should earn the credit.

Rather, it's the human mind and creative spirit that are responsible. Likewise, artistic failures are not attributable to the medium alone. Despite our society's constant attempt to blame the computer for this or that, ultimately it is a "people problem." We are the artists forming art, not the machines.

We will soon address some of the common misconceptions that lead to questionable attitudes about technology, but one needs to be mentioned immediately. This is the myth that machines, like computers or electronic music keyboards, are somehow smarter than people.

There is little doubt that a digital computer can accomplish amazing things. For some time now, computers have been able to do routine (and sometimes not-so-routine) mathematical calculations, item sorting, and data transformations—often at remarkable speeds. Computers can make informed decisions, communicate at a basic and even a not-so-basic level with other computers, and—most importantly for musicians and artists—display, sound, and print a wide variety of information. More recently, there have been major advances in the ability of computers to record and play back music, control external sound devices, and recognize speech and the printed word.

In all of this, three important points must be remembered. First, each major achievement has been created by people. Programmers and engineers have created these abilities; the computer is entirely at the mercy of the software that controls it. Actually, computers are very ignorant. You will see in the next viewport, that all a computer understands inherently is whether a switch is on or off. Granted it knows about millions of these switches, and it can accomplish this switching with extreme speed, but there is simply no more ability than this. It takes human intelligence, sensitivity, and creativeness to make the computer offer its power to others.

Second, central to this creativeness is the human ability to think with the added complexity of feeling—or what is commonly referred to as the *affective* or *aesthetic* dimension. Yes, we can imagine programming a machine to respond to us in subtle ways that simulate the simplistic surface indications of affect. Remember *Hal*—the computer in Arthur Clark's *2001: A Space Odyssey*? We can imagine code being written to do just what *Hal* did—perhaps even more impressively. But no amount of programming imaginable today can simulate the deep emotional feeling in Isaac Stern's mind during the closing moments of a live performance as he shapes a musical phrase in one of Bach's unaccompanied partitas. It is quite doubtful that any machine can replicate the complex web of thought and feeling that must have occurred in the mind of Igor Stravinsky as he conceived the "Sacrificial Dance" in the *Rite of Spring,* or Charlie Parker as he improvised the classic solos that so influenced the jazz world, or of Nadia Boulanger as she thought of new and subtle ways to teach students like Aaron Copland, Darius Milhaud, and Elliott Carter.

Third, and maybe most important, it is inconceivable at this point in history that we can create hardware and software systems that come close to the human ability to think, feel, and understand to a level that can approximate the creation of music as art. We freely admit that advances in artificial intelligence research have given computers and connected devices some extraordinary capabilities, as we shall see in the coming modules on music notation and composition. But the ability of humans to make intuitive leaps and links as they store and process information is vastly superior to even the most advanced computer system today and in the foreseeable future. Consider this, as well: if it were possible to come reasonably close to the complexity of thought and feeling in human cognition with a machine, what about our machine's ability to communicate these subtleties to other machines in ways that parallel our ability as humans to exchange ideas, create art, pass on culture—in short, to contribute to society?

So what's the point? Simply this: because of the genuinely human attribute of affect, musicians as creative artists are acutely aware of that *unexpected turn* in the creative process that is inspired by the complex mingling of rational thought with intuition, feeling, and imagination. It is this fascinatingly human mixture that makes people far more important in the creative process than the technology itself. Hardware and software will constantly improve and will continue to be tremendous aids to the creative musician, but such technology remains out of reach and quite apart from the capacity of humans to conceive and execute great art or to understand and convey its import.

Given all of this, it seems far more meaningful to consider the role of technology in the hands of musicians who have demonstrated their ability to use it in a creative way. Such people will serve as inspirational guides for us as we set our course through the maze of computers and music technology in the sections that follow.

Featured Musicians

It takes little effort to find examples of people who have demonstrated stunning success in working with technology. In the viewports that follow in the book, you will read the words of ten extraordinary musicians whose accomplishments with technology are well known to the music world. They will provide you with some fascinating insights into music technology in action.

Diversity Abounds!

Edward Asmus
(Courtesy of Busarth
Photography)

Henry Panion, III
(Courtesy of the University
of Alabama at Birmingham
and Marc Bondarenko,
photographer)

The first thing that strikes home as you become acquainted with these musicians is the amazing diversity of the technology they use. Part of this is because of the differences in their professional work. Christine Hermanson and Timothy Smith are interested in software for music skills and use a wide assortment of computers and software to meet the needs of their students. Multimedia computer workstations are very significant in the work of Fred Hofstetter, Edward Asmus, and Dale Olsen, as well as Hermanson and Smith. They want to explore the diversity of learning environments that can be created through technology.

Pierre Boulez uses predominately Macintosh and Unix workstations but needs special software written to meet the real-time, live performance needs of his composition and performing. Boulez, Max Mathews, and David Cope all use larger and much more complex computer and MIDI-based music systems than Hermanson and Smith, and they are interested in researching fascinating ways to merge traditional instruments with electronic ones and to invent new instruments.

Libby Larsen works hard at finding a comfortable balance between her need for unrestrained creative productivity in composing, and the use of her Macintosh to assist with notation, orchestration, and the design of new digital sounds. Henry Panion uses music technology both in his studio and on the road to meet the extraordinary demands of the professional popular music scene, where time and quality are of the essence.

Cope, Hofstetter, Olsen, and Panion do a great deal of word processing and desktop publishing to facilitate the many writing and administrative projects in which they are involved. And Asmus and Cope use larger and faster computer workstations to handle the number crunching for their statistical and numerical analyses of music data.

Not only are the applications and computers different, but so are the software packages that they use. Because each has a particular need in mind, as well as different hardware power for that need, each has chosen a different software solution. There is simply no "best" software program for any need. Keep this fact in mind when we come to the discussions of software choice in many of the viewports that follow.

Music Hardware. Nearly all our featured musicians are heavy users of MIDI-based equipment. All need quick access to the best quality sound possible for their needs, in a format that is standard across hardware and software platforms.

Christine Hermanson
(Courtesy of Picture Me, Inc.)

David Cope
(Courtesy of UCSC Photo Lab,
Don Fukuda)

Dale A. Olsen
(Courtesy of The Florida State
University School of Music)

Pierre Boulez
(Courtesy of IRCAM and
Pierre Boulez)

For MIDI equipment, some favor keyboards with onboard sequencers and special effects. This feature, built into the keyboard, lets a musician construct a composition in layers of sound, and alter and modify those sounds. Others prefer "keyboardless" sequencers that are part of their computer software. As Mathews stresses in his interview, there is a "big step ahead" when all the "sound sources or sampled files will be stored in the computer disks or memory rather than on the synthesizers." This will create considerably greater "flexibility in the realm of what sounds a performer or composer can draw upon," and all the "transformations of samples that are done currently on synthesizers can be done on sound files."

Many of the teachers in our profiles have CD-ROM drives that also serve as audio CD players attached to their computers. Asmus and Smith are excited about the use of CD players to demonstrate real music excerpts—as opposed to contrived, isolated examples—for classes. Asmus designs his own software using authoring systems and Smith uses the Internet to control remote CD-ROM drives as he teaches about the music of Bach over the Internet. Hofstetter has invested considerable creative energy in laser technology for teaching and learning, and his music videodisc series and PODIUM software show the wonderful potential for video as well as the emerging DVD technology.

In reviewing the music hardware use of our invited musicians, you will see that Mathews and Boulez are both experimenting with alternate ways to link computers with music devices. Mathews continues to experiment with controlling devices like his MIDI Radio Baton and with writing software for "expressive sequencers" that offer new possibilities for performing artists. Boulez is also interested in linking the conductor and performer to electronic sound in ways that can be blended with acoustic instruments, and in real-time computer manipulation of the performing environment. He speaks of "triggering," "automatic scores," and "score following" by computer. As he says, the technology needs to respond to the "interaction between performer and machine," the "particular playing style of the performer," and the "performance gestures."

Similarities. Most of these musicians did not come from a computer background. Each came to music and technology from a slightly different path, but nearly all were trained as musicians in high school and college. With the exception of Mathews and Larsen, none of our guest musicians claimed a strong background in mathematics, physics, or engineering. As Maestro Boulez tells young composers who fear technology because of their deficiencies in math: "Don't even think of that. Think about the sound! That is what is important."

It is not surprising how many of our musicians use other software in addition to music applications. Many are engaged in administrative work, especially those who run their own music businesses and those who direct research activity. Word processing and desktop publishing seem to be a shared interest, as does electronic communication through e-mail and the Internet.

One of the most used music software applications is music notation. Hermanson, Olsen, Smith, and Asmus use notation software to produce

Libby Larsen
(Courtesy of Libby Larsen)

Max Mathews
(Photo by Patte Wood)

Fred Hofstetter
(Courtesy of the University
of Delaware, Jack Buxbaum)

small excerpts for printed handouts for class and modest-sized music arrangements. Larsen, Cope, Panion, and Boulez need more powerful packages that print longer scores and large numbers of parts. They also require custom notation formats and symbols as well as standard features. Panion needs a very portable solution that lets him do overnight arrangements for Stevie Wonder while traveling with Stevie, his musicians, and his sound and recording engineers.

Many of the musicians noted how the technology helped them do their jobs. Perhaps Smith said it best: "The process of telling the computer how I want it to portray what I think is the musical structure invariably gives me new ideas about what the structure actually is—new ideas that would not have been generated without this creative interplay between mind and machine."

Needed Changes and the Future. Each of our featured musicians feels deeply about what needs changing in current music technology. The common themes that emerge are the impact of technology on teaching, the development of intelligent music systems, the opening of the music creative enterprise to everyone, and the expansion of collaboration through real and electronic means.

Hermanson and Smith reflect on the need for technology to play a larger role in the education of musicians in the music classroom. Olsen feels that the access to digital audio and video will continue to improve, and Panion expects more cross-platform improvement.

A few of our distinguished guests predict the emergence of intelligent interactive music systems. Cope asks for compositional devices that are "integral rather than external to music instruments, so that all input and output is intrinsically musical." Larsen asks for computer systems that "don't physically get in the way of the creative process, simulating more closely what a composer does when sketching by hand on music paper." Asmus sees the need for these intelligent systems to break away from traditional notation with a more "intuitive system for the production and notation of sound that doesn't require years of technical study." Hermanson and Hofstetter see these systems becoming more interactive and using laser-disc technology to its fullest. Cope goes even further in recognizing the significance of virtual reality environments, where we can even create "holodeck-Mozart" or, perhaps, go so far as to bring virtual-Beethoven into the classroom to admonish students to practice more!

On the creative front, we hear Mathews and Boulez argue for the emergence of live computer music—real-time performance with computers. As Boulez and Hofstetter point out to us, however, these music creativity machines will also open up the capability of anyone, young or old, to create "music sketches" at home, "using computers to make the music they like," in Hofstetter's words, "instead of having to like the music others make." Larsen also anticipates the permanent addition of an electronic section to the symphony orchestra. Panion reminds us that "some fairly successful attempts are being made to have notation and sequencing software interpret meaning over action." As he says, "transcription algorithms," for example, "are far superior—in fact, they are amazing."

Tim Smith
(Courtesy of Silver Image Photography, Flagstaff, Arizona)

Collaboration and networking is also a common theme. Boulez wants to see a greater "synergy" between computer-music efforts worldwide, connecting centers, small and large, through the Internet and sharing information and experimentation. He sees the need for a richer dialog between musician and scientist; musician and engineer. We need to keep emphasizing, he says, the importance of people "working with musical ideas, not computer ideas."

Smith feels that students will soon have the ability to experience most music instruction remotely from anywhere in the world. He argues that, even now, the power of the Internet is changing the way we think about education and is challenging views of classroom instruction, financial aid, registration, and the whole mission of our teaching institutions. Olsen sees the use of the Internet for teaching as a way to help expand the awareness and diversity of the world's musics.

We hope you enjoy learning about these amazing people and their musical accomplishments.

Misconceptions and Attitudes

Before we take a more systematic look at the procedures that people employ to use computers and music technology, we must deal with a few misguided ideas that might slow you down. We have already dealt with a major one in the Introduction: that *computers are somehow smarter than humans*. There are a few others. Some of these misconceptions have a grain of truth. In general, though, they may lead to major attitude problems toward music technology.

Ten Misconceptions

No. 1   Technology refers only to hardware

The decision to purchase a computer or music keyboard is not where the story begins and ends. Hardware is part of a *system* in which there is much more to be considered. What are the needs (people and procedures), the information to be treated (data), and options to treat it (software)? Hardware is an important (and perhaps the most talked-about) part of all this, but hardly the only thing to think about. Think, instead, of the *big picture*.

No. 2   There is hidden "knowledge" inside the hardware that is intimidating

This misconception often creates fear in the person using hardware (what some call *cyberphobia*). In Viewport II, we will deal with how a computer works. This will help you grasp just what *is* or *can be* put inside a computer. Yes, there is a certain amount of "knowledge" built into a computer by the manufacturer, but only to get things going when you turn it on. Then the machine sits there, dumb and happy, waiting for you—the boss—to tell it what program to run, what data to treat, what tasks to do. This is generally true for music keyboards and other devices. Just knowing a little bit more about the inside workings and realizing that you are in charge will go a long way.

No. 3   The hardware might break if something is done incorrectly

Short of hitting a piece of hardware with a hammer (an urge that is certainly possible at times of frustration!), there is not much you can do to hurt a piece of equipment by using it normally. No computer or music device of which we have any knowledge broke because a button was pushed or a key depressed in error. There are times when the software can cause the computer to crash and require restarting. However, the machine did not break, and it is likely that whatever happened can be corrected easily. Except for rare equipment failures that are usually out of your control, you cannot damage hardware by normal use.

No. 4   Computer technology is reserved for the technical elite

At one time, this was true. In the period when computers were large and delicate and required trained systems operators, and during the time of the first sound devices that relied on complicated procedures to connect one element to another, you needed to know a good deal about technical things. This has all changed. Newer computers and music devices offer much easier to use *interfaces* between people and the hardware. Mice, touch-sensitive screens, light pens, and microphones have made working with computers much easier. Computers are more portable for use on the job. Liquid crystal displays, slider bars, and simple switches have made music devices easier to use. Software designers have become aware of issues of user friendliness.

There are, of course, certain concepts and procedures that need to be understood. And there are times, regardless of our level of understanding, when we must turn to more technically knowledgeable people. Yet it is far easier these days to use technology than at any point in our history. If you have learned to play a musical instrument or sing, you can use a computer or a MIDI keyboard quite effectively.

No. 5   Computer technology takes too long to learn

If you are impatient, computers and music technology may not be for you. However, if you have achieved any success in music, it is likely that you have learned how to live with small but important gains from practice. If you approach computers and music technology in the same way, rich rewards will follow. It is true that some computer software programs take longer to learn than others, especially if you are learning basic computer operations at the same time. Try to do this work in stages. You set yourself up for failure when you try to accomplish a complex technology task, such as entering and printing a score and parts, with an unrealistic deadline. You may find that you are spending a lot of time at the beginning of your work, but you will quickly find the time very well spent.

No. 6   Computer technology is only for the young

Thinking this is like deciding not to listen to music composed after 1919 or refusing to vote in a presidential election. We have seen no biological or psychological evidence that demonstrates that older people cannot learn to use technology productively. Perhaps this misconception has more to do with open-mindedness and willingness to change than with age and technology themselves.

No. 7   Using technology removes the creative spirit from music experience, producing music that is antiseptic or sterile

Sometimes this is true, especially if there is a lack of imagination in the musician responsible or if the technology doesn't allow for subtlety. (If the latter is true, get better technology; if the former, don't blame the technology!) There *is* a good deal of poor music that gets created with technology. From the "boom-chic-a-boom" sounds of trite preprogrammed drum tracks to the insipid melodic dribble that pours out of Joe Cool's synthesizer, there's plenty of bad music created by people with machines. What's more, this is not restricted to any one genre; we've heard just as much uninspired and tiresome music from "serious" electronic music studios as we have from the pop scene. Bad music is bad music! Of course, this is true for traditional acoustic music as well—a point that seems to be lost on some of technology's harshest critics.

No. 8   Computers, MIDI, and CD-ROMs, when used for teaching about music, are just another expensive set of technological gimmicks that take time and money away from the real business of music education

This complicated misconception probably has less to do with technology itself and more to do with beliefs about what teaching strategies and the *real* business of music education should be. To us, the focus should be on *expressive sound* and its role in music experiences. We believe that the technological tools described in this book provide powerful support to open up the world of music to as many people as possible. MIDI devices provide effective ways to teach about timbre, melodic and rhythmic subtlety, dynamics, and articulation. They offer extraordinary ways to engage students in the creative process of sound shaping through improvisation and composition— experiences that, until now, have been rarely considered. CD and DVD players attached to computers provide elegant support for focused listening experiences, together with supportive visual information. For us, these tools are not fads, but major advances in teaching. The expense in time and money seems well worth the investment.

No. 9   Technology, not music, becomes the focus

This can be true when technology is used poorly. If the most interesting aspect of a performance was the performer's ability to play both keyboard and wind controller while working the mouse on a computer, apparently the music itself didn't capture our interest. If we attend a talk about music in which the graphics displayed on the overhead projector were more interesting than the content, we should blame the speaker, not the technology. Musicians who spend inordinate time engaged in the frills of technology perpetuate this misconception. Again, place the blame where it belongs.

No. 10   Technology replaces musicians' jobs

Yes and no. It is true that certain employment opportunities are affected by music technology, but what often is not considered is the number of new jobs created *because* of technology—and the time saved for more creative work.

Resulting Attitudes

Each of these misconceptions, considered as a whole or in combination, leads to rather deeply held, negative attitudes about technology and the music experience. We meet many in the music enterprise who have great suspicions about technology. Some flatly refuse to consider its merits, citing technology's impersonality, technical complexity, and unmusical qualities. When pressed to say why they feel this way, we find that often they base their feelings on a number of bad experiences at concerts or in school. Most are uninformed about technology and unwilling even to consider its merits. Others can't seem to say why.

On the other hand, we also meet a number of musicians who have gone too far in the other direction—often relying so heavily on technology that they lose sight of the point of fine music making. They often buy the latest software or MIDI device merely to have the latest gimmick. They hold the potentially dangerous attitude that any new idea is a great development for the art, without much careful consideration.

We suggest a middle ground. There are legitimate concerns about the present role of technology in music and we must keep a careful eye on all new trends. Here are a few tips that might be useful in forming your attitudes:

▶ Work from a position of knowledge. Try to learn as much as you can about technology and how it is used in the aspect of music that most interests you. Do this by reading sources and by talking with others who use technology in music.

▶ Plunge right in! Start working with technology yourself by experimenting with a few projects.

▶ Be patient at first. Avoid making your first experience with technology center around an unreasonable deadline.

▶ Try not to rush to judgment. Develop your opinions after as many experiences as possible. Be open-minded!

▶ Keep your focus always on the artistic and pedagogical end product. Use technology to improve the music experience.

Procedures and Applications

The first section of this viewport on *People and Procedures* has introduced you to a number of people actively using computers in one fashion or another for their daily music making. The many ways these musicians use computers provide you with a wonderful repertoire of ideas for putting computers to use in your work as a musician. This is what we will focus on next: the procedures or tasks that computers perform for us. We can use computers to:

► Organize music information and communicate with musicians

► Learn about music

► Publish information about music

► Compose and notate music

► Perform music

► Create music software and multimedia

► Conduct historic, analytic, and systematic research

► Play games (preferably music ones!)

Categories of Computer Mastery

We've also discussed some misconceptions people have about using computers. These could be translated into fears about computing. Music technophobia is not as prevalent today as it once was, but many musicians are still reluctant to experiment with computer technology. One reason for this is that they have the impression that being computer-knowledgeable means knowing how to program or write your own software. Nothing could be further from the truth. We suggest that you approach computers through three levels of application, or, if you will, of mastery: Buy-and-Run; Fill-Your-Own; and Roll-Your-Own. The second level, Fill-Your-Own, has three aspects of its own: instructional, administrative, and creative. We will explain these in a moment.

A comparison to swimming pool psychology might help clarify these levels. Based on our experience, we wisely select the low end of the pool (we are only wet up to the waist or wading), the middle of the pool (we can still touch bottom if we need to), or the deep end of the pool (where the high divers doing triple somersaults hang out). There is satisfaction attainable at all three depths. The last thing a sane wader would do is to head for the diving board. Therefore beginning users of computers should never start by programming a computer on their own. They should pick an appropriate level of wading (Buy-and-Run applications), work their way up to swimming with the bottom in reach (Fill-Your-Own applications), and finally, take on high-diving techniques (Roll-Your-Own applications).

Programming a computer is not the only example of high diving. You can take any of the three levels of Fill-Your-Own software and advance to a high-diver's level of sophistication. There are wading-pool as well as high-diving skills that can be mastered in word processing and music notation. When you are first starting to find your personal level of computer skill, the Buy-and-Run to Fill-Your-Own to Roll-Your-Own path is a good way to start. Everyone should seek a comfortable level to swim or work in.

Buy-and-Run Applications

Buy-and-Run applications are those for which the only experience you need is knowing how to insert the computer disc and turn on the machine. This level is just about as easy as using a videotape recorder or a compact disc player. There are software applications for music fundamentals, for ear training, for music history and literature, for music analysis, for instrumental skill development, and for supplementing textbooks. Most of the music applications in this category are called computer-assisted instruction or CAI software. As we will see in Viewport III, there are different types of CAI software.

Figure 3.1 shows a typical music computer laboratory with students receiving computer instruction.

Figure 3.1
The computer lab at Illinois State University shared by art, music, and theater students (Courtesy of Rhondal McKinney)

Fill-Your-Own Applications

Fill-Your-Own applications are those that are contentless. That is to say, someone has already programmed the logic of the computer software but has left it empty of content so you can fill in your own information. This level of computer mastery requires more skill than Buy-and-Run because you need to learn enough about the mechanics of each Fill-Your-Own application to add and edit your music content—you have to keep your head above water. As we noted earlier, Fill-Your-Own programs fall into three categories: instructional, administrative, and creative. There is a large array of software in each of these groups to meet almost every need.

Instructional

These are programs that let you build instructional materials by simply typing in the content of the review materials and the possible correct answers. Programs of this type are sometimes called instructional *shells*. This means that the software provides an empty shell to be filled. Many commercial aural music skills programs come with a shell or editor so the instructor can add or customize items.

Administrative

This category includes word processors, spreadsheets, database software, grading and scheduling software, various music-inventory applications, and communications software that lets us link computers over the Internet or the telephone. Each of these applications assists us in becoming better managers of information. They work similarly to shells in instructional Fill-Your-Own software.

Here is a typical scenario that a musician like David Cope or a musicologist or music theorist, for example, might follow to produce or desktop-publish a newsletter. They begin by typing up the material for the newsletter with commercial word-processing software or by inserting word-processed files that people have sent them. They then design artwork using a graphics software package, and perhaps a scanner. Switching to desktop publishing software, they integrate the text and graphics, and design the layout of the newsletter. When they are done, the image on their screen looks just like the final printed copy. Now, by means of an inexpensive laser-quality printer attached to their computer, the final newsletter is printed. One stop at the local copy shop for 500 copies and the newsletter is ready for mailing.

In Viewport IV, we will explore desktop publishing along with graphics applications that are useful for musicians in publishing documents. In Viewport II we will introduce you to how you can connect one-on-one with other musicians to share information or to connect through commercial computer networks, electronic bulletin boards, and the Internet.

Among our featured musicians, David Cope, Fred Hofstetter, and Dale

Olsen have produced several well-known books using word processing and desktop publishing. Ed Asmus could not conduct his music education research without the aid of administrative and communications software for word processing, databases, and spreadsheets to perform statistical computations on his research data. He also makes extensive use of the Internet for keeping in touch with other researchers.

Creative

To Be or Not To Be		
	Binary	**Decimal**
T	01010100	84
O	01001111	79
	00100000	32
B	01000010	66
E	01000101	69
	00100000	32
O	01001111	79
R	01010010	82
	00100000	32
N	01001110	78
O	01001111	79
T	01010100	84

The creative category includes software that lets you design graphics, newsletters, and posters; compose and notate music; design marching-band charts; and produce a host of other music products. Many of these creative products come from manipulating computer-generated sound and graphics with a computer and from the use of music devices controlled through the Music Instrument Digital Interface or MIDI.

The software applications in this category are the more exciting and, perhaps, the most complex of the Fill-Your-Own applications in music. For a person like Henry Panion, they represent powerful creative resources. Your imagination, be it visual or aural, can be expressed in a neutral, unbiased form—binary numbers in the computer. As binary numbers—a topic to be discussed in more detail in subsequent modules—all sound, text, and graphics are stored in the computer as alternating sequences of ones and zeros. The figure in the margin shows Hamlet's well-known phrase transformed first to the decimal numbers (ASCII codes) used to represent letters by all computers and then to the binary values the machine understands.

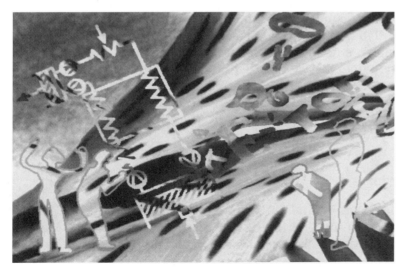

(a) "Differential Morphology" by Joan Truckenbrod
(© Joan Truckenbrod, courtesy of Williams Gallery, Princeton, NJ)

Figure 3.2
Computer-generated art
and music

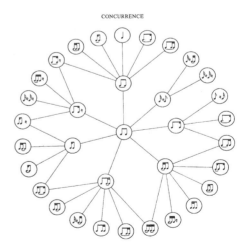

(b) "Concurrence" by Charles Ames
(*Interface: Journal of New Music Research*, 17, n.1, 1988; courtesy of Swets & Zeitlinger Publishers)

As a tantalizing aside, think of some interesting possibilities. A computer image of Andy Warhol could be *heard* by playing the image back through MIDI sounds. Or, the computer codes for the sounds of the Grateful Dead could be seen by displaying the music as graphics. Pretty far-out stuff but certainly possible. Visual artists like Joan Truckenbrod and musicians like Charles Ames are using fractals, artificial intelligence, expert rule systems, and other techniques to transform mathematical structures into music and art. Figure 3.2 shows samples of Truckenbrod's computer-generated art, which she calls a "diagrammatic dialogue," and Ames's computer-generated music, "Concurrence." Ames's diagram for his solo violin piece represents a relational network or knowledge base used to guide closeness or distance between rhythmic patterns.

Desktop Publishing, Graphics, and Notation. To teach you more about these applications, Viewports IV and V will introduce you to the underlying concepts of how graphic images and music notation are stored and manipulated in a computer. Using common commercial software, musicians can do professional-level music notation easily on a computer. Preparing the individual parts for each musician is automatically done by the notation software as well. No more pen and ink scores and late nights copying parts! Libby Larsen and Henry Panion make extensive use of music notation programs for composing, orchestrating, and preparing work for performance and publication.

Music Sequencing and MIDI. MIDI, or the Music Instrument Digital Interface, is the industry standard for controlling the incredible array of electronic music equipment that includes keyboards, drum machines, wind controllers, guitar controllers, and computers. Viewport VI discusses the mechanics of MIDI and music sequencing software. Figure 3.3 shows a typical all-MIDI music studio set up for student work in a college music lab, illustrating the wide variety of MIDI equipment that can be attached to a small personal computer. Chris Hermanson uses MIDI capabilities somewhat differently from what might be experienced in a college MIDI music lab. As a studio music teacher, she uses MIDI keyboards and computers to teach keyboard and improvising skills. Figure 3.4 shows young children working with computers and MIDI keyboards much as Hermanson would do.

Digital Audio. Viewports VI and VII will take you inside the techniques of digital sound and sampling. Three of our featured musicians, Maestro Boulez, Max Mathews, and Libby Larsen use digital audio in their work and have played key roles in the development of electronic music and digital sound.

Here is a typical scenario for using digital audio capabilities. A violinist is playing into a microphone attached to a PC. The screen shows a three-dimensional analysis of all of the elements of the live sound that has been captured by the computer. A commercial software application will let the

Figure 3.3
A view of the Electronic Music Studio at Illinois State University
(Courtesy of Rhondal McKinney)

violinist view, manipulate, and transform the sounds captured by the computer through the microphone. The captured digital images can now be reproduced on the computer with fidelity equal to that of any commercial compact audio disc; in fact, you could create your own CDs with such a computer.

In Viewport VII we will introduce you to the techniques and concepts for capturing sound and music using your personal computer in much the same way that the violinist captures digital sound samples from the violin.

Figure 3.4
Professor Maud Hickey (foreground) working with young composers at Northwestern University's School of Music MacLab

Roll-Your-Own Applications

This is the final category for computer applications. We are now at the deep end of the swimming pool in terms of expertise required. At this level you need to learn how to design and write your own software. Even here there are varying degrees of expertise depending on how much control you want over the machinery.

At the more advanced level, you can choose to work with sophisticated programming languages such as Pascal, C++, and Java. You can also find easier software development paths especially designed for instructional applications with authoring languages like Logo or with multimedia language environments like HyperTalk, Lingo, HTML, JavaScript, or Visual BASIC.

Fred Hofstetter and Tim Smith work extensively with multimedia authoring languages on computers. Ed Asmus accomplishes many advanced techniques with Excel spreadsheets and HyperCard by programming in the scripting language available for both applications. Two other music software programmers, David Zicarelli and Laurie Spiegel, use the Pascal and C languages in their commercial development of the music software Max and Music Mouse.

We will help you develop a variety of multimedia music projects in Viewport VIII. This viewport will present concepts behind programming languages and multimedia development tools including CD-ROM and DVD players and slow-motion video and animation. The Internet will be featured as both a delivery system and as a multimedia development environment in its own right.

Module 4 | Finding Help

Software Activity: "Tracking Down Campus Computing Resources."

Before venturing out into the waters of computer music technology, it is a good idea to know where the lifeguards are stationed. They can come to your rescue if the computer application gets too "deep" for you or if your computer freezes up—what computer people call a computer "crash."

Let's look at some places where you are likely to find computer lifeguards. In general, we find that people who work around computers and technology are friendly and willing to share their expertise. Many computer scientists and engineers are fascinated with producing music on a computer and are often eager to get involved when they have a chance. Don't hesitate to seek them out for help.

There are three sources where you can look for help and support as you begin your study of computer and music technology: people with technical skills, computer facilities, and published materials. This list summarizes some of the sources you should consider:

People with Technical Skills

► Computer technical support staff on campus or at work

► User groups

► Friends and fellow students with computer expertise

► People at the local computer stores

► On-line help from people on network services and the Internet

Computer Facilities

► Campus computer lab(s)

► Campus computer store or resource center

► Music computer lab(s)

► Electronic and/or MIDI music lab(s)

▶ Public and campus libraries

▶ Local computer stores

Published Print and Non-print Materials

▶ Computer books and magazines

▶ Manuals for software and hardware

▶ Video- and audiotape training materials

▶ This book

People with Technical Skills

Begin with those closest to you. If you are on campus, this means your instructor, fellow students or friends, teaching assistants, and technical computer staff. In the community, seek out friends who use computers and look for help from the local computer store where you purchased your computer. (This is one of the best reasons to buy your computer locally!) The next step is to seek out local or regional computer user groups that are compatible with your interests. Usually they form around certain computer types (e.g., Macintosh, Wintel, etc.) or application types (e.g., business, graphics, music, etc.). Then get connected via your modem to local electronic bulletin boards or networking services (e.g., America Online and the Internet). There is a tremendous number of resources on network services—including personal, one-on-one assistance. We will talk more about the technical aspects of networking in Viewport II.

When looking for computer assistance, be sure to take a quick reading on the technical competence of your volunteer lifeguard. Make sure that your resource is at least several yards ahead of you in the swimming pool and that your problem matches his or her repertoire of skills.

Computer Facilities

Again, find the physical resources closest to you. You never know when you may need a printer, a scanner, a faster computer, or MIDI equipment.

If you are on campus, find out where the computer labs are located and what resources they have. Check what restrictions apply. Find out if your campus has a store or resource center where you can purchase computers and supplies, perhaps at reduced cost. Then do a survey of what your music department or school has available in the way of a computer lab, an electronic music studio, a MIDI studio, and so on.

If you are in the community, see if a local college or public school will let you use their facilities. It may be worth signing up for a computer class just to gain access to campus computing resources. The continuing or adult education program on a campus may be able to help you as well. See what facilities your local computer store will let you use gratis or on rental. Many copy shops provide computers and printers for use on an hourly basis. Computer resources are becoming standard offerings at public libraries, which may also provide computer books, software, and hardware.

Print and Non-print Materials

There is an abundance of computer books, magazines, videos, and audiotapes to choose from. There are books for almost every major commercial software application. Take some time to scan through books before you buy. Check that the technical level matches your own. Computer books are expensive, so ask for recommendations and read the book reviews in the computer magazines, or try to find the books at the library. There are several firms that specialize in developing videotape and audiotape training materials for computers and software. Some libraries and video rental stores may stock them.

Viewport II

The Initial Plunge: Your Computer and the Internet

"I shall sit here," he said, "on and off, for days and days."
—The Footman to Alice, in Lewis Carroll's *Alice in Wonderland* (1865)

Computers don't actually think. You just think they think. (We think)
—Ted Nelson, *Dream Machines* (1974)

The most useful technology in the last 20 years served human needs; it did not replace or mimic human styles. The World Wide Web, digital libraries, news groups: these are attractive because they enable users to find information and communicate thousands of times faster than they could with other media.
—Ben Shneiderman, author of "Designing the User Interface: Strategies for Effective Human-Computer Interaction," *Forbes* magazine (April 20, 1998)

World communications . . . virtually extend our psychical environment, providing a constant stream of moving, fleeting images of the world for our daily appraisal. . . . Through these devices we can telescope time, move through history and span the world a great variety of unprecedented ways.
—John McHale, "The Plastic Pantheon," *DotZero* magazine (1967)

Overview

This viewport deals with key issues for becoming acquainted with your computer workstation and getting it connected to the Internet for access to music and other on-line resources. Module 5, on software, begins with basic concepts related to computer operating systems: navigation of the graphical user interface (GUI); maintenance of computer files on various storage media including network storage; and the practice of safe computing. Module 6 then focuses on the key elements for successful use of the Internet for Web resources, e-mail, news, and file transfer. Module 7, on data, concentrates on how the computer represents information, on how this information is structured for transmission over networks and the Internet, and on the file formats that are used for universal exchange of data. Module 8, on hardware, describes how a computer is designed internally to process data though the various stages of Input, Process, Output, and Storage (IPOS). Then, we examine the various options for getting a computer workstation physically connected to networks and the Internet, either remotely through modems or directly through various network protocols and wiring. In this viewport we will:

▶ Present the key features of the graphical user interface (GUI), including mouse gestures, icons, windows, and menus

▶ Discuss procedures for storing your computer data on floppy, hard, and removable disks, as well as network storage.

▶ Stress the issues of legal software distribution, viruses, and software backup

▶ Discuss how a person establishes an Internet address and account

▶ Present the World Wide Web and the use of Web browsers and Internet search tools for locating music resources

▶ Review the Internet concepts of e-mail, news groups, listservs, threaded discussion groups, and FTP of files over the Internet

▶ Distinguish between analog and digital information and the ways in which computers connect to the external world through parallel and serial connections

▶ Study the data structures for remote networking through modems, local area networks, and the Internet with TCP/IP

▶ Discuss the common file formats and compression techniques used to universally share text, graphics, and sound across networks and the Internet

▶ Present the Input, Process, Output, Storage (IPOS) model for how computer systems work

▶ Discuss hardware issues for CPUs, RAM, CRTs, and disk storage devices

▶ Review networking hardware for remote modem connectivity, LAN topologies and wiring, and connecting PCs to networks and the Internet

HISTORICAL TIMELINE
The Technology of Computing Machines

3000 BC	Babylonian abacus performs numeric calculations with beads on rods
1 BC	One of the first known analog computers used by the Greeks for astronomy
1600s	Logarithms invented; computers use them to multiply by addition
1620s	Schickard invents the Calculating Clock, the first machine using mechanical representation of numbers
1660s	Leibniz develops concept of binary numbers and rules of logic
1720s	Electronic pulses first sent over a wire
1830s	Babbage designs the Analytical Engine, a model for today's computers, including programming with punched cards
	Samuel Morse develops the Morse telegraphy code
1860s	Transatlantic telegraph cable laid
1870s	Alexander Graham Bell patents the first telephone
1880s	Felt's calculator becomes the first use of a keyboard to enter data
	Edison invents the vacuum tube

1890s	Hollerith invents a system for coded punch cards used on computers into the 1970s
	Burroughs invents a calculator with keyboard and built-in printer
1910s	Edward Kleinschmidt invents the first teletypewriter
	Bendicks discovers that germanium crystals can convert AC to DC current, which leads, forty-five years later, to the integrated circuit chip
1930s	RCA demonstrates the first TV with a CRT or cathode-ray tube
	Zuse's Z1 with electromechanical relays is one of the first computers using binary numbers
	Shannon proposes that information can be treated quantitatively and manipulated by a machine
1940s	The Atanasoff-Berry Computer (ABC) and the ENIAC are some of the first electronic computers built that used vacuum tubes
	Transistor, discovered by Shockley and others at Bell Labs, will later replace vacuum tubes to miniaturize computer switches
	Magnetic-core memory (precursor of modern random-access memory) invented by Jay Forrester for the Whirlwind
	Introduction of first printed circuits laid out on board covered with copper
1950s	EDVAC computer built; a model for today's computers with stored programs, CPU, RAM, binary numbers, and logic
	IBM 701, first commercially successful computer (used by Max Mathews for first music sampling work)
	First magnetic media for storing data on metal-backed tape and plastic-backed tape
	Jack Kilby of Texas Instruments invents the first integrated circuit (IC)
	MIT Whirlwind real-time computer was the first to use CRT displays and interactive monitors
	Sputnik satellite launched (started US space program, which brought with it ICs and small electronics)
	The first *chip* or mass-produced integrated circuit built by team led by Robert Noyce
	First commercial TV sets and pocket radios as well as first satellites launched
1960s	First inexpensive minicomputers built with transistors, like DEC's popular PDP-8, appear
	IBM System/360 computers becomes the first major family of mainframe computer systems
	CDC-6000 Series computers introduced (PLATO instructional system later developed on CDC)
	Mouse invented by Douglas Engelbart at the Stanford Research Institute
	First 256-bit RAM chip based on magnetic core concept of Forrester
	Paul Baran at the Rand Corporation develops the decentralized, packet-switching concept that forms the basis of the Internet
	First commercial modems and acoustic couplers produced
	ARPANET, the precursor of the Internet, is installed by the Department of Defense with four nodes based on the RAND design
	Thompson and Ritchie at Bell Labs develop UNIX
1970s	Floppy disks introduced
	Winchester design for magnetic hard discs invented (head floated on a cushion of air above the disk platter)
	The Intel 8008 designed, the first 8-bit microcomputer on a chip
	First working personal computer is Ed Titus's Mark-8 home-brewed machine built around the Intel 8008
	TCP/IP becomes the primary networking protocol for connecting networks to the ARPANET, which has 37 nodes by 1974

	Robert Metcalfe at Xerox PARC conceives of Ethernet networking for sharing data between computers
	Internet e-mail emerges at the University of Wisconsin
	Mailing lists and USENET news groups appear on the Internet
	CompuServe and The Source commercial on-line services begin
1975	MITS Altair 8800 was first commercial personal computer in a kit with 256 bytes of RAM
	Apple II personal computer introduced for $1195 with color and sound, 16K of RAM, 6502 CPU, TV as monitor
	Apple introduces first floppy disk drive for personal computers
	Xerox Star workstation is the precursor of computers with icon-based operating systems, mouse, menus, and windows
	Shugart announces Winchester hard drives for microcomputers
1980s	First popularized computer virus attacks (the Cookie Monster Worm virus displayed "I'm a worm, kill me if you can")
	Copyright reform for computer software
	IBM PC marks IBM's first entry into microcomputer field
	Microsoft develops the MS-DOS Operating System for the IBM PC
	Apple introduces the Macintosh computer with icon-based operating system and digital sound synthesis
	Optical disk drives introduced
	1-megabyte RAM chips appear
	SCSI interface for drives and peripherals becomes a standard
	First intercity fiber-optic phone systems appear
	BITNET created to connect IBM computer centers worldwide
1985	Microsoft Windows extension to DOS (brings an icon-based operating system to IBM PC and compatibles)
	The year of the viruses: Brain, Bell Labs, Israeli, MacIn, Scores, and Trojan, with the Morris worm the first well-known Internet virus
	America Online goes into service, soon followed by Prodigy
	NSFNET added to the Internet to connect national supercomputer centers, and the Internet has 33,000 computer nodes in 1988
	Apple creates the first low-cost local area networking with AppleTalk
	The original ARPANET formally expires in 1989, marking the departure of the original military influence from the Internet
	Tim Berners-Lee proposes the World Wide Web as well as HTML and HTTP Web servers
1990s	Microsoft Windows 3.1 breaks the 640K RAM barrier on PCs
	4- and 16-megabyte RAM chips
	Personal Digital Assistants or PDAs appear as small, hand-held computers with writing and drawing tablets
	NREN (National Research and Education Network) approved as a 5-year, $5 billion upgrade to the Internet, and the Internet has 1.8 million host computer nodes in 1993
	Gopher is introduced at the University of Minnesota
	NCSA Mosaic client opens the Internet to on-line multimedia applications
1995	PowerPC chip brings RISC processors to PCs and portables
	Microsoft's Windows 95 marks the end of DOS with over one million copies sold in the first week; Windows 98 on the way

Netscape and Microsoft browsers become the two most used software applications for surfing the Web

Web TVs merge personal computing and television for plug-and-play Internet access

56K modems and the potential for Internet service from cable TV make Internet access better and cheaper for home computing

Apple Computer acquires NeXT software, Gateway acquires Amiga computers, Commodore goes out of business, Steve Jobs returns as CEO of Apple Computer, and Apple unveils the iMac.

Iomega brings removable storage to the masses with its Zip (100-MB) and Jaz (1-GB) drives

Java and Javascript, dynamic HTML and XML, all contribute to Web pages that are interactive, more attractive, and more sophisticated in their ability to be customized to each person browsing the Web

The Internet2 is developed for universities and research centers as a new, state-of-the-art network to provide a very-high-speed, greater-bandwidth Internet

2000   Firewire and the Universal Serial Bus (UBS) provide simple, high-speed connections between computers and peripherals with only one wire for storage, video, audio, and more

Computers have CPU speeds in the 1-gigahertz range, and commercial resolution digital audio and video are standard features of a computer, as is a DVD disc player

THE PEOPLE

REAL-WORLD PROFILE #1:   EDWARD (ED) ASMUS

Role: Professor of Music Education at the University of Utah

Dr. Asmus has extensive experience working with computers and computer programming, growing out of his work in music education, music education research, and measurement and evaluation. He has worked with mainframes and PCs, has programmed in FORTRAN, Pascal, and Visual Basic as well as HyperCard, and has developed many tools and aids for researchers working with such applications as Excel spreadsheets and HyperCard. He is a major advocate for the use of the Internet in research, maintains an Internet server at the University of Utah, and electronically publishes a directory of e-mail addresses for music researchers.

Interview

How did you become interested in computers and music technology? As an undergraduate at The Ohio State University. I was assigned to Dr. Henry Cady doing statistical analyses of music data with mainframe computers, punch cards, and soft-ware written in FORTRAN. Our first connection to the mainframe was with a teletype at 33 characters per second!

What computers do you use? On my desk at school is a Macintosh PowerPC 8500AV with a color monitor, extra hard drive, a second CD-ROM, and a scanner attached. The system, as with any desktop system, is too slow and too small. I have an ancient Macintosh PowerBook 160 that has complete fax and communications capabilities and, through our cam-

Edward Asmus working with students
(Courtesy of Edward Asmus)

pus network, I use VAXs, Sun workstations, and the facilities of our Center for High Performance Computing, which includes IBM RS/6000 workstations, a Cray Origin 2000 with 60 processors, and an IBM SP with 64 processors. I also have an HP Palmtop that I carry around for a wide variety of scheduling and research purposes.

Three ways you use computers and music technology? Communication is important for me. I maintain a worldwide e-mail list of music researchers and a Web server for music education and research. Computers support my teaching (classroom presentations and lectures, computer-assisted learning, music education simulations, handouts), my music education research work (statistical analyses, database, graphic analysis), and software development to solve teaching and research problems.

A unique way you use computers for music? I have developed computer-assisted learning materials that lead students to an understanding of various computer applications without having to be instructed in how to do the application. Students are required to use local and national Web sites for their class projects. In addition, I have developed software for efficient use of computer technology within traditional public school music ensemble classes.

If you could change one thing about how computers are used, what would it be? Get people away from traditional music notation. We can toss the cumbersome notation out the window. We need a more intuitive interface for the production and notation of sound that doesn't require years of technical study.

The one most significant change 10 years from now? I foresee more people being able to do music because the interfaces will be more intuitive and easy to use. Artificial intelligence built into music systems will allow a range of human involvement from completely hands-off to completely hands-on. The users will set their own level of involvement in the music production process.

One word of advice you have for musicians interested in computers? Do not plan on knowing everything. Identify a task, then learn the technology that will best perform the task. Ask questions. Be a bit skeptical of what you are told about computers. Don't glorify the computer beyond what it is—a tool.

REAL-WORLD PROFILE #2:   DALE A. OLSEN

Role: Professor of Music, Director of the Center for Music of the Americas, and head of ethnomusicology and world music studies at The Florida State University

Dr. Olsen, besides his extensive experience as a researcher and teacher of ethnomusicology, has performed flute in a number of symphony orchestras, and also plays the Andean kena, siku, charango, Peruvian harp, and Japanese shakuhachi. As a shakuhachi artist he has performed widely throughout the United States, Argentina, Brazil, Paraguay, and Peru, as soloist and with American and Japanese artists. Dr.

Dale Olsen holding a muhusemoi (deerbone flute) of the Warao Indians of Venezuela, and sitting in front of him is a hebu mataro (calabash spirit rattle) used by a Warao wisiratu shaman.
(Courtesy of the School of Music at Florida State University)

Olsen has numerous publications including two books: *Musics of Many Cultures: Study Guide and Workbook* (1995), and *Music of the Warao of Venezuela: Song People of the Rain Forest* (1996). His interest in the development of an Internet-based distance learning version of his popular "Music Cultures of the World" began in 1995. He developed a study guide for a popular world music textbook and then undertook the Internet design of his course. He considers his greatest contribution in Internet-based distance learning to be his knowledge of the content of world music.

Interview

What do you do as a musician? I'm an ethnomusicologist. I do fieldwork, write, teach, and perform. I research the music of South America, the Caribbean, and the South Pacific, especially among the Warao from the Venezuelan rain forest; among the people of the Andes; among the Japanese immigrant communities in Argentina, Bolivia, Brazil, Paraguay, and Peru; and others. I have written a number of books about my fieldwork. The courses that I teach are geographic area courses that include Music of Latin America, Music of the Caribbean, Music of Japan, and Music Cultures of the World; introductory and theoretical courses in ethnomusicology; and several world music ensembles (Music of the Andes and Japanese Shakuhachi). I perform numerous musical instruments from the Andes, the Japanese shakuhachi, and the Western flute.

How did you become interested in computers and music technology? I became interested in computers, music technology, and the Internet because of my desire to disseminate knowledge of world music to as many people as possible. Specifically, I desire to fill a void in community colleges and other small colleges, where there are no teachers of world music and no means to hire teachers of world music.

What computers do you use for your writing, research, and teaching? I use Macintosh almost exclusively for my personal writing, and a Gateway PC for my Internet involvement and distance instruction development. In addition, I use an IBM Thinkpad for classroom projection of Internet materials and CD-ROM playback.

What ways do you use computers in your ethnomusicology research and teaching? I use a Gateway Wintel computer for all my distance instruction development on the Internet, which includes Web site construction, slide and photograph scanning, video capture, audio editing, and "burning" of a CD-ROM for a master (published with my study guide entitled *Musics of Many Cultures: Study Guide and Workbook*).

Would you briefly describe how your "Music Cultures of the World" Internet course works? The course provides a general overview for studying music in a world context and offers specific examples from particular music cultures. The distance learning version of this course provides access for students from statewide campuses and has the potential for being administered throughout the United States and, indeed, the world. Through this distance learning course on the Internet, multiculturalism through music can be taught to larger numbers of students than ever before. This may be the first world music cultures course to be offered on the World Wide Web.

The course requires the purchase of two textbooks, one of them containing the CD-ROM of materials I

have compiled. A home page on the Internet, accessed by password, includes: the course syllabus; an index; 40 lessons; communications for announcements, news, instructions, and feedback from the professor based on e-mail comments and concerns from students; e-mail access to the professor and teaching assistant; instructions for writing assignments; and multiple choice examinations on line. Included in the 40 lessons are a multitude of visual examples that are comparable to what a student would see in a classroom via slide presentations. Audio and video examples of performances and demonstrations of musical instruments from the regions pertaining to the course contents, comparable to what a student would experience in class via film, video, and live performances, are included on the CD-ROM. The uniqueness is the method in which these examples are addressed via the Internet instruction: they are all linked to the objectives within individual lessons. Additional links to URLs around the world provide additional visual and audio examples, along with more information on the musics of the world's peoples.

If you could change one thing about how computers are used, what would it be? I would like to see better development of built-in Internet playback systems for audio and video. Presently, few students have the hardware to download audio and video from the Internet. For that reason, I am producing a CD-ROM to handle audio and video examples for my distance learning course.

The one most significant change 10 years from now? I suspect it will be the ability to download audio and video with ease.

One word of advice you could offer for musicians (ethnomusicologists) interested in using the Internet and the Web? Beware of wrong information presented on Web sites about music cultures of the world. There is a tendency for some Web designers to oversimplify and even falsify multicultural musical data, perhaps for the following reasons: treatment of music as tourism or as a new-age phenomenon; interest in making money by "exoticizing" musics of the world; or lack of interest in or knowledge about how to study world music as a social science, a fine art, or one of the humanities.

<table>
<tr><td>

Module

5

</td><td>

Operating System Software

</td></tr>
</table>

In reading this and other viewport modules, there is nothing magical about the order of things. There are times when you might benefit from reading ahead or looking back at previous sections. Links between software, data, and hardware ideas for computers and music technology are often very strong. Feel free to explore, especially when you see this icon in the margin!

Modules 5 and 6 present information on the software that runs your personal computer and its connections to the outside world. We will consider how this software represents not only the data that are part of your local computer, but also how it helps manage data that are available to you from remote servers and the entire interconnected community of computers around the world that we have come to call the Internet. Right from the start, we urge you to consider your computer as a tool for local information and as a "window" to the entire world.

After a few preliminary observations about your computer and hardware environment, we will discuss what to expect in a typical operating system, how to save and manage your files on your local hard drive and on a network, and how to practice safe computing. Module 6 addresses what to consider as you connect your computer to the Internet and how to use Internet software effectively.

Your Computer and Music Hardware

We begin with the assumption that you are working with some kind of computer and music hardware system either in your own living area or in a computer lab. Such systems vary greatly in design, but we imagine that Figure 5.1 comes close to representing what you have. We recommend that you take a moment to study the back of your computer and the connections that lead from it to your network, printers, audio gear, and MIDI equipment. In subsequent sections of the book that deal with hardware, we'll cover the specifics of how the connections are made for this equipment. For right now it's important that you simply get an overall sense of the environment in which you are working.

Streams of Information: Local Storage

There are five important streams of information going in and out of your computer: *local storage, network, printing, MIDI,* and *audio.* We will present local storage first and the others in the next section.

37

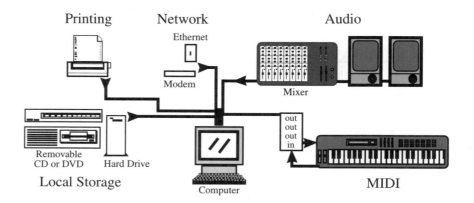

Figure 5.1
A basic music and
computer system

We assume you have a
basic knowledge of how
to physically set up your
computer system and
other hardware. If not, be
sure to follow the direc-
tions in your hardware
manuals or seek advice
from others.

See Modules 6 and 8 for
more about the Internet,
Modules 11 and 21 for
MIDI, and Module 8 for
storage hardware.

The local storage stream contains information that flows in and out of your computer from devices connected directly to it. There are many options for local storage, and you will learn more about them in Module 8. Figure 5.1 displays different kinds of "drives" either connected to or contained within your computer. Each kind uses a particular drive technology. The first is your hard drive that contains all of the operating system software and most of the software applications that you will use. This drive is usually built inside your computer, but in Figure 5.1 it is pictured outside. If you are in a computer lab, the storage area on this drive may be open to all who use the computer. If you are at home, this is a more private space for your work.

You may have a second disk drive that is external and has a removable cartridge. This kind of storage might be used for backing up your internal hard drive and for very large sound or movie files that you create or find on the Internet. Having a few of the removable cartridges on hand would allow plenty of flexibility.

A third kind of drive is an internal floppy. It may be one of the older varieties that contain only a small amount of information (about 1.4 megabytes), or it may be one of the newer Zip drives from Iomega that have nearly 70 times the capacity of the older floppy drives. Some machines might have both kinds of floppies. These drives use diskettes that are also removable and can be transported from computer to computer.

Finally, you may have some sort of laser-based drive that plays media. This drive accepts both audio compact discs (CDs) and CD-ROM discs that contain other forms of data such as words, digital audio, still images, and movies. This drive may also be a Digital Versatile Disc (DVD) that hosts a wide variety of laser-based media. You generally cannot store information on this kind of drive, but you do have access to the information that comes from discs inserted into it.

Other Streams

A second stream of data is provided by your network connection. If you are at home, this link might be through a modem that uses a telephone line. If

More on drive technologies in Module 8.

More on the difference between the terms "digital" and "analog" in Module 7.

you are in a computer lab or in a building that has a direct connection to the Internet, your link is a direct one managed by the institution. It is likely that this direct link also offers access to shared printers and other local computers called "servers." Servers offer storage for your projects and often contain software and data of importance to your work. If you are at home, it's likely that you have a printer that is attached to your computer and independent from your modem connection to the Internet.

The third stream of information is data that flows to your printer. In Figure 5.1, we imagine that you have a printer connected directly to your computer, but print data might also flow from your network connection to a remote printer on a network.

The last two streams are related to music: the Music Instrument Digital Interface or MIDI network, and audio analog audio signals. We describe MIDI at length when we introduce computer-assisted instruction and music notation and sequencing. This network allows your computer to exchange digital information with music keyboards and other MIDI music equipment that you might have.

Analog audio can be captured and sent out of your computer. Your computer is capable of recording audio through a microphone and can also send audio signals out to be heard through headphones or a sound system.

Manager Needed

The universal systems model, Input-Output-Process-Storage (IPOS), is used many times in this book.

These various network streams and storage options provide quite a challenge for those new to music and computers. These software modules on operating systems, Web browsers, and the Internet are designed to help with the management of all these resources. Perhaps the best way to think of this environment is to realize that information flows in, is processed, and then sent out to be used immediately or stored for the long term. We use this model throughout the book in our modules on hardware. The software that controls this information flow is the operating system of your computer. The better you understand its design, the better you can deal with computers and music technology.

What Does an Operating System Really Do?

Right from the Start

The operating system begins work the very moment you turn your computer on. In these initial seconds as the machine is "booting up," internal instructions are being carried out including a check of the important circuitry inside the computer, the sending of initial messages to the screen and appropriate sounds to the speaker, and the loading of routines that control the work of the computer.

The word *boot* comes from the very early days of computing when the idea of starting a computer was likened to the idea of "pulling yourself up by your own bootstraps."

More in Module 8 on CPUs.

A small part of the operating system is actually designed right into the circuits of the computer's hardware. For the most part, however, the operating system is written as software by programmers familiar with the hardware design. The decisions they make regarding how the computer screen looks and what the user must do to make the machine start, run, and stop can differ somewhat from computer system to computer system. This gives each operating system its particular personality. However, as we will soon see, the vast majority of operating systems for personal computers have a similar look and feel.

Incidentally, you might wonder why all these instructions can't simply be built into the computer so that it knows what to do without needing to seek out software from a disk. After all, computers inside washing machines, ovens, and cars don't need software to be loaded each time they turn on. The answer lies in the need to make computers more flexible. Computer designers purposely decide not to embed in the hardware all the decisions about the way the computer operates. This permits flexible approaches to the computer's functions and longer life for the hardware. All the system files are in a key system folder or directory installed on your computer by the manufacturer. We will explain folders shortly. When it comes time to update your system, these are the files that will get replaced by the installation software.

Four Key Roles for Your Operating System

The operating system is a set of programs that act as a link or bridge between you and your application software (music printing, word processing, etc.) and between you and the hardware. Figure 5.2 displays this relationship. Whatever you choose to do is sent through the operating system to the computer itself. The operating system is a kind of silent manager or conductor that is responsible for the smooth operation of the computing enterprise.

There are four types of management:

▶ At the very basic level, the operating system translates your command into something the hardware in the computer can understand. A simple gesture by the mouse, for example, travels through the application you are using to the operating system and on to the hardware itself. Even when you are doing nothing at all, the operating system is busy humming away, constantly looking for information to pass along to the hardware.

▶ On another dimension, the operating system has routines ready to perform commonly requested tasks. These include such things as printing a document, saving your work, opening work that you have saved before, launching an application, and closing down the computer for the day. You issue commands to do these sorts of things within the application in which you are working, but what really does the work is the operating system routines that are always on call.

▶ The operating system also manages multiple applications that you may run simultaneously. You may want to have both your music notation software and your word-processing software running together at the same time. You

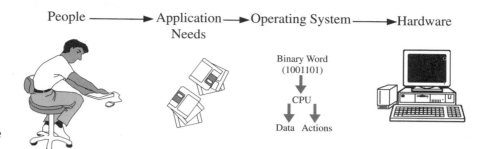

Figure 5.2
Operating system software
in context

can be writing about dominant seventh chords using your word-processing program, then flip over to a music program to create your notation example, then back again to your document to paste in the music notation. The operating system keeps these two different programs in order so the hardware can share its power between them.

▶ Finally, the operating system manages your interaction with external networks. You can be reading your electronic mail or surfing the Internet at one moment, then switch back to a local music aural skills program the next. Modern operating systems manage these transitions. Many operating systems have links to the Internet built right into them so that you can have seamless connections to remote resources located either in the same room, building, or campus, or around the world.

Graphical User Interface (GUI)

Historically, "Wintel" stands for Windows and Intel. It's an easy term to refer to all computers that use the Windows operating system.

So what does an operating system look like? Figure 5.3 represents two typical operating systems from personal computers. One figure comes from a Macintosh (*a*) and the other from a Wintel computer (*b*). Both screens use a *desktop* metaphor where small pictures (icons) represent data files, software applications, folders, printers, local storage drives, remote servers, and links to the Internet. In the Wintel example, we have also opened a music application which is on the desktop. These pictures and windows are what the graphical user interface (GUI, pronounced "gooey") is all about. The GUI model is the predominant approach to representing the operating system, regardless of the brand of computer you own.

Here are five components of a GUI that you can expect to use as you navigate around electronic desktops:

▶ Mouse gestures

▶ Icons

▶ Windows

▶ Menus

▶ Buttons and dialogs

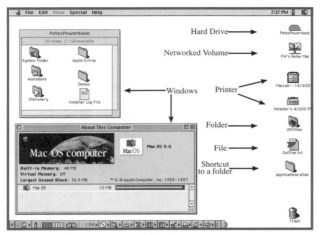

(a)

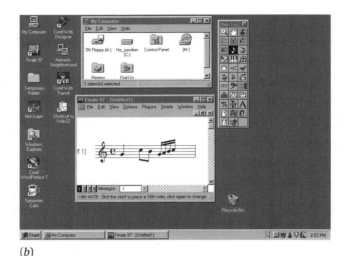

(b)

Figure 5.3
Macintosh OS 8 (a) and Windows (b) operating systems

Mouse Gestures

The mouse is really a pointing device with buttons that add additional control features. A ball inside the mouse rides against the surface of the table (or mouse pad if you want a flat and friendly surface). The ball records the slightest movements of the mouse and sends them on to the operating system routines that are written to watch over the mouse movements. This translates into movement of a pointer, usually an arrow, on the screen. The pointer is called a "cursor." You will quickly get a sense of the relationship between your hand movement with the mouse and the movement of the arrow on the screen. This is not unlike the kind of psychomotor skill we learn as musicians when we coordinate our eyes with our hands while playing a musical instrument.

In addition to movement from side to side and up and down, four classic gestures are important to have in the mouse repertoire: single-click; double-click; multiple-click; and click-and-drag.

If you run out of mouse space on the table, just pick up the mouse and move it!

▶ Single-click is simply moving the cursor over the top of an object such as an icon and clicking the mouse button once. (For those mice that have two buttons, the left button is the one that applies here.) Single clicking is usually used to choose an object for some other command or to place a marker at a particular spot on the screen.

▶ Double clicking (two clicks in quick succession) is also performed while the pointer is on top of an object. This usually is a request for activating some process like opening an application.

▶ Multiple clicking (more that two clicks) is also possible. Triple clicks are sometime required to choose a full paragraph of text or to select a large portion of material. Two and one-half clicks (two clicks and then holding down the mouse button) can also be used for special commands and options on certain computers. The right button on two-button mice also provides for special options; usually the right button brings up a menu of options for the object being clicked.

▶ Click-and-drag is probably the most frequently used mouse gesture. If you want to move an object from one position to another, you move the pointer to that object, push down on the button, hold the button down, and move the mouse. The object moves along with your gesture. Another use of click-and-drag is when you want to highlight a passage of text, a set of music notation symbols, or a string of numbers. The general rule is simply to place the pointer to the upper left of the objects you wish to highlight and drag (with the mouse button down) to the lower right. Each situation is a little different, so experimentation is called for.

These gestures may sound confusing, but they really are not once you have some practice. Much of what is said below about icons, windows, and menus offers an excellent opportunity for mouse practice.

Icons

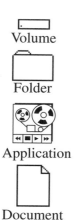

Volume

Folder

Application

Document

True to the meaning of the term, icons often take on the appearance of the entity or idea they represent. A typical operating system uses icons to represent many of the components of a music and computer system. Take another look at Figure 5.3. We have labeled icons that represent hardware such as drives, printers, and servers. We have also noted icons that represent software such as application data files, the applications themselves, and links to software for accessing the Internet. Hardware icons resemble the devices they represent. The folders look like file folders that you might find on your real desktop, and they resemble pieces of paper. Software companies invent distinctive icons to represent their applications and data files.

Icons are movable and "clickable." If you need to reposition one, just click-and-drag it to the place you want. Certain movements with icons mean particular things to the operating system. For instance if you move a floppy diskette icon on top of a hard disk icon, this instructs the system to perform a copying task. Dragging a data file on top of its application will launch the application. Dragging a file on top of a printer icon will cause the printer to print the file. Dragging a server icon to the trash can or recycle bin disconnects you from the server; however, moving an icon that represents a file to the trash/recycle bin will be a signal to the operating system that you wish to erase the file. Learning these movements is important for your computer health (and personal sanity!)

Windows

Another concept that you will find useful in the graphical user interface is the use of windows. When opened, each application runs in a particular window (or set of windows) on the screen. For example, the digital audio

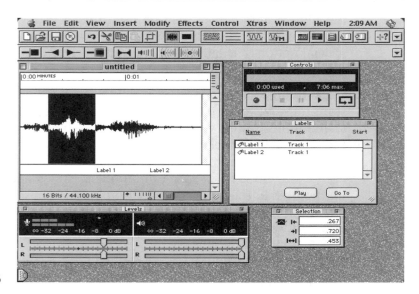

Figure 5.4

Multiple windows for Macromedia's SoundEdit 16

program pictured in Figure 5.4 has several windows open. The main editing window is the one named Untitled. The others are supportive of the work being done.

With the presence of so many windows on the screen at once, it is easy to see how the GUI uses a layering effect. Windows can be layered on top of one another like playing cards in a deck. Multiple applications opened at one time will create sets of windows that can be displayed at one time. To help bring order to the desktop, most operating systems will allow you to "hide" and "show" sets of application windows.

Windows are marvelously flexible. Most can be moved, closed, or resized. You can also move material that is within the windows. Click-and-dragging the title bar of windows will move them around the screen. Boxes are offered for closing and resizing. Many times, there will be more information in a window than the space of the opening will allow. Most windows come with vertical and horizontal scroll bars that allow you to adjust the viewing area in the window.

Figure 5.5 displays the parts to windows commonly found on Wintel and Macintosh computers. The top box is from a Wintel machine and the bottom from a Mac. Notice that the boxes for closing, growing, and hiding are, in some cases, positioned in different locations but the functions are similar.

There are limits to the number of windows you can have open and the number of applications that can be running at the same time. One limitation is physical space on the screen. The other limitation is the amount of *random access memory,* or RAM, space that is available on your computer. This will be described further in Module 8.

Menus

Menus are lists of commands that instruct the computer to do things. To choose these commands, you simply use the mouse pointer to navigate to

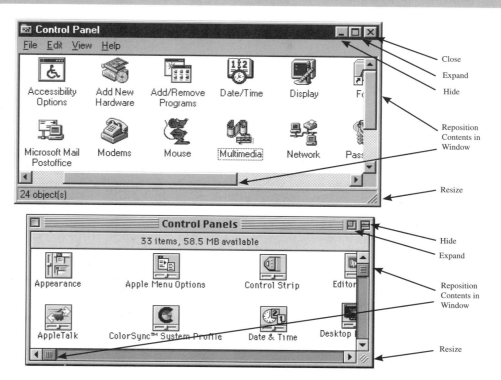

Figure 5.5
Windows on Macintosh
and Wintel Machines

an item you want. Let go of the mouse button and the command is chosen. Sometimes this results in an immediately executed action. Other times, it establishes a setting that will determine how later actions will be executed. In the latter case, often a check mark appears next to the command item to let the user know that it has been chosen. Many menu items have *keyboard equivalents,* or ways to use the computer's keyboard to issue these same commands rather than pointing and clicking with the mouse. The many menus we have displayed in Figure 5.6*a–c* have these equivalents displayed to the right of many of the menu items.

Menus take many forms. A common type of menu is the *pull-down* variety that can be noted in Figure 5.6*a*. The Macintosh operating system has a number of pull-down menus, as do many applications written for Macintosh and Wintel. The menu bar at the top of your computer screen lists the various menus, and this changes often as you move from one application to another. If you become familiar with names of menus for your favorite applications, you can easily tell which of these applications is "active."

Single, pull-down menus are not the only kind used. *Contextual* menus are also common.These are menus that appear next to a file, folder, or volume icon when you make some action with your mouse or keyboard. For any chosen icon, clicking on the right button of a Wintel machine's mouse displays a menu of choices for that icon. This kind of contextual menu also appears in certain operating systems for the Macintosh when you click on the mouse button while holding down the "control" key. Figure 5.6*b* displays a contextual menu for a Wintel machine.

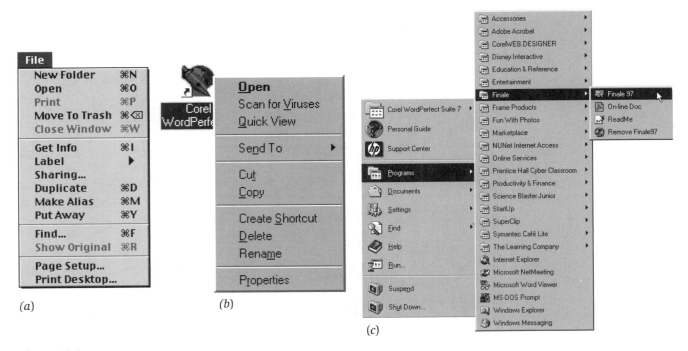

Figure 5.6
Typical menus for
Macintosh and Wintel

There are *submenus* that are really menus within menus. We have included one of these as Figure 5.6c. A software author who wants to have one menu item lead to another would place an arrow to the right of a menu item to indicate the presence of another menu. When you come to this command item, another menu comes up next to it and you move the pointer over and choose from that menu.

Sometimes menus *pop-up* from different places on the screen. This is also displayed in Figure 5.6c. In this screen from Windows 95, the item "Start" at the bottom left of the screen is a pop-up menu name that leads to the menus and submenus that are pictured to the right of the first menu. Macintosh systems have pop-up menus as well, but they come from inside either windows or dialog boxes. One major difference between the Mac and Wintel operating systems is that for Wintel systems running Windows 95 there are no pull-down menus in the operating system itself; rather, there are pop-up menus such as the one pictured in Figure 5.6c. In terms of applications for both operating systems, menus can appear in many different places.

Finally, some menus *tear-off* to become separate windows. This is handy for menus used a great deal, like those in graphics and music notation applications. They are sometimes called *palettes*.

Dialogs and Buttons

Additional navigation devices you will learn to use are dialog boxes and buttons. Dialog boxes appear when the computer needs to be informed about certain choices. Often they will appear when you ask for some task to be

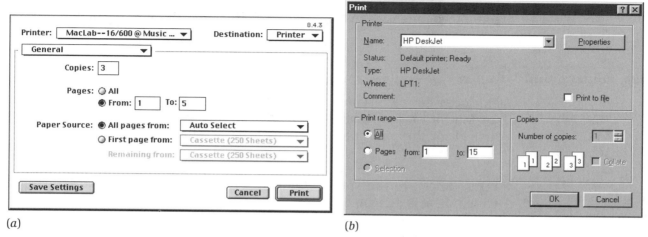

(a)   (b)

Figure 5.7
Dialog boxes for Macintosh
and Wintel computers

executed, and once a choice is made, they disappear. Sometimes you can tell when they are coming. For example, in the Mac OS, menu command items that have an ellipsis (. . .) trailing after the item generally invoke a dialog box. An example of this is the dialog box given as Figure 5.7a for a Macintosh machine. It is displayed when the "Print Desktop . . ." item in the File menu in figure 5.6a is chosen.

The dialog box in Figure 5.7a asks for information before printing. It begins by providing the name of the device to which the print job is headed—in this case a laser printer called "Mac Lab 16/600." We have asked for three copies of the first five pages only. We have placed these numbers into their appropriate box by using the mouse pointer to position a cursor or by using the tab key to move from box to box. The round buttons are called *radio buttons* because they resemble push buttons on old-fashioned radios. They are typically used when mutually exclusive choices are required; when one radio button is clicked, others in the same set are *deselected*.

Another style of button is the *check box,* which we see in a similar print dialog box in Figure 5.7b for a Wintel machine. When you click on the check box next to the Print to File box, you send a message to the printer to print the pages to a file rather than to paper. When all the options are to your liking, you click on the button labeled Print to execute the operation.

Learning To Be a Good Housekeeper

Learning to use the operating system includes learning how to manage resources. One problem that all musicians face is how to organize and manage the growing number of files that become part of your computer's environment. Your local applications (e.g., word processors, notation packages, graphics programs) all generate files. Internet applications like e-mail programs and Web browsers all contribute to the growing number of files that you need to manage. In this section we will consider how files, folders, and volumes work in the GUI operating system. We also include some recommendations for naming these structures and for how to format volumes.

Files, Folders, and Volumes

Lots of detail on file formats is provided later in the book for music files, graphics, the Internet, and more.

You need an understanding of the terms *file*, *folder*, and *volume*. The GUIs for Macintosh and Wintel machines use these terms in similar ways. Note that all of this information relates to how data are organized within the computer.

Files. Files are the smallest unit of organization, or *data structure*, for which there is an icon on a disk. There are three basic kinds of files:

▶ An application (e.g., aural skills program, sequencing and notation packages)

▶ Data files created by these applications

▶ Resource files such as special fonts or other special files that make the application work smoothly

Software activity: "Organizing Your Desktop and Software Backup."

The application itself is the file that contains all the instructions for doing the job. An example would be a music notation program such as Coda's commercial software, Finale. These applications are often designed to create data files; for example, a short music excerpt for a paper or a new composition you are writing for a recital. The icons for data files resemble the icon for its parent application. The data files that an application creates are usually designed to be used by that application alone. For example, a Finale notation file cannot be automatically used by Cakewalk's Overture program. However, there are translation programs that allow for certain popular file types to be exchanged. There also are generic formats that are supported by many companies; for example, a generic MIDI data file format that allows one company's sequencer files to be opened by another company's software.

If any resource files come with an application, they are often automatically placed somewhere on the computer (usually with the operating system software), and probably will not be noticed in day-to-day operation of the software.

The term "directory" is used in the Windows 95 and Unix world, the term "folder" in the Macintosh world.

Folders or Directories. As more applications and data files are added to the computer's storage, there needs to be some way to organize them. Without some plan, files of all types would be scattered about the computer desktop and it would be very difficult to find things when you needed them.

For this reason, the operating system allows the creation of a folder or directory. You have seen these icons in many of the figures presented before. As noted, they emulate real file folders from a filing cabinet, and they can contain any type of file. You can include a folder within another folder in as many hierarchical levels as you wish. You can drag data and application

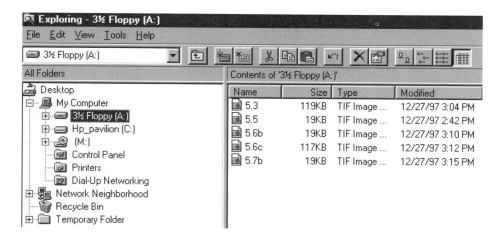

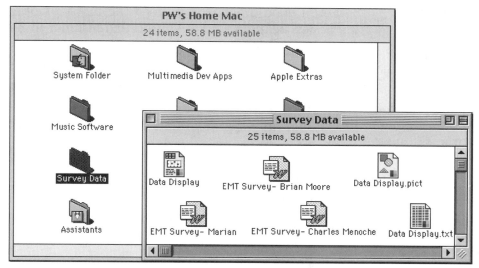

Figure 5.8
Folder hierarchies in operating systems

files into different folders and label these folders in ways that make sense for you.

Volumes. Files and folders are located on local hard disks, on floppy diskettes, on laser-based discs such as CD-ROMs, and on remote servers that might be located in the same building or around the world on the Internet. These storage areas are considered as volumes by the operating system. Why is this important? As you save more and more files to different locations, the operating system needs to keep track of where folders and files are located in such a complex environment. Volume names help do this. Once a name has been given to a file, its folder, and its volume, the operating system keeps track of the location of files by internally assigning each file a specific *pathname*.

In Figure 5.8 we have created two different views of the hierarchy in operating systems. The top view shows Windows displaying its files and folders by name. The left side displays the volumes that the operating system knows about, and the right side shows a detailed view of the floppy "A" drive. The bottom window is an example of a Macintosh operating system displaying its files and folders by icon.

Naming Things

It's possible to define more than one volume on a physical disk. This is known as partitioning, and it makes one physical disk drive look like two or more disk drives to the operating system. Also, be aware that people sometimes use the term "disk" to mean a volume, but this is technically not correct.

Generally, you have reasonable freedom in naming files, folders, and volumes. However, there are a few conventions that we will pass along to you that will make your work easier:

▶ Keep the names of volumes, folders, and files within 10 or 15 characters for readability. You can use as many as 30 characters, but such names are very difficult to work with. If you intend to save files for use on the Internet, a good practice is to keep the first part of a file name (characters to the left of the period if you use extensions) to 8 characters with no space or punctuation.

▶ Avoid using the right slash "/" and a colon ":" in the titles of files or folders. These symbols may interfere with the creation and readability of pathnames.

▶ Develop the habit of naming files with extensions. For instance, it's a good idea to name word processing files with a ".doc" extension or a general MIDI file with a ".mid" extension. You might for example name your resume: "vitae.doc" and the General MIDI version of your school song "almamatr.mid". This becomes quite important if you are developing files that will eventually be transferred to the Internet as part of Web pages. We offer more about these file conventions in Module 7.

Formatting. Storage media like floppies and hard disks cannot accept the information that the computer wants to place on them without preparation. Unlike analog audio tape that is ready to accept anything your cassette tape deck gives it, these media must first be formatted. This means that electronic *tracks* must be placed on the diskette to accept the digital data that come from the computer. Most blank storage media come preformatted from the factory. However, you might occasionally need to format new media or perhaps reformat (completely erase and start from scratch). After selecting the particular media, the "Erase Disk" or "Format Disk" items in the operating system's menus will begin the reformatting process.

See Module 7 for technical information on formatting and disk tracks.

When the operating system encounters some unformatted media or you ask the machine to reformat, a dialog box asks if you want to start the process. At this point you can decide on a name for the volume and (in some operating systems) decide on the kind of format (Macintosh or Windows). Generally, Macintosh and Wintel machines use different formatting schemes. Regrettably, the computing industry has not established a single standard for disk drive formatting. Macintosh machines will read, write, and format Wintel media. The reverse is true only if certain utility programs are in use on the Wintel side.

Working with Files

Now that you have a firm grasp on what the GUI is and how you can use it to organize your desktop, we turn to actually working with files that you either create or obtain from other sources such as the Internet. We cover very important information about opening, closing, deleting, saving, and duplicating files. We conclude this section with cautions about legal file distribution.

Opening, Closing, and Deleting. An important part of the operating system's duties is to allow the opening, closing, and deleting of files. There are many options for doing each of these procedures.

Opening files. If you wish to open an existing file, you can double-click on the file icon directly. The file automatically finds and starts up its parent application. This gives the impression that the data file *is* the application. Not so: the operating system has simply retrieved the application for you. A second common way to open a file is to first open its parent application and then use the "Open" item in the application's File menu. This creates a dialog box that allows you to locate the file in question. A third way is to drag the file icon on top of the parent application icon. This technique is called "drag-and-drop." Most applications will let you open more than one file at one time.

Closing files. You can usually close a file without closing its application by clicking on the *close box* in the window in which the file is displayed. However, in certain Wintel operating systems if you click the close box to close an application's last open window, the application may quit. You can also click on "Close" in the File menu of most applications. You can close the application by choosing the "Quit" item from the File menu in the application. If there is any work that has not been saved, the application will pass on a message to the operating system to ask if you wish to save your work. The entire concept of saving is discussed shortly.

Deleting files. GUI operating systems have convenient ways to delete files. A *trash can* or *recycle bin* icon, to which files can easily be dragged, is displayed on the desktop. Once the file icon is in the trash, you must tell the computer to "empty trash," and it deletes the file. Until it is empty, the trash can continues to hold the files, just in case you change your mind. Only files and folders can be deleted this way. Icons that represent volumes are not erased but are either disconnected from the operating system or ignored.

Saving, Duplicating, and Stealing Files. *We cannot stress enough the absolute importance of developing good habits for saving files.* In our years of experience working with hundreds of students and colleagues, we can safely say that there is nothing so discouraging and frustrating as the loss of critical digital data. This almost always happens because of carelessness with saving and backing up critical data. Please read this section carefully.

Basic Saving. As you are using computers to create data, this informa-

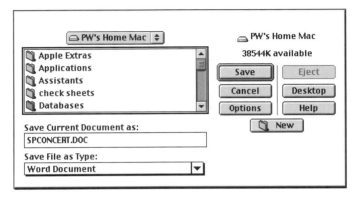

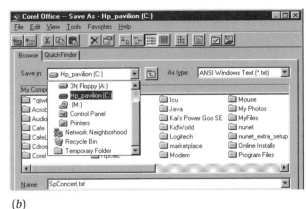

(a)

(b)

Figure 5.9
Save dialog boxes

A common goof is to forget where you have saved a file, or to save a file in the wrong folder. Each operating system provides a helpful menu command to "Find" a file.

Remember that you can save only to those volumes to which you are connected by way of your networking hardware and software.

tion is stored *only temporarily* in the computer's short-term, random-access memory (RAM). It is not generally stored on disk immediately. The computer waits until you tell it to save. A dramatic interruption of the computer's work before you have saved can result in the loss of this work. For instance, if your cat jumps on your power strip, turning off the switch, your computer will shut down and whatever you have done since the last time you saved will be lost. More frequent than a power loss is a software glitch that causes the machine to *crash* (stop operating correctly) or *freeze* (not respond to your commands). Often the only solution is to restart your machine, only to have lost the data that were temporarily in RAM.

This means that you must establish a regular routine of saving work. There are many ways to save your data to hard disks and floppies. Applications that create data always offer a Save menu option, usually under the File menu. When instructed to save, the operating system looks to see if there is a document already established. If the operating system finds that you have saved the file at least once already, it will simply overwrite the old file with your current work. If not, if presents a dialog box that most often demands *three* important bits of information: what you want to *call* your data file; *where* you want to save it; and what *file format* to save it in.

Figure 5.9 presents two Save dialog boxes, one from a Macintosh and the other from a Windows operating system. In the Macintosh box (*a*), we have decided to save a file named "SPCONCERT.DOC" to a hard disk volume called "PW's Home Mac" using the file format "Word Document." Notice that the window under the volume name provides a listing of folders on that volume that are possible locations for the saved file. You can double-click on these to choose them as locations.

In the Windows dialog box (*b*), we have used the ".txt" extension in the name and have asked the software to save the file as a "Text Only" file. The Windows example includes one other change. We have chosen to consider a different place to save the file. To see our options, we have revealed the names of connected volumes to our computer by clicking on the top volume name box and holding the mouse button to see other options. We can save to the local drives, plus we can save to remote servers. You may do this often, saving files in many different places according to the needs of a project or other assignment. Notice how the list always begins with local locations and then lists more remote volumes.

Another option in the operating system's File menu is the "Save As" item. This allows you to save a new version of the file under a new name, in a new location, or perhaps under a different file format. This option is very handy for making backup copies—a most important technique that will be discussed presently. *It is very important to think through these saving options carefully each time you save.*

Cloning files. Each operating system offers another interesting feature—duplication. If you need to create multiple copies of a file, a Macintosh user might use the "Duplicate" item in the File menu for a chosen file. Windows users might use the right mouse button and contextual menu items to accomplish the same thing or use the copy and paste features.

Illegal rip-offs. All of this information about saving and duplicating is very important for successful computing. Software owners should make copies of their legally obtained application software for use on their computers and should never use their original software in their disk drives. Original software should be placed in a safe place so that it can be used to reinstall files if the applications are accidentally deleted or the disk fails.

But—and this is a big *but*—software owners like you do *not* have the right to duplicate commercial software applications and give them away to friends! Although there are a number of gray areas in the legalities of technology, this is not one of them. This is a clear violation of copyright law and is absolutely illegal. *It is stealing!*

This sort of activity has many consequences for computer use. Its widespread practice forces computer software companies to create software protection schemes that make the software difficult and cumbersome to use by legitimate owners. It also drives the price of software higher and creates a vicious circle of pirating when software becomes expensive. (When companies decide on price, many figure that four out of five software copies used will be illegal!)

Some categories of software can be freely distributed. For example, all of the data files that you create with your software are fine to give away to others (provided that it isn't homework for a class!). Certain applications, called *freeware,* are distributed free of charge by individuals who are not interested in commercial gain and simply want to offer a service. A third kind of software is called *shareware.* These files are distributed freely among computer users, but on the honor system. You may try out the software and, if you like it and want to use it frequently, you send the author a modest fee for its use. This fee usually provides support from the author in the form of updates and perhaps help on its use. Freeware and shareware can be found in several places, especially on the Internet and from local software user groups.

Think about where you want to save the file, what you want to name it, and what file format you wish the software to use.

Be sure to also check out "academic" versions of commercial software for which you may be qualified!

Practicing Safe Computing

Backup

The point of backing up files, copying, and duplicating is safety. If you maintain and operate computers correctly, they generally are quite reliable. Unfortunately, there are times computers fail because of outside variables or simply from fatigue. If a backup system is followed, losses will be minimal.

A safe system of backup requires a consistent approach to saving data. We have noted the usual safeguards during the actual time you use the computer to create data—largely the practice of saving frequently. We have suggested installing application software on your hard disk and putting the original diskettes away for safe keeping. We have also mentioned making duplicate copies of data files. But here we suggest that you establish a routine of backing up data files to some additional volume.

How is this routine established? Perhaps the most economical approach is, at the end of each computing session, to insert some sort of removable media and save a copy using the "Save As" menu item provided in the application. This would insure that a copy exists on both the hard drive of your computer and an external volume. Put this backup volume in a safe place and use it each time you create important data.

If you are working in a public site such as a library or school lab, or perhaps on another person's computer, keep *two* volumes with your work on each. When you return to your own system at home, transfer it to your own hard disk. (Hard disks are more reliable than some removables simply because they are not portable. Removables can become damaged, so protect them as much as possible.)

A good rule to follow is always to have a copy of important data on at least two different physical volumes at all times. This guards against the possibility that a drive failure or a corrupted file will wipe out hours of work because there was no backup.

Other approaches to backup require a greater investment of time and money, but they may become important as valuable data become more extensive. Software utility programs are available to automate the backup process. The Windows OS includes a backup utility. These programs allow you to specify which files are to be backed up (for instance, all your data files). When you run this utility, the software determines the number of "removables" you need and then manages the whole operation by prompting you to insert the removable media at the appropriate time. If your backup volume is large enough, you can automate this process without even being around. You can tell the software to back up important files at 3:00 AM on every Sunday and just leave your computer running while you sleep.

The best advice we can give is to first establish a routine system for backing up software inexpensively while you are working on a daily basis, then graduate in stages to more elaborate systems as time goes on. All this backing up may seem time-consuming, but it will pay off in a big way the first time a major disaster (that lost final report or an all-night project) has been averted because of your vigilant approach to data protection.

Viruses

Software activity: "Formatting a Disk and Checking for Viruses"

A section on safe computing practice would not be complete without mention of computing viruses and other malicious problems associated with shared disks and networks. Measures to protect your operating system, application, and data files are now standard practice for active computer users. In your environment, you need to be most careful right from the start.

Viruses are fragments of software designed to attach themselves to other applications or to files. They attack application software, data files, and system software, depending on their nature and intent. Viruses transfer from one computer to another by exposure to other pieces of software and by finding a host as a base of operations.

Possible ways to become infected are:

▶ Through use of other people's volumes that might contain a virus (such as shared floppies)

▶ Through use of a public computer that supports software that has not been routinely monitored

▶ Through use of the Internet and network software that is not well controlled

▶ From commercial CDs, especially those that come with free shareware

Put all your documents in one folder and at least back these up to a Zip or other source on a daily basis—you can always reinstall the software if there is a system crash.

Viruses are not funny. Some are designed to be humorous and not do much damage to files, presenting what may seem to be humorous remarks or events. Others are much more malicious, doing serious damage to important data. Whether malicious or not, computers and software do not function well when foreign code is introduced, and such mischief is completely unacceptable.

Making matters worse, there are other demons afoot. Destructive software such as *worms* and *Trojan horses* is also of concern. Worms are mainly spread through connection to networks. They differ from viruses because they do not require a host and do not attach to legitimate code. Rather, they are self-contained replicating programs that simply clog up the operation of the computer, often bringing it to a halt. Worst of all, Trojan horses are programs disguised as harmless software, but really designed to do something harmful, like erasing a hard disk drive.

Of most concern to the average user are viruses, however, because they are the most common and most easily "caught." Points to remember:

▶ Viruses on computer systems are *not* biological or caused by natural events. They are created by people, some having malicious intentions.

▶ Most viruses are not meant to destroy hardware. Software is the major target of viruses.

▶ There are instances of viruses for all operating systems.

▶ Commercial software is *not* immune from possible viruses, although their presence in such software is rare.

▶ Internet and well-maintained public computer sites are *not* immune from possible viruses; in fact, these are among the most likely places to pick up a virus.

▶ Just because someone says a volume is virus free, don't take their word for it.

Protection. Virus protection software and careful use of volumes and networks are the best protection against virus attack. There are many excellent virus software packages available, many distributed at no cost by computer experts who wish to fight destructive software. This software accomplishes two tasks. First, it scans your hard disks and floppies for any *known* viruses and attempts to repair the damage. Second, it may provide protection against the intrusion of new destructive software, either by providing a small operating system file that watches for suspicious activity or by actively scanning diskettes each time one is inserted into the drive. In choosing which software to use, be sure that there is a clear policy about updating the product when new viruses are detected in the computing community. Such software is only as good as the latest update.

If you are connected to a network, make sure that your files are not open to the public. Do not allow others to write to your hard disk. The software you use to link with other computers will allow you to do this; learn how to use this option.

Other Operating Systems

In this module, we have focused on important concepts for the operating systems that run on Macintosh and Wintel machines. They represent the major operating systems for personal computers today. As important as these operating systems are, there are others in current use that are worth noting.

UNIX

Perhaps the most important of these is the UNIX (pronounced "you-nicks") operating system, developed by the AT&T Bell Research Laboratories in the early 1970s. It was designed initially for powerful scientific workstations. With the increased power of today's personal computers, UNIX can now realistically be used on personal machines, and it continues to be used for high-end workstations such as those from Silicon Graphics, Hewlett-Packard, Sun, and IBM. In its basic form, it employs a "command-line" user interface much like the operating systems used prior to GUI systems.

A few important music applications for UNIX machines have been created by music researchers, theorists, and electronic music composers. These applications are generally designed for advanced technical work with sound. Figure 5.10 displays an example of a sound-editing program that uses the IRIX operating system, a version of UNIX that runs on Silicon

ASIDE

Linux is a popular UNIX-like OS that can be installed on Macs and Wintels as an alternate OS.

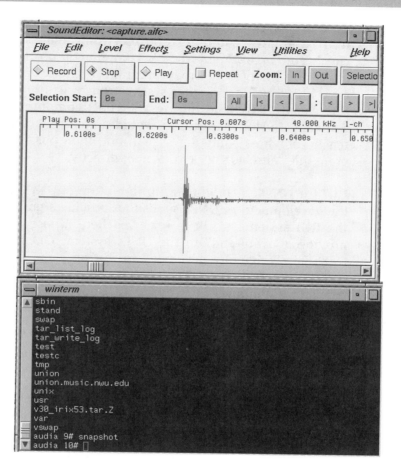

Figure 5.10
Sound editor using a
UNIX operating system

Graphics, Inc., computers. Notice the command line interface in the lower window.

UNIX's strength lies in its ease of use for those with advanced programming knowledge. It uses an *object* approach, where units of software create flexible building blocks for designing applications that run under the system. It also supports multiple users and advanced multitasking capabilities that permit the computer to work on more than one job at the same time. Its weakness is its difficulty for the normal computer user to learn. It also has been plagued by multiple versions that compete with each other for general acceptance.

UNIX and the Internet. You may encounter some UNIX as you use the Internet. Many of the servers that provide Web page support, electronic mail, newsgroups, or file transfer services use UNIX as their operating system. Although Internet software clients for Macintosh and Wintel machines are designed to receive data from such servers and present information to you using the GUI, there are times when you may need to know a little UNIX and be able to find a listing of UNIX commands for the computer to which you are connected.

For example, perhaps you are visiting a friend at a location far away from your own computer and electronic mail account and you want to check your mail. Your friend's computer is on the Internet, but you can't easily use his personal mail program to check your mail. You could, however, link to your computer system from your friend's by using a UNIX routine called "Telnet" to link to your host computer that has the mail server software. In doing this, you would actually be using UNIX commands to reach your host computer system and then possibly run a UNIX mail program like "elm" to check your mail directly.

GUI for UNIX. A bright star in the future of UNIX as an operating system is the development of UNIX shells that provide a graphical interface much like the GUI systems we have reviewed here. These are add-on programs that provide a "front-end" to the UNIX system. One example is a shell called NeXTStep, originally developed to run on NeXT computers (now a part of Apple Computers). Other GUI UNIX implementations of interest are IBM AIX and XWindows (a freeware GUI operating system for UNIX originally developed at MIT).

Software for Communication

"May I send you an e-mail with my rehearsal dates?"

"What did you think about that posting on the comp.music.midi newsgroup the other day about copyright permission?"

"Why don't I send you this notation file over the network?"

"Did you download that Beatles MIDI file from some Internet source?"

"Have you seen the new audition schedule on the Chicago Symphony's Web site?"

A few years ago, questions like these might have seemed like pure nonsense to musicians. Today, such questions are commonplace as individuals go about the daily business of making music. The focus of this module is on the software that supports computer-based networking. It directly follows our opening module on operating systems because computer communication is directly related to how the operating systems are designed. Today's operating systems have communication as a major part of their mission.

Figure 6.1 displays the desktops for typical operating systems that we studied in Module 5. In 6.1*a*, the Macintosh OS 8 displays links to the Internet along the right side of the screen. Notice the icons that represent browsers and mail programs as well as helper programs that are designed to assist in the setup of the computer to reach the Internet. In 6.1*b*, we see a Windows 95 operating system with links to Netscape's Internet browser as well as to other specialized services on the Internet that we will discuss in this module.

The Power of Networks

Why is computer-based communication so important to the musician? The answer lies in the richness of information that is available "out

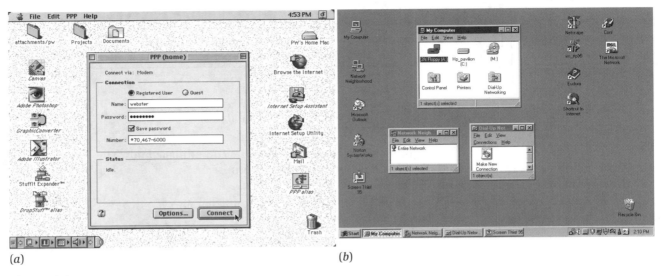

(a)   (b)

Figure 6.1
Network links in operating systems

The Internet's history is noted in the timeline for this viewport, and details of its operation are covered in Module 7.

there." Improving the way we teach, perform, create, and experience music is the primary reason for exploring music technology and the links to people and data that technology provides. This is all possible because of the network resources that are being created, the musicians that "serve up" the information, the computers themselves, and the rethinking of time and space.

Individuals nationally and internationally are being linked by cables, radio frequencies, fiber optics, and satellites. You are able to "reach out and touch someone" anywhere, anytime from a phone, TV, computer desktop, or even—before long—through a Dick Tracy-type digital watch! The basis for the information superhighway of connectivity for computers is already here: It's called the *Internet*. The Internet is a collection of networked computers around the world that are linked to each other, forming a huge network of networks. Government and industry want to further integrate the networks into a cohesive system with enough power to make digital video and sound communication commonplace.

This is why computer operating systems are being made with built-in network links. As this trend continues, your desktop will come to represent a large metacomputer, a computer of computers, that not only organizes your local computer space but also puts the many resources of the Internet at your disposal.

Serving Up Information from Servers to Clients

Computers can be *servers* or *clients*:

▶ A computer as a *server* maintains data and deals with requests from other computers for these data. Server computers can be as large as mainframes or as small as a personal computer on your desk. Musicians around the world are pouring information into server machines that help us all understand our art better. You yourself may soon become a server of information as you develop Web pages, contribute to news groups, and make files available.

▶ Other computers and software fill the role of *client*. You have access to an array of client software that has the intelligence to navigate the Internet and access servers to retrieve and exchange data. It is this software that will be explained in the coming pages.

Another major advantage of client-server relationships is the independence of machines. It matters little what kind of machine is doing the serving and what kind of machine is doing the receiving. A UNIX machine might provide services to a Macintosh or Wintel machine or vice versa. Client and server software are designed to handle these multiple platforms.

Small and Fast Computers

The computer world is rapidly downsizing, moving from desktop computers to transportables, transportables to laptops, and now laptops to personal digital assistants, or PDAs. Examples of these include the Palm Pilot and small WindowsCE palmtop computers that fit in the palm of your hand. Companies have already designed small, network computers (NCs) for TV. Your pocket calculator is giving way to an intelligent PDA with full word processing, spreadsheet, database, communications, and personal management software. It doesn't even have to be plugged into the wall; wireless connectivity will let it connect to the Internet as you stroll in the park, sit in your favorite coffee house, or relax during a concert intermission. Think about what impact this has on the way you may communicate with your fellow musicians.

Changing the Way We Collaborate: New Ideas of Time and Space

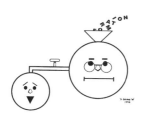

© 1995 D. Brian Williams

© 1995 D. Brian Williams

Can you imagine where this is heading? There will be servers all over the world (you won't care where they are) holding rich digital resources of documents, video, imagery, recorded music, MIDI and sound samples, music notation, and multimedia instruction modules. The globe will be encompassed by an international networking infrastructure to provide connectivity to these multimedia servers. You will be able to plug in or tune in to the network at any place or any time, by using your desktop computer or PDA, and then run your client software to access anything or converse with anyone in the world.

These advances in communication change the way we learn from one another. In years past, learning was designed in a hierarchical style where most information was passed down from an expert to the unknowing learner. This model was designed for the industrial age to insure a disciplined work force that could follow directions. Thankfully, this model is now giving way to a more cooperative, collaborative one that values networking and more informal, nonlinear working relationships. New technologies facilitate cooperative learning and mentorships with any authority you can find in cyberspace! Plus, you can learn from any location. Such technology helps us rethink the time and place matrix of collaborative work.

The matrix in Figure 6.2 shows how education might change over the coming years. Each cell represents a different environment that could be constructed, by use of networking and other technology, to facilitate sharing

	Same place	**Different place**
Same time	Class & meeting space	Virtual class & meeting space
Different time	Virtual labs, libraries & media space	Remote coordination & collaboration

Figure 6.2
The time and place matrix of collaborative activities

We present more about wireless connectivity in Module 8.

Some network surfers call the universe of connectivity "cyberspace;" others call it the "telecosm." "Cyberspace" was coined by William Gibson in his sci-fi novel *Neuromancer*; "telecosm" was coined by futurist author George Gilder.

information. Let's imagine that you are in charge of a conference on piano performance and plan to use technology to help with its design.

Same time/same place. The first cell represents the most traditional way to share information. Conferees all gather in one room at one time to hear a presentation. However, computers are already changing even the way a traditional same time/same place meeting is conducted. Local computers could be used by the participants to communicate with one another. An electronic whiteboard (video display similar to a traditional chalkboard) in the room accepts input from any participant's computer; you could create your own windows on the whiteboard, draw diagrams, and/or modify the ideas and contributions of others. Traditional presentation software, such as the ones described in Viewport VIII, could be used to highlight talks. Internet access could be provided to attendees for their consultation.

Same time/different place. Under this model, the presentation is still held at the same time but the attendees are not required to be in the same place. Using the power of network connectivity and advances in cable TV and telephony, collaboration takes on an expanded meaning. Any group of people can be brought together for a meeting at the same *time*, without regard to *place*. We can hold text-based conferences, audio conferences (i.e., phone conferencing), and full audio and video conferencing right from our desktops. We could offer tutoring remotely. Mentors or experts can be brought into a classroom, a meeting place, or a "virtual meeting room" from anywhere in the world.

Figure 6.3 displays two Northwestern University technology students who have worked with a team of professors and programmers to create an interactive *netjam* using MIDI. Using the Internet, musicians can improvise together with MIDI devices at the same time but in vastly different places. Imagine a bass line coming from England, percussion from the United States, and the piano solo from Ghana, with everyone hearing what the other is doing in real time!

Figure 6.3
Matt Moller (left) and Canton Becker working with their MIDI program that allows jam sessions with other musicians on the Internet
(Chicago Tribune photo by John Bartley)

Different time/different place. Computers enable us to ask the question: Why must all the "attendees" gather around their computer screens at the same time? Couldn't we use computers to allow them to access the presentation information whenever they want?

Electronic mail (e-mail) is the most widely used of any of the different-time, different-place technologies. Through service providers for the Internet, we can communicate with any of our fellow musicians. E-mail has a great social leveling or "equalizing" effect. When you interact only through text with people whom you have never met, the exchange is free from visual stereotypes. Students can talk with professional artists, performing musicians, and composers anywhere in the world. A 12-year-old could maintain an e-mail conversation with some of our distinguished musicians such as Ed Asmus, Libby Larsen, or David Cope without ever revealing his or her identity. The ability to initiate and maintain a person-to-person conversation depends solely on the level of expertise and credibility demonstrated in the electronic exchange. Of course, it is possible too that negative biases can result from a lack of face-to-face dialog.

You could set up a newsgroup about the material for your piano conference. Via e-mail, this might create a long-lasting exchange on the topic of piano performance and new developments in techniques and scholarship. You could publish the conference program on your Web site (more about Web sites in a moment), and anyone could connect to the Internet and obtain a copy of any one of the presentations, text and graphics, from your server. Through hyperlinks, more than one server could be involved, so that information could be shared from various presenters around the world.

Different time/same place. As a variation on the last model, all of the conference materials could be stored at one site, the Internet server at your institution, for example. You might include virtual libraries and museums about piano performance at the site—any application that lets musicians access a common location remotely any time they choose. You could connect to thousands of servers featuring full-text documents, abstracts, on-line library catalogs, MIDI-music files, digital-sound samples, and software applications. You could also include electronic information kiosks that might offer music instruction and multimedia software that is available for self-study. You might include creative projects, either individually or collaboratively. Traditional research papers are becoming augmented by hypermedia projects that allow participants to express concepts that represent the rich information resources available to them. "Drop" folders that act as a gathering place for conference documents could be maintained.

Connecting Your Computer to the Internet and Setting Up the Software

Modules 7 and 8 contain more detailed information on options for connecting to the Internet and the hardware to make this happen.

So how do you begin to take advantage of all this power? The first step is to physically link your computer to some kind of Internet connection: establishing an on-ramp to the superhighway of information. Internet service is provided to us by some kind of Internet Service Provider (ISP). If you are in an academic setting or in business, it is likely that your institution will provide you with this service without cost. If you are on your own, you will need to secure the services of a commercial ISP such as EarthLink or SprintNet. Some commercial services such as America Online and Microsoft Network provide both an Internet connection and additional services such as special databases and electronic mail systems.

Once connected physically, you will need to inform both your operating system software and the client software about the details of your ISP connection. We provide some basic information below about how to do this; however, each particular personal computer and service provider will have its own specific instructions.

Physical Connection. Figure 8.3 in Module 8 provides an overview of the four principal ways that you can connect to other computers. In this module, we will assume that you will be connecting to the Internet either remotely from home using a modem (Route C) or directly from your school of office network facilities (Route D).

It's quite likely that your Internet service provider will give you all this information or supply you with prepared software or installation programs that will take care of this procedure for you. We take the time to include an overview here so that you can understand just how your computer becomes a part of the Internet.

Setting Up Your Software. Figure 6.4 provides a sense of how to complete the setup of your operating system for Internet access. Machines on the Internet, including your own computer if it is connected directly and not through a modem, must have unique numerical addresses for all the connections to work properly. Sometimes these numbers are permanently assigned, as is often the case with direct connections, or they are temporarily assigned, as is often the case when you use a modem connection. These addresses are called Internet Protocol (IP) numbers and unique Internet names (Domain Names). Each operating system has a small program which will need specific information about how you are going to connect to the Internet (remotely or by direct connection) and what IP number approach is correct for your computer. Figure 6.4 displays the route taken to establish this connection for a typical Wintel computer.

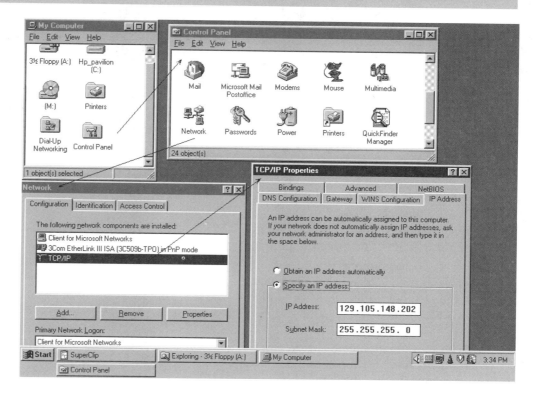

Figure 6.4
Setting up the operating
system with an Internet
Protocol (IP) number

Client-Server Model: Web Browsers and Other Clients

Now let's take a closer look at a few of the Internet clients that you might
find useful, not only for the imaginary conference profiled above but also
for your personal growth as a musician.

In Table 6.1, we have provided a selection of the major software services that run on the Internet, together with the names of typical clients
with their associated servers that support that service. We also include a
brief description of the network services themselves. Understand that
these client-server services run independently on the Internet. The Internet is the transmission vehicle, and these client-server programs and their
respective data are the content of the Internet. It's really amazing that all
this different content doesn't get confused and that everything works as
well as it does! Module 7 explains just how the messages over the Internet
work.

The first kind of Internet service that we list, World Wide Web—commonly known as "the Web"—is the most pervasive service on the Internet
today. So popular are these Web browsers that they are beginning
to include other Internet services such as electronic mail, file transfers, and newsgroups as an integral part of the browser software. The
other kinds of Internet services that we list are still important parts of the
Internet scene in their own right and deserve our attention as independent clients.

Be sure to check Module 8
for more information on setting up your operating system software for connection.

Table 6.1

Internet Services	Wintel Clients	Macintosh Clients	Server
World Wide Web Interactive text and graphic information, as well as supportive audio, video, and animation	Netscape Navigator Microsoft Internet Explorer	Netscape Navigator Microsoft Internet Explorer	Web or HTTP
Electronic Mail and Listservs Exchange of private messages; Listservs automatically forward mail from others interested in a particular subject	Eudora	Eudora	POPMail
File Transfers Ability to exchange files of text, graphics, sounds, music scores, and other file formats	WS_FTP	Fetch	FTP
Newsgroups Public messages that center on a particular topic of interest; questions can be submitted and members can respond	NewsXpress, Gravity	NewsWatcher	USENET News
Push Technology News and information delivered to you each time you log in. You subscribe to "channels" of information	PointCast	PointCast	Specialized Servers
Chat Groups Interactive conversations based on a particular topic	PERCH, WSIRC, AOL Messenger	Ircle and AOL Messenger	IRC or MUD

Web Browsing Software and Web-Based Multimedia

ASIDE

This idea had been considered before, as we will note in Viewport VIII. Vannevar Bush wrote about this concept in 1945. Ted Nelson's Xanadu hypermedia project was first proposed in the 1960s.

Perhaps the most exciting service on the Internet is access to multimedia resources. Servers connected by the Internet that provide text information augmented by still graphics, animation, sounds, and movies are called *Web servers*, and the clients that access the servers are called *browsers*. Web servers support links between each other and can support links embedded *within* documents. You might be reading about Scott Joplin's ragtime music on a New Orleans server and encounter a *hot link* that links you to a Web server in Paris that has some digital pictures of Joplin as a youth. Still other buttons might play sound clips of early ragtime music, show a score, or perhaps play a short movie—all of which might be "served" from different locations in the world.

This whole concept first began with linking text information only. Created at the European Particle Physics Laboratory (CERN) in Switzerland in the early 1990s, the idea of a net-based hypertext system quickly caught the imaginations of computer scientists around the world. The idea was to have *hot links* within documents on one computer that would call into action documents on another computer. The idea soon began to expand to include not only hypertext, but also graphics, sounds, and digital movie technology.

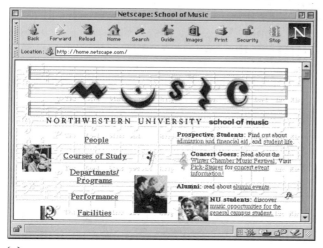

(a)　　　　　　　　　　　　　　　　　　　　(b)

Figure 6.5
View of (a) a typical home page with (b) its HTML source codes.

We will deal with HTML in greater depth in Viewport VIII.

We will provide more information on how to create Web pages in Modules 8 and 27.

Thus was born the concept of a World Wide Web (WWW) of computers connected by the Internet to share multimedia resources.

How Are Web Sites Made? If you wanted to promote your piano performance conference, you might create a *Web site* on your ISP or campus Web server. A Web site is simply a folder that contains files of text, graphics, sounds, and movies about the conference that are designed to be shared on the Internet. You might also build in some links to other Web sites that contain information related to the conference.

Your ISP would provide you with an account and space on a particular computer that was established as a Web server. You would develop files of information locally on your computer, then transfer them to your account on the ISP computer. You, of course, would have complete control over the content of your Web site, and only you would be able to change it.

The key documents in this folder are text files that use a combination of your text information and special codes or tags called HyperText Markup Language (HTML). These tags help merge your text with media such as pictures, sounds, and movies. One HTML document is your *home page*, the first thing a person sees when they connect to your Web site. From there, the home page would direct the person visiting your site to other HTML documents in the Web site or to other HTML documents in other parts of the world.

Figure 6.5 displays an example of a typical home page. The first graphic (a) displays the page as you might view it from a typical browser client. Note the text, graphics, and underlined words that represent the links. Screen (b) shows the document that actually created this home page. It looks a little strange, but once you understand some of the codes, it makes sense. It is actually a HyperText Markup Language (HTML) document that defines the layout of the page and the location of graphics, sounds, and movies. You will need to learn the simple codes to do this in order to create Web pages.

More on IPs and URLs in Module 7.

Software activity: "Surfing and Searching the Web"

Graphics on the Internet are in either the GIF or the JPEG format. See Module 7 and Viewport IV for more information on graphics formats.

Basic Browser Operation. *URLs.* As you might guess from the description of Web sites, browsers locate and display the contents of files from locations around the world. The key to this is the browser's ability to manage the addresses of files and the servers on which they are stored. Remember our description of IP addresses for machines on the Internet? Web files also have addresses, and they are called *Uniform Resource Locators* (URLs). URLs point to the Web servers that store the files.

Look again at Figure 6.5*a*. The line of information just below the navigation buttons contains an example of this kind of address. The URL is the key to traveling around the Internet when you are using the World Wide Web service. If you read the URL from left to right, the "http://" is the code that identifies the address as Web-based. The remainder of the address pinpoints the Web server computer and the exact pathname (folders and subfolders) to the file to be displayed. This is why some URLs are very long and cumbersome, especially if you are trying to reach a specific file that is deep in the server's hierarchy. Fortunately, browser software, with special "bookmarks," helps to minimize the need to always type these addresses.

Where is Home? A special URL is the "home" location, a site from which you would like your browser to always begin its journey. For the browser software in Figure 6.5*a*, the edit menu contains a "Preferences" item that in turn contains a place for you to specify the home location. When you install a fresh copy of the browsing software, the home location may be the URL for the company that produced the software, created the operating system, or made the computer. These home locations can all be changed, or you can specify that no home location be used in favor of a blank page.

Navigation Buttons. A line of buttons just above the URL is the most often used feature of browsers. These are the buttons that aid basic navigation. As you explore various links to sources of information, you will need ways to move backwards and forwards and perhaps return to the home page. You are also given a Stop button to terminate the search for a link or the downloading of a file. You can print a complete page of information at any time (the whole page created by the author, not just the portion of the page you are viewing), and you can ask the browser to load or reload images to the screen from the remote server. The File menu provides an option for opening a dialog box into which you can type a particular URL if you already know it.

Viewing Window. If you have had any experience with using Web browsers, you have quickly discovered that the authors of Web pages usually create more content for a page than can fit on your screen. You may need to adjust the size of your viewing window to see the entire page and, if that doesn't do the trick, you may need to use the vertical and horizontal scroll bars to see everything. The scrolling of windows is very common when you explore Web pages.

Two other points about viewing windows. Some Web authors make use of multiple scrolling windows within one page. These are called "frames," and they will require the manipulation of multiple sets of scrolling bars. Also, realize that it is possible to have multiple Web sites open at once with multiple windows—much as a word processor allows multiple documents to be open.

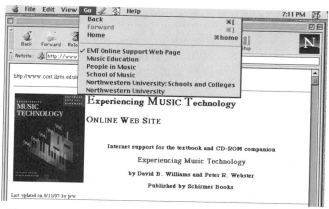

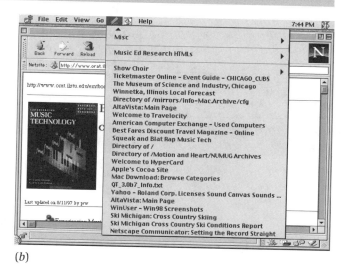

(a)

(b)

Figure 6.6
Saved links and bookmarks

Saving. The File menus on most browsing software allow you to save a page that you are viewing. Two formats are possible. One format is the text of the actual page you are viewing; the second format is the HTML code that created the page that also includes the text, but surrounded by markings similar to those in Figure 6.5*b*. The former option would be appropriate if you are doing research and need the basic text information for documentation. The latter option would be useful if you wanted to see how a page was constructed.

What about saving the graphics you see? You can save any graphic by clicking on the graphic (hold the mouse button down on a Macintosh or use the right mouse button on a Wintel machine) and using the pop-up menu to save it to your preferred location.

Previously Visited Links and Bookmarks. As you use your browser, visiting different URLs, the software keeps track of where you have been. This "crumb trail" of site addresses is kept in a menu. The menu actually displays the written titles of the pages the Web author assigned; the software retains the URL for these pages safely out of view. Figure 6.6*a* displays a menu from a typical browser that contains the names of sites visited since the browser has been open. Revisiting these locations can be accomplished by simply choosing the desired menu item. These menu items are good only until the browser window is closed or you quit the browser.

If you want to keep track of visited sites on a more long-term basis, you can create *bookmarks* or *favorites*. Figure 6.6*b* displays the bookmark menu system for a typical browser. You see the titles of pages that we have asked the software to save as bookmarks. It's also possible to save the bookmarks in a separate file. This creates an HTML document that is made up of the bookmark names and their URLs for finding the locations of the sites. Web browsers provide bookmark editors for helping you manage large numbers of bookmarks. Bookmark files can be exported and imported for easy exchange with others.

Preferences. Each major browser allows you to set the viewing and operation preferences desired. You can choose font type, size, and color. This is

Saving sounds and movies can be more difficult. When you ask to audit or view sound and movie files, your browser downloads these files to a location in your system folder called the cache.

ASIDE

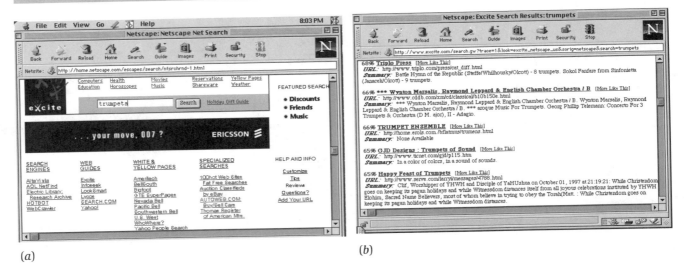

(a)   (b)

Figure 6.7
Typical search engine

We will present the use of Web browsers as multimedia authoring tools in Viewport VIII.

As Web browsers merge with your operating system, you may soon find that you cannot tell the difference.

possible because the HTML code that creates the page does not specify such matters, so the user can specify these options. Preferences can also be set for the appearance of the buttons and the way you wish images to be loaded (if at all).

You can also set how long you wish links to be active. The software "remembers" what sites you have visited in the more recent history of using the browser by coloring that link a different color from a link that has not been visited. For example you might be working on a project dealing with the history of trumpets, visiting as many sites each day as you can. Browsers keep track of these sites (even after the software has been quit) to help you remember where you have been. You can set the expiration date of these visited links in the preferences section of the browser.

Opening Local Files. A very useful feature of browsers is their ability to open HTML files locally. You can actually run an entire Web site right on your own machine for your own use. This is useful in two ways. First, you can "try out" the files that might make up your own site before you mount them on a server somewhere in cyberspace for everyone to see. The other way is that you can use your browser as a kind of local, multimedia authoring system. If you wanted to use the browser as a presentation system with multimedia extensions, this would be a cost-effective way to do it.

Searching the Web. Among the many amazingly powerful services found within the Web are the search engine servers. These are actually Web sites that are dedicated to helping you find other sites of interest. They employ a highly efficient system of indexing using the names and initial text contained in Web pages from around the world. To find a list of search engine sites, you click on the browser's "Search" button. This brings you to a particular search engine site that the browser chooses. The page also contains a link to other search engine sites, just in case you don't like the one that automatically comes up.

Figure 6.7a displays the search engine "Excite" called into action by clicking on a browser's search button. Notice the listing of other search engine sites and other sources of information on the Internet. In this example, we have decided to use the "Excite" site. We are interested in trumpet playing in Vienna, Austria, and have typed in the term "trumpets" to learn about all the sites that might help us. Figure 6.7*b* reveals a portion of the first page of *hits* for the term "trumpets." Ten links are supplied at one time, and we have the option of exploring the next ten and the next until the 9,450 sites are explored!

Searches can return literally thousands of hits on an entered term if it is as general as this, so the more specific you are the better. Using quotation marks around a descriptive term is a much better strategy. This will force the search engine to look for that exact phrase. We entered the term "trumpet playing in Vienna" on a second search and this produced only a few hits and led to the exact sites we wanted.

Some search engines have advanced search features that let you narrow your search with other strategies. The AltaVista search engine from Compaq is a good example of a site that offers sophisticated search options. If you have never used a search engine on the Web to investigate something of interest, try it!

Utility Applications and Plug-ins. Web browsers often require help to play and display certain types of multimedia files. Clients by themselves may not have the ability to play all types of audio files, display digital movies, and uncompress various data files. Programs or utilities written to work with browser software are often required.

Utility applications are generally independent software programs that are called into action by a browser to accomplish a particular task. For instance, if you stumble upon a Web site that offers a large number of compressed files concerning the music of Haydn for you to download, you might be tempted to ask the site to send them to your hard drive. The browser software will likely not be able to automatically uncompress all the files for you, unless it is helped by an independent decompression application like Alladin's Stuffit Expander.

"Plug-ins" are similar in function to utility applications except that they are small programs designed to work exclusively with the browser and cannot be used by themselves. They are actually extensions of the browsers, and you rarely know that they are even in use. Such plug-in programs are placed in a special folder next to the browser application itself. Typical plug-ins for music include RealNetwork's RealPlayer plug-in for playback of compressed audio files and Apple's QuickTime plug-in for digital movies. You must tell your browser software to use these programs to help out. Figure 6.8 displays the preference window from a typical browser, which "maps" the use of both applications and plug-ins. Notice that you must identify the file type and then the application or plug-in to use. In this example, an audio file in AIFF format is routed to a plug-in called "LiveAudio" and graphics in TIFF format will open with the application "JPEGView."

In order to "play" multimedia programs on the Web, companies like Macromedia and Microsoft provide plug-ins for their authoring software; see Viewport VIII.

To find the latest applications and plug-ins for your browser software, check the home page for the company that distributes your browser.

Web-Based Newsgroups, E-mail, and Interactive Capabilities

Additional Internet Services. An important trend in modern browser software is the addition of other Internet services besides Web browsing. For

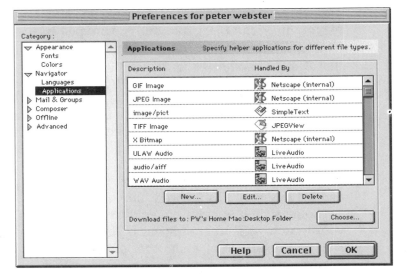

Figure 6.8
Web browser preference settings for applications and plug-ins

instance, you can join, read, and contribute to newsgroups as well as send e-mail messages to others—all from your Web browser.

In Figure 6.9*a* we display the Message Center from Netscape's Communicator. Here, you can subscribe to newsgroups and manage your e-mail. The other graphic (*b*) displays a message from one of the newsgroups that appears in a separate window. In order to use mail and newsgroup capabilities with browsers, you must supply the names of the servers for mail and news as part of the setup for the browser.

It's clear that Web browser companies would like to have all your Internet services rolled into one product or set of interrelated products. The downside to all this is that the browser application continues to get larger in terms

Figure 6.9
Browser support for news reading and e-mail

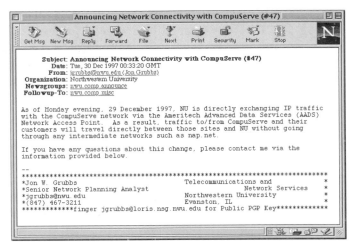

(a)   *(b)*

of application size and the amount of RAM needed to operate. Because of this, compromises are often made in the special features that independent e-mail and newsreader clients routinely offer (see below). Nevertheless, basic news reading and e-mail services make Web browsers more versatile for those who want a basic, all-in-one application. This is especially appealing if everything is integrated into the operating system of the computer.

Interactive Capabilities with Java and JavaScript. Web browsers support interactivity by offering Web authors the opportunity to write small programs embedded in their Web pages. For instance, if you wanted to write a routine that might offer an interactive lesson on structure in the music of Bartók, you could create some JavaScript that would give users the power to see animation, receive feedback on entered information, and hear and see custom music excerpts based on information provided. You would likely use the Java programming language developed by Sun Microsystems to create this program, called an *applet*. The applet would call into action the Java interpreter that is built into the browser. There are also premade applets created by programmers using the Java programming language that can be plugged into your Web page.

One downside to Java is that it is a relatively complicated, high-level language, similar to C^{++}, and it may be difficult to learn for a novice. To help with this program, Netscape Corporation developed JavaScript to work as a scripting language within its Netscape browser software. JavaScript is much easier to learn and provides the interactive capabilities needed by many Web developers. JavaScript is officially endorsed by Sun as a complement to Java and is supported, at least in part, by many other browsers.

Figure 6.10 displays a screen from a Web page that teaches how to connect MIDI devices to a computer. In addition to providing graphics and text that explain what is connected to where, an interactive animated quiz is written as a Java applet that allows you to test your knowledge of the connections. The author asks you to click on the places you think the connections should be made, and the Web page responds by drawing in the cables for the connection (if you were correct). This kind of intelligence is built right into the Web page and the host browsing software. It requires no interaction with the original Web site that supplied the page.

We will present more information about the details of Java, JavaScript, and ActiveX in Viewport VIII.

Other Internet Clients

Web browsers are not the only clients that work on the Internet. Return to Table 6.1 and note the other five services that we have included. Three of the five services (news reading, e-mail, and file transfer) are also supported by Web browsers to some extent as we have noted; however, we include more robust examples of each as found in independent clients. We end this module with the two other Internet services of interest, push technology and chat groups.

Software activities: "Using E-mail, Listservs, and Newsgroups on the Internet"

Electronic Mail and Listservs. Figure 6.11 displays a screen with the Windows version of an e-mail client program from Qualcomm called Eudora Pro. Eudora Pro works with a mail server computer provided by your ISP.

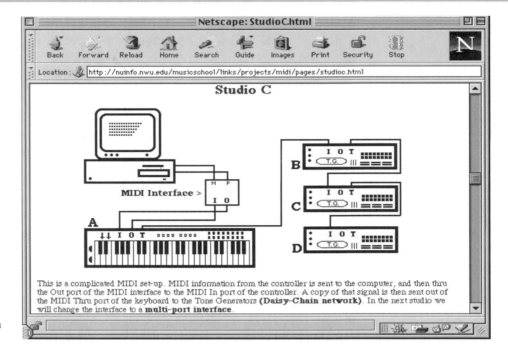

Figure 6.10
Example of a Java applet
embedded in a Web page
to interactively build a
MIDI network
(Peter Raschke, Northwestern
University)

The server is always on the lookout for incoming mail from the Internet. If it gets a message intended for you, the server simply waits for you to log in to check your mail. The server sends the complete message immediately to your client software, in this case, Eudora Pro. Some of the more advanced features of e-mail clients are:

▶ Multiple mailboxes for messages coming in and going out

▶ The option of creating different signatures and personalities for outgoing mail

▶ The ability to attach files with an e-mail message. (The client will automatically translate the file to a format the Internet will understand. When the same or similar client receives a file, it will automatically translate it back to the original format!)

▶ Reports of received messages, with information about who sent them, time of arrival, and relative size

▶ Quick ways to forward, redirect, or copy files

▶ Nicknames for correspondents

▶ Filters that allow you to direct mail to specific mailboxes depending on defined variables

As in many client programs, editing a file is like working in your favorite word processor. There is no need to resort to cumbersome line commands. You can easily cut and paste from one kind of document to another, as well. Printing support is quite flexible, as are the settings for screen dis-

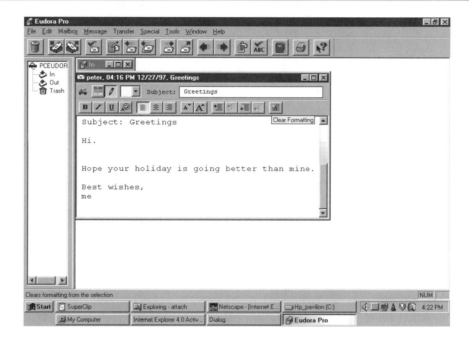

Figure 6.11
Eudora Pro
(Qualcomm Inc.
[Mac/Windows])

Music and technology
periodicals frequently
publish listings of the
many listservs in music.
The number grows expo-
nentially each year!

play. If you leave your computer on for extended periods of time and you have a continuous connection to the Internet, the client program can be configured to run continuously in the background, checking the mail server at specified intervals to look for new mail.

A *listserv* is a listing of e-mail addresses of people who want to automatically receive e-mail messages about a particular topic. You may be interested in the latest news in the music theory profession. You learn that there is a listserv on this subject at Harvard University. This means that someone at Harvard has placed a simple piece of software on one of their computers (the server) that maintains a directory of e-mail addresses of people like you (the client).

To subscribe, you send an e-mail message to this machine, asking that you be placed on the list. You will soon get a response back from the Harvard computer confirming that your name has been added, together with instructions about how to unsubscribe from the list if you want. From that moment on, you will receive a copy of every e-mail message sent to this particular listserv at Harvard, whether you want it or not! Each time you check your mail, you will see the activity on the list. You can read the messages and reply to a few if you want. Your response is sent to everyone on the list. If you subscribe to a number of listservs, you will likely need the help of intelligent e-mail clients to help filter and sort your mail because of the large amount of mail listservs can generate.

File Transfers. We have already noted that browser and e-mail clients can support the transfer of files. This can also be done by independent clients designed for this purpose, often more efficiently. Two such programs are Fetch for the Macintosh, Figure 6.12*a*, and WS_FTP, Figure 6.12*b*, for Windows.

These clients are designed to access computers on the Internet that are set up to be FTP (File Transfer Protocol) servers. FTP sites support the pub-

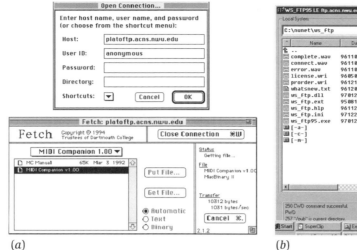

(a)

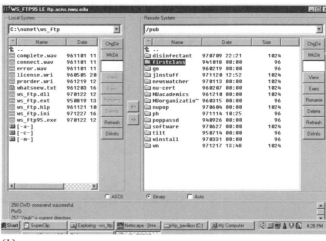

(b)

Figure 6.12
FTP clients for accessing files
(a) Fetch
(Trustees of Dartmouth College [Mac])
(b) WS_FTP
(Ipswitch, Inc.)

You might use FTP clients when you develop a Web page. This software may offer the best way to transfer files from your computer to the account at the ISP. Web authoring software may also have FTP capabilities built in.

lic distribution of files, usually on the basis of a theme or topic. Suppose you decided to make a number of files relating to your piano performance conference available before the meeting. You could use FTP server software on a computer provided by your ISP. You would establish folders with files related to the conference on the server computer. Registrants would point their FTP client software at your server by entering the address of that machine, and fetch, or FTP, the files.

The Fetch program, Figure 6.12a, begins by having the user enter the name of the host (top screen). Also required is a user ID and password. Most public FTP servers are set up to be *anonymous* sites so that no password is required; however, they can also be made private by establishing specific users and passwords.

The bottom screen shows how Fetch is used to select a specific folder, *MIDI Companion 1.00* in our example, and then a specific file. Clicking on the Get button to the right begins the transfer. Notice the status section to the right that indicates that the file is being transferred at a rate of 1,031 bytes per second. The speed depends largely on the kind of connection to the Internet. The Put button is used if someone wants to add a file to your computer.

The same kind of support is offered by WS_FTP (Figure 6.12b). Notice the two columns of information, *Local System* and *Remote System*. A conference registrant could specify your host as the remote system, select the file, choose a location on his or her local computer, and use the arrow buttons in the middle to download a file. The process would be reversed for transferring a file to your system.

Groups of files can be transferred at once. As with e-mail clients, translation of files from one format to another can be handled by the clients. Shortcuts can be easily created by the user to represent frequently visited sites. Once created, the shortcut can be used to automatically link to remote locations with one point of the mouse.

Newsgroups. Newsgroup clients are similar to listservs because both provide an opportunity for individuals to contribute to a discussion about topics of interest. Newsgroups, however, provide opportunities to contribute to threads of thought by using a client-server structure separate from e-mail. You can choose when and how to read the messages. Newsgroups are also listed in a central place, and you can choose to subscribe to the ones you want to read.

Software running on computer servers throughout the Internet provides points of distribution for various newsgroups. For instance, your ISP likely provides a news server whose main job is to distribute news to your software. Your ISP may choose to subscribe to a certain set of newsgroups and make those available to everyone. Common sets are those distributed under the voluntary rule structure known as USENET. USENET groups are maintained by common understanding among the Internet community. You might want to establish a local newsgroup for your piano performance conference or for follow-up discussion that would come after the conference. You would need to get the cooperation of your ISP to do this.

Newsgroup client software works with the news server by first providing a list of all the groups available, and then allowing you to choose which ones you want to read on a regular basis. Each time you open a newsgroup client, it links to the server to see what articles in a group you have not read. The server is constantly being replenished by the Internet as people contribute.

Take a look at the displays in Figure 6.13. These are newsreader clients for both Wintel and Macintosh machines. The Mac news client is Northwestern University's NewsWatcher (Figure 6.13a). The three screens show the path taken by someone reading an article. Reading from left to right, we see the window "My News," which represents those particular groups this person is interested in following. NewsWatcher has just checked the server for new articles since the last time the person opened the client. This person subscribes to 20 newsgroups of various interests. Notice the numbers next to

Newsgroup names start with a general category like k12.ed for kindergarten–12th grade education and then .music for the more specific category of music.

Figure 6.13
Newsreader clients
(*a*) NewsWatcher
(Northwestern University
[Mac])
(*b*) NewsXpress
(Ng Wang Lui [Windows])

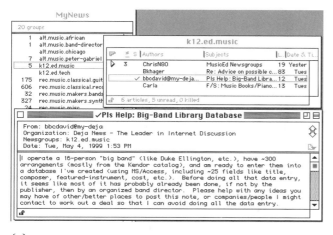

(*a*)

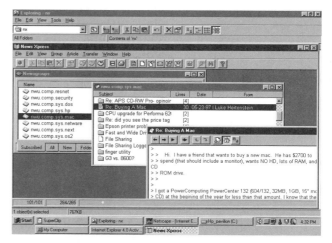

(*b*)

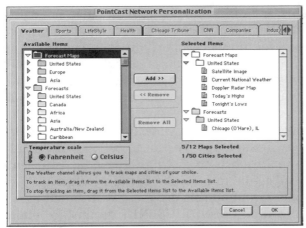

(a)

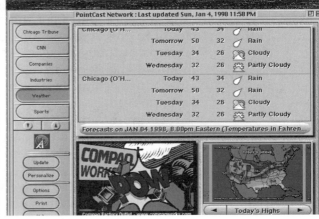

(b)

Figure 6.14
Examples of push
technology clients:
PointCast Network
Viewer
(PointCast, Inc.
[Mac/Windows])

the names of the groups. This represents the number of articles in that group that have not yet been read.

If we double-click on the *k12.ed.music* group, we can see the subject of each thread displayed in a separate window. We can then read the message that is of interest. If the subject is not of interest, we can skip it. Before closing the client, we can easily mark all those articles that we wanted to skip as "read" so that we will not see them again.

The Wintel client is NewsXpress (Figure 6.13*b*). The three windows demonstrate the path taken to read the messages.

Newsgroup clients offer a number of features that allow convenient and powerful ways to keep track of information and to get help with problems. It is quite common to post a question within a newsgroup and have a dozen answers back in a matter of a few hours! This is just one example of the power of the Internet.

Push Technology. Push technology is an emerging client-server service that provides automated data delivery to your desktop. Unlike e-mail and newsgroup readers, which must be activated and managed by you, a push client sends you new information on particular topics immediately when you ask to be brought up to date. There is also no interaction, no chance to reply. You get the information "pushed" to your computer. You subscribe to "channels" (not unlike broadcast television) that are devoted to a special topic such as concert events in your town or the latest arts news in Vienna, Austria. Such channels also can carry complete software applications or updates directly from a publisher. Some push technologies can even alert you to new items of interest without the client even running. Figure 6.14 includes screens from PointCast, Inc.'s PointCast Network Viewer. Screen *a* displays a window in which the Weather channel has been chosen. The user can elect to see weather information from a number of cities. Screen *b* shows the weather for the Chicago area.

Chat Groups. Using the same concept of "channels" as noted above, chat group clients allow you to subscribe to groups with topics assigned to a par-

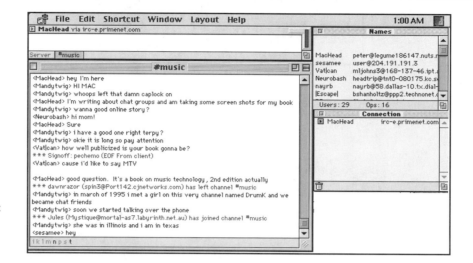

Figure 6.15

Example of a chat client:
Chris Bergmann's
MacIRC

(Chris Bergmann [Mac])

ticular channel. Unlike e-mail and newsgroups, you do not have to wait for a reply. The interaction is relatively instant, although you do need to learn how to wait for the typing of others to conclude before you jump right in. One popular live chat system on the Internet is called Internet Relay Chat (IRC). Some chat clients allow you to exchange files, play sound files, and exchange Web pages.

Figure 6.15 includes an example of a chat conversation. The user "Mac-Head" (a nickname) has joined the group called "Music" and has entered into the conversation. The window on the left contains the chat interchange, and the windows on the right provide information about the server that is connected and the people in the chat group. The top window is the area where MacHead composes the next line of text for the chat. When all is ready, MacHead hits the return key and the message is transmitted.

Moving On

In Modules 5 and 6 we have provided much information on operating systems, Internet connections, and software. In Modules 7 and 8, we give a more detailed picture of how all this works by examining the data structures and hardware of computers and networking. This should establish a wonderful base for understanding how your music and computer environment will work to support music software and hardware.

Data Structures for Computers and Networking

Mix your study of the data and hardware modules with practical software experiences.

In Module 5 you've been introduced to the Graphical User Interface or GUI operating system on personal computer workstations, and techniques for storing your computer files on your floppy or Zip disks, hard disk storage, other removable drive formats, and on network storage. In Module 6, you discovered how your computer can make use of the Internet for Web browsing and searching, e-mail, news, chat, and file transfer. We hope you have had an opportunity to try out some of these concepts and skills on your own.

Now that you've begun to learn how to drive with a GUI operating system and navigate the Internet, as it were, it is time to look under the hood. In this module we will first look at how the parts of a computer communicate: the *data structures* a computer uses for its operating system and peripherals. Then we will look at the data structures computers use to communicate with other computers over networks and over the Internet. Grappling with these concepts will increase your confidence in using computer technology.

Analog to Digital and Back

Let's examine two important, very basic notions associated with computers and computer music: *analog* and *digital* representations of events; and *binary numbers*. To understand how a digital computer works and how it interacts with instruments and events in the real world, you need to be aware of the difference between *analog* events and *digital* ones. In the simplest terms, *analog* represents events that are recorded as continuous, as opposed to events that are recorded as discrete steps or numbers.

Our timepieces provide a good illustration. A traditional analog watch measures time by visually circling the dial in a smooth, continuous motion. Time is relative and infinite in the analog dimension and we describe it accordingly: "half past four"; "ten till the hour"; "almost eleven." Digital watches, on the other hand, dramatically shift our perception of time and the symbols we use. Time is measured in precise increments, commonly down to the unit of a second. We now say: "4:31"; "9:50:02"; "2:15"; "10:59 and 32 seconds." Time is no longer continuous

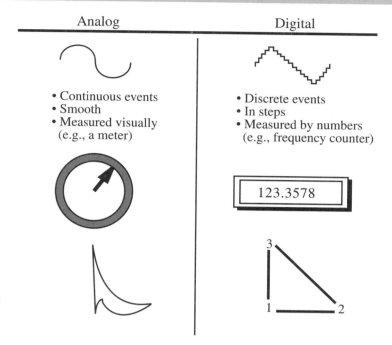

Figure 7.1

Comparisons of analog and digital events

revolutions around a circle but a precise, numeric point within a twelve- or twenty-four-hour frame.

Computers perform in digital; that's why they are called digital computers. People perform in analog. How a computer translates analog events to digital and, in turn, translates digital events back to analog is a key to your understanding of computer and music technology.

Figure 7.1 illustrates in several ways the difference between the two dimensions. Notice how the drawing of a simple sound vibration is represented by a smooth curve on the analog side and by stair steps on the digital side. Here the computer has translated analog sound into numeric values, each representing a step in time or samples of time. The analog and digital meters illustrate the analog and digital clocks. The bottom of the figure shows the path of a baton while conducting a ¾ meter pattern. On the left is pictured the smooth analog path of the baton; on the right is a digital representation of the meter pattern: 1–2–3.

Counting and Thinking with 1 and 0

We made the point that computers are digital machines. When a computer translates analog information into digital, those data are represented in a very simple numeric form. Back in 1666, philosopher-scientist Wilhelm Leibnitz came up with a system for representing numbers and performing logic decisions that required only two values, 1 and 0. This system is referred to as the *binary* or *base-2* number system. The system that we are most familiar with is the *decimal* or *base-10* number system that we inherited from India and Arabia around 700 AD.

Binary	Decimal
0000	0
0001	1
0010	2
0011	3
0100	4
0101	5
0110	6
0111	7
1000	8
1001	9
1010	10
1011	11
1100	12
1101	13
1110	14
1111	15

The figure in the margin shows you how you would count from 0 to 15 using both the decimal (base-10) and the binary (base-2) system. Counting in base 2 is very tedious for humans, but machines—especially computers—revel in it. Why? For two reasons. First, the beauty of the binary system is that 1 and 0 can be represented mechanically in many ways: holes punched in paper or metal (1 = hole and 0 = no hole), switches turned on or off, light reflections (1 = light and 0 = no light), gears in or out of position, pins inserted or not in a board, and so on. All of these possibilities have been used over the past 300 years for number calculating machines and even for some music machines. The present-day computer uses millions of microscopic semiconductors for binary switches that are either on or off. Compact audio discs and DVD discs of video and audio use light reflected off a laser beam for creating their ones and zeros. Floppy and hard disks use the position of magnetic particles to define binary numbers.

The second feature of binary numbers that make them ideally suited for computers is that machines can use them to perform simple logic. You may remember from your algebra class that the concept of binary logic is called Boolean logic, named after George Boole (c. 1830). We will revisit the concept of binary numbers and logic many times throughout the book, as well as the concept of translating from analog to digital information, and from digital back to analog information.

Computer Bits and Bytes. There are a few terms related to the binary nature of a computer that you should be familiar with: bits, bytes, and words. These elements are the basic building blocks of how a computer represents information:

▶ The terms *bit* and *byte* are based on binary numbers. A bit (Binary digIT) is the most fundamental unit in a computer. It is one electronic switch that can be on or off, and is represented by a single binary digit, 1 or 0.

▶ A group of bits is referred to as a *byte*. A byte is a group of eight bits, with the smallest byte value being 00000000_2 (represented as 0_{10} in decimal), and the largest byte value being 11111111_2 (or 255_{10} in decimal). (The subscript 2 tells you it is a base-2 or binary number; the subscript 10 tells you it is a base-10 or decimal number.) In computer lingo, eight bits make a byte.

▶ As the number of bits a computer uses increases beyond 8, the term *word* is used to generally refer to a group of bits. The early Apple II personal computer was an 8-bit machine. This means that the largest word it could computationally represent was eight bits long. When the IBM PC was released, its word size was 16 bits. Many present-day computers have 32- and 64-bit word sizes, and it is not uncommon to find 128-bit machines among large mainframe computers.

Base 16 or hexadecimal comes in handy when working later with MIDI. "11111111" in binary is "FF" in hexadecimal, where each of 16 digits (0–F) equals four bits.

Chatting among Computers, Drives, Printers, and More

Computers are always talking with the external, analog world, translating analog information into digital form and then back to analog. Here we look

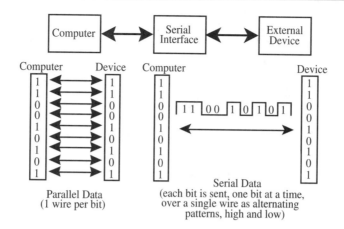

Figure 7.2
Serial and parallel data structures

As you will see in Module 8, knowing the word size of a computer is important when it comes to filling it with memory.

at the data structures a computer uses to communicate with its own devices such as disk drives, keyboards, printers, modems, and even MIDI music keyboards. On an elementary level, all devices that connect to a computer do so either through a serial or a parallel connection.

Expressing Data in Parallel Form. Figure 7.2 illustrates a *parallel* connection between a computer and an external device. It is called parallel because the binary bits in the computer are connected in parallel with the bits in the external device on a one-to-one basis. You might say that physically a wire connects each bit of the computer with the parallel bit of the device. This is a fast, neat way to connect devices.

If a computer uses 32-bit words, then every parallel connection requires a bundle of 32 wires going from the computer to the device. This is what happens when a disk drive is connected to a computer. The industry standard SCSI interface used for disk drives, video scanners, and some printers is a parallel interface. There is a weakness in the parallel solution, however. The cables get cumbersome, especially for a long-distance connection.

Expressing Data in Serial Form

Figure 7.2 also shows the *serial* alternative to parallel data. Here only one wire is used between the computer and an external device. Serial exchange of data presents a classic problem, however. How do you take data stored in a computer and transmit them to another computer or device at a distant location? The answer is to convert the data into a serial stream of information, which then can be translated back into parallel information by the receiver.

For sending computer data over telephone wires or through direct wiring, the serial form is a stream of binary (on and off) electrical voltages in specific patterns to represent the numerals, punctuation, and letters of the alphabet. The standard code for computer text data is ASCII. The original ASCII had seven possibilities or 7 binary bits in its code to work with; that gave 128 possible combinations of characters, both upper and lower case.

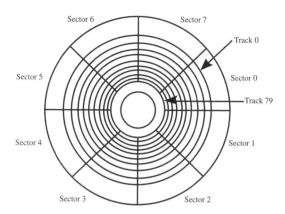

Figure 7.3
Data structure for disk formatting

Storing files on disks is discussed in software Module 5.

Therefore, when you deal with any form of computer networking and communications, the data in your computer must be packaged and sent as a stream of binary 1s and 0s to be transferred over the network to another machine. At the other end, the data must be unpackaged from its serial form and translated back into parallel bits of data for use by the receiving computer. Typical devices that communicate through serial interfaces are printers (some printers also use parallel connections), modems, your mouse or joystick, keyboards, other computers, and all MIDI music instruments.

What is the downside of transferring data serially between devices? Speed. It takes time to take apart each character your computer needs to send, bit by bit, send it serially over a wire, and then reassemble the bits back into a character at the other end. Serial data are most often used for sending information over a telephone where long distances are required. Distance and single-wire simplicity are the advantages of serial connections.

When you get a Disk Full message from your computer, the computer is telling you that there are no empty sectors remaining on the disk. Different computer operating systems and disk formats vary in the number of tracks available on a floppy or hard disk and the number of sectors on those tracks.

Expressing Data in Disk Form. Most disk drives use some form of parallel connection to exchange data between the computer and the drive. When we are talking gigabytes of data storage, it is also critical that the disk itself use some systematic means for placing data on the storage medium. This is referred to as the *disk format*, and a computer and its operating system may support multiple formats for disk volumes and storage. Windows computers typically use what is called a DOS formatting for its disk storage; Macintosh has its own special formats for storage devices.

You cannot use a disk for storing files without first formatting the disk. Figure 7.3 shows a schematic representation of how a disk is formatted and organized. The primary organizing elements are *characters, sectors,* and *tracks*. Characters are the letters of the alphabet and numerals represented as ASCII binary numbers. As you can see, the surface of the disk is divided into concentric circles called tracks, starting with Track 0 closest to the outside of the disk and ending with the last track, Track 79, nearest the center. The disk is then divided into eight wedge-shaped sectors such that each track is segmented into eight parts.

Chatting among Computers over Telephones

To use the telephone to talk between computers you need a device called a *modem,* no matter whether your computer is talking over the phone to another computer, to an on-line service like America Online, or over the Internet. We'll talk more about the hardware characteristics of modems in Module 8. Let's look at the data structures or *protocols* for getting computers to talk to one another through modems.

The purpose of a modem is to translate serial computer data that are digital into analog serial codes that can be sent over the phone lines. Phone lines carry analog signals like our voice conversations. The name modem comes from modulate/demodulate. This means that modems modulate digital data to analog tones at the sending computer's modem, and then demodulate the analog data back to digital codes at the receiving computer's modem. (The receiving end could be a bank of hundreds of modems for an on-line service or a college campus dial-in port to the Internet.) Figure 7.4 illustrates serial conversion (step 1), the addition of modems to the chain (step 2), the conversion from digital to analog sounds (steps 2 and 3) and back to digital (steps 3 and 4) for the transfer of data between modems, and the final translation back into parallel bytes (step 5) at the receiving end.

You might find it useful to think of modem sounds going over the phone lines as musical tunes made up of two tones, a high tone for a *1* and a low note for a *0*. The modems handle the translation between digital *1*s and *0*s and the two tones. If you've picked up a phone while two computers are playing these tunes, back and forth to each other, you've heard their familiar hissing or screeching noise. When two modems are communicating they each use a different pair of pitches for their tunes; this is how the modems identify which modem is sending and which is receiving.

Baud Rates and Compression. A key issue with modems is the rate of transmission (the tempo of the tune) or *baud rate/ bits per second* (bps). This refers to how many bits are sent through the modem per second. The earliest modems were 300 bps; 9,600- and 14,400-KBps modems have been commonplace for a number of years. Transmission rates of 33.6 and 56 KBps are the standards of 1999, but the rates keep getting faster as the technology gets more sophisticated.

You can calculate the number of characters per second that can be transmitted by dividing the bps speed by 10. The ten comes from the total num-

Emile Baudot invented the first teletype and the Baudot code, hence the term *baud* rate.

Figure 7.4
Using modems to convert serial data to analog phone transmission

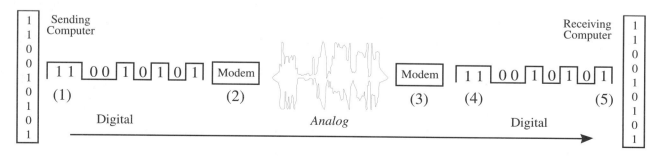

ASIDE

The terms *bits per second* and *baud* do not, technically speaking, mean exactly the same thing, but common practice in the PC world finds people using the terms interchangeably.

ber of bits in each character, from start bit to stop bit. Thus, at 33.6 KBps, you will send about 33,600 ÷ 10, or 3,360, characters per second.

Speeding Up the Transmission Process. It is all going digital, even voice phone transmissions. The POTS, or plain old telephone system, is giving way to new, high-speed methods to move more data over phone lines in digital form. ISDN (Integrated Services Digital Network) can provide speeds of 64 KBps bits per second over a regular phone line at almost the same cost as a normal phone call. The quality of sound you hear from a vinyl LP record versus that from a compact disc is a good analogy to the comparison of transmission qualities between a regular sound-based telephone line versus an all-digital ISDN line. Another high-speed alternative is Asymmetrical Digital Subscriber Line (ADSL) technology, or one of the other varieties of DSL transmission. ADSL technology has been clocked at speeds up to 6.14 KBps downloading data. Also to be considered are cable modems, modems designed to use the television channels on your cable TV service. With technologies like cable, ADSL, and ISDN, phone modems as we know them today may become obsolete. Computer data in its digital form will be able to be mixed with voice and television broadcast data flowing over the same lines.

Chatting among Computers over a Local Area Network (LAN)

It is possible to have computers talk to each other without the use of modems and phone lines. Over a *Local Area Network* or *LAN* computers can converse with their own special communication protocols in digital form without the need of analog conversion. Such protocols include those named Ethernet, Token Ring, FDDI, and ATM. When you use a computer in a school lab or in an office space that is chatting with other computers, there is a good chance that the data structure used for the network protocol is one of these common types of network protocols. Ethernet is one of the most common of the network protocols.

▶ *Ethernet* is one of those marvelous inventions that came out of the Xerox PARC "think tank" in the early 1970s. It is called *Ethernet* because its networking environment is passive, or "ether," and it is by far the most prevalent networking data structure in use today. Ethernet sends packets of data at 10 megabits per second over a single-lane highway called a *bus*. It uses what is known as a *contention* network strategy because the network has to deal with collisions between data packets traveling both ways over a one-lane road. Newer technologies for Ethernet, or Fast Ethernet, will provide transfer rates up to 100 megabits per second.

▶ *LocalTalk* is a poor-person's network developed by Apple Computer for the Macintosh that works very much like Ethernet. Its transfer rate is much slower than other networking protocols, but a reasonable trade for its use of very inexpensive twisted-pair or telephone-like wiring.

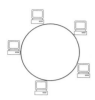

▶ *Token Ring* avoids the collision problems of Ethernet and LocalTalk using tokens to move data packets in an orderly fashion around a ring. Even though several other commercial parties have released Token Ring networking, it is still thought of as an IBM solution. Its transfer speed is 16 megabits per second. Token ring is one of the most reliable and fastest network protocols. However, be prepared to pay for it in terms of the installation, materials, and support.

▶ *FDDI* (Fiber Optic Distributed Data Interface) is a newer ring protocol for networking that takes advantage of the high speeds and long distances possible with fiber optic cable. FDDI speeds are a fast 100 megabits per second. FDDI is also expensive to implement, however, and is primarily used for network backbones that link other LANs and networking services over long distances.

Indiana University was one of the first to use ATM for high-speed delivery of CD-quality digital audio recordings over the Internet. Through the Variations Project, music students can listen to music recordings for class assignments over an ATM LAN network from computer workstations in the School of Music's library.

▶ *ATM* (Asynchronous Transfer Mode) is one of the more recent networking schemes and is not an upgrade to an existing standard like Fast Ethernet. Token Ring uses a ring topology and Ethernet uses a bus topology. In both designs, data packets compete for space and time on the same network channel. ATM uses a packet-switching topology similar to the phone systems. When you need to transfer data to another computer, a virtual circuit is established between the two machines, and that data path is reserved for your use until the exchange has been completed. ATM also uses a fixed size for data packets, thus facilitating real-time video and audio applications where accurate, consistent transmission rates are critical. With ATM networking, digitized voice, data, and video can be transferred at gigabit speeds. Many see ATM as the key to wide bandwidth over the Internet.

Chatting with TCP/IP among Computers over the Internet

Using either a modem or a direct connection like Ethernet, a computer can also chat with other computers over the Internet through either an on-line service, a school or college campus, or a local Internet Service Provider (ISP). The Internet is a worldwide consortium of networks connecting government, university, commercial, and other computers. It truly is a network of networks! The Internet also has a special data structure that is used so that all computers talking over its network can understand one another. This data structure is known as *TCP/IP* or *Transmission Control Protocol/Internet Protocol*. It is the language that your computer must speak if it is to use the Web, e-mail, news groups, or transfer files over the Internet.

Internet software that uses TCP/IP is discussed in Module 5.

To get a perspective on how the Internet and TCP/IP originated, we have to go back to the 1950s. Understanding its history helps you to see both its technical operation and the philosophy of its environment. The RAND corporation was given the task of inventing a communications system that would connect all the strategic military and research sites in the United States. This communications system would have to be able to keep lines of communication open in spite of the malfunction of any node or site. While the phone system relies on central hubs and switching stations to route its

As the government seeks to use the Internet to create its National Information Infrastructure (NII), many fear the unregulated spirit will be lost.

calls, this communications network could not risk having communications lost if a key hub was destroyed.

The solution was the network that has expanded, since the first four nodes were connected in the 1970s, to become what is now known as the Internet. As it was initially designed, the Internet is a communications system that is virtually indestructible. It is more like the postal service than like a phone service: your electronic data will be delivered come rain, sleet, snow, or any conceivable network breakdown. The design assumes that the network is unreliable and the worst delivery conditions exist. No one manages the Internet; the operation is completely distributed with no central authority controlling or managing or censoring data; it is a democracy with all nodes created equal.

Now that you see the big picture of how the Internet and TCP/IP works, we need to get "under the hood" to understand how data are exchanged between computers, or between a computer and a server. Let's create our own fictional postal service to illustrate how the Internet works: our post office will use carrier pigeons to deliver the mail. We will create two fictional people for a moment, Bruce Baudtalk and Ester Email. Bruce wants to send Ester a Microsoft Word file with graphics included. Follow Figure 7.5 as we trace its route to Ester's desktop.

The Word file is packaged for mailing in a special electronic envelope (sometimes called a *datagram*) with the Internet addresses (called the *IP address*) of both Bruce and Ester's computers. Bruce's address is *baudtalk@ecsa.edu* and Ester's is *e_email@oum.edu*. Some error-checking code is also added to the envelope, and a code that will let Bruce's machine know if the envelope has been received successfully by Ester's machine.

Next, we are going to tear or fragment this datagram into tiny strips (called *packets*) and mail them each individually. We will assume that each packet stands a better chance of getting through individually than one large envelope sent alone. Each packet has the addresses of the sender and the receiver, as well as the error checking codes.

Some refer to packets and frames instead of datagrams and packets.

Now Bruce's network hardware translates each packet into a serial stream of bits to be sent out on the Internet (similar to the modem's role discussed earlier). Here is where our carrier pigeons come in. Imagine a slip of paper (each packet) given to a carrier pigeon to be delivered to Ester's Internet address. We don't care how the pigeon gets the packet there, just as long as it is delivered in good condition. The Word file exists on the Internet as independent fragments of the original file, encapsulated into packets addressed to Ester at e_email@oum.edu.

At the receiving (Ester's) computer in Figure 7.5, the datagram (envelope) is reassembled as the pigeons arrive with their slips of paper. Should pieces be missing, a pigeon can be sent back requesting that a duplicate of the packet be sent. When the datagram is completely received, Ester's operating system will translate that datagram back into a familiar Microsoft Word file on her desktop.

It is a simple and elegant system. All the packets that make up a datagram are broadcast out on the Internet to find their own best route to the receiving node or computer. Packets take flight from node to node on the

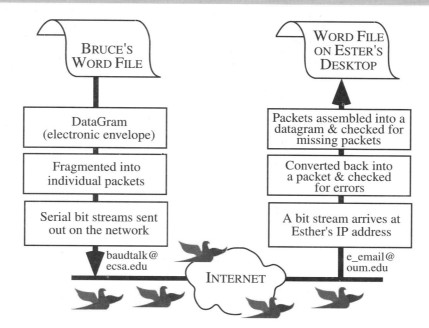

Figure 7.5
Sending a file over the Internet from desktop to desktop

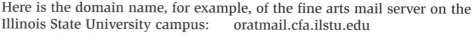

network. Should one node be out of operation, another will suffice. The packet of data couldn't care less what path it takes through the maze of networks that make up the Internet; it only cares that it gets to its destination.

Internet Addressing. Internet addresses have a fixed format and exist in both a numeric form (IP addresses) and a labeled form (domain names). Using names is much easier for people to read and remember. Every node and every activity on the Internet has a unique address. We will examine personal Internet addresses, addresses for Internet Web sites or URLs, and addresses for various servers such as e-mail, Web, news, etc.

Server Internet Addresses. Here is the structure for an Internet server address: machine.subdomain.organization.domain

Here is the domain name, for example, of the fine arts mail server on the Illinois State University campus: oratmail.cfa.ilstu.edu
And the IP address is: 138.87.136.5

Most domain name addresses are written in lower case even though case is not important. A dash can be used in the address as well as the digits 0 to 9, but no other punctuation is allowed.

The IP address (the one that computers use) is in reverse order from the domain name address (the one that people use). Thankfully, most people rarely encounter the IP address; a software program called a Domain Name Server (DNS) translates the domain names into IP addresses so that the computer can understand it.

The domain portion of the address categorizes network users into distinctive categories: universities (.edu), commercial users (.com), government users (.gov), nonprofit organizations (.org), and networking organizations (.net). International codes include such domains as Australia (.au), Canada (.ca), United Kingdom (.uk), and so on. The organization name, coupled with the domain, is the unique identifier for this site on the Internet, that is to say, ilstu.edu or 138.87.

Addresses for computer workstations and servers at any Internet site, such as the ones on the Illinois State University campus, have a common numbering scheme. Further, common services like mail, news, and Web have a common naming scheme. The Illinois State campus is no exception. The IP numbers all start with 138.87 to match the domain names that end with ilstu.edu, and the names of Internet services follow common practice. To illustrate:

If you know the IP number you can use this in any Internet address. An e-mail address of "baudtalk@128.40.6.2" would work just fine, especially if the DNS at your site is not working.

The news server domain name is:	news.ilstu.edu
And its IP address is:	138.87.1.6
The phone book or Ph server name is:	ph.ilstu.edu
And its IP address is:	138.87.1.7
The campus Web server is:	www.ilstu.edu
And its IP address is:	138.87.1.2

Personal Internet Addresses. Personal e-mail addresses on the Internet are made up by taking the domain name of one's e-mail server and generating an ID that is unique to that mail server. We can use Bruce Baudtalk's e-mail address as an example.

Here is the structure for a personal Internet address: userid@machine. subdomain.organization.domain

Bruce's address is:	baudtalk@mozart.music.ecsa.edu
His full domain name is:	mozart.music.ecsa.edu
His abbreviated domain name is:	esca.edu
And his IP address is:	128.40.6.2

The ID "baudtalk" only has to be unique to the e-mail server running on "mozart.music.ecsa.edu." If a Ph server (electronic phone book of e-mail addresses) is running on a host computer for an Internet service, a person can use the abbreviated form of the address (e.g., ecsa.edu) for some activities, such as e-mail, because the campus Ph server knows the full address locally. In fact, outside a local networking organization, all the Internet world needs to know is the organization.domain portion of any e-mail address.

URLs from Web browsers were first presented in Module 6.

Web Internet Addresses or URLs. Web browsers use a variant of the domain name address called URLs or Uniform Resource Locators. In front of a server's domain name is added the prefix "http://" to tell the Web browser that this server is a Web server. If the URL is an FTP server for downloading files, then the prefix to the domain name would be "ftp://", and for a Gopher server, gopher://, and so on.

Exchanging Files between Computers over Networks

Consider one more time the serial nature of data over networks and the Internet. In all forms of networking, we are moving a large volume of bits across great distances, and we want to move them as fast as possible. One technique for increasing speed is to increase the bit or baud rate of the transmission. The range of modem transmission can start with 56K bits per second and increase up to 6M bits per second with ADSL transmission. And, with direct Internet connections, the speed can range from a usable 2 to 3 MBps of Ethernet up to 100 MBps or faster speeds of Fast Ethernet and ATM networks. Only with Fast Ethernet and ATM do we approach the speed necessary to directly deliver audio and video data over networks and the Internet.

Thankfully, there are other ways to increase the transmission speed of files you are transferring over a network: *file compression* and *optimized methods* for file transfers. When you access FTP servers abundant with freeware and shareware files on the Internet, most of these files will be stored in some compressed format. When your Web browser goes to download graphics, sounds, and movie clips that are needed to create the multimedia Web pages on your browser's desktop, the files will also be optimized and stored in some compressed format.

Packaging and Compressing Files. Table 7.1 gives you a list of some of the more common file schemes you will find on the Internet for packaging and exchanging files. Some provide compression to reduce the file size. The column on the left indicates the file extension that will be appended as a suffix or *extension* to the file name (e.g., myfile.uue, or myapp.zip, or muscode.sea). The second column indicates the computer that originates each file type. And the remaining column briefly describes the packaging or compression scheme.

Table 7.1. File Formats and Extensions for Exchanging Files Over the Internet

File Extension	Computer	Description
sit and .cpt	Mac	Mac format created with either StuffIt or CompactPro
.zip	Win	DOS/Wintel format created with PKZip or other similar software
.sea	Mac	Self-extracting version of StuffIt format
.exe	Win	Self-extracting DOS/Wintel compressed file format
.bin	Mac	Binary format that includes Mac file with key desktop information
.z, .Z, .gz, .tar	Unix	Common Unix file compression formats
.hqx	Mac	Binhex format that converts Mac binary files to a text form
.uu or .uue	Unix	UUCoded format that converts binary files to a text form

Compression of graphics and sound and video files is discussed elsewhere in the book. Check out Modules 14, 23, and 28, respectively.

Shrinking File Sizes. In its simplest form, file compression works by replacing patterns of redundant information in a file with more efficient coding. There are many different software algorithms for accomplishing this. Error checking is also built into the process, so when a file is uncompressed there is a validity check to see if any data were lost in the exchange.

Extensions like .sit and .zip are for compression schemes developed around early software utilities that have become pervasive through common use: Stuffit and CompactPro for the Mac and PKZip for DOS and Wintel computers. Self-extracting compression files (.sea and .exe) are frequently .sit or .zip files that have extra code added to the file so that it is intelligent enough to uncompress itself when downloaded to your computer without the need for special software.

MacBinary is unique to the Macintosh world. MacBinary (or technically, MacBinary II) with the .bin extension is a file compression format that includes all of the binary data from the file plus key Mac resource and Finder information. This added information insures that the file, when uncompressed, appears on your Mac desktop with the correct icon. Most Mac programs, Fetch for example, decode MacBinary automatically.

Files with extensions like .z, .Z, .gz, and .tar are compressed files that originated on a Unix system. A "tar" file is actually a collection or library of several files that are compressed into one package for file transfer.

Packaging Binary Files as Text. An early method of sending binary files (i.e., applications, graphics, and sounds) that is still in use today is the conversion of binary codes to ASCII text. This technique, called *binhex conversion*, is very common on the Internet and among UNIX installations. When a file is *binhexed*, the binary codes are translated into hexadecimal values and the numbers are written as the ASCII characters for each digit in a text file. Sometimes, files are both binhexed and compressed. For example, a file labeled, *macFile.sit.hqx*, or more simply, *macFile.hqx*, was first compressed with the StuffIt application (.sit), and then binhexed (.hqx). To unpack this file, first it will have to be un-binhexed and then un-stuffed.

Remember, techniques that create .zip, .sit, or .z files are "compression" techniques that reduce the size of a file; techniques that create .hqx or binhex files are not compression techniques but a procedure to "package" a binary file as an ASCII text format with no compression involved.

Uucoded files are, like the Mac binhex format, binary files that have been coded in an ASCII text form for easier transmission over the Internet. Binhex and the uucode format are not compression formats, but if you want to be sure your files can be read by just about any server on the net, this is the safest way to go. Because binhex or uucoded files are ASCII text, it is possible to include a binary file as a string of codes in an e-mail text file or as an append file to a newsgroup posting. If you ever receive an e-mail message with a long block of strange numeric codes appended at the end, it is a sure bet that if you run the e-mail through a utility to unpackage either the binhex or uucoded format of the file, an application or document will appear on your desktop.

File Compression Utilities. There are many different software utilities for compression, and the more popular ones dominate the networks. To compress or uncompress a file you need a software utility program to create a compressed file or to uncompress a file back into its original state. There is a

7.2. Universal File Formats and Their Extensions

File Extension	Types	Description
.txt	Tex	Universal ASCII text file format
.ps	Postscript	Postscript file format
.pdf	Document	Portable document format for electronic publishing
.html or .htm	Text	HTML document format for the World Wide Web
.gif	Graphic	8-bit compressed graphic format
.jpeg or .jpg	Graphic	32-bit compressed graphic format
.mov, .mpg, avi	Movie	Quicktime, MPEG, and Video for Windows movie files
.au or .wav	Sound	Compressed sampled sound files
.ra and .rm	Sound	RealAudio high-compression format
.mid	MIDI	MIDI music files (usually type 0)

Universal file formats are discussed in Module 14 (JPEG and GIF), and Module 24 (AU and WAV).

wide variety of software available for uncompressing files that you can download off the Internet (Unzip, PKUnzip, UULite, StuffItExpander, WinZip, SuperZip, etc.). Similar software exists for compressing files in these formats as well, notably StuffIt for the Mac and WinZip for Windows computers. With either of these on your computer, you can translate just about any of the file formats in Table 7.1, including the Unix files.

Exchanging Documents With Universal File Formats. General file compression is one important issue when transferring files over networks and the Internet. Another is cross-platform independence once the files have been uncompressed: the ability to exchange application files across any computer or software platform. This need for the universal exchange of files has become especially critical with the growth in the World Wide Web. Media files such as sounds, video clips, and graphics are automatically downloaded to a person's Web browser with the server having no knowledge of the browser's computer platform. Table 7.2 notes a few of the more common universal file formats used for exchanging media across the Internet. Other application file formats like TIFF, EPS, and AIFF, for example, will be covered in later modules.

Exchanging Text Documents. The first set of files shown in Table 7.2 include ASCII text and PostScript. The common denominator among all computer software and machines is the ASCII text file. There is even a cult of users on the Internet that specialize in ASCII graphics and art; images are created using patterns of ASCII characters spaced out on a page. When in doubt, send an ASCII text document; most word processors will provide the option of saving or creating documents in this form as "text only" documents. The drawbacks to using ASCII files, of course, are that: all style and formatting information (e.g., bold, underline, fonts, font sizes, paragraphs, margins) is lost, and, if word spaces or space runs (a series of spaces) were used to create tables or formatting effects, alignment can be easily destroyed if margins and fonts do not match at the receiving end.

Because Postscript is used on many current-day printers, many documents are being exchanged as Postscript files noted with the .ps (Postscript). Using the Postscript format insures that the printed copy at the receiving end is a good replica of the original fonts, styles, document formatting, and even graphics. Postscript files are text files containing the codes or instructions used to generate desktop-published documents. After downloading one of these files, you can use a Postscript utility to print the file.

Adobe's Portable Document Format (.pdf) is a special document type that encapsulates the Postscript data from an electronic document along with graphics, hyperlinks, and other elements, and creates a portable file for exchanging the document with a large number of computer platforms that support the Adobe Acrobat Reader. Acrobat Reader is a free application. It will display the original word-processed or desktop-published document just as it appeared on the screen or printer of the computer that created it. The file may then be printed and, again, it will look the same as it did on the original computer. A special application from Adobe is required to create the PDF file initially. PDF files are very popular not only on the Internet for exchanging documents, but also for printing services, industry, and publishers. A good deal of printed documentation for software manuals are distributed on-line in the PDF format.

Exchanging Web Documents. The HTML (HyperText Markup Language) document uses a special file formatting language developed from an earlier markup language called SGML. It is used to exchange complex documents with styles, graphics, and even data links over the Internet through World Wide Web (WWW) document servers. HTML files are Web files that can be read by any Web browser regardless of the computer platform. HTML files are simply text files, but imbedded within the text are HTML tags enclosed in brackets like < A HREF > or < IMAGE > or < P >. The Web browser uses these tags as instructions for formatting the Web page, displaying the graphics and other media, and creating links to other HTML documents on or off the Internet.

Exchanging Graphics and Video. GIF (Graphic Interchange Files) and JPEG (Joint Photographic Experts Group) are universal formats for graphic files. GIF provides compression for 8-bit or 256-color graphics and is one of the most prevalent graphic file types on the Internet; the JPG or JPEG format provides high-resolution graphic compression and up to 32-bit color, and is especially suitable for photographic images. A variety of GIF/JPEG readers are available that allow translation of images into the common formats used by painting and drawing programs on Wintel, Macintosh, and UNIX computers. Many graphics applications and most Web browsers will read both formats directly. If you need to transfer a photographic image, choose JPEG. For any other graphic image, try the GIF format if the reduction to 256 colors doesn't affect the quality of the image.

There are three competing formats for digital video over the Internet,

There are two forms of the HTML extension for Web documents: .html is the most common one used on Unix and other computers; .htm is a form used with the Windows operating system where only three-character extensions are allowed for files. Web browsers and servers usually accept both forms.

Designing Web pages and coding HTML tags are covered in depth in Viewport VIII.

MOV, AVI, and MPEG, with the most common currently being MOV or QuickTime. Though developed for the Macintosh as a proprietary format by Apple Computer, Inc., QuickTime can be used on Wintel computers with the addition of the free QuickTime for Windows software. AVI video files are primarily a Wintel format designed by Microsoft. MPEG, short for Moving Picture Experts Group, video will play on most platforms, but may require special hardware or software for playback.

Stay tuned for more to come on file formats. Graphic file formats are covered in more detail in Module 14, audio file formats in Module 24, and video file formats in Module 28.

Exchanging Digital Audio and MIDI. The remaining set of universal files in Table 7.2 are for digital audio and MIDI music file exchange. The earliest universal digital audio format on the Internet was the AU file. It offers some degree of compression, but less than satisfactory quality for audio and music sound samples. WAV files, very common in the Wintel world, have also proliferated on the Internet, and most Web browsers will play WAV as well as AU audio files. Not noted in the Table are also AIF and SND files, two Macintosh-specific audio formats, that can also be found on the Internet. Given all of these formats, however, the AU file is the most universally accepted across all computer platforms.

MIDI files (.mid) provide a standardized way for transferring MIDI performance codes across computer platforms. Most MIDI applications will read the standard, type-0 format, MIDI file no matter what software it was created on. Netscape and Microsoft Explorer Web browsers will both play type-0 MIDI files without special software. Given the small size of MIDI files in comparison to digital audio files, MIDI files are a good choice for Web page music clips.

<table>
<tr><td>Module
8</td><td># The Mechanics of Computers and Networking</td></tr>
</table>

Module 7 acquainted you with the concepts of the binary logic of computing machines, and the protocols used for networking. We will use these concepts now to gain some insight first into computer hardware operations and then into networking operations.

Computer Hardware Operations and the IPOS Model

There are four stages to the mechanics of any computer system: input, process, output, and storage (IPOS):

▶ The *input* stage represents those devices we use to get information into the system, e.g., a computer keyboard and a mouse.

▶ The *process* stage stores and transforms the information. Here we have the central processing unit (CPU), memory (RAM and ROM), and the timing clock.

▶ The *output* stage of a computer represents those devices that are used to get information out of the computer, e.g., video displays.

▶ The *storage* stage includes devices like floppy, optical, and hard disks for saving and transporting your computer work.

Between each of these stages are *interfaces* that translate the signals coming from the input, output, and storage devices to the process part of the computer, oftentimes performing analog to digital and digital to analog conversions. Figure 8.1 shows the IPOS model, along with the interfaces used for the computer and for networking. We will deal with the networking issues later in the module.

All present-day computers have all four IPOS stages. In this module, we will discuss each of these stages and the mechanics of their operation. With each stage, we will also discuss the *interfaces* used to connect various devices.

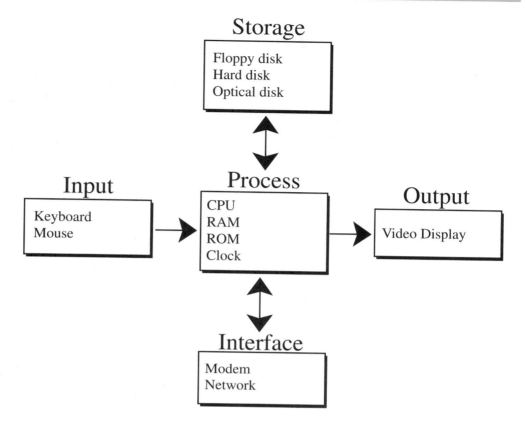

Figure 8.1
The Input-Process-Output-Storage (IPOS) model of a computer

Process

Software activity: "Setting up Your Computer and Diskettes"

The process stage is what some people call the "brains" of the computer. It is here that computers do what they are designed to do: transform or change information. Numbers are added, text is manipulated, music codes are arranged and modified, and decisions are made. The diagram in Figure 8.1 shows three important components of the process stage: the central processing unit or CPU; memory; and a clock. We will discuss each in turn.

Central Processing Unit (CPU). In today's computer, the CPU is an electronic circuit called the microprocessor integrated circuit or *chip*. The CPU is the "brain" of a computer and coordinates the flow of data in and out of the machine.

In a computer, the main flat plastic board on which the CPU chip and other electronic circuitry is located is called the *motherboard*. Other chips for memory, video, sound, and so on are also located on the motherboard. Each chip is a small wafer mounted in a frame of plastic and metal pins. The wafers are made by etching nearly invisible wires onto slivers of ultra-pure silicon. Each wafer contains numerous transistors, or tiny switches, that perform a given function. Chip manufacturers like Intel, IBM, and Motorola keep increasing the complexity of electronics that are placed on smaller and smaller silicon chips.

HISTORICAL PERSPECTIVE

Over 350 years have passed since William Schickard designed his Calculating Clock. Except during the period 1940–1970, most calculating machines have been small desktop units. With the appearance of the first personal computers and microprocessor chips in the 1970s, the small, personal calculating machine returned with power for logic and computation that far surpassed the designs of any of the "big iron" mainframe computers from the middle of this century.

With Charles Babbage's design of his Analytical Engine in 1834, certain critical components of the computer were born. Babbage's mechanical computer had a "store" for numbers, a "mill" to perform calculations with those numbers, a "barrel" to control the flow of numbers, and punched cards to program the machine's mechanical gears—an idea Babbage borrowed from the Jacquard weaving loom that used punched cards to remember patterns.

The ENIAC (Electronic Numerical Integrator and Computer) realized Babbage's design on a huge scale. Completed in 1946, the machine was the first all-electronic computer. It used 19,000 vacuum tubes, covered a city block, and consumed so much electricity that the lights in its section of Philadelphia dimmed when it was turned on. In addition to the drawback of its size, the ENIAC lacked the ability to store or remember instructions, its *program*.

Working with the designers of the ENIAC, the mathematician John von Neumann conceived of the computer as we know it today. The design concept of the EDVAC, built in 1951, is used in present-day personal and desktop computers and is known as the *von Neumann machine*. *Input* devices (corresponding to Babbage's punched cards) bring information into the machine. The *process* (Babbage's "mill") carries out the computations and controls the information flow ("barrel"). The *storage* component (Babbage's "store") holds the results of the computation or data waiting to be processed, and *output* devices display the results of the computer's calculations. The unique element that von Neumann added to this design was the idea of a stored program. Just as data are stored in the computer, so is the program, or instructions for processing those data. Programs can be changed just as easily as data.

Around the same time as the EDVAC, Forrester and Everett built the first real-time computer, the

Dodd, Forrester, Everett, and Ferenz with the Whirlwind I Computer at MIT
(Courtesy of The MIT Museum)

Whirlwind, at MIT (see the 1951 photo). This later became the SAGE computer used for the nation's air defense and early-warning system. Several of its innovations were precursors of features in today's computers. The Whirlwind used the first *magnetic core* memory (an ancestor of today's random-access memory) for storage. Because of its interactive nature (e.g., monitoring aircraft flight patterns), techniques were developed for controlling external devices and visualizing the results. We see this today in any computer controlling a MIDI music system and visualizing music notation on a screen. The Whirlwind was the first computer to use CRT video display monitors and light guns for pointing to enter commands.

Several important developments led to the miniaturization of computers: the inventions of the transistor at Bell Labs in 1947; of the integrated circuit (or *chip*) at Texas Instruments in 1952; of the first RAM chips in 1968; and of the first microcomputer on a chip at Intel in 1972.

Other developments led to the look and feel of the personal computers we use today. The first personal computers with sound and graphics as standard features (Apple II and the Commodore PET among others) were introduced in the late 1970s. The Xerox Star computer developed at the Palo Alto Research Center (PARC) was the precursor to graphic-based systems with windows, icons, pull-down menus, and the mouse. This design first appeared commercially in the Apple Lisa computer, followed by the Apple Macintosh and then the OS/2 and Windows operating systems for Wintel personal computers.

The sixth generation Pentium Pro CPU chip contains 7.5 million transistors connected by wires less than 1 micron apart; by comparison, a human hair is 100 microns thick.

If your computer has battery power to support RAM, as do many laptops, you will not lose your data in memory.

Memory. In the simplest terms, there are two kinds of *memory* in a personal computer:

▶ *Random-access memory* (or RAM)

▶ *Read-only memory* (or ROM)

More appropriate names for RAM are *read-and-write memory* or *changeable memory*. You can retrieve data stored in RAM and you can write data back to RAM memory.

RAM memory is what you use the most in a computer; it's your best friend. However, your best friend has one bad character trait: as soon as you turn off the power to the computer, all the RAM data are lost! This is why we have storage.

The first RAM chips appeared around 1968 and contained 256 bits of read-and-write memory. A 1-KB memory chip soon followed. The KB stands for *kilobits* or 1,000 bits of memory; note 1,000 bits, not bytes, in this case. In an 8-bit machine like the old Apple II, it would take eight 1-KB chips to give you 1,000 bytes of RAM.

By the 1990s, personal computers were using 32-bit word sizes for computation and memory addressing, and total memory installations of 16 to 32 megabytes. SIMMs or *single in-line memory modules* were created to greatly reduce the components required to install this much memory. SIMMs are sized by word size, not bits, so that a 16-megabyte SIMM is truly 16 megabytes of memory on a 32-bit computer. With the introduction of the newer 64-bit PowerPC and Pentium II machines, DIMM memory chips were created by combining two SIMMs.

Let us now examine *read-only memory,* or ROM. This type of memory can only be read. You cannot change the contents of ROM. When you turn on the computer, the information stored in ROM is always there. The main kernel of the operating system is placed in ROM by the manufacturer to ensure that your computer has some intelligence when you first turn it on. Programs stored in ROM are called *firmware* rather than software because they cannot be erased.

Clock. The third component of the process stage is the *system clock.* For musicians this is a simple concept. Every computer has the equivalent of a metronome that synchronizes all events that take place within its various stages. The metronome in a computer is a precision quartz clock. The tempo of the metronome is the computer's *clock speed;* each CPU has a range of clock speeds that it can support; clock speed is also dependent upon the rate at which memory can read and write data. Clock speed is measured in *Hertz* (Hz), or cycles per second; the abbreviation MHz indicates *MegaHertz,* or millions of cycles per second. Clock speeds have increased from 1 MHz to 350 MHz and are going higher. IBM and others are experimenting with CPU chips running at the 1-gigahertz speed.

Instead of using simple clock speed to determine the efficiency of a computer, it is more accurate to refer to the number of instructions a computer can execute per second. If an average instruction on a Pentium II chip takes 3 clock cycles and the CPU's clock speed is 300 MHz, then the number of instructions per second is 100 million. In computer jargon one could say that the Pentium II is capable of 100 MIPS, or million instructions per second.

Interfaces. Inside the process stage of a computer, the CPU, memory, and clock communicate and connect with each other through an internal parallel *bus* on the motherboard. This is a pathway of small etched wires that connects various chips. Most computers provide slots or connections that enable external devices or circuit boards to access data, controls, and clock signals on the bus. Terms like NuBus, MCA bus, ISA or Extended ISA (EISA) bus, and PCI bus refer to different bus designs used in different computers.

The Peripheral Component Interconnect or PCI bus is now commonly used by the industry across all computer platforms. Following the PCI standard makes it easy for you to purchase a new device for your computer, like a hard drive or video board, for example, without worrying whether it is a Macintosh or a Wintel computer. PCI is a 32-bit bus but supports a 64-bit extension for new processors, such as the Pentium or PowerPC.

Another standard, especially among laptop and portable computers, is the PCMCIA (Personal Computer Memory Card International Association) card interface. PCMCIA is a standard for small, credit-card-sized devices, called PC Cards. From your laptop you can pop in and pop out PC Cards for modems, Ethernet networking, fax, SCSI interfaces, video digitizers, and more.

Input

In order for the CPU to process information, the data must be entered into the computer. Charles Babbage proposed using punched cards. Other input devices that have been used at one time or another include punched paper tape, magnetic tape, typewriter-like keyboards, music keyboards, musical instrument controllers, and a host of pointing devices. Pointing devices include light guns, light pens, touch panels, graphics tablets, joysticks, and the one in common use with GUI operating systems today, the mouse.

Keyboard. The keyboard has a long association with communications and computers dating back to the teletype machine. The impetus for the ASCII system came from the need to standardize the codes for each key so that teletypewriters and computers could communicate. Many of the names for ASCII keys stem from their teletype heritage. For example, the return key is known as the *carriage return* from older typewriter technology where the carriage physically moved across the page when a new line started. Each computer manufacturer maintains the standard QWERTY layout and then adds special keys: escape (esc), control (ctrl), enter, cursor movement keys, and function keys (F1, F2, . . . F15). Wintel keyboards have certain idiosyncratic keys like the ALT, INS, and function keys. Macintosh extended keyboards also have function keys and "enter" as well as

ASIDE

The QWERTY (pronounced "kwerty") keyboard layout was devised about 1870. Its name comes from the series of letters reading from the left in the top row of letter keys. If you know how to touch-type, you are familiar with the QWERTY keyboard by feel alone.

The feel of a keyboard is very important.

"return." The one unique Macintosh key is the Command key, also known as the Open Apple ⌘ or Flower ⌘ key.

Physical features to consider are the placement of the keys in terms of typing comfort, the action of the keys when pressed (a lot like keyboard action on a piano), and the number of special keys provided. Most keyboards have what is called *n-key rollover*. This means that the keyboard will let you press another key before your finger has released the previous key—a must for fast typists.

Mouse. The *mouse* gets its name because it looks like a little creature with a tail. It was invented as a *point-and-click device* by Douglas Engelbart at the Stanford Research Institute in 1964, and was made popular by the Macintosh.

There are two mouse designs, mechanical and optical:

Mouse devices now offer a scrolling wheel between the two buttons for fast scrolling through long documents and Web pages.

▶ The *mechanical* mouse uses a rubber-coated ball that rotates within the mouse case as you roll it over a flat surface. It can be used on any surface but requires regular cleaning.

▶ The *optical* mouse uses optical sensors within the case to track the movement of the ball. It requires a special reflective pad. The mouse directs a light beam down on the reflective surface, and the reflections are used to track its position. The optical mouse provides a smooth, frictionless feel, and requires little maintenance.

The traditional Macintosh mouse has only one button for selecting options from pull-down menus, check boxes, and the like; the traditional Windows mouse has two buttons. The left button behaves like the Macintosh button. The right button, when clicked, usually brings up a pop-up menu with various options that can be selected from the object chosen. For example, right-clicking on a disk drive icon will give you options for Open, Copy, Format, and Properties, among others.

Output

After data have been manipulated by the computer, the results must be translated back into human-readable form. Output devices include color and monochrome video displays, and printers of different varieties including laser, ink-jet, color, and others. Video displays go by many names including CRTs (cathode ray tubes), VDTs (video display terminals), monitors, screens, displays, and terminals.

We will discuss printers and video displays in more detail in Viewport IV.

Interfaces. Printers use either a direct parallel connection or a serial network connection; many offer both as an option. A Hewlett-Packard (HP) laser printer, for example, may come with both a Centronics parallel connection and an Ethernet or TCP/IP network serial connection. The network connection provides the capability of sharing the printer with other computers. Computers commonly connect to video displays in accordance with either of two industry standards: NTSC *composite* video or *RGB* video; both are serial methods.

Storage

LINK

Modules 5 and 7 also discuss features of disks.

The remaining stage of the IPOS model is storage of programs and data on devices including floppy disks, hard disks, and optical disks. On each type of storage device, binary information is recorded in a permanent form external to CPU and memory.

Floppy Disk Technology. Figure 8.2 shows a common 3.5-inch floppy diskette. Inside its outer plastic shell is a circular disk coated with the same magnetic material as audio recording tape. This inner disk is thin and flexible; hence the name *floppy*. The computer cannot use the diskette unless it has been formatted into tracks and sectors. Floppies hold as little as 160 KB on older 5.25-inch diskettes, up to 1.4 MB or even 2.8 MB on 3.5-inch diskettes.

Through improved technology, new super-floppy disks offer an attractive alternative to conventional floppy diskettes. The Iomega Zip is a good example with its 100-MB, inexpensive disks that look like fat floppies. Competitors to the Zip disk permit reading of the older 1.4-MB floppies as well as the newer 100-MB or greater flexible disk format. The super-floppy technology may soon replace the old 3.5-inch floppy diskettes as the flexible storage medium of choice.

Winchester Hard Disk Technology. Floppy diskettes are great for transporting data; a 3.5-inch floppy fits nicely into your shirt pocket and is reasonably safe from damage. But eventually you will need more storage space and faster access to data and applications. Enter the Winchester hard disk, developed by IBM in 1973 and first appearing for personal computers as the Shugart drive in 1978 (see the diagram on the right of Figure 8.2).

A Winchester hard disk uses an inflexible, rapidly spinning platter; hence the name *hard disk*. The platter is coated with magnetic material similar to that on recording tape and floppy diskettes. Its storage capacity is typically somewhere in the 1- to 9-gigabyte range. The drive gets its

Figure 8.2
Workings of floppy and hard disks

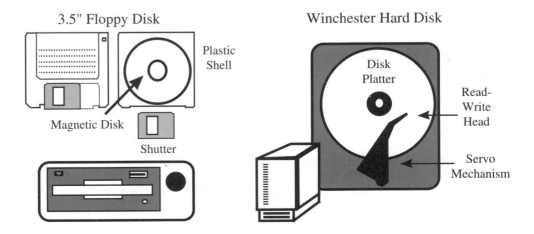

3.5" Floppy Disk

Plastic Shell

Magnetic Disk

Shutter

Winchester Hard Disk

Disk Platter

Read-Write Head

Servo Mechanism

name from the Winchester recording head that floats on a cushion of air, never touching the platter. The entire mechanism is sealed from the environment.

Figure 8.2 shows the outside case of a hard disk and a schematic diagram of the sealed drive mechanism. Note the disk platter, the servo mechanism that moves the drive heads around the platter, and the read-write head. As with floppy diskettes, the hard drive platter must be formatted before any computer data can be stored on the disk.

The key factors to consider when evaluating the performance of hard drives are:

Slipped dis(c)(k)(ette)s: Would you believe? Use *disc* with laser discs; use *disk* with all other disks; use *diskette* when referring to conventional floppy disks. Sorry!

▶ Access time: How long it takes a drive to position the drive heads over the correct track and sector in order to read or write data. Hard drives have access times in the range of 4 to 16 milliseconds.

▶ Data transfer rate: how long it takes to get data from the computer to the drive and back again. This rate is difficult to assess because it depends on many other design factors. In modern PCs, you should expect data transfer rates of 5 megabytes per second or higher. Hard drives especially designed for recording digital video and audio in real time typically have much faster access times and transfer rates, but the increased performance makes them more expensive.

▶ Storage capacity: how many bytes of data you can store on the disk. Capacity most commonly is at least 1 gigabyte and can go up to and beyond 9 gigabytes.

Removable versions of hard disk technology also exist to provide portability and flexibility in storage. With the *hard drive cartridges*, the Winchester disk platter is sealed in a removable case or cartridge, which you can remove and replace with another. Access time is generally slower than with fixed-platter hard drives. Syquest has made cartridge drives for many years which have become a standard for the printing industry with cartridges from 44 to 200 MB in storage. Iomega makes a Jaz cartridge removable drive that provides 1 GB of storage with fast enough access that it can be used for recording digital audio and video.

CD-ROM and DVD Technologies. Optical discs use a different principle for recording information. Instead of magnetic particles arranged on a spinning surface, optical devices use light reflected off minute crystalline particles. To write binary codes to an optical disc, a laser beam heats or changes a spot on a disc from a random or amorphous spot (binary 0) to a crystalline or ordered spot (1). To read the data back, the laser beam looks for reflections from the crystalline particles. The process is similar to that of consumer compact audio and video laser discs. Consumer laser discs, however, can only be read. Many computer optical discs can be written to as well as read. Those are known as CD-Recordable or the newer CD-ReWritable (CD-RW) discs.

Optical disc drives are becoming a reliable primary means of computer storage. They exist in many forms:

There's more to come on CD-ROM and DVD applications in Viewports III, VII, and VIII.

▶ The *CD-ROM drive* is, like its close relative, the compact audio disc, a read-only storage device. You can purchase CD-ROMs filled with clip art, digitized and MIDI music clips, fonts, encyclopedias of information, library retrieval indexes, and more. A CD-ROM disc can hold up to 640 MB of data, 600 times more than a floppy diskette.

▶ A more recent offspring of the CD-ROM disc is the DVD (Digital Versatile Disc). The DVD offers far greater storage capacity, up to 7 times the capacity of a CD-ROM or 4.7 GB per disc, with enough space to put a digital copy of a full-length feature film on one disc. The second generation of DVD drives offer a fast 200-ms or greater access time. More notable, though, is the fact that this generation of DVD drives supports the playback of standard CD audio, CD-ROM, DVD, and CD-RW or CD-R recordable formats. Your next purchase of a computer may include a DVD drive built in, or even, a DVD-RW drive (also known as DVD-RAM).

Erasable optical drives are ideal for storage of large graphic and music files.

Optical drives are available that write as well as read data. The CD-R and CD-RW drives are CD-ROM drives that will create CD-ROMs on the fly. The CD-R technology uses a blank CD-ROM disc to write or "burn" a CD-ROM that cannot be changed. The CD-RW drives do the same thing, but allow you to rewrite the CD-ROM disc (hence the RW for ReWrite). DVD-R or DVD-RAM drives perform the same functions with the DVD format. Both of these are excellent alternatives for backup of large amounts of data, including various multimedia files like digital video, graphics, and digital audio. Another attractive option for storing large amounts of data is the erasable or magneto-optical (MO) cartridge. Most of the optical cartridges are the same size as a 3.5-inch floppy disk and hold 120 to 240 MB of data each.

Tape Technology. Magnetic and digital tape recording systems are used with computers as alternative storage devices. The most common application for tape systems is for backup. For personal computing, quarter-inch magnetic tape cassette drives are inexpensive and popular. A digital audio tape (DAT) cartridge is slightly larger than a credit card and contains a magnetic tape that can hold from 2 to 24 gigabytes of data. Tape systems are not random-access like a magnetic disk. They are linear, and to find a file you may have to search all the way to the end of the tape before you locate it. For archival backup purposes, however, tape systems are inexpensive and hold considerable quantities of data.

A competing interface standard for hard drives is EIDE, short for Enhanced IDE. Because of its lower cost, EIDE has replaced SCSI in many areas. With an EIDE device, however, you lose the ability to chain multiple devices that SCSI provides.

Disk Drive Interfaces. Disk drives are interfaced to computers for the most part using parallel data transfer. The critical nature of data transfer rates demands the most direct route possible between the CPU and the disk drive head. Many computer manufacturers have proprietary interfaces and cabling for their disk drives. The one interface that has achieved standard acceptance is the *small computer system interface,* or SCSI. Optical disks, floppy disks, hard drives, CD-ROM and DVD drives, and even printers and scanners use the SCSI interface. It has a cable and connector that is quite distinctive. Up to seven SCSI devices can be successively connected in a *daisy chain.* Newer versions of the SCSI interface providing faster transfer rates between SCSI devices include FastSCSI and UltraSCSI.

Networking: Four Routes to Connectivity

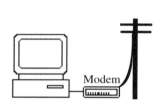

We turn our attention now from the mechanics of computers and their peripherals to focus on the mechanics of getting connecting to networks and the Internet. Network hardware enables our computers to expand beyond the desktop with worldwide access to other computers and servers.

Figure 8.3 illustrates four ways that two people might connect and communicate through their computers over phone lines or a direct network connection. We will bring back Bruce Baudtalk and Ester Email from Module 7 to help explain these options. These routes use three solutions for establishing communication:

▶ modems and standard phone lines

▶ direct-wire connection through a local area network (LAN)

▶ the Internet

We will briefly trace each route for you.

Route A. In Route A, Bruce and Ester are directly connected over tele-

Figure 8.3
Four routes for network connectivity

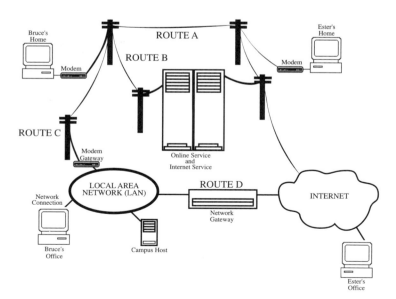

Client and server concepts were first discussed in Module 6.

phone lines from their home, computer to computer. In its simplest form, this is peer-to-peer networking. Both of their workstations have modems to translate computer data into the appropriate signals required to convey data over phone lines. This is one of the oldest and simplest connections to implement. However, it requires them to dedicate their personal phone lines while they are connected, pay long-distance phone rates, and personally arrange the time for connecting and exchanging information. This is also one of the slowest ways to transfer electronic information between two computers.

Route B. Bruce and Ester continue to use a modem and personal phone lines from their home. Instead of a direct peer-to-peer link, however, they use a commercial on-line service or an Internet Service Provider (ISP) as an intermediary. This is an example of client-server networking, where the computers of Bruce and Ester are *clients* accessing a commercial or ISP *server* that provides a variety of services including access to the Internet.

Route B uses exactly the same modem setup as Route A, but now they can avail themselves of the data storage, electronic mail, newsgroups, Web hosting, conferencing, and other features provided by the ISP. On-line services like America Online (AOL) also provide many additional features like on-line magazines, shopping malls, stock information, educational references, news feeds, and so on. Bruce and Ester can dial into the on-line service at a time that best suits them and leave files and mail for each other. They can use a local phone number to reach the service, avoiding long-distance calls. The on-line services do charge a monthly fee, but this is way below the cost of long-distance charges.

Network Connection

Route C. Bruce's campus has a *local area network* or LAN connecting all of the campus computers together. Bruce uses the local phone lines and his modem to dial in from home to the campus LAN. He can gain access to the LAN through a modem gateway, or bank of modems, connecting local phone lines to the campus network wiring. With special software on his home computer that uses the Internet TCP/IP protocol, Bruce Baudtalk's home computer can respond and navigate over the Internet just as his office computer directly connected to the network can. However, using modems and local phone lines, transmission of data will be much slower than when working from his office connected directly to the LAN. For this arrangement, Bruce has the advantage of being part of a college campus that provides ISP services for its students and faculty. Without this service, Bruce would have to use a commercial ISP service as noted in Route B.

Figure 8.3 shows the computer in Bruce's office connected to this LAN, as well as a computer connected to the campus network as a network *host* for campus e-mail, Web pages, FTP files, and other Internet services. Notice that the campus LAN is connected, through a network *gateway,* to the Internet. This provides another route for Bruce to reach Ester's computer. The Internet connects computer workstations (the network clients) and host computers (the network servers) around the globe through high-speed telephone and fiber optic connections.

TCP/IP was discussed in Module 7.

Route D. Bruce and Ester can directly exchange information between their office computers over the Internet (peer-to-peer computing). This gives them the fastest, most flexible way to exchange e-mail and files and carry

on electronic conferencing. It also gives them access to each other's personal Web pages that they have placed on the campus network server, and to the e-mail or Web pages worldwide of any of their colleagues who are also connected to the Internet. Should either Bruce or Ester have their computer workstation turned off, Internet mail and files will be left on their campus host computer (network server) and can be retrieved at their leisure when they are back in their office.

Now that you have a view of the ways in which computers can physically connect to each other and the Internet, we will examine some of the hardware for modems, LAN connections, and wireless networking.

Modems. Routes A and B in Figure 8.3 require two key hardware components: a modem and a phone line. The phone line is a standard plain old telephone service (POTS) analog phone line. The line should not be a party line and, if you do a lot of computer networking, you many want to install a second phone line to keep your computer conversations separate from your voice conversations. Modems offer a wide variety of options to choose from. We will review the basic characteristics of modems, and what is required to connect one to your computer.

Networking protocols for modems was covered in Module 7.

Flavors of Modems. There are a number of factors to consider when examining the different flavors of modems, including:

▶ Speed (14.4, 28.8, 33.6, and 56 K bits per second): Modem speed directly determines modem cost. Fortunately modems are getting faster and cheaper. At the slow end, 9.6K and 14.4K modems fall in the cheapest category. In the midrange, 28.8K and 33.6K modems provide greater speed. The top-of-the-line modems at the moment are the 56 KBps. Typically, a top-of-the-line modem costs about $200. Which speed should you purchase? As fast as you can afford and your ISP supports! In 1999, the 33.6K and 56K modems were the upper limit. You also want the fastest speed possible to handle the moving graphics and sound files that are commonplace on Internet Web pages.

▶ Physical packaging: Two popular modem packages are the classic desktop modem, which is external to your computer, and a small portable modem. Another option is to purchase a modem as an internal card. If you have a laptop with the PCMCIA interface discussed earlier in this module, small credit card modems can provide top-of-the-line modem speeds.

Modem manufacturers include, Zoom, Diamond/Supra, 3Com/USRobotics, Global Village, Motorola, and many others.

Installing Your Modem. Figure 8.4 shows a typical setup for installing a external modem; the accompanying margin diagram illustrates a back panel of a modem. A standard phone wire (with RJ-11 plug and jack) is connected from the wall jack to the line jack on the back panel of the modem. Your

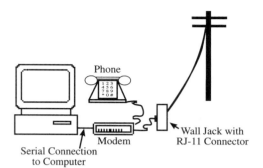

Figure 8.4
Setting up a modem

analog phone then plugs into the phone jack on the modem panel. To connect the modem to your computer, use a modem cable with a D-25 plug on one end (like the Serial Port connector shown in the diagram) and whatever your computer requires at the other end (for example, a 9-pin DIN or another D-25). Your computer must have a serial port for you to connect your modem. On Wintel computers, this is the serial COM1 or COM2 port, and on the Mac, it is your modem or printer serial printer port. Connect the power to your modem and the hardware setup is complete.

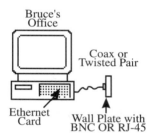

Connecting Computers to LANs. When communicating through a LAN, no modem is required (because phone lines are not being used), but networking hardware is needed. Figure 8.5 gives you a global view of the networking environment for Bruce, and the illustration shows you how his workstation is connected to the campus LAN. Let's examine some of the options for network connectivity from a personal computer. Protocols for network connectivity were discussed in Module 7. These included Ethernet, LocalTalk and EtherTalk, Token Ring, FDDI, and ATM network protocols.

The hardware required to connect a workstation to a LAN includes:

▶ A network interface card appropriate for the network protocol being used and for the physical network interface (or one already installed in your PC)

▶ The appropriate wiring from the card to the wall

▶ A wall jack or network tap that will make the connection to the LAN

See Module 6 for the settings for setting up your network software. A variety of network protocols were also discussed in Module 7. There are many good books and information on the Internet should you wish to delve deeper into this topic.

Bruce's computer shown in Figure 8.5 is connecting into an Ethernet LAN, one of the more common protocols for LAN networking. The computer is using an Ethernet interface card. Many PCs come with Ethernet already built into the computer without the need for an additional card. Vendors providing Ethernet network cards include 3Com, Dayna, Asantè, Farallon, and Xircom. Like modems, Ethernet network cards come as internal cards, as external boxes that can connect to a SCSI (or sometimes a parallel) port, and as PCMCIA credit-card sized versions. Figure 8.6 shows a variety of Ethernet cards. Most networking cards like these come with the standardized PCI bus discussed earlier in the module so that they can be used interchangeably on Macintosh and Wintel computers.

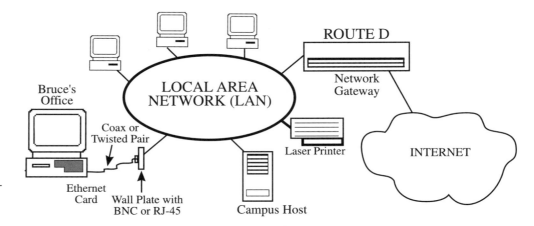

Figure 8.5
Peer-to-peer and client-server networking activities on a local area network (LAN)

Now for the wiring. Bruce's LAN uses 10Base-T Ethernet with RJ-45 connectors that look like fat telephone connectors. His office phone jack was already wired for telephone and 10Base-T, so all he had to do after installing his Ethernet board in his computer was to connect the cable from the card to the wall. After installing the appropriate software, he was ready to surf the Internet.

Wireless Connectivity. The future vision for computer networking is an environment where "anywhere-anytime computing" prevails. For education as well as business, achieving this goal will have tremendous impact on the way we use technology to enhance our daily personal and professional affairs. A key ingredient necessary to make anywhere-anytime computing a

Figure 8.6
Ethernet networking cards for desktop and portable computers
(Courtesy of 3Com)

In 1941, Actress Hedy Lamarr and the early 20th-century American composer George Antheil patented the concept of "frequency hopping" that is used in today's wireless computer networking.

(Courtesy of Metricom)

reality is wireless connectivity. Exciting things are happening to free us from the tyranny of wires, cables, plugs, and jacks. Wireless technologies offer both an attractive cost and a physical alternative to drilling holes and pulling wire to network classrooms, dorms, and the like.

Three technologies provide anywhere-anytime wireless computing:

▶ Infrared

▶ Cellular

▶ Radio

Infrared is provided with many computer workstations. Using the same technology as TV and VCR remote controllers, infrared signals can broadcast data at 230K bits per second or higher throughout a room. Its only drawback is that it cannot go through walls or floors. With the infrared feature, your computer can exchange data with printers, other computers, or a personal digital assistant or PDA computer like the Newton. Devices that can talk infrared are known as IRDA devices; HP and Citizen IRDA printers, for example, can print from an IRDA computer. This is just the wireless solution needed for a computer lab-on-wheels, and even for cable-free MIDI music setups. Direct, line-of-sight infrared networking can move data at 16 MBps or higher, the same speeds of Token Ring and Ethernet.

Cellular wireless networking piggybacks computer data on top of cellular voice transmissions. It takes advantage of unused air time during cellular phone calls. With transmission rates around 20 KBps, cellular is one solution for local community-wide wireless networking. It is an excellent solution for communicating from the mall, park, home, school, car, or airport from your portable computer or a personal digital assistant like the US Robotics' PalmPilot.

Radio wireless networking solutions broadcast much like a radio from an assigned radio frequency. Metricom is one commercial venture that provides this type of computer networking to several cities and university campuses. You subscribe to Metricom's service much like signing up for cable TV. They provide a Ricochet wireless radio modem like the one shown in the margin at the left that easily attaches to your computer or laptop and picks up Metricom's broadcast from 902 to 928 MHz on your modem's "radio dial." You can check your e-mail, surf the Web, or submit your homework assignments from anywhere on campus or within range of its radio broadcast.

LAN Topologies and Other Networking Issues

The balance of this module will touch on more general issues related to networks: LAN topologies (arrangements), peer-to-peer and client-server networking, and network gateways. These concepts are helpful as you face decisions about connecting your computer to networks.

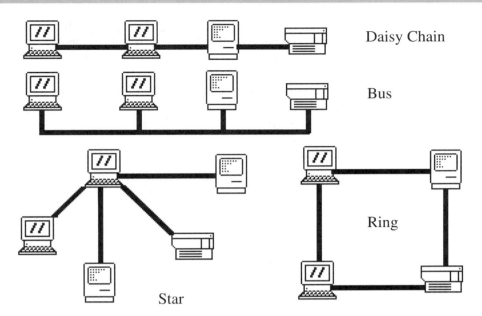

Figure 8.7
Four networking
topologies

Topologies. There are four layouts or *topologies* for constructing a local area network. These, shown in Figure 8.7, are:

▶ daisy chain

▶ bus

▶ star

▶ ring

Each topology describes the wiring configuration for connecting hardware on the LAN. That hardware can include any clients or nodes on the LAN: computer workstations, printers, file servers, modem servers, and the like.

Network concepts like Ethernet and LocalTalk, and Ring and Bus, are covered in Module 7.

Daisy Chain. The *daisy chain* topology is the simplest LAN to implement. Just connect network wiring from one workstation to the next. One computer client hands off the data to the next client in the chain. This topology is recommended for small LANs of a few workstations in close proximity to one another. However, this topology is only as good as the next client in the chain; if a workstation is disabled, the chain stops there. LocalTalk or EtherTalk LANs are easily and cheaply configured as daisy chain topologies. The simplest MIDI networks use a daisy chain topology.

Bus. As you start to expand a LAN, you can improve upon a daisy chain by using a *bus* topology. It is simple to implement and maintain. A bus topology lays down a primary wiring pathway (often called a *backbone* on larger LANs), and all the clients on the LAN then tap into this network bus. Each message is sent out on the bus in search of the address of its destination. Ethernet LANs commonly use a bus topology, as well as LocalTalk LANs.

LANs built upon a bus topology use a minimum of wiring and are easy and inexpensive to implement. Their major advantage over daisy chain topologies is that any node on the network can be taken out of operation, or a new node added, without disabling the rest of the network. The disadvantages are traffic jams, network security, and maintenance. All clients on the bus use the same backbone and, as the LAN expands and the number of nodes increases, there is greater competition for space on the bus. Furthermore, it is difficult to pinpoint problems on a bus topology, and security is hard to maintain when every network client on the LAN can potentially see all the data flowing across the bus.

Star. In the *star* topology, all the clients on the network radiate out from a hub or central workstation (see Figure 8.7). In fact, a star LAN works just like the phone system with all messages flowing through a central switchboard.

The star configuration provides a highly controlled network environment. Each client has its own private wiring to the central hub for fast and reliable data transfer. New clients can be easily added. Maintenance and security are excellent, because data can be traced to each specific node. The disadvantages include that this topology takes considerably more wiring to implement and, more importantly, that the workstation that serves as the main hub has a lot of work to perform. If the central hub goes out of commission, the entire star is shut down.

Ethernet LANs can be implemented with a star topology. Stand-alone *hubs* or network servers can be the central hub on the star, instead of a computer workstation. On large LANs, the bus and star topology can be combined with mini-star LANs at each node on a bus—some call this a *tree* topology. The Internet is undoubtedly the biggest, most extensive tree topology of all!

Ring. In a ring arrangement, the data are passed from node to node (or client to client) around the circle until they find their destination. You might view the ring topology as a daisy chain where the last node is connected to the first. Data in a token ring are passed in tokens that move around the ring much as automated people movers on a tram or subway.

An advantage the ring shares with the star topology is high-performance speed and reliability, because there is a dedicated path to and from each workstation on the LAN. As with the bus and daisy chain topologies, wiring is minimized. A primary fault of this topology, however, is the weakness caused by a break in the ring. This can be overcome by the use of wire centers for each node that keep the ring intact even though a machine is removed from the ring. This configuration is most often associated with IBM token ring and FDDI networks. They have a reputation for being some of the most secure and stable network LANs, but the most expensive and complex to implement and maintain.

Peer, Client, and Server Relationships. *Peer-to-peer* or *client-client* networking, and *client-server* or *file-server* networking, are terms used to

Consider these same topologies and issues when configuring a MIDI network. As you will see in Module 22, a good MIDI network is one that uses a star topology with the MIDI interface or patch bay as the central hub.

Web, e-mail, FTP, and news clients are used to perform many Internet client-server activities.

describe both software operations over a network and hardware relationships where a computer can take on the role of a client, a server, or both in a network topology.

One mode of network activity takes place directly between clients. Files can be exchanged, and text, audio, or video conferencing can take place. The clients all have equal status on the LAN, with the workload distributed among them. That is why this mode is called peer-to-peer or client-client networking.

Refer again to Figure 8.5. Bruce can perform peer-to-peer activities with any of the other clients or workstations on the campus LAN; he can also perform peer-to-peer activities over the Internet with workstations on other LANs. Computers that are used as clients on a network can run the gamut from Wintel and Macintosh PCs to SGI, Sun, Hewlett Packard, and Digital workstations.

The other mode of network activity is *client-server* or, to use an older term, file-server networking. Notice the campus host computer on the LAN in Figure 8.5. This computer maintains a variety of databases and servers for the campus information system: student records, course offerings and syllabi, a campus phone book, e-mail, Web pages, Usenet news, shareware, and the like. Any of the other clients on the campus LAN can carry out client-server activities with the campus host by accessing the servers on this machine. Through the campus gateway to the Internet, client-server connectivity can also be established with other Web, news, and e-mail servers throughout the world.

Creating servers on networks can be as simple as dedicating a Wintel or Macintosh computer workstation. However, those machines that act as servers for a large number of users, especially with Internet access, are typically machines with faster and more sophisticated processors, memory, and storage. When you log onto servers on the Internet, you are likely to find a computer such as an RS6000, VAX, Sun, SGI, or Hewlett-Packard, or even larger mainframe systems.

Gateways, PPPs, and More. The last hardware topic that we will touch on related to LANs is the issue of connecting LANs to LANs and connecting remote users to LANs via phone lines and modems. The campus network shown in Figure 8.8 has a gateway between the campus LAN and the Internet, and a modem/PPP server providing remote access from modems off-campus.

Figure 8.8 shows a *gateway* between the campus LAN and the Internet. The campus link to the Internet is a high-speed telephone service over fiber optic cable, a 1.54-MBps T1 line through a provider like MCI or Sprint. Gateways are used when a wide variety of networking protocols must be translated in order to link with many different LANs and the Internet. The gateway in Figure 8.8 translates TCP/IP over Ethernet networks to meet the requirements for sending data packets over the high-speed T1 phone line.

Another form of connectivity noted in Figure 8.8 is the *Point-to-Point (PPP) server*. This server provides a link between remote users dialing in over modems and provides access to TCP/IP resources on the campus LAN.

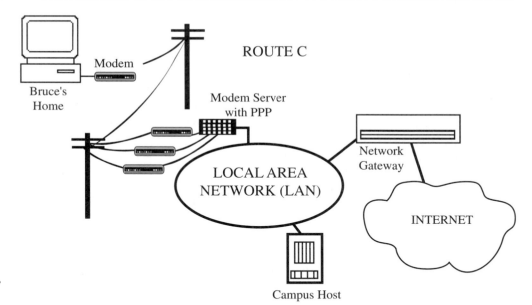

Figure 8.8
Remote Internet access
through a PPP server, LAN,
and Internet gateway

Modem servers act as bridges between modem and network protocols, and permit a large number of dedicated phone lines and modems to serve as a dial-in port to a network. Typically one number is used for dial-in, and the telephone hardware rolls the incoming call over to the next available number in a pool of phone lines and modems.

PPP connectivity is very important to you! With this form of network access, your remote computer is a full and active Internet client. You can use FTP, Web, e-mail, and news clients over the modem just as you would with a direct connection to the network. Once PPP is configured on your computer, all Internet client software will function properly without the need for setting modem communication parameters for every application. Pardon the expression, but PPP is "the greatest thing since sliced bread" for supporting Internet computing from remote locations!

Viewport II

Summary

Learning to use computers and the Internet for musical experiences is a bit like learning your first musical instrument. At first, you just want to know what needs to be done to make nice sounds. Later on, you discover that knowing something about how the instrument is designed and how music works makes you more independent and musical. These modules have introduced some of the important concepts about getting started with computers and linking to the Internet and the World Wide Web. In doing so, we stressed not only how to get started with a few simple tasks but also how to think about the design and structure of computers and their connections.

We have covered a good deal of detail in this viewport that you will want to refer to again. To help with this, the chart below shows the key concepts related to computer systems and to the Internet. Refer back to this any time you need to look up this information.

Table 7.3

Category and Topic	Module 5	Module 6	Module 7	Module 8
Historical Perspective				√
Computer Setup				
Your computer and music environment	√			
Three streams of digital information (Network, MIDI, and audio)	√			
Local and networked resources	√			
Storage Options				
Storage media, including floppy, hard, optical disks	√			√
CD-ROM and DVD technologies	√			√
Tape technology				√
Networked storage options, including linkages with the Internet	√	√	√	√
Data Structures of the Computer				
Digital representation and binary numbers	√		√	

Category and Topic	Module 5	Module 6	Module 7	Module 8
Bits and bytes			√	
Digital to Analog and Analog to Digital	√		√	
IPOS Model				
IPOS model and the operating system	√			
IPOS model and hardware				√
Central Processing Unit (CPU)				√
Random-access memory (RAM)				√
Storage memory				√
Read-only memory (ROM)	√			√
System clock				√
Hardware bus				√
QWERTY keyboard and mouse				√
Disk formats and formatting media	√		√	√
Drive Interfaces (Parallel and serial data structures)		√	√	√
Function of the Operating System				
Linking the user with local and networked resources	√		√	
Graphic User Interface				
Mouse gestures	√			
Icons	√			
Windows	√			
Menus	√			
Buttons and dialogs	√			
Files, folders, and volumes	√			
Folder hierarchies in operating systems	√			
Working with Files				
Opening, closing, and deleting	√			
Saving, duplicating, and stealing	√			
Naming conventions for files and folders	√			
Freeware and shareware	√			
Safe Computing				
Approaches to backup	√			
Viruses and other forms of mischief	√			
Alternative Operating Systems				
UNIX	√			
Power of Networks				
Network connections built into operating systems	√	√		
Client-server model	√	√		√
Trends toward smaller and faster computers		√		
Effects on concepts of time, space, and collaborative learning		√		
Configuring operating system software and Internet client software for Internet	√	√		
E-mail		√		
News readers		√		
FTP		√		

Category and Topic	Module 5	Module 6	Module 7	Module 8
Connections to the Internet		√	√	√
Physical link of the computer to a Internet Service Provider	√	√		√
Remote (modem) and direct connections to the Internet		√	√	√
Data over telephone lines—modem protocols		√	√	√
Modem setup				√
Baud rate and compression			√	√
ISDN and other digital transmission formats with phone lines			√	√
Ethernet, LocalTalk, Token Ring, Fiber Optic Distributed Interface (FDDI), and Asynchronous Transfer Mode (ATM)			√	√
10BaseT and other options				√
Wireless connectivity				√
LAN Topologies: daisy chain, star, ring				√
Data Structures on the Internet				
Transmission Control Protocol/Internet Protocol (TCP/IP)			√	
Internet Protocol (IP) numbers			√	
Packets and Datagrams			√	
Domain Names			√	
File transmission and compression: .sea, .exe., and other formats			√	
File compression utilities			√	
Universal file formats for text, sounds, images, and movies	√		√	
Binhex conversion			√	
Web browsers				
World Web Web browser software and its characteristics		√		
Basics of how Web sites are constructed		√		
Links between Web sites		√		
Hypertext Markup Language (HTML) as the code for Web pages		√		
Universal Resource Locators (URLs) as the addresses for files		√	√	
Search engines and their role in finding resources on the Web		√		
Bookmarks as saved links		√		
Browsing software's ability to open local files for inexpensive multimedia presentations		√		
Helper applications and plug-ins for Web browsers		√		
Incorporation of e-mail and news reading as part of Web browsers		√		
JavaScript as part of Web browsers		√		
Other Internet Clients				
Push technology		√		
Chat groups		√		

Supplementary Readings

Ackermann, Ernest, and Karen Hartman. *Search and Researching on the Internet and the World Wide Web.* Wilsonville, Ore.: Franklin, Beedle & Associates, 1998.

Danuloff, Craig. *Mac OS8 Book: The Ultimate Macintosh User's Guide,* Research Triangle Park, N.C.: Ventana Communications Group, Inc. 1997.

Dictionary of Computing, 4th Edition. Oxford: Oxford University Press, 1996.

Giordan, Daniel. *The Whole Mac.* Indianapolis, Ind.: Hayden Book Co, 1996.

Hafner, Katie and Matthew Lyon. *Where Wizards Stay Up Late: The Origins of the Internet.* New York: Simon and Schuster, 1996.

Honeycutt, Jerry. *Using the Internet* (4th edition). Indianapolis, Ind.: Que Press, 1998.

Joyce, Jerry, and Marianne Moon. *Microsoft Windows 95 At a Glance.* Redmond, Wash.: Microsoft Press, 1997.

Levine, John, and Margaret Levine Young. *Unix for Dummies* (3rd edition). Foster City, Calif.: IDG Books, 1997.

Mash, David. *Musicians and Computers.* Miami: Warner Brothers Publications, 1998.

Ohara, Shelly. *Discover Windows 95.* San Mateo, Calif.: IDG Books, 1997.

Perelman, Lewis J. *School's Out: Hyperlearning, the New Technology, and the End of Education.* New York: William Morrow and Company, 1992.

Pogue, David. *MacWorld: Mac & PowerMac Secrets.* San Mateo, Calif.: IDG Books, Inc., 1996.

Quercia, Valerie. *Internet in a Nutshell.* Sebastopol, Calif.: O'Reilly & Associates, Inc., 1997.

Reid, Robert. *Architects of the Web: 1,000 Days That Built the Future of Business.* New York: John Wiley, 1997.

Rheingold, Howard. *The Virtual Community: Homesteading on the Electronic Frontier.* Menlo Park, Calif.: Addison-Wesley Publishing, 1993.

Schrage, Michael. *Shared Minds: The New Technologies of Collaboration.* New York: Random House, 1990.

Turkle, Sherry. *Life on the Screen: Identity in the Age of the Internet.* New York: Simon and Schuster, 1995.

White, Ron. *How Computers Work, Deluxe Edition.* Emeryville, Calif.: Ziff-Davis Press, 1997.

Williams, Robin. *The Little Mac Book* (5th edition). Berkeley, Calif.: Peachpit Press, 1998.

Viewport III: Computer-Assisted Instruction in Music

> If the computer is a universal control system, let's give kids universes to control.
>
> —Ted Nelson, *Dream Machines* (1974)

> The conventional "technology" of the classroom is a thousand-year-old invention initially adopted to discipline an esoteric cadre of ascetic monks. The institution of contemporary, "public" education is a 19th-century innovation designed as a worker-factory for an industrial economy. Both have as much utility in today's modern economy of advanced information technology as the Conestoga wagon or the blacksmith shop.
>
> —Lewis Perelman, *School's Out: The New Hyperlearning, Technology, and the End of Education* (1992)

> The present uses of computers and related technologies in music education, often limited to noncreative skill development, can expand to new horizons of musicality if they fulfill their potential of giving people direct access to creative decision making with sounds, storage and instant retrieval of those sounds, and devices to alter and refine the previous decisions: all the conditions that would enable genuine compositional creativity.
>
> —Bennett Reimer, music educator and philosopher, *A Philosophy of Music Education* (1989)

Overview

This viewport is devoted to technology that supports the teaching and learning of music. Module 9 deals with computer-assisted instruction (CAI) software that provides support for aural skills, theoretical and historical understanding, and performance; also of importance are programs that seek to simulate music experiences associated with composition and improvisation. This is followed by a primer on acoustics in Module 10, the essential properties of sound critical to understanding sampling and music synthesis. Modules 11 and 12 provide the first introduction to the data and hardware concepts related to digital audio and sampling, laser video and audio, and MIDI technology. We shall:

▶ Review the historical basis of CAI software and hardware

▶ Describe categories of CAI software according to music content and style of instruction: drill-and-practice, flexible practice, guided instruction, games, exploratory, and creative

119

▶ Use examples of commercial software to illustrate desirable features of music CAI

▶ Consider software choice in term of both the instructor's and the student's needs

▶ Review the acoustical properties of sound and sound synthesis

▶ Introduce data structures for digital audio, MIDI, and laser audio and video

▶ Examine the mechanics of hardware devices common to educational settings, including digital audio, MIDI, CD-ROM, and DVD-ROM

HISTORICAL TIMELINE
The Technology of Music and Instruction

1800s	Fourier establishes that any periodic motion can be represented as a sum of harmonically related sine waves
	Helmholtz publishes landmark work on the physics and acoustics of sound
1940s	Frank Cookson develops ear training drills using music examples on magnetic recording tape
1950s	Earliest experiments in digital synthesis conducted by Max Mathews and others at Bell Labs
	B. F. Skinner proposes that instruction can be divided logically and behaviorally into a number of small, linear steps leading to mastery
	Presser invents first automated teaching machine based on Skinnerian concepts of behavioral modification
	Norman Crowder proposes branching in programmed instruction to customize instruction to different ability levels
	Don Bitzer invents PLATO, a mainframe CAI system with touch sensitive panel input
1960s	Moog and Buchla design first popular commercial analog synthesizers
	Spohn and Poland develop a programmed instruction series for teaching music ear training using tape recorders
	James Carlsen devises first commercial programmed instruction for melodic dictation with prerecorded patterns on magnetic tape
	Edward Maltzman, working under Skinner, develops programmed instruction materials with a teaching device for pitch matching
	Ted Nelson coins the term *hypertext* to refer to linking and navigating through text information
	Kuhn and Allvin use an IBM 1620 with pitch-extraction to train melodic sight singing
1970s	Placek, Peters, and Eddins develop a library of music programs for the PLATO system
	David Shrader develops a rhythm teaching machine that is later marketed as the TAP Master
	Ned Deihl's ear training program for an IBM 1500 uses computer displayed music examples and prerecorded music tapes
	National Consortium for Computer Based Music Instruction (now the Association for Technology in Music Instruction) begins with a newsletter

	The low cost and portable design of the ARP 2600 makes it a popular synthesizer for the university music classroom
	Seymour Gooch designs digital sound generation device (Gooch Box) for mainframe music CAI, including PLATO and GUIDO systems
	Minnesota Educational Computing Consortium (MECC) is the first state-sponsored computer consortium to distribute and produce instructional software
	Fred Hofstetter develops GUIDO ear training curriculum for Burroughs 6700 mainframe, PLATO system (1975), Micro PLATO (1980), and then IBM PC (1985)
	Kuhn develops ear training instruction using a PDP-10 time-sharing system linked to a Thomas organ
	David B. Williams develops first music CAI software for a PC, Melodious Dictator (originally for a Poly 88)
	The Apple II, Commodore PET, Radio Shack TRS-80, and other home PCs appear
	MECC publishes Music Theory, one of the first music programs for the Apple II
1980s	CD-ROM and CD Audio (CD) format establishes worldwide standards for mass-produced CD-ROM discs
	First commercially successful pitch extraction device, Pitch Master, is marketed by Temporal Acuity Products
	David Williams and David Schrader's Micro Music, Inc. (MMI) produces first commercial library of music CAI for PCs, followed by G. David Peters's software library from Electronic Courseware Systems (ECS)
	Bruce Benward produces software series for Apple II to parallel his music theory textbooks
	The Melodious, Rhythmic, Harmonious, and Jazz Dictator series is the first rule-based music CAI designed for PCs by David Williams, Tim Kolosick, and others
	Mountain Music System is the first advanced digital sound for Apple II with light pen and 8 voices per stereo channel
	Music Instrument Digital Interface (MIDI) established by the MIDI Manufacturers Association and others
	Silver-Burdett publishing company produces first elementary basic text series to use software
	Brian Moore creates Sir William Wrong Note, first music error-detection program for PCs
	Sony produces first commercial compact disc player four years after idea developed by Philips and Sony
	Martin Lamb's Musicland Games for the Apple II is first creative composition tool on PCs for children
1985	Ted Nelson coins the term *hypermedia* to refer to linking and navigating through graphics, sound, and text
	Delaware Videodisc Music Series offers the first music videodiscs for interactive instruction
	Laurie Spiegel's Music Mouse is the first improvisation-based software that turns the computer into a musical instrument
	Bill Atkinson's HyperCard for the Macintosh is the first popular commercial hypertext authoring system
	ECS Keyboard Skills is the first MIDI teaching software that interacts with a piano keyboard
	Practica Musica and Listen become the first and most often used ear training and theory music CAI for Macintosh
	John Schaffer develops Harmony Coach using an expert artificial intelligence system designed for music CAI on a PC

1990s	Band-in-a-Box is the first commercial software to use MIDI instruments and a PC to provide automated accompaniments for improvisation
	Beethoven's Ninth Symphony CD (The Voyager Company) developed by Robert Winter is the first commercial instruction software using interactive CD audio
	Goodwin produces Pitch Explorer, an inexpensive pitch extraction package designed for the Macintosh
	Apple introduces QuickTime and Microsoft introduces Video for Windows for playing video and audio clips in desktop applications
	Coda's Vivace (SmartMusic) is one of the first computer-based accompaniment programs for the mass market that can follow the tempo and the notes of the performer
1995	Morton Subotnick's Making Music, followed by Making More Music, is one of the first children's composing software programs that uses a visual drawing metaphor
	Harmonic Vision's MusicAce I and II use guided instruction, game, and creative techniques to teach the basics of music to young children
	A 1997 survey at the University of Illinois found that 36 percent of teachers and students use some kind of music software in their school, and 27 percent use music CAI software (most commonly Music Ace, Professor Piccolo, Practica Musica, and Microsoft Musical Instruments)
	The first Web-based music instruction software appears and uses plug-ins like CDLink, Beatnik, Crescendo, and MIDIPlug for interactive MIDI, CD audio, and digital audio music
2000	Commercial DVD discs provide access to extensive libraries of digital video and audio for interactive computer-based music instruction
	Music CAI on demand becomes available over the Internet to create a universal library of software for a broad range of music skills and concepts

THE PEOPLE

REAL-WORLD PROFILE: CHRISTINE HERMANSON

Role: Private studio instructor and software designer in St. Louis

Christine Hermanson first used a personal computer for music instruction as an independent keyboard instructor in 1980, and has since become nationally known for her work in the use of technology in music education. She has been a frequent lecturer and clinician at state, regional, and national professional meetings, including the conferences of the Music Teachers National Association and the Music Educators National Conference. She has developed music curricula around the use of technology, has written articles about technology, and has organized and conducted the MTNA National Symposium on Technology in Music since its inception in 1988. She

Christine Hermanson working with CAI software
(Courtesy of Christine Hermanson)

is the author of the eleven award-winning software courses in the Musicware PIANO series, the Alfred's Basic Adult Piano Courses for Windows, and Musicware's newest product, SING!

Interview:

What do you do? I am a jack of all trades in music teaching! I have taught music in the public schools, have had a large privately-owned fine arts academy, have directed large and small choral ensembles, and I am a pianist and organist. I have been spreading the word about music technology as a clinician at conventions and consultant for school districts and colleges since 1983. In 1989, I had the opportunity to begin developing some of my own music instruction software, and have been working at that since then.

How did you become interested in computers and music technology? In the mid-70s, my dad built a PC from a kit (1K RAM)! I could see the potential for the PC in education, and had some specific applications in mind for use in my music studio. In 1980, we bought our first Apple II+ when the MECC Apple Music Theory software was first introduced. I already had a learning center set up in my music studio where each student spent time (in addition to regular lesson time) doing ear training tapes and theory worksheets. The computer replaced the pencil, paper, and tape recorder.

What computers do you use? I use both IBM-compatible and Macintosh computers. Our home contains multiple computers: several Windows 95 machines, a few Macs, and even an Apple II GS that we bought new way back when.

Three ways you use computers and music technology? Teaching: My piano students have used music technology in virtually every phase of their music experience with building music skills, applying those skills in performance, and creating music. Currently one can find tools in music technology to assist in the teaching of each of these skills. Music publishing: I use both IBM and Mac systems for music publishing and desktop publishing. My composition/notation software of choice: Nightingale (Mac) and Cakewalk (Windows 95). Writing and software development: I use my Mac and Microsoft Word to write articles, books, and manuals; I use the Windows 95 machines for software development.

A unique way you use computers for music? This past year I developed Musicware's SING!, and the latest release: Musicware PIANO Course Four. SING! uses microphone input in unique ways to give the student visual feedback of what they are singing. Each product is a complete course that includes music reading, ear training, theory, technical skills, and real-time vocal and piano performance which can be used to enhance private

instruction or as an independent study course for busy adults. A unique feature of these products is the fully-orchestrated accompaniments that provide an ensemble performing experience for users of both PIANO and SING! Each program includes a state-of-the-art accompaniment delivery system that features interactive teaching guides, pictures of each instrument used in the accompaniment, and feedback that indicates pitch and rhythmic accuracy, along with many other features.

If you could change one thing about how computers are used. what would it be? People's state of mind! In my work with schools and institutions of higher learning, I have been disappointed with the snail's pace at which the use of computer-assisted music skill development has been adopted. Our progress has been very slow! I am hopeful that as more states continue to reassess their music competency standards, it will become self-evident that the most effective and efficient way to develop the music reading, writing, and performance abilities in our students is through the consistent use of quality music instruction software that has been integrated into the day-to-day music curriculum.

The one most significant change ten years from now? I see the continued development and commercialization of the Internet and interactive TV as the next wave of technology that will affect the way music is taught in the schools and the home. Music courses available over the Internet, and distance learning/video conferencing technology that is allowing students to link up with master teachers from around the world, are already underway, and will continue to push music technology into even more advanced applications.

One word of advice you have for musicians interested in computers? Take advantage of every resource you can find: courses, workshops, and sessions on music technology in education, visit schools with successful programs, visit the Web sites of the various music software publishers, and try out the software demos. If you don't already have a computer of your own or computers in your classroom, don't make any computer purchases until you have selected the software you want to use. Don't be rushed in your decision by well-meaning friends or computer sales personnel who don't know music applications or your specific needs.

<table>
<tr><td>

**Module
9**

</td><td>

Instructional Software for Musicians

</td></tr>
</table>

Computer-assisted instruction, often referred to as CAI, is the subject of this viewport. As we noted in Module 3, this software falls into the Buy-and-Run category because little has to be done to make the software productive for your needs.

Who Cares about CAI?

See Module 12 for a historical overview of the development of CAI.

The quick answer is, "All musicians!" We are certainly concerned with the hundreds of music teachers and soon-to-be music teachers who make informed decisions about the use of software and hardware in the studio, rehearsal hall, and classroom. We know, too, that professional educators are not the only people concerned with good CAI. We all are students of music, no matter what our age, level of sophistication, or professional emphasis. Good musicians are always looking for ways to improve their understanding and ability, whether they are in formal classes or not. As the variety and quality of CAI technology grow, so does the independent use of this technology by all of us interested in self-improvement.

As we will see, the simple drill software that offered sometimes boring and often *amusical* exercises has long since given way to more intelligent, musically sensitive, and exciting software. Just as modern computer and music technology systems provide each of us with powerful ways to produce and notate music, so too have advances in hardware and software provided new ways to work with CAI.

Getting Started with CAI

You may have basic equipment already, including a computer that has a CD-ROM drive and a keyboard synthesizer that has MIDI capability. You may feel relatively comfortable with the way your computer works, but you may not understand your keyboard synthesizer and how it links with the computer and music software. You need a good mini-course in CAI technology! It should include information about:

▶ The variety of CAI software in music

▶ The acoustical properties of sound itself

▶ Music data structures used in software

▶ Hardware used in music CAI

We will touch on each of these topics in this viewport. *Software choice* is not always an easy issue. Remember in Viewport I we noted that software is one of the first things to consider in assembling a technology system. "What do I want the technology to do?" is the primary question, and it relates directly to a philosophy of music teaching and learning that should drive all curricular decisions. The question is: "As a music teacher, what kinds of music experiences do I want the software and hardware to support in order to make my teaching more effective?"

You need to ask yourself how the available technology will match your own philosophies about music teaching and learning, rather than just buying what seems to be the newest equipment or software. You also need to consider the individual student's personality, learning style, and motivation. This module will help describe some of the software possibilities that will match your needs as a teacher.

Module 10 lays the foundations for understanding how computers and music devices represent the *acoustical properties of sound*. You won't be able to use a synthesizer or a computer to its full potential if you don't understand these properties. We will explore both analog and digital concepts and provide a short introduction to the kinds of sound synthesis.

Module 11 explains how *data structures for music CAI software* are designed. This includes an introduction to MIDI and sound sampling, two important data structures of music technology that are used extensively for teaching as well as many other applications that will be explained in future viewports.

Finally, Module 12 addresses *music hardware* issues. It is here that we explain some of the mechanical issues of MIDI devices and laser discs such as CD-ROMs, CD audio, and Digital Versatile Disc (DVD). We will present our first version of a model computer workstation designed for music instruction activities (Figure 12.12); we call this music system the Keep It Short and Simple or KISS music system. The system will grow in complexity as we use it to describe other hardware setups in later viewports. To help tie all of this together in the viewport summary, we present a short description of how this information can be used to make initial decisions about music CAI software and hardware.

Drills to Thrills: Toward More Realistic Music Experiences

CAI has a long historical tradition. Early experiments with teaching machines began in the late 1940s. As important as the developments in sound and computer technology have been, perhaps the most important advances are in the design of the software itself. Traditional drill-and-practice software continues to be produced today, taking full advantage of increased processing speed and vastly improved sound. However, five new approaches in music software design emerged toward the end of the 1980s and continue today in increasingly elaborate form. We call these newer approaches:

▶ Drill-and-practice

▶ Flexible practice

▶ Guided instruction

▶ Games

▶ Exploratory

▶ Creative

In the pages that follow, we will list important characteristics for each category and offer a number of software examples from the many contexts that use CAI.

Drill-and-Practice. Because a large part of music education focuses on skills in aural perception (listening) and theoretical knowledge, and because computer software can be written relatively easily to exercise these skills, traditional drill-and-practice remains a common category of CAI. Software in this category is largely *computer-determined*, providing instruction in a manner dictated entirely by the software authors and the computer itself.

For example, software can be written that makes the computer display or sound a series of chords. The student is asked to respond by indicating the chord types or perhaps their function. If the student answers correctly, the software might provide a new set of chords that is more challenging. If the responses are incorrect, the software might branch off to an easier set. The music stimuli themselves are often quite short and are presented outside of a musical context. For many, this software provides an efficient and direct means to improve specific skills.

See Modules 11 and 12 for more about digitized sound and MIDI.

Flexible Practice. Software in this category has the purpose of skill development, but adds features that allow flexibility of use for an instructor and for the musician seeking self-improvement. Many of these features are a result of both the increased power of technology and of more creative, and perhaps more musical thinking by software authors. Software in this category is student- and teacher-centered in that choices permit individuals to have a hand in engineering their own music education. For instance, students might use their own understanding of weaknesses in chord identification to establish a special set of drills.

Flexible practice software typically provides menus and dialog boxes that let students choose the settings for a series of exercises that best suit their needs. In a similar way, teachers can use these features to create a tailor-made curriculum for an individual or class. These flexible options allow musicians to work with more realistic musical materials, while giving the software more depth of content.

Both drill-and-practice and flexible practice software often support multiple sound sources (internal digitized sound and MIDI sound). Because this software is often used for individualized instruction in large classes, it also provides some form of record-keeping in a networking environment.

Guided Instruction. Instead of offering a series of tasks for completion, some music software leads the student through tutorial instruction. An idea is presented through demonstration using text, audio, graphics, animation, movies, or some combination of all these. Often the software asks the student to interact with the tutorial in order to verify that the ideas are understood. Material is presented in levels of complexity and may contain related games to test mastery. Guided instruction software can be very imaginative and entertaining. As with drill-and-practice software, music content is nearly always defined by the author of the software.

Games. Some of the most motivational software for music teaching and learning, especially for younger children, is found in this category. Here the emphasis is placed on basic skill development and knowledge of the music elements such as melody and rhythm. This is done in a competitive way, often allowing more than one user to have turns at the correct answers. Sometimes the games are more like adventures in which a single user is asked to solve a puzzle or arrive at some defined plateau. Such adventures often have music tasks to solve on the way to the final goal. Game software generally makes extensive use of graphics and animation to accompany its many uses of sound. It might also contain elements of the exploration and creative categories.

Exploratory. The software in this category encourages the student to explore resources about a topic in a free way, moving from one topic to another in any approach that makes sense. The accent is less on mastering a particular skill or knowledge set and more on gathering information about a topic through the use of links. Exploratory software does not expect the user to work in a linear fashion from the beginning of the program to the end. This software often is organized in chapters or units of instruction with content between chapters interrelated. Links to a glossary of terms are common, as are connections to relevant content found on the Internet's World Wide Web. The focus of this category of software is on music history and listening experiences. Many titles in this category use audio CDs, CD-ROMs, and DVDs (as that technology emerges).

Creative. The most recent category to emerge in CAI software is what we have called "creative." Here the idea is to encourage students to create music as a way of better understanding the art. For example, creative CAI might provide an opportunity to compose music with graphic representation or to improvise original music with accompaniments provided by the software.

See Modules 11 and 12 to learn more about audio CDs, CD-ROMs, and DVDs.

Still other titles might provide an accompaniment to a traditional solo work. To support listening, creative software might offer a construction kit for creating images and words that demonstrate the organization of the music. The software provides an opportunity to interact with the technology in a way that is as similar as possible to the ways people create musical experiences: listening, performing, composing, and improvising. Through this simulation, the student is given a great deal of creative control. MIDI-based sound is often used with this software, as are other multimedia resources.

Use of Multimedia

Viewport VIII describes authoring systems and multimedia software development that are at the heart of much CAI software.

We return to digital video in detail in Modules 27 and 28.

Modules 12 and 25 provide greater detail about DVD and its role in replacing video tape, laser videodiscs, and audio CDs.

Text, Graphics, and Sound. The last four categories of CAI software are all likely to use multiple forms of media to achieve their goals. Experiments in mixing sound, images, and text, both with and without computers, date back to the 1970s. However, it was music software that accessed the audio CD (such as Voyager's Beethoven Symphony No. 9, published for the Macintosh in 1991) that helped set the example for others to follow. This merger of media, together with the parallel development of MIDI, provides a powerful set of aids for teaching about the subtleties of music.

Digital video. One additional medium that is used frequently in the last four categories is digital video. With this technique, you can feed a video signal from a videotape machine or other video source such as a digital camera directly into the computer. The computer samples the video and audio information into a digital video file which can be used for teaching.

One popular file format for digital video is QuickTime, developed first for the Macintosh, but now widely available for Windows. QuickTime and other movie formats like AVI (Video for Windows) and MPEG (used with DVDs) use special software routines that compress the large amount of complex digital information that video requires into a smaller space. Because the QuickTime file format supports digital sound, MIDI, text, still graphics, and even programming codes as well as video, the possibilities for software development in music CAI are many.

Digital Versatile Disc. Before leaving the subject of multimedia and digital video, we need to note the importance of the Digital Versatile Disc (DVD) media for CAI. Instead of creating software files for video that can be played back from a hard disk or from a CD-ROM, it's likely that more and more authors will rely on DVD players to play back video and other forms of data. DVD is destined to replace both traditional videotape and compact audio discs as the preferred way to distribute audio and video. Computers will soon have DVD-ROM players as standard equipment.

Examples of Computer-Assisted Instruction in Music

Armed with a general sense of software categories, you are now ready to review examples of what's out there. From the six categories of CAI, you will gain a sense of what matches your philosophy as a music teacher and what matches the growing needs of each of your students.

We cannot describe all the CAI music software available for personal computers, but we can discuss a representative group. Our inclusion of these programs does not necessarily constitute a listing of the "best" CAI software available, because this determination is always a very personal one based on individual circumstance. What we offer here is a cross-section to serve as a model for comparison. Actually, this is the approach we follow for all commercial products mentioned in this book.

Table 9.1 includes a selected set of titles sorted by the six CAI categories and by their instructional content. The content categories are based in part on the ways people participate in the music experience: listening (aural skills, theory, and extended listening), performing, composing, and improvising. We also include a separate section on software that's appropriate for beginning music experiences with younger children who have not gained a great deal of word reading ability.

Before we view each of these examples more closely, it is worth noting two "holes" in our matrix that are striking. Exploratory software seems to exist primarily for the history/extended-listening category. This is because linkages to outside sources and free exploration designs lend themselves best to historical and listening experiences. As multimedia software continues to grow and as the Internet begins to support more commercial applications, we feel confident that the exploratory category will expand to other instructional content.

Composition/improvisation content is most evident in the creative category, as might be expected. We found few examples of flexible practice, guided instruction, or gaming software that address composition and improvisation in music. As both composition and improvisation become more important in music instruction in coming years, we expect that this situation will change dramatically.

Drill-and-Practice for Beginning Music Experiences. As educators and researchers discover the importance of music learning in the early years of life, quality software for this age group is becoming more common. In most software categories, we have found excellent examples of computer-aided instruction that place less emphasis on word reading and that use instead engaging graphics, animation, and speech. Most titles are appropriate for primary school ages, but some can be used with even younger children.

Using internal digitized sound, Adventures in Musicland is a set of four activities that can be used singularly or between two players. The Sound Concentration program, pictured to the left in Figure 9.1, is a matching activity that exercises the young child's aural memory. Options are included that allow the child to modify the difficulty level, the number of rounds, the speed of the example, and the kind of sound: single pitches; intervals; triads; scales; and sound effects. Other programs in the set present drills for aural memory with a "growing" melody, much like the familiar Simon game. Interesting graphics provide motivational interest throughout.

Placement of a software example in each category is based on our judgment of its primary function. Some software actually could be considered in multiple categories.

Remember this use of sound as you read Modules 10 and 11.

Table 9.1 Matrix of CAI Categories by Instructional Context

Instructional Context	Drill-and-Practice	Flexible Practice	Guided Instruction	Games	Exploratory	Creative
Beginning Music Experiences	Early Music Skills (Mac/Windows)	Toney Music Games (Mac)	Music Ace I (Mac/Windows)	Menlo the Frog (Mac/Windows)		Making Music (Mac/Windows) Thinkin' Things (Mac/Windows)
Aural Skills/ Music Theory	Music Lab (Mac/Windows) Listen! (Mac) MiBAC Music Lessons (Mac/Windows)	Practica Musica (Mac) MacGAMUT (Mac) Musica Analytica (Mac)	Music Ace II (Mac/Windows)	Musicus (Mac/Windows) Juilliard Music Adventure (Mac/Windows)		
History/ Extended Listening	Music Terminology (Mac/Windows)		Discovering Music (Windows)	Xplora I (Mac/Windows) Pianist (Mac/Windows)	Apple Pie (Mac/Windows) Classical Notes (Windows) Stravinsky Rite of Spring (Mac) Living Jazz (Mac/Windows)	Enhanced CD (Mac/Windows) Crazy for Ragtime (Mac/Windows)
Performance	Rhythm Tutor (Windows)		Piano (Windows) Teach Me Piano (Windows)			SmartMusic (Mac/Windows)
Composition/ Improvisation						Music Mouse (Mac) Band-in-a-Box (Mac/Windows) Sound Toys (Mac/Windows) Making More Music (Mac/Windows)

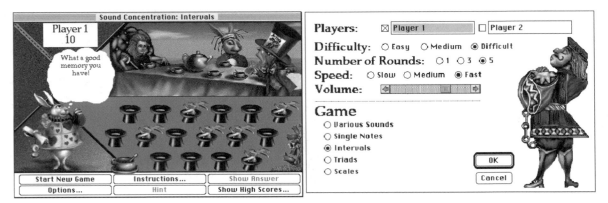

Figure 9.1
Adventures in Musicland
(Electronic Courseware
Systems Inc. [Mac/Windows])

Early Music Skills provides experiences with note movement and identification of lines and spaces. The example in Figure 9.2 shows two colorful tasks, one that teaches about lines and spaces and a second that deals with interval direction and movement. The program supports both MIDI and digitized sound.

Drill-and-Practice for Aural Skills/Music Theory. As we noted earlier, drill-and-practice software has had the longest history in CAI. The content of the software has focused on aural skills and music theory, with literally hundreds of programs developed for all ages. Much of this software is customized, designed to support a particular curriculum or instructional strategy. An example of this kind of proprietary system is the Music in Education software modules developed by the Yamaha Corporation to offer systematic instruction with Macintosh computers and specially designed MIDI keyboards in a laboratory environment.

Many software products, however, have been developed independently and are designed to be used by both teachers and independent musicians in a variety of settings. We provide examples of three of these programs which are designed to offer comprehensive coverage together with some degree of flexibility.

Music Lab is a drill-and-practice program that provides many options for

Figure 9.2
Early Music Skills
(Electronic Courseware Systems, Inc. [Mac/Windows])

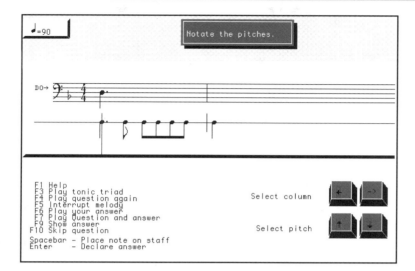

Figure 9.3
Music Lab
(Musicware, Inc. [Mac/
Windows])

A MIDI sound module for high-quality sound is particularly powerful for teaching music with computers. Check out MIDI hardware in Module 12.

developing basic musicianship skills. The program provides a main menu that displays the drills, the twenty levels of skill associated with each, and an indication of those levels where mastery has been demonstrated. Figure 9.3 shows a session in progress. We just completed notating the melody played for us and are about to notate the pitches. Other modules include singing both isolated pitches and pitches in a melodic context, identification of note names by sound and pitch, and the tapping of rhythms. Teacher options include the setting of acceptable time limits and mastery scores. Record keeping includes the establishment of class rosters and passwords. The student interacts with the software using the computer keyboard and the microphone that comes with both Macintosh computers and Wintel machines with sound cards.

Figure 9.4
Listen
(Greg Jalbert, Imaja [Mac])

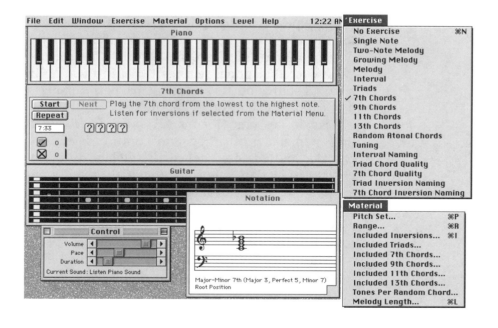

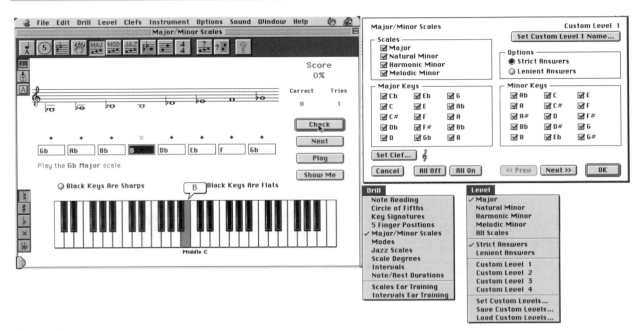

Figure 9.5
MiBAC Music Lessons
(MiBAC Music Software, Inc.
[Mac/Windows])

Listen (Figure 9.4) makes powerful use of the graphical user interface by employing both piano keyboard and guitar graphics upon which you may click to supply answers to questions. The guitar offers players of that instrument a particularly friendly response mode. The seventeen drill sets are accessed from the Exercise menu and include a heavy emphasis on melodic memory (e.g., the identification of pitches in a "growing" melody similar to the Simon game approach seen in Adventures in Musicland), together with interval and chord recognition. The Random Atonal Chords exercise is a unique option among such software. The program offers many options on how the material is presented, including specifying the melody range and chord types. A level option offers increasingly demanding difficulty levels for the exercises. Listen does not offer collective record keeping, and is designed as a more personal tutorial that can be used independently in a variety of educational settings. MIDI is a feature in this software not only as a sound source but as an interactive performance source for playing through a MIDI keyboard or other controller.

Music Lessons (Figure 9.5) includes twelve drill sets beginning with note name identification and continuing through interval identification, chords, and scales. Each drill set has different levels of difficulty, and choices of clef are offered. Individual progress reports can be saved. Extensive on-line help is available, and the user can choose several options for response including on-screen piano, guitar, and alphabet blocks as well as attached MIDI devices and QuickTime instrument sounds in the system folder.

Music Lessons also provides many possibilities for custom level definitions for aspects of the lessons themselves. Subtleties for choosing acciden-

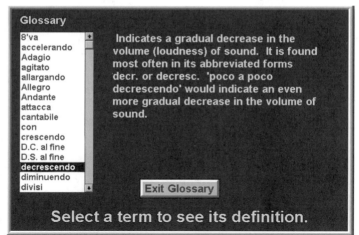

Figure 9.6
Music Terminology
(Electronic Courseware Systems,
Inc. [Mac/Windows])

tals are well supported, as are details for scoring. It also comes with a program for generating help documents.

Drill-and-Practice for Music History/Extended Listening. Drill-and-practice is not limited to beginning experiences or aural skills and music theory. Music Terminology is a set of five independent programs for improving a student's knowledge of music terminology. Content is based on the *Harvard Dictionary of Music* and typical testing formats include True/False, Multiple Choice, and Fill-In. A glossary of terms (Figure 9.6) is provided as a reference point before the drills begin. The routines randomly choose questions from a pool of over 100 terms, and feedback is provided at the end of each session for terms that should be reviewed.

Drill-and-Practice for Music Performance. In the performance content category, drill-and-practice software offers assistance in mastering certain psychomotor skills. Rhythmic performance is a common subject for computer software because it is relatively easy to create programs that use the computer's keys to tap rhythm patterns. The computer assesses the accuracy of the tapped rhythms. This is the approach taken by Rhythm Tutor. Figure 9.7a displays exercise #28, which contains quarter and eighth notes tied to other eighth notes. The patterns are scrolled along in the window while you perform. You indicate how long you wish the exercise to go and how fast you wish the tempo to be. After you are finished, the evaluation button returns a report similar to the one in Figure 9.7b. Notice that you are given an overall accuracy score and some information about how early or late you were in the entire time period. You can choose to have the beat played and the rhythms sounded as you tap or turn these off for a more challenging exercise. MIDI is supported, allowing tones to sound on a selected MIDI timbre, and the MIDI device can be used for input. The program offers 54 exercise sets, including reviews that combine patterns in more complex ways.

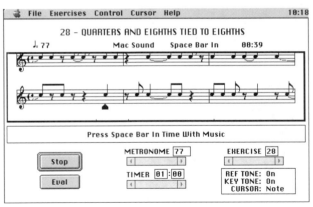

(a)

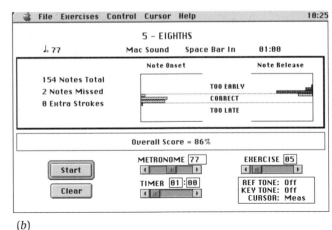

(b)

Figure 9.7
Rhythm Tutor
(Copperman Software
[Mac/Windows])

Flexible Practice

Guard against the idea that flexible-practice titles are always "better" than drill-and-practice. It all depends on the person and the purpose!

See Module 12 for more information about audio CD technology.

Flexible Practice for Beginning Music Experience. The flexible-practice category is closely related in overall intent to drill-and-practice, but has the important distinction of special flexibility. A prime example of this is Toney Music Games, a set of three programs ("Boxes," "Puzzles," and "Clubhouse") for young children that helps develop music memory and tonal perception. The games use movable icons (boxes or cans) that represent either full melodies or melodic fragments; when you click on the icon, you hear the melody. "Boxes" presents the child with a target melody in a main box and a series of additional boxes that contain that melody plus a few others that sound like it (Figure 9.8a). The task is to match the right box to the target and, by so doing, help to develop same/different discriminations.

In "Puzzles," the target exists but the boxes represent partial fragments of the target arranged in random serial order. The task for the child is to identify the fragments and order them in the correct serial order to match the target. This exercises the ability to hear order and to reconstruct the melody. With Clubhouse, the target is compared with boxes in the "clubhouse" that have similar music (Figure 9.8b); however, one box is quite different in terms of either its melodic shape or its rhythmic design. The task is to identify the odd box and pull it out. Here the child needs to grasp the overall dimensions of music structure. (The tasks are based on the Piaget concept of *conservation,* as applied to music.) In all of the games, enjoyable animation and sound effects support motivation.

Although Toney may seem to be better placed in the games category, we have placed it in flexible practice because of its unique customization. In addition to allowing the musician to set difficulty levels with a library of supplied music examples, the application offers a built-in editor that lets you create your own music patterns. The sound source may be the computer's internal sound, or it may be precisely defined clips from an audio compact disc. This means that teachers can create not only simple music patterns,

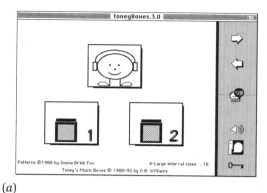
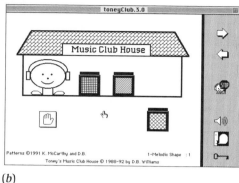

Figure 9.8
Toney Music Games (David B. Williams [distributed by ORAT, Illinois State University] [Mac])

(*a*)   (*b*)

but full audio examples from any kind of music recorded on compact disc. One additional intelligent attribute in this software takes the form of a sophisticated record-keeping option.

Flexible Practice for Aural Skills and Music Theory. We now highlight three flexible-practice programs for aural skills and music theory that offer powerful options for creating custom content. MacGAMUT offers drills for intervals, scales, chords, melodic dictation, and harmonic dictation. Several levels within each drill set are offered. For the interval exercises, melodic and harmonic voicings are given in both simple and compound design. Scales are provided in both ascending and descending form, in both major and minor keys. Modes are also an option. Chord drills use both triads and seventh chords with different inversions. For melodic and harmonic dictations, 18 and 20 levels are included, respectively, that range from very simple to quite complex. Over a thousand melodies and chord progressions are included across all levels.

In addition to all these choices, teachers using MacGAMUT can set parameters for mastery for each level before the student can progress to the next level. If the teacher doesn't care for the melodies or harmonic progressions provided, the instructor's disk contains routines to create completely new examples.

Users can also choose to practice any level for any drill set without the pressure of showing mastery. Perhaps the most exciting option is the ability for users to create their own drill examples for intervals, scales, and chords. This allows users to take charge of their own learning. There are even options to practice notating and playing exercises similar to the ones in the program.

Figure 9.9*a* displays a screen from the scales drill set. Here we have identified the correct scale and added the correct accidentals. We are also ready to move on to the next level, having reached mastery. In Figure 9.9*b*, showing the screen from the chord drills, we were not so skillful. Notice how the program provides diagnostic comments in the box in the lower left. The program provides options to hear your answer and the correct one. The screen shown in Figure 9.9*c* offers similar help, but this time from the har-

ASIDE

In many of the programs that use MIDI, authors have added the QuickTime musical instrument sounds as an option for both Mac and Windows computers. We noted the importance of the Quick-Time software for video earlier. But this same set of system software extensions offers synthesized sounds that conform to the General MIDI sound format that we describe in Module 11. This means that software authors can have the MIDI sounds played by the software resources of their Macintosh or Windows computers without the need for MIDI hardware!

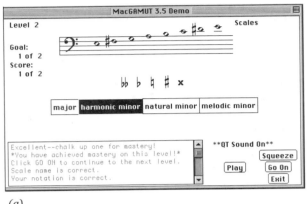

(a)

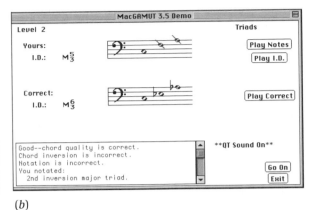

(b)

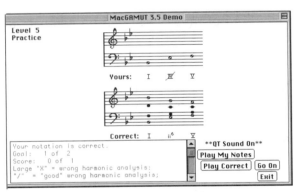

(c)

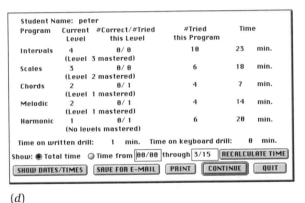

(d)

Figure 9.9
MacGAMUT
(Ann K. Blombach,
MacGAMUT Music Software International [Mac])

monic progression drill set. Notice we heard the bass line correctly but did not get the chord quality. Finally, Figure 9.9*d* shows an example of the record keeping in MacGAMUT. Detailed information is given for the teacher and the student. Notice the option to save the progress as a simple text file for an e-mail message to the teacher.

MacGAMUT offers MIDI input and output as well as digitized sounds from the computer. The QuickTime musical instrument sounds are also supported, including the option to change timbre for the drill sounds.

Practica Musica is representative of a flexible-practice program that merges the comprehensive approach to aural skills and music theory offered by Listen with the customization features of MacGAMUT. The program offers drills on sight-reading, scales, intervals, and chords, all with four levels of difficulty. Generally, the student responds to drills using a detailed on-screen piano keyboard graphic that offers options for displaying pitch symbols with enharmonic equivalents (Figure 9.10*a*). MIDI input and sound output are a recommended option in this program, especially for the sight-reading exercises that help develop performance competency. However, Practica Musica also offers excellent internal sound samples with options for piano, harpsichord, and organ timbres. A unique feature is the ability to

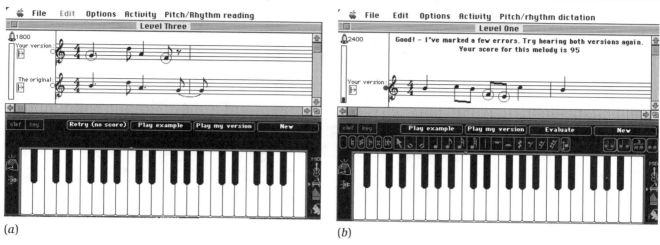

(a)   (b)

Figure 9.10
Practica Musica
(Jeffrey Evans, Ars Nova [Mac])

Software activities: "Practice Your Aural Skills with Music CAI: Practica Musica and MiBAC Music Lessons"

choose internal tuning systems, such as just intonation and mean-tone tuning, as well as the standard equal-temperament system.

The features that make Practica Musica valuable as a flexible-practice program are the melodic dictation options. The program offers a choice of pitch-only, rhythm-only, or both simultaneously (the usual approach). An onboard editor for selecting rhythmic values and MIDI input for pitch identification are options favored by users (Figure 9.10b). Practica Musica supplies melodies in various styles and also allows for computer-generated tunes, and there is a useful editor for creating customized melodies. Additional options include a metronome sound and the ability to work on smaller sections of a long melodic series. Both MacGAMUT and Practica Musica offer on-line help for questions musicians might have about content.

Finally, Musica Analytica is a flexible practice program that is really a toolkit for constructing theory and aural skills assignments. Unlike other software we've described, Musica Analytica comes with no content defined but instead provides a set of text, graphics, and music notation tools to allow a teacher to construct all tasks. The teacher begins by creating tasks such as the one begun in Figure 9.11a. Here, we have created some text instructions and a set of chords with the tools provided. We are about ready to have the program construct a file that contains the display of these chords with boxes that the student will use to answer questions about chord quality and position. Once the file is to our liking as teachers, we can make it available for students to "check out." This means that they log in to Musica Analytica as enrolled students, copy the file on to one of their floppy diskettes, answer the questions, and then check the file back into the teacher's program for analysis. The teacher can evaluate the work, add comments, and return the work. Figure 9.11b displays a box of possible assignments that the student might see as a result of the construction by the teacher.

Teachers can construct six tasks, including: pitch, interval, triad, chord, and scale identification. Each task has a few built-in options that the program will render. The sixth task is more complicated. Labeled "Advanced

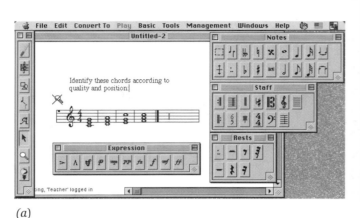

(a)

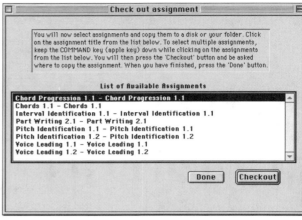

(b)

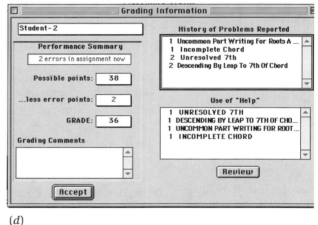

(c)

(d)

Figure 9.11
Musica Analytica
(ER Technologies [Mac])

Analysis," this task allows the construction of part writing, voice leading, and chord progression assignments. Each of these assignments have settings which can be edited to help make for further flexibility.

Figure 9.11*c* displays a chord progression assignment. Notice that playback is provided. Sounds from the QuickTime Music Instruments are used. Figure 9.11*d* displays a typical analysis that is returned to the student. Musica Analytica can do the analysis, but the teacher can also add to the feedback and tailor it to meet the needs of the student.

Guided Instruction

All the software examples noted thus far have had mastery of specific skills as their major goal. Guided Instruction also has this as its mission, but does so with ongoing guidance in the form of tutorial instruction. As software distribution moves to CDs, DVDs, and the Internet, more space is available for content. Speech, music, text, and graphics will be used more creatively, and we are bound to see growth in this category of software.

(a)

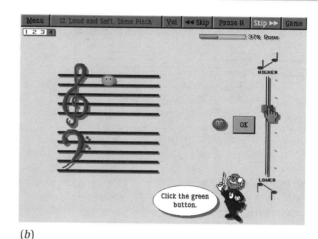

(b)

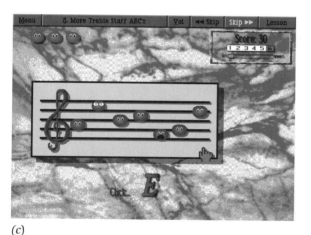

(c)

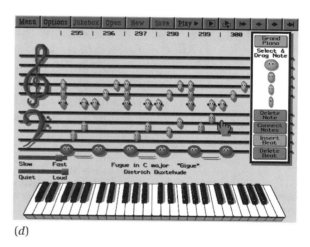

(d)

Figure 9.12
Music Ace I
(Harmonic Vision, Inc.
[Mac/Windows])

Guided Instruction for Beginning and for More Advanced Work. A software series that demonstrates guided instruction for young and more advanced students is Music Ace I and II. Music Ace I is appropriate for younger children, especially those without strong word reading skills. Music Ace II provides more advanced lessons and falls more into the aural skills and music theory category of instructional content.

Both programs offer a similar design approach. Figure 9.12*a* displays the opening screen for Music Ace I. Notice that the user can choose to work with a lesson and that a lesson has a game that can also be played. To the left of the screen are options for the "Doodle Pad" and for checking progress.

The lesson material is the central feature of the software and the guided tutorials that give Music Ace its power to teach. Figure 9.12*b* shows Lesson 12, devoted to the relationship between volume and pitch. The lesson begins with the Little Professor explaining how pitches heard at different loudness levels might confuse the hearing of pitch. The lesson provides opportunity to match pitch at different loudness levels by using the slider bar to match the pitch. There are multiple levels to each lesson. Other

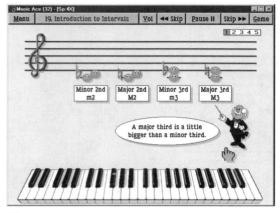

(a)

(b)

Figure 9.13
Music Ace II
(Harmonic Vision, Inc.
[Mac/Windows])

Notation and sequencing
software is described in
more detail in Viewports V
and VI.

lessons include an introduction to the keyboard, staff, timbre, pitches, sharps and flats, key signatures, and major scales. Games are provided for each lesson and they, too, have various levels. Figure 9.12c displays a note identification game that comes from Lesson 8.

The Doodle Pad is always available to allow users to experiment by creating their own compositions. Different timbres are possible, and notes can be dragged into place for each timbre. Speed and volume can be controlled. Figure 9.12d contains an example of a gigue by Buxtehude that has already been composed as an example from the "Jukebox" group of supplied tunes.

Music Ace II follows the same approach but uses more advanced lesson content. Figures 9.13a and b display lessons on intervals and chords, respectively. Notice the use of more sophisticated ideas while still maintaining the guided lesson approach. Music Ace I and II both use MIDI sound and the QuickTime musical instruments. Progress charts are maintained for each user. Multiple users are supported for both family and large class use.

Guided Instruction for History/Extended Listening. Discovering Music provides a helpful set of guided lessons on a number of music topics. Figure 9.14a provides a view of the main menu of this program. Notice the four sets of activities, including the sections called "Jammin' Keys," "Recording Station," and "Music Write." "Jammin' Keys" offers opportunities to arrange sound clips provided by the program and to do so in different popular music styles.

"Recording Station" is an elementary sequencer program that allows the user to arrange tracks of original MIDI and audio data. The "Music Write" portion of the program works like a beginning music notation program. These three portions of the program allow for the easy creation of music and, in some cases, Discovering Music provides an interactive tutorial for the activities.

We included this program in the History and Extended Listening category, however, because of its "Music Conservatory" chapter. Figure 9.14b provides a view of the many options in this part of the program. The sections on Great Composers, History of Music, and Music Glossary lead the

(a)

(b)

Figure 9.14
Discovering Music
(Voyetra Technologies, Inc.
[Windows])

The data structure for
Enhanced CDs includes
both audio tracks and digital data for text and graphics. See Module 25 in
Viewport VII for more
information.

user through many experiences about music presented in text, graphics, and sound. For example, 15 composers are featured in the Great Composers section, beginning with Baroque through to the start of the twentieth century.

Although some links are made among items—which might make this software appear to be more exploratory in nature—the major emphasis is on guided instruction. This is particularly true in the Music Theory section, which introduces the nature of sound and then the elements of music in a clearly designed order.

Another example of guided instruction in music history and listening comes from the many "enhanced CDs" that are now produced. These audio CDs are multipurpose. You can simply use them as regular discs as part of your stereo system, enjoying the music recorded on them; or you can also use them in your computer and take advantage of the extra multimedia material included, which "enhances" your listening pleasure.

As an example, we include information about *A Musical Odyssey: A Journey through the Classics.* The CD contains 12 audio tracks, which include works selected from the Baroque, Classical, Romantic, and Twentieth-Century style periods. Figure 9.15*a* displays a view of the screen that allows you to listen to these works from your computer, but you can also simply play these tracks in your audio CD player. As a bonus, however, this enhanced CD allows you to explore four other options: learn about notation and do a little composing; watch some of the music notation scroll by as you listen to the music; explore the instruments of the orchestra with a guided audio tour; and take a guided audio tour of the music history periods themselves. It is the last two options that make this enhanced CD a good example of guided instruction.

Figure 9.15*b* provides a view of one of the typical screens during the music history tour. The text is narrated, and the music used comes from the pieces that are featured on the CD, in this case the Bach Orchestral Suite No. 3. The Meet the Orchestra section provides a similar tour through the orchestral instruments.

Enhanced CDs of this sort are available for many styles of music. Popular music titles are becoming more common, building on the popularity of

(a)

(b)

Figure 9.15
A Musical Odyssey
(Intersound, Inc.
[Mac/Windows])

televised music videos that are often produced to accompany a recording. In this case, the goal is more to entertain than to educate, but the technology to create enhanced CDs is similar.

Guided Instruction for Performance. Guided instruction programs for guitar and piano are popular examples of this type of software applied to performance. The software Piano, for example, is part of a body of interactive MIDI software that will certainly increase as traditional and nontraditional instrument technology embraces the MIDI standard. Much of the performance software developed to date is centered on keyboards and guitars, but devices that transmit MIDI codes from other string, woodwind, and brass instruments will likely prompt development of guided instruction software for these instruments. Figure 9.16*a* is a typical screen from Piano. The software teaches finger position and correct pitch execution in context. Rhythm is not evaluated, although there are rhythm exercises that provide a graphic representation of sustained durations. Piano provides three units of instruction that are filled with exercises that increase the technical ability of beginning players.

Figure 9.16*b* displays a screen from Teach Me Piano. This program sacrifices the large range of exercise material in favor of more multimedia resources. Digital movies provide introductions to each of the chapters within the five sections. Some videos can actually be used as an accompaniment to your playing. For each piece that is practiced, the user can play along with one hand or the other. The software also evaluates performance accuracy. A "perform" option allows the user to play the piece with an accompaniment.

ASIDE

Guided instruction software often uses elements of other categories such as creative activities and links between content areas, but the core purpose of the program is to lead you through a set of activities.

Games

Game software is very motivational for a number of people. We have seen a major growth in this category in the last few years as authors have tried to capitalize on the power of computers to render musical material in new ways.

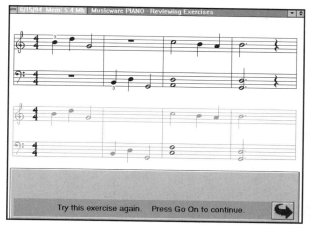

(*a*) Piano
(Musicware [Windows])

Figure 9.16
Examples of guided
instruction for performance

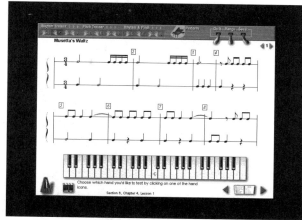

(*b*) Teach Me Piano
(Voyetra Technologies, Inc. [Windows])

Games for Young Musicians. Menlo the Frog is an example of a musical adventure game for very young children. Termed "A Musical Fairy Tale," this software features a frog named Menlo and his frog friend, Princess Winnicent, as they try to recapture a key stolen by the evil King of Later. The key is necessary to keep the Melody Man singing. The adventure leads to different scenes that make use of music games that focus on music theory and composition.

Figure 9.17*a* displays the Clam Game portion of this scene. This game asks the child to recognize five pitch sets ranging from very low to very high. There are three levels that can be played depending on where the child clicks in the scene. The basic idea is to help develop pitch recognition.

Figure 9.17*b* shows a composition activity. The little animals play predefined patterns, and they can be arranged on the 32 spots on the marimba keyboard. For example, the mouse plays a simple tonic sound and the raccoon plays a dominant to tonic pattern. The little bird actually represents a rest. The child can arrange the animals on the marimba in any order. The tempo can be controlled with the "tempo crank," and the instrument timbre can be changed between piano, flute, and violin. Other activities include beat and rhythm tapping. As the child plays with the software to help Menlo on his mission, the activities help to make the game more interesting and teach ideas about music.

Juilliard Music Adventure is similar to Menlo but is meant for a much older person. Here, the adventure centers on the need to free a queen who has been locked away by an evil character. The idea is to travel through the rooms of a castle in search of keys to unlock the place where the queen is hidden away. In doing so, you must solve musical problems presented to you along the way. To get you started, the program presents a rhythm and melody maker similar to the one pictured in Figure 9.18*a*. Here, you can create rhythm and melodic patterns and arrange them in tiles to play a song. The tasks throughout the game ask you to solve musical problems with

(a)

(b)

Figure 9.17
Menlo the Frog
(Windy Hill Productions
[Mac/Windows])

rhythm and melody, starting with fairly simple tasks in Level I of the castle to much more difficult ones in Level III.

One task in Level II requires the creation of syncopated patterns. Figure 9.18*b* displays a scroll that helps you figure out what syncopation is and how it might be used to solve the puzzle. Juilliard Music Adventure explores other aspects of music as well at various points in the program. By the time you reach the goal of freeing the queen, you will have had a great deal of experience working with the rhythm and melody tools provided.

A very different kind of music game is Musicus. Falling note blocks must be maneuvered into measures of specific meters. Figure 9.19 shows the progress of a game in the early stages. We have just successfully scored points by filling the entire bottom line with correctly placed notes. The game is timed, and the speed of the falling notes can be changed. At the conclusion of the game, the user has the option of hearing the complete

Figure 9.18
Juilliard Music Adventure
(Theatrix Interactive, Inc.
and The Juilliard School
[Mac/Windows])

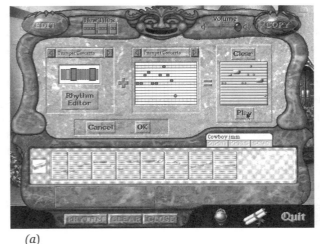

(a)

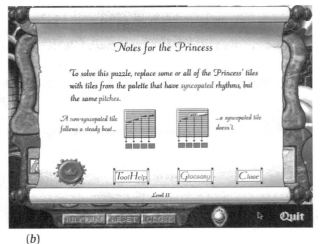

(b)

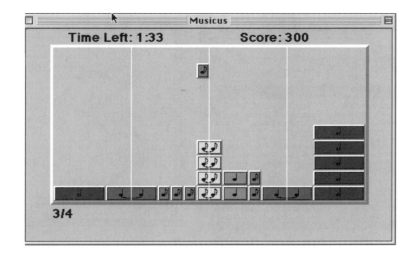

Figure 9.19
Musicus
(Electronic Courseware
Systems [Mac/Windows])

rhythmic lines. Five levels of the game provide increasingly difficult sets of meters. A more advanced version of the game uses more complicated meters and note values.

Games for History/Extended Listening. Pianist uses the power of MIDI for flexible music listening and historical understanding. This software is really a kind of MIDI jukebox of piano classics, with more than 200 famous piano solos captured in MIDI file format, created by concert pianists performing live. Subtleties of phrasing are all captured in real time. The solos can be played in any order and can be chosen on the basis of composer, style of music, or difficulty level. There are even options for changing keys, adjusting tempos, and setting different loudness levels.

We have placed this software in the game category, however, because of the "Guess" and "Trivia" options. Figure 9.20*a* displays a screen that is used for guessing the identity of the piano work being played. You can restrict the pool of pieces to choose from or you can go for broke and use the hundreds of works included in the software. Figure 9.20*b* shows a typical screen from

Figure 9.20
Pianist
(PG Music, Inc. [Mac/
Windows])

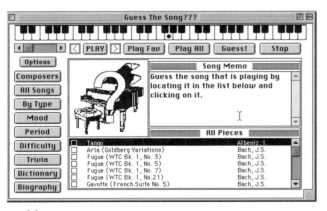

(a)

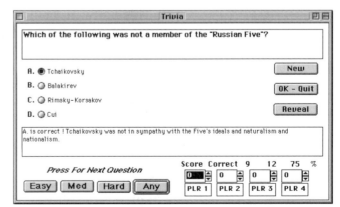

(b)

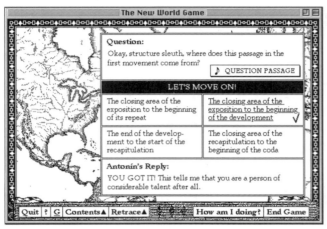 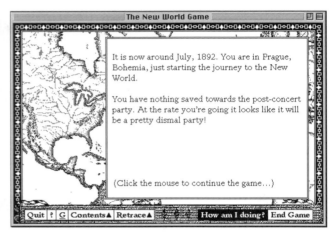

(a)   *(b)*

Figure 9.21
Antonín Dvořák
Symphony No. 9
(The Voyager Company, Inc.
[Mac])

Hybrid CD-ROM music
software is software for
Mac and Windows, both
formatted on the same
disc.

the trivia section of the software. Here, the user can be asked questions in three difficulty levels and play against other users. The questions not only cover piano-related issues, but also include queries about music that is covered in the written material about each piece.

A final example of gaming software is the Antonín Dvořák Symphony No. 9. We placed this work in the gaming category because of its final chapter, "Can You Get Dvořák to Carnegie Hall?" The idea of this game is to answer questions about Dvořák's music, life, and times based on the content of the other chapters of the software. In so doing, the player advances a position on a map that plots Dvořák's famous trip in 1892 from Prague to the United States. This trip is related, of course, to the Symphony No. 9, subtitled *From the New World.*

Figure 9.21*a* displays a typical question format. Notice that the question uses an excerpt from the CD recording of the work itself. Many questions do this, making the game quite educational and musically more valid than if the questions were all based on factual items. As the game progresses, you can inquire about your progress to Carnegie Hall (Figure 9.21*b*), which is the goal of the game. You can play against a partner, and the software provides three levels of complexity, which can be selected at the start of each game.

This software could also have been easily placed in the next category, Exploratory. The earlier chapters make use of many internal links and encourages exploration in a nonlinear fashion much as Apple Pie, Beethoven and Beyond, and the Stravinsky Rite of Spring do. Detailed information about the work and the historical context of the music are included. Of special interest is an interesting description of Dvořák's stay in the "New World," which includes sound clips of people talking about his visit and his music.

Exploratory Software

Exploratory software is largely centered in one instructional content area: history/extended listening. We imagine this will change as more authors

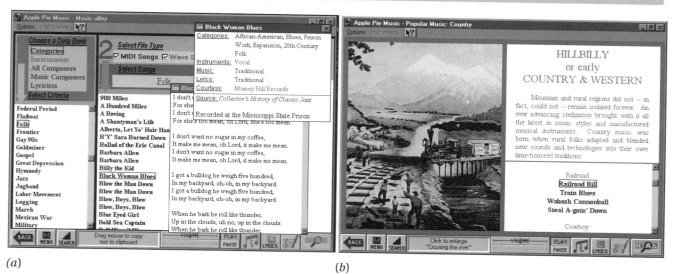

(a) *(b)*

Figure 9.22
Apple Pie Music: A History
of American Music
(Queue, Inc.)

Exploratory software uses
hypermedia linking
approaches much as Inter-
net browsing clients do. Be
sure to check out these
similarities in Module 6
and in Viewport VIII.

use the Internet imaginatively and as the authoring tools for exploratory software get easier to use. The titles we include here all require a CD-ROM or DVD-ROM drive in your computer and make extensive use of audio clips or complete audio recordings. All make extensive use of text and graphics and some use digital movies and MIDI sound. Links are included by using either underlined or colored words.

Our first example in this category features content from the history of American music. Apple Pie Music provides over 1,000 screens of information about American music history, concentrating on popular, religious, and folk literature. There are links to audio recordings of over 400 songs, and the program contains hundreds of pictures. Figure 9.22*a* shows a typical screen. We have chosen a shot from the "Music Alley" chapter with a section from the "Categories" submenu. We have opened the link to the folk section and the specific song "Black Woman Blues." Notice that the software provides the lyrics to read as you listen. MIDI and digital sound are both supported by this program. Figure 9.22*b* represents a screen from the history section, featuring popular music. Note the written material about the music and the artwork which relates to the context of the music. The chapters are interlinked and provide for hours of exploration.

Other examples of exploratory software come from the "classical" music scene. We have already noted the Antonín Dvořák Symphony No. 9 package in the game section; here are two other examples. Beethoven and Beyond comes from the "So I've Heard" series. Unlike the Dvořák and the Stravinsky titles that are intended for more advanced music listeners, this software is intended as an introduction to Beethoven's music and the Romantic era of music history that he ushered in. The software highlights the innovations of Beethoven's music and then features the compositions of Schubert, Chopin, Brahms, and others. More than 100 musical examples are sampled and indexed, including links to the sources for full recordings and recommendations for further listening. Figure 9.23*a* displays a typical page. Notice the links to other composers and terms. If there is a particular screen that you

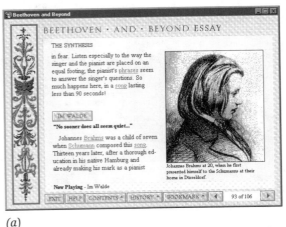

(a)

(b)

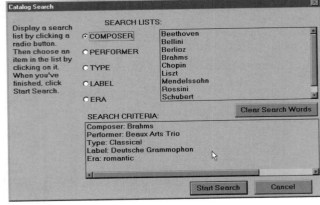

(c)

(d)

Figure 9.23
Examples of "classical" music exploratory software: (a) and (b) Beethoven and Beyond (Voyager Music, Inc. [Mac/Windows]); (c) and (d) Igor Stravinsky: The Rite of Spring (Voyager Music, Inc. [Mac])

wish to "bookmark," you can do so in order to return to it directly another time. Figure 9.23b shows another approach to the software by searching for a particular work using different criteria.

Igor Stravinsky: The Rite of Spring features extensive information to support the study of one complete masterwork. This CD contains a full performance of the Rite of Spring ballet score, plus a number of short excerpts from other works that are designed to explain important aspects of the music. Figure 9.23c shows the main menu screen, typical of many of exploratory applications. Notice the major sections on historical background (Stravinsky's World), specific music content (A Close Reading), and the on-line Glossary. The Pocket Guide option reveals a list of subsections of the ballet score that can be accessed interactively on the CD. You can toggle back and forth between any two subsections to compare music characteristics. There is even a multiple-choice quiz that uses excerpts from the CD, similar to that in the Dvořák program described earlier. You can take a journey through any of these sections, one screen after another, and return to the main menu for other work; or, more typically, move around in a nonlinear manner.

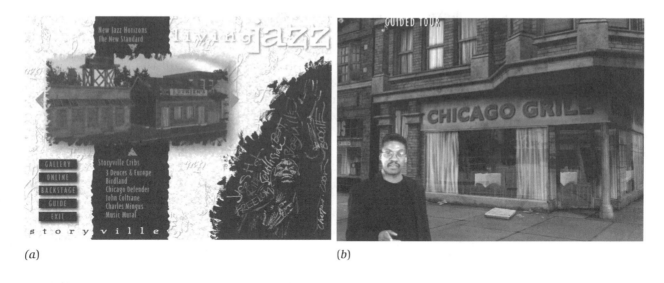

(a)   *(b)*

(c)   *(d)*

Figure 9.24
Herbie Hancock Presents
Living Jazz
(Graphic Zone, Inc., Hancock
and Joe Productions, Inc.
[Mac/Windows])

Figure 9.23*d* illustrates a screen in the Close Reading section that offers a detailed look at the music structure. Text description is combined with music notation and sound excerpts from the performance. The software highlights each measure during the playing of the excerpt (the last measure of the excerpt was playing as this screen was captured). The button choice on the lower right allows the musician to hear only one line (solo) or the entire orchestra. Notice the links to other parts of the program that help to explain the concept.

Our final example of exploratory software comes from the world of jazz and is a tour de force for multimedia integration. Herbie Hancock Presents Living Jazz is a CD filled with music, artwork, poetry, narration, and text that provide highlights of the history of jazz music. Figure 9.24*a* provides a view of the opening screen. In the center, notice the graphic with arrows on either side. This is called the "Navigator" and is one way to get started exploring the CD and its contents. The graphic is actually a "virtual reality" movie. Clicking on the arrows moves the scene along a street of buildings, much like moving a video camera. The buildings are actually 3-dimensional renderings of the real buildings that once stood in Storyville, a section of New Orleans before World War I that was the heart of the early jazz scene. The section of the movie that you see here is of the Storyville "cribs" where artists lived. Each section of the movie provides a menu for exploration deeper into the history of jazz.

Another way to get started is to click on the "Guide" option from the main menu. This leads to text material about the design of the CD. An option is to have Herbie Hancock give you a personal guided tour. Figure 9.24*d* provides a view of Hancock talking about a scene that features the jazz music of South Side Chicago as the CD chronicles the movement of jazz to northern cities. By clicking on illuminated hot spots, additional digital movies appear featuring early jazz artists performing.

Returning to the main menu page (Figure 9.24*a*), note the menu under the central movie again. If you click on the "Storyville Cribs" link, you are taken to a screen that is a closeup of the cribs. From here you can explore links to Birdland, the famous New York jazz club (Figure 9.24*c*). Links on this screen bring you to still more movies, graphics, and audio clips. One link in the upper left-hand corner brings you to New York in the 1960s and a digital movie of John Coltrane performing (Figure 9.24*d*).

A most interesting link off the main menu page (graphic on the right hand side) leads you to a poem by Quincy Troupe that is accompanied by original music by Hancock and digital movies of dancing. The program also provides links to Web sites on jazz, provided your computer is connected to the Internet.

Creative Software

Software in Viewports V, VI, and VII can also be used in a creative teaching environment. Check those titles out too!

Our final category in CAI is what we have termed "creative." Recall that this category requires users to interact with software by creating their own music structures. Each title we review here offers an opportunity to make aesthetic decisions about sound as a way to understand music better. This category is closely linked to the software reviewed in Viewports V, VI, and VII on music notation, sequencing, and sound sampling, respectively. There, the software reviewed is meant for professional production of music, not necessarily for a teaching and learning environment. Here, the software is designed to allow creative work in music listening, performance, improvisation, and composition for the purpose of teaching about sound.

Creative Software for Young Musicians. Morton Subotnick's Making Music and Making More Music allow the musician to actually draw music gestures on the screen and manipulate them much as a composer does. Making Music is best suited for preschool and early elementary-aged children; Making More Music works best for older students who are beginning to learn traditional music notation and would like more advanced work.

In Figure 9.25*a*, we see the central screen for "making music." Here, we have drawn two musical lines, each assigned to a different timbre by using

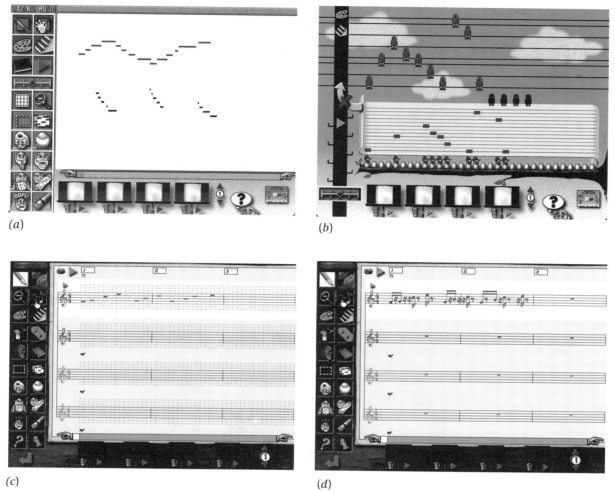

(a)   *(b)*

(c)   *(d)*

Figure 9.25
Morton Subotnick's Making Music (*a* and *b*) and Making More Music (*c* and *d*)
(The Voyager Company, Inc. [Mac/Windows])

one of the buttons on the left side. The important aspect here is the drawing approach. By using the mouse to sketch, a child can create a musical gesture. Other buttons allow a chosen portion of the gesture to be altered for dynamic change, pitch, or tempo. You can ask the program to make global changes such as inverting the intervals, playing the line backwards (retrograde), or some combination of both. Smaller sections of the musical gestures can be "picked up" and moved around to different pitch levels. The user can even alter the underlying scale structures by electing to have minor, pentatonic, chromatic, or whole-tone scales. You can even create your own scales.

Figure 9.25*b* shows another option for composition. This approach has you deciding first about the rhythm structure with the little eggs at the bottom of the screen, then the pitches you want by moving the birds in place on the staff. Once you have both of these established, you can put the two together to make your melody. You can save these melodies and use them in the main portion of the program. Making Music allows the saving of multiple compositions into libraries of creative work and also offers a number of supportive games for aural skills training.

Making More Music is similar in structure, but much more advanced in terms of traditional notation. Instead of an open structure for drawing, the user works with a chamber music metaphor of either four independent instruments, a solo instrument and piano, or two pianos. Figure 9.25c displays the main screen of Making More Music with a view of the four independent instruments. Notice the similarity in the tools on the left-hand side of the main screen to the options in Making Music. Drawing the music gestures is similar too; however, you draw on a traditional staff.

Figure 9.25d shows what happens in Making More Music when you ask the program to translate the drawings to traditional notation. This conversion from drawing to traditional notation is a powerful feature. Of course, you can also decide right from the start not to draw but actually to work with traditional notation.

Making More Music also has a melody maker that allows you to choose the length of a melody, the complexity of the rhythm, and the general intervallic structure. You can make changes in tempo, dynamics, meter, and scale. The program comes with a Rhythm Band which uses percussion instrument timbres and allows the creation of rhythms for your compositions by tapping a rhythm. There is a Theme and Variations maker as well as more advanced games that use full compositions in more sophisticated ways than Making Music. Both programs use external MIDI devices or the built-in QuickTime sounds.

Thinkin' Things is a series of three programs for young children that are designed to encourage exploration of arts and ideas. Music plays a major role in each set of programs. We have chosen two parts from Thinkin' Things Collection 2 to highlight here. Each of these parts present opportunities for young children to compose and experiment with sound. Compositions that are created can be saved and reviewed later.

Figure 9.26a shows "Oranga" and his band. The Oranga character (and his friends) serve as performers for the sequence that can be created in the three "tracks." This can be done by simply clicking on the cells in each track to have a sound occur and then by clicking on the Play button. The characters play what has been composed. The instruments that the characters play can be changed to other timbres, and there is even an option for recording your own sound by using the computer's microphone. Sounds can be changed, and custom sounds can be recorded. Two perception games are also included. One game asks the user to listen to a sequence and tell which character played a highlighted track; the second game reverses the task and asks which track was played by the highlighted character. A range of difficulty levels are permitted.

Figure 9.26b displays "Tooney," a bird that plays music! You can teach Tooney to play your own tune by clicking on the keys of the instrument in any order or at any speed possible using the mouse. We show the tuba-like instrument here, but Tooney can play other interesting instruments as well. The software remembers the pitch and rhythm choices and has Tooney play back the music as it was entered. Tooney will also teach you to play back a

The structure of this program is similar to that of sequencing software, which we will present in Module 19.

(a)

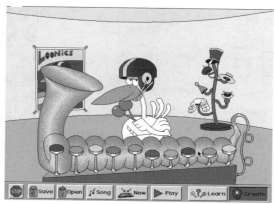

(b)

Figure 9.26
Thinkin' Things Collection 2 (Edmark, Corp. [Mac/Windows])

selected familiar tune from a set of fifteen provided by the software. The character first plays the entire tune, then plays each phrase one at a time, waiting for you to play back the correct pitches. In our figure, we see Tooney teaching us the University of Michigan fight song, complete with football helmet.

Creative Software for History/Extended Listening. The three software packages we feature in this category all encourage the user to experiment with sound as a way to better understand a particular style of music or to learn more about the listening experience. Crazy for Ragtime focuses on the history and development of ragtime music and is very exploratory in nature. We include it here because of a special section that allows users to create their own rags. Rock Rap'n Roll allows users to add improvisatory material to ten different rock and pop music styles. Eine Kleine Nachtmusik has users experiment with the compositional structures of this famous Mozart serenade.

Figure 9.27*a* displays a screen from the "Ragtime Sampler" portion of Crazy for Ragtime. Here we are listening to the "Kansas City Rag" by James Scott and watching the notation at the same time. The highlighted box that surrounds the first measure will change as successive measures are played. The CD offers both MIDI sound and digital audio for the more than 50 complete rags that the program provides. Notice that at the bottom of the screen you have options for changing speed, key, timbre, and loudness. This kind of experimentation is what this category of software is all about.

A more dramatic example is shown in Figure 9.27*b*. This is another chapter from Crazy for Ragtime, "Make Your Own Rag." This comes as a later chapter in the software and builds on the information about rags that has been presented previously. You begin by choosing the kind of form you want to use. Here we chose "Free," but you also can choose the "Classic" or "Successive Phrase" forms, which are real form types that exist in rag music. Next, you choose the basic material to work with. Notice that we have again used the "Kansas City Rag" as our source, and the top row of tiles represent the basic sections of this rag. The tiles in the bottom row represent our new

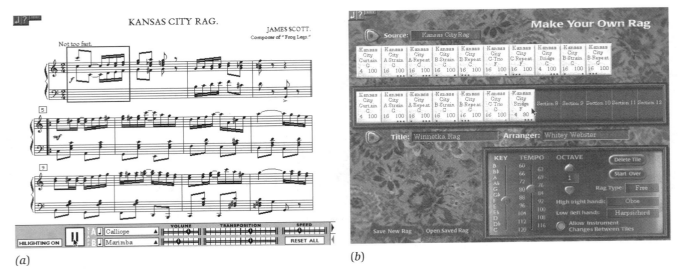

(a)

(b)

Figure 9.27
Robert Winter's Crazy for Ragtime (Calliope [Mac/Windows])

form. Key and tempo are indicated on each tile. The dots supply information about the rhythm structure. We are composing the form and much of the content of the rag. We can use the controls on the bottom right to change key, tempo, octave, and timbre for each tile or section of our rag. Notice that we have started to change these parameters for the last tile that we added.

Rock Rap'n Roll allows the user to construct a composition from digitized sound excerpts. Several styles of popular music are offered, including blues, techno-pop, rap, and soul. After picking a style, you are given a screen to construct the composition. Figure 9.28a shows a screen for the blues. The excepts listed on the left can be dragged into the circles at the bottom to create a sequence. Once the sequence is chosen, clicking on the start button will play the excerpts in order. As the music is playing, you can add shorter sound licks with other buttons and keyboard options. As shown in Figure 9.28b, you can even add your own custom sounds using the microphone of your computer.

The software allows you to save your actions with this program in the form of a file. When you do this, you are not saving the sounds but rather the decisions you made. Opening the file at a later time reconstructs the decisions and allows you to hear what you did. The program allows teachers and students to study the nature of the style and to experiment with sound combinations that are appropriate to that style.

The program Eine Kleine Nachtmusik uses the power of MIDI to provide active experimentation with Mozart's music. The software uses standard MIDI files of the piece as the basis for a number of listener-selected options. The files are treated in various ways in order to demonstrate what the piece sounds like when you "mess around" with Mozart's music.

Mozart originally wrote *Eine Kleine Nachtmusik* as a quintet for two violins, viola, cello, and string bass. The author of this program created a MIDI file with each instrument's music written on a separate line or track. The listener can control the way these tracks are played. For instance, if you want to hear the MIDI file with brass instrument sounds instead of strings, you can use the software to tell the MIDI device to use the brass sounds.

(a)

(b)

Figure 9.28
Rock Rap'n Roll
(Paramount Interactive [Silver
Burdett, Inc., distributor]
[Mac/Windows])

The same is true for a number of other attributes, including loudness, over-all key, tempo (including ritards and accelerandos), and even the pitch and rhythmic values themselves. Any device that conforms to MIDI standards will respond to these changes instantly.

This software allows for experimentation with music properties within a previously composed work. Figure 9.29*a* illustrates one of the "feeling" screens from the software. Here you can ask that the score be played in a number of different ways to create quite different musical effects. In a group setting, a teacher might use the software to generate a discussion about aesthetic choice.

Figure 9.29*b* is a screen from one of the "Messing with Mozart" options that allows the musician to substitute different timbres.

The software provides a number of other features including:

► Turning off selected tracks to focus listening on one or two lines

► Changing the rhythmic values and melodic order

► Instantly altering tempo to evaluate music effect

► Moving phrases around in different order

Creative Software for Performance and Composition/ Improvisation. We end this category by presenting information about four programs that help musicians perform and improvise. The SmartMusic software and hardware package deserves special note as an example of creative software for performance. The system is designed to allow the computer to accompany instrumentalists and vocalists as they work on performance literature. Using either the QuickTime sounds in the computer or a special sound module, the SmartMusic system intelligently accompanies the player or singer by following the tempo variations. As the musician performs, the software "listens" to the solo line by way of a supplied microphone, identifies the pitch patterns, compares these with the data that represent the score, and produces the accompaniment. The system is sophisticated enough to "find" the soloists if they skip ahead or back in the score.

Figure 9.30 displays some of the screens from the system's software. In

The concepts of MIDI
"track" and "patch" are
described in detail in
Viewport VI, Module 19.

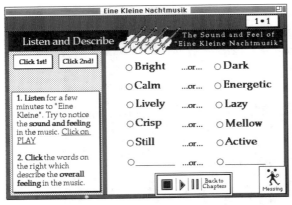

(a)

(b)

Figure 9.29
Eine Kleine
Nachtmusik
(Sam Reese [distributed
personally, School of Music,
University of Illinois]
[Mac])

the upper left, we show the main screen from SmartMusic. This version is called the Practice Studio and uses the computer's internal sounds. To use this version, your Macintosh or Wintel computer must be a recent model with relatively fast processing speed. If you have an older computer, you may need to buy the version of SmartMusic that provides its own sound module.

In addition to the basic software and hardware for the system, the user must also buy the cartridges or disks that contain the files for the solo literature. A wide variety of repertoire is available for elementary, intermediate, and advanced performers. In our example, we have chosen to load the first movement of the Haydn Trumpet Concerto in E Flat. Notice that this main screen has controls for stopping, starting, rewinding, and fast forward. A foot pedal is also included in the package to help with starting and stopping for mouse-free operation. The software displays the measure and beat as the accompaniment is played. Here we have set the tempo to a quarter note = 126 and have asked for one measure of countoff.

The upper right screen is a tuner option that allows the soloist to tune up with the computer's sound. A "linear" tuner option is also included that displays variations in pitch along a straight line. Both types of tuner displays offer interesting possibilities for instruction in their own right.

SmartMusic provides many ways to customize the accompaniment. The screen on the lower left displays options for doing this. We have entered some information for the percentage of intelligent accompaniment for a given section. This percentage figure governs the extent to which the software responds to tempo variations. A selection of 100 percent means that the software is sensitive to every nuance in your playing and may return false information based on just the slightest variation in rhythmic performance. A selection of 10 or 25 percent would mean that the software would ignore certain changes in tempo. The performer can experiment with different settings to find the right balance.

Notice also the options for marking sections in the score for easy access, establishing cuts in the score to ignore long introductions or interludes, and setting tempo markers, breath marks, and note markers. Still other options exist for reverberation in the sound of the accompaniment, skips over rests, and transpositions. It's also possible to ask SmartMusic to play the melody line along with the accompaniment.

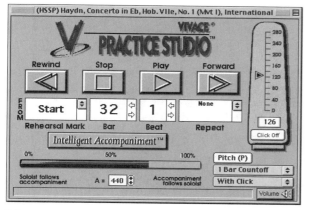

(a)

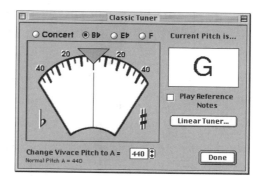

(b)

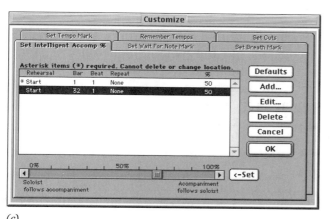

(c)

(d)

Figure 9.30
SmartMusic
(Coda Music Technology
[Mac/Windows])

Finally, the software provides text information about the composer and the music itself. The screen on the lower right displays a text block about Haydn and leads to links about the composition and the symbols and terms used in the music.

Music Mouse was one of the first computer improvisation packages. It is also one of the first *intelligent instrument* programs because it turns the computer itself into a performance instrument. Although it uses MIDI as a sound source along with the QuickTime musical instruments sounds, the real performance instrument is the computer itself, because the mouse and computer keyboard are the controllers of music expression. For this reason, it might rightfully be argued that the software is actually a performance rather than an instructional product. We include Music Mouse here, however, because of its potential for CAI in the shaping of expressive music.

Figure 9.31*a* illustrates the main screen showing the performance grid where all the action takes place. The mouse controls the movement of the vertical and horizontal lines that are the performer's guide to what harmonic and melodic material is being manipulated. To the left of the grid is a summary of the modifiers and controllers that have been chosen. These can all be changed on the fly during the performance by using the computer

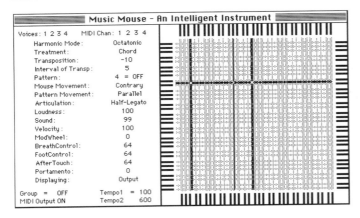

(*a*) Music Mouse
(Laurie Spiegel [available as shareware from http://www2.factory.com/spiegel] [Mac])

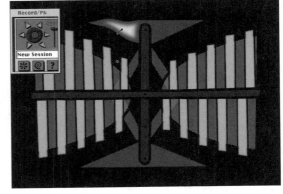

(*b*) Sound Toys
(C. Todd Robbins [published by Voyager Music, Inc.]
[Mac/Windows])

Figure 9.31
Examples of creative software for improvisation

Software activity: "Simulate Improvisation with a Computer Using Band-in-a-Box"

keyboard. Strictly vertical movement of the mouse causes the harmonic parameters chosen to remain constant but the melodic material to change. Horizontal movement causes the melodic value to continue while the chosen harmonic material changes, and diagonal movement causes everything to change at once. These motions, together with the computer keyboard options noted in the figure, provide for a surprising amount of variety. Several scale systems are supported, including pentatonic, quartal, and Middle Eastern, as well as different textural styles. The benefits for instruction in the subtleties of musical expression are obvious.

Sound Toys works very much like Music Mouse by providing ways to improvise using the mouse. Figure 9.31*b* displays one of the five main screens for Sound Toys. As the user moves the mouse over the graphics, different sound patterns occur. Clicking the mouse button creates a slightly different result. For additional interest, an ostinato pattern can also be started to give the sound patterns a background and a basis for organization. All of this can be recorded for playback using the graphic in the upper left corner. Each of the five main screens uses different patterns and sounds. One screen uses primarily folk guitar sounds while another uses more "heavy metal" timbres. Still another uses "new age" sounds and allows the musician to construct the graphic blocks that are used for the improvisation.

Band-in-a-Box, our final example in this category, adds still more variety to creative CAI for improvisation. This program turns your computer and any MIDI device (or devices) into a music ensemble devoted to supporting your solo improvisations. Like many of the programs described in this module, you can also run this program without external MIDI devices by using the QuickTime sounds.

Figure 9.32*a* illustrates the main improvisation screen, showing measure numbers that highlight what measure the accompaniment is playing. Notice the chord symbols that we have added for the pop tune "Yesterday." After adding the chord changes, we have chosen the "pop ballad" style from a list of 24 standard styles (Figure 9.32*b*). Once this is done, we can select a tempo and then define the form by telling Band-in-a-Box which measures make up the introduction, chorus, and ending. Clicking on the "play" but-

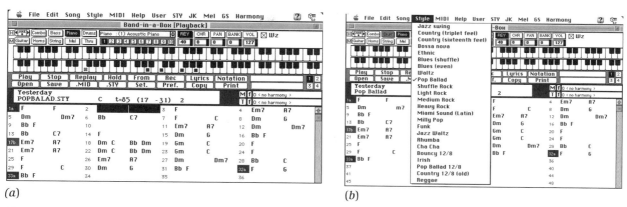

(a)   *(b)*

Figure 9.32
Band-in-a-Box
(PG Music, Inc.
[Mac/Windows])

ton causes the program to give a two-measure introduction and then to start to play an accompaniment that uses drum set, bass, piano, and guitar tracks. If you have a MIDI device such as a keyboard synthesizer attached to your computer, you can add a melody line with improvisational patterns. The program allows you to change the accompaniment timbres instantly if you don't like what is given. Changes in the style will create new rhythms and timbres as appropriate for the style chosen.

The program provides several hundred precomposed arrangements with chord changes for you to use with your own tunes. You can even see the instrument parts in notated form and print the arrangements if you wish. Another valuable feature is that all accompaniments and melodies can be saved as standard MIDI files to be either played in a traditional sequencer program or treated in a special way with advanced music notation software.

What to Choose: A Matter of Content and Need

It should now be clear that you have many choices for adding computer-assisted instruction to your studio. The individual musician who wants to use the computer for self-improvement has a similar array of options. Before we continue our mini course on CAI, let's summarize this module on software by considering content and student need.

What Do You Want as a *Teacher*? In the opening pages of this module, we pointed to the important first question that you need to ask: "What do I want the technology to do?" Software choice is really an extension of your philosophy of music teaching and of what you want the music experience to be. Now that we have seen some examples of software in different categories with different music content, consider these questions as a guide:

▶ What can the software best help to teach when I'm not around?

▶ Do I want the software to stress factual information, aural skills, or creative thinking?

▶ Am I only interested in software that reinforces performance ability?

▶ What is an acceptable balance between sound and visual information?

▶ Do I want the software to concentrate on shorter units of sound or longer ones?

▶ Do I want to be in control of the content and the order of that content, or do I want to allow the student a good deal of freedom?

Software activity: "Evaluate Two Music CAI Programs"

These are also good questions to ask if you are trying to choose software for self-improvement. Each raises fundamental issues about CAI software and its match to your own perspective on technology and the music experience.

What Do You Want As a *Student*? Each learner is in a different place. Good teachers sense this and adjust their teaching style accordingly. You know yourself and, as an independent learner, you know what works best for you. Today's CAI software in music is diverse enough in design and content to offer a wide selection based on individual needs.

Here are some more factors to consider:

▶ *Age.* This is the most obvious factor, but often the most misunderstood. With the exception of software that is specifically designed for young children, no single program or program set should be considered appropriate for one age level only. For example, drill-and-practice software should not be considered as appropriate only for adolescents and exploratory or creative titles as suitable only for adults. The reverse may actually be true for certain people. A decision to use a particular software title should not rest on age but on *readiness* and *internal motivation*, which often comes from natural curiosity.

▶ *Learning style.* Research continues to demonstrate that individuals learn in different ways. Some learn best when sound is augmented by visual cues, others when sound is augmented with words, still others when it is augmented with physical movement. Choice of software to match learning style preference is important.

▶ *Flexible choice.* Some individuals learn best when given choices about such things as drill criteria, length of software use, style of music, and aesthetic decision making. Others just want to be told what to do, and still others like a combination of these two methods.

▶ *Transfer.* We hope, and sometimes incorrectly assume, that we transfer understanding about one aspect of music to another (e.g., transferring rhythmic understanding to the ability to sing melodies). A good question to ask about music software is how well does it help the transfer of music learning between skills.

▶ *Technology itself.* Some of us just don't like using technology to learn, period. If this is the case, we should consider not using it. Computer-assisted instruction in music is not for everyone!

Module 10 — Acoustics Primer

Modules 10–12 will discuss how computers generate sound. Many traditionally trained musicians have little understanding of how music can be created with electronic devices and computers. Why does a musician need to know about acoustics? Acoustics is the study of the physics of sound. Generating music with any machine, computer or otherwise, requires manipulating, editing, mixing, and controlling the physical properties of sound. When you are using software to capture a digital sound image in your computer, you will have the power to change the pitch or loudness of all or parts of the sound you hear, alter its articulation, and use filtering and other techniques to change the color of the sound. When you are learning to program the controls provided with a MIDI synthesizer to create new sounds, you will have to make similar choices.

When you look "under the hood" of computer music synthesis you will find the basic physical elements of:

▶ Frequency

▶ Amplitude

▶ Harmonic spectrum (frequency and amplitude)

▶ Envelope (harmonic spectrum over time)

We will discuss each of these elements in turn and then conclude by applying them to various forms of music synthesis.

Acoustical and Perceptual Properties of Sound

Recreate in your mind for a moment a favorite piece of music. Perhaps you hear the opening movement to Beethoven's *Eroica* symphony, or the Beach Boys singing "Surfin U.S.A.," or Glenn Gould playing the Bach *Goldberg Variations*, or Béla Fleck and the Flecktones playing "The Flight of the Cosmic Hippo." Can you hear the music in your mind?

Freeze a moment of that music in your mind. That brief moment holds the complex array of vibrations that make up what you hear. We can study that captured sound acoustically, examining all of its physical properties.

Figure 10.1
Two three-dimensional views of a single clarinet tone from James Moorer's research at Stanford University (1975): on the left (a) a perspective plot of a clarinet tone showing time (x), amplitude (y), and frequency (z) for each harmonic; on the right (b), a spectrographic plot of the same clarinet tone showing time (x) and frequency (y), with the width of the bars indicating amplitude (Graphs courtesy of James Moorer)

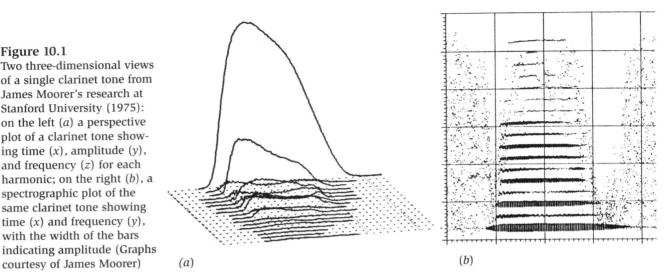

(a)   (b)

This is like taking a drop of water from a pond and examining the contents under a high-powered microscope to see beyond what we see with the naked eye.

The graphs in Figure 10.1 show two computer views of the elements of a single clarinet tone. They are among an extended series of graphs developed by James Moorer at Stanford University in the 1970s, using a computer to show the acoustical complexity of single instrument tones. You can see that there is a lot going on. Can you imagine what a single moment in time from a full symphony orchestra might look like?

We can study the *acoustical* properties of sound to determine its physical characteristics independently of how we hear it. We can also examine the music in terms of its *perceptual* properties: what we hear. Table 10.1 shows the acoustical properties of sound and their parallel perceptual properties.

It is important to keep a clear distinction between these two ways of examining sound. When we use terms like *pitch, loudness, articulation,* and *timbre,* we are describing how we hear and perceive the sound. We can describe sound as getting higher or lower, louder or softer, brighter or duller, and so on, with an infinite variety of adjectives. These properties are not physically quantifiable by measuring devices like frequency counters, sound-pressure level meters, oscilloscopes, and computers.

Table 10.1. Comparison of Acoustical and Perceptual Properties of Sound.	
Acoustical	**Perceptual**
Frequency	Pitch
Amplitude	Loudness
Envelope	Articulation
Harmonic spectrum	Timbre

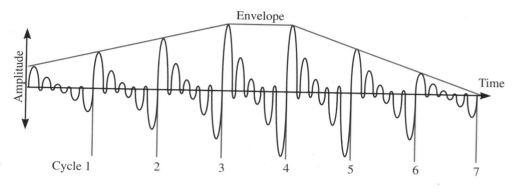

Figure 10.2
A wave sample showing the acoustical properties of amplitude, frequency, and envelope

Frequency = cycles per second

Observing the distinction between acoustics and perception, you know that a computer or a synthesizer does not generate pitch, loudness, and timbre. Rather, it generates and manipulates frequency, amplitude, envelope, and harmonic spectrum: the physical properties of sound. Figure 10.2 depicts a sample of sound showing a number of its acoustical properties. We will discuss each in turn.

Vibrations, Frequency, and Amplitude

Figure 10.2 represents the vibrations in a frozen moment of sound. Sound is produced when something vibrates or oscillates. There must be a vibrating source of energy, or *oscillator*, to create sound: think of striking a metal pipe, blowing across the top of a soda pop bottle, plucking a string, buzzing your lips, or moving your vocal cords by speaking or singing. Electronic devices can also serve as oscillators to create sound.

When anything vibrates, it sets the molecules around it into motion, starting a chain reaction through whatever media surround it. When you hear a sound, its oscillation has passed through air, a vibrating membrane (your ear drum), vibrating bones (your middle ear), fluid motion, and vibrating hair cells or cilia (your inner ear or cochlea).

Vibrations produce alternating patterns of change in molecules as they are pulled apart and pushed together—an increase and decrease in energy or pressure—graphically represented in Figure 10.2 by a curve that is shown repeatedly going above and below the center line. The curve above the line represents an increase in pressure; below the line, a decrease in pressure. Each pattern of increase and decrease is one *cycle* of the vibration. The graph of the pattern is called the sound's *waveform*, and, because the waveform contains similar patterns that repeat over and over, it is called a *periodic* waveform.

Frequency. Frequency is a measure of the rate of an oscillation: how many cycles occur in a certain frame of time. The standard orchestral tuning note A is a vibration at 440 cycles per second (cps). We can indicate this as 440 cps or 440 Hz. (Hz represents Hertz, the international standard unit for

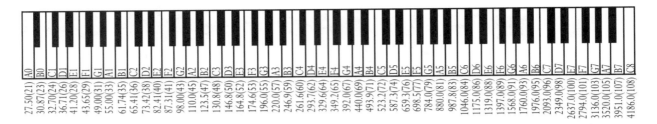

Figure 10.3
Frequencies of notes on the piano keyboard (MIDI note values in parentheses)

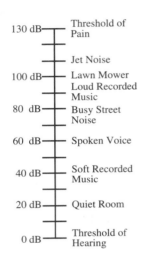

cycle per second.) Just as we use the letters *K* and *M* to mean thousand or million bytes in the size of memory chips, we use them to abbreviate *Kilo-Hertz* and *MegaHertz*. For example, we could say 2 KHz or 5.5 KHz instead of 2,000 Hz or 5,500 Hz.

Figure 10.3 shows the range of frequencies the 88-key piano keyboard covers. Next to each white key we have also indicated the MIDI music code; the frequency and MIDI values will be useful to you when you begin working with MIDI software for sequencing and other tasks.

The human ear is responsive to frequencies from 20 Hz to about 20 KHz, depending on how acute one's hearing is. When the frequency of oscillation increases, we hear the pitch getting higher. When the frequency of oscillation decreases, the pitch we hear gets lower.

Amplitude. Amplitude is a measure of the magnitude of the oscillation: how great an increase and decrease in pressure is produced by the vibration. When the amplitude of a sound increases, we hear it get louder. When the amplitude decreases, we say that the sound gets softer. The distance the curve's rise and fall above and below the middle line in Figure 10.2 represents the amplitude of the sound.

Amplitude can be measured in many ways depending upon the vibrating medium. Most commonly, we measure amplitude using a relative scale of *decibels,* or dB. This scale begins at zero, the point at which the ideal human ear can just perceive a 1,000-Hz tone, and extends to the point where the amplitude of sound causes pain to the human ear, roughly 130 dB. The figure in the margin gives you a general idea of how the decibel scale works by correlating various environmental sounds to the scale from 0 to 130 dB. You will encounter the concept of amplitude again when we discuss digital audio and sampling of sound, and when we look at how MIDI translates amplitude information from instrument controllers (also called *velocity* information in MIDI).

Envelopes

Notice in Figure 10.2 that the amplitude of each cycle is not the same: it gradually increases, then stays constant, and then decreases toward the end of the sound sample. This pattern of amplitude change over time is the *envelope* of the sound. Each musical instrument has a distinctive envelope that can be described by a number of time points from the sound's start until its end. The simplest envelope can be described by its *attack, decay, sustain,* and *release,* or ADSR:

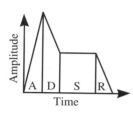

▶ *Attack* is the initial onset of the tone when the oscillator or instrument begins to vibrate.

▶ *Decay* is the brief decrease in amplitude immediately after the attack.

▶ *Sustain* is the amplitude during the middle portion of the envelope just prior to its release.

▶ *Release* is when the instrument stops producing a sound—the time it takes the instrument to stop vibrating or come to a state of rest.

ADSR describes only four points of the envelope. The more points that can be defined, however, the more accurate the description. To accurately recreate the envelope of the clarinet tone in the Moorer and Gray diagram would take hundreds of amplitude points. Envelopes can be generalized into a few common shapes; for example:

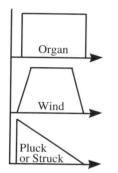

▶ Rectangular envelopes are typical of mechanical devices, like organ pipes opening and closing.

▶ Trapezoidal envelopes are typical of instruments in which air is blown through a pipe, for example, wind and brass instruments.

▶ Triangular envelopes are typical of plucked or struck instruments like pianos, guitars, and dulcimers.

What we perceive as timbre is due, in part, to the shape of the envelope. Most of the information that we used in identifying a unique timbre comes from the attack phase of the envelope. Later we will see how this property is used in the design of computer music samplers. We also perceptually describe the envelope of a sound by its articulation, using such terms as staccato, legato, and marcato.

Harmonic Spectrum

Envelope accounts for only part of what we perceive as timbre. We also need to analyze the amplitude of each of the frequencies that make up the sound. This is called the *harmonic spectrum* of the sound. Where the envelope represents changes in amplitude over time, the harmonic spectrum represents the amplitude of each frequency at a given point in time.

To understand the principle of the harmonic spectrum, we will examine the concepts advanced by three important scientists:

▶ Sauveau's overtone series: In the early 1700s, Joseph Sauveau discovered the *overtone series*: the phenomenon that complex sounds contain frequencies following a common pattern of ratios.

▶ The Fourier theorem: Some 100 years later, Jean Baptiste Fourier proposed that any periodic vibration can be represented as a sum of harmonically related sine waves that follow the overtone series.

▶ Helmholtz's theory of harmonic analysis: In the mid-1800s, Hermann von Helmholtz, using hollow vibrating glass spheres, was able to demonstrate the first harmonic analysis (known as *spectral analysis*) of complex sounds fol-

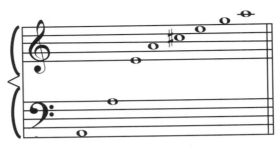

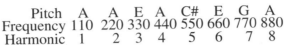

Pitch	A	A	E	A	C#	E	G	A
Frequency	110	220	330	440	550	660	770	880
Harmonic	1	2	3	4	5	6	7	8

Figure 10.4
The overtone series starting on the pitch A

lowing the Fourier theorem. The details of Helmholtz's experiments resulted in the landmark book, *On the Sensations of Tone,* published in 1863.

Each of these concepts is important to your understanding of how computers create music, so let's examine them in greater detail.

Overtones. Figure 10.4 shows Sauvier's overtone series for a pitch sounding on A. The initial frequency in the series is called the *fundamental,* in this case 110 Hz, or A. All periodic vibrations contain frequencies or overtones above the fundamental, with the same intervallic relationships. A sound with no overtones, only the fundamental, is known as a *sine* wave.

If you know the frequency of the fundamental, you can always calculate the overtones above the fundamental using this standard set of ratios. When blowing through a brass instrument like a bugle or trumpet, you can produce many of the notes in the overtone series simply by changing the rate of vibration of your lips and the air pressure.

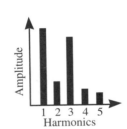

The closest natural sound to a sine wave—a sound with no overtones—is a human whistle; a pure sine wave can only be produced with an electronic oscillator.

Overtones are also called *harmonics,* with the first harmonic being the fundamental. You will also encounter the term *partial,* a synonym for *harmonic.* The first overtone is the *second harmonic* or *second partial,* the second overtone is the third harmonic and partial, and so on.

Harmonic Spectrum and Fourier's Theorem. Fourier's theorem states that any periodic vibration can be expressed as a series of sine waves. We can add sine waves to make increasingly complex sounds (additive synthesis); we can take a complex sound and subtract sine waves to make simpler sounds (subtractive synthesis); and we can analyze any sound by identifying the amplitude of every sine wave in the overtone series present in that sound (spectral or harmonic analysis).

For a dramatic demonstration of Fourier's theorem in operation, try this experiment with a grand piano. First hold the damper pedal down, lifting all the dampers off the strings. Then try singing or playing different instruments into the open piano. You should hear an echo of the same timbre you played. Each string in the piano *sympathetically vibrates* to match the ampli-

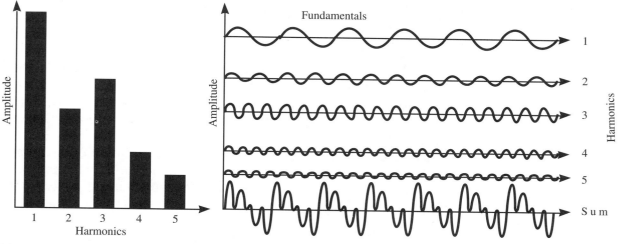

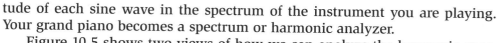

(*a*) Harmonic spectrum of the complex wave on the right

(*b*) Five individual sine waves, one for each harmonic, that add up to a complex wave ("sum")

Figure 10.5
The construction of a complex wave

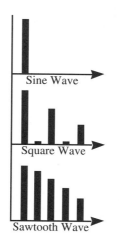

tude of each sine wave in the spectrum of the instrument you are playing. Your grand piano becomes a spectrum or harmonic analyzer.

Figure 10.5 shows two views of how we can analyze the harmonic spectrum of a complex sound. On the left (*a*), you see a graph indicating the amplitude of each harmonic in the overtone series up to the fifth harmonic. On the right (*b*), you see the sequential addition of five sine waves, one for each harmonic, that add up to the complex wave at the bottom (the "sum" of the sine waves). The graph on the left can be produced with a spectrum analyzer; the one on the right with an oscilloscope—devices that measure and represent physical phenomena.

Electronic oscillators used in analog synthesizers are commonly sine, square, and sawtooth oscillators. The figure in the margin shows the harmonic spectrum of each. Notice that the sine wave has no overtones, the square wave has only the odd harmonics, and the sawtooth generator contains the full spectrum of harmonics.

Changes in the harmonic spectrum of a sound are perceived as changes in timbre. The timbre of each instrument has a unique, characteristic harmonic spectrum. Clarinet sounds favor the odd harmonics like the electronic square wave. Rich sounds like the oboes have lots of harmonics at strong amplitudes. Flute sounds favor the octave harmonics.

Understanding the harmonic makeup of sounds is absolutely critical to working with digital sound synthesis. Altering harmonics is the key to techniques of synthesis, filtering, sampling, and many other notions related to computer music.

Summary of the Acoustic Properties of Sound

Let's summarize the acoustic elements we have discussed. Any complex sound can be analyzed in terms of three physical properties: frequency, amplitude, and envelope. The Moorer and Gray graph of the clarinet tone in

Figure 10.1 shows these three dimensions. Frequency measures the rate of vibration and amplitude the amount or intensity of the vibration. Frequency is measured in cycles per second (cps) or Hertz (Hz), and amplitude is measured in dynes/cm2 or decibels (dB).

You can look at changes in amplitude over time to analyze the envelope of the sound. Envelopes typically follow a pattern of attack, decay, sustain, and release (ADSR). You can look at the amplitude of each sine wave present in a sound at a point in time to analyze its harmonic spectrum. This is the basis of Fourier's theorem.

You now have the basic concepts necessary to fully interpret the Moorer graphs in Figure 10.1. Figure 10.1*a* shows time on the horizontal dimension. Harmonics are shown across the bottom of the graph starting with the first harmonic or fundamental at the back and the highest harmonic at the front. Amplitude is shown in the vertical height of the graph. Each harmonic has its own envelope. You can view the changes in the harmonic spectrum of the sound by comparing the amplitude for each harmonic at various points in time. Notice that the clarinet harmonic spectrum emphasizes the odd-numbered harmonics.

Figure 10.1*b* gives a different view of the same tone, a spectrographic view. Time is still on the horizontal dimension. Frequency for each harmonic is shown on the vertical dimension. The width of each of the bars then represents changes in amplitude for each harmonic over time.

Forms of Synthesis

If you read some commercial ads for various synthesizers you will notice that they use such terms as FM synthesis, additive synthesis, digital wave synthesis, and physical modeling. What do these mean? Any time we create sounds using electronic oscillators, we are engaged in electronic music synthesis. Analog techniques for music synthesis use analog electronic oscillators like sine, square, and sawtooth wave generators as the sound source. A typical analog synthesizer requires three components:

▶ *Oscillators*: To create the sound source

▶ *Filters*: To allow modification of the harmonic spectrum of the sound

▶ *Amplifiers*: To allow the envelope of the sound to be modified

These are all of the controls necessary to manipulate the acoustical properties of sound.

In simple terms, there are three methods for creating analog synthesis. Figure 10.6 illustrates these three techniques: *additive, subtractive,* and *distortive* synthesis.

Additive synthesis combines oscillators to build up more complex sounds. Recall the Fourier theorem. By adding sine waves at varying amplitudes, we can create different harmonic spectra. So, by changing the amplitude of different electronic oscillators in various combinations, we can change the harmonic spectrum of a sound and therefore the timbre we perceive.

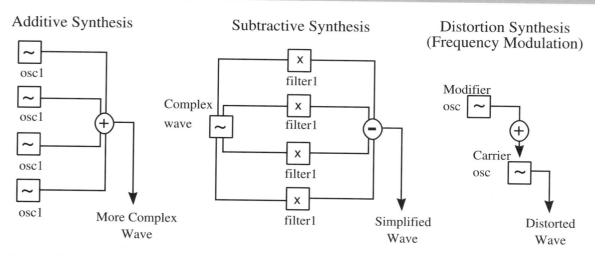

Additive Synthesis   Subtractive Synthesis   Distortion Synthesis (Frequency Modulation)

Figure 10.6
Three forms of music synthesis: additive, subtractive, and distortive

Cahill and the Teleharmonium are mentioned in the Timeline of Viewport VII and in the Historical Perspective on digital audio presented in Module 23, as are other early pioneers of digital audio and music synthesis.

The early Telharmonium (around 1900) was an additive synthesizer that used immense electronic dynamos weighing tons to create complex waveforms. The Hammond organ used mechanically controlled devices called tone wheels that mixed various waveforms to create complex sounds. Additive synthesis became the basis for digital synthesis when Max Mathews showed how additive synthesis could be implemented on a computer in 1957.

Subtractive synthesis starts with a complex sound, like that of a sawtooth electronic oscillator. It then employs electronic *filters* to subtract selected harmonics. Again, Fourier's theorem comes into play. Subtracting selected harmonics from the overtone series alters the harmonic spectrum. Subtractive synthesis was a common technique used by analog synthesizers such as the Moog, Buchla, and ARP synthesizers of the 1960s.

Distortive synthesis takes several forms; one of the more common is FM or frequency modulation synthesis. Distortion means that one physical property of sound is used to distort or modify the same or a different property of sound. (Some also use the term *multiply* synthesis because one sound may multiply properties of the other.) With FM synthesis, the sound generated by one oscillator (called the *carrier*) is distorted by another oscillator (called the *modulator*) to produce unique and rich harmonic spectra of sounds. John Chowning at Stanford University refined this method of analog synthesis and licensed the techniques to Yamaha. Many of Yamaha's electronic synthesizers in the 1980s, among them the FB-01 and the DX-7, used this technique. Yamaha called the carriers and modulators *operators*.

Digital wave synthesis. Another way to create oscillation is to use a computer to generate a series of numbers (digital) to create an image of the shape of a single cycle or wave of a sound's vibration. This series may be described as a table of numbers representing the wave shape, or a wavetable. The numbers can then be changed back into an analog vibration by using a digital-to-analog converter. The principles of additive, subtractive, and distortive synthesis can be applied to these tables of digital numbers to create new sounds just as they are applied to analog synthesis. The table of numbers can be recomputed to subtract out harmonics from a table, or to add two tables together to create new wavetables, which, when fed to a digital-to-analog converter, will create new analog sounds. We will devote much of the discussion of synthesis throughout the book to various forms of digital synthesis.

Physical Modeling. One of the newer techniques for sound synthesis, *physical modeling*, attempts to simulate the acoustic properties of a sound through mathematical formulas. A model is a simulation that enables a computer to physically recreate the acoustical behavior of a vibrating body and then alter that model by altering the mathematical formula. No image of the sound is stored in the computer, only the model of its acoustical vibrating behavior. So, instead of having 88 unique synthesized sounds to create the sound of a Bösendorfer grand piano, one model could be created that simulates the acoustical behavior of a key striking on the Bösendorfer grand, and then the model could be adjusted to fit the changing acoustical traits of each key as you move up the 88 keys of the piano. It is only with the newer computer CPUs, and their fast processor speeds, that physical modeling as a means of sound synthesis is possible.

Module 11 | Data Structures for Digital Audio and MIDI

As a musician goes about building or expanding a computer music system, different techniques for music generation will need to be evaluated. One quickly discovers that understanding MIDI and digital audio is essential. These concepts are the basis for most of the electronic music systems popular today. To help you become a more discriminating user of MIDI and digital techniques, this module will discuss the fundamental data structures, or the way that music information is organized, for:

▶ Digital music and sound

▶ MIDI messages

▶ General MIDI

Digital Sound Structures

Digital audio is important for use with CAI software because most of the electronic music devices produce their sound through digital audio and sampling techniques. This includes computer sound devices, keyboards, MIDI sound modules and synthesizers, and laser audio technology and discs. Digital audio is so pervasive, in fact, that there is a good chance that when you use your telephone to speak with family and friends, much of the phone communication is digital.

In Module 7, we introduced the concepts of analog and digital information. *Analog* represents events that are recorded as continuous in nature, as opposed to *digital* events that are represented as discrete steps or numbers. Let's see how that distinction applies to analog and digital sound representations.

All the acoustic concepts discussed in Module 10 describe sound in its analog form. Vibrations and changes in amplitude are analog events. Figure 11.1 represents sound vibrations being transformed by analog *transducers*.

The analog vibrations begin as rapid movements of the singer's vocal cords, then are transformed into fluctuations in air pressure, then to changing electrical voltages by the microphone, then to rapid movements in the cone of a speaker, and then once again to fluctuations in air pressure. The

Figure 11.1
Analog transformations of sound from voice, to air, to microphone, to speaker, and back to air

Transformations of analog vibrations ⟶

Figure 11.2
Adding analog recording to the chain of transformations

Recording with analog tape ⟶

vocal cord, air, microphone, and speaker cone are all analog transducers of sound. They convert acoustical vibrations and energy from one analog form to another.

How can we store or capture analog sound vibrations? A phonograph recording or a magnetic tape recorder are two examples. Figure 11.2 adds a magnetic tape recorder to our chain of transducers. Now the electrical voltage oscillations from the microphone are transformed by the tape recorder's recording head into patterns of magnetic particles along the length of recording tape. For playback of the tape, the magnetic particles are converted back into voltage changes through the playback head of the recorder. Again, all of these transformations are analog representation of sound.

Phonograph recordings are also analog events. The oscillations are carved into grooves in the vinyl of the record. The figure below shows what magnetic patterns on recording tape and groove patterns on a vinyl phonograph record look like under high magnification.

Figure 11.4 replaces the tape recorder with a computer, a digital device. The continuous changes in voltage from the microphone are now converted into a series of numbers that the computer stores. *Analog-to-digital* conversion has been performed. The box marked ADC represents a device that per-

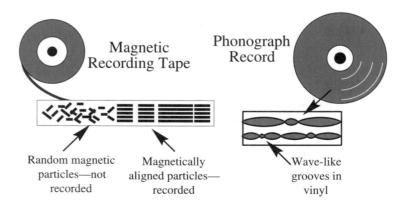

Figure 11.3
Analog patterns on a phonograph record and a magnetic tape

Magnetic Recording Tape

Phonograph Record

Random magnetic particles—not recorded

Magnetically aligned particles—recorded

Wave-like grooves in vinyl

Figure 11.4
Converting analog sound to digital (ADC) and digital back to analog (DAC)

The term *sample* is used in two different ways. It may refer to a single point: one number in the ADC process. However, a series of samples that create a set or series of numbers is also referred to as a sample.

forms the analog-to-digital conversion. To change the number series back into analog data, a *digital-to-analog* converter (DAC) is used.

Let's convert a sound from its original analog form to digital and back again. Figures 11.4 and 11.5 represent this process. From left to right, the original analog vibration passes through the analog-to-digital converter (ADC) and produces a series of numbers. Each number is a discrete point or *sample* from the analog sound. Next, a digital-to-analog converter (DAC) converts the numbers back to analog form, enabling the speaker to produce the analog sound as shown at the right of the figures.

Note in Figure 11.5 that the illustration representing the final analog pattern on the right does not look quite like the original sound. The curve has the unsmooth edges that in computer jargon are called *jaggies*. The presence of jaggies shows that some data from the original sound have been lost in conversion. Your ear hears what is visually represented by these jaggies as a loss in audio fidelity.

The extent to which digitized sound samples match the original sound is dependent upon the accuracy with which the computer samples the analog sound data. This accuracy depends upon two factors: sampling rate and sampling width (also known as *quantizing*). We will go into these concepts in greater detail later, but for now we offer a simple explanation.

Sampling Rates and Quantizing. The *sampling rate* is the speed at which the computer can convert analog changes to numbers: the number of samples per second. Ideally we'd like a sampling rate that is as good as the upper limits of human hearing, or 20 KHz. A sampling rate of 44 KHz will

Figure 11.5
The digital sampling process from an analog waveform, to a waveform table, then reconstructed again as an analog sound

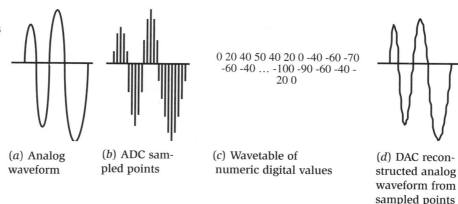

(*a*) Analog waveform

(*b*) ADC sampled points

(*c*) Wavetable of numeric digital values

0 20 40 50 40 20 0 -40 -60 -70 -60 -40 ... -100 -90 -60 -40 - 20 0

(*d*) DAC reconstructed analog waveform from sampled points

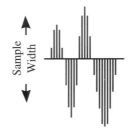

Sample Width

When you capture digital audio in stereo, you have two separate streams of audio data; hence, a stereo digital audio file is typically twice the size of its monaural equivalent!

Concepts and terms like frequency, envelope, and amplitude are covered in Module 10's tutorial on acoustics.

give us an upper frequency limit of 22 KHz on playback. The frequency limit on playback is always half the sampling rate.

Sampling width or *quantizing* refers to the *resolution* of the sampling: how large a number is used to represent each data point or sample. (Note: *quantizing* here has a different meaning from the same term as used with MIDI data.) Typical number sizes are 8-, 12-, or 16-bit numbers. With sampling rate and quantizing size, faster and bigger is better—if possible. In reality, however, memory and speed constrictions limit the ability to digitize all sound at 44 KHz with 16-bit resolution. Music can be digitized with reasonable quality with 8-bit resolution and 22-KHz sampling rates, comparable to AM and FM radio.

Bear in mind, however, that when sampling on a computer system, there is a direct relationship between the sampling rate and width you use and the amount of storage space you need. With a 16-bit width and a 44-KHz sampling rate, a one-minute sample of analog stereo sound will consume about 11 MB of hard disk space. Using an 8-bit width and 22-KHz rate, a one-minute sample uses about 2.5 MB of space—a dramatic difference.

Techniques for Digital Sound Production. Digital sound structures are used in computers and digital synthesizers in four general forms:

▶ *Complete sample.* A digitized sample is made of a complete segment of music or speech. To reproduce the sample, the complete series of digitized, numeric values is played back through a DAC device or a digital oscillator. This offers the best computer realization of an analog sound sample, but consumes large amounts of memory and storage. Therefore, this data structure works best where short portions of music or speech are needed, especially as in music CAI software. Hardware and software that both record and play back complete samples are called *samplers*. Those that only play back prerecorded samples are called *sample players*.

▶ *Single-tone sample.* A digitized sample is made of one complete musical tone. The sample contains all the envelope and harmonic spectrum information needed to produce a real-sounding single tone of an instrument. For best realism, however, multiple samples, one for each pitch, need to be created to represent an instrument's full range of timbres. This data structure works best where a degree of realism for various instrument timbres is needed. If you play on a digital or sampling keyboard, single-tone sampling is most likely the way it creates its sound. The kinds of CAI music software that use single-tone sampling include computer drill-and-practice software for ear training, and improvisation software.

▶ *Single-cycle waveform.* A series of numbers are created that represent one cycle of a waveform. This series may be sampled from an analog source or computed mathematically. It contains only the harmonic spectral information. To produce a tone in the computer, the series, or *wavetable,* is repeatedly cycled through at the rate of the desired frequency, and the resulting numeric values are played back through a DAC. A computer or synthesizer using this technique is called a *digital synthesizer;* it uses *digital oscillators*.

The wavetable in this case contains no envelope information to shape the attack and decay of the sound. The amplitude information for the envelope needs to be added from a separate DAC device and an *envelope table.* The single-cycle waveform data structure works best for situations where memory is critical. Like the single-tone-sample data structure, this form works well for uses like simple CAI drill-and-practice software for ear training. It does not provide the realism offered by the other two structures.

▶ *Wave shaping.* Since digital audio first appeared in PCs in the late 1970s, engineers have experimented with the first three forms of digital sampling to continue to improve the quality of the musical sounds that a computer can produce. What has emerged is increasingly complex techniques for capturing audio and sound sampling that combine the best of these three forms to minimize the memory needed to store the waveform samples and, at the same time, strive to produce the most realistic digital instrument sounds. Combining these forms can be termed *wave shaping.* Wave shaping refers to more complex digital sound generation where algorithms are used to *shape* the digital waveform through various combinations of digital oscillators, digital-controlled amplifiers, digital-controlled filters, and digital effects processors.

Several different wavetables can be combined to create the final instrument sound generated by the digital device. As a simple example, the attack portion of an instrument's sound envelope may be one wavetable, another may be used for the decay of a sound's envelope, and a third wavetable may be repeated many times or *looped* to create the sustained portion of the instrument's envelope. More complex shapes can be constructed when the envelope is described by many wavetables to create subtle nuances in the shape of an instrument's waveform.

Digital synthesizer manufacturers tend to have proprietary techniques for the hardware and algorithms used to shape a digital sound. Examples include Korg's AI2 (Advanced Integrated sample synthesis), Yamaha's AWM (Advanced Wave Memory), Kurzweil's VAST (Variable Architecture Synthesis Technology), and Alesis's QS Composite Synthesis, among others. Except for the very low-end MIDI keyboards and samplers, most use some form of wave shaping in creating their digital instrument sounds.

MIDI Sound Structures

Our discussion so far has focused on structures for representing analog sound vibrations in a computer: The computer is making the sound. We now turn to data structures that represent *performance data,* or instructions for playing music. By performance data we are talking about the numbers generated by a MIDI keyboard, for example, when keys are pressed while playing some music. These numbers, sent to a computer, communicate the frequency of the key played, the intensity with which the key was pressed, and the time that each key was held down. Only these performance data are stored in the computer, not the actual sounds of the music itself. The performance data can then be sent to other MIDI music

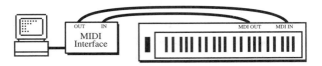

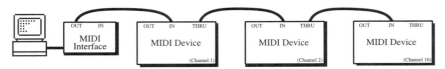

(a) Simple, two device network

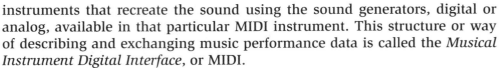

Figure 11.6
Two MIDI networks

(b) A daisy chain of MIDI devices

There is much more to come on MIDI in this book, especially in Viewport VI.

The MIDI standard is voluntary, not mandatory. Each MIDI device has idiosyncrasies and may not implement all MIDI specifications. It is important to read the manuals that come with each device, especially when you begin to explore its more exotic options.

instruments that recreate the sound using the sound generators, digital or analog, available in that particular MIDI instrument. This structure or way of describing and exchanging music performance data is called the *Musical Instrument Digital Interface*, or MIDI.

MIDI (rhymes with "city") is an industry standard for communicating music performance data between music devices such as computers, synthesizers, drum machines, instrument controllers, and even tape recorders, mixers, and effects generators. MIDI was adopted in 1983 by the MIDI Manufacturers Association, and has since undergone several revisions. The *General MIDI* format is a recent addition that we will discuss shortly.

The MIDI standard includes both the performance language for communicating among MIDI devices (data structures) and the specifications for how MIDI devices are electronically connected (hardware). We will provide a general introduction to the data aspects, then follow with a discussion of the hardware features in Module 12. We will return to discuss MIDI in greater depth in Viewport VI.

Figure 11.6 illustrates two simple MIDI networks. Figure 11.6a shows two MIDI devices, a keyboard and a computer, communicating with one another. You need a minimum of two MIDI devices to create a network: two synthesizer keyboards, a computer and a keyboard, a keyboard and a drum machine, etc. Most MIDI devices can send MIDI data (OUT), receive MIDI data (IN), and pass MIDI data on through the network (THRU). A very basic MIDI system, with a computer connected to an electronic keyboard, looks like the one in Figure 11.6a.

Figure 11.6b shows an expanded MIDI network in which a series of MIDI devices are connected in a daisy chain. This diagram helps illustrate the notion of *channels*. The MIDI language can transmit performance data over 16 discrete MIDI channels, similar to TV channels. Any MIDI device can tune in to one or more of these channels to receive the performance commands being broadcast over them.

Potentially you can have 16 MIDI devices receiving data over the MIDI network. Most MIDI devices default to Channel 1 as the base channel, but can be retuned to any of the 16 channels. Notice that the first MIDI device is the *master* unit and all of the others are *slave* devices. Each slave passes the network MIDI data on to the next device with its MIDI THRU connection. A musician would consider this type of a network if there was a need for adding more MIDI devices: perhaps a sound module, a drum machine, or another keyboard.

MIDI Performance Language. MIDI performance codes are just a simple computer language with commands and data. Combinations of commands and data are referred to as MIDI *messages.* MIDI messages allow considerable control over performance on any MIDI devices.

There are two major sets of MIDI messages:

► *Channel messages* are commands broadcast to a MIDI device on any one of the 16 available channels

► *System messages* are commands broadcast to *all* devices on *all* MIDI channels

Channel Messages. Channel messages are commands broadcast on a specific MIDI channel. These commands include playing notes, expressive properties, and monophonic versus polyphonic performing modes. There are two types of channel messages, *voice* and *mode*.

Channel voice messages. Most channel messages are voice messages. These commands are the "fingers" that do the playing, and they require certain data. Because they are channel messages, they require a channel number (1 to 16) to identify the unique channel for broadcasting the data.

The most used MIDI channel voice messages include:

► Note On

► Program Change

► Control Change

Note On produces the notes that are to be played on a MIDI device connected to the system. It is the most often used command in the MIDI language. This message requires data that specify which note is to be turned on or off. The notes are numbered on a continuum from 0 to 127; the 88 keys on the piano keyboard span from the values 21 to 108 with middle C being number 60.

The Note On command also requires a *velocity* value that controls the volume or dynamics of the note, including turning the note off. On a MIDI device without velocity sensing keys, no matter how hard you strike the keys you will always get the same loudness. These devices produce only two values, 0 (off) and 64 (on). When the MIDI device does have velocity sensing, the data values can range between 0 (off) and 127 with 1 being pianissimo (pp) and 127 being fortissimo (ff). Figure 11.7 illustrates MIDI note on and note off data being sent to a keyboard from a computer.

The *Program Change* message sets the instrument or *patch* to be used on

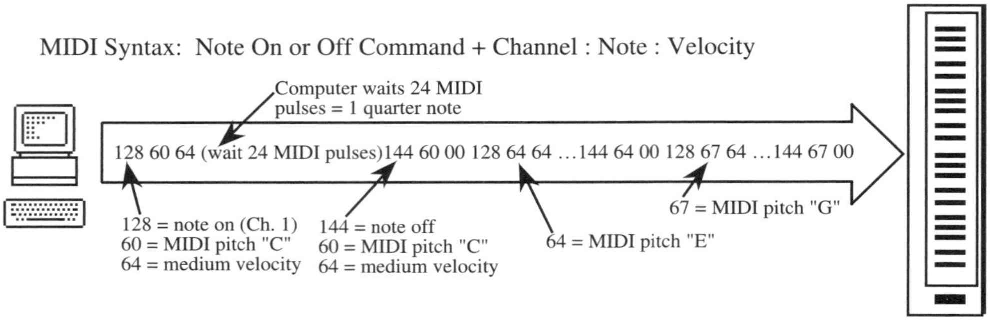

MIDI Syntax: Note On or Off Command + Channel : Note : Velocity

Computer waits 24 MIDI
pulses = 1 quarter note

128 60 64 (wait 24 MIDI pulses)144 60 00 128 64 64 ...144 64 00 128 67 64 ...144 67 00

Figure 11.7
The flow of MIDI channel voice messages from a computer to a keyboard: the Note On and Note Off commands

128 = note on (Ch. 1)
60 = MIDI pitch "C"
64 = medium velocity

144 = note off
60 = MIDI pitch "C"
64 = medium velocity

64 = MIDI pitch "E"

67 = MIDI pitch "G"

devices tuned into a channel. The message is accompanied by data indicating the channel and instrument numbers. Originally, instrument numbers were not standardized. You had to know the unique number for a given timbre for each MIDI device; a clarinet sound did not necessarily have the same number, for example, on Roland and Yamaha synthesizers. Later, the *General MIDI* format introduced a standardized numbering system for MIDI instruments so that piano timbres, string timbres, wind timbres, etc. would have the same patch or program number regardless of the MIDI synthesizer being used. However, the actual sounds may still vary from device to device; one device's clarinet sample, for example, will not sound exactly the same as another's (depending on the quality of the sample, the original sampled instrument, etc.).

The *Control Change* message provides performance control over a variety of expressive properties. These include vibrato, sustain or release time, overall volume on a channel, and so on. Like the other messages, the Control Change command is accompanied by a data value to set the degree of control.

Channel mode messages. Mode messages control how many channels a MIDI device receives (Omni On or Omni Off) and how many voices it plays or transmits (Monophonic or Polyphonic; in MIDI, the term "voices" refers to the number of notes you can play simultaneously on any one channel). There are four combinations of Omni On or Off and Monophonic or Polyphonic; these combinations are known as Modes 1 through 4. Mode 3 (Omni Off/Polyphonic) is the Poly mode and is the most frequently used mode with music CAI, sequencing programs, and the like. Many MIDI devices have a default setting of Mode 3. In this mode, each MIDI channel contains specific, polyphonic performance data. We will deal with mode messages in more detail in Module 20.

An additional channel mode command that can be handy is All Notes Off. MIDI devices sometimes get stuck in play mode, and this command will turn off all sound.

System Messages. System messages do not contain channel codes. These commands affect *all* devices in the MIDI network and are broadcast over all channels. There are three types of system messages: common, real time, and exclusive. These commands control the timing events, sequences of performance data, and special effects unique to MIDI devices.

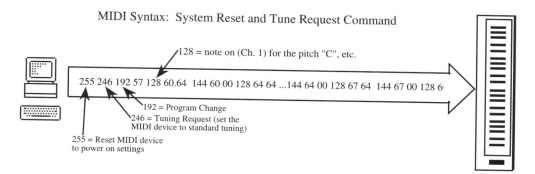

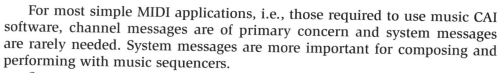

Figure 11.8
The flow of MIDI system messages from a computer to a keyboard

Stay tuned for Module 20 and more details on the MIDI language.

For most simple MIDI applications, i.e., those required to use music CAI software, channel messages are of primary concern and system messages are rarely needed. System messages are more important for composing and performing with music sequencers.

System common messages provide indexing control over sequences of MIDI performance data. The common commands permit the selection of various sequences, the indexing of specific locations within a sequence (song pointers), and real-time indexing of sequences with MIDI time codes. MIDI devices generate a timing code of 24 pulses per quarter note that all of the devices on the MIDI network can use to synchronize performance and performance effects. Under the system common messages is a command that turns the General MIDI format on and off.

The system messages serve the same function as controls on a tape deck. They provide commands for starting, stopping, pausing, and continuing the performance of MIDI sequences. Figure 11.8 illustrates two system real-time messages: System Reset and Tune Request.

System exclusive messages offer each MIDI manufacturer exclusive codes or patches for their device. These are termed SysEx messages (pronounced "sis-ex"). A unique identification number is assigned to a given manufacturer's device and only that device will acknowledge SysEx messages addressed to it.

Pay attention to General MIDI. It is very important for CAI! There's more on General MIDI in Module 20, including a complete table showing the numbers for all 128 instruments.

General MIDI Format. General MIDI is an attempt to "standardize the MIDI standard." It goes beyond the original MIDI standard to establish a common denominator for a number of music and device controls. Musical instruments, timbres, and percussion sounds all have a common numbering system among General MIDI devices. There is an agreed-upon mapping for the use of channels 1 to 10, with channel 10 reserved for the rhythm or drum track. MIDI channels 1 to 6 are recommended as the main channels for data.

General MIDI also requires that each instrument have 16-channel support, the ability to play 16 simultaneous instrument timbres, and the ability to play 24 notes simultaneously (24-note polyphony, or 24 voices). Default settings of MIDI devices are also defined in the General MIDI format.

General MIDI is very important for musicians. Before General MIDI, you had to configure every piece of software for each MIDI device before it could be used. In some cases, software simply would not work on certain synthesizers. When purchasing a new MIDI device, software setups had to be reconfigured. Channels had to be reset, timbres redefined, etc. Most music software, especially music CAI software, will be written to conform to the General MIDI format, thus insuring that MIDI keyboards and synthesizers will work when the software is run right out of the box!

<table>
<tr><td>

Module 12

</td><td>

Hardware Devices for Music CAI

</td></tr>
</table>

Refer back to Module 8 if you need a review of basic computer operations

So far in Viewport III you have studied a variety of software applications that fall into the category of music computer-assisted instruction (CAI), and a few of the important data structures that underlie music sound generation in these applications. In this module, we will focus on the music hardware necessary to implement music CAI software. At the conclusion of the module, we will introduce the first of several models for a computer music system, the KISS music system for CAI music activities.

IPOS Model

In our discussions of hardware in Viewport II, we introduced the input-process-output-storage or IPOS model. Let's use the IPOS model as shown in Figure 12.1 to categorize the different hardware possibilities for music applications. In this module, our interest is in hardware devices for inputting music performance data and generating or controlling music output. In order to optimize the use of computers for music instruction, we are especially interested in MIDI keyboard controllers, high-quality sound generation devices, and the ability to use commercial CD and DVD audio discs, and video recordings for instructional applications.

Figure 12.1
IPOS model for music CAI hardware, with the storage component omitted

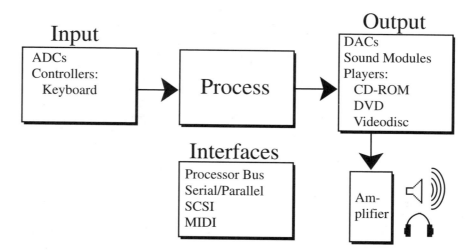

For *input*, we will consider the need for MIDI keyboards, briefly mention other music controllers, and discuss the use of analog-to-digital converters (ADCs) for capturing analog sounds as digital files. On the output side of our IPOS model, we will take a first look at music sound modules; laser-disc players for CDs, DVD discs, and videodiscs; and digital-to-analog converters (DACs) for reproducing digitized sound samples.

Figure 12.1 contains a separate box for hardware *interfaces*. The type of interface required for connecting music devices, especially MIDI devices, to computers is critical. The *output* box indicates the need for audio equipment with a typical Buy-and-Run music application. Stereo earphones or a small amplifier and speakers are the minimum requirement. The *process* stage in this chart represents any computer system. The *storage* stage of the model is omitted for the sake of visual convenience, because it is not necessary to discuss storage here. Should you need more information on the process and storage stages, refer back to Module 8.

Instead of discussing each of the IPOS stages in order, it is easier to group music hardware by sound-generation techniques. We will examine

HISTORICAL PERSPECTIVE

A student studying music CAI on a PLATO terminal with its distinctive touch-panel screen
(Reproduced by permission of Fred T. Hofstetter)

There is a fascinating historical interplay between music instruction, automated teaching machines, electronic music synthesizers, and the concepts of programmed instruction (PI) and computer-assisted instruction (CAI). CAI and its paper-and-pencil predecessor, PI, evolved from the behaviorist theories of Skinner in the 1950s. The history of this interplay shows a quest among music educators for developing automated music training that provides instant access to realistic, high-quality sound production and intelligent sensitivity to individual learning needs. The devices that accompany automated music instruction can be divided into audio playing devices and electronic music devices.

Audio Playing Devices and Music Instruction. The early 1960s were marked by the use of the tape recorder and the large mainframe computer in music instruction. The PLATO system was invented at this time by Don Bitzer at the University of Illinois. PLATO, implemented on Control Data mainframe computers, is one of the most extensive commercial CAI systems developed, and a large library of music teaching materials has been written for the system.

Experiments with programmed instruction and audio recording devices included the extensive ear training series developed by William Poland and Charles Spohn at Ohio State University, and James Carlsen's commercially successful melodic dictation drills in the early 1960s. As computer-assisted instruction replaced PI in the late 1960s, music PI migrated to mainframe computer systems and computer-controlled audio tape recorders, both reel-to-reel and cassette. Tape recorders for automated music instruction met with mixed success, however, due to the slow, sequential nature of the medium.

Notable early experiments with computers and audio recording devices for music CAI include the music training materials developed by Ned Deihl, Robert Placek, G. David Peters, and John Eddins. Deihl used an IBM 1500 mainframe and computer-controlled prerecorded tapes. Placek, Peters, and Eddins used the PLATO system and a special-built computer-controlled magnetic disc recording device.

Laser discs, in the form first of the videodisc in the 1970s and then of the compact audio disc in the early 1980s, provided a much needed boon to automated music instruction. The Philips-Sony standards for commercial laser-disc production quickly changed music education's focus from tape to disc.

CD audio discs, videodiscs, and more recently, DVD discs, surpassed the capabilities of tape recording by providing fast, random access to music examples with audio and video fidelity that met the critical demands of the human ear and eye. Present-day music instruction now benefits from the combination of inexpensive and increasingly more powerful personal computers and extremely accurate control over laser-disc recordings of exceptional quality.

Electronic music devices. One of the first uses of an electronic music device interfaced to a computer for music teaching was in Wolfgang Kuhn's work at Stanford in the late 1960s. An electronic organ and a pitch extractor were interfaced to an IBM 1620 mainframe computer for automated aural skill and sight singing training.

In the early 1970s, using another CDC PLATO installation at the University of Delaware, Fred Hofstetter designed the GUIDO CAI music curriculum using a customized digital synthesizer interfaced to a computer. Many others used minicomputer systems (especially the popular DEC PDP systems) for music training in the 1970s by connecting just about any electronic music device imaginable to a minicomputer.

The cost barrier to the mass application of music CAI to education was broken in the early 1980s with the introduction of the personal computer (Apple II, Commodore PET, and TRS-80), and the soon-to-come MIDI standardizing of electronic music devices. The Apple II personal computer with the addition of the Micro Music DAC card or the ALF three-voice analog synthesizer provided a platform for the development of hundreds of music CAI software programs. Through the pioneering efforts of Micro Music Inc. (MMI), Temporal Acuity Products (TAP), and Electronic Courseware Systems (ECS), schools and universities could now offer an expansive library of CAI applications for music training used on low-cost microcomputers with simple polyphonic synthesizers, both digital and analog.

With the entry of MIDI music devices in the mid-1980s, the quality and control of music sound improved by leaps and bounds, as did the sophistication of input devices, like keyboard, wind, drum, and string controllers, for training in music performance. While the Micro Music DAC card (1978) provided the first low-cost solution to digital audio technology and music CAI, digital music synthesizers developed with astounding sophistication over the next ten years. Computers like the Apple IIGS, Macintosh, Amiga, and NeXT came with digital audio as part of the hardware, while companies like AlphaSyntauri, Creative Labs, Digidesign, Ensoniq, Korg, Mountain Music, and numerous others, using bus-extended music boards, matched the digital performance of CD audio by the 1990s.

Check out Module 8 if you need some help with some of the computer hardware terms used here.

the various devices in our chart in the following order: digital sampling devices, MIDI devices, and laser-disc players.

There can be some confusion, when discussing music hardware for a computer, as to where the hardware is located or installed. There are three alternatives to consider. Each of these will be discussed as the interface requirements are addressed for digital, MIDI, and laser hardware:

▶ *Built-in sound.* The computer itself contains the hardware necessary for sound input and output as part of its standard circuitry.

▶ *Bus-extended sound.* A sound input or output device is built on a circuit card and added to a computer by plugging that card into an expansion slot of the computer, i.e., the computer's expansion bus, or into a PCMCIA or PC Card slot on a laptop computer.

▶ *External sound.* An interface and cable are used to connect the sound device to the computer using MIDI, SCSI, USB, Firewire, or simple parallel or serial communications with the computer.

Digital Audio Devices

Digital audio was first discussed in Module 11 and will be discussed in more advanced terms in Module 24.

(Courtesy of E-Mu Systems)

Interfaces. Let's review our explanation of the digital sampling process in Module 11. Analog vibrations are sampled or captured by an analog-to-digital converter (ADC) and stored in a computer as a series of numbers, a *sample*. To play a digital sound sample back, the series of numbers is sent to a digital-to-analog converter (DAC), which converts the numbers back into analog voltages. These voltages oscillate the cone in a speaker or a set of earphones so you hear the reconstructed analog sound. Both the ADC and the DAC are special hardware devices in the form of integrated circuit chips. Some chip companies like Lucent Technologies and Motorola build special *digital signal processing* chips, or DSPs, which are used to handle the demands of high-resolution digital audio.

Speed is of the essence in moving between analog and digital information. Hence, ADC and DAC devices are usually built directly into the computer's hardware or mounted on a circuit card that plugs directly into the computer's bus. The Macintosh computer has built-in ADC and DAC chips. Bus-extended digital sound cards are available for both Macintosh and Wintel computers using the industry standard PCI bus architecture from companies such as Creative Labs, Ensoniq, Diamond Multimedia, and Voyetra/Turtle Beach. PCMCIA or PC sound cards, such as the E-Mu sound card shown in the margin, are also available for laptop computers.

Digitizing hardware, ADCs and DACs, can be components of a synthesizer as well. When both ADC and DAC digital recording and playing capabilities are built into a computer or synthesizer, it is called a *sampler*. A device implementing the DAC process only, using prerecorded samples from disk or in ROM, is properly called a *sample player*.

ADC Input. To digitize sounds with a computer, you need an ADC and a means of connecting it to the outside analog world (Figures 12.2 and 12.3). Two common methods for inputting sound to an ADC are a microphone (to digitize live music and sound) and a line input similar to the inputs on any tape recorder or amplifier (to digitize recorded music). Microphone input jacks are usually miniature phone plugs, stereo or mono, similar to those found on portable cassette tape recorders (Figure 12.4).

In our discussion of digital audio in Module 11, we noted two variables that are key to the quality of the captured sampled audio: *sampling rate* and

Figure 12.2
Computers or synthesizers as samplers and sample players

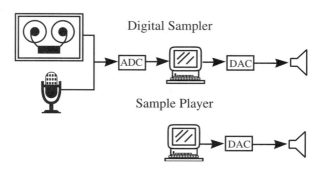

Figure 12.3
Digidesign's Audiomedia III package with hardware and software
(Courtesy of Digidesign, a Division of Avid Technology, Inc.)

sampling width or *quantizing*. Sampling rate can vary from 2,000 samples per second (2 KHz) to 48,000 samples per second (48 KHz); sampling width can vary from 4- to 32-bit values for each sample. Remember that you must divide the sampling rate in half to determine the maximum frequency of the sound you will hear: a 44-KHz sampling rate will give you an upper frequency response of 22 KHz, just above the upper limit of human hearing.

Typical ADCs in PCs are of 44-KHz/16-bit stereo resolution, comparable to the quality of CD audio. Under software control, it is possible to select the sampling rate in a range from 4 to 44 KHz; speech samples often can be sat-

Figure 12.4
Three configurations of audio jacks and plugs

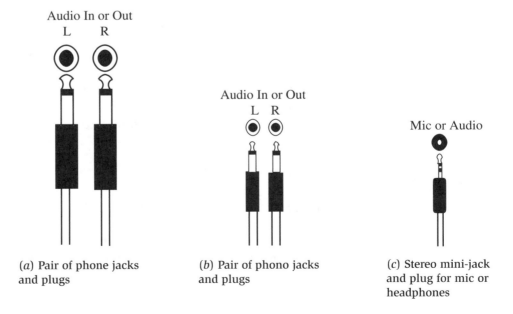

Audio In or Out
L   R

Audio In or Out
L   R

Mic or Audio

(*a*) Pair of phone jacks and plugs

(*b*) Pair of phono jacks and plugs

(*c*) Stereo mini-jack and plug for mic or headphones

One minute of stereo 44-KHz/16-bit sampling consumes 11 MB of storage; at 22 KHz/8-bit sampling, 2.5 MB of storage.

isfactorily digitized at sampling rates around 11 KHz. The built-in ADC on the current Macintosh PC systems matches this resolution, and microphone and line jacks are included to encourage the use of digitized speech and music. A bus-extended card is required for Wintel PC systems to provide ADC capabilities, and many multimedia Wintel computers come prepackaged with a sound card with an ADC chip for sampling digital audio.

High-end ADCs have a resolution of up to 48 KHz sampling rate and up to a 24-bit sampling width, with multiple channels of sound. This level of quality is comparable to that of systems for commercial CD audio recording. Most of the special audio DSP chips provide this quality of resolution. Fast and voluminous hard disk storage—several gigabytes in size—is required in any system doing digital audio sampling at this rate. Various techniques for compressing audio files, fortunately, are available and improving, so that greater sound resolution can be stored in smaller and smaller file space.

For both the Macintosh and Wintel computers, digital audio cards like the Digidesign Audiomedia III card provide bus-extended ADC of this quality, as does the Pinnacle Pro Series from Turtle Beach (Voyetra).

More on digital hard disk recorders and sound file compression in Modules 24 and 26.

DAC Output. Digital sound output on most computer systems is comparable to ADC input resolution. For digital-to-analog conversion, 44-KHz/16-bit sound quality is standard. DAC-only or sample players have been available for personal computers since the late 1970s. The sound chip in Macintosh computers produce sampled sound at the 44-KHz/16-bit resolution. The MPC or Multimedia PC Level 3 standard for Wintel systems suggests a minimum of a 44-KHz sampling rate and 8- or 16-bit samples. The high end, as with the ADC, can provide as much as 48-KHz/24-bit resolution. This level of quality can be obtained through the same bus-extended cards already mentioned.

Output from DAC devices is usually provided as a stereo line-out connector suitable for an audio amplifier. Some may also provide stereo mini-jacks for headphones. Some of the digital cards even provide Dolby Digital 5.1 sound with six discrete channels of audio.

The quality of resolution possible with present-day analog-to-digital conversion puts the power of compact disc recording at your fingertips. Personal computers with the addition of ADC and DAC hardware can sample analog speech and music at the same resolution that appears on compact disc recordings. Sampling rates of 44 KHz and quantizing widths of 16 bits are the industry standard. Decreases in the cost-to-size ratio of disk storage media, increases in the speed of CPU processors, and the industry-wide acceptance of multimedia are helping to make digital sampling hardware essential to any personal computer.

MIDI Devices

Beginning MIDI users are often overwhelmed by the task of connecting the devices, matching INs to OUTs and THRUs and generally becoming tangled in a spaghetti bowl of wires. Therefore, we will begin this section by showing you how the MIDI interface works and typical setups for MIDI equipment. Then we will discuss some of the features of MIDI instruments with

Be sure to read the MIDI sections in Modules 9–11 of this viewport as well.

enough depth to cover the needs of a typical music instruction setting. Our emphasis will be on MIDI controllers and sound modules. Synthesizers and various MIDI instrument configurations are basically some combination of these two components.

MIDI Interfaces. The key item of hardware needed for any MIDI setup is a MIDI interface and the accompanying cables. For CAI music applications, only a basic interface is needed. It can come in the form of a bus-extended card that plugs into your computer (or PCMCIA card for a laptop), a stand-alone box with a cable that plugs into one of the serial or parallel ports of your computer, or as an additional feature of your computer's sound card. Figure 12.5 shows a simple MIDI interface box and a MIDI cable with its distinctive connector.

The MIDI interface is an electronic translator between the computer and MIDI devices like keyboards and synthesizers. It translates the MIDI data sent from the computer into the standard electrical signals and timing recognized by other MIDI devices, or translates MIDI signals coming from other MIDI devices back into numeric data that the computer can understand.

Let's look at an inexpensive interface suitable for most music CAI applications. Basically, an inexpensive MIDI interface has the following attributes:

Pick up any MIDI publication and you will see how quickly MIDI offerings and features change. Supplement your study with articles in the key periodicals like *Electronic Musician* and *Keyboard*.

► It is a serial device

► Data rate is the standard 31.25 KHz

► It broadcasts on 16 MIDI channels

► It has one MIDI IN and one to three MIDI OUT ports

► Optionally, it has one MIDI THRU port

► It is *dumb* rather than *smart*

► It is powered by either the computer or its own power source

► It uses MIDI standard 5-pin DIN plugs, jacks, and cables for connections

See Module 7 for help with serial and parallel data.

MIDI interfaces are serial devices, sending or broadcasting data out serially (one bit at a time) at the rate of 31,250 bits per second over 16 channels of the MIDI network. A simple MIDI interface usually has one IN port for receiving MIDI data from an external device, and one to three OUT ports for

Figure 12.5
A simple MIDI interface box with a MIDI cable

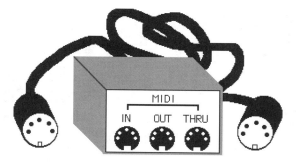

Remember that a MIDI sound generator or keyboard with 16 channels is really 16 different MIDI sound devices in one box, each channel able to generate a different instrument playing different notes and rhythms. It is sort of like having 16 musicians in one box!

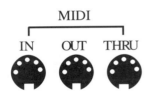

sending data to external MIDI devices. Some interfaces also include a MIDI THRU port for passing on MIDI data over the network to another device.

If the interface is *dumb,* it simply makes the electronic conversions necessary to convert parallel computer data into serial data with the correct timing. *Smart* interfaces, on the other hand, have their own microprocessor chip, are able to interpret MIDI data on their own, provide timing information and more control, and store some of the data in their own RAM. For most CAI applications, the less-expensive dumb interface is all that is needed.

The handiest MIDI interfaces get their power directly from the computer. Others, however, require a separate power source, usually an AC/DC power supply that plugs into a 120-volt wall socket. If possible, opt for an interface that does not need a separate power supply. The fewer cables and cords that are required, the better.

The MIDI standard requires all devices to use the same type of cabling and connectors: *5-pin DIN.* These connectors are unique to avoid confusion with other connectors, like those for your printer or audio amplifier. Figure 12.5 and the illustration in the margin show what a MIDI cable and its connectors look like. Notice that the connectors have five pins. This style of connector is known as a DIN connector, hence a 5-pin DIN connector.

MIDI Networks. Now we need to consider how MIDI cabling and interfaces are used to set up a MIDI network. Figure 12.6 shows three simple configurations that would be appropriate for music CAI settings. The first setup (*a*) shows a computer and a sound-generation module. This would be suitable for music CAI applications in which MIDI sound only is required, e.g., aural skills training or algorithmic improvising software where no input is required. Notice that only the MIDI OUT port of the interface is used.

The second setup (*b*) adds a MIDI controller to the network; for music CAI this most likely would be a keyboard controller. But the power of the MIDI standard makes it possible for you to substitute almost any controller,

Figure 12.6
Three basic MIDI setups with a computer

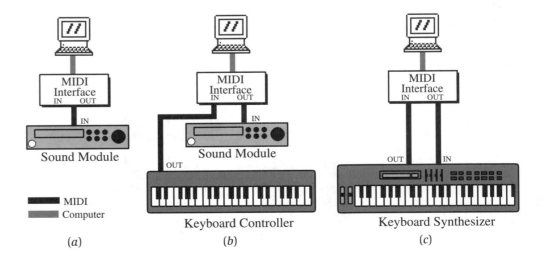

be it a wind, string, or keyboard device. Notice that the keyboard is connected to the MIDI IN port of the interface.

For the last setup (*c*), the computer is networked to a common synthesizer that has a keyboard controller and a sound generation module combined into a single unit. Notice the cabling. The IN of the interface is connected to the OUT of the synthesizer; the OUT of the interface is connected to the IN of the synthesizer. One of the most common "gotchas" is to connect INs to INs and OUTs to OUTs. They must be flip-flopped: IN to OUT and OUT to IN.

The third setup (*c*) is probably the most common arrangement; the self-contained keyboard and sound generator is compact, portable, and cost-effective. However, if you were purchasing a new MIDI system, the second setup (*b*) would have advantages worth considering, especially for flexibility. When one uses CAI software that requires only a sound-generating source, the keyboard is not needed and can be conveniently removed from the computer workstation. Also, you are not locked into one keyboard controller. Different keyboard, wind, or string controllers can be substituted.

MIDI Interfaces: Good News and Bad News! Up to this point, you might have the impression that selecting a MIDI interface and connecting MIDI devices to your computer is very simple: just purchase an inexpensive MIDI interface and you're ready to set up your MIDI network. But we've got bad news and good news. The bad news is that it is not quite that easy; not all MIDI interfaces talk to computers the same way. The good news is that the situation keeps getting better with greater acceptance of a few industry standards.

The problem is in how the computer talks and connects to the MIDI interface. It is not a MIDI standardization problem, but a computer one. A special piece of software is required to link hardware devices to music applications that use MIDI. This piece of software is called a *device driver*, and there are two flavors: *device-dependent* and *device-independent*.

If all drivers were device-independent, we would not have a problem. Any MIDI interface could be connected to a computer and it would work with any software on that computer that conformed to the device-independent driver. This is the case with most MIDI interfaces used on the Macintosh platform, because the Macintosh uses device-independent drivers. Whether you use an inexpensive Apple, Opcode, or other MIDI interface, your Macintosh music software should be able to communicate with the interface. Macintosh MIDI interfaces connect to one of the serial ports on the computer, either the printer or the modem port.

Some MIDI interfaces, especially those for the Wintel platform, use device-dependent drivers. This means that you need to match the software application to the MIDI device driver it supports. In a device-dependent software environment, a few manufacturers usually win out and set the de facto standard. For the Wintel, it has been the Roland MPU-401 standard; most Wintel music software conforms to this device standard. You will see many MIDI interfaces that are MPU-401 compatible. The Windows 95 operating system has helped simplify the device driver issue with its plug-and-play

When connecting MIDI devices, connect INs to OUTs and OUTs to INs!

Select the music software you want to use, then match the MIDI interface to the software.

Figure 12.7
Two simple MIDI interfaces
from Opcode
(Courtesy of Opcode Systems)

(*a*) Macintosh MIDI Translator II   (*b*) PC MIDI Card II

See Module 19 in Viewport VI for more information about establishing links from software to MIDI interfaces.

solution to hardware installation. You should see a statement in the specifications for a MIDI interface that indicates that it uses an MCI-compatible Windows 95 driver.

Common vendors for Mac and Wintel MIDI interfaces are Altech, Opcode, and MIDIMAN. Figure 12.7*a* shows a simple MIDI interface for a Mac that connects to the printer or modem part, and then a Wintel interface (Figure 12.7*b*) that plugs into an internal bus-expansion slot or connect to the parallel port.

Input: MIDI Controllers. A MIDI controller is a device that translates music performance actions into MIDI data. Fingers pressing down keys; sticks hitting a drum head; bowing, strumming, or plucking strings; air and lip pressure; foot pressings on a pedal; and possibilities we haven't even thought of yet are among such performance actions. All MIDI devices translate performance data into an unbiased code: the computer does not know whether the MIDI note data were from a drum pad or a violin. MIDI controllers can be flexibly interchanged among voice and wind, string, percussion, and keyboard instruments in any type of computer-based music learning environment.

There are two approaches to MIDI controller design: *acoustic* and *synthetic*. Traditional acoustic musical instruments can be equipped with sensors that translate analog actions or vibrations into digital MIDI data. Synthetic MIDI controllers are designed from scratch as electronic performance instruments. They may simulate acoustic instruments or be created as new and unique instruments that optimize the electronic translation of performance actions to MIDI. Acoustic controllers give you the natural feel of a traditional instrument with a tradeoff in electronic accuracy. Synthetic controllers give you the best electronic accuracy with a tradeoff in traditional performance realism.

Table 12.1 shows the common types of acoustic and synthetic MIDI controllers available. For the purpose of this viewport, we will focus on keyboard controllers and leave the others for Viewport VI, where we return to a discussion of MIDI hardware.

Table 12.1. Common Types of MIDI Controllers.

Controller	Mechanism
Keyboard	Touch-sensitive switch
Drum	Trigger-to-MIDI converters
Voice	Pitch-to-Voltage (PVC) and Pitch-to-MIDI (PMC) Converters
Wind	PVCs and PMCs
String and guitar	PVCs, audio pickups, and electronic switches

The composer Jean-Claude Risset created his *Duet for One Pianist* using a Disklavier piano and a computer.

The first Disklaviers did not do true MIDI, and a translator program was needed to convert MIDI files into Disklavier MIDI files.

Keyboard controllers. Keyboard controllers are the most common type of MIDI controller. Most MIDI synthesizers come as a self-contained package with a built-in synthetic keyboard controller. The translation mechanism for both acoustic and synthetic keyboards is some type of touch-sensitive switch or, in some cases, optical sensors on each key. Note On and Note Off data are provided by the on-off state of the switch or sensor. Some inexpensive keyboards provide only Note On/Off data. Velocity and aftertouch data come from the voltages provided by touch-sensitive switches that measure the time it takes for a key to move from one position to another. With the additional sophistication of velocity and aftertouch data, you and your software can be creative with expressive properties like dynamic, envelope, and timbral changes.

Acoustic MIDI keyboard controllers are attached to the action of a standard acoustic piano. There have been only a limited number of experiments with acoustic piano controllers; there are too many variations in the physical dimensions of pianos and piano actions to make this a widely accepted method of control. Pre-MIDI experiments at blending acoustic with electronic technology include the Neo-Bechstein piano of the 1930s and the more recent Bösendorfer computer-based piano. Yamaha modified several of their acoustic pianos, most notably their Disklavier grands and uprights, in the 1980s to provide MIDI control.

Present-day acoustic MIDI piano controllers include the Gulbransen KS kits and the Yamaha Disklaviers. Each offers a different solution to providing MIDI performance data from an acoustic instrument. The Gulbransen kits add optical sensors to the keys to turn the piano into a MIDI keyboard controller. The computerized optical scanning board fits onto the keyboard frame directly underneath the keys. The sensors track MIDI note-on and note-off data as well as velocity, sensitivity, and aftertouch data. It is only a controller; you can send MIDI data from your piano, but playback will have to come from a MIDI sound module, not the piano.

The Yamaha Disklavier is more than an acoustic controller. It is a true MIDI-ized, electronic player piano that still provides the action and feel of a traditional, acoustic piano keyboard. The Diskclavier sends MIDI data, records the data on 3.5-inch PC diskettes, and plays back the data as well as using Yamaha's latest tone generator, General MIDI technology. The Disklaviers come in a variety of models and sizes from grand pianos to upright studio pianos. A computer interface on the Diskclavier permits full access to all of its features from a personal computer.

Figure 12.8
Fatar ST-49 Velocity Sensi-
tive Keyboard Controller
(Courtesy of Music Industries
Corporation)

Synthetic MIDI keyboards are what most of us will use when doing MIDI work for CAI. The keyboard mechanism of the electronic pianos of the 1970s, with its plastic keys and light touch, serves as the basis for most synthetic MIDI keyboard controllers. These controllers are designed to favor electronic switching and portability, while attempting to simulate the feel of a piano keyboard. The Fatar shown in Figure 12.8 is a good example of an inexpensive keyboard controller.

MIDI keyboards come in sizes that range from 25 to 88 keys, using both miniature and full-size keys. The more expensive synthetic controllers simulate the key mechanism of an acoustic piano by using wooden, weighted keys. (This is the type most music teachers would like for their students but they tend to be expensive.) Every manufacturer of MIDI synthesizers (Yamaha, Casio, Roland, Kawai, Korg, Ensoniq) provides a variety of MIDI keyboards integrated into a MIDI synthesizer or digital keyboard. Fatar and Novation feature keyboard-only controllers. The Fatar MIDI keyboard controller shown in Figure 12.8 is a typical keyboard-only controller; it has 49 velocity-sensing keys. Novation makes a small, portable keyboard controller with only 25 keys, two controller wheels, and a sustain pedal input.

Output: MIDI Sound Generators. When people first become interested in MIDI, they often pick up an assortment of computer music magazines and catalogs to read. If you do this, don't be frustrated if you find yourself feeling overwhelmed. The incredible mixture of labels that are used to describe MIDI music devices and their operation can be very confusing. Some terms found in advertising copy and reviews include multitimbral synthesizers, digital pianos, MIDI sound modules, tone modules, music sound stations and wavestations, samplers, sampler/synthesizers, drum machines, and so on.

We will do our best to help you sort these out. Manufacturers of MIDI equipment create new MIDI systems that combine basic components in new ways and, for market appeal, create new labels for them. Table 12.2 is a short list of MIDI devices found in music systems, with a description of their function.

All of these devices can be packaged in various ways: some in small,

Table 12.2. A Variety of MIDI Sound-Generating Devices.

MIDI Device	Function
Controllers (Keyboard, Wind, Drum...)	Translate performance actions
Synthesizers	Modify and manipulate sounds, analog and digital
Samplers	Record and play back digital representations of analog sounds
Tone Generators	Generate tones with analog or digital oscillators
Sample Players	Play back digital representations of sounds
Drum Machines	Create and sequence percussion sounds
Sequencers	Record and manipulate sequences of MIDI performance data

portable cases, others as part of a keyboard or controller, many as rack-mountable units for studio use, and some as bus-extended cards to be installed directly into your computer.

MIDI keyboards are often combined with tone generators or synthesizers. In fact, most synthesizers have a keyboard. This is probably what you have if you own a MIDI keyboard. Guitar synthesizers are a combination of guitar controller and synthesizer. Digital pianos are a combination of keyboard controller and sample player. By understanding the unique function and design of each of the devices in Table 12.2, you will be able to intelligently sort out and select the best combination for your needs.

We are not going to cover all these components now. MIDI controllers have already been presented in this module. Sequencers, synthesizers, samplers, and drum machines will be explained in more depth in Viewports VI and VII. What is important to our understanding of music hardware for Buy-and-Run music applications is MIDI music-generation devices. Music generation can be obtained through tone generators and sample players, and by simply using the built-in presets of synthesizers.

Here is a list of the features you would look for in a sound-generating module:

▶ Number of timbres that can be played at once (multitimbral preferred)

▶ Number of voices that can be played at once (24-voice polyphony as a minimum)

▶ Number of instrument and percussion sounds in RAM or ROM (more is better)

▶ Sound generation technique (digital, analog, or hybrid)

▶ General MIDI standards

▶ Audio support and connections

▶ Packaging (device combined with controller, rack mounted, in standalone case, or as computer card)

▶ Power (battery and/or wall-plug)

We've created two make-believe MIDI devices to illustrate these features. Below is a description of a MIDI sound module as it might appear in a manufacturer's ad:

Problems following some of the MIDI jargon here? Review the MIDI discussion in Module 11.

> The WAM-II WolfieBox is a 24-note polyphonic sound module with 16-part multitimbral capability, 192 sampled instrumental sounds, and eight drum kits. The half-rack sound module is General MIDI-compatible with audio in/out, stereo headphone jack, MIDI IN, OUT, and THRU provided.

You would classify the WolfieBox sound module as a sample player because the ad says that it has "192 sampled instrumental sounds and eight drum kits." These sampled sounds are stored in ROM memory in the module. There is no keyboard controller with this unit. It is designed to be MIDI-networked to a computer, a keyboard, or a MIDI controller of another type.

This sample player has "16-part multitimbral capacity." This means that a unique timbre can be assigned to each of the 16 MIDI channels. If you were doing harmony training in a CAI program, each voice could have a different timbre; if you were so inclined, you could create sixteen-part instead of four-part harmony.

The module also is a "24-note polyphonic sound module." With a 49-key keyboard connected, you could press all 49 keys at once and would hear only the first 24 notes: 24 notes can be played on a MIDI channel at one time. General MIDI sound modules must have as a minimum 24-note polyphony and be 16-channel multitimbral.

The ad indicates that the WolfieBox is General MIDI (GM) compatible. The sampled instrumental and percussion sounds would conform to the same timbres used on any other GM sound module by any manufacturer. If you create and save an improvisation with a different MIDI keyboard and it conforms to the GM format, then the MIDI music file should play similar timbres on the WolfieBox for each of the parts. The rhythm track would have been created on MIDI channel 10, and the percussion effects would be similar.

What does the ad tell us about its physical characteristics? "Half-rack" indicates that its size is half that of a full-size rack-mounted MIDI device; the full size is 19 inches wide and about 1 inch high. This size is very portable and fits conveniently next to a computer, ideal for a music CAI system. It provides the essential audio connectors for using earphones or connecting to a stereo amplifier and speakers. The standard MIDI ports are available as well.

Figure 12.9
Korg X5DR AI2 General
MIDI Synthesis Module
(Courtesy of Korg USA, Inc.)

Figure 12.10
Korg X5D Music
Synthesizer
(Courtesy of Korg USA, Inc.)

Here is another fabricated description, this time of a MIDI synthesizer with a keyboard controller:

> The Igor-20 multitimbral synthesizer features 61 velocity- and aftertouch-sensitive weighted keys; 16 multitimbral parts; 24-voice polyphony; 300 presets plus 128 user-programmable tones; 8 drum kits; effects including reverb, chorus, delay, and band pass filtering; one envelope generator and two LFOs per tone; it is General MIDI compatible.

This unit has several components that we will need to sort out: controller, sound module, and synthesizer. The description does not mention "sampling" or "digital," so we can probably assume that it an analog synthesizer. It is not clear what type of tone oscillators are used to create the 300 preset sounds; perhaps FM synthesis.

The Igor-20 has 61 keys that are "velocity and aftertouch sensitive," and the keys are weighted to give a more traditional piano feel.

Like the WolfieBox, the sound module will play 24 notes simultaneously on any one channel, and up to 16 different timbres can be assigned to the full complement of 16 MIDI channels. The Igor-20 is General MIDI compatible as well. Any work you had done with the WolfieBox should sound quite similar on this synthesizer. Caution is in order, however: if you use all of the 300 tones on this synthesizer and then go back to the WolfieBox, the WolfieBox with only 192 timbres will not be able to handle them all. The Igor has many timbres that are not available on the other sound module and in this respect exceeds the GM format.

The Igor-20 is a synthesizer. Synthesizers give you the ability to create unique sounds by modifying and manipulating the acoustic properties through a set of synthesis tools. The ad gives us a hint at what some of those tools are.

This synthesizer will let you create 128 tones or timbres of your own. You may mix different sounds together (additive synthesis) from the 300 preset tones provided in ROM. You could then further modify these new sounds. The *band pass filter* offers subtractive synthesis by letting you filter various harmonics to change the harmonic spectrum. The LFOs (low frequency oscillators) let you apply distortive synthesis by modulating sounds to create vibrato and other effects. The envelope generator shapes a sound's envelope, and then you can sprinkle in a little reverb, chorus, or delay effect for the finishing touches.

Laser-Disc Players

Should the laser-disc jargon confuse you, check out the information on laser discs in Module 25.

Computer workstations set up for music CAI applications can take advantage of three types of music-generating devices: digital sampling, MIDI, and laser-disc players. We have discussed the first two, so we will now look at the third type of device, laser-disc players. To begin, we will examine computer CD-ROM players and the variations that allow them to be used with CD audio, PhotoCD, and other CD formats. Then, we will look at DVD-ROM players. And, to conclude, we will take a quick look at videodisc players. We will discuss hardware needs for interfacing CD-ROM, DVD-ROM, and videodisc players to a computer as we progress.

Output: Variations on CD-ROM Players. If you go shopping for a laser-disc player for your computer workstation, you will find that there is one essential piece of hardware needed, a CD-ROM player or its next of kin, a DVD-ROM player. A general purpose CD-ROM player, with the right interface and software device drivers, can read several variations of CD discs including commercial audio CDs.

There are many manufacturers of CD-ROM players. Companies like Toshiba, Pioneer, and NEC manufacture the CD-ROM drives that are packaged by others like Creative Labs, NewCom, or Diamond Multimedia. CD-ROM players can be installed inside the computer or connected externally through a SCSI port. What are the common characteristics of a full-featured CD-ROM player suitable for multimedia applications? Here is a brief list:

Before you go shopping for a CD-ROM or DVD-ROM player, make sure you don't already have one in your computer; most computers come bundled with these installed and ready to use!

► Reads computer CD-ROM discs. The Philips-Sony Yellow Book standard for CD-ROM discs specifies *how* computer data are stored on the disc, but not how the data are *formatted*. The data format usually conforms to the operating system of the computer using the CD (e.g., DOS or Mac OS) or follows the International Standard ISO 9660 (High Sierra) format. Therefore, a given CD player may be used on Macintosh and Wintel computers, but you need to select the appropriate CD-ROM discs for each machine. Many discs are hybrid CD-ROMs that hold both Mac and Wintel versions of the documents or applications.

► Plays CD audio discs. Simply plug in a set of earphones or connect the CD-ROM player to an amplifier and speakers to play any of your audio compact discs. In order to interactively control an audio CD disc from the computer, however, you will need to have audio CD device drivers installed on your computer. With this element of control, the computer has precise access, down to $1/75$ of a second, to any portion of a CD audio disc at random. Most music multimedia CAI software, like that from LTI/Voyager or that from Warner NewMedia, make intensive use of the ability to control CD audio

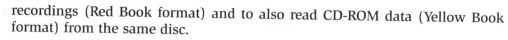

Appropriate software device drivers (similar to MIDI device drivers) may be required to read CD-ROM formats and to control CD audio and PhotoCD from a computer.

recordings (Red Book format) and to also read CD-ROM data (Yellow Book format) from the same disc.

▶ Reads Kodak PhotoCD discs in multisession format. You can take a roll of 35-mm film to be developed and request that the images be put on a CD-ROM instead of receiving prints. The CD-ROM that you get back is known as a Kodak PhotoCD disc. Given the appropriate software, most CD-ROM drives will read at least single-session Kodak PhotoCD discs, but multisession is preferable. A multisession disc is one where additional sets of photos can be added to the disc after the initial set. Multisession PhotoCD discs require the drive to be able to read special CD-ROM *XA formats* that include the capability of having additional information written to them.

▶ Multiple transfer rates: Up to 24 times (24X) the base speed of 150 kilobytes per second. With the use of CD-ROM for multimedia, graphics, sound samples, motion video, and animation, the speed of CD-ROM drives has continued to increase up into the 24X or higher range. A 24X CD-ROM drive transfers data between the computer and the CD-ROM disc 24 × 150 KBps, or 3,600 KBps.

▶ SCSI computer port, with cables and computer interface if needed. CD-ROM players use the parallel SCSI interface when connecting to a computer system to maximize transfer speed. With computers that do not provide a SCSI port, a separate SCSI card will be required.

▶ Stereo audio jacks, headphone jack, and volume control.

To play audio CDs in most CD-ROM players, you must have special audio software to control the player.

Output: DVD-ROM. The latest kid on the block, and next of kin to the CD-ROM player, is the DVD-ROM player. DVD stands for "digital versatile disc." A DVD can hold, at a minimum, seven times the amount of data as a CD-ROM disc, or 4.7 gigabytes. And, there is the potential to record on two layers on a side, and both sides of the disc, to increase that to 28 times the storage of a CD-ROM, or 17 gigabytes. Additionally, DVD-ROM players, like the PC-DVD Encore from Creative Labs shown in Figure 12.11*a*, can read CD-audio discs, CD-ROM, CD-ROM/XA, PhotoCD, VideoCD, DVD-ROM, and DVD-Video, among other formats.

The DVD-ROM player is so "versatile" that it performs all the functions of a CD-ROM player and stands a good chance of replacing the CD-ROM as the laser player of choice in any computer workstation. The same manufacturers that make CD-ROM drives also make the basic DVD-ROM mechanism. These units are then packaged by companies like Creative Labs and Diamond Multimedia with software, a computer interface board, and additional hardware into DVD packages. A Creative Labs DVD drive is shown in Figure 12.11*b*.

DVDs were initially used as a laser format for digital video to distribute movies for home entertainment. DVD movies are digitally coded in MPEG-2 format, and much of the audio is coded in AC-3 Dolby Digital format. The details of these formats are discussed later in Modules 24 and 25. For this reason, a DVD-ROM package like the ones shown in Figure 12.11 comes with the hardware for playing MPEG-1 and MPEG-2 video and

 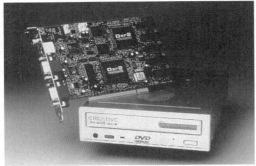

Figure 12.11
Creative Labs
(Courtesy of Creative Labs, Inc.)

(*a*) PC-DVD Encore package and   (*b*) DVD-ROM drive and interface card

Dolby Digital 5.1 channel audio, as well as PCM and MPEG audio. S-video as well as NTSC and composite video output is provided, and digital or S/PDIF audio output.

DVD transfer rates are computed differently from CD-ROM rates. The basic DVD transfer rate is 2,700 KBps and, for reading CDs, 3,000 KBps.

Output: Videodisc Players. Videodisc players have been around since the late 1970s. The most popular application of videodisc, and the medium in which it excels for interactive instruction, is the recording of film, opera, and ballet. This older format stored video imagery in analog format on the disc. Videodisc players output their analog video signal in a form suitable for TV display, not computer screens. Again, this works well for videos. The problem for interactive CAI is that this requires either a separate video display next to the computer screen or a special video *overlay* board for the computer. The video overlay digitizes the analog video onto a window in the computer CRT screen. This adds additional expense to the multimedia system.

There is a considerable repertoire of material recorded on videodisc. It remains to be seen how soon this content will be remastered to DVD disc. Because DVD is completely digital, this means that the video and the audio will have to be converted to MPEG digital video, and the audio to PCM or Dolby Digital audio. Furthermore, any computer-based instructional materials developed for videodisc will need to be reworked to take advantage of the newer and faster technology required for accessing information from a DVD-ROM.

Music CAI Keep It Short and Simple (KISS) System

Digital audio, MIDI devices, and laser audio and video provide a rich palette of options for music computer-assisted instruction. With continued demand for multimedia computing from business, education, medicine, science, and entertainment, the standardization and integration of all these elements by the computer industry continue to improve.

To help bring together the various hardware components discussed in

Music CAI KISS System

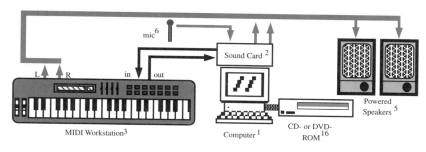

Figure 12.12
The CAI KISS Music
System for Classroom
Instruction

▬▬▬▬ **Audio**
▨▨▨▨▨ **Computer**
▬▬▬▬ **MIDI**

this module, we will complete this viewport by presenting a model computer workstation designed for CAI. We call this music system the *Keep It Short and Simple* or *KISS* music system. We will revisit the KISS music system several times throughout the course of the book as we apply computer, MIDI, and audio technology to applications in music, each time with a different application in mind.

Figure 12.12 presents the Music CAI KISS system for instructional applications. All of the components of this system have been discussed in this viewport. The CAI KISS workstation will let you use CAI music applications that require General MIDI or digital audio sound, CD-ROM or DVD-ROM discs, or a MIDI keyboard. With the microphone provided, this setup would enable you to use applications like Musicware's MusicLab where singing can be analyzed with software-based pitch conversion.

Here is a rundown on the various features in the CAI KISS system:

▶ Computer (1) with a 200–300 MHz Pentium or PowerPC, 32 MB RAM, and 4 gigabytes of disk storage

▶ General MIDI keyboard synthesizer (3), a minimum of 16-part multitimbral and 32-note polyphonic, with 49 or 61 full-sized, velocity-sensitive keys. (Note: if the digital sound card has General MIDI capabilities, then a basic MIDI keyboard controller could be substituted for a MIDI keyboard synthesizer to save on cost.)

▶ Digital sound card (2) with 16-bit, 44-KHz sampling resolution for stereo analog-to-digital and digital-to-analog conversion (addition of General MIDI useful); may not be needed for a Macintosh computer

▶ MIDI interface (2 or 3) either built into the sound card or into the MIDI keyboard, or as a separate MIDI interface box

▶ CD-ROM or DVD-ROM drive (16) capable of reading DVD video, DVD audio, CD audio, PhotoCD, and CD- and DVD-R (with 24X transfer rate for a CD-ROM player)

▶ Pair of powered speakers (5) with a built-in amplifier

▶ Microphone (6) connected to the ADC port of the sound card for pitch conversion

▶ 56K modem or Ethernet card and a connection to the Internet (not shown)

▶ Serial, parallel, SCSI, mouse, stereo audio, composite video, and joystick ports

Viewport III | Summary

Never before have we had such rich possibilities for learning about music. This is a real blessing. But with these possibilities come new information, the need to make tough choices, and the potential for confusion. We hope this mini-course on CAI in music has contained valuable information.

By way of summary, let's now sketch out an initial approach that you might take as you invest in software and hardware for your teaching. We are not trying to prescribe a "best solution" that all musicians must follow, but to suggest a possible path for one person based on the information in the modules.

Approach to Software

You may not be able to buy all you want right away, but it is possible to create a plan for how to start and to expand in the future. Philosophically, let's assume that you believe in encouraging your students to explore music independently right from the start. You understand the need for structure in your teaching and have a healthy respect for fundamentals, but ultimately you want pupils to apply this knowledge by making their own musical and aesthetic decisions right away. For these reasons, you choose software in the categories of flexible practice, guided instruction, and creative activities. You are also interested in exploration packages, particularly for students whose learning style is difficult to discern and who might enjoy taking a wider view of music experience.

You want a broad base of programs that address composition, improvisation, and listening. Because your students will likely range in age from very young children to adult learners, a wide variety of levels and challenges within each program are quite important. You also want software that supports excellent sound quality and longer, more realistic music examples. MIDI capability is important, as is audio CD. Using examples from the software table (Table 9.1 in Module 9), your choices to start might be the following:

Beginning Music Experiences	Thinkin' Things, Music Ace I, Making Music
Aural Skills/Music Theory	MiBAC Music Lessons, Making More Music
History/Extended Listening	Apple Pie Music, Beethoven and Beyond, Living Jazz
Rock	Rap'n Roll
Performance	SmartMusic
Improvisation	Band-in-a-Box

Notice that this software will work on both Macintosh and Wintel computers and that titles might be added as time goes on.

Approach to Hardware

If necessary, refer back to Viewport II for hardware help.

On the basis of the software chosen, and armed with information in Modules 10 through 12, you can make some hardware decisions. You begin first with your computer, then investigate MIDI and CD-ROM or DVD-ROM issues.

Computer Suitability. You are delighted to learn that your machine can run all the programs you now own and there is enough storage space to install the software, but you quickly discover a common problem: memory. The version of the operating system you would like to use, together with requirements of some of the more recent music software, require more RAM than you now have. Your first hardware purchase is a set of memory chips that expand your computer's random access memory.

The CD-ROM drive that comes with your computer is perfectly suitable for your disc software. Programs like the Dvořák New World and Living Jazz should work very well. Also, because some of your software has built-in links to the Internet, you will want to make sure your computer has a modem or is connected to the Internet in some other way. This will ensure that your students can make use of the World Wide Web and e-mail services for their CAI work. You might want to add to your wish list a DVD-ROM player, because the quality of your music experiences will increase with this technology.

MIDI Equipment. For sound, you can use QuickTime resources; however, the electronic keyboard that you have been using is a possible sound source as well. After reading its manual, you realize that the keyboard is a digital synthesizer and that some limited synthesis is possible. This may be useful as you create interesting sounds for students to use, but you also know that other synthesis techniques in more modern keyboards would be valuable. However, because you are relatively happy with the feel of the keyboard, you think that perhaps you may stick with it, as a sufficiently adequate device, for the time being.

You know from your mini-course that there are other MIDI considerations. Remembering the features of the Igor-20 from Module 12, and MIDI implementations described in Module 11, you might check out: (a) touch sensitivity; (b) multitimbral capability; (c) type of MIDI interface needed; and (d) MIDI implementation including send and receive channel options, addressability of timbres or presets, and channel mode support. "Not too bad!" you say. "It's not an Igor-20, but the keyboard has enough capability to be a reasonable support device for my CAI software." You are gaining an impressive knowledge base about music technology!

You may want to keep your older keyboard as a controller and purchase a small sound module. Be sure that it supports the General MIDI format so that you can use your software more easily. Using the KISS MIDI model as a guide, you also decide to buy the MIDI interface box and cables needed to link all this together.

After trying out all your music software, you discover that some titles require careful MIDI setup. For example, the improvisation software Band-in-a-Box requires the assignment of MIDI data to specific channels and presets. Clearly you must know the MIDI language and your equipment well enough to do this. The readings in Modules 11 and 12 will help here.

Audio Equipment. A few pieces of audio equipment remain. You already have a set of speakers and an amplifier. You simply add a small audio mixer so that all the sound equipment can be routed to the amplifier together. You may want to count the number of sound lines coming out of all the equipment: two lines out of the keyboard, sound module, and computer. A mixer that can support at least six lines "in" would be perfect. You connect the mixer to the stereo system and you are in business. Consult that CAI KISS workstation one more time to be sure that you have all that you need!

The Future

The foundation for an exciting teaching environment is in place for you. As new software is written and new hardware to support it comes to the marketplace, additions can be easily made. Remember to stay true to your beliefs as a musician, teacher, and lifelong learner using music experience as the guiding light!

Supplementary Readings

Berz, William, and Judith Bowman. *Applications of Research in Music Technology.* Reston, Va.: Music Educators National Conference, 1994.

Hill, Brad. *Going Digital: A Musician's Guide to Technology.* New York: Schirmer Books, 1998.

Mash, David. *Computers and the Music Educator.* Melville, N.Y.: SoundTree, 1996.

MTNA Guide to Music Instruction Software (3rd edition). Cincinnati, Ohio: Music Teachers National Association, 1996.

Murphy. B. (ed.). *Association for Technology in Music Instruction Technology Directory.* Knoxville, Tenn.: Association for Technology in Music Instruction, 1998.

Peters, G. David, and John Eddins. *A Planning Guide to Successful Computer Instruction.* Champaign, Ill.: Electronic Courseware Systems, Inc., 1996.

Rothstein, Joseph. *MIDI: A Comprehensive Introduction.* Madison, Wis.: A-R Editions, 1995.

Rudolph, Thomas. *Teaching Music with Technology.* Chicago: GIA Publications, 1996.

Rudolph, Thomas, et al. *Technology Strategies for Music Education.* Wyncote, Pa.: Technology Institute for Music Education, 1997.

Stanley, Jungleib. *General MIDI.* Madison, Wis.: A-R Editions, 1995.

Wiggins, Jackie. *Synthesizers in the Elementary Music Classroom.* Reston, Va.: Music Educators National Conference, 1991.

Viewport IV

Desktop Publishing for Musicians

It would appear that we have reached the limits of what it is possible to achieve with computer technology, although one should be careful with such statements, as they tend to sound pretty silly in five years.

—Comment reportedly made by John von Neumann, originator of the concept of stored computer programs (ca. 1949)

Most teachers surveyed took at least five years to learn how to use computers in creative and effective ways. . . . If they use computers at all, [they] do so primarily for drill and writing assignments.

—Survey by the Center for Technology in Education at the Bank Street College of Education (1980s)

Overview

We begin a series of four viewports based on Fill-Your-Own software that provide musicians with an environment for creating their own content and creative products. These might be best conceived as "productivity" or "creativity" packages. Music software that fits this category includes music printing programs, music sequencing programs, sound sampling programs, and multimedia shells. A number of nonmusic software packages that offer important uses for musicians also fit into this category: word-processing, desktop publishing, database, graphics, and communications programs, to name a few.

This viewport deals with desktop publishing and the word-processing and graphics software that relate to it. Various kinds of word-processing, page layout, graphics and integrated software are reviewed that may be useful for the musician. We give special consideration to how graphics software can be used to enhance a musician's written materials, including publicity materials and desktop-published documents. We illustrate these features through the design of a newsletter on medieval music. In the data and hardware modules of this viewport, we explore some of the technical issues underlying the display and printing of text and graphics: data structures for bitmapped and object-oriented images and fonts, and hardware features for printers, scanners, digital cameras, and video displays.

In this viewport we shall:

▶ Review the historical developments leading up to "what-you-see-is-what-you-get" (WYSIWYG) word-processing, desktop publishing, graphics, and integrated software technology

▶ Provide hints in using word-processing software

▶ Examine the features of graphics paint and draw applications

▶ Illustrate features common to word processors and graphics software with a music newsletter project

▶ Explore fonts (Postscript, TrueType, and bitmapped) for display and printing

▶ Explore file formats for text, word processing, and graphics data

▶ Provide guidelines for calculating printing and scanning resolution in black-and-white and color

▶ Review special desktop publishing concerns for musicians, including integrating notation

▶ Study the mechanics of hardware devices critical to desktop publishing: printers, scanners, digital cameras, and video displays

HISTORICAL TIMELINE
The Technology of Writing and Publishing

3200 BC	Egyptians first use ink for writing
1300 BC	Date of a wooden writing tablet found in a Bronze Age ship in the Mediterranean
105	Tsai Lun invents paper
1440s	Gutenberg Bible printed with movable metal type
1800s	Alois Senefelder invents lithography, whereby an image is printed from stone slabs (later metal plates)
1820s	Babbage's Difference Engine records its navigation tables on metal plates for publishing
1870s	First commercially successful typewriters, like the Remington, appear
	QWERTY keyboard invented with its layout still used on keyboards today
1880s	Othmar Mergenthaler invents the linotype for mechanically setting type for printing
1890s	Herman Hollerith's tabulating machine reads data on punch cards for the U.S. Census
	William Burroughs invents a calculator with keyboard and built-in printer
1930s	Chester Carlson invents xerography, leading to the Xerox machine and laser printers
1950s	Phototypesetters appear
	Early Optical Character Recognition (OCR) for computers developed

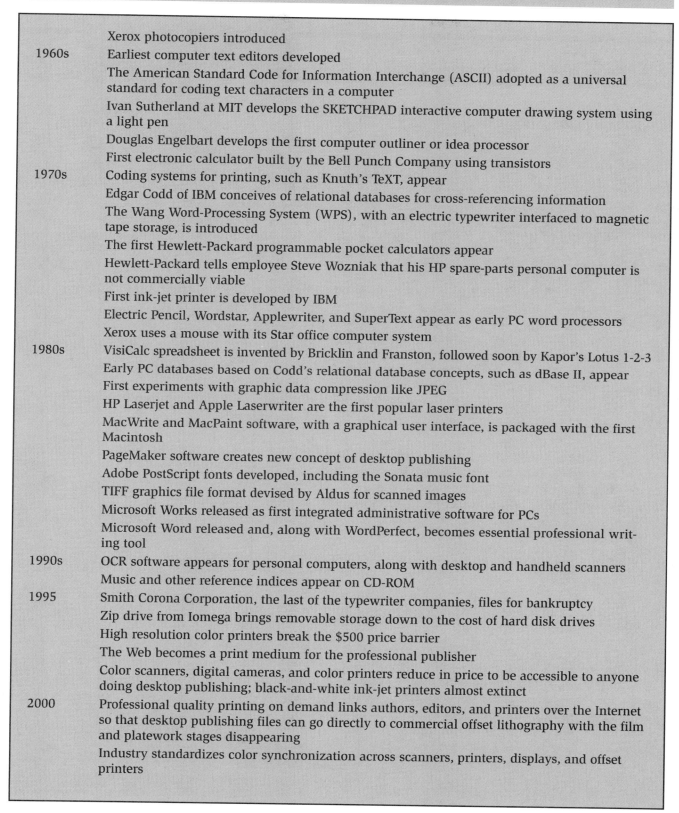

1960s	Xerox photocopiers introduced
	Earliest computer text editors developed
	The American Standard Code for Information Interchange (ASCII) adopted as a universal standard for coding text characters in a computer
	Ivan Sutherland at MIT develops the SKETCHPAD interactive computer drawing system using a light pen
	Douglas Engelbart develops the first computer outliner or idea processor
	First electronic calculator built by the Bell Punch Company using transistors
1970s	Coding systems for printing, such as Knuth's TeXT, appear
	Edgar Codd of IBM conceives of relational databases for cross-referencing information
	The Wang Word-Processing System (WPS), with an electric typewriter interfaced to magnetic tape storage, is introduced
	The first Hewlett-Packard programmable pocket calculators appear
	Hewlett-Packard tells employee Steve Wozniak that his HP spare-parts personal computer is not commercially viable
	First ink-jet printer is developed by IBM
	Electric Pencil, Wordstar, Applewriter, and SuperText appear as early PC word processors
	Xerox uses a mouse with its Star office computer system
1980s	VisiCalc spreadsheet is invented by Bricklin and Franston, followed soon by Kapor's Lotus 1-2-3
	Early PC databases based on Codd's relational database concepts, such as dBase II, appear
	First experiments with graphic data compression like JPEG
	HP Laserjet and Apple Laserwriter are the first popular laser printers
	MacWrite and MacPaint software, with a graphical user interface, is packaged with the first Macintosh
	PageMaker software creates new concept of desktop publishing
	Adobe PostScript fonts developed, including the Sonata music font
	TIFF graphics file format devised by Aldus for scanned images
	Microsoft Works released as first integrated administrative software for PCs
	Microsoft Word released and, along with WordPerfect, becomes essential professional writing tool
1990s	OCR software appears for personal computers, along with desktop and handheld scanners
	Music and other reference indices appear on CD-ROM
1995	Smith Corona Corporation, the last of the typewriter companies, files for bankruptcy
	Zip drive from Iomega brings removable storage down to the cost of hard disk drives
	High resolution color printers break the $500 price barrier
	The Web becomes a print medium for the professional publisher
	Color scanners, digital cameras, and color printers reduce in price to be accessible to anyone doing desktop publishing; black-and-white ink-jet printers almost extinct
2000	Professional quality printing on demand links authors, editors, and printers over the Internet so that desktop publishing files can go directly to commercial offset lithography with the film and platework stages disappearing
	Industry standardizes color synchronization across scanners, printers, displays, and offset printers

THE PEOPLE

David Cope working in his studio
(Courtesy of UCSC Photo Lab, Victor Schiffrin)

REAL-WORLD PROFILE: DR. DAVID COPE

Role: Professor of Music at Porter College, University of California, Santa Cruz

Dr. Cope is professor of music at the University of California, Santa Cruz. He is well known for his writing and research on new trends in music technology and music intelligence. His unique work in machine composition, or, as he terms it, "Experiments in Musical Intelligence," is presented in his books *Computers and Musical Style* (1991) and *Experiments in Musical Intelligence* (1996), published by A-R Editions. David is also a composer who performs on cello, piano, and self-made instruments. He uses PCs for word processing and MIDI work, but prefers the more powerful Sun workstations with their UNIX environment for the massive number-crunching needed for his composition work.

Interview:

What do you do? I am a composer who also performs on cello, piano, and self-made instruments. My recordings include *The Way* and *Concert for Piano and Orchestra* (Opus One Records) and *Arena* and *Margins* (Orion). I write books and articles on various topics related to new music, composition, computers, and the like. My *New Directions in Music* (Waveland), *Techniques of the Contemporary Composer* (Schirmer), and articles for the *Computer Music Journal* are good examples. More recently I have developed techniques for machine composition in various classical and contemporary musical styles.

How did you become interested in computers and music technology? As you can see, I do a good deal of writing. As an author I became interested in computers for their extraordinary potential for text and graphic editing. I can now edit and spell-check my writing, create professional diagrams and related graphics, and insert nearly engraved-quality music wherever I wish—changing my mind as frequently as I desire with virtually no constraints whatsoever. But also, as a composer, I became interested in the possibilities computers offer for timbre production,

exploration, and the potential to automate certain aspects of composition. I can now test-sound an orchestral piece without the need of an actual orchestra, or assign certain compositional parameters to the computer while retaining overall control of my compositions.

What computers do you use? I currently use a combination of Macintosh computers (upgraded Mac IIs and Quadra 950s) and Sun workstations using UNIX. I use the Macs for all text, graphic, and MIDI interfaces, and the Sun for massive number crunching required for compositional endeavors.

Three ways you use computers and music technology? I use computers as a text and graphic tool, as a music notation editor, and as an assistant for music composition.

A unique way you use computers for music? I use the computer to model musical intelligence with my project called "Experiments in Musical Intelligence." My programs analyze the music of a given composer and then produce new music in that same style. The program then outputs the results to both notation and sound, using MIDI-controlled samplers. The results are often both aesthetically valuable and of scholarly importance, leading to deeper research into the nature of musical style itself.

If you could change one thing about how computers are used, what it would be? The computer is a natural extension of the way in which writers write. Spell checkers, cutting and pasting, and so on, all enhance the writers' approach to their craft. Computer and typewriter keyboards are virtually identical. The same is not true, however, of the ways musicians relate to music. While MIDI keyboards, Disclaviers, and other MIDI-fied instruments have developed more touch sensitivity and hence more musical interaction with computers, we are far from reaching a parallel to that of writers. I would very much like to see the development of music-specific computational devices which are integral rather than external to musical instruments, so that all input and output is intrinsically musical rather than computational by nature.

The one most significant change 10 years from now? I believe the single biggest future change for music and computers will be Virtual Reality. VR simulations will have us playing first horn in Beethoven's Third Symphony without a moment of practice, composing massive orchestral works in real time by simply conducting what we hear in our inner ear, or becoming a "holodeck-Mozart" as he composes a new symphony. The effects of VR on music and, for that matter, almost everything we do, will be enormous and psychologically challenging. I cannot image a more promising future!

One word of advice you have for musicians interested in computers? One should not use a computer simply because it is the thing to do. If a clear-cut objective definitely requires computers, set aside time and learn how to achieve that objective. Otherwise, let computers evolve as harmlessly as we allow microwave ovens and CD players to evolve in our lives.

Up to this point, we have dealt with software in which most of the content is already defined. Operating system software and much CAI music software is ready to be used right out of the box. Some of these programs offer customization features and even some built-in editing, but these software titles are essentially Buy-and-Run applications with most decisions already made.

Creative Frameworks: The World of Fill-Your-Own

See Module 3 for an overview of Buy-and-Run, Fill-Your-Own, and Roll-Your-Own.

Not all software is like this. Fill-Your-Own titles offer no content, just frameworks for content. Desktop publishing (including word-processing and graphics programs), database, spreadsheet, and statistical software are examples of Fill-Your-Own software outside of music; music notation, composition, and sampling software are examples within music. In all of these applications, *you* must supply the creative thinking to make them produce anything useful. They are simply sophisticated tools standing ready to support creative work.

The time it takes to learn a new program is referred to as the *learning curve*. Certain programs have steeper curves than others, but this should not be the sole reason to reject a program. Some are well worth the investment of time! In this viewport and the three others that follow, we will lead you through the creation of a newsletter about music, a printed score, some sequenced compositions, and a set of digital audio samples.

Desktop Publishing Technology

Desktop publishing is not a topic that deals with thinking in sound, but it is important for musicians as creative people. Grant applications, recital programs, program notes, brochures, newsletters, and even a custom holiday card home to family can all be accomplished more quickly and more effectively with desktop publishing and supportive software. You may have decided to buy a computer and printer primarily for the preparation of words and graphics.

HISTORICAL PERSPECTIVE

The Sholes and Glidden typewriter was the first Remington typewriter, marketed in 1874. Mark Twain purchased one of these the same year. He was quoted as saying "it piles an awful stack of words on one page." His *Life on the Mississippi* was the first known typewritten manuscript submitted to a publisher.
(Photo from *The Typewriter and the Men Who Made It* by Richard N. Current)

Technology has always played a major role in supporting the written word in our culture. During the first half of the fifteenth century, the Western world began using movable metal type in early printing presses. Germany's Johannes Gutenberg is generally cited as the first European to use printing systems with movable type, although the Chinese experimented with similar systems before the twelfth century. Gutenberg and his followers used converted wine presses to create printed pages with metal type characters cast from hand-carved steel forms. The flexibility of the system for producing multiple copies and resetting new publications was a major achievement for Western civilization. It marked the movement from the Middle Ages to the Renaissance. Music printing soon followed during the late fifteenth and the early sixteenth centuries.

The nineteenth century marked the continued development of printing presses as well as mechanized typesetting machines such as the linotype, invented by Othmar Mergenthaler. The personal typewriter emerged in the late nineteenth century as a logical extension of movable type for personal text processing. Typewriters still exist, of course, but are quickly becoming a relic of the past. The 1950s saw the development of photographic processes where individual type characters were transferred to film grids or film strips. Typesetting machines would shine bright light through the film's clear letter images, and the image would be captured on photosensitive paper. Photographic processes also figure in today's photocopy machines. Development of these photographic processes has steadily continued into the present time, merging with digital computer control systems in common use by professional publishers of books, magazines, and newspapers. Such digital computer technologies as scanning and laser printing are rapidly replacing many of the traditional photographic techniques used by professional publishing houses.

LINK

See Modules 14 and 15 for more information on page-description languages and printing hardware.

We all process words and deal with images each day. We often think in words and images, and, of course, we use words and images to communicate. Capturing words and images on paper for others to see is a natural way to communicate, pervasive in our culture. In fact, many would argue that these symbol systems, along with music, are central to understanding a culture.

The computer has not only changed the way professional publishing companies do their business but has had a profound effect on personal communication. Desktop publishing is common today because of these innovations:

▶ *Advances in Computer Design.* Affordable personal computers can display and edit both text and graphics with ease.

▶ *Printing Technology.* We now can afford high-resolution personal printers that use laser and ink-jet technologies, even in color.

▶ *Software Advances.* We now have page-description languages like PostScript and TrueType that are designed to translate information from the computer to the printer—just as MIDI translates music information from the computer to MIDI devices.

▶ *Flexibility.* The computer screen can display exactly what the page looks like, allowing the individual to spot errors or to lay out the words in different ways. *What-you-see-is-what-you-get* (WYSIWYG, pronounced "wiz-e-wig") provides great flexibility.

▶ *Speed.* Word-processing software allows the quick entry of text by direct typing or by *pasting* from other documents. Unwanted text can be cut quickly or moved to other parts of the document. Revisions can be done right up to the moment of printing.

▶ *Intelligent Analysis.* Most word-processing software offers a built-in spelling checker, thesaurus, and grammar checker. These features can check for errors in real time as you type, and in some cases can automatically correct the errors. Many programs offer special features like alphabetical sorting and column calculation for numbers.

▶ *Integration.* Graphics and text can be integrated into publishing programs, and some types of software also support the integration of database and spreadsheet functions. Audio and video data can be integrated, too, as desktop publishing software becomes more supportive of multimedia extensions.

Creating a Newsletter

Software activity: "Putting Together a Music Newsletter"

The remainder of this module will be devoted to the creation of a newsletter that a musician might produce for professional work. We have chosen a music history topic, a newsletter about music during the twelfth and thirteenth centuries in medieval Europe. We will imagine that you are an expert on secular song and that you have agreed to edit this newsletter for a professional organization. You have a large collection of facsimile manuscripts, reproductions of artwork that contain musical instruments, and a vast bibliography of scholarly works. In the past, you have relied on a card file, typewriter, photocopier, scissors, and tape for your scholarly work. Your professional organization has given you enough funds to purchase a desktop computer system including both hardware and software. You also have a small budget for production and mailing.

The Finished Product and What Is To Come. Figures 13.1*a* and *b* display two pages of a typical newsletter that you might produce. Notice that there are both text blocks of various types and images of many different kinds. On the first page (Figure 13.1*a*) there is a heading section, followed by two columns of text. There is a table of information at the bottom and some "footer" material on both pages that includes the title of the newsletter and the page number. On page 2 (Figure 13.1*b*), there are graphics in the form of music notation.

In terms of graphics, notice that we have added a freehand drawn image

Adam de la Halle Society Newsletter

A Forum for Information Exchange on Secular
Song and Poetry of Medieval Europe

Volume 1, No. 1   **Fall, 1998**

Welcome to the Adam de la Halle Society Newsletter!

This quarterly publication is devoted to the exchange of scholarly information and lively speculation about the secular monophonic music and poetry of Medieval Europe. We intend to feature articles on extant music as well as performance practice during the twelfth and thirteenth centuries. We welcome not only contributions that focus on the music, but also on the social and political influences that were so important for the times.

In this first issue you will find an article on a newly discovered chansonnier by Pierre Pagier. Professor Pagier discovered the document in a French monastery only recently opened to the public. He is preparing a major paper on the collection, but shares with us some of his early findings.

Russ Diffan offers speculation on the origins of the Renaissance lute by tracing the development of the vielle and other stringed instruments during the late thirteenth century. Little is known of course about how the troubadours and truveres used instruments to accompany their sung poetry, but Diffan presents an interesting theory about the use of stringed and wind instruments.

Finally, I include a brief reminder about our Society's namesake, Adam de la Halle. Like many important figures in the history of music, Adam plays a pivotal role between centuries. The variety of his compositional style highlights the rich monophonic secular song of the thirteenth century and the beginning of the three-voice polyphonic song of the next century.

Our Winter issue is already full, containing contributions by noted musicologists and medievalist. For example:

- Gerry Ludkin presents a study of vernacular texts such as the Chanson de Roland.
- Henry Rayner and Beth Simon contribute an essay on the social history of twelfth century Germany and the rise of the Mastersingers.
- Ted Krep clarifies terminology to be used when discussing pastourelles and other ballad songs.

We hope that you subscribe to the Newsletter and also contribute from time to time.

Donald Debase, Editor
School of Music
Northport University

Direct Inquiries and Submissions to:

Specialty Area	Name	School	Email
Performance Practice	Beth Simon	McHenry College	simon@hey.ca
Instruments	Russ Diffan	Eastern Outward College	rd@eou.edu
Music Structure	Jan LaRow	Town College of New York	janie@tcny.edu
Poetry	Gerry Ludkin	Westman School of Music	lud@west.edu
Life and Times	Henry Rayner	Hellene Institute	hr2@bigie. bitnet
Subscriptions	Ruth Schure	Northport University	ruthie@nu.edu
General Editor	Donald DeBase	Northport University	pausaum@nu.edu

(a)

Figure 13.1
Two pages from a completed music newsletter

Instruments of the Troubadours

Russ Diffan
Eastern Outward College

Little is known about the use of instruments by the thirteenth century Troubadours. We do know from accounts of their singing that they were masterful musicians and poets of their time and that their work was highly valued by their court employers. There are no writings which describe how their songs were accompanied, if at all.

The twenty chansonniers which are currently know are of little help either. Even the newly discovered chansonniers by Pierre Paige, described for the first time in this Newsletter, holds no clue to instrument use. Did these troubadours really sing their wonderful poetic tunes without the aid of any

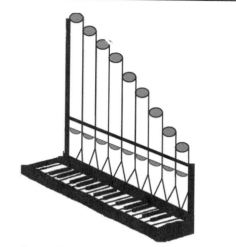

Portatif organ played on the knee

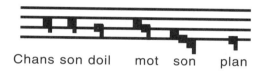

Chans son doil   mot   son   plan

accompanying instrument? Some scholars argue that this is exactly what they did, basing their opinions more on the absence of data than on anything else.

I believe that this is nonsense and that it can be easily assumed that troubadours did use many different instruments as part of their music making. Iconographic evidence is clear that keyboard instruments such as the portatif organ (shown above) and stringed instruments such as the rebec and the lute (scanned photo opposite) were commonly used.

Let me suggest how these instruments might have been used to accompany the troubadour chanson, "Chansson Doil Mot." I have included (above) both the medieval and modern notation of the first few measures.

Adam de la Halle Newsletter

Page 2

(b)

of a medieval trumpet in the upper left corner of the heading material on the first page. This graphic is added here to give the opening page some visual interest. The second page contains several graphics. The top picture of a portatif organ is also a drawn image, but uses a technology for drawing that is different from what was used for the trumpet. Next we see some inserted notation. At the lower left is a scanned image from some original artwork photographed in a book.

We begin the module with a description of what software you might use to create this newsletter, then continue with a few tips about creating the page layout and entering the text. The remainder is devoted to working with graphics. We assume that you have had some experience already with text entry, and we spend most of our time explaining graphics.

Why Not Use Photographs and a Print Shop? Why can't we just turn the text and a few photographs over to the print shop and be done with it? There are two big reasons. The first reason is cost. Remember that musicians typically have a small budget. If you take your text and some photographs to a print shop and ask that they put it all together for you including the graphics, the costs will be very high. You will need to spend money for a graphic artist's time, photo offset for the pictures, typesetting, and then the duplication costs. You may be reasonably happy with the final result, but not the price tag.

The second reason is content. Even if you could afford to go the professional production route, you may not want to do so. Much of your graphic needs center on illustrations of instruments, instrumental and vocal techniques, and music notation itself. Photographs don't work for many of these needs, and you, yourself, may want complete control over the graphic images and text formatting. By the time it takes to explain to a print shop what you want, look at page proofs, edit and then make the usual second round of edits, you might as well do it yourself with today's powerful computer technology. When a photograph is really needed, you can either use a good quality scan of a traditional photograph or use a digital camera. This is what desktop publishing is all about!

Software Choices for Processing Words and Graphics

Let's review the choices for both word-processing and graphics software that will offer support for the creation of this newsletter and other publishing projects that musicians require. In no way will you need all of these programs for your work, but we will review all options to start.

On the word processing side, there are separate programs on both the low and high ends in terms of features offered. Then, there are page layout programs that offer special features for desktop publishing and for the preparation of documents for professional print shops. There are also integrated packages that come with tools that do both words and graphics and also include spreadsheet and database capabilities. These programs also allow for some page layout functions.

Turning to graphics, we have separate graphics software for both painting and drawing. There are also graphics packages that support special functions such as scanning and three-dimensional rendering. We begin with word processing and page layout.

Word Processing, Page Layout, and Integrated Software.

Low-end text editors are used for HTML and Web page editing. See Viewport VIII.

Word-Processing Software. Bargain-basement word processors are available for the simplest of text editing and printing tasks. Often these programs are referred to as *text editors* rather than word processors. Many are available as part of your operating system software, or from freeware or shareware sources. Examples include SimpleText for the Macintosh and Notepad for Windows. These elemental text editors offer little more than the chance to enter, save, and print simple text files with minimal options. You might find these programs useful at times when you need to print a quick memo or to read a text file, or write some computer programming code, but you will need something more sophisticated to put together a newsletter or to write those important scholarly papers on music.

Another useful kind of text editor is a program like BBEdit for Mac or Arachnophilia for Windows. This kind of editor gives you special extensions for editing Web pages and high-level program code, but not for desktop publishing.

Higher End. On the other end of the spectrum, we find separate word-processing programs, costing hundreds of dollars, that offer extraordinary power. Such full-featured word-processing programs offer options for:

► changing characters, lines, and paragraphs

► creating footnotes, headers, footers, and tables

► automatically generating a table of contents or an index

► searching for and replacing text

► providing special utilities that check spelling, merge documents, write mathematical formulas, and print special effects.

We used Microsoft Word for Macintosh and Windows in the preparation of the chapters of text for this book.

These programs often support the integration of graphics files such as those created by music notation software and contain tools for creating such graphics as lines, boxes, and shaded areas. Examples of such programs include Microsoft Word and WordPerfect, both available for Macintosh and Windows.

Figure 13.2 provides a display of a text page from an article that we imagine you would write for the newsletter if you were using Microsoft Word. We have displayed several menus for you to see the options that such higher-end software provides. Notice the options for editing, viewing, inserting, and formatting, and tools for special processing. This sort of program is excellent for the preparation of scholarly papers and extensive book chapters that require custom dictionaries, predefined style templates, and other special utilities. You can do some page layout too, but that is not the strength of higher-end word processors.

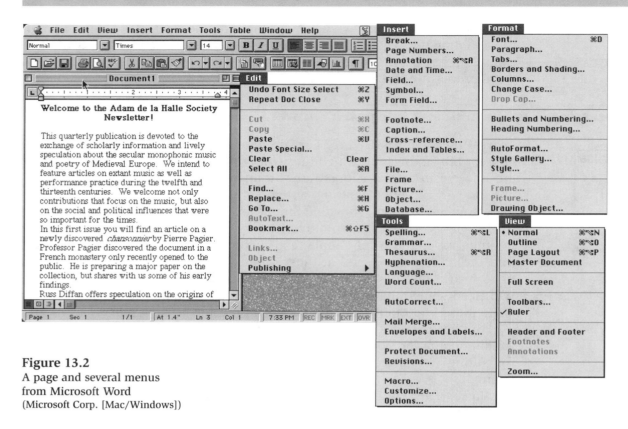

Figure 13.2
A page and several menus
from Microsoft Word
(Microsoft Corp. [Mac/Windows])

ASIDE

Our publisher used
QuarkXPress to do the
final preparation for
this book as it went to
production.

Page Layout Software. This kind of program has some word processing features, but its strong point is in flexible approaches to integrating text with graphics. Similar to a graphic artist using a large board to paste up a page for printing, page layout software allows the individual to place a graphic image in a particular spot and then *pour* text around it for visual appeal. Other powerful features include extensive control over text spacing, shading, and distortion for special effects. Often these programs have special support for color printing and offer some graphics tools for drawing. An example of this kind of software is QuarkXPress, available for Macintosh and Windows.

QuarkXPress would be especially useful for creating a newsletter requiring multiple pages, graphics, color, and special effects. The downside for this type of program is its cost and complexity. Although this program offers you the widest range of options for page layout, you might not need all this power right away. The complexity of learning the software and the high costs in money and time are factors to consider, especially considering that it may not supply the painting, drawing, and scanning software you need to create graphics.

Integrated Packages. Another approach to word-processing software is the integrated package that offers modest word processing capability along with software modules that create spreadsheets, databases, and graphics. In addition, these packages often contain a communications module that lets you use a modem. All these options are included in the same program, which serves as a kind of Swiss Army knife for business and personal productivity.

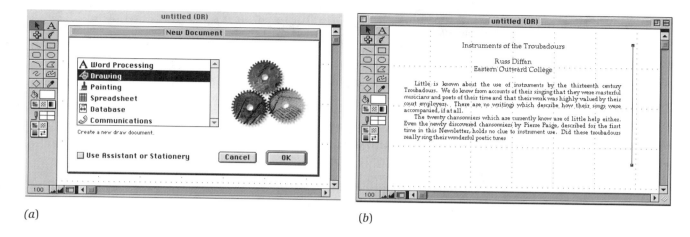

(a)   *(b)*

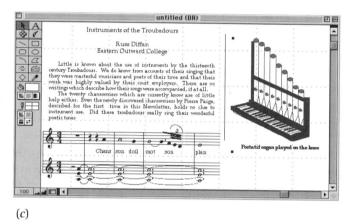

(c)

Figure 13.3
AppleWorks
(Apple Computer, Inc.
[Mac/Windows])

A nice feature of this all-in-one approach is that you can do some simple page layout tasks, as you will see in a moment.

How can all this fit into one program? The answer lies in the art of compromise. The word processor portion of the program doesn't offer all the bells and whistles of a high-end program, and similar compromises are made in all the other modules. For instance, the word processor might include plenty of text-entry and printing options, but not include such powerful features as outlining, custom styles, special dictionaries, a thesaurus, a table of contents or index generator, a grammar checker, or a word counter. Similar compromises in graphics, database, spreadsheet, and communication software are also made.

What you do get are the basic components of each of the software types for the cost of a single software package. This might be all you need to get started, especially on a small budget. You might find that relatively simple text files integrated with graphics and spreadsheet layouts are an attractive solution for your small-scale newsletter needs and for other projects such as concert programs. A simple database to hold subscriber information might be another useful feature. Examples of integrated packages are AppleWorks and Microsoft Works, both available for Macintosh and Windows.

Figure 13.3 shows an example of an AppleWorks project—actually the

Table 13.1. Bit-Mapped versus Object-Oriented Programs

Type	Strength	Weakness	Common Software Packages
Paint/Bitmapped	Direct control of each pixel. Versatile tools (such as charcoal and calligraphy brushes) and special effects (smudging and pressure sensitivity). Color and shades of gray (called grayscale) are fully supported.	Images are difficult to manipulate without distortion. Printing results do not get any better than the original resolution of the bitmapped image. Resizing can cause distortion.	MacPaint for Macintosh; Fractal Design Painter and Adobe Photoshop, available for both platforms.
Draw/Object-Oriented	Graphics can be resized or "scaled" without distortion. Printed resolution will be as good as the printer permits.	Works best where the components of the image are largely geometric shapes that can be generated by definable formula. It is difficult to use draw software for irregular shapes and more subtle image elements. Draw software is not useful in editing scanned images or adding special visual effects. It is far better to work with paint programs to achieve these results.	MacDraw for the Macintosh; Corel Systems' CorelDRAW is a more sophisticated package for Wintel machines; two advanced titles include Adobe Illustrator and Deneba Canvas for both Macintosh and Windows. These excellent drawing packages work especially well as complements to page layout software and Internet design tools.

files we used to create the finished newsletter shown in Figure 13.1. We began by opening AppleWorks and choosing the "Draw" option (*a*). We then integrated some text blocks and some simple separator lines (*b*). Finally, we added in the graphics (some created in AppleWorks and others created by other programs) (*c*). This worked well for us, and you might consider this approach for similar projects.

The Graphics Software Scene. So far we have reviewed mainly word-processing software with some ability to insert and generate graphics. Now we turn to primarily graphics software that you might use. Look again at the graphics used in the finished newsletter shown in Figure 13.1. Notice how the medieval trumpet and the scanned picture look painted or freely sketched, and the organ and the music notation look more like illustrations with fewer curved lines and subtle shadings. The trumpet and scanned picture are called "bitmapped" images, and those to the right are called "object-oriented."

Two Approaches to Graphics: Paint (Bit-Mapped) vs. Draw (Object-Oriented) Programs. Graphics on a computer are really about turning on and off *pixels* (the little dots that form images on your computer screen) to create patterns. There are two types of programs that accomplish this: bitmapped or *paint* programs that offer a set of tools and menu options that allow direct control of each pixel (the trumpet in the newsletter was drawn in this way); and object-oriented or *draw* programs, which use mathematical formulas to define objects (the organ was created by use of drawing techniques). Table 13.1 compares the two types of programs and gives their strengths and weaknesses.

Musicians will find that drawing packages offer significant advantages for poster preparation, technical drawings, flowcharts, and images that use arrows and text. Most draw programs can integrate paint images when needed.

Combining Paint and Draw. Some programs merge paint and drawing together. AppleWorks has both a paint and draw mode that made it an obvious choice for our work with the newsletter. We created the trumpet as a painting and included it as a separate object into the drawing mode (see Figure 13.1). We then used the drawing tools to create the organ. We imported the music from a music notation package (more on this later) and inserted the scan after it was treated by other software.

There are different ways for integrating paint and drawing tools. For instance, Deneba's Canvas for both Macintosh and Windows is designed to allow painting and drawing to be applied to the *same* image by alternating between each set of tools and options. This is not always simple to do, however, and there are compromises and issues about the order in which work is done. Combination programs offer many of the basic tools of both kinds of software but sacrifice a few of the more powerful options in each.

Special Categories of Graphics Software. Professional musicians like yourself might find use for other kinds of graphics software. The following use either a draw or paint approach as their basis, and each has a specialized capability.

► *Charts and graphs.* Music is a business as well as an art, and some professionals in our field find specialized graphics programs that support charts and graphs to be very useful. Such formalized graphics are usually possible as options in standard spreadsheet programs like Microsoft Excel for both Macintosh and Windows. Statistics programs also include charts and graphics. Even some of the high-powered word processors have a small set of graphing tools. Separate programs for graphs and charts, such as Deltapoint DeltaGraph, also exist.

► *3-D.* Three-dimensional drawing gives images a sense of depth and realism that may be needed in certain circumstances. Such 3-D images can often be moved along three dimensions so that objects can be viewed from different

ASIDE

Most music notation software works as draw software, using fonts and other technology that are remarkably parallel. The music notation in our newsletter is a good example of this.

perspectives. Multimedia software and Web pages are beginning to use more three-dimensional graphics. Extreme 3D is an example of such software.

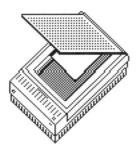

▶ *Scanning.* One of the most effective ways that you can use previously created art, like photographs and complicated line drawings, is by means of a scanner. The software necessary to use scanners may be sold separately or included with the scanner itself. Advanced graphics software like Adobe Photoshop also supports simple add-on modules, or plug-ins, for scanning. This modular approach is common. Scanning software often includes built-in intelligence that helps choose correct brightness and contrast settings and also allows for custom choices. The scanned image from the newsletter was created using such software.

▶ *Digital Camera Software.* Digital cameras are much like scanners. The software required to link them with the computer comes bundled with the camera itself. Be sure to verify that the camera comes with software for your particular computer platform and operating system. In most cases, the camera stores its graphic picture files either on a small removeable disc or on a fixed hard disk. A cable may come with the camera to attach it to the computer, and the software transfers the images right to your hard drive. Other cameras come with diskettes, PC cards, or flash memory cards that can be removed and inserted into your computer.

Be sure to read Module 14, which brings you up to date on digital cameras and scanners. Read about the new "TWAIN" technology that lets your camera and scanner work directly with your desktop publishing or multimedia software.

Digital cameras are a wonderful addition to desktop publishing and multimedia. Imagine that you are in Vienna, touring the State Opera on the Ringstrasse. You have brought along your digital camera and laptop computer with modem. You are given permission to take a few photos of the opera house with your camera. That night, you log into your local Internet account and update your Web site with photos from your trip. Instantly your family and friends are made aware of your day's events. This will surely solve the problem of postcards that arrive weeks after you're home!

The Final Choice for Our Project. To review, we have chosen to use the integrated software program AppleWorks to create our newsletter (Figure 13.1). It contains enough word-processing, painting, and drawing tools to meet our needs; its page layout possibilities are sufficient for a basic design. The spreadsheet function can help us create the table at the bottom of page 1, and the database part of the program will help with the mailing labels and subscriptions. We also need some scanning software to help import our picture.

We could have used a higher level word-processing program or page layout package, but our time and budget did not allow this. Perhaps this will be different later on as our needs change and as our resources increase.

Creating Text for the Newsletter

Figure 13.1 displayed a page from the newsletter that demonstrated how some of the text and graphics pieces fit together in AppleWorks. We used the "draw" part of the program as the central focus and placed the pieces together as objects. We will soon find out how to actually create the graphics parts of this puzzle, but how about the text?

Your Own Word Processor. First off, you can simply create the text for the newsletter in your own favorite word-processing program and enter it into a program like AppleWorks or QuarkXPress. We are betting that you already know how to:

▶ set margins and tabs

▶ choose fonts, font styles, and sizes

▶ set spacing between lines

▶ chose to justify the text to the right, left, or center

▶ cut, copy, and paste text

▶ find and replace text

▶ use page breaks

▶ check spelling.

Much of the formatting and text preparation that you already know can be put to good use here. The text that you paste into these desktop publishing programs will retain much of your formatting.

A Few Tips. Here are a few additional tips about word-processing software that you might not know and that can help with desktop publishing efforts.

Hidden Characters and Tabs. Figure 13.4 displays the last portion of the text of our lead story. We have highlighted the text and have asked the program to reveal the "hidden characters" that control text and formatting. We have done this to make clear to you how word processors organize their approach to text formatting.

Hidden Characters Tell All. If your text simply is not behaving properly or if someone has given you a text file that is not responding properly to your formatting efforts, it probably is because of extra spacing characters or unwanted hard returns. Take a look at the third paragraph of the text in Figure 13.4. Here we have added a number of extra spaces to form a spacing for the indent of the paragraph and a few incorrect hard returns at the end of a line. These incorrect uses of the space bar and the return key might first appear to be harmless, but when a font size changes, a margin tab is increased, or new formatting is applied, the original text will become quite distorted. Avoid the use of the space bar to format text; always use tabs or other control characters. Never use hard returns at the end of a line unless you want a new paragraph; always allow the computer to create an automatic line wrap.

Power of the Paragraph Hidden Character. The paragraph character contains much meaning for the style of the paragraph. Take a look at the bulleted items that follow the third paragraph. The hidden paragraph character

ASIDE

The word *return* comes from the days of manual typewriters when you had to physically return the carriage in order to type the next line.

maintains the information about the bullet, text tab, line spacing, justification, and margin tabs. If that hidden paragraph character was copied and was pasted in to another line replacing its paragraph mark, the line would respond to the pasted character. This can be used as a short cut when formatting paragraphs with different styles and can be a very powerful feature.

Wrap-around Margin with Tab. A ruler feature that is not often used by novices is the wrap-around margin with the tab. We use this in the bulleted items. The entire series of bulleted items starts to the right a few spaces. This is set up by the bottom margin character. The bullet is placed there, then the tab character controls the start of the text. The top margin character controls the wrap-around point. This allows a crisp appearance with the list and is entirely done with control characters.

Styles. Most casual users of word-processing software are unfamiliar with the ability of most programs to save overall style characteristics of documents. Look once more at Figure 13.4 and the bulleted items. Notice that we have chosen to use a predefined style for these bullets, as noted in the popup box in the ruler on the left. Other styles are displayed as well, including "Heading 1" and "Normal." These styles contain the specific formatting instructions for the paragraphs that are specified. For example, a set of bulleted items might have a particular indent scheme, set of font characteristics, tabs, and justification. Once you have these many characteristics set for a document, define these styles using the edit function once and simply call upon them again later in the writing as needed.

Can you see the time savings here for documents that have special formatting requirements that continue to occur? You can define these in a "dummy" document that can serve as a template for other documents you may need. Some word processors will also allow you to import styles from other documents. Styles are very useful in setting up a series of headings that serve as the titles for sections, and for headers, footers, and footnotes.

Sections in Documents. Most word processors allow you to define formatting characteristics for multiple sections. Let's say you are working on a concert program that has four principle parts: a front page that contains some graphics; the body of the concert program that has the names of compositions, composers, and the order of performance; a section that lists personnel and credits; and finally a set of program notes. All of these parts have distinct formatting requirements that may include different font characteristics, centering, tab types, and overall styles. One temptation might be to create four different documents or to insert page breaks and try to define different styles.

Another way might be to define separate sections in your word processor that are formatted separately for the four different parts. Once you have done this for the first time, you can save the document as a template and have your setup done for the next concert! Headers and footers are actually small sections in a document that repeat from page to page. Most word-processing software allows you to set the format design of footers and headers in the same way as the design of larger sections.

Tables. Our newsletter has a table on page 1 (Figure 13.1). This was created in AppleWorks by using the spreadsheet portion of this integrated pro-

A *template* is a model file that has no real content, but does have all the settings created—ready for the content you enter. Templates are useful in desktop publishing and in many other music software applications such as music notation and sequencing.

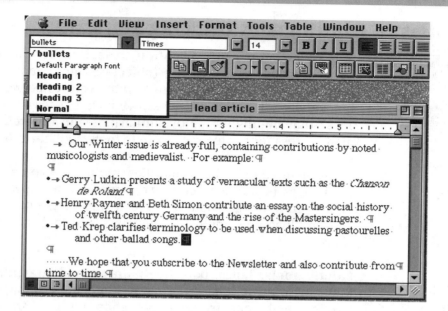

Figure 13.4
A page of text from Microsoft Word

gram. Figure 13.5 displays this technique. We created a table with the cell dimensions of 8 × 4 and filled in the information. Other programs use built-in table generators. We show this for Microsoft Word in Figure 13.5. Notice not only the fast creation option in the ruler, but also the entire menu devoted to formatting the table's construction (also see Figure 13.2). Options for borders and shadings for each cell are also possible. Take a look at the tables throughout this book for examples of table construction.

Insertion of Clip Art and Original Art. Our last tip has to do with inserting graphics. In our newsletter, we inserted graphics into the draw portion of AppleWorks; however, we could have inserted clip art directly into the word-processing part of the program. Many word-processing programs come with a clip art library that can be used for ready-made insertion. This is true for AppleWorks as well as Microsoft Word.

If you are not happy with the art collection, you can use a graphics program to create your own designs and insert them where needed. This is what we did in our newsletter to create notation on page 2 (see Figure 13.1).

Figure 13.5
Creating tables in Apple-Works and Microsoft Word

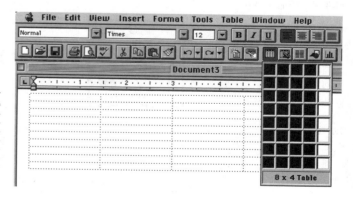

Similarities in Painting and Drawing Software

Line and Shape Tools

We now turn our attention to techniques for using painting (bit-mapped) and drawing (object-oriented) tools in graphics software. Let's first observe some of the *common* features between painting and drawing software. To guide ourselves, we have created a comparison table (Table 13.2) that highlights major similarities and differences. Comparisons are made across four categories: palette tools, tool attributes, menu options, and layout.

To help you see the similarities and to give you a sense of how to create the images in the newsletter, we placed the trumpet (paint image) and the organ (draw image) that we used in the newsletter side by side in Figure 13.6 to illustrate some of the similarities in tools and their attributes in our chart.

Palette Tools. Lines, both freely drawn and straight, are possible in both kinds of software. Shapes of many kinds are also supported, including rectangles, ovals, and irregular polygons. Figure 13.6 shows how these are used in each image. Remember that, even though both kinds of programs support these tools, they create graphic patterns with lighted pixels in different ways. In the margin, we've placed two versions of the oval found in our paint and draw programs. The top one is a paint oval drawn with the oval tool. The pixels that form this line are turned on by the point of the pencil. The bottom one is drawn with the draw oval tool. We've clicked on top of this image and the draw program surrounds it with little square boxes or *handles,* indicating that it is a draw object that is defined by a formula.

Tool Attributes. To dramatize the fill and line characteristics of paint and draw programs, we have placed in the middle of Figure 13.6 the options used to specify color, fill patterns, gradients, line thickness, and arrows. If you decide to draw an oval colored in with a solid color or filled with a special pattern, you can use the options displayed in Figure 13.7. One special

Figure 13.6
Common features of paint
and drawing programs

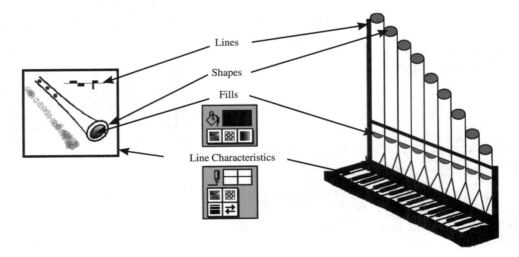

Lines

Shapes

Fills

Line Characteristics

Table 13.2. Comparison Table of Standard Features for Painting and Drawing Programs

	Similarities	Differences	
	Painting and Drawing Programs	**Painting Programs**	**Drawing Programs**
Palette Tools	Lines (Pencil and line tools in painting; freehand and line tools in drawing) Shapes (rectangle, rounded rectangle, ovals, regular and irregular polygons)	Marquee/Lasso Eraser Paint Brushes Spray Can	Arc Curves (Bezier)
Tool Attributes	Fills Within Shapes (patterns, colors, and gradients) Line Characteristics (thickness, color, gradients, arrowheads)	Paint Brush Shapes Spray Can Patterns	
Menu Options	Text Insertion and Formatting Selection and Duplication (copy and paste in painting; object selection and duplication in drawing) Rotation Flipping (horizontal and vertical)	Invert Darken/Lighten Shear Distort Perspective Resize	Reshape Smooth and Unsmooth Scale
Layout	Zooming In and Out Grids and Grid Alignment Rulers	Resolution	Layers (options for moving layers) Group/Ungroup Align Lock/Unlock

kind of fill pattern is a gradient. This is a series of grayscale or colored textures that gradate from one to another. We've used one of these in the middle of the bell of the medieval trumpet.

Fills can be done after an object is created as well. The paint-can tool can be used to designate a fill by first choosing the style of the fill from the options in Figure 13.7, then using the paint can's *hot spot* (the end of the dripping paint!) to designate the area. We provide an example in the margin. The paint can is outside the area in the top image, then it is dragged over the area to be filled and the mouse is clicked. Voila!

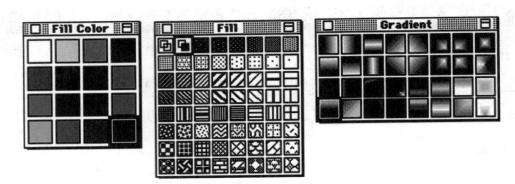

Figure 13.7
Options for colored, textured, and gradient fills

Text

Marquee   Lasso

Pointing Tool

Some programs will let you hold down the option (Mac) or control (Windows) key and drag the selected item. It creates a clone of the selection automatically!

Menu Options. *Text insertion and formatting.* Text can be included in both paint and draw programs. Options for style, font, and font size are similar to those in word processors. Keep in mind that painted text can *not* be easily edited, because you're only lighting a set of individual pixels that represent letters. Text entered in draw programs *can* be edited easily because the letters are objects. This makes insertion of text as a draw object much more desirable.

Selection and duplication. Both paint and draw programs can select and duplicate portions of an image. Portions of the image that require duplication need to be selected first, then duplicated by using the standard menu commands. Once duplicated, these new portions can be dragged to new locations using the mouse pointer. There are some differences between paint and draw programs in how to do this. Try to understand how the distinctions below relate to the bitmapped versus object-oriented nature of paint and draw images.

▶ *Paint.* Two special tools particular to paint programs, the *lasso* and *marquee*, allow selection. Each tool chooses a portion of the lighted pixels in a paint image. The lasso is used to trace around a selected portion of an image and selects only those pixels that are lighted. The marquee tool chooses a rectangular area and includes all pixels, lighted or not. This tool is quicker to use than the lasso, but less selective. Figures 13.8*a* and *b* show how each tool was used as we worked with the medieval trumpet. The marquee allowed us to select and duplicate the button images, and the lasso allowed us to grab the inner oval in the trumpet bell for copying and for manipulating if needed.

▶ *Draw.* Because draw images are groups of objects, you must decide which objects to select. To select, you simply click on a portion of the object. Holding the shift key down while selecting objects will keep them all selected. You can tell that an object is selected because it has the handles displayed. Once all the objects are selected, you copy and paste as usual. Figure 13.8*c* demonstrates the duplication of the objects that make up the organ pipe to the right. You simply alter the new objects to make them a little smaller and then paste them in as the next smaller pipe!

Rotating and flipping. Both paint and draw programs usually include menu options for rotating and flipping an image. Rotation moves the image

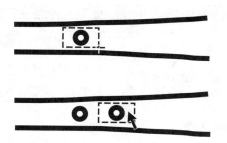

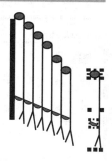

Figure 13.8
Selecting and duplicating in paint and draw programs

(*a*) Selecting and duplicating with marquee in a paint program

(*b*) Selecting with lasso in a paint program

(*c*) Selecting and duplicating in a draw program

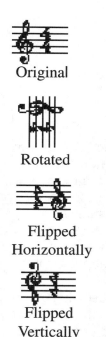

Original

Rotated

Flipped
Horizontally

Flipped
Vertically

around a center point, usually in 90-degree increments. Flipping, however, is different, as the music staves in the margin illustrate. Imagine a line running up and down through the center of a selected image. If you flip horizontally, the image flips along the center line so that the left side is now on the right and the backside of the image is revealed. For vertical flipping, the imaginary line runs through the middle and the bottom back flips to the top front.

Layout. Both paint and draw allow magnification (zoom in) for fine editing, and reduction (zoom out) for seeing the layout in a larger perspective. In addition, *grid* and *grid alignment* options are also offered in graphics programs. Grids are vertical and horizontal lines imposed on the working area to help line up images. You can adjust the scale of the grid pattern to suit your task.

Grid lines can be made visible or not at will, but the grid is always there whether visible or not. Grid alignment is an option that allows the program to automatically *snap* the selected image into alignment with the nearest visible or invisible grid line. This option can be turned off and on, so you can move images between grid lines if you wish.

Finally, all graphics software offers rulers in order to measure size. You can opt for rulers expressed in inches, centimeters, or other units of measure. You can hide rulers at any time.

Special Characteristics of Paint Software

We have seen a number of operations that are common to all types of graphics software. Now we shall examine some that are special to paint packages.

Eraser Tool

Tools. *Eraser.* We have already seen how the marquee and the lasso capture individual pixels. Another tool that complements the marquee and lasso for editing is the *eraser*. As you drag it over a graphic, it erases it pixel by pixel. Although there are ways to turn off lighted pixels with other tools, the eraser is the most direct. It often cannot be used in intricate designs, and the image must be magnified several times normal size to use the eraser effectively. Double clicking on the eraser tool in most programs is a shortcut for

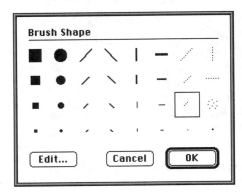

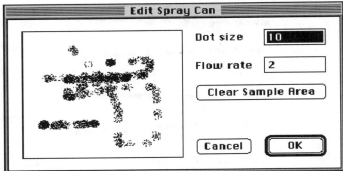

Figure 13.9
Brush and spray can options

Paint Brush
and Spray Can

erasing the entire screen, so treat the eraser with respect. By the way, don't forget that any action can be undone by choosing the Undo option under the Edit menu. This feature gets people out of more jams then any other command! Some advanced software offers multiple levels of Undo so that you can back out, step by step, of a problem that you have created.

Paint brushes and spray can. The paint brush and spray can are enjoyable to use. Just as you might expect, the paint brush acts as a real artist brush for freehand painting. The spray can is used to apply a spray pattern of paint.

What makes these tools so much fun is that the brush shapes and spray patterns can be edited. Double clicking on each icon calls up a dialog box for this purpose. Figure 13.9 (left box) shows a selected brush shape of only three diagonal pixels; it allowed us to make the flag patterns in the image below the dialog boxes. We next edited the spray can's pixels and flow rate (right box), tested it in the sample area, and drew the ground under the flagpole. Other controls are possible using the fill, pattern, and gradient options in Figure 13.7. We used the spray can to make the shadow for the medieval trumpet.

Menu Options. Most paint programs offer some special effects menu options. We did not choose to use any of these, but Figure 13.10 shows some of the possible options. Invert, Darken, and Lighten act on an original image without changing its dimensions. The other options change the dimensions dramatically. Shear slants a corner of the image on the same plane. Distort allows portions of the image to be moved flexibly in space. Perspective changes the image proportionally to provide a sense of depth. Resizing makes the image smaller or larger by stretching and shrinking; dis-

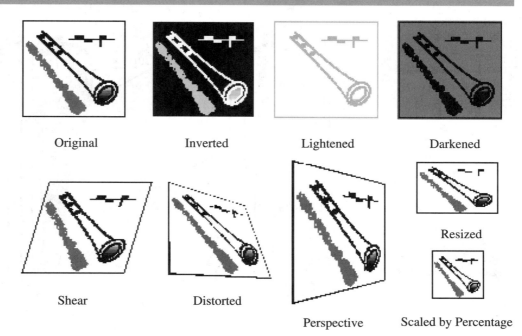

Original   Inverted   Lightened   Darkened

Resized

Shear   Distorted

Perspective   Scaled by Percentage

Figure 13.10
Menu options for special effects in paint programs

tortion is particularly noticeable here. The Scaling by Percentage approach keeps dimensions in proportion.

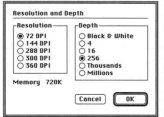

Layout. Most paint programs will allow for changes in both resolution and depth, because the quality of the printed image is usually critical. As we said before, the higher the resolution and depth, the better the image. Early paint programs supported only 72 dpi and minimum depth, but today's software is more flexible. Low-resolution paint images will look poor when printed on a laser printer. You will probably want to print on at least a 600-dpi printer and have some shades of gray for a quality image, so you will need to set your software options accordingly. This may mean that some adjustment will need to be made in document size and memory allocation to support these more demanding conditions.

Special Characteristics of Draw Software

Palette Tools: Arcs and Bezier Curves. In the image in Figure 13.11*a*, we used a draw program to create another medieval trumpet. This one has more complicated curves drawn by use of the *arc* tool. We have pulled apart the parts of the trumpet drawing to illustrate how the arc segments work together to form the instrument. Arcs are based on a formula for drawing graduated curves, and the results are far more precise than those of hand drawing. If your figures have a number of arcs in them, a drawing program might be a better choice than a paint program.

Draw programs can also create complex polygons that include arc shapes with frequent direction changes. Figure 13.11*b* shows our approach to creating a medieval harp. Here, we used the *Bezier tool* to draw the spe-

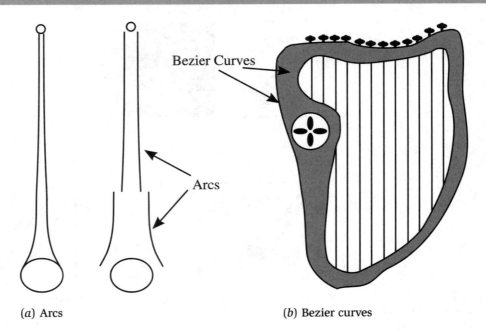

Figure 13.11
Bezier and arc curves

(*a*) Arcs   (*b*) Bezier curves

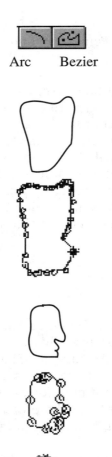

Arc   Bezier

cial shapes that form the body of the harp. It's used much like a freehand tool, but with every mouse click a *control point* is added. You can drag control points to add more angled effects. Smooth curves are drawn between control points to form the shape.

A miniature version of the harp body curves appears in the margin showing the original curve (top) and the curve with control points. These control points can be reshaped to adjust the shape as we have begun to do at the lower right of the bottom figure. The Bezier tool is tricky to use at first, but becomes easier with practice.

Menu Options. *Smoothing and reshaping.* Draw programs offer several options to make figures look more like paint objects. Two important ones are the Reshape and the Smooth/Unsmooth commands. We have already seen how reshaping can be used with Bezier shapes. This same approach can be used with polygons, arcs, and freehand shapes. Simple examples of this are illustrated in the margin. The top image of a person's head was drawn with the freehand tool and smoothing turned on. The middle figure is the same head, but with the reshape options turned on. The circles are added by the software to allow the shape to be redesigned. The bottom figure is the same head, but with smoothing turned off. Most draw programs assume you want the smoothing option on when you use the freehand tool, but you can turn it off easily. Notice that, with smoothing turned off, the lines are straighter and the curves more angular.

Scaling. Scaling is similar to the resize option in paint programs, but with an important difference. Scaling in draw programs preserves the exact characteristics of the original image, so it will print beautifully on a good printer. Word-processing programs have scaling features too for inserted graphics.

Layout. *Layers and groups. Layers* are quite special in drawing programs. As Figure 13.8c showed, individual objects in a draw figure can be selected and copied, deleted, or altered. This ability to select individual objects in a draw program is the basis of the layering idea. Instead of working on a single surface as a painter does on a canvas, the user of draw programs can work in layers placed on top of one another. Figure 13.12 shows our medieval harp drawing with the strings (center) selected and pulled out. The strings are, in fact, layers that we added after the body of the harp was created. So too are the little tuning pegs at the top of the harp. These layers can be made transparent (layers underneath can show through) or opaque (layers on top hide what is underneath). Layers can also be moved forward and backward like playing cards in a deck. All of this adds flexibility to the drawing process.

Grouping works a little differently. A series of objects can be made into one object for convenience. This creates a *group.* For example, we drew each harp string separately, but then grouped all the strings into one group so we could move them around as a unit, or single object. The single set of handles on the rightmost figure indicates that we have regrouped the strings into one object. Grouping can be undone at any time for special editing of individual objects.

Aligning and locking. Other layout options in most draw programs include alignment and locking. Alignment snaps an object or group of objects into line with another object or to the underlying grid. This is useful when you want portions of the figure to look uniform. Locking objects protects them from possible changes; they can be unlocked if you want to manipulate them.

Layers also exist in paint programs like Photoshop.

Special Graphics Considerations for Musicians

In Figure 13.1, page 2 of our newsletter contains a kind of graphic that we have said little about: music notation. Both traditional and medieval notation have been added to the page layout. How did we do this? There are no music tools in AppleWorks, so the notation must have been imported into

Figure 13.12
Layers and groupings in a draw image

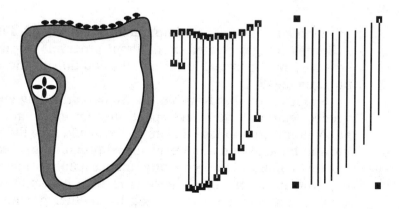

If you don't have a special *capture* program, you can ask the operating system of your computer to copy a complete picture of your screen to your disk. This usually gives you more than you need, but you can edit it with graphics software.

the newsletter somehow. How do musicians import graphic music notation into word-processing, page layout, or integrated software files?

Your first guess might be by cutting and pasting from a music program, using the clipboard of the computer or by saving small files from your notation program in the proper file format for your word processor. Good thinking! Unfortunately, many music notation programs don't support these options. You can cut and paste within the notation program itself, but many don't support the clipboard for other programs or offer the ability to generate standard file formats outside their own world.

How about just printing the excerpt and scanning it in like a photograph? Interesting idea, but there are two big problems with this approach. First, it only works if you have a very high-quality printer and scanner. Second, and most importantly, you probably won't like the results even with expensive equipment. Scanned music graphics simply do not have the clarity that musicians demand.

Capturing the screen. There are two more possibilities, one better than the other. The first possibility is to *capture* an image of the music notation screen in some way and include that in the word-processing file. Special utility programs do this easily. Just create the music excerpt the way you want in the music notation program and then use the utility program to take a snapshot of the music as it appears on the screen and save it in a usable file format. Once the file is created, it is easily imported into your word processor or graphics program.

This approach works, but there is one problem. The snapshot is of the *screen of your computer* at a resolution no better than 72 dpi, so the quality of the image will be less than ideal. It will probably be better than a scanned image, but still not acceptable on a high-resolution printer.

Exported draw formats and EPS. Perhaps the best solution for including music notation in another file is to use a notation software package that *exports* its internal files in either a draw format (PICT is generally used on Macintosh, WMF for Windows) or encapsulated PostScript (EPS) format. The EPS format is generally best because it guarantees that all of the elements are perfectly scaleable and will print well on PostScript printers of any resolution.

File Formats Galore

File formats are covered in more detail in Module 14.

Graphic file formats are important to understand. Bitmapped or object-oriented images created by different programs on different computers can be saved in different file formats in addition to the native ones that each program creates.

Suppose you discover that the AppleWorks drawing tools cannot create a needed feature. If you have spent an hour creating a draw image, you certainly don't want to lose this time! You could save the work as a AppleWorks file and hope to find a more advanced program that reads this native format, but this happens less frequently among graphics than among word-processing programs. Your best choice is to save it in one of the several standard graphics formats that can be read by another program. AppleWorks on the

Macintosh, for example, can save paint and draw images as PICT files, so your best option is to save the work in that format and then open the file in another program. With Windows, AppleWorks will save files in BMP (paint) or WMF (draw) file formats for exporting to other Windows software.

This works in reverse too. Suppose a friend of yours sends a diskette containing a graphic of a lute that would be perfect for the next issue of the newsletter. It is produced by a fancy image-processing program that you do not own. Can you incorporate it into AppleWorks? Yes, because your friend was smart enough to save it in a file format that can be read by Apple-Works.

Standard file formats make life a lot easier in the graphics world, but you must learn about them and know which ones your software can work with. As you might expect, expensive full-featured programs like Photoshop, Illustrator, and CorelDRAW support a large number of these formats while less expensive products are less comprehensive.

A Special Word about Color and Grayscale. Finally, we haven't said much about color or shades of gray (except that paint and draw software usually supports them). Musicians do not often need to deal with color in graphic displays. Of course, most computers now come with color displays, and color scanners and color printers are becoming more affordable. If musicians want to add color to their images, it certainly can be done with today's software and hardware.

But be forewarned. Color demands a great deal from computer technology. It can be a complex and expensive proposition. Color graphics require increased RAM, hard disk storage, and CPU power. We spoke earlier about pixel resolution (dpi or dots per inch) as an issue for screens and printers. The companion concept is *depth,* or the amount of digital information needed to represent each pixel. With black-and-white pixels, depth is not a problem because the pixel is either on or off. With different shades of color and gray, however, we have increasing demands on the size of the number that must represent each pixel, taking a toll on the hardware required to support it. A full screen of realistic color can take a huge amount of memory and of processing time. We will see this again in Viewport VIII when we discuss digital video, animation, and compression techniques.

Graphics software must be smart enough to represent color accurately on both screens and printers. If images are to be printed in color by a professional print shop, the software must communicate just what shade is required. Advanced graphic software to do this job is there if you need it.

Module 14

Data Structures for Desktop Publishing and Graphics

See this viewport's time-line for key historic points.

The newsletter desktop publishing project from Module 13 is completed. It is time now to look below the surface of desktop publishing and graphics software. The importance of understanding data structures that tell us something about how graphics and fonts are represented and processed in a computer also extends to music notation software (Viewport V), networking applications and especially the World Wide Web (Viewport II), and multimedia authoring (Viewport VIII).

Let's begin by putting the topic into perspective. The years 1985–1986 mark the advent of desktop publishing. In one quick blink of an eye, typewriters disappeared from the publishing and graphic arts. About that time, the Macintosh with its graphical WYSIWYG interface was introduced; the first low-cost personal laser printers appeared; Aldus began marketing Pagemaker, the first microcomputer-based desktop publishing software; and Adobe standardized laser printing and font technology with its PostScript page description language.

No one planned this desktop publishing revolution. It just happened. This set of events enabled your personal computer to produce publishing-ready documents that increasingly, each year, approached professional printing quality. Overnight, ordinary people began talking about fonts, kerning, bitmaps, PostScript, and leading: the jargon of the professional typesetter, artist, and printer.

Integrating all the publishing elements into one page on the desktop of a computer requires an understanding of some of the following concepts:

▶ Bitmapped graphics

▶ Object-oriented graphics

▶ Text and characters

▶ Font technology, both bitmapped and outline

▶ File formats for text and graphics

▶ Representations for black and white, grayscale, and color images

238

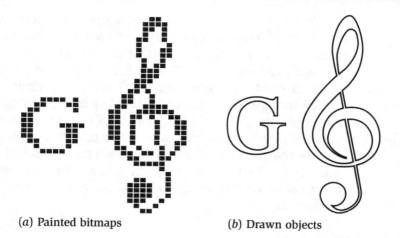

Figure 14.1
Text and graphics represented as bitmaps and objects

(*a*) Painted bitmaps (*b*) Drawn objects

Over the next several pages we will tackle each of these in turn. We will focus more on WYSIWYG graphics structures than on text-based structures common to the past-generation of computers and computer editors. At the conclusion of the module, we will show you how all of these concepts come together to create a desktop-published page with graphics and text combined for display or printing.

It's All Either Dots or Polygons

Review the terms *bits, bytes,* and *binary* in Module 7 if you need to.

In a WYSIWYG publishing environment, there are three key data elements: text characters, bitmapped graphics, and object-oriented graphics. As you will see, your written page becomes bitmaps or dots, and objects or polygons, as words and images are digested by the computer.

Bitmaps represent analog events in a computer as digital patterns of 1s and 0s. Module 10 showed how music could be sampled or digitized as bitmaps of sound. We can shape letters in text as bitmapped patterns, draw images as bitmapped shapes, and scan or convert pictures into bitmaps. Notice how the letter and music symbol in Figure 14.1*a* have been represented as bitmaps.

Objects represent analog events in a computer as mathematical formulas or instructions for drawing a shape. Objects represent the shapes of text and graphics as curves, lines, circles, and polygons. Because most object-oriented graphics are complex images, the polygon is often the most frequently used geometric object. Figure 14.1*b* shows how the shapes in Figure 14.1*a* would be represented as computer objects in contrast to their bitmapped counterparts. Notice how much smoother the object-oriented graphics are.

If bitmaps are to graphics what sampling is to music, then objects are to graphics what MIDI messages are to music. Objects are the instructions, the formulas for directing a graphics device like a printer in creating a graphic image. The computer only stores the instructions, not the event itself. With bitmaps, on the other hand, the computer is storing an actual replica or image of the analog event.

ASCII was discussed in Module 7.

Text represents characters and signs as numeric values in the computer. Every letter and sign has a standardized numeric value which is correlated to the keys on a computer keyboard. The standardized numbering system is the ASCII coding system. The text that you type into the computer is stored as ASCII codes. However, in a WYSIWYG computer system, text is transformed into either bitmapped (*fixed*) or object-oriented (*outline*) fonts when displayed or printed. Because ASCII text values are translated into bitmapped or outline fonts, any shape can be assigned to an ASCII value. Do you see the power in this? The letter *A* can be the letter *A* graphically, but it can also be the hand sign for the letter *A* in sign language, a Kanji symbol in Japanese, or the music notation for a whole note on the note A on the music staff.

Text: Saying It with Characters

Computers use ASCII standard numeric values for coding text. Each code represents a unique character or nonprinting key like the TAB (09), RETURN (13), or DELETE (127) keys. ASCII coding is the most widely used format for representing text in computers of any size. Most computer books have a complete ASCII code chart should you have need for one.

Files. There are several different structures for representing text in a computer file, from the simplest to the complex:

▶ ASCII text files (TEXT or TXT): An ASCII text file is nothing more than a string of ASCII codes. There is no image formatting coded into this file, or information about margins and indents, fonts, font size, and styles. Italics and bold will not be communicated in any ASCII file.

▶ Tab-delimited ASCII text files. Tab-delimited ASCII files are used for spreadsheet and database data; an ASCII TAB character (09) separates each field in the spreadsheet or database and a RETURN character (13) ends each record. If you need to send a file to someone else and didn't know what kind of computer or word processor they use, an ASCII text file would always be a safe bet.

If you have people submitting articles for a publication, have them send either a Word or WordPerfect file as well as another copy as an ASCII text file, just in case there is a problem in file translation.

▶ Rich text formats that include layout codes (e.g. RTF, DIF, and SYLK). These files are standardized file structures that have formatting information added to them. RTF stands for *rich text format,* a text format with layout data added. This file type, devised by Microsoft, contains information about font choice, style, and size as well as other formatting information related to indenting, margins, and page breaks. If you are considering exchanging files with somehow who has a different word processor, the next level of sophistication above ASCII files is to see whether your application and that of the other person can read any of the RTF-like formats.

▶ Application-specific files (e.g., Word, WordPerfect). These are files written using the codes of specific programs. Some word processors, like WordPerfect and Word, and desktop publishing software like QuarkXPress and Page-

Maker, are so commonly used on personal computers that they typically come with translators for reading each other's files.

Painting: Saying It with Dots

Computers and computer devices use bitmaps to represent many things. Bitmapped images for graphics are best suited for painting and scanning activities: the kinds of artwork where you sketch, brush, shade, and erase pixel by pixel. Bitmapped images do not work as well for activities where rotating, scaling, and cutting and pasting are required; object-oriented graphics are better for these tasks.

Resolution. There is a close parallel between sampling music sounds as bitmaps and painting or scanning visual images as bitmaps. The two critical issues related to bitmap graphic resolution are density and depth. These correlate with rate and width in music sampling. Density in a graphic image is calculated in dots per inch, or dpi. Typically, density is on a continuum from the 60- to 72-dpi resolution of a CRT screen through the 300-dpi resolution of low-end laser and ink-jet printers to the 1200 and 2450 dpi of professional-quality imagesetters for publishing. Depth refers to the number of bits used to describe the color for each dot or pixel. Table 14.1 shows the common bit depths.

Just as with music sampling, the trade-off for increased resolution is memory consumption. A 1-bit, black-and-white image scanned at 72 dpi consumes less than 1K of memory; the same image at 300 dpi consumes over 10K of memory. To come to the aid of your pocketbook and your hard drive, several compression schemes to conserve storage space for graphics exist; JPEG and GIF compressed files are two common schemes.

Aliasing and Jaggies. The bitmapped trumpet graphic in Figure 14.2 shows perceptible jaggies on the curves of the bell and tubing. Object graphics are not susceptible to jaggies. The technical name for this phenomenon is *aliasing*.

Aliasing occurs in music sampling as well; see Viewport VII.

On the left side of Figure 14.2 is shown the trumpet graphic, painted at 72 dpi. It has been scaled and rotated. Note the distortion that occurs. Figure 14.2 shows, on the right, the trumpet drawn as an object and scaled and rotated. Note how it retains its shape and dimensions.

Table 14.1 Common Graphic Bit Depths	
Graphic Bit Depth	**Color Application**
1-bit	Black-and-white, monochrome graphics
4-bit	16 colors or grayscales
8-bit	256 colors or grayscales
16-bit	65.5 thousand colors
32-bit	16.7 million colors (24 bits for color, 8 bits for control values)

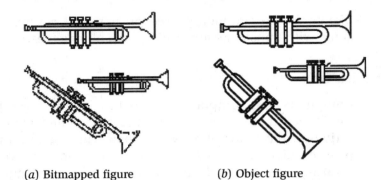

Figure 14.2
Comparison of trumpet
images in original form,
scaled, then rotated

(*a*) Bitmapped figure   (*b*) Object figure

Bear in mind that as the dpi density of a graphic increases, perceived aliasing decreases. The better the resolution, the less likely our eye will see the digitized edges of the image. If you scan images at 150 to 300 dpi and print out the final copy for publication at least at this density, very little aliasing should be apparent.

Graphic File Formats. Unfortunately, there is not a universal file structure for graphics comparable to the ASCII text file. There are several that have been used in enough applications that they approach being industry standards and, with a translation software utility that will convert across platforms such as Mac and Wintel, many bitmap graphics files can be exchanged.

TIFF and EPS. The cross-platform, printing industry standards are TIFF files for bitmapped graphics and EPS for object graphics. TIFF (Tag Image File Format) or TIF was created specifically by the Adobe and Microsoft companies for scanned, bitmapped images in color or black and white. Scanning and photo-imaging software like Photoshop use TIFF files. EPS (Encapsulated PostScript) is unique to PostScript applications. It stores a bitmapped image *encapsulated* or wrapped in the page description language commands. Most page layout programs, like QuarkXpress and PageMaker, are entirely PostScript based. When creating music notation or graphics for desktop publishing projects, always look for an option to save your graphic in EPS format rather than PICT or TIFF in order to retain the PostScript precision.

GIF, JPEG, and PNG. The two cross-platform compression formats for graphic files are GIF and JPEG. GIF is optimized to handle 8-bit, 256-color file compression; JPEG will handle 32-bit color graphic compression and is best suited for photographic images. If you need to place your TIFF scans on the Internet, then JPEG is a good choice for compression. The more complexity in the graphic image, the better JPEG works to compress the file; the less complexity, the better GIF works.

PNG is short for Portable Network Graphics and is pronounced "ping." It is one of the newer bit-mapped graphics formats similar to GIF. PNG is completely patent- and license-free and will become a common compression standard for bitmapped graphics showing up in graphics software and on the Internet. PNG's big advantage over GIF is that it will compress color resolutions up to 48 bits per pixel, way beyond the 8-bit limitation of GIF files.

Platform specific formats. The most common file types for bitmapped graphics on the Mac are PAINT and PICT files. On a Wintel machine, BMP, CGM, or WMF will handle bitmapped images. For object graphics, PICT is the most common format on the Mac; on Wintel computers, CGM or WMF. PICT and CGM or WMF files will store bitmapped and object-oriented graphics in black-and-white, grayscale, and color.

Drawing: Saying It with Shapes

Graphic objects are descriptions of shapes by mathematical instructions. Where bitmap images are ideal for painting and scanning, objects are best suited for draw- and shape-intensive activities. The shape is always alive: you can scale it, rotate it, resize it, re-shape it. The world of an object-oriented draw program is based on lines, arcs, circles, polygons, and other geometric figures. Shapes have selection handles, end points, anchor points, and direction points by which they can be manipulated.

Resolution. The variables of image density and depth that apply to bitmap graphics also apply to object graphics. Refer back to Figure 14.2, where the trumpet image was shown in both bitmapped and object versions. The difference is that the resolution of an object-oriented graphic ultimately depends on the device it is displayed or printed on. The resolution density and depth is always optimized to fit the output device, be it a 72-dpi display screen, a 150-dpi dot matrix printer, or a 600-dpi PostScript-based laser printer. Furthermore, you can change the shape and size of an object without distortion because the application is simply changing the formula used to construct the image, not the image itself.

Files. Object graphics are stored primarily as PICT, WMF, or EPS files or in a file format specific to an application like Freehand, CorelDRAW, Illustrator, or Canvas. There is a close affinity between object graphics, EPS files, and PostScript. They are all object-oriented systems.

Fonts: PostScript, TrueType, and More

Describing Fonts. When you enter the world of desktop publishing, you enter the world of typography: the art of designing and printing with type. With this world comes its own terminology, dating back to Gutenberg and the early days of printing in the 1400s.

Letters are called *upper* and *lower case* because the capital letters were stored in the upper storage case and the other letters in the lower storage case in front of the person doing the typesetting. The *leading* (pronounced "ledding") between lines was so called because a strip of lead was placed between the rows of type. You will find that your software gives you control over the more obvious features of font type, size, and style, but also the finer controls of *kerning* (separation of letters) and leading as well. Font *size* is determined in *points*, for example, 9, 10, 12, 24, and larger. Any font size is possible.

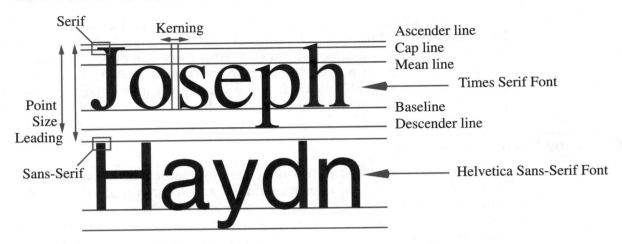

Figure 14.3
The anatomy of a font

Figure 14.3 illustrates some of the common terms used to describe the features of a character in a font. The term *typeface* is synonymous with the term *font,* and a *font family* includes all the font styles and sizes that share a common typeface. *Serif* fonts are characterized by the presence of *serifs,* small horizontal crosslines attached, generally, to the tops and bottoms of the main strokes of a character. Serif fonts are usually easier to read. Times is an example of a serif font. Fonts with no serifs are called sans-serif ("without serifs"). *Display* fonts, like Franklin Gothic, Bubbledot, Holiday, and Playbill, are especially made for emphasis or special effects.

Fixed-Scale or Bitmap Fonts. Just as there are bitmap and object graphics, there are bitmap and object fonts. Generally they are known as fixed-scale and outline fonts.

Each fixed-scale font requires a unique set of bitmaps, one for each character in the font. Fixed-scale fonts also consume lots of memory. (Many printers come with several font families in ROM for this reason.) What advantage are fixed-scaled fonts? Speed. The computer doesn't have to take time to build the font from an outline. For displaying fonts on a screen, especially with slower personal computers, this can be the determining factor in choosing fixed-scale over outline fonts.

Outline Fonts. An outline font is a set of descriptions of how to draw each character. These descriptions for font shapes are written in a Page Description Language (PDL). The advantages of outline fonts are quality of resolution, savings in memory space, and the ability to scale and change the style of the font without distortion. The disadvantage is lack of speed. The computer must calculate each character it has to print, although some systems are smart enough to remember recently created characters. There are two common PDLs or outline font systems in use: Adobe's Postscript font system and TrueType, an outline font system developed by Apple and Microsoft.

Printing versus Screen Fonts. The fonts that you see on your screen are not necessarily the same as those that are supported by your printer. It is

Times Plain 10 Point

Times 12

Times 14

Times 18

Times Italic

Times Bold

Times Outline

Times Shadow

TIMES SMALL CAPS

Franklin Gothic

BUBBLEDOT

Playbill

Fixed-scale font

Outline font

necessary to match printer fonts with display fonts to truly have WYSIWYG technology in which screen display and printer output are identical. Depending on the equipment you own—including software, operating system, and printer capabilities—you can come close to achieving this ideal situation. In general, with slower personal computers and non-PostScript printers, you are better off using fixed-scale display and printer fonts. Usually the fixed-scale printer fonts are optimized for best quality on the printer. Beginners should stick to the fonts that are included with their system and printer; today, you will find an ample supply of fonts are available to you.

Creating a Desktop-Published Page

Don't overuse fonts. Watch out for copyrights on some fonts.

We have examined all of the basic elements that go to make up a WYSIWYG page, including object and bitmapped graphics as well as fonts. In order to present these elements in context, we will look at a common application where they are combined to make up a word-processing or desktop-publishing page—one that you can view on your computer screen or print on a printer. Figure 14.4 shows how these elements work together to create a page of text with graphic scans, music notation, and bitmapped graphics. This page is much like a page of a report you might create for a project of your own. Bear in mind the point that in WYSIWYG software, all imagery is essentially bitmaps in one form or another.

The Page. The center of the diagram is the *page bitmap*. In a computer's memory when this page is displayed, or in a printer's memory when this page is printed, a major data structure is created to represent each page of the document. This page is one large bitmap made up of any mixture of elements from text, bitmaps from scans and painting, and objects from drawing and music notation.

The Fonts. Text is stored as ASCII character codes. However, when the *page bitmap* is constructed those character codes must be converted to bitmaps. The diagram shows the computer using its *font library* to retrieve predesigned shapes for these bitmap images. A font is a set of images or directions for creating graphic shapes for characters. A *font library* is a collection of all the different fonts stored in the computer, available for use from within different software applications.

This is why many programs have a text or normal view, and a page layout or graphics view.

Fixed-scale fonts are fixed bitmap shapes for each ASCII code. If 12-point Times Roman is selected for the font, a predefined set of bitmaps is retrieved to create Times Roman images for the text in the *page bitmap*. When fixed-scale fonts are used, a separate font is needed for each font type, size, and style.

PostScript and TrueType are examples of outline fonts. The font library for these contains the object formulas to direct the computer in building a bitmap for the shape required for any letter or ASCII code. With outline fonts, only one set of font instructions is needed for each font type. The computer can use the instructions to generate different sizes and styles of bitmaps as needed. Don't expect the computer to create the bitmaps as fast as it accesses fixed-scale fonts, however.

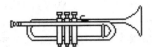

The Paintings and Scans. The *page bitmap* in Figure 14.4 contains a scan of the composer Handel and a sketch of a trumpet from a paint program. Paint graphics software works on the basis of bitmap data structures, so paint images can be pasted directly into the *page bitmap* without conversion. The trumpet illustration, however, shows jagged lines around the curves in the tubing and bell. These are the notorious *jaggies* typical of bitmapped images. The scan also has some jaggies as well but they are not as noticeable because the dots that make up a scanned image are more diffuse than those in a line drawing like the trumpet.

The astute student might wonder why, if the entire page is a bitmap just like the trumpet, we don't see jaggies around all the text letters and the music notation. A simple answer is that the graphic resolution of these objects is different. The printed page was produced on a printer with 600-dpi resolution. The trumpet was created at 72-dpi resolution. The font bitmaps and music notation were created at 600 dpi. And the scan was made at 100 dpi. In general, the quality of any image added to the *page bitmap* is as good as the resolution of the application that created that image.

The Drawings. The *page bitmap* contains a graphic of music notation created with a music notation program that saves its images as objects: unique objects for each note shape, the clef, the staff and barlines, and so on. Notice how geometrically smooth the curves are in the G clef. This graphic also could have been drawn with a drawing program, like the organ for the newsletter in Module 13.

One of the most beneficial features of the data structure for object graphics is that the computer can apply an object's formula to the best quality resolution available. When you move from a screen with 72-dpi resolution to a printer with 300 dpi and then to a publisher's imagesetter (a device like a super-high-quality printer) at 2450 dpi, image quality gets better and better. Furthermore, if we want to resize or rotate an object graphic, because the object is stored as a mathematical formula, the computer customizes and draws a new bitmap that produces an accurate rendition of the transformed image.

Displaying. What do we see displayed from the *page bitmap?* Another bitmap. The computer sends the *page bitmap* to the computer video RAM memory. The video circuitry then performs a digital-to-analog conversion (just like the DACs used to convert sound samples to audio) to create voltages that control the electron guns in the video CRT display and change the image on the screen. The screen image, called a *raster* image, is just another bitmap represented by the activated pixels on the CRT tube. It makes no difference whether the screen is black and white, grayscale, or color.

The mechanics of CRTs are discussed in Module 15.

Printing. Now we come to the important final step, printing to the page. The diagram in Figure 14.4 shows two printing paths: bitmapped printing and PostScript printing.

Bitmapped printing. The printer driver takes the page bitmap and formulates a printer bitmap of the page that conforms to the data structure

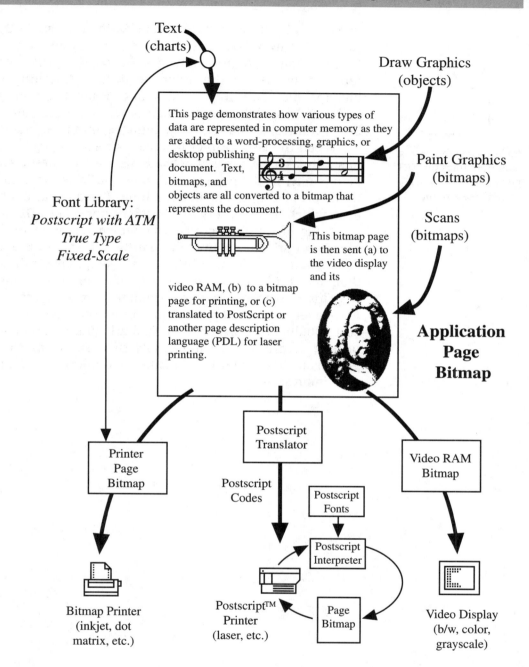

Figure 14.4
The makeup of a
WYSIWYG application
page with bitmaps,
objects, and text

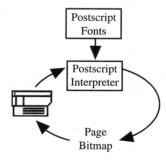

required by the printer. Each dot in the printer bitmap conforms to a dot on the printed page created by the printer.

PostScript printing. PostScript is a page description language designed as an object-oriented graphics system. The diagram in Figure 14.4 shows the PostScript PDL translator taking the *page bitmap* and converting all of it into PostScript codes (similar to creating MIDI codes to control a music synthesizer). The PostScript codes are sent to the printer, typically a laser or ink-jet printer. The PostScript printer contains its own computer, including a microprocessor and memory. Its PostScript interpreter takes the codes and trans-

Raster refers the zigzag pattern of lines the CRT's guns draw across the screen. See Module 15.

lates them back into a page bitmap in the printer. As the diagram notes, the Interpreter uses PostScript fonts to create the shapes necessary for text. Graphics that were originally created as objects, like the music notation, get redrawn by use of the object formulas. Anything that was created as bitmaps, like the trumpet and scan of Handel, get encapsulated in the Post-Script codes as bitmaps: the jaggies will not necessarily disappear, but Post-Script can resize and rotate the bitmaps, often without distortion.

When the laser printer has reconstructed a *page bitmap,* it translates the bits into laser beams that activate a supply of plastic *toner,* like that used in xerography, in the printer. The toner particles are then heated, fusing them to the printer paper one dot at a time. The dots have a high resolution, however, which is the beauty of a PostScript or other PDL printer.

A file of the PostScript codes which represent our *page bitmap* can be saved and printed on any other PostScript printer; the file is device independent. The file could be printed on a 300-dpi laser printer for proof copy, and then on a 1200- or 2450-dpi professional imagesetter for final copy.

This is what we would recommend if you were publishing your own newsletter. You could prepare and proof the newsletter on an ink-jet or low-cost 300-dpi laser printer, then find a higher-quality 600- or higher-dpi laser printer, or a printing shop locally that has an imagesetter at 1200 dpi or greater, to have final copy made for duplication. Your subscribers will be very impressed.

<table>
<tr><td>Module
15</td><td># Hardware Devices for Music Publishing</td></tr>
</table>

This module considers hardware needs for setting up a computer for desktop publishing. Let's revisit our IPOS universal systems model in light of a desktop publishing workstation by examining Figure 15.1. Some of the items shown in the model are technically software, but they are critical in discussing memory and the mechanics of printer hardware.

Figure 15.1 provides an overview of the features of printing and display hardware that are essential to present-day desktop publishing. These are features that you need to consider when expanding a computer to handle your graphics and publishing needs. Because final output is so critical for desktop publishing, we will consider printers first. Then we will discuss scanning technology, followed by video displays. Graphic DSP chips will be discussed under video displays, PDL interpreters, and storage under printing.

Printers

The quality of your printed output is a sign of your desktop publishing skill. One person can have a slow, out-of-date computer with a small display screen and a simple word processor, but a 1200-dpi laser printer. Another

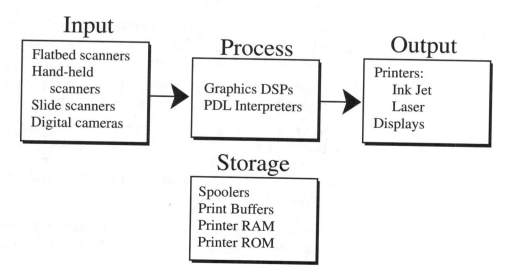

Figure 15.1
The IPOS model showing input, process, output, and storage for desktop publishing

Input
- Flatbed scanners
- Hand-held scanners
- Slide scanners
- Digital cameras

Process
- Graphics DSPs
- PDL Interpreters

Output
- Printers:
  - Ink Jet
  - Laser
- Displays

Storage
- Spoolers
- Print Buffers
- Printer RAM
- Printer ROM

can have a fast, state-of-the-art computer with lots of memory and industry-strength desktop publishing software like QuarkXPress, but a 150-dpi ink-jet printer. Who will have the best-looking finished product? The person with the 1200-dpi laser printer will come out ahead. Don't sacrifice on the quality of your printed output if you want to do music publishing on a computer!

Printers and the IPOS Model. Our input-process-output-storage model can be used to understand how printers work. We will outline the important features here and then discuss each stage as we specifically examine common ink-jet and laser printers.

Input. The input stage of the printer is concerned with the form in which data are received from the computer. These were discussed in Module 14. They include:

▶ ASCII coded text characters (character-based printers)

▶ Lines of bitmapped patterns (line printers)

▶ Pages of bitmapped patterns (page printers)

▶ PostScript or other page description (PDL) codes (PostScript or other PDL printers)

Process and output. The process stage is concerned with the *print engine:* how the printer translates desktop publishing data into a form that can be imprinted on the paper. There are two print engines in common use with personal computers, ink-jet and laser. Ink-jet uses drops of ink sprayed on the paper; laser fuses dots of toner to the paper. The output stage is concerned with how, physically, the printer imprints the image on the paper. Several other print engines that we will not devote attention to include: dot matrix, thermal, and imagesetters.

Storage: Printers use memory, both RAM and ROM, for a number of operations including:

Buffers: Memory for temporarily storing a line or a page of data being processed for printing.

Fonts: Memory for storing tables of font descriptions: either fonts that are downloaded into RAM from the computer or fonts that are permanently installed in the printer.

Spoolers: Memory (in the computer or in the printer) for storing lines or pages of data waiting to be sent to the printer.

Paper input and output. Printers can deal with a variety of media including sheet paper in various sizes and weights, envelopes, labels in various sizes and shapes, and transparencies. The more common mechanisms that printers use to move print media through a printing device include: single sheet feed, paper tray feed, and tractor feed.

Measures of Printer Performance. There are a number of industry standards for measuring printer speed and printer resolution. Printing speed is

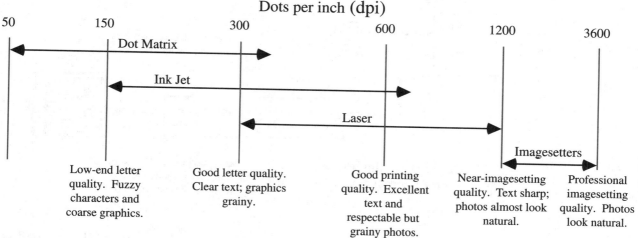

Figure 15.2
A comparative chart showing the range of dpi (or ppi) performance across printer engines

measured in *pages per minute* (ppm) with ink-jet and laser printers. It measures how fast a printer can process a complete page. The range can be from 0.25 to 8 ppm for ink-jet and from 4 to 12 ppm or higher for a good laser printer. Caution: printing graphics, especially color graphics on ink-jet printers, can be very slow even though the rated black-ink text speed may be 8 ppm. A color 8×11 photo image may take up to 10 or 15 minutes to print!

Dots per inch (dpi) or pixels per inch (ppi) is a measure of resolution for printing any bitmapped image, whether text or graphic. The chart in Figure 15.2 illustrates the resolution of common printer engines and gives you an indication of the benefit of increasing the dots per inch on the final printed output. The chart shows the considerable variation in resolution among dot matrix and laser print engines. It also shows that for most projects short of professional printing, a resolution of 300 to 600 dpi is suitable, especially if you are not using scanned photographs. Thirdly, although you might conclude from the chart that greater dpi resolution is better, cost is a significant factor to consider. Few of us can afford to purchase professional imagesetters. You must ask yourself: Given your budget for a printer, what is the highest dpi resolution affordable?

Lines per inch (lpi) is an important unit of measure when you are doing lots of graphics printing, especially with scanned and photographic images. Printers and video displays *rasterize* their data onto the page or screen. This means that the images are printed a line at a time as the print head or laser scans across the page and down. The number of levels of gray or color within the dots that make up each printed or scanned line influences the overall resolution of the process. On a 300-dpi laser printer, 70 lpi would give you about 16 levels of gray. To put this in context, photographs in newspapers are around 70 lpi and are usually grainy with little richness of grays; magazine photographs are around 100 lpi and have little perceptible grain and good richness of grays; and the highest quality, coffee-table books, with glossy paper, give you 200 to 300 lpi.

ASIDE

Raster and rasterizing refer to creating images by lines. Printers and video displays are raster devices and create images line by line.

LINK

Module 14 discusses printer resolution in terms of lines per inch (lpi) and pixels or dots per inch (ppi and dpi).

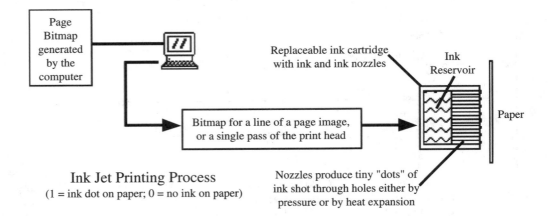

Figure 15.3
The operation of an ink-jet print engine

Ink Jet Printing Process
(1 = ink dot on paper; 0 = no ink on paper)

Having considered printers in general terms, let's look in more detail at two recent types: ink-jet and laser. We will discuss the mechanical features of their operation, consider their speed and resolution, examine the positive and negative aspects of their design, and cite a few examples of popular commercial models.

Ink-Jet Printing: Spraying Drops of Ink. Ink-jet printers are nonimpact printers. IBM released one of the first commercial ink-jet printers around 1976. The concept is quite simple and elegant. Bitmaps of characters and graphics are sprayed onto the paper as minuscule droplets of ink.

Figure 15.3 illustrates the operation of an ink-jet printer. Most ink-jet printers are not character-based; they are bitmap-based printers. In other words, the ink-jet printer only sees patterns of bits and has no concept of ASCII text codes as do the older, character-based dot matrix printers. The computer sends to the ink-jet printer, one line at a time, a bitmap of each page of your document. The ink-jet print head moves across the page, dropping ink dots in vertical columns. Ink comes from the reservoir of a disposable cartridge and is dispensed onto the paper either by pressure or heating to form a droplet of ink. The drop of ink is about one millionth of a drop from an eyedropper.

Photographic images are also created with patterns of dots. Grayscale images are created with black and white dots, and color images with dots of the four basic colors cyan, magenta, yellow, and black (CMYK). Most color ink-jet printers are based on CMYK color. By printing combinations of these colors close to each other, CMYK can simulate most other colors. This is the same technique used in printing most commercial books and magazines. Some lower-price printers use only three colors: cyan, magenta, and yellow.

Most ink-jet printers use a paper tray that feeds single sheets of paper through the printer one at a time. This system lets you use letter-sized paper, personalized stationery, and envelopes for printing.

One early ink-jet printer, in particular, captured a large part of the personal computing market: the 300-dpi Hewlett-Packard DeskWriter (for Mac) and DeskJet (for Wintel). The HP and Epson color ink-jet printers in various configurations provided the first low-cost color printing solutions for per-

Table 15.1 A Comparison of Ink-Jet and Laser Printers

Ink-Jet	Laser
Up to 600 or 720 dpi resolution	Up to 1200-dpi resolution
Slower (up to 8 ppm; very slow with color)	Faster (up to 16 ppm)
Color at modest price	Grey scale common; color expensive
Quality varies with ink and paper	Copy machine quality printing or better
Personal networking possible	Workgroup networking possible
Lowest cost printer to purchase	More expensive than ink-jet
Quiet operation	Moderately quiet operation
Small and lightweight	Larger and heavier
Low cost to feed except for color ink	More expensive to feed with paper and toner

Modules 7 and 8 cover TCP/IP and Ethernet, if you need some help with these concepts.

Xerography was invented in 1937 by Chester Carlson. It wasn't until the late 1950s, however, that the first commercial photocopy machines appeared, with the Xerox machine among the best known.

sonal computing as well. Other alternatives include the Apple Stylewriters, the newer HP ink-jet series, the Epson Stylus series, the Canon BJCs, and the ink-jets from Okidata and Lexmark.

Table 15.1 compares ink-jet with laser printers. Ink-jet printers are an excellent low-cost solution for desktop publishing, with resolutions up to 600 dpi and print speeds up to 8 ppm for text but much slower for color graphics. It is hard to find anything but a color ink-jet printer, just as it is hard to find anything but a color video monitor because the price has dropped so low. The latest ink-jets can also be networked in case a few people need to share a printer over Ethernet or TCP/IP for small personal networking needs.

A primary drawback to this print engine is its very nature: spraying ink. The ink flows into the pores of the paper and some fuzziness can occur. Using high-quality paper and paper coating can greatly improve the quality of the printed output. When printing large areas of black or color, you can see the wet ink. Be careful not to smear it until it dries. Only a few higher-end ink-jets will print oversized paper. Caution: if you plan to do a lot of printing of high-resolution photo images, the color ink cartridges and the special paper can be very expensive. Typically, color ink-jets use one cartridge for black ink and another cartridge for the three or four colors (CMYK).

Laser Printing: Melting Dots of Plastic. The laser printer ushered in desktop publishing in the mid-1980s. It is a direct descendent of the Xerox photocopy machine. The boon to personal printing began in 1983 with the first Hewlett-Packard (HP) LaserJet and, shortly thereafter, with the Apple LaserWriter. Both these printers used the Canon laser engine and achieved printing resolution of 300 dpi. The HP LaserJet IV released in late 1992 provided 600-dpi laser printing for a very reasonable cost, and the newest lasers are offering 1200 dpi.

Figure 15.4 illustrates the operation of a laser printer. To begin, the computer sends to the laser printer a bitmapped image for an entire page to be created on paper. The printer processes one line of a page at a time, sending that line of bit patterns to the laser engine.

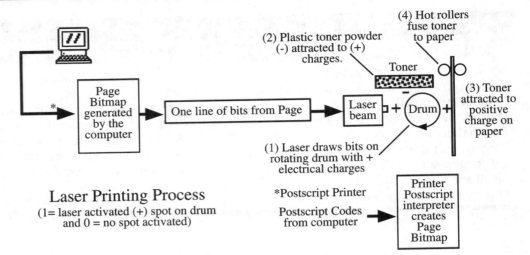

Laser Printing Process
(1= laser activated (+) spot on drum
and 0 = no spot activated)

Figure 15.4
The operation of the laser
printer engine

Put as much memory as
you can in your printer.
The larger the memory
buffer, the faster the printer
will deliver your output.

We discussed the use of
scanners for desktop pub-
lishing in Module 13.

A laser beam draws the bits on a rotating drum by creating positive electrical charges. The toner, a negatively charged fine black plastic powder, is
attracted to the positive spots on the drum like fleas jumping onto a dog.
The toner particles on the drum are then attracted to the paper, which has a
static electrical charge (the fleas just jumped off the dog onto a passing
hand). The paper with its toner particles passes through a pair of heated
rollers that fuse the toner to the page. The result is a professional-quality
print job that looks far superior to a photocopy and, in most cases, is suitable to be printed directly.

Laser printers, like ink-jet printers, control paper flow using paper trays
(see Table 15.1). Options are available for envelopes, transparencies, and
labels; legal as well as letter-size paper can be used. Multiple trays may be
available options to permit various combinations of plain paper, letterhead,
and envelopes to be software-selected from the application. High-speed, networked lasers can offer shared network printer access for a computer lab or
office area from either TCP/IP or Ethernet.

A laser printer, though costing a few hundred dollars more than ink-jet,
offers the best quality printed output possible from a personal computer.
Maintenance and toner supplies are more expensive and involved than with
ink-jet printing, but the increase in cost per page is more than made up by
the quality of output. With 600 dpi the standard resolution for laser printers,
and the higher-end lasers offering 1200 dpi, most routine publications do
not need high-end imagesetters for the final output. Music notation generated on a 600-dpi laser printer will rival any commercial music printing.

Plotters. Not all printing devices are based on bitmaps. Plotters are object-
based systems that draw lines, circles, polygons, and so on, with a computer-
controlled pen. They are essential to any drafting tasks that might be used by
an engineer or architect. In music and the arts, they are used in scene design,
costume design, and marching-band charting. These are all applications
where imaging by line drawing is much more efficient than bitmaps.

Mechanically, plotters are very simple. Plotters are essentially a remote-controlled ink pen driven by commands from the computer. Some allow selection among multiple pens of different colors. Plotters come in flatbed or table models and in freestanding forms that can hold very large sheets of paper.

Hardware for Digital Imagery

Two key tools for incorporating live images, photographs, sketches, and artwork into your desktop publishing projects are scanners and digital cameras. These tools, for relatively little expense, let you capture timely material in the computer as a bitmapped graphics image. This image can then be edited and transformed with image manipulation software such as Adobe Photoshop.

Scanners. Scanners come in flatbed, sheet-feed, hand-held, slide, overhead, and drum varieties. We will focus on the flatbed scanners. Let's revisit xerography: the familiar photocopy machine. The first stage of the photocopy machine is the mechanism that captures the image from the original page, using light reflection. When we sampled audio images in Module 10, we converted sound frequencies into digital bitmaps using analog-to-digital converters (ADCs). A scanner samples *light* frequencies using ADCs to produce bitmaps of video images. As you can see, so many operations in a computer are similar: the machine really doesn't care if it is dealing with a visual or an audio image.

Figure 15.5 reduces the operation of a scanning device to a very simple form. The diagram shows a light source illuminating the image. Have you noticed the light beam that scans the page any time you make a photocopy? That's the same type of light beam scanning the scanner's page. Using a system of mirrors, the reflection of the light is then magnified, focused, and aimed at a strip of photocells.

The resolution of the scanner is determined by how many photocells are along a strip that is as wide as the scanner's page size. Scanning density can range from 150 to 1200 dpi, or 150 to 1200 photocells per inch. If the photocells can only detect the presence or absence of light, then the depth of the resolution is a 1-bit image known as *line art* in scanning nomenclature. A 1-bit image is simply black and white. If the photocell can detect multiple lev-

Figure 15.5
The mechanics of a computer scanner

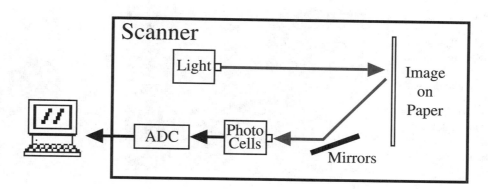

els of light, then the depth of scanning resolution can be from 4 to 24 bits of gray or color. A 24-bit color scanner can capture millions of shades. However, to scan color, many scanners actually make three scans of the image filtering out the reds, the greens, and then the blue colors to build an RGB (for Red, Green, Blue) file image.

With a *flatbed* scanner, the image lies on top of a plate of glass just as with a photocopy machine. This setup results in well-controlled and accurately aligned scanning. Flatbed scanners come in standard page sizes from 8.5×11 to 11×17 inches, with resolutions from 300 to 1200 dpi.

The Hewlett-Packard ScanJet was one of the first commercially successful low-cost scanners. A later HP ScanJet is shown in Figure 15.6a. Models from such firms as HP, Apple, Microtek, Agfa, Visioneer, and Nikon now populate the market.

A variety of other scanning devices are available for translating photographic images into computer bitmaps. There are also scanners especially suited for scanning text from documents through what is known as Optical Character Recognition (OCR). The Visioneer Paperport sheetfeed printer (shown in Figure 15.6b) and the Microtek PageWiz are examples of these. There are also hand-held scanners like the Logitech Scanman for quick on-the-fly work and high-end slide scanners like the Nikon CoolScan for capturing images from photographic slides. Sheetfeed scanners pull the paper image through the scanner much as a printer feeds through paper.

TWAIN Drivers. Scanners, as well as digital still and video cameras, commonly use a standard driver software known as TWAIN or EZ-TWAIN. This makes it possible to use them with a wide variety of software. Digital imaging hardware that uses the TWAIN interface should be readable by most of your photo and video editing software that supports TWAIN, regardless of whether you have a Macintosh or a Wintel computer and software.

Digital Cameras. Scanners work great for existing photographs and printed documents. There are times when you need to capture a live image for publication, such as photos of music events, a group photo shot, or a portrait photo. Here is where a digital camera comes to the rescue. The digital cam-

PhotoCDs offer the least expensive way to transfer photographs and slides to digital form. These are discussed in Modules 12 and 29.

Figure 15.6
Two scanners:
(*a*) Hewlett Packard Scan-Jet 5100C color flatbed scanner
(Courtesy of the Hewlett-Packard Company)
(*b*) The Visioneer Paper-Port Strobe sheetfeed scanner
(Courtesy of Visioneer)

(*a*)   (*b*)

Figure 15.7
(*a*) Minolta Dimage V digital camera with its detachable lens
(Courtesy of Minolta Corporation)
(*b*) Canon Optura digital video camcorder
(Courtesy of Canon USA, Inc.)

(*a*)

(*b*)

era is like a traditional camera only it doesn't need film, and the images don't have to be developed. Take a snapshot, download it to your computer, and place it immediately in your desktop published document!

Digital cameras work somewhat like the scanner operation detailed in Figure 15.6. Light enters the lens and a charge-coupled device (CCD) captures the image. The CCD is a computer chip of sorts with several layers that react to different features of light. As with the scanner, these electrons are passed to an analog-to-digital converter.

Different digital cameras offer various solutions for storing the digital image: direct transfer to the memory of a computer; internal memory to the camera; removable memory cards in the camera; or 3.5 inch floppy or other compact disc medium.

Typically the low-end digital cameras capture either 16-bit or 32-bit color images in a 640×480 format. You can usually choose the resolution size. The number of images you can capture depends on how much memory is provided internal to the camera and what resolution size you have selected. Removable memory cards or floppy diskettes allow you to capture a greater number of images. A basic digital camera will come with a built-in flash and an LCD display of some type so you can see the images without having to be connected to a computer. The camera may use the TWAIN software drivers, noted above, when connecting to your PC.

The more expensive cameras provide a larger resolution screen size, more memory for images, and special features like a zoom lens, color LCD viewing monitor, and large, removable memory cards for storage of images. Many companies traditionally known for their film cameras, including Agfa, Canon, Fuji, Kodak, Minolta, Nikon, Ricoh, Olympus, and Sony, produce a line of digital cameras. Figure 15.7 shows a digital still camera, the Minolta Dimage V with its distinctive detachable zoom lens, and a digital video camera, the Canon Optura.

Displays

You will be spending long hours in front of a computer screen whether you are doing desktop publishing or surfing the Internet. What your eyes see and how they feel after several hours of work is the primary test of a video display. We will briefly look at the various types of video displays, the critical subjective issues in picking a monitor that will wear well on your eyes, and the mechanical issues that explain how a video display draws your computer image on the screen. We will conclude this section with a discussion of issues related to video performance, and a look at flat-panel video technology.

Types and Sizes of Displays. Video monitors come in all shapes and sizes, from the old Macintosh classic 9-inch screen to the basic 15-inch color monitors up to the 21-inch and larger monitors. A 17-inch monitor is a popular size for most general computer work. The larger screen sizes give you lots of visual desktop space, with the 21-inch displays providing the equivalent of two complete 8.5×11 desktop-published pages of text and graphics. If you are desktop publishing large documents, composing large musical scores, or charting marching band performances, a display as large as 21 inches may be worth the extra cost to you.

Not too long ago, monitors came in monochrome (black and white), grayscale, and color. You have to look pretty hard to find anything other than color these days, because the cost of color displays has dropped so low. Color monitors are sometimes called RGB monitors because they work with three separate signals: red, green, and blue.

There also used to be a wide variety of video interfaces, cards, and cables for connecting your monitor to your computer, especially on Wintel computers. Today the video standards are simplified to only a few interface standards. VGA and SVGA are two key display systems for Wintel machines; Macintosh has its own video interface. There is a simple adapter for connecting an Apple Macintosh monitor to an SVGA Wintel computer, and likewise an adapter for connecting SVGA monitors to Macintosh video.

Subjective Factors. As your repertoire of computer software and music technology expands, you will be spending more and more time in front of a display screen. You will be reading lots of text on this display. Subjective factors include:

▶ focus and clarity

▶ brightness and contrast

▶ image fidelity and distortion

▶ color quality

▶ the layout of the screen and controls

The ultimate test is not the numbers for a display's specifications but your personal sense of look and feel after using the screen. So, be sure to try it before you buy it.

The Mechanics of a CRT. How does a video display work? The screen in a computer display or a TV set is the front of a large, glass cathode ray

Figure 15.8
(*a*) NEC's multisynch 17-inch CRT display
(Courtesy of NEC Technologies, Inc.)
(*b*)NEC's LCD flat screen
(Courtesy of NEC Technologies, Inc.)

(*a*)

(*b*)

tube (CRT) that tapers off toward the back. At the back of the CRT is an electron gun that aims a narrow beam of electrons at the screen. Phosphors on the screen glow when the beam strikes them. To create a complete image, the electron gun scans the complete screen starting at the top left, following a pattern of left to right and down. In Figure 15.9, the diagram in the lower right corner illustrates the path of the electron gun. A metal mask or grid of dots keeps the beams focused on the correct spot of phosphor.

To create a variety of colors, the CRT uses three primary colors—red, green, and blue (RGB)—each projected from one of three electron guns. As the guns scan the screen, they strike each of these three colors with varying intensities, and the mix of shades for red, green, and blue provide the color you see on the screen. This is known as *additive* color synthesis. When all three colors are at full intensity, you get the color white.

Scan rate. Note that the pattern in Figure 15.9 is *interlaced,* meaning that it scans the even-numbered lines and then the odd-numbered lines to draw and refresh the screen image. As the beam moves across and down the screen, it *rasters* the screen in lines. This procedure conforms to National Television Standards Committee (NTSC) specifications for 525-line frames that are drawn 60 times per second (60 Hz) in an interlaced pattern. The extent to which you can see the redrawing or *refreshing* of the screen is called *flicker.* You may not consciously see a 60-Hz refresh rate, but your eyes feel it.

Better quality video display monitors are *not* NTSC compatible, for good reason. Using faster refresh rates, a greater number of lines per frame, or no interlacing creates clearer, sharper video images that minimize flicker and reduce eye strain. A refresh rate nearer 72 Hz on video displays is kinder to your eyes and results in much less fatigue.

Most video monitors today are *multiscan* monitors. This is a type of monitor that can automatically adjust to the scan frequency of the video display board to which it is connected. Multiscan monitors give you much more flexibility and can display images based on almost any graphics dis-

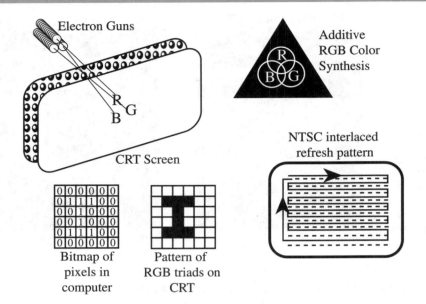

Figure 15.9
The inner workings of
color CRTs

A pixel is *not* the same as
the phosphorous dot
which the CRT makes
glow on the screen. Hun-
dreds of phosphorous dots
may make up one pixel,
and as you change the
pixel dimensions of your
screen or the pixel depth,
the number of phospho-
rous dots that make a
pixel also changes.

play system, including MDA, Hercules, EGA, VGA, XGA, SVGA, and Macintosh video. NEC's 17-inch multiscan monitor is shown in Figure 15.8*a*.

Key Factors Determining Image Quality. All video displays used with personal computers are graphics-based. In order to work in a world of the
graphical user interface and Windows, a display screen must operate on the
same concept of bitmaps as graphic imaging and printers do. In selecting a
monitor, the most basic issues are the screen area available (screen size),
how much memory is provided for video display (pixel density), how many
colors you want on the screen (pixel depth), and how fast the computer can
get the information displayed. These factors work together to deliver a nice,
crisp, readable image on your computer monitor.

Pixels. The basic visual unit in computer graphics is the picture element
or pixel. Each pixel represents one square or dot on the CRT screen. The
computer builds the image it wants to display in memory by creating a
binary *bitmap* of pixels that corresponds to the image as it is painted on the
CRT by the electron guns. This is illustrated in Figure 15.9 by a bitmap of
the letter *I* constructed on a screen. This technique is the same described
earlier for transferring a bitmapped image to a printer.

Pixel depth. The depth of a pixel is determined by how much information the computer stores for *each* pixel. The lowest depth is a 1-bit pixel, or
a black-and-white image, also known as a monochrome image. The only
information stored is whether the pixel is white or black, on or off. Pixel
depth can be increased to 16 colors with a 4-bit depth, 256 colors with an 8-
bit depth, 65,536 colors with a 16-bit depth, or millions of colors with a 24-
bit depth. If you look at your computer system's control panel for adjusting
the video display image, you will probably have some options for changing
the pixel depth of your video image, depending on how much video memory is in the computer.

Remember, resolution *density* refers to dots per inch (dpi) and *depth* to how many bits represent each dot.

Screen size and pixel density. The physical size of a display screen is the diagonal distance from the top left-hand corner to the bottom right-hand corner, e.g., 15 inches for a 15-inch monitor. However, not all of the screen space is used for the image, hence a 15-inch monitor may only use an area of 11.5×8.5-inch viewable space. That's the physical space used.

Within that physical space is the screen size as defined by the number of pixels across and down the screen space. This is the *pixel density* or the monitor's *resolution*. Generally monitors have 72 ppi or pixels per inch, some a little higher. On a 15-inch monitor, the largest pixel screen size may be 1024 × 768. On a larger, 21-inch monitor, the largest pixel screen size may be 1280 × 1024. Whether you call it a *dot* or a *pixel*, it refers to a logical point on a screen that is determined by the computer's software and by the video circuitry. A VGA video screen, for example, can have a size of 640×480 pixels, an SGVA video screen an 800×600 pixel screen size, and a Macintosh a video screen size of 832×624.

The screen size, like the pixel depth, is usually adjustable in software up to the amount of Video RAM or VRAM available. It is possible to stretch the screen sizes, given enough video memory, up to the screen's maximum pixel density, but this will have other, undesired effects: The text on the screen will be so small that you won't be able to read it!

Many word processors or DTP applications let you hide the graphics on the screen to increase performance speed while working with text.

Video Performance. Remember that these factors all interact with one another to determine video performance. Your computer interface has a finite amount of Video RAM (VRAM) to hold the bitmapped image to be displayed on the CRT screen. There is a limit to how fast the computer's video interface can send pixels to the display. As you increase the pixel depth from 4 to 24 bits, the computer has to use more VRAM for each pixel, so it has less memory for screen size. It may also take longer for it to display this picture.

With lots of text or music notation to move around, screen size will be at a premium; therefore, the lowest pixel depth possible may be the most efficient resolution. When color quality is more important than screen size, as it is in editing 24-bit color images with Photoshop, opt for a small screen size with full 24-bit color resolution.

A number of devices, including video accelerators and graphics DSP (digital signal processing) chips, enhance video performance, in addition to adding more VRAM. Video accelerators using graphic DSP chips are special video boards that add large amounts of VRAM and CPU processing as well. Adding a video accelerator is like adding a small microcomputer that does nothing but video tasks for your personal computer. Video accelerators are optimized for moving graphics information to the CRT device and for enhancing the speed of typical graphics operations like rotation, redrawing, and resizing where there are significant amounts of math computation involved. All these functions may be rolled into one single chip, called a *graphics DSP chip.*

Flat-Panel Display Alternatives. Not all computer video displays are based on the CRT design inherited from television. Some, especially the displays in laptop computers, use some form of flat-panel display technology.

Computer projectors for displaying images in a large room are also an important topic; see Module 24, where we discuss the features and alternatives for projection systems.

LCD or *liquid crystal display* flat-panel solutions are the same as those first used in digital watches. Present day LCD is known as active-matrix LCD, and full-color display is possible.

The LCD screen is a matrix of thousands of tiny rod-shaped crystal dots, and turning on a pattern of dots creates the image on the screen (with the addition of some form of backlighting to provide illumination). The scoreboard at a baseball or football game works in an analogous way.

Flat-panel displays are increasingly being used for desktop monitors as well. An NEC desktop flatpanel display is shown in Figure 15.8*b*. The latest flat-panel displays use a version of active-matrix technology called TFT or *thin film transistor* display. Incredible quality display resolution, comparable to 300 to 600 dpi of printer technology, is possible with TFTs. The color active matrix displays for computer desktops are now available in the 14- and 15-inch flat-panel sizes. A screen size of 1536×1024 with a TFT display provides some 6 million pixels for display, and the speed needed to refresh this screen size is considerably less than for the older CRT technology.

The cost of desktop flat-panel displays, however, still is significantly higher than that of CRTs. When manufacturing costs come down, the flat-panel technology may well replace the common 15-inch CRT video display used today.

Viewport IV | Summary

We have presented some basic information about how computers process words and graphic and introduced the broad category of Fill-Your-Own software. Musicians quickly discover that the same computer workstation and printer that helps with sequencing, printing, and studying music can also process letters, papers, grant applications, concert programs, and teaching materials. In fact, many musicians may have first purchased computer equipment for word and graphics processing only to discover music applications later.

Most people have discovered the flexibility, speed, and features of word processing. Perhaps less obvious, however, are the graphics software programs that we found so useful in producing pictures for the newsletter. This graphics software can be used for creating interesting concert program covers, posters that advertise events, and visual aids for instruction.

Besides the obvious practical payoffs that this viewport presents for day-to-day work, there were a few overarching conceptual lessons to be learned. These topics not only help us summarize the important content of this viewport, but they also lay a foundation for what is to come.

Levels of Software

In assembling a desktop publishing system, we are confronted with many levels of sophistication in both word-processing and graphics software. Word processors range from simple text editors to powerful programs with advanced features. Simple text editors are cheap and effective at doing quick memos or at reading documentation but are of less help with projects like a newsletter. High-end programs offer wonderful support for footnotes, indexes, tables of contents, and grammar checking; these options may be useful for large-scale projects like books and major research articles, but they are overkill for many projects.

A similar situation exists on the graphics side. Simple draw and paint programs can be found for working with black-and-white or simple color images. At the other extreme, we noted several advanced graphics titles that allow special features like charcoal drawing, smudging, and shadowing effects.

263

Our choice was to work with software that offered a reasonable compromise in word-processing and graphics features. Given our need to create a newsletter that required some layout of text and graphics, and our hope of setting up a database of addresses, we opted for an integrated package that had word processing, graphics, spreadsheet, database, and communications capability. As our comfort with technology grows and our budget changes, we may move to more powerful software, and hardware to support it. For right now, a midlevel approach seems in order.

The important lesson here is to balance the levels of software complexity against the needs of the task at hand. There is little sense in buying an expensive carbon-fiber touring bicycle if you are only riding it to work once a week! We will see this balance at work in each of the remaining viewports.

Bitmapped and Object-Oriented Graphics

In Modules 13 and 14 we presented the important topic of bitmapped and object-oriented graphics. There is probably no other issue in digital graphics more fundamental than this one. We created both kinds of graphics in the newsletter example and learned that they play an important role in font technology as well.

We choose paint as a mode for original art when we want absolute control over each pixel. Like the medieval trumpet in the newsletter, graphics of this sort often require special shading, coloring, or other nuances that paint programs do beautifully. We also deal with pixels when we work with scanned photos such as the lute in the newsletter. More advanced image-processing software is used to work with these images, but the concept of pixel control remains the same.

We used an object approach for original art when the image was more of a line drawing, like the organ. Object-oriented software becomes especially useful if we have to create repetitive elements in an illustration. The ability to more effectively resize and print on different quality printers is an important consideration. As we have noted, music notation software uses a object-oriented approach for exactly these reasons. Software packages with both drawing and painting approaches are now available, but each has its own strengths. We will likely need to move from this integrated software approach to a dedicated graphics program at some point in the future.

The distinction between bitmapped and outline fonts becomes important for us as we print the final newsletter. Object-oriented or outline fonts offer the most flexibility for excellent printing and screen images.

Conventions

You discovered a few conventions that, when followed, resulted in fewer problems. With word processing documents, the ruler provides important options for controlling the behavior of text characters. The use of tabs rather than spaces created with the space bar makes a big difference in the consistency of the printed page when variables like fonts or margins change. Hard returns should be avoided within a paragraph.

Graphics software offers similar sets of conventions, often tied to the nature of the bitmapped or object-oriented approach itself. For instance, with bitmapped painted images, you immediately discovered that working in a magnified view was frequently necessary for careful editing. With object-oriented graphics, choosing objects to move about within the layer approach provided certain challenges for the handling of the mouse.

Each kind of software program has a set of procedures particular to it. Learning to work in graphics, music notation, or multimedia applications requires time to learn the conventions of the software data structures and the hardware on which it operates.

Features

Closely related to conventions are feature sets. You discovered quite early that software packages have sets of features that save time and allow for customization. In word processing, some of these include the ability to define style settings for paragraphs, hidden characters that control text flow, definable menus, multiple ways to view a page, defining sections, and creating tables.

In graphics software, we noted certain similarities between painting and drawing tools, even though the images being created by the tools are represented internally in quite a different way. For example, pencil, line, and shape tools are quite similar and act predictably. Fills within spaces, line characteristics, text insertion and formatting, selection and duplication, rotation, flipping, and zooming in and out all behave in a similar way in both paint and draw programs.

Of course, a number of other features, particularly more advanced ones, are peculiar to each specific software program, but the point is that a person develops certain expectations with experience.

We will discover similar functions in music sequencing and notation software as well. In fact, many of the techniques developed with word processing and graphics software are applicable to music software, including:

► Cutting and pasting

► Deleting

► Choosing

► Moving and selecting

► Font and font attributes

► Object selection

► Custom style groups

► Options

► Preferences

► Printing controls

Resolution and Depth: Hardware Issues

The concepts of resolution and depth are mentioned in several viewports, and they appear here in our descriptions of printers, scanners, and displays.

You have a small budget, so you must look for the best compromise between cost and quality. As far as the computer itself is concerned, you can take just about any PC that has a reasonable amount of memory, CPU speed, and disk storage and upgrade it to a desktop publishing workstation with the addition of a printer, scanner, and perhaps an enhanced display. A digital camera will also come in handy.

Choices for this peripheral equipment, however, require careful consideration in terms of resolution and depth. For instance, resolution for printers is important for black-and-white printing. Depth applies if color or grayscale printing is required. After considering all the options, you will probably decide on at least a 600-dpi, grayscale laser printer with PostScript capability. This may cost a little more than you want to pay, but the advantages for printing your scanned photos, original art, music notation, and text will be great. You will also need to be sure that the software and hardware you choose support each other.

For scanners and displays, depth has to do most directly with the presence or absence of color and grayscale. Most affordable scanners will allow grayscale and color up to at least 24 bits. You will definitely want this capability. Because the newsletter will be reproduced on black and white equipment, color is not too important to you, but grayscale is. Nearly all displays sold today will support grayscale and color. More important is the size of the screen area. A 17-, 19-, or 21-inch display will provide more area to see your work. Larger displays are very useful for newsletter production and for working with music scores!

File Formats and Integrating Music Notation

We come face-to-face again with the importance of understanding file formats. For text, the situation is relatively simple. But for graphics, the options are much more complex. You will likely decide to work with PICT, TIFF, and EPS file formats if you are working on the Macintosh. They print well on your PostScript printer and can be resized as necessary. Should you work in the Windows environment, you would use CGM, WMF, TIFF, or EPS file formats for graphics. If you want to stick to the cross-platform, industry standards, use TIFF for bitmap images and EPS for object-oriented graphics.

This is important for integrating music notation into documents like your newsletter. The concepts of importing files created by another program and of exporting files created by one program into another are important here. As you edit your newsletter using files submitted to you from others, you must be aware of what can be handled. For example, are you able to use a WordPerfect word processing file in native format or must you ask that it be in text-only (ASCII) form? How about a Finale music notation file as opposed to an EPS version? You must inform your contributors about which file formats you can use, given the desktop publishing system you have.

Armed with the information covered here, you should be on your way to a new level of professional productivity. Your desktop publishing system is matched to your needs as you make the transition away from typewriters and file cards. Now, where did you leave that sackbut . . .

Supplementary Readings

Campbell, Alastair. *The New MacDesigner's Handbook* (2nd edition). Philadelphia: Running Press, 1997.

Ihrig, Sybil, and Emil Ihrig. *Scanning the Professional Way.* Berkeley, Calif.: Osborne Books, 1995.

Joyce, Jerry and Moon, Marianne. *Microsoft Word 97 At a Glance.* Redmond, Wash.: Microsoft Press, 1997.

McClelland, Deke. *Macworld Photoshop 4 Bible* and *Photoshop 4 for Windows 95 Bible.* Foster City, Calif.: IDG Books, 1997.

Meehan, Tim. *Introducing Desktop Prepress.* New York: MIS Press, 1995.

Murray, James, and William VanRyper. *Encyclopedia of Graphic File Formats* (2nd edition). Sebastopol, Calif.: O'Reilly & Associates. Inc., 1996.

Robinette, Michelle. *The Clarisworks Reference for Teachers* (2nd edition). Foster City, Calif.: IDG Books Worldwide, Inc., 1997.

Spiekermann, Erik, and E. M. Ginger. *Stop Stealing Sheep and Find Out How Type Works.* Mountain View, Calif: Adobe Press, 1993.

Schwartz, Steven. *Macworld ClarisWorks Office Bible.* Foster City, Calif.: IDG Books Worldwide, Inc., 1998.

Williams, Robin. *Beyond The Mac is Not a Typewriter.* Berkeley, Calif.: Peachpit Press, 1996.

Viewport V

Music Notation

We need a way of getting music read automatically for machine use rather than first translating into an input language. . . . It seems to be perfectly within the possibilities of today's techniques. . . . Such an optical reader would read the whole process. . . . You could have an entire repertoire stored in the memory of the machine.

—Arthur Mendel at the first symposium on Musicology
and the Computer (1965)

Any music notation program that thinks it can tell what its users *really* want is going to do them a lot of favors they would have been better off without.

—Donald Byrd (author of Nightingale), in
Yavelow's *Music and Sound Bible* (1992)

Overview

This viewport is the second in our series dealing with Fill-Your-Own software applications. Here our focus is on desktop music publishing and music notation. Music notation software is represented by a large number of titles across various computer platforms, with capabilities ranging from freeform graphics programs that do not use MIDI to sophisticated MIDI-based applications that use traditional notation rules. We present the features of MIDI-based notation programs using illustrations from a wide selection of software. In the data module we present a historical perspective of music notation devices and computer coding systems for music. We then discuss data structures for representing music in a computer, making an important distinction between coding for performance and coding for display. The viewport concludes with a glimpse at traditional and alternative hardware for entry of music notation. In this viewport we will:

▶ Place music notation software in context with sequencing and digital audio software, and give an introduction to the full scope of music production software

▶ Examine strategies for the design of computer notation software: entry systems, rules and control of notation, layout and format, playback options through MIDI, and printing and file output

▶ Study the features of notation software

▶ Provide illustrations from commercial software to demonstrate common features as well as more advanced, specialized features

▶ Recommend a sequence for preparing a desktop notation project: note entry, editing, and printing

▶ Provide a historical perspective for music notation devices and coding systems for music

▶ Study ways of representing notation in a computer for performing and displaying music

▶ Expand our treatment of font technology and provide important tips for music printing

▶ Describe new efforts to define a standard file format for notation

▶ Review hardware devices for note entry, including new experimental systems

HISTORICAL TIMELINE
The Technology of Music Notation

1800 BC	A human song, apparently about love among the Gods, is the earliest known music notation
100 AD	Oldest known Chinese music notation
1400s	Earliest appearance of mensural notation and the first printed music
1500s	Ottaviano dei Petrucci, the "Gutenberg of music printing," prints first music with movable type
1550s	Round notes appear in music notation and music is printed in one single-impression printing
1690s	Beaming (new tied notes) appears in music typography
1750s	Mosaic music fonts developed by Breitkopf in Leipzig become standard for music typography
1810s	First music boxes, with music coded as metal pins on cylinders
1850s	The pianola (player piano) uses music coded as hole punches on paper rolls
1880s	First successful commercial music typewriter (Tachigrafo Musicale) by Angelo Tessaro
1890s	Music for the calliope is coded as punched holes on metal discs
1920s	Walton invents music typewriter with transposing key and printing of instrumental parts
1950s	Max Mathews develops the first computer music language (MUSIC 1) at Bell Labs, using holes in computer punch cards (later versions at Princeton, MIT, and Stanford)
	Commercially successful Musicwriter invented by Cecil Effinger
1960s	MUSICOMP composition language developed for Lejaren Hiller's IBM 7090 computer at the University of Illinois
	Barry Brook devises the Plaine and Easie Code notation system for music cataloging, using a single-line, ASCII code
	The graphic input computer is built at Bell Labs and used for drawing and editing scores
	Classic paper by Mathews and Moore, "Pitch Quantizing for Computer Music" (1965), related to graphic input of music notation
	First symposium on computers and musicology is held, *Musicology and the Computer I and II*
	MUSTRAN music analysis language developed by Jerome Winkler as a comprehensive text-based coding system, including non-Western music
	Photon is used for music printing with a rotating disc of symbols projected on film

	DARMS (Digital Alternate Representation of Musical Scores) developed by Stefan Bauer-Mengelberg for computer-based music printing
	Leland Smith of Stanford develops SCORE notation software as a score preprocessor for Music 10 (based on Music 4)
1970s	Structured Sound Synthesis Project developed by William Buxton (University of Toronto) uses computer graphics for score manipulation with digitizing tablet and a slider box for note entry
	MUSICOMP dedicated computer-based music typesetter developed by Armando dal Molin, using Photon for printing
	Notation software (later called "Lime") developed by the CERL group at the University of Illinois for the PLATO system
	First consumer music composing software appears for PCs: Micro Music's Music Composer and ALF's software for the Apple II
	John Maxwell and Severo Ornstein develop Mockingbird music notation software at Xerox PARC; precursor to later notation software
1980s	First popular laser printers appear with the Hewlett-Packard LaserJet printer and Apple LaserWriter
	Passport's Polywriter introduced as an early PC-based notation software using a combination of keyboard input and graphic editing
	Jack Jarrett's Music Printer Plus, starting on the Apple II and then the IBM PC, is one of the first widely used notation programs for the PC
1985	Deluxe Music Construction Set (DMCS) by Geoff Brown is the first commercially popular music notation software for the Macintosh
	Leland Smith's SCORE software adapted to IBM PC
	Synclavier music notation software provides professional music printing using laser printers
	Personal Composer by Jim Miller is the first widely used sequencer/notation program for the IBM PC
	Mark of the Unicorn's Professional Composer is the first serious notation software for Macintosh using a graphic-editing system
	Adobe's Sonata, the most widely used music font, developed by Cleo Huggins
	ENIGMA notation engine developed by Phil Farrand and Tim Strathlee of Opus Dei, and used for Coda's Finale notation software
	CERL's LIME notation software adapted to Macintosh
	Coda's Finale notation and composing software becomes first professional integrated sequencing and notation software for the PC
1990s	Musicware/TAP's Nightingale music notation software developed by Donald Byrd and others for the Macintosh as graphic-based music notation and composing system to rival Coda's Finale
1995	Optical character recognition for music using common graphic scanners becomes an option for entering notation with software like MidiScan
	Notation windows appear within sequencing programs starting with Mark of the Unicorn's Performer and Steinberg's Cubase
	Notation Interchange File Format or NIFF is defined by an industry group to create a universal notation file format to make it easier to collaborate on notation projects across competing applications
	Plug-in technology that makes it easy to add special, customized features comes to notation software like Finale 98
	Sibelius notation software, adapted for Macintosh and Wintel from the Acorn computer, presents a commercial challenge to Finale.
2000	Printing on demand comes to the Internet; browse the scores on-line and purchase and print what you like

THE PEOPLE

Stevie Wonder at his Bösendorfer MIDI Grand with Henry Panion (Courtesy of Marc Bondarendo, Bondarenko Photography, Birmingham, Ala., and the University of Alabama)

REAL-WORLD PROFILE: DR. HENRY PANION, III

Role: Composer, arranger, and college music professor and administrator

Dr. Panion is professor of music and chair of the music department at the University of Alabama at Birmingham. Since 1992, he has served as conductor and arranger for superstar Stevie Wonder and has led his performances and recordings with many of the world's most notable orchestras, including the Royal Philharmonic, Boston Pops, Bolshoi Theatre Orchestra, and the Tokyo Philharmonic. Dr. Panion's own works for orchestra have been performed by such orchestras as the San Francisco Symphony, Cleveland Symphony Orchestra, National Symphony, and the Detroit Symphony. His work has produced two Grammy Awards, two Dove Awards, and a host of other national music awards and nominations. He uses Macintosh computers extensively with his composing and arranging. When he's on the road he has a Mac laptop loaded with Finale, Freestyle, Performer, AOL, Netscape, and Word, along with a small printer and portable MIDI gear.

Interview

What do you do as a musician? I am the head of the music department at the University of Alabama-Birmingham (UAB) as well as professor of music. I serve as director of UAB Entertainment!, a university-run record label. And, I also work with Stevie Wonder as an arranger and conductor. My arrangements have won two Grammy Awards. The Winans album "Let My People Go" won Gospel Album of the Year and Gospel Song of the Year. Stevie Wonder's "For Your Love" from *Conversation Peace* won R & B song of the year. I served as arranger on both recordings.

How did you become interested in computers and music technology? I've been using computers to score my music since the mid-80s. It was during this time that commercial software and hardware became available that enabled individuals to print professional looking scores. As much as I love the process of composing music, I've never enjoyed

copying parts. There was one particular event that really got me using the first computer notation software at this time. I was a graduate student at Ohio State and in need of extra change in my pocket. The James Cleveland Gospel Workshop is a big national event and gospel choirs come from all over the country. Some really talented arrangers for gospel music would bring their scores to the workshop to be read, but the notation was pretty bad. They were self-taught musicians who did most of their work by ear. So I started earning really good money using my computer and my musical training to clean up their music, making it look really professional!

How does someone get to be an arranger and conductor for someone like Stevie Wonder? Could you do this gig without the aid of technology? Stevie is considered a pioneer in field of music technology. He was one of the first major artists to use synthesizers heavily in his recordings. Stevie had heard about my arrangements and compositions for orchestras and was familiar with some work I had done on the Quincy Jones–produced project "Let My People Go" by the Winans. Without question, if I didn't have the help of computer tools for notation and sequencing, it would be next to impossible for me to compose, arrange, orchestrate, and then, produce the parts within the short time frame that is required in this industry, and, at the same time, maintain the level of quality that is absolutely necessary. I may have to produce a new arrangement for Stevie, on the road, literally overnight!

What computers do you use? Macs, Macs, and more Macs (and my PalmPilot that is always with me!).

What ways do you use computers and music technology? Every aspect of my musical activity involves using computers, from using spreadsheets, databases, word processors and contact managers to run the music department, to using software for authoring, CAI, and notation and sequencing for teaching theory, composing and arranging, and multimedia production.

Do you actually do arranging with a computer on the road? A lot of my arranging for Stevie is done on the road. I remember one of our tours to Japan, the one in which we recorded the album *Natural Wonder*. An auto manufacturer had begun to use Stevie's "Stay Gold" in a commercial. By the time we got to Japan the song had become a hit. One day before the show (after the rehearsals with the orchestra were completed) Stevie said, "I have this idea. Let's perform this tomorrow night with the orchestra." So, I arranged it. We rehearsed it at sound check and performed it that night. That tune has become one of my favorites from the *Natural Wonder* CD. Most importantly, if necessary, the technology allows me the opportunity to preview all my arrangements, visually and aurally, before printing and rehearsing with the orchestra.

When you travel with Stevie Wonder, what kind of software and hardware do you take on the road with you? I have put together what must be the most powerful and smallest rig known. It includes a Mac laptop loaded with Finale, Freestyle, Performer, AOL, Netscape, and Word. Then add an Apple portable Stylewriter printer, Novation 2-octave controller, Yamaha MU-5 tone module, Acoustic Research "palm size" speaker, Fostex MNO6 mini-6-channel mixer, Sony TCD-D7 DAT Recorder, and a Panasonic SL-S170 portable CD. Then throw in an assortment of cables, MIDI interfaces (including one that is 1.5 inches in diameter that I found in Australia), and I believe every adapter that Radio Shack makes. All of this fits into an Anvil case I had designed that's only 27 inches wide, 16 inches tall, 13 inches deep. Believe me!

Are there times when the computer and the notation software get in the way of your composing or arranging? Some fairly successful attempts are being made to have notation and sequencing software interpret meaning over action in notation. One example of this is Mark of the Unicorn's FreeStyle. While I can't imagine giving up the power, sophistication, and flexibility of Finale, transcription algorithms in FreeStyle (and now in Performer 6.0) are far superior—in fact, they are amazing. This is the direction I feel all software development should take.

If you could change one thing about how computers are used, what it would be? From a pedagogical point of view, the computer is only a tool. While it can serve to enhance one's musicianship, it cannot take its place. Just because the combination of the tuba and oboe patch seems to work well on the 2-inch internal speaker of your computer, this doesn't mean it will work with a full orchestra performing on a concert stage.

The one most significant change 10 years from now? The particular software and hardware one uses will not matter. Cross-platforming will be as seamless as driving different cars.

One word of advice you could offer musicians interested in computers? Be prepared to devote yourselves to a lifetime of learning.

<table>
<tr><td>**Module**
16</td><td># Music Notation Software</td></tr>
</table>

As we start this music notation software module, let's consider the broader picture of music production software that encompasses notation, sequencing, and digital sound sampling. Viewports V, VI, and VII will deal with each of these approaches to music software separately, but there are important reasons to start with a more unified view.

Music Production Software: The Big Picture

Return to this section at the start of Modules 19 and 23.

Music notation software begins with the assumption that your main goal is a score: a written representation of your music. This software supports the printing of full scores, individual parts, lead sheets, jazz charts, and other printed material. Sound capabilities are very handy to have, but that's not the main focus.

Sequencing and sound sampling software, however, have sound as their main focus. In sequencing, the power of MIDI codes is used to create sound files that can be played and refined. Sampling software allows for the digitization of live performances in real time and provides several ways to process the sound.

These basic approaches to the creation and representation of music are not exclusive; in fact, the tendency in the last few years has been for software companies to merge the capabilities of each approach as computers become more powerful. There is no single product that "does it all," although some come close.

Table 16.1 shows many music production software titles that are representative of these basic approaches. You can see how many of them have capabilities that run across at least two of these three categories. Software is listed alphabetically within each category, except where it makes sense to include a program with its "family." Notice that we have shaded some of the software titles to indicate these families of products from one company. For example, G-VOX Entertainment (formally Passport Designs) has three levels of their notation software product, each offering different feature sets.

In this Table, we divided the software into three categories, basic, midlevel, and advanced:

▶ "Basic" means that the software provides entry-level capabilities. For example, basic sequencing capabilities for music notation software would mean that you could create tracks of MIDI data that would be used as a way to enter note values. Basic notation capabilities for sequencing software would mean that traditional notation is provided as a way to view the MIDI data.

▶ "Midlevel" means, in addition to the basic functions, that there are quite powerful, near-professional level features. For instance, midlevel sampling capabilities in sequencing software means that not only can you add digital recordings, but you can also process these digital tracks by moving segments of the audio data around or editing those data. Mixing the balances of both digital audio and MIDI may be possible. You might also be able to apply some software-based, digital sound processing for a reverb effect or for moving a sound from the left to the right stereo speaker (panning).

▶ "Advanced" means that the level of sophistication for notation, sequencing, and sampling is appropriate for professional work and represents "state-of-the-art" for that category. Advanced-level sequencing software, for example, might include unlimited tracks, special manipulation possibilities for MIDI data, and the ability to edit the data in real time without interrupting the music performance.

The Music Notation Scene

Just as word processors and graphics software have changed the way writers and artists work, music notation software has changed the work of musicians. Perhaps no other software development has touched the lives of so many musicians, whether they be jazz, rock, pop, folk, or classical composers, arrangers, performers, educators, theorists, or historians. Nearly 50 notation titles exist today, written for nearly every kind of computer on the market. Even more are being planned as you read these words.

Why is this so? Western culture has always valued written music, from the earliest examples of Gregorian chant to the more recent music of Pierre Boulez and Garth Brooks. Composers and arrangers use notation to represent their musical thinking for performers to recreate. Educators, theorists, and historians constantly use notation in their work to help illustrate creative ideas about music.

This emphasis on written symbols has certainly ensured that the record of music creativity is preserved and celebrated in study and performance, but it also has introduced a number of nonmusical problems. Chief among these is the tedium of writing scores and parts, the chance for errors in notation and transposition, unreadable manuscripts, and major expenditures of time and money that might be better spent in other ways. Technology offers an attractive solution to these problems, while providing the contemporary musician with new tools for the creative process.

The Ultimate Notation Technology? Well, Not Quite Yet. Arthur Mendel's statement, quoted at the beginning of this viewport, suggested that, in 1965, technology would soon permit the input of music codes by directly scanning a sheet of music. Perhaps you have seen this process done with words to

Table 16.1. Music Production Software—Support for Notation, Sequencing, and Sampling

Product	Company	Platform	VP	Notation			Sequencing			Sampling		
				A	M	B	A	M	B	A	M	B
ConcertWare	JUMP! Music	Mac/Win	V		x				x			
Desktop Sheet Music	Midisoft	Win	V		x				x			
Music Time	G-VOX	Mac/Win	V			x			x			
Rhapsody	G-VOX	Mac/Win	V		x				x			
Encore	G-VOX	Mac/Win	V	x					x			
Finale	Coda	Mac/Win	V	x					x			
Music Maid	Signature	Mac	V		x							
Nightingale	Musicware	Mac	V	x					x			
Scorewriter	Cakewalk Music	Mac/Win	V		x				x			
Overture	Cakewalk Music	Mac/Win	V	x					x			
Personal Composer	Personal Composer	Win	V		x				x			
SongWorks	Ars Nova	Mac	V		x				x			
SpeedScore	Fred Noad	Mac	V		x							
QuickScore Elite	Sion	Win	V		x				x			
Score	San Andreas	Win	V		x				x			
Sibelius VMP	Sibelius	Mac/Win	V	x					x			
Home Studio	Cakewalk Music	Win	VI	x				x				x
Professional	Cakewalk Music	Win	VI	x			x				x	
Pro Audio	Cakewalk Music	Win	VI			x	x			x		
Cubasis AV	Steinberg	Mac/Win	VI	x				x				x
Cubase VST	Steinberg	Mac/Win	V			x	x			x		
Cubase Score	Steinberg	Mac/Win	VI	x			x			x		
Digital Orchestra Plus	Voyetra	Win	VI			x		x				x
Digital Orchestra Pro	Voyetra	Win	VI			x	x				x	
FreeStyle	MOTU	Mac/Win	VI			x		x				
MicroLogic	Emagic	Mac/Win	VI	x					x			
Logic Audio Discovery	Emagic	Mac/Win	VI	x			x				x	
Logic	Emagic	Mac/Win	VI	x			x					
Logic Audio	Emagic	Mac/Win	VI	x			x				x	
MasterTraks Pro	G-VOX	Mac/Win	VI				x					
Metro	Cakewalk Music	Mac	VI					x			x	
Musicator Win	Musicator	Win	VI	x			x					x
Performer	MOTU	Mac	VI		x		x					x
Digital Performer	MOTU	Mac	VI				x				x	
PowerTracks ProAudio	PG Software	Win	VI			x		x			x	
Musicshop	Opcode	Mac/Win	VI			x		x				
Vision	Opcode	Mac/Win	VI				x				x	
Studio Vision Pro	Opcode	Mac/Win	VI				x			x		
Cool Edit	Syntrillium	Win	VII								x	
Deck II	BIAS	Mac	VII						x		x	
Peak LE	BIAS	Mac	VII								x	
Peak	BIAS	Mac	VII							x		
SAW	Innovative	Win	VII								x	
SAW32	Innovative	Win	VII							x		
Samplitude Studio	SEK'D	Win	VII							x		
Sound Designer II	Digidesign	Mac	VII							x		
Sound Forge XP	Sonic Foundry	Win	VII								x	
Sound Forge	Sonic Foundry	Win	VII							x		
SoundEdit 16	Macromedia	Mac	VII								x	
WaveLab	Steinberg	Win	VII							x		

x, level of support; A, advanced; M, midlevel; B, basic

create text files and assume that it surely must be possible today with music. In Christopher Yavelow's writings on music technology, he has suggested that WYPWYP, or "What You Play Is What You Print," is an ultimate goal for music notation from live performance. You may have seen something like this done in a music software demo at a music store or at a conference. You may have also seen or read about attempts to create commercial sheet music kiosks that allow you to pick the music you want from a selection described on a screen and then have it instantly printed in the key and arrangement you select!

If you are only casually familiar with music technology, it may be tempting for you to think that we are able to scan written music into sound, create accurate scores directly from live performance, and manipulate written music at the touch of a key. Many advances toward these goals have been made as this century ends, but we are not quite there with 100-percent accuracy.

Why not? The answer lies in the enormous complexity of these tasks. As you will soon see, data structures that are necessary to represent accurate music notation and subtle, time-sensitive performance data are difficult to harness in software in ways that are required by the professional musician. As an example, imagine the machine intelligence and raw power necessary to (a) record complex MIDI data generated by a composer playing a keyboard in real time; (b) sort out and reconstruct this information so that individual streams of symbols can be assigned; and (c) display these symbols as quickly as possible on the screen while accounting for subtle changes in time and performance style that may or may not have been intended.

There are hundreds of nuances in the human experience of performance and notation that our brains process instantly but that are extremely difficult for machines to process correctly. It is a wonder that we have come so far in the last few years—a real tribute to the software engineers whose work we now address more carefully.

You may have already noticed some impressive characteristics just by casually observing the work of others using notation software:

▶ Notation can be entered by several methods, including real-time entry with a music keyboard

▶ Powerful editing and layout capabilities can save precious time and money

▶ Scores can be played back by MIDI instruments with realistic timbres, often in musical ways, so that errors can be caught. This "proof-hearing" capability alone seems well worth the investment of time and money

▶ The printed quality of the scores is excellent and so, too, are the printed parts

▶ Because notation programs can save files in the Standard MIDI File (SMF) format, these files can be exchanged between different programs and across the Internet for collaborative work.

You have also heard a few negative grumblings from these same people. They complain about long learning times for some software, tedious editing, slow printing for scores and parts, graphic elements in the score that don't

Be sure to read Module 17 on data structures to help grasp the concepts discussed here.

Si dedero

Jacobus obrecht

Venice, 1508

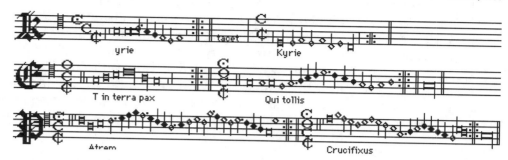

(*a*) Chant example produced by computer

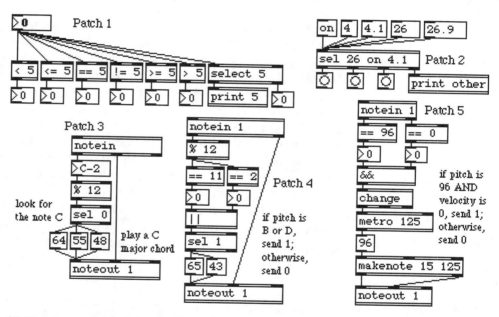

Figure 16.1
Examples of
nontraditional notation

(*b*) Diagram score produced with Max (Opcode Systems [Mac])

work just right, unmusical MIDI playback with some software, and the inevitable computer crashes and data loss. All this is true to some extent, but the advantages far outweigh the occasional problems, as most experienced users will argue.

Traditional versus Nontraditional Notation. This module is concerned with conventional music notation, but some mention should be made of music symbol systems that are not so conventional. Figure 16.1 displays music fragments, one quite old and the other quite new. Each uses symbol systems that are not traditional, but each is supported by music technology. The piece of chant uses an early form of our current notation system and is produced here by a special software program designed for printing this type of music.

You may not be interested in alternative notation schemes for work right now, but you may be in the future. There are certain well-known problems with traditional notation, and other approaches may well develop in generations to come.

The other example looks much more foreign to our eyes, but represents sound nonetheless. It comes from a software program designed to represent music gestures as *objects* that can be manipulated, linked, and transformed. Named after Max Mathews, the distinguished music engineer featured in Viewport VII, the Max program takes an alternative approach to score production by using very different graphic symbols and arranging them in very different ways. Admittedly, you can't "read" this notation and internally hear the sounds the way that you can with traditional notation; however, we include it here as an example of a system of representation that is different from our traditional one. We will present more information about Max in Module 19.

To MIDI or Not to MIDI. The vast majority of music printing software does support MIDI, allowing musicians to use instruments such as MIDI keyboards and wind controllers to enter music and to hear the score played. Many packages allow the importing and exporting of standard MIDI files (SMF) as well. To many musicians, this is a major advantage for entering music and for hearing its realization for editing purposes. Table 16.1 reinforces this by showing the number of notation programs that include sequencing options for note entry.

However, such capabilities may not always be needed. For instance, musicians who want to have complete control of the graphic appearance of the music by using the mouse to click and drag elements into precise alignment would have little interest in MIDI options for music entry. Figure 16.2 displays Music Maid, a utility that allows the construction of musical examples. Here, we have constructed a task for a person to complete using the tools provided by the program. There is no playback of sound offered by programs like this one, but sound might not be of interest to those primarily concerned with graphic issues. Music Maid has built-in support for the con-

Figure 16.2
Music Maid
(Signature Music Software [Mac])

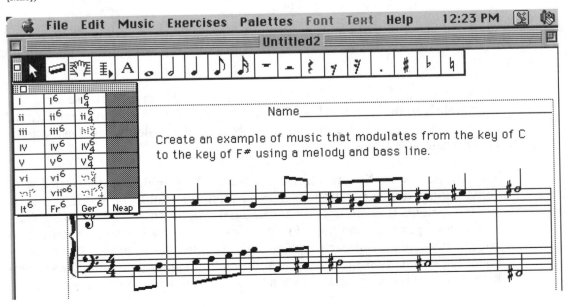

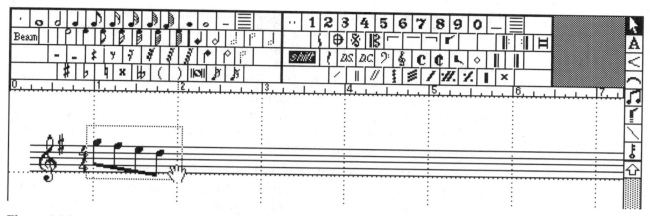

Figure 16.3
SpeedScore
(Frederick Noad [Mac])

Refer back to Modules 11 and 12 for a review of MIDI and MIDI equipment.

struction of exercises most appropriate for instructional settings, but we include it here because it does provide relatively flexible scoring options for a wide variety of uses.

Another example of this kind of notation software is SpeedScore (Figure 16.3). Here, the author has provided a more complex palette of notation symbols which can be easily moved into place to exact locations for the creation of scores. SpeedScore is especially good for rendering guitar music and tablature.

Total Freedom, Strict Rules, or Something In-between? Directly related to the MIDI support question is whether a package conforms to a rule structure. SpeedScore, for example, is a program that is completely free of internal rules that guide note entry. The person using the program must specify each graphic event. This has the advantage of putting a person completely in charge of the score, but it increases the likelihood that extensive work will be tedious and repetitive.

Most music notation software available today takes the opposite approach, providing us with rule structures that automate note entry. For instance, a music notation program might (a) look for consecutive eighth notes and automatically beam them; (b) keep track of the number of beats in a measure and alert the musician in some way about a possible error; or (c) position note stems in the proper direction. Such rule systems work in tandem with MIDI note entry and playback as well.

You will likely choose to use one of these rule-based programs for your first major experience with notation software largely because of the time that it can save. It's important for you, though, to find a program that will allow rules to be turned off, because there will always be occasions when this will be necessary. This is especially true for placement of graphic elements like articulations and dynamic markings. It's fine for a program to make its most intelligent guess about such placements, but the ultimate power to make these decisions must be left in the hands of the musician. Early examples of music notation software rarely allowed this, but many of today's high-end programs allow for rule-based features to be turned off and on as needed.

Music Context: Just What Do You Need, Anyway? As with other software discussed in this book, no one product is perfect for all situations. If you are interested in writing lead sheets for printing songs, an expensive notation package that offers over a hundred staves per system and extensive MIDI channel assignment for playback makes no sense. Similarly, if you are interested in writing jazz charts for Saturday night's gig, or studio music that will be read only once or twice, it is unlikely you will need a program that is designed to produce engraved-quality manuscript for publication. Here are a few context issues to consider:

▶ *Numbers of staves.* The full-featured programs like QuickScore Elite and Finale offer almost unlimited options for staves and systems. If you only need a few staves of music within each system, consider a program like Songworks or Music Time. These packages may provide all the power and elegance needed, while offering features for special needs like song writing, jazz charting, or single-line excerpts for exporting notation into word-processing files.

▶ *Engraving quality and special effects.* Music is read in different contexts, and the need for graphic quality varies greatly. Programs like Overture, Nightingale, and Sibelius VMP offer power over the spacing between graphic elements, tuplet schemes (an uneven number of notes, such as a triplet, played in the space usually taken by an even time value), beaming, complex key and metric combinations, and other special requirements that are necessary for the highest standards of traditional notation. These programs often provide special tools to generate and save custom graphics that many contemporary concert music scores require. If you don't need this level of power, however, you may find the program cumbersome and too complex for quickly generating legible scores and parts.

▶ *Text, lyrics, and chord symbols.* Most programs offer some sort of text and lyric insertion, but there is a wide range of techniques used. If the music context requires a large amount of text material, especially lyrics that are tied to notes, this might have a profound effect on your choice of program. Finale, for example, offers several approaches to lyric insertion, including the use of a word processor. In certain music contexts, chord symbols and even guitar fret notations are necessary. G-VOX's Encore supports both chords and frets, but other programs may not offer both.

▶ *Part extraction.* In some contexts, creation of separate parts from a score is a must. Although most notation packages support part extraction (there are some notable exceptions), there is a wide difference in how this is handled. For instance, Finale and Nightingale not only print parts but also create separate files for each part so that special editing can be done if needed. These programs also combine measures of rests so that the resulting parts look more professional. Many other programs simply print out the parts directly and include repeated measures of rests.

▶ *Logic in design.* Finally, consider the logic of how the software is designed. Does it seem to be comfortable to use after you have learned most of its design features? Do you constantly need to refer to documentation to perform standard operations? Does the software seem comfortable to use? Does it make sense?

Many companies provide free or inexpensive demo copies of software for trial use.

Cost and Learning Curve. Musicians also need to consider their pocketbooks and the amount of time they can give to learning a new program. Usually the price of software varies according to capability, but this is not always the case. The best thing to do is shop carefully and read comparative reviews in books and magazines.

Probably a more important issue is learning time. Clearly the feature-laden programs take longer to learn. If such packages contain important capabilities needed for your music project, they may be well worth the investment in time and money.

We want to stress something that you may already have learned. Traditional music notation is very complicated and particularly difficult to capture in a software tool. Notation programs that have reasonable capability will take time to learn. Deciding to use such software a day or two before the score is needed for performance is totally unrealistic.

Common Characteristics of Notation Software

L et's make a few assumptions. You probably want a program that:

Musicians' styles of working differ. For example, you may like to work away from the computer, then use the technology to enter the music. This is similar to the way that Libby Larsen described her work in the opening of Viewport VII. Other people like to work right on the computer screen all the time, while others start with sequencing files and translate them to notation software later. Both of these techniques are used by Henry Panion, the featured musician who opens this Viewport.

▶ offers traditional music notation and supports MIDI input and playback

▶ is based on rule structures that can be customized if you want

▶ includes the full range of ensembles from small chamber groups to symphony orchestras with voices

▶ can support a wide set of parameters including text entry, part printing, and excellent print quality

There is actually a large number of programs that meet your needs, and it would be inappropriate for us to suggest a specific program for you. What we will do is present a set of common characteristics found in music notation software today, choosing from a variety of Macintosh and Windows packages. These common characteristics will be tied to procedures that you will use to create your first major score with the aid of technology. We will end the module with a look at some special features in the most advanced notation software, which you may not need right now but may want in the future.

Sample Sketch. Figure 16.4 displays a handwritten sketch of the first few measures of some music that a student composer has created. The score calls for five instrumentalists and a vocal solo. Figure 16.5 reveals these same opening measures, but now realized by notation software (in this case, Finale). The score presents some interesting challenges that older and less advanced notation software couldn't handle. For instance, notice the use of both changing and mixed meters, beamings across staves and bar lines, the independent scoring of both trumpet parts on a single staff, and the use of a

Figure 16.4
Original sketch

one-line staff for the percussionist. Let's note a few of the steps that the composer followed.

Working Order. Unlike working in other categories of music software, the order that you follow in working with notation programs can be very important. For instance, it could be a mistake to begin by immediately notating the top flute part only. Because the overall design and instrumentation of the score are known, it's much better to set up the staff framework of the full score first, without adding notes. This is particularly true in this case because the spacing between staves varies, as do the barline groupings and meters. Setting up the score in this order also allows for smoother real-time note entry. Other possible errors of order include adding articulation markings and lyrics too soon, because major changes in note placement can often require reformatting the markings and words.

Here's a suggested order to follow within each of the major phases of notation software used when a sketch of the music is already made. If you were working from a previously created sequencing file or from scratch with the computer, the steps might be different.

Note Entry Stage

If the score setup is one that you intend to use again, save a copy as a template for later use! A music notation template is a score page designed with everything but the notes and markings of a composition. Many of the more advanced packages already come with templates written for you!

► Design the score and take a rough guess at the layout. Decide on placement of instrument names and of bodies of text such as the title and headers and footers.

► Establish the attributes (instrument names, MIDI assignments, clef, time and key signatures, and so on) of each staff.

Figure 16.5
Sketch rendered in
Finale
(Coda Music Technology
[Mac/Windows])

▶ Some programs offer more than one way to enter notes. Begin by adding notes with a note entry system that is comfortable. Entry approaches will vary according to the musical context. This is where you will also use the built-in sequencing capabilities of notation software (Table 16.1).

▶ If the work is a long one, consider working with major sections as separate files and later merging the work together. This makes navigation much easier.

▶ Work linearly through important melodic lines. When appropriate, use these lines as the basis for copy-and-paste techniques with repetitive or similar motives and phrases.

Careful Editing Stage

▶ If possible, use MIDI playback to audit each line for possible errors or for possible changes in original aesthetic decisions.

▶ Make any global editing changes that affect transposition or note and measure attributes.

▶ If your notation package has options for adjusting spacing of notes globally according to predefined rules, make those adjustments. Check for any subtle adjustments in spacing for individual staves that may be necessary.

▶ Enter lyrics, using options in the software to link words with notes.

▶ Add markings such as articulations, dynamics, chord symbols and guitar fret symbols (if desired), and rehearsal numbers or letters. Subtle changes in

Refer back to Figure 16.5 as needed.

individual beaming, stem length, and note spacing would also be appropriate at this stage.

▶ Finally, check page layout and make adjustments. Check for acceptable page breaks and margin settings. Do a final MIDI playback to check for errors.

Printing Stage

▶ Decide on page printing options such as page orientation and reduction.

▶ Print one page of the score to test for proper fonts and page setup.

▶ Print score.

▶ Edit parts if possible before printing. Print parts.

Note Entry Stage

Let's take a closer look at each of these stages and examine some of the actions that you might take to realize your score. We will use examples from many different software programs.

A quick tip before we begin. Notation software generally allows for two *views* of a score: *scroll view* and *page view*. Scrolling view provides a continuous line of music in linear fashion, much like the old piano rolls on player pianos. This approach is more suitable for note entry and would probably be the best in the initial input stage. Page view, however, reformats the music so that you can see each page of the score, much as it would normally be printed. This view is best in the careful editing and output stages when you are making adjustments to the visual appearance.

Software activity: "Beginning Note Entry Skills with Encore or Finale"

Score Setup. It's often said that music notation programs are like word processors for musicians. Actually, desktop publishing programs may be a closer analogy, especially in the initial phases of use.

Spacing. The first order of business is to lay out the appropriate number of staves and to connect them to form a system, with special attention to spacing between the staves because of the range of various melodic lines and the need to leave room for inserting lyrics. Most programs allow great flexibility in setting up these parameters and in changing them if needed. Figure 16.6 shows a developing template for the sketch. Notice how this program provides small boxes or *handles* to aid in moving graphic elements, in this case the staff. Bar lines can be vertically extended to form groups for the wind players and the grand staff for the piano. Choice of clefs, key signatures, and time signatures might also occur at this time, assigned by staff.

Be sure to choose text fonts that are supported by the printer you are using; otherwise unpredictable placement of text can occur.

Text. Text blocks might be added at this point to include the title, composer, and instrument names. As with word processors, notation packages offer the full array of fonts that are installed in the operating system, and they also support various styles and point sizes.

MIDI management. Once the basic layout is complete from either a fresh design or a template, the next step is to begin assigning attributes to the staves. Because MIDI-assisted entry and playback of your score are features you will probably want to use, it's a good idea to tune up your software

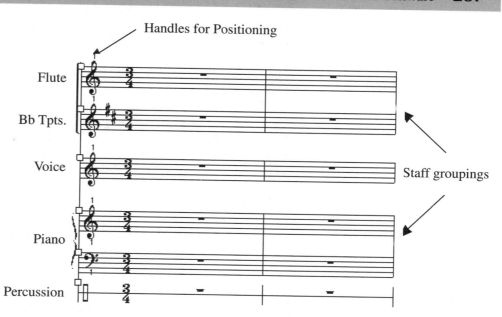

Figure 16.6
The sketch's template using Finale

You may want to return to Module 11 and study the descriptions of MIDI data structures. There will be much more about this throughout Viewport VI as well; also note that we have already mentioned QuickTime in Viewport III (CAI) and will learn more about it in coming viewports on sequencing, sampling, and multimedia.

with your MIDI resources. Figure 16.7 shows Finale's MIDI setup box as an example of a dialog box that is common in most MIDI-based notation software.

There are different systems that the computer can use to manage the flow of incoming and outgoing MIDI data. Here, we have chosen to use the Open MIDI System from Opcode as our MIDI management system (see Module 19).

Notice too that we have told Finale to use the Korg X5D external keyboard synthesizer for input and output on channels 1–16. We have also asked that output from channels 17–32 be played by the QuickTime music instrument sounds that are resident in the computer's system resources. With information in this dialog box, Finale can now support sound playback and be ready to record real-time note entry from our keyboard.

MIDI channel and timbre assignments. Next, we need to assign staves to MIDI channels and timbres. A different MIDI channel must be assigned to each discrete timbre. In Figure 16.5, we used five different timbres (flute, trumpet, voice, piano, and suspended cymbal). Five different MIDI channels would be needed to have a MIDI device or the system's MIDI resources play back correctly. We also need to inform the notation software what timbre ("patch" or "program") should be assigned.

Figure 16.8 displays Encore's approach to assigning MIDI channel and timbre to a staff. We have created a single violin staff and have chosen the "Staff Sheet" window in this software program. This window contains a great deal of information and is very important for working with this program as a sequencer (as we will soon see). At this point, we are concerned with the setting of the staff line's name (which will appear as part of the score) and the MIDI channel and timbre information. Notice the column for the instrument which we have assigned to Channel 1.

We have clicked on the "Program Name" column for that staff, and the dialog box in the center of the figure appears. In this box, you first specify the

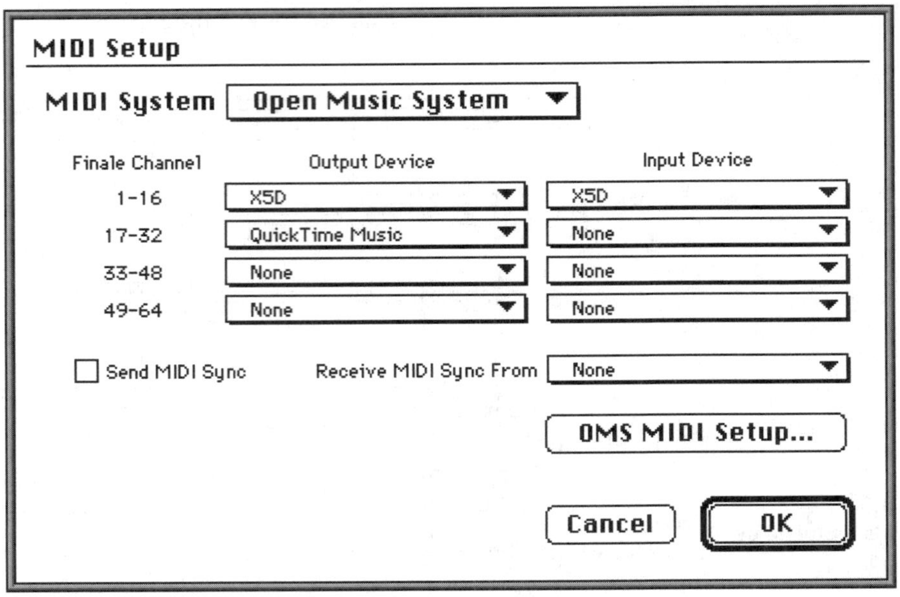

MIDI Setup

MIDI System [Open Music System ▼]

Finale Channel	Output Device	Input Device
1–16	[X5D ▼]	[X5D ▼]
17–32	[QuickTime Music ▼]	[None ▼]
33–48	[None ▼]	[None ▼]
49–64	[None ▼]	[None ▼]

☐ Send MIDI Sync   Receive MIDI Sync From [None ▼]

[OMS MIDI Setup...]

[Cancel] [OK]

Figure 16.7
MIDI Management in
Finale

Check out the history of
note-entry systems in
Module 17.

kind of instrument you are using for the playback of this staff. We have chosen
the General MIDI option; other options might be a specific brand of keyboard
that Encore knows. If you are using a device that Encore does not have in its
list of supported devices, it's an easy matter to create your own custom names.

We have assigned #41, the violin sound from the dialog box. Notice that
this gets recorded in the Staff Sheet in Encore. When you play back the score,
this staff will sound on the General MIDI device you have, using its violin
sound. Each program has its own kinds of menus and dialog boxes to accomplish this, but the procedures we have described here will be the same.

Additional attributes. Key and time signatures (if needed) are obvious
examples of other attributes that must now be set. Also important are such
items as number of measures in the piece (if known) and initial decisions
about note spacing. All of this can be changed later, but it is always good to
define as much as possible ahead of actual note entry.

In our sketch, we opted to enter key and meter changes after designing
the staff layout. In the case of the trumpet parts, the transposed parts were
entered right from the start, and the key for the trumpet parts was established as "D." For MIDI playback, we needed to set the staff to actually send
MIDI data to the synthesizer a whole step lower, so the resulting ensemble
would sound correct. Most notation software can easily do this.

Another way to deal with the issue of transposing instruments would be
to enter transposed instrument parts in concert pitch as if you were creating
a "C score," then transpose the staves to appropriate keys just before printing. This might be a better solution if all music lines are to be entered in
real-time by way of a MIDI device. Some advanced packages also allow you
to work the other way as well: return a transposed score to concert pitch.

Note Entry Options. In the early days of notation software, musicians had
a limited set of options for entering notation. They could pick graphic elements from a palette or use a MIDI keyboard in a limited way.

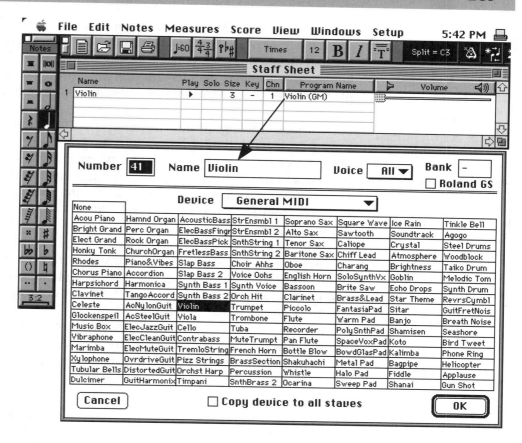

Figure 16.8
Staff setup windows in Encore
(G-VOX Entertainment [Mac/Windows])

Today, the more common approaches include:

► Mouse input using a symbol palette

► Step-time entry

► Real-time note entry

Character codes such as those described in Module 17 can occasionally be found in current systems, such as San Andreas Press's Score software written by Leland Smith.

Mouse input. Each software package provides a set of traditional note and symbol palettes for use in entering music. You simply select the symbol and place it where desired. In the case of notes, the correct rhythmic duration is chosen from the palette and the location on the staff is chosen by clicking where you want the note placed. This may sound like a laborious process, but actually you may find that you can do this quickly, especially if you use the typewriter keyboard to choose note durations from the palette, along with the mouse to enter the pitch locations. This is a common approach for non-MIDI notation programs. Palettes also are used to enter information other than notes. Dynamics, articulation, and other markings are easily placed with the mouse.

We used this entry method for some of the more complicated piano figures in the second measure of the sketch. Figure 16.9 displays a collection of symbol palettes from four notation programs. These palettes also may lead to other options; for instance with Personal Composer in Figure 16.9(*a*), you could click on the rest, whole note, shaped notehead, dotted note, triplet, accent, and accidentals to open sublayers of palettes.

A palette in software most often refers to a table of choices that can be selected by the mouse. These boxes are often floating windows that can be moved to different locations on the screen for convenient use.

Step-time note entry. Another approach is to use the palette of symbols and/or a typewriter keyboard together with a MIDI device that indicates pitch. The MIDI device is used simply to signal pitch, while the typewriter keyboard or palette signals durational values. We used this technique in places where there are a number of identical durations in a row, such as in measures one and two of the first trumpet part in Figure 16.5. Here one could choose the eighth-note duration from the palette and enter the consecutive pitches with the keyboard. In passages where there are, say, 48 consecutive sixteenth notes in a bass line pattern, this technique is very fast and quite accurate! By the way, this method can be used to enter the block chords in the piano part in measures one and three. Figure 16.10 displays an example from Desktop Sheet Music. Notice the tools available for entry and editing of notes in step-time.

Real-time note entry. Perhaps the most powerful and inherently musical of the note-entry systems is real time. We used this method for entering all of the vocal line and much of the flute and piano score. This is done by indicating at which measure and staff to begin and then playing the music in real time on the music keyboard.

But how does the software figure the correct durational values? The program needs a beat reference of some sort; different programs approach this problem in different ways. Some programs supply a metronome beat, much

Figure 16.9
Symbol entry boxes for various software packages

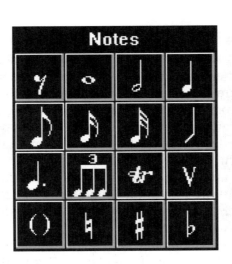

(*a*) Personal Composer
(Personal Composer System [Windows])

(*b*) Overture
(Cakewalk
Music Software
[Mac/Windows])

(*c*) Nightingale
(Musicware [Mac])

(*d*) Finale

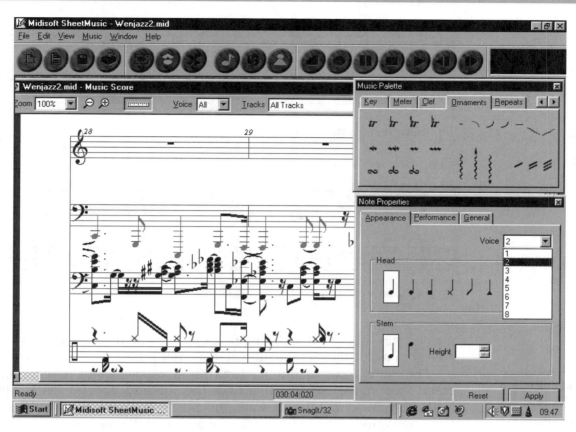

Figure 16.10
Editing in Desktop Sheet
Music
(Midisoft)

Quantization is treated further in Module 19.

as many sequencing packages do (see Viewport VI). The metronome beat is often referred to as a *click track*. You can specify a tempo, the software will offer a countoff, and you are off and playing. The closer you come to conforming exactly to the beat reference in the playing, the more accurate is the notation.

Nobody plays exactly on the beat (in fact, to do so would be terribly unmusical!), so many software packages offer a way to adjust for this. The software can "interpret" the playing by locking in the notes played to an underlying time grid (much like turning on the automatic grid in a graphics software program). If you are a little early or late in the attacks and releases on the keyboard, the software will take its best guess as to what was intended. This approach of rounding off to the nearest exact beat is called *quantization*. You can specify how exact this rounding off needs to be. This approach works quite well in most cases.

Figure 16.11 displays two moments in time during a musician's real-time entry of the opening measures of the famous G-Major Sonata of Mozart. The top line captures a point in time during the actual playing, as this particular software program places noteheads in rough proximity to the correct locations. The second line occurs right after the recording has stopped and the software has had an opportunity to quantize and display its best guess as to what the performer meant. Note that the release of the third note of the

(*a*) Display during real-time note entry

Figure 16.11
Real-time entry using
Encore

(*b*) Display after recording and quantization

Software activities: "Notating Your First Score with
MIDI Playback for Encore
or Finale"

melody was a little quick during performance and the software has inserted an eighth rest instead of the full-value quarter note.

The more accurate the playing, the more successful is real-time note entry. Most musicians find that once they become accustomed to both the MIDI instrument and the software, this note entry approach is quite successful. Small errors can easily be repaired by use of the mouse.

For real-time input to work well, not only does the playing need careful attention, but also the settings within the software need to be made correctly. Figure 16.12 is a dialog box from a software package that offers real-time note entry. Many of the settings are quite typical:

▶ *Metronome tempo settings.* A full range of tempi are provided as well as the option to just turn it off after the opening countoff.

▶ *Transcription settings.* Choose the smallest value of note and rest in the passage being played. This establishes the *quantization value,* which provides for more accurate notation.

▶ Options for dealing with grace notes and triplets.

▶ *Split point setting.* This is important when using two-hand playing in order for the computer to understand which notes belong on which staff.

Another approach to beat reference, offered by only a few programs, is to enter the music any way you want, then return to the beginning of the passage and, while listening to the playback, enter your own beat reference in real time. With this approach, *you* rather than the computer are supplying the beat reference. (A variation is to supply the beat reference yourself during performance by using a pedal or a key on the keyboard.) The real value of this is that you can play at any tempo you want and naturally perform phrases with subtle rubato, knowing that you can return and tell the computer just where the beat reference points are.

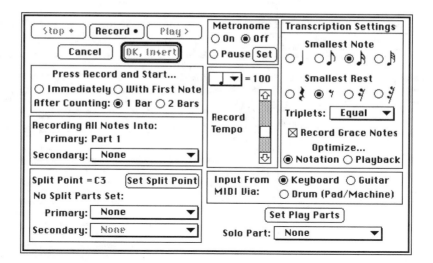

Figure 16.12
Record options from
ConcertWare
(Jump! Music [Mac/
Windows])

Copy, paste, and paste again! It's no secret that music is repetitive. Not only do themes return, but often whole sections of accompaniment patterns repeat. Sometimes there are subtle changes, but the basic structure is the same. Computers can help enormously with repetitive tasks. Just as in word-processing or graphics programs in which words and objects can be copied and pasted, notation software offers these same features.

You can probably guess where we used cut and paste in Figure 16.5. Look again at the opening measures. In the flute part, the descending eighth-note passage just before the double bar is exactly like the piano line, except three octaves higher. You can copy the piano line, paste it into the flute, and then ask the program to transpose the passage up three octaves. Another example is the rolled chords in the piano. They are not exactly the same notes; however, copying the first chord and pasting it in as the second, followed by some simple adjustments with the mouse, is really all that is needed. Most software will let you simply click on a note and drag its location up or down.

It turns out that we made extensive use of repetitive eighth-note patterns and piano chords such as those in the opening measures. This often occurs in music, no matter what the style. A great deal of time can be saved by understanding the similar structural content of the music and using the copy and paste tools. Some notation programs will support diminution and augmentation of both pitch and rhythm, offering even more opportunity to save valuable time on repetitive tasks.

Sequencing and music notation software. We end this section on note entry by reminding you again of how basic sequencing software relates to notation packages. Figures 16.13, 16.14, and 16.15 are drawn from notation programs that display their sequencing capabilities. Each display shows how note entry is enhanced and controlled by use of a number of different track and editing windows.

Figure 16.13 demonstrates how Encore's Staff Sheet provides a view of the MIDI options for all the staves of music in this large score. Notice the

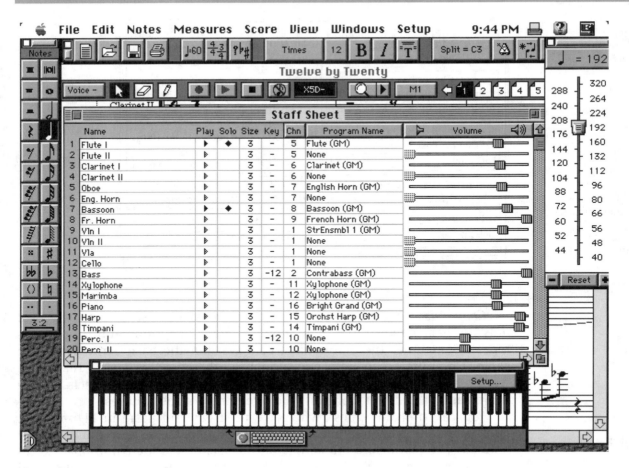

Figure 16.13
Sequencer-like options for Encore

ability to "solo" or hear only one or two staves during playback. Control for the volume of each staff is also provided in the form of sliderbars. This virtual mixer idea will appear several times in the screens that we will see in Module 19.

In addition to the Staff Sheet, notice the playback controls in the upper menu bar. You can also control tempo with the metronome graphic to the right and use the keyboard representation on the bottom of the figure for note entry.

Figure 16.14 shows similar controls for the Finale program. The large palette to the left is the main one for the program. The note entry mode is highlighted. The central windows are very similar to Encore for MIDI options and for playback.

Figure 16.15 is a picture of the many options offered in QuickScore Elite. Notice the bar graph notation view. We will see this as one of the most-common graphic representations used in sequencing software. The options that we have displayed in the pull-down menu are not often found in notation software. For example, QuickScore supports options for filtering unwanted MIDI data when importing a MIDI file and for linking the score to movies and film, and it supplies special options for drum notation. This program also supports volume mixing.

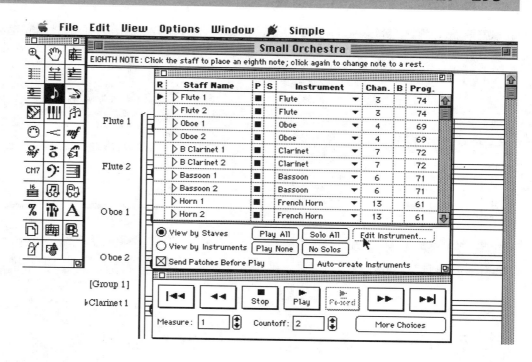

Figure 16.14
Sequencer-like options for
Finale

Careful Editing Stage

Inserting the basic music content is a major achievement, but much of the
time spent using notation software is consumed by careful editing. At this
point in the process, we recommend moving to page view and using the following five-step approach:

(a) sound check via MIDI

(b) global editing

(c) lyric placement

(d) micro-editing

(e) final page layout and sound checks

Moving to page view at
this point in entering your
music is an option. You
can stay in scroll view
until the final output stage
if you want.

Sound Check. Use that MIDI power to check your work! You will find this
an enjoyable part of using notation software, as do many composers and
arrangers who used to rely only on imagining the sound of their writing.
The use of MIDI with notation software allows musicians not only to check
for errors that might have escaped the eye but also to listen to each line of
music in context so that aesthetic decisions can be verified and possibly
altered. You will find that most MIDI equipment has acceptable flute, trumpet, piano, and percussion sounds, so that you can hear a version of the
sketch with timbres that approximate the live performance. If the muted
trumpet parts are not a good choice with the flute sound, for instance, we
might make a decision to alter the score. Better to do this during the editing
stage of the score than to make these costly changes during the first live
rehearsal or recording session.

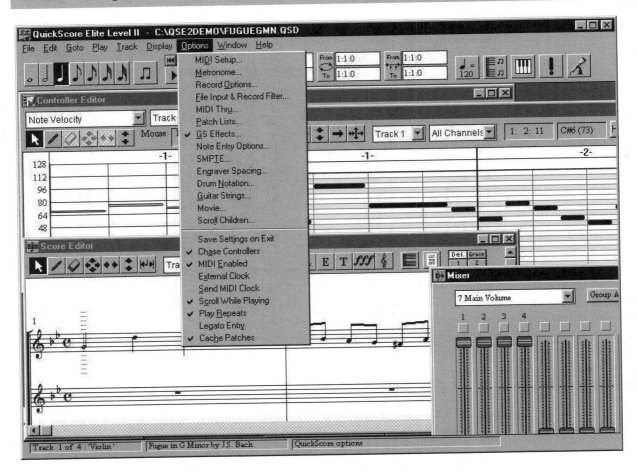

Figure 16.15
Sequencer-like options for QuickScore Elite (Sion [Windows])

Some software will also allow you to globally change different modes. For instance, you can change E major to E minor or to other custom-defined scales.

Global Edits. Once all the notes have been checked for accuracy, a number of global edits can be completed. These include possible changes in transposition, note and measure attributes (graphic appearance and playback), and global spacing.

Transposition. Most notation software offers at least three types of transposition: global, diatonic, and chromatic. Figure 16.16 displays the first measure of the first trumpet part in four different forms. The (a) measure is the original before it was transposed, and the (b) is the result when the key was changed. The (c) measure is the original transposed up a third diatonically. Notice that there is no systematic attempt to keep the intervals exact, just to move the notes up a third. That is not the case with the chromatic transposition (d). Here the integrity of the intervals remains intact. The ability to transpose chromatically and diatonically is quite helpful if composers are creating sequential patterns based on a core idea.

Note and measure attributes. Other scoring features can be globally controlled in most notation programs. Figure 16.17 shows typical dialog boxes from one program. Box (a) offers control over stem height, placement of accidentals, notehead style, and type of rest. All you need to do is select a region of music or the entire score and use the dialog box to choose your settings. Box (b) controls changes in playback. In this case, tempo is altered

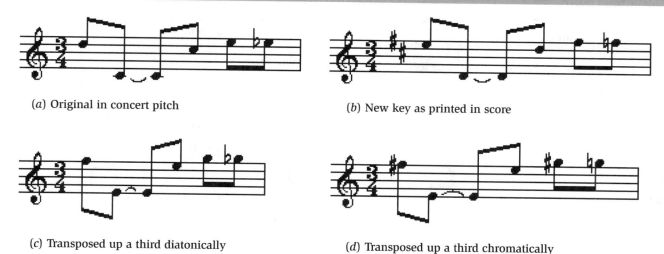

(a) Original in concert pitch

(b) New key as printed in score

(c) Transposed up a third diatonically

(d) Transposed up a third chromatically

Figure 16.16
Transposed passages from the sketch

either at a specified measure or gradually over time to create accelerandos and ritardandos. A similar box might be used for dynamic changes. Box (c) displays changes that can be made for barline types.

Other global attributes for notes include stem direction and thickness of beams. You can also indicate if you want rests to be inserted globally in staves that contain no music.

Global spacing. In the early days of music notation software, programs rarely offered many options for note spacing. Either you were given complete freedom to move graphic elements (as is the case with graphics-based notation programs today) or you were given no freedom at all. Most notation software programs today offer flexible spacing options. Figure 16.18 presents two spacing arrangements. The first measure is typical of the appearance of notes when one is first entering notation; it is proportional spacing that is quite generic. The second measure is nonproportional spacing that conforms to a set of rules similar to that which professional engravers use when setting music by hand. When you have determined that all the music is entered correctly and all the note and measure attributes are in place, you can tell the software to space the music to reflect professional notation spacing before adding lyrics and other markings.

Lyric placement. If the score contains lyrics, this would be a good time to add them. Notice that the sketch does have a vocal line that enters in the third measure. Early notation software simply let you enter words under notes. This was fine, except that it required a great deal of fine tuning to align the placement of noteheads and syllables.

woods -- I know to

Most software today offers intelligent linking of words to notes. This means that spacing of notes is automatically adjusted as you enter the words, and subtle adjustments in alignment are simple because notes and syllables operate as a linked unit. We simply indicated that lyrics were to be entered under a staff, and the software provided a text entry box right where it was needed. In the case of the third measure of the sketch, we clicked under the D quarter note and typed the word *woods*. Then we hit the space bar, and the cursor advanced to the point under the next quarter note where

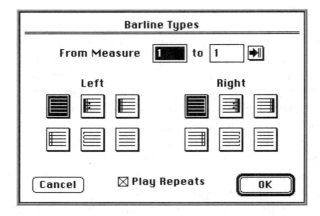

(a) Note attributes

(b) Tempo changes

(c) Measure changes

Figure 16.17
Dialog boxes from Encore

the word *I* would be entered. After pressing Tab to the next word *know,* which occurs under the eighth note B, we simply hit the space bar a second time to move to the note "B♭" for the word *to.*

Another approach to note entry is displayed in Figure 16.19 from the Overture software. Here you enter the words in a special lyrics entry box; once typed, the software flows the words automatically under the notes of the specified staff. Some packages even offer the option of using a word processor to enter all the lyrics and then to import them right from the word processing file into the score with all the links automatically made.

If the placement of any of the notes that are linked to lyrics changes position, the words automatically move with the changes. You have the freedom to use whatever font or font size you wish, and you can enter multiple lines of text if there are repeated stanzas.

Micro-Editing. Now that most decisions have been made about global editing and lyric placement, we can turn to the careful placement of markings such as articulations, dynamics, chord symbols, guitar frets (if desired), and rehearsal numbers or letters. Subtle changes in individual beaming, stem length, and note spacing are also appropriate at this stage.

Figure 16.18
Spacing options

(*a*)   (*b*)

Knowing *where* to place markings needs to be understood ahead of time. Musicians need to know the conventions!

Markings. There are two kinds of markings: those that occupy a single point and those that extend over longer spaces. In our Figure 16.5, good examples of single-point markings are the accents and articulation markings in the flute and trumpet parts and the dynamic indications in each part. Examples of markings that stretch over space include the crescendos and decrescendos in the flute, trumpet, and piano lines, and text blocks such as *with authority* and *with feeling.*

Most single-point markings occupy a position above or below a notehead, such as an articulation or bowing marking, while others are placed above or below a measure to designate a repeat or a change in dynamic. All were placed after the basic layout of the music was established.

Each notation program offers a different approach to entering markings. Tempo indications, rehearsal letters or numbers, and text blocks that offer performance guidelines are often established by use of menu options. Most markings, however, are entered from palettes of symbols. Figure 16.20 displays examples of palettes from three different notation programs. Notice the support for traditional articulation markings such as staccato, tenuto, and

Figure 16.19
Lyrics entry in Overture

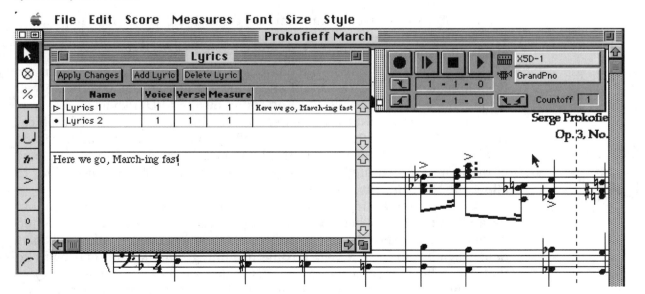

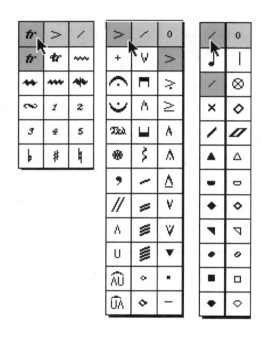

Figure 16.20
Articulation and
symbol palettes

(a) ConcertWare

(b) Encore

(c) Overture

accents. You simply choose the marking desired and attach it to notes or to staff locations. In the case of crescendo and decrescendo markings, you can choose the symbol from the palette, click on the score at the beginning spot of the marking, and drag to the end point. There are additional options for flexible placement and reshaping after they are placed. Some software will actually reflect the symbol's effect on sound during MIDI playback.

Some programs offer a simple set of drawing tools (see the "Graphics" palette in Figure 16.20b). Tools for drawing boxes, ovals, and lines can be used for special purposes, often to highlight performance directions. Some of the more sophisticated software packages also provide a custom editor to allow you to create any symbol you want.

One kind of marking that extends over space deserves special mention: tie and slur marks. These can be tricky. Because ties and slurs are often unique in shape and placement, software developers need to allow this particular symbol to have a very flexible beginning, middle, and end point so that it can be shaped accordingly. This makes the necessary hand-entry of most slurs and ties somewhat tedious. As both the real-time recording abil-

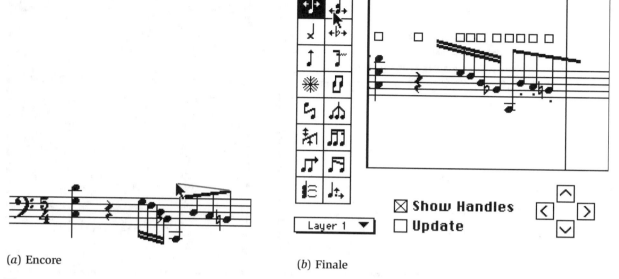

(*a*) Encore

(*b*) Finale

Figure 16.21
Approaches to individual adjustments

ity and the built-in intelligence of software improve, this marking will become easier to manage.

Individual adjustments. Complex music requires special attention to detail. Not all musicians need to tinker with subtle adjustments in their music, but we did in our example in Figure 16.5 because some of the measures were complex and the best possible appearance was required. For instance, look at the sixteenth-note piano figure in measure two of the music. When the notes were first entered for that portion of the score, things were fine. But after the other music was entered and the global spacing rules were applied, there were a few subtle spacing decisions that were not correct. No software program, no matter how intelligent, can be expected to handle every situation. For this reason, most packages provide some means for subtle adjustments of note spacing, beams, stems, and measure lines. These subtle adjustments should be made close to the time of final printing, after the major decisions about the score are in place.

Figure 16.21 demonstrates how two software packages handle these adjustments. In the first (*a*), you can grab part of the graphic and manipulate it by dragging with the mouse. In this case, we caught a moment in time when a stem length is being adjusted to improve the angle of the beam. The B♭ will also need to be pulled to the right to make for better spacing.

In the second example (*b*), the software uses a set of palette tools to manipulate note elements such as beam angle and extension, note spacing, and custom stems. The tool highlighted is the spacing tool, and the handle boxes above the notes can be dragged to adjust spacing.

Beaming adjustments are particularly common. As you enter your music, the software guesses how you want the beaming scheme to work. For instance, if you entered two eighth notes in a row, the notation software assumes that these are to be beamed. You could turn off this automatic feature if you want the software not to guess.

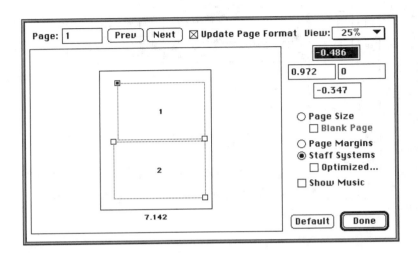

(a) Finale

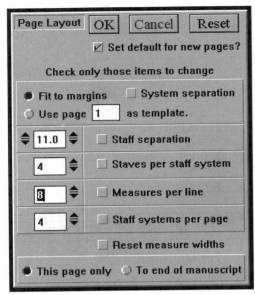

(b) Personal Composer

Figure 16.22
Page layout dialog boxes

If you intend to do a good deal of notation work, consider buying a large monitor! Check out Module 15.

Final Page Layout and MIDI Check. The last steps are checking for page layout and listening to a final playback. This is a good place to choose the page view option so that you can see the entire screen. In shifting to this view, the page may go off the screen to the right. Often notation software includes some kind of Page to Fit or Fit to Window command that lets the musician see the page layout on the screen. There may also be an Update Layout command, much like the global note spacing update described earlier, that reformats the entire page layout.

You can check how the margins and systems appear on each page and make any last-minute adjustments. Figure 16.22 shows how this control is accomplished in different programs. In dialog box (a) on the left, you can grab the boxes that represent the individual systems and move them around. You can also enter numbers that define the dimensions of the staff in the fields provided at the upper right. Notice that this dialog displays the box that represents the first system slightly indented on the left side to allow for text or other graphics that might be added because this is the first system of the piece. In dialog box (b) on the right, a different program uses settings for staff separation, staves per system and page, and measures per line. You can control these and other settings and watch the effects in the page preview window, as noted below.

Some software provides a *page preview* or *print preview* option similar to that found in word-processing programs. The layout of the final measure often requires some readjustments so that it doesn't look either too cramped or too spread out. If the software provides the Update Layout command noted above, it is always a good idea to use this option just before printing.

Finally, this is also the time to review each part for placement of graphics. You might like to use the MIDI playback options to audit each part separately, as well as the entire composition. This will help to catch any errors that may still remain.

Printing Stage

Refer to Modules 14, 15, 17, and 18 for more information on fonts and printer technology.

The last stage is printing the score and parts. Many of the steps in this stage resemble printing techniques for any document created by a computer. Let's begin with how you want to print the score.

Score. Some important decisions about printing a score still need to be made. They may affect page layout issues discussed earlier. Among these are printer choice, page resizing, and page orientation.

Printer choice. Different printer types may be used for music printing. Inexpensive ink-jet printers will produce acceptable results, particularly if the printing technology supported by the printer works with the software. You must keep in mind that most notation packages use the PostScript page-description language that uses a PostScript font for music symbols. This provides a powerful language for defining complicated graphics and for rendering them on high-resolution laser printers.

If you choose to print the work on an inexpensive printer, you must use a printer that works effectively with your software. An alternative is to use TrueType technology or add-on software like Adobe Type Manager (ATM). If you find that the software works well with these alternatives, you probably can achieve good results with an inexpensive printer. The print resolution may still not be what you want, but the score will be quite readable.

Laser printers are probably the best choice, even if you need to pay a small printing charge at a copy shop or a college lab. Resolution quality is quite high on most laser printers (600 dots per inch, or more), and most of them support PostScript technologies.

There is, however, one problem with laser printers for music printing: paper size. The vast majority of laser printers offer only 8.5×11 or 8.5×14 paper sizes. Larger laser printers exist and are becoming more affordable, but they are hard to find and often require a hefty per-page cost. If the score being printed is too large for standard paper sizes and an oversized laser printer is not available, there are alternatives.

Laser printers add a small margin around a printed area. If your notation software supports tile printing, be sure to turn off this margin default within the software.

One alternative is to print the score in *tiles* or panels, as you would a large poster or sign. Printing in tiles produces sections of the score printed on single sheets of paper. The whole score is eventually printed, but in several parts. This will require some physical cutting and pasting, but the final result can then be photocopied onto larger paper. Some notation software will not support this approach, however.

Page resizing. Another approach is resizing the score. This can be done in two ways. The first is to ask the notation software to reduce the individual size of all or selected staves. This might save some space and have the added effect of being appropriate musically, as in the case of a vocal and piano score or with percussion parts in an orchestral arrangement. Not all programs support this procedure. The other way is to ask the part of the

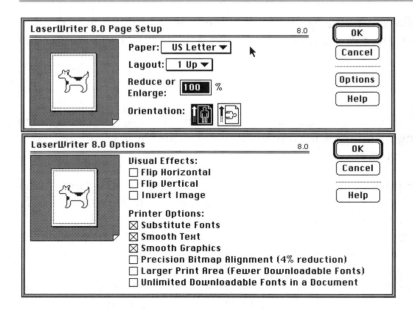

(a) Macintosh Page Setup box

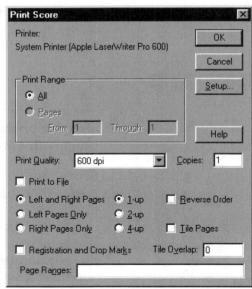

(b) Windows Page Setup box

Figure 16.23
Page setup boxes

It would be wonderful if music software allowed the score to reflect changes made in the parts. This dynamic linking in the opposite direction is poorly supported even in the most expensive packages.

operating system software that governs printing to reduce the entire printed image during the print process. This can be done with all software. Figure 16.23 displays the Page Setup dialog boxes that accomplish this on Macintosh and Wintel machines.

You need to remember that methods of resizing may alter page layout. After indicating the settings desired for resizing, you should review the page layout to check how the page will look when printed.

Page orientation. The dialog box in Figure 16.23a also has an *orientation* option. The default orientation, the left box, is the normal vertical page arrangement, but you can choose to have the image rotated 90 degrees and printed so that music is printed across the longer dimension of the paper. This is, in fact, what we chose to do for the sketch in Figure 16.5. Because the music has only six staves and somewhat complicated measures, this choice allowed the score to easily fit on a piece of regular paper without reduction. This page orientation especially suits jazz charts.

We'll make one last point about score printing. Most laser printers allow for *manual feed*. This option allows the musician to feed paper into the printer one page at a time and is useful for printing on both sides of a single sheet. Some packages allow the printing of only odd and only even pages, which means you can bypass the manual feed option and just put your pages through a second time.

Parts. Certainly we all want to have software print individual parts. This is one of the great advantages of music notation software. Even if your program does not automatically do this, it may be possible to work around this limitation by instructing the program to hide all but one line of music and print each staff separately, or by copying and pasting a staff to a new file and printing it. Fortunately, today's software packages offer options for

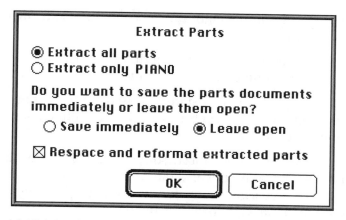

(a) Nightingale

(b) Finale

Figure 16.24
Dialog boxes for part extraction

printing parts automatically. Figure 16.24 offers examples of dialog boxes for the printing of parts. Notice that the word *extraction* is used in most programs to indicate that the parts are *extracted* from the score and printed separately. (Hopefully this won't be like an extraction in a dentist's office!)

Most programs allow for some editing of parts before printing, but the options vary. Some programs offer the option of creating separate files for each part; this adds flexibility. Editing of parts is important because special indications may need to be added to certain parts, or the process of part extraction may change certain note and measure formats. Ideally, music notation software should take care of this automatically, but extraction does not always happen as expected.

A good notation package should provide a part that reflects consecutive measures of rests accurately. You probably want to have a program automatically concatenate measures of rest with a figure indicating the total number of measures printed above the concatenated measure, as in professionally printed parts. You want the software to design these concatenations to visually reflect changes in tempo or major section changes within these measures as well. You may also want to add cues in certain parts. Advanced notation software will do all this.

Some Advanced Features

Much of what has been described so far can be done with the majority of MIDI-based music notation software available today. However, there were a few features used that are available only in certain software. We provide a listing of these and other features not commonly available. If you require one of these particular capabilities or features, be sure to check the software you are considering: check the manuals with the dealer or publisher or with software users on campus or on the Internet.

Newsgroups and list-servs on the Internet are a great source of information on notation software. See Viewport II.

Graphics

▶ *Beaming* Our music in Figure 16.5 required the use of special beaming effects in the piano part in measure two. The beams were extended to link the sixteenth notes *between* staves and the eighth-note beams were extended *across* the barline to measure three.

▶ *Polymetric systems*   Measure three required the superimposition of a 12/8 meter in the flute part over common time in the rest of the score.

▶ *Flexible options for lines per staff*   A one-line staff was used for the percussion part. A few notation programs allow such staves, plus additional staff lines beyond five to accommodate special needs.

▶ *Variable staff size*   One nice feature of advanced software is the ability to change the size of each staff—not only globally but within a system. One application of this would be in preparing scores for an accompanist, where the solo line is smaller and the piano's grand staff is regular size.

▶ *Flexible horizontal spacing*   Although most software spaces notes according to globally defined rules, a few packages allow many such rule definitions within one file. This allows each measure to have its own spacing conventions, if necessary.

▶ *Flexible vertical spacing*   Most software will allow global adjustments of distances between each staff and between systems, but some software provides this kind of adjustment only for selected systems.

▶ *Nonstandard key signature*   Custom mixtures of this sort are needed in some contemporary scores.

▶ *Linked measures*   Some programs will allow sets of measures to be *linked* so that changes in a particular set of measures will affect changes in all the others. For instance, if you copied and pasted a cello passage from a string bass line and linked it to the string bass line, changes in the string bass line would automatically be mirrored in the cello line.

▶ *Staff sets and hidden staves*   In a complicated score with many staves, it often becomes difficult to work on the whole score on the screen. Certain software allows temporary *hiding* of staves. It's also possible to group staves in sets, like all the string or wind parts, and work only with those visible at one time.

Screen redraw speed can also be enhanced by turning off color and making a smaller window for the score. Computer enhancements include increasing RAM and adding more video memory (VRAM). See Module 15.

▶ *Merging and unmerging staves*   Staves can be merged and unmerged to save valuable note entry time. This feature is particularly useful if you use standard MIDI files from sequencing packages.

▶ *Custom shape designer*   Palettes may not contain all needed symbols. A custom shape designer allows you to create custom symbols with graphics tools. Symbols can then be grouped into custom sets for use in more than one score.

▶ *Screen redraw options*   Screen redrawing slows down the operation of graphics software like notation packages. If you are working with a large score with a large displayed image on a big monitor, the computer's processing time is taxed severely when it constantly has to redraw the screen. Some software offers options for postponing complete redrawing until you are ready for an update.

▶ *Options for common defaults*   Options for globally controlling graphic elements such as beam thickness, stem length, and articulation offsets are useful. Some software provides extensive user-defined preferences.

▶ *Search and replace*   This is similar to search and replace with word processors. Instead of words, pitch and rhythm patterns are sought.

▶ *Automatic slur formatting*   Click on one notehead and the software connects a preformatted slur to the next notehead.

▶ *Smart linking of expressions to notes*   Expression marks are often attached to a single notehead and then dragged to a particular location. The origin of that attachment is often forgotten by the program, making it hard to locate the original notehead when changes are necessary. Some software allows the musician to double-click on the expression mark to reveal the mark's origin.

See Modules 14 and 17 for more information on these file formats.

Printing

▶ *Separate files for part extraction*   We have already noted how this special feature can help.

▶ *Error checks for incorrect number of beats in a measure*   The software will flag measures with too few or too many beats before printing.

▶ *Staff suppression*   If a section of a score contains systems with only certain instruments playing, the software will create systems that use only the staves for those instruments that are playing.

▶ *Score Reduction*   Some software allows for score reduction, allowing individual staves to be combined for a smaller sized score.

▶ *EPS and PICT or WMF output format*   Surprisingly few programs offer flexibility in how they print or save graphic formats, which has special importance when you want to insert scores into word processors and desktop publishing programs. The ability to save a small selection of notation as a graphics file is also a handy feature.

MIDI Support

▶ *Multiple channels for each staff*   All MIDI-based software packages offer at least one MIDI channel for each staff. Some offer considerably more, especially for multiple voices per staff and for additional MIDI effects.

▶ *MIDI playback sensitivity and MIDI capture*   How notation programs work with MIDI playback and MIDI capture vary from the bare bones to the elegant. The more expensive packages try to play back as much performance expression as possible from the symbols in the score. Similarly, they try to capture as much subtlety as possible when the musician is entering music in real time. If sensitive MIDI playback is important when working from a notation package, shop carefully.

▶ *Option to edit MIDI data*   Some programs actually offer ways to edit the MIDI data directly to help the playback achieve desired results. Some of the sequencing packages that we will cover in Module 19 have notation options advanced enough for you to use sequencers as a starting point if subtlety of playback is an important need.

▶ *Extensive beat referencing*   Nearly all MIDI-based programs support real-time note entry, but few offer options for helping the computer find the beat. Usually a self-generating metronome is used to establish a click track. Some programs offer options for player-generated beats during performance. Still others provide the option of adding a beat structure after the music has been entered into the computer.

Useful Additions

Plug-ins and Custom Fonts. In Modules 19 and 23, we will speak more about the trend in recent times to allow music production software to be expanded with plug-ins. We mentioned this trend for Internet clients and for graphics programs. Plug-ins are possible with notation software as well. For example, Finale allows you to add plug-ins for checking instrument ranges. If you know how to program in a high-level language like C^{++}, you can even create your own plug-ins!

There may be times when the fonts supplied with the notation software do not meet all your needs. It is possible to purchase custom fonts as add-ons to notation software. Good examples of this are John Clevenger's ChordSymbol and CSTimes fonts. These are available in both TrueType and PostScript formats for both Macintosh and Windows operating systems.

Utilities. As you become more confident with music notation technology, you will use it not only for your composition work but also for other purposes. For example, a good screen-capture program for either Macintosh or Wintel computers will allow for the insertion of screen clips from notation programs into word-processing or page-layout files. This will not give you as elegant a printout as inserting PICT, TIFF, or EPS files from notation programs, but it is faster and often more convenient.

Another useful kind of utility allows for the construction of custom-designed fonts for those notation packages that do not include a built-in editor to do this. These utilities are often available as shareware from computer networks and user groups.

Music Scanning. Perhaps the most innovative addition to music printing software in recent years is scanning technology for music. The ability to use a scanner to create digital music notation files from previously printed music is now a reality. This provides very powerful options for you. Suppose you have a previously printed score that is not in digital form and you need to have a printed copy that is written in a new key. Instead of entering all the music into the computer by hand, you could scan the score and make the changes quickly using the software!

Nightingale uses an add-on program called NoteScan to scan music into that particular software. Separate music-scanning programs, such as Musitek's Midiscan for Wintel machines, are also available. These programs provide standard MIDI files that can be used in the music notation program of choice.

Some Final Thoughts

Notation software is constantly improving, providing the flexibility necessary to support many sophisticated needs. The complexity of graphics in traditional notation is well known, and much software is available to meet these demands. The ultimate program that blends this power with exceptional ease of use and near-flawless note entry has not yet been written. What we do have is a wide assortment of software that is appropriate to various needs and offers excellent support for most tasks. You will find the time required to master such a program well worth the effort, especially when it comes time to check for errors and print the score and parts.

Module
17

Data Structures for Coding Music Notation and Performance

Why can't all notation programs do all things? Why can't a musician just play some music patterns and have them appear on a printer all properly notated? This would ideally be accomplished by what Christopher Yavelow has termed WYPWYP or "What You Play is What You Print" software. We can also turn this around and ask for "What You Print is What You Play" software.

The answer for these questions lies in understanding the difference between how we represent music performance data and how we represent music printing or notation data in a computer. When this distinction is understood, you will more fully grasp the underlying design issues of notation software and gain some insight into the topic of Viewport VI, music sequencers for performance.

How Is Notation Represented in a Computer?

To begin our discussion, let's define the smallest music element we would want to store and manipulate in a computer. For the sake of dis-

Figure 17.1
A model of a music object

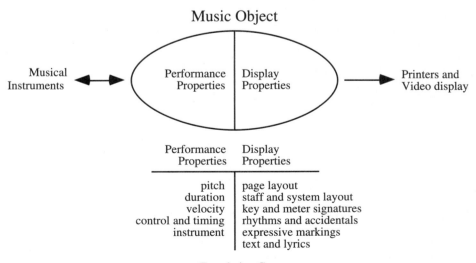

Music Object

Performance Properties	Display Properties
pitch	page layout
duration	staff and system layout
velocity	key and meter signatures
control and timing	rhythms and accidentals
instrument	expressive markings
	text and lyrics

Translation Gap

cussion we will call this a *music object*. Such an *object* may represent any pattern of music, from a single note to a complex phrase. Our object needs to describe everything that is required to both perform the music and print or display its score. Figure 17.1 provides a simple model to illustrate.

We can see that to describe a music object's performance and its notation requires a data structure with two sets of properties, and that the information or data needed for performing music are very different from the data needed for displaying or printing music.

Data Structures for Performing and Display. Our discussion of MIDI showed us that the data required for performing music is the same type of data that we are able to represent with MIDI control codes. With MIDI or any performance codes, we are concerned with recording and playing events over time: pitch, duration, velocity or amplitude, control changes, and so on.

The data needed for displaying music on the printed page are very different. Here we are concerned with locating symbols within the space of a printed page. We need information that is unrelated to performance data, like:

▶ Page and staff layout

▶ Changes in key and meter signatures

▶ Enharmonic spellings

▶ Beaming, slurs, and spacing of notes

▶ Expressive markings and other performance directions

▶ Lyrics and text

Translating Between Performance and Display Data. The elements needed to describe performance and notation are so different that translation between the two domains has many problems. That is why we have labeled the line separating the two domains as the *translation gap*. As we move from performing to notating and back, critical elements that provide the essential interpretive elements for performing and the essential elements for rendering the printed page are lost in the translation.

When software has to translate MIDI performance codes into notation codes, it must cross the translation gap. It can use the chromatic MIDI pitch information to decide what notes to put on the page. But durations are more complicated. What you play is not necessarily what you want to print. The performed durations have to be *quantized* or rounded off into rhythmic values or symbols: the traditional symbols for sixteenth, eighth, or quarter notes, and so on. When we quantize duration we throw away lots of very detailed performance information.

What about the key signature and accidentals, spacing on the page, beams, and stem direction? Either all these notation elements must be added by human intervention, or the computer software needs rules to guide it in inferring these elements from the performance data.

What happens when the software needs to reconstruct a performance?

The Mozart example in Figure 16.11 illustrates the translation gap with (*a*) performance and (*b*) notation graphics.

When the software goes back across the gap to reconstruct a performance based solely on notation codes (without performance data), the performance sounds amusical and sterile. Even if expressive markings like *rubato* and *andante* had been added to the printed score, the computer would have to have rules to translate those notation codes into performance codes.

Table 17.1 helps to summarize the key contrasts between structures for printing and for performing. Take particular note of how pitch is represented. With display codes, pitch is coded by graphic positions in relation to the staff. With traditional Western music this is a *MOD-7 system,* meaning that the staff positions are coded in seven numeric steps (0 to 6, or A to G) across octaves. With performance codes, extremely accurate performance information is required. Here pitch is traditionally coded in a *MOD-12 system,* where there are 12 chromatic steps to the octave (0 to 11, or C to B).

Is WYPWYP Music Software Possible? Are you beginning to get an idea of the difficulty of the task at hand? The data structures and the rules for translation are incredibly complex. Notation software designed solely for printing doesn't need any rules for translation; it's strictly "What You See is What You Print," but you lose the ability to perform the score even on a very rudimentary level for proofreading.

On the other hand, notation software designed for composing relies heavily on rules programmed into the software for translating between the performance and notation domains. We do need to see what we are creating and would like to have a printed score when done. The more refined the rule structures, the better the translation.

The problem is that, technologically, we keep getting closer, but we aren't there yet. The rules are not refined enough to give us Yavelow's WYP-WYP music software. What typically happens in current notation software is that the designer makes an *a priori* decision about the program's bias, toward either composing or printing. If the notation software is composing-biased, then the software design will depend greatly on rules for inferring the notation from the performance data. The notation will operate in a time-based rather than a space-based environment. When and if we do finally achieve the level of sophistication required for high-quality translation between notation and performance (WYPWYP software), we will probably no longer find it necessary to distinguish between sequencing software and notation software; they will be one and the same.

Table 17.1 Contrasts in Music Coding for Performance and Display

Performance	Display
Controlling instruments	Controlling symbols on a page
Time-based systems	Location- or space-based systems
Optimized for performance accuracy	Optimized for notational accuracy
Pitch coded as chromatic (MOD-12)	Pitch coded as display position (MOD-7)
Rhythm coded as temporal duration	Rhythm coded as shapes
Interpretation embedded in pitch, duration, and velocity	Interpretation coded in signs and labels

(a)   M.M. ♩ = 120

(b)   !F !K3B !M34 !T120 G3Q / C4 E G / C5H EQ / DH F4#Q / GH. //

Figure 17.2
Music example: (*a*) with
Simple Music Coding, (*b*)
from Beethoven's Sym-
phony No. 5, 3rd Movement

A Simple Example of Coding Music Notation

How does a computer programmer actually create coding instructions for music display and performance? To see how this might be done, it would be instructive to walk through a simple example.

Look at the music pattern notated in Figure 17.2. We want to code this in the computer. We are not sure whether we want to use the music data for performing or notating, so let's start by describing the phrase using an alphanumeric or ASCII music code that we will call our Simple Music Code. Part *b* in the figure shows the music phrase coded in our Simple Music Code. If you examine it for a moment, you can probably figure out the syntax on your own. Here is how it works.

Simple Music Code. Each note is represented by its pitch name (*n*), octave (*o*), accidental (*a*), and rhythm (*r*), always in that order: *n–o–a–r*. Where:

$n = a, b, c, \ldots g$

$o = 1, 2, \ldots 8$

$a = $ # or ♭

$r = s, e, q, h,$ and *w* (standing for sixteenth through whole notes); a dot (.) can be added to any rhythmic value.

(Note: once stated, an octave, accidental, or rhythmic code carries through until a new code is used.)

Expressive and interpretative markings follow an exclamation mark (!):

!G or !F for treble and bass clef

!K*na* for the key signature, where *n* is the number of sharps or flats, and *a* is # or ♭

!M*nb* for the meter, where *n* is the number of beats and *b* is the beat value (e.g., 4 = quarter note)

/ alone is a single-bar line and // is a double-bar line

!T*nnn* is the tempo, where *nnn* is a three-digit M.M. value

This code is simple and readable for humans. For the computer to create a performance of these codes it has to translate them into MIDI values. To notate them, it has to translate them into symbols positioned on a staff. Let's take on translating the codes for performing first.

Performing the Simple Music Codes. We will need to *parse* the music codes, one character at a time, to determine what MIDI pitch to play. *Parse* is a term used in programming to refer to examining each character of a string of codes, one character at a time. We will just look at parsing the MIDI pitch for one note to give you a idea of what's involved. We can skip over all of the notation coding except the tempo, because we do not need to know the clef, meter, key signature, and barlines in order to perform the music.

To determine the MIDI pitch, a MOD-12 system (0–11) is used with 0 representing the pitch C and 11 representing B. We can use a *lookup table* to translate the note symbol or pitch name (e.g., G) into a numeric pitch code. Visualize the Pitch Names (*pn*) A, B, C, D, E, F, and G in one column of the table, and the corresponding Pitch Codes (*pc*) of 8, 11, 0, 2, 4, 5, and 7, respectively, in the parallel column. A *lookup table* lets you or your software look up a value in one column of a table (e.g., the pitch *F*) and find its equivalent in the other column (e.g., the value *5*).

To determine the MIDI pitch code for any number we:

1. Look up the pitch name (pn) in the table, and determine the pitch code (pc)

2. Alter the *pc* value by the accidental:

    $pc = pc + a$; where $\# = +1$ and $\flat = -1$

3. Add the *pc* value to 12 times the octave code (12 semitones per octave):

    $pc = pc + (o \times 12)$

To illustrate, take the first note code, *G3Q*, in the Beethoven example (*b*):

1. Looking up *G* in the table, $pc = 7$

2. There is no accidental, so $pc = 7 + 0 = 7$

3. The octave code is 3, so $pc = 7 + (3 \times 12) = 43$

We could then send the value 43 through a MIDI interface as a Note On message and expect to hear performed the note G in the correct octave. Viewport III, Figure 10.3, shows a piano keyboard with corresponding MIDI codes; MIDI code 43 is G in the correct octave. The complete series of MIDI pitch codes for the Beethoven excerpt is: 43–48–52–55–60–64–62–53–55.

This should give you a idea of how music codes can be translated into MIDI performance codes from a notation program. The next part of our exercise will be to translate these same codes into display locations on the page for notation.

Notating the Simple Music Codes. This translation is considerably less straightforward than the performance translation. For our exercise here, we will just give you a snippet of an example as to how one might develop a structure for representing notation on the computer screen or the printed page.

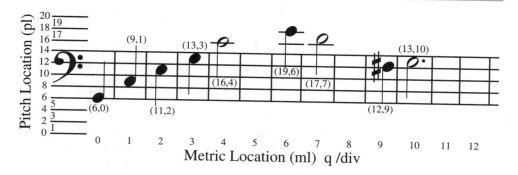

Figure 17.3
Notation matrix for displaying the Simple Music Codes from Beethoven's Symphony No. 5

Study Figure 17.3 for a moment. Notice how we have changed the music staff into a matrix of *pitch location* by *metric location*. The notes from our Beethoven example have been overlaid on the matrix, which represents the bass clef.

The vertical axis of this matrix represents display locations for pitch (pl) with a MOD-7 scale; it starts on A (0) and goes up by steps on the staff until you get to G(6). We will need another *lookup table* here for the computer to use in translating the Pitch Name (*pn*) into Pitch Location (*pl*) values. Visualize a column of Pitch Names, A, B, C, D, E, F, and G, and a parallel column of Pitch Locations, 0, 1, 2, 3, 4, 5, and 6. Then we factor in the octave code to continue the Pitch Location scale. The series of seven notes (A–G) starts over again, with the next A or Pitch Location (*pl*) as:

$pl = pl + (o \times 7)$ or, for the next octave A,

$pl = 0 + (1 \times 7) = 7$

Thus, A(7) to G(13) is the next octave, and A(14) to G(20) is the last octave represented on this matrix. Compare this with our formula for translating the octave for the Pitch Code (*pc*) earlier. The only difference is that we are using 7 as the constant rather than 12.

OOPS! A slight oversight. The octave range we are using for the Notation Matrix and the one designed into the Simple Music Code do not match. The matrix has a restricted range, so we will need to offset our octave code (*o*) by a constant of 3.

Metric location. The horizontal axis in notation matrix for the Beethoven example represents Metric Locations (*ml*). We have divided time along the axis into divisions of the quarter note; that is to say, quarter-note time slices. If we needed finer resolution we could have used an eighth or sixteenth note. The rhythm code is coded as the number of divisions or places along the Metric Location axis required for that symbol. A quarter note is the smallest value, so it represents one (1) division, a half note represents two (2) divisions, and so on.

Displaying the notes. Given our system for coding pitch and rhythm, all we need to do to display any note is to locate its position within this matrix (*pl, ml*) and draw the necessary symbols at that point. Notice that we have indicated the coordinates (*pl, ml*) next to each of the notes in Figure 17.3. The interpretive codes in the Simple Music Code could be used here as well to instruct the computer to perform the following tasks:

!F = Draw a bass clef staff on the page

!K3B = Draw a key signature with 3 flats

!M34 = Draw a meter signature with {3/4} time

!T100 = Draw a metronomic marking of M.M. = 100

Remember that in a display system, everything is referenced as coordinates in space. In our example here, the displayed items were coordinates within the staff. A display system has to deal with many issues that we have skipped. Among the especially difficult ones are stem position; barlines; slurs, beams, and ties; nuances of note spacing; multiple voices; and more complex staff systems. If you want to know more about programming music structures on your own, the text *PASCAL Programming for Music Research* by Alexander Brinkman, is a good resource.

Tour of Computer Music Coding Systems

Let us further expand our view of data structures for coding music by taking a brief look at some of the attempts that have been made in developing music notation systems using the computer. Musicians, engineers, and others have devised ingenious systems to mechanically code music events.

Pre-1950s: Mechanical Music Coding. As best we know, music notation has been around since the Chinese first used notation for their lute tablatures (100 AD or earlier). The emergence of the Western music notation system we use today dates to around 1400 AD with the beginnings of mensural notation. Petrucci of Fossombrone (see example in Figure 17.5*a*), Breitkopf of Leipzig, and other early music typographers including Pierre Attaignant and Tylman Susato developed the traditions and techniques of printing music from movable type. Music typography as it evolved from the 1400s on forms the basis for much of current computer-aided notation. This lineage is present in the fonts, layout, rules, and techniques used to move music symbols around the computer screen and onto computer printers. Figure 17.5*b* shows examples of the Diamond mosaic font for piano and chant music. Each notation element was assigned a unique numeric code. A sample of these notation codes from an 1873 book of typefaces is shown in Figure 17.6.

Until the middle of the nineteenth century, most music notation was done by hand by calligraphers or typesetters. Early attempts at automating the process were proposed in theory by Johann Unger in 1745 with the design of his Machina ad Sonos et Concentus. The Machina was to print lines on paper with ink pens connected through rods and levers to the keys on a clavichord. Miles Berry's 1836 music-writing machine realized Unger's design with limited success, printing a music code of dots and dashes on a roll of paper. Successful music typewriters appeared in the late 1800s along with the invention of the first Mergenthaler linotype. Examples include Angelo Tessaro's Tachigrafo Musicale (1887), and Noco-Blick's (1910) and

Coda named its Finale music font *Petrucci*.

Figure 17.4
Two music typewriters from (*a*) the 1920s and (*b*) the 1950s

(*a*) The Blick Music Typewriter (ca. 1910) from Gamble's *Music Engraving and Printing*
(Photo courtesy of the Newberry Library)

(*b*) A later model of the Musicwriter orginally developed by Cecil Effinger ca. 1955
(Courtesy of the Music Print Company, Inc.)

J. Walton's (1920) music typewriters (see Figure 17.4*a*). Later, Armando Dal Molin (1948) and Cecil Effinger (1955) developed more sophisticated music typewriters, with Dal Molin's system turning into his Music Reprographics printing business in New York City and Effinger's Musicwriter (Figure 17.4*b*) becoming one of the most popular music typewriters for amateurs and professional musicians.

Music coding for performance. Attempts at automating music performance in the late 1700s brought about the first mechanical music coding systems. Music boxes, calliopes, mechanical orchestras, and the immensely popular player pianos coded their music with systems of pins on metal drums, punched holes in paper rolls, and holes in circular metal discs. Some consider Givelet and Coupleux's programmable organ (ca. 1929) to be one of the first programmable synthesizers; the organ's four oscillators were controlled by codes on punched paper rolls.

The data structure for these devices consisted of pitch and duration coded over time on a revolving drum, paper roll, or disc; some of the more advanced player pianos provided coding of different dynamics through separate holes or tracks for pitch and velocity. The data structures have changed little over the years; just the delivery and storage technology. Today's music sequencing software still uses the piano player roll, now graphically portrayed on the computer screen.

ASIDE

Hiller and Effinger collaborated in 1960 to interface the Musicwriter to a computer.

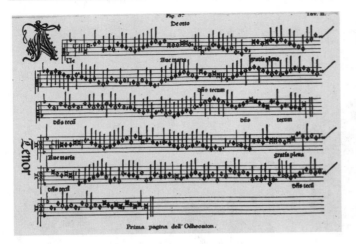

(a) An example of Petrucci's music typography from Vernarecci's *Ottaviano de' Petrucci da Fossombrone: Inventore dei Fipi Mobili Metallici Fusi Della Musica*, 1882 (Photo courtesy of the Newberry Library, Chicago)

(b) Two examples of the use of the Diamond music font for piano and chant notation from Shanks & Co.'s *Specimens of Printing Types and Music Founts*, 1873 (Photo courtesy of the John M. Wing Foundation, The Newberry Library, Chicago)

Figure 17.5
Examples of (a) Petrucci's music typography and (b) mosaic printing with the Diamond music font

See Module 28 for an explanation of machine language and other computer languages.

Figure 17.6
A sample from a mosaic music font with small, equal-sized parts used much as computer font parts are today; from Shanks & Co.'s *Specimens of Printing Types and Music Founts*, 1873 (Photo courtesy of the John M. Wing Foundation, The Newberry Library, Chicago)

1950s to 1960s: Notation to Feed the First Computer Music Synthesizers. In the 1950s, Mathews at Bell Labs, Olson and Belar at Columbia and Princeton, and Hiller and Isaacson at the University of Illinois built some of the earliest computer music synthesizers, including the ILLIAC and the RCA Mark I and II synthesizers. The only language available to program these machines was the native machine language, and input was through punched cards or punched paper tape—not much different from coding on piano rolls. Expressing music codes in a readable form was the least of one's concerns; just the ability to control a computer synthesizer with any notation system, no matter how cryptic and unfriendly, was sufficient reward.

Max Mathews developed a music input language called MUSIC 1 at this time that quickly went through several transformations, MUSIC 3 through MUSIC 5. Other versions of this code were developed at various universities like Princeton, Stanford, and Queens College.

Let's examine how Mathews's machine-friendly (music-unfriendly) system worked. In Table 17.2, you see the coding for our Beethoven excerpt from the Fifth Symphony (see the original notation in Figure 17.2a). The chart is fairly self-explanatory. This is strictly a performance coding system. Pitch and loudness are coded in physical terms as frequency and amplitude, permitting considerable freedom in the intonation and intensity of each

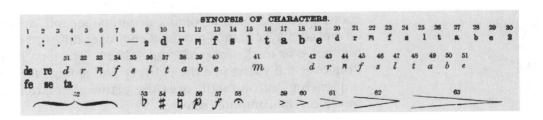

Table 17.2 Mathews's MUSIC 5 code for the Beethoven excerpt (c. 1965)

Instrument	Starttime (secs)	Duration (secs)	Frequency	Amplitude
NOT 0	0	1	098	20,000
NOT 0	1	1	131	20,000
NOT 0	2	1	165	20,000
NOT 0	3	1	196	20,000
NOT 0	4	2	262	20,000
NOT 0	6	1	330	20,000
NOT 0	7	2	294	20,000
NOT 0	9	1	185	20,000
NOT 0	10	3	196	20,000

note. Duration is expressed in seconds (or fractions of a second), and the cumulative Starttime works similarly to MIDI timing in most sequencing software.

In the design of Mathews's music system, there were two operations: creating the instrument definitions or algorithms for generating sounds, and creating the score of codes for the music sequence as shown in Table 17.2. You can see that composing an extensive composition by working directly with the numeric codes would be very tedious.

To check the frequencies against the notes for the Beethoven excerpt, use the keyboard diagram (Figure 10.3).

MIDI timing is discussed in Module 21.

Mid-1960s to Mid-1970s: Friendlier Text-Based Music Coding. In 1963, the ASCII standard was defined for keyboard devices like computers and teletypes. The first generation of friendly notation systems for the large mainframe computers of that time appeared, with such names as DARMS (or Ford-Columbia Input Language), MUSTRAN, Plaine and Easie Code, Score, and other derivations and inventions.

Stanford University was using the Mathews's MUSIC system adapted for their computer-music synthesizer MUSIC 6 and 10. Leland Smith developed one of several preprocessors to follow that let musicians use a text- or ASCII-based coding system in place of the numeric codes we saw for MUSIC 5. Table 17.3 demonstrates Smith's Score language for the Beethoven excerpt.

Again, the example is self-explanatory. Notice that it is, indeed, a much friendlier notation language, permitting greater efficiency for entry and edit-

Table 17.3 Smith's preprocessor, SCORE, for Music 10 coding for the Beethoven excerpt (c. 1970)

Code	Comments
Tempo 13 120	120 beats per minute
i1 0 13	instrument 1 begin at time 0 and play for 13 beats
p 3 rhythm 4 / 4 / 4 / 4 / 2 / 4 / 2 / 4 / 2.;	rhythm codes
p 4 notes g2 / c3/ e / g / c4 / e / d / fs3 / g ;	pitch codes
p 5 numbers 20000 * 13 ;	amplitude for 13 notes
end;	

Table 17.4 Bauer-Mengelberg's DARMS code for the Beethoven excerpt (ca. 1965)

Code	Comments

Single line code:
!F !K3- !M3:4 1Q / 4 6 8 / 31H 33Q / 32H 7#Q / 8H. /

Analysis:

Note: Display or space codes indicate unique location on the staff

!F !K3- !M3:4	Bass clef; key signature with 3 flats (3-); meter of 3/4
1Q / 4 6 8 /	Staff display locations 1, 4, 6, and 8 with quarter notes
31H 33Q /	Space codes 31 and 33; half and quarter note
32H 7#Q /	Space codes 32 and 7; half and quarter with a sharp sign
8H. /	Space code 8 with a dotted half note

Smith's Score notation software will reappear later!

ing. You may notice some similarity to the Simple Music Code, shown in the sidebar earlier in this module, in the way that pitch, rhythm, and octaves are coded.

In 1965, musicologists gathered for the first time to discuss computer applications at two symposia, Musicology and the Computer I and II. Several music notation systems for music analysis, printing, and cataloging were presented. Most of them were single-line, text-based entry systems using alphanumeric codes that bore some resemblance to the music symbols.

In Table 17.4 you can see an illustration of the comprehensive DARMS (Digital Alternative Representation of Musical Scores) code developed by Stefan Bauer-Mengelberg. Its particular design was optimized for music printing. The coding system was centered around space or location codes graphically related to the printed staff. This system is very much like the Simple

Table 17.5 Brook's "Plaine and Easie Code" for the Beethoven excerpt (c. 1965)

Codes	Comments

Single line code:
(Allegro, bBEAminor, 3/4) ,,4G/ ,C E G / '2C 4E / 2D ,4#F / 2.G /

Analysis:

Note: Octaves are designated ,, , ' "

(Allegro, bBEAminor, 3/4)	Tempo Marking Key signature: 3 flats which are B, E, and A, and A minor key Meter in 3/4
,,4G/ ,C E G /	4 = quarter note; pitches GCEG with octave markings
'2C 4E / 2D ,4#F /	2 = half and 4 = quarter note; pitches are CED and an F #
2.G /	Dotted half note G

Figure 17.7
Wenker's MUSTRAN code (Adapted from "A Computer Oriented Music Notation" by J. Wenker in *Musicology and the Computer*, B. Brook (ed.), The City University of New York Press [New York, 1970])

GS,2E,4(+1)F,8$(-3)G,8(+5)A,8N(+7)C,1D

(a) Micro-Accidental Coding

GS,6=4,4D(++),4*F(+),8G(+),8C+(-),8C+(-),4G.
JH+H(-),4G(-),//,END

(b) Estimated pitch coding

Music Code example presented earlier, where pitch codes were translated to display codes in much the same way. You will note other similarities as well.

In his report on the DARMS code at the 1965 musicology symposium, Bauer-Mengelberg also talked about the Photon, a device interfaced with the computer performing the DARMS translation, that had remarkable similarity in concept to present-day laser printers and phototypesetters. The Photon was a revolving glass disc with 1,440 symbols; the computer selected the symbol to be printed and then optically imaged that symbol onto film for printing.

Barry Brook's Plaine and Easie Code was designed for cataloging music scores. Its objective was to provide a human-readable code using standard keyboard characters on a single line. The Beethoven excerpt is coded in Table 17.5 with the Plaine and Easie Code. This system contains many features of future text-based computer notation systems. Several direct spin-off languages from Brook's code were Gould and Loge Mann's ALMA (ca. 1970) and Hofstetter's MUSICODE (1972).

The 1965 Musicology and the Computer symposia presented other notation systems besides Bauer-Mengelberg's and Brook's. Above is an illustration of Jerome Wenker's feature-laden notation language, MUSTRAN (called MUSAN at the symposium). It was unique in its ability to code music required for ethnomusicology research and cataloging. Figure 17.7 shows how MUSTRAN codes micro-accidentals and subtle nuances of pitch change in the documentation of performed music.

1970s: Experimentation and Graphic Display of Notation. Many different developments were occurring during the 1970s. Musicians had minicomputers, graphic displays, early interactive operating systems, and voltage-controlled synthesizers to play with. Punch cards and tape were being replaced by magnetic tape and hard-disk storage. With minicomputers readily available, greater experimentation occurred with music composing and notation systems. Just about any musician on a college campus with access to a computer could experiment with computer music analysis, composition, or cataloging using text-based coding systems like DARMS, Plaine and Easie, and MUSTRAN. The missing link for notation at this time was a low-cost, high-resolution music-printing device. History was waiting for the laser printer!

Graphic display devices and interactive computer systems began to offer the opportunity for text-based notation systems to be augmented and enhanced with graphic display and editing of notation symbols. Mathews and Rosler at Bell Labs had started experimenting with graphic entry of notation with Graphic 1 and an IBM 7094 around 1965. That device is por-

Figure 17.8
The Xerox PARC Mocking-
bird music workstation
(Photo courtesy of the Charles
Babbage Institute, University
of Minnesota, Minneapolis)

trayed in the action photo of Mathews in Viewport VII. William Buxton at
the University of Toronto created one of the first entirely graphics-based
music score systems; the Structured Sound Synthesis Project (SSSP), using a
digitizing tablet and custom slider box (early equivalent of the mouse) for
music entry and editing.

The MUSICOMP system developed by Armando dal Molin for his Music
Reprographics music printing firm was a custom computer system with a
special music symbol keyboard and graphic display of notation. Later in the
1970s, John Maxwell and Severo Ornstein designed the Mockingbird music
notation system at Xerox Palo Alto Research Center (PARC). The Mockingbird system (see Figure 17.8) took advantage of the features of a graphical
user interface with a mouse, invented at PARC, and laser printing to create a
complete graphic environment for manipulating music symbols. This system, like those of Buxton and dal Molin, was a precursor to much of the
music notation software to come in the late 1980s on personal computers.
Donald Byrd's Nightingale notation program, published in 1993 after many
years in development, has design ties to the Xerox Mockingbird software.

Also during the '70s, the Dartmouth group of Sydney Alonso, Cameron
Jones, and Jon Appleton built their minicomputer-based Synclavier music
system, which provided one of the first professional music composing and
publishing systems for small-frame computers. And the CERL PLATO computer group at the University of Illinois, with their video displays and touch-
sensitive panels, developed the LIME notation software.

Early 1980s: Personal Computers and Consumer Music Systems. With
the introduction of the first personal computers in the late 1970s—the PET,
Apple II, TRS-80, and others—the development of computer music systems
rapidly accelerated. Computer engineers and hackers, driven in part by their
desire to create video games, designed impressive graphics features as well
as simple sound generation into the first PCs. The sound capabilities were
quickly enhanced by add-on cards and boxes that appeared in the late
1970s, like the ALF 3-voice analog music card and the Micro Music (MMI)

four-voice digital sampling card for the Apple II, and the MTU digital music card for the Commodore PET. The next generation of sound systems for these early PCs included the Mountain Music System, the Wenger Sound-Chaser, the AlphaSyntauri music system, and a wide variety of software for the Commodore 64's SID sound chip.

Music coding systems and graphic display of music notation that had been reserved for mainframe and minicomputers quickly found their way to the early PCs. The MMI Music Composer software for the Apple II used a text-based, command-line notation system for entering up to four voices of polyphonic music. The notation appeared on screen and would scroll in time with the music. The command-line music code bore a resemblance to Brook's Plaine and Easie code. David B. Williams designed the software (Music Experimenters Package or MEP) that processed the music sound and graphics coding used in the Music Composer and in the large library of music CAI software produced by Micro Music in the early 1980s.

Other similar music software quickly appeared, and coding music for composing jumped from an esoteric pursuit of selected musicians in studios and colleges to an activity accessible to anyone. The software became more sophisticated, and true notation software appeared with such systems as Passport's Polywriter software and Jack Jarrett's MusicPrinter for the Apple II (originally published by Temporal Acuity Products). These systems used combinations of command-line input, custom music keyboards, and graphics display. A major limiting factor to computer music notation remained the lack of low-cost, high-resolution printing.

Mid-1980s: The Birth of Desktop Music Publishing. Several significant events surfaced in the period from 1984 to 1986 that, when combined, changed music composing and notation and made high-quality music printing accessible to anyone:

▶ The Macintosh personal computer provided the ideal operating system with its graphical user interface and mouse; music could now be manipulated by symbols without the need for intervening text or numeric codes just as on the earlier Mockingbird system at Xerox PARC

▶ The MIDI music standard provided interchangeable input and output devices and a standardized data structure for the entry and performance of music code

▶ The HP and Apple laser printers provided the low-cost, high-resolution printers that were needed

▶ Cleo Higgins of Adobe Systems created the first PostScript music font, Sonata, for the new laser-printer technology

▶ Mark of the Unicorn's Professional Composer software, Deluxe Music Construction Set, and Concertware provided graphics-based consumer and professional music notation software

The IBM PC, with its traditional, command-line DOS operating system, was also rapidly gaining in popularity. Jim Miller's Personal Composer, for the IBM platform, was the first widely-used sequencer and notation program using graphic display and command-line input of notation. Jarrett's Music Printer for the Apple II was given a major overhaul and emerged as Music Printer Plus for the IBM PC. Leland Smith's Score notation software resurfaced as one of the more sophisticated music-notation programs available; however, in this case, its lineage back to the days of the MUSIC 5 family also gave it a very complex text-based input language. Similarly to Smith's Score software, LIME notation software was dusted off by the CERL group and adapted to the Macintosh and Wintel PCs of the 1990s. And Keith Hamel's Notewriter and Frederick Noad's Speedscore provided music printing software designed for free-form placement of music symbols on the music page, with little concern for performance.

Music data structures go underground. There is a significant point to be made here in terms of the study of notation coding systems for music. The musicians of the 1960s who developed DARMS and other programs were concerned with developing computer data structures for music that could be easily understood by musicians. With the proliferation of graphic display of notation on the computers of the 1980s, the data structure could now become transparent to the user: the user no longer needed to be aware of the complex codes that make possible computer notating or performance.

Late 1980s and 1990s: Intelligent Rule-Based Music Coding Systems. Key developments in the design of music coding systems in this period are total graphic notation systems, rule-based integration of performance and notation activities, greater input and performance options, and machine independence. One of the premiere notation programs in the late 1980s was Coda's Finale, first released for the Macintosh and then for the Wintel computers. Finale is based on the ENIGMA notation software developed by Phil Farrand and Tim Strathlee of Opus Dei. Rule-based operations in the software enable accurate quantizing of performance data to notation data; transposition; error checking for meter and rhythm; and intelligent placement of notes, beams, and many other layout features. Donald Byrd's Nightingale (originally published by Temporal Acuity Products) rivaled Finale in its design sophistication and features, but it is more sensitive to the user interface and ease of use. Others to come on stage include G-VOX's Encore, Concertware by Jump!, Mark of the Unicorn's Mosaic, and Overture from Opcode (now Cakewalk). Sibelius (originally for the British Acorn computer) and Graphire MUSIC PRESS are two other sophisticated notation systems.

The trend appears to be toward software that integrates both the performance and display domains. In practice this means that sequencing (performing) and notation (display) software are merging. Such programs will depend on increasing refinement in the intelligence of the software's rules to carry out the translations needed to cross between the display and performance domains. Much of the present-day notation software is heavily dependent on rule-based structures for quantizing performance. To the person solely interested in music printing, this may be more of a hindrance than a gain. As Donald Byrd noted, "any notation program that thinks it can tell what its users *really* want is going to do them a lot of favors they would have been better off without." Notation software like Notewriter II, SpeedScore, and Sion Copyist may be the last of the notation programs that provide a free-form, space-oriented graphics environment (with no rules) for creating printed scores where the musician is in complete control. The challenge to the next generation of software is to provide highly intelligent rule-based environments in consort with a free-form graphic environment that lets musicians choose the degree of control desired whether they are performing or printing music.

Music Fonts and Files for Notation

Revisit Module 14 to review data structures for fonts.

Parallel to music coding is the issue of structures for the files and fonts that support music performing and notation activities. Common problems occur when someone is trying to learn a new notation program: the notation generated by the printer is a curious jumble of alphanumeric characters instead of music symbols; or an imported notation is displayed with the beaming, spacing, slurs, page layout, and other features lost. Both of these situations can produce a very frustrated musician! These problems—and many others—can be explained by understanding the data structures behind music fonts and files.

Music Fonts: Bitmaps and Outlines. Music notation fonts are a little different in design from other printer fonts. Keep in mind the difference

Table 17.6 Petrucci and Seville Music Symbols Compared with ASCII Characters		
ASCII Font	**Petrucci Font**	**Seville Font**
U	⌒	🎸
?	𝄢	🎸
&	𝄞	
e	♪	🎸
h	♩	🎸
F	*mf*	🎸

between bitmapped fonts, which are created from patterns of digitized dots, and outline fonts (PostScript or TrueType), which are created from mathematical outlines that describe the shape of each font symbol. Bitmapped fonts are typically used for screen display and for printing on dot matrix or other printers that do not support PostScript or TrueType fonts. Typically, outline music fonts come with a bitmapped equivalent for the computer to use for screen display.

The first PostScript music font was the Adobe Sonata font, designed by Cleo Huggins in 1986. It remains one of the most commonly used music fonts. Table 17.6 shows a sample from two music fonts: the Petrucci font used in Finale notation software and the Seville font for notating guitar tablatures. The music symbols are matched to the ASCII alphanumeric set. The keystroke for letter *e*, for example, gives you an eighth-note symbol, stem up in Petrucci; by adding the Shift key with the *e* you get the same value with stem down. The letter *h* gives you a half note, *w* a whole note, and so on. Likewise, any guitar chord can be indicated by choosing the ASCII letter associated with the appropriate tablature. One could actually construct some music notation or provide guitar tablatures within any word processor document by selecting a music font and looking up the corresponding ASCII keystrokes.

With this background on music fonts, let's see if we can resolve the common problem with printing music that results in alphanumeric jumble on the printer page. If you do not have the PostScript version of the font required by the notation program installed on your computer, the printout will be a string of alphanumeric characters. In the absence of the necessary music font, the printer substitutes its default font (which uses ASCII characters) for the music symbols. Remember, the music symbols are mapped onto the ASCII character set used by all fonts. Perhaps the software doesn't provide the PostScript font but only the bitmapped version. If this is the case, you will have to buy the font yourself.

If you have to purchase a PostScript music font, or if you try to use one from your other music programs, you need to be aware that many notation programs do not let you use music fonts other than the one for which the software was designed. If a program is designed for Sonata, then Sonata may be the only font you can use. Even though the music symbol may correspond to the same ASCII code, the form of each symbol in terms of height and width and other typographical factors may vary. Substituting a music font usually results in a printout where the music symbols are out of alignment and stems are not connected to notes, along with other signs of printing disaster!

Lots of Music Fonts. Several music fonts have been designed since Sonata in 1986, some created to add extra features and others to sidestep licensing fees with Adobe. Coda's Petrucci font and Passport's (G-VOX's) Anastasia font are two examples. Others include Mark of the Unicorn's Vivo music font and Sibelius's Opus IV font.

Music fonts that have the look of handwritten music charts are popular. Nightingale has added Tom Williams's Blue Notz handwritten font, Sibelius

Remember that most music fonts are copyrighted!

Figure 17.9
An example of music printed with a set of fonts designed to simulate handwritten music notation, the JazzFont collection.
(Image provided courtesy of Sigler Music Fonts at www.jazzfont.com)

has its Manuscript font, and the GoldenAge font provides the look of professional, hand-copied sheet music. Figure 17.9 shows a handwritten notation example created with the JazzFont collection designed by Richard Sigler.

Besides standard music printing fonts, there are a host of specialty fonts. For shaped notes there are Willard's Doremi font; Hindson's fonts for harp pedals; recorder fingerings, and saxophone fingerings; Clevenger's ChordSymbol font, which features a wide variety of analytical symbols including roman numerals and letter names, and figures and slashed figures in three tiers; and the Gregorian chant font, StMeinard, from the Saint Meinard Archabbey. For old-style printed music one can use the Rameau font. Additionally, some notation programs like Finale let you create your own symbols within the notation software.

Music File Standards: SMF, ETF, NIFF, and SMGL. A common music file format that will transfer between all music software and exchange performance as well as display data does not exist. With music notation scanning software on the market the problem becomes more intense, because this software needs to be able to store the music codes in a form accessible to a large number of notation programs.

There are basically two sets of file types we will consider:

▶ MIDI performance files (SMF or MID)

▶ Display or notation code files (ETF, NIFF, and SMGL)

More on MIDI files in Viewport VI, where we discuss sequencing software and exporting and importing music files.

To understand the uniqueness of each set, we must return to the distinction between performance and display data structures made at the beginning of this module. MIDI performance files store only performance events that happen over time: MIDI events like pitch, velocity, control codes, and so on. Display files are space or location oriented and generally store information about symbol placement on the printed page. The translation gap

Table 17.7 Three Types of Standard MIDI Files

Format	Structure
Format 0	All MIDI data combined in one track
Format 1	MIDI data remain in unique tracks, tempo and time signature in first track only
Format 2	MIDI data remain in unique tracks as well as tempo and time signature

remains when you try to move performance files into display code environments and vice versa.

MIDI performance files (SMF or MID). SMF or *Standard MIDI File* formats were adopted by the MIDI Manufacturers Association in 1988. These files have the extension .SMF or .MID. Most notation programs permit importing and saving SMF files. There are three types of SMF files: Formats 0, 1, and 2 (Table 17.7).

Because MIDI SMF files are a performance data structure, SMF files do not contain text or graphic data, with the exception of track names. When you save a notation file as an SMF file with the intent of importing it into another notation program, key information is lost, including: slurs, accents, articulation markings like staccato and legato, dynamics, measures per system, systems per page, all layout information, correct spellings of enharmonics and chords, and, to some extent, rhythmic values and patterns.

When you go to import the SMF file back into another notation program, the software has to be smart enough (i.e., have enough rules) to infer the display elements from the performance SMF data file. Rhythmic values are another major problem. The MIDI Note On and Note Off data have to be re-quantized back into rhythm codes. Meter and barlines may translate accurately provided that the software has rules to accommodate this translation, but any problems with mixed and compound meters, tied notes, or complex rhythm patterns will have to be corrected manually.

Why have SMF files at all, you ask? Three reasons come immediately to mind. First, SMF files work fine when going from performance environment to performance environment, as with sequencers, for example. Second, SMF in a notation environment can be used similarly to ASCII text files in a word processor. If you need to go between notation programs you at least can import and export the basic content: pitch and, with some limitations, meter and rhythm. Third, as we shall see, all notation programs seem to support the MIDI SMF standard, even given its glaring deficiencies.

Developing music notation file standards. There have been a few attempts at standard file structures for transporting display codes between software applications. However, those developing and designing notation software have yet to embrace any one standard file type throughout the industry (except the SMF standard noted above).

Each notation program seems to have its own unique format. To make matters even more difficult, many of the notation programs that now exist on both platforms, Macintosh and Windows, do not translate successfully across platforms. Notation software typically does not have built-in translators, as word processors do, to enable you to read display codes from a competitor's file (e.g., Word to WordPerfect in word processing compared with Finale and Encore in music notation). This tells us something significant about the structural design underlying the different commercial notation products. How they represent music display elements is radically different and in a proprietary format. This makes it a very difficult task to write translators between notation programs.

Finale's file format could become a common standard that all notation programs would read, simply because of the large installed base of Finale software in the music industry and in education. Finale is based on the Enigma notation engine, and Finale files can be saved in *Enigma Transportable File* or *ETF* format. However, in early 1998, other than Coda's Finale, only Musicware's Nightingale offered the option of importing ETF notation files.

There are two major attempts at developing standard industry formats apart from existing music products: NIFF and SMGL. The *Notation Interchange File Format* or *NIFF* was completed in 1995 through the sponsorship of a large number of music industry participants, among them Musicware, Mark of the Unicorn, Cakewalk Music Software, Passport Designs, and Opcode.

The data structure for NIFF was designed to be very flexible, allowing the simplest to the most complex of music notation, even MIDI performance codes, to be stored. The designers of NIFF considered both the DARMS music coding system and the Score structure. SGML (noted below) was also examined, but SGML was not completed at the time. In the end the NIFF format modeled its features on Score, added many useful functions from DARMS, and used the most current format conventions, namely Microsoft's Resource Interchange File Format (RIFF) for its file structure.

NIFF seems like a wonderful cooperative venture that draws on the historical lineage of music notation formats. However, as of 1998, none of those sponsoring the development of NIFF had included the facility for importing and exporting the file format in their notation software. Only CERL's Lime notation software and Musitek's MIDISCAN music scanning software had NIFF import and export features, as well as some music braille translation software.

Another possibility exists for standardization in notation data files, SDML or *Standard Music Description Language*. A team of IBM researchers led by Charles Goldfarb developed a Generalized Markup Language (GML) in the 1960s. A *markup language* is a set of codes for "marking up" or formatting. This language was adopted by the International Standards Organization (ISO) in 1986 as Standard GML (SGML). SGML is used by government agencies and industry as a document standard and appears as a file format option in some word processors.

HTML (HyperText Markup Language), used to lay out documents for the World Wide Web, is also a derivative of SGML. HTML was designed by Tim Berners-Lee, working at the CERN research lab in Switzerland at the time, for linking research documents over the Internet. SGML and HTML use a

The HTML markup language, used for the World Wide Web on the Internet, is a relative of SGML (see Viewport VIII).

series of *tags* to specify the format and layout of a document. These tags are similar to those used in printing and typesetting and in early word processors for PCs, like Applewriter and WordStar. The tags indicate placement and format of text, graphics, Web links, and the like.

In 1986, Goldfarb, along with Steven Newcomb, headed a committee to define a music markup language based on SGML, the *Standard Music Description Language* or *SDML*. The first meeting of the committee was hosted by Passport Designs. Several key persons from the historical overview of music notation presented in this module contributed to the project, among many others. With the rapid growth of multimedia applications, however, the HyTime (Hypermedia/Time-based Structuring Language) standard for multimedia applications emerged from the early efforts of SGML and was officially sanctioned by ISO in 1992. The SMDL markup language for music exists as a proposed subset of HyTime. However, as of 1998, the McGill University "Music Library of the Future" project and the Thesaurus Musicarum Italicarum (TMI) project editing Italian Renaissance and early Baroque music treatises plan on using SGML markup codes for documenting music.

Module

18

Input Devices for Music Notation

A variety of techniques are currently used for music notation software to enter music codes into the computer. None of them reach either Arthur Mendel's goal of going directly from printed music to music codes or Yavelow's goal of going directly from performance to the printed page. What we do have is a variety of entry techniques that can be combined in various ways to suit the skill, needs, and preferences of the musician.

Music entry systems include:

► Text codes or key codes entered from a computer keyboard and numeric keypad

► MIDI controllers (keyboards, wind controllers, guitar controllers, etc.)

► Pitch-to-voltage or pitch-to-MIDI converters for singing or playing

► Graphic palettes with a mouse or other pointing device

► Alternative nonmusical input devices

► Music optical character recognition

Let's take a quick tour through these options. Most musicians like working with a MIDI keyboard and a mouse, but one is always looking for faster ways to produce a clean, professional-looking music score.

Text and Key Codes from the Computer Keyboard

Text-based music coding systems have been around since the DARMS code was introduced. These coding systems are based on ASCII text commands and codes associated with the computer keyboard. Some notation programs still offer a text-based music code, at least as an alternative to graphic entry of notation. There are composers who still find text codes a fast and desirable entry system. (See Tables 17.4 and 17.5 for examples of text-based codes.)

Just about all of the music notation programs offer single keystrokes for entering pitch, rhythm, and other music symbols. The layouts for the keystroke alternatives are complex enough that you need a template as a guide. Notation programs make effective use of the numeric keypads that are available on extended computer keyboards. A detachable numeric keypad is very handy for this type of entry system.

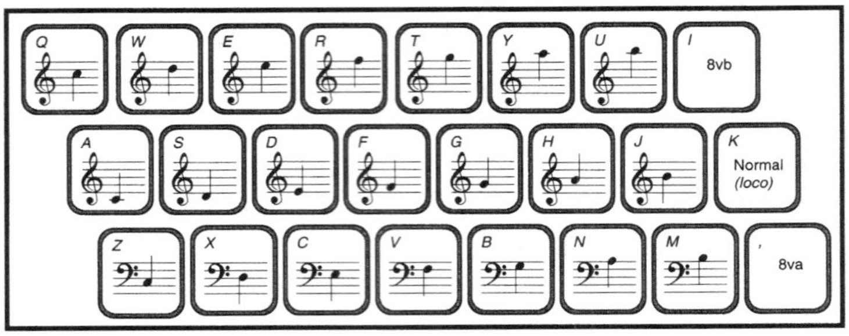

Figure 18.1
The keypad codes for
Speedy Entry pitch in
Finale.

Pitch can be associated with key names, oftentimes either the corresponding letter of the alphabet or through a physical relationship to the keyboard. Rhythms can be associated with numeric values on the keyboard. Figure 18.1 shows the Speedy Entry keystrokes used in Finale for pitch in different octaves. Rhythms are associated geographically with the numeric keys across the top of the keyboard: 1 equated with the 64th note, across to 8 being associated with the double whole note. Key coded systems like Finale's Speedy Entry can be used alone or in combination with a MIDI music keyboard for quick notation input.

You can create your own custom key codes or commands as well. Keyboard macro editors like QuickKeys for Macintosh or Perfect Keyboard for Windows 95 are utilities that let you define a series of commands with one keystroke. A single keystroke can easily be programmed for any complex set of operations from within your music notation software. For example, you can create a single keystroke command to play the music that will automatically save your work before it starts playing.

MIDI Controllers

MIDI keyboard controllers are discussed in Module 12 and other MIDI controllers in Module 21.

Pitch-to-MIDI and Pitch-to-voltage conversion is covered in Module 22.

The use of a MIDI keyboard is a standard music entry option with music notation software. Don't overlook the obvious, however, that any other MIDI controller such as a guitar or wind controller can be used for music entry. Pick the MIDI controller that best fits your music performance talents. Most notation programs permit *real-time entry* of music through a built-in sequencer in the software. As we found in Module 17, the software must be sophisticated enough to quantize or round off the rhythmic values as you perform the music so that you don't end up with a lot of strange rhythmic values for every bit of rubato you put into your playing.

Step-time entry with a MIDI keyboard is a much simpler entry system and gives the user greater control and accuracy over the notation process. Step-time entry uses the MIDI keyboard for the pitch values, and keystrokes or mouse selections for the rhythm values. No rhythm or timing is required in the entry of notes. Hit a key on the computer keyboard to set the rhythm as you strike a key on the MIDI keyboard, or blow the note on your wind controller, or pluck a string on your guitar controller.

Singing in the Notes

If you are looking for an alternative to "singing in the rain," you can try singing in your notes: singing notes to your music notation software, that is. Software like Wildcat's Autoscore uses the microphone or microphone input built into your Mac or Wintel computer and the computer's sound card. As you sing—or play—into the microphone, the software converts the sound vibrations into MIDI codes. You can then save your sequence as a standard MIDI file and load it into any notation program for further editing. A hardware pitch-to-MIDI device is an even better alternative because it will let you use the hardware as a MIDI controller directly with the notation package.

If singing isn't to your liking, then you could try talking to your computer in music notation. Acoustical analysis of your voice works somewhat like the computer's analysis of music pitch. Several voice-recognition devices are available for the Macintosh and Wintel PCs. The Mac OS has voice recognition built into its operating system. These devices let you teach the computer to recognize your voice commands for any operation. If you are using step-time pitch entry with a MIDI keyboard, you can use voice commands for the rhythm values in place of keystrokes. Rehab Designs' IntelliTalk is a special software package for those with physical and visual disabilities that allows spoken entry of keyboard commands.

Graphic Palettes and a Mouse

Few notation programs remain that do not use the GUI interface and provide for the use of a mouse as a pointer device to select music symbols from an array of graphic palettes. Module 16 provided many examples of palettes from a variety of music notation software. However, some musicians prefer to work with step-time entry using keystrokes, finding this entry system faster than pointing and clicking with a mouse. Mouse entry is more suitable for the novice or for small notation tasks where visual representation of music symbols is beneficial. The learning curve is steeper for step-time and key entry systems, but, once acquired, it can be a more direct means for encoding music than point-and-click techniques with a mouse.

Several notation programs have devised clever systems for expanding upon the basic mouse gestures of point-and-click, double-click, click-and-drag, and so on. The goal is always to reduce the number of actions required to enter a note. Nightingale especially has some unique mouse gestures. For the Macintosh, shaking the mouse at a speed you specify toggles the cursor between the arrow pointer and the previous tool you've selected. When you've clicked on the screen, hold down the Command key and you can cycle through the duration values, or hold the Shift key down and cycle through the accidentals.

Alternative Input Devices

There are many other possibilities for entering data into a computer, be they music, words, or graphics. An incredible variety of devices provide alternatives to fit unique entry needs, especially for the disabled. They can also be applied to training, entertainment, and research applications for music.

Figure 18.2 shows two interesting devices that could be used to facilitate music notation entry. Logitech, a major manufacturer of many different strands of computer mice, produces a 3D Mouse (Figure 18.2*a*) that could

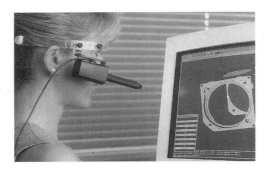

Figure 18.2
(*a*) The Logitech 3D Mouse (Logitech)
(*b*) Vision Control Systems Eye Tracker (Vision Control Systems, part of Ferranti Technologies, Ltd., Lancashire, UK)   (*a*)   (*b*)

be very useful for step entry of music using the numeric keys for the rhythm codes and the controller for cursor placement. The controller, much like a joystick, can be programmed to be responsive to movement along three dimensions, pitch, roll, and yaw. For something a bit more exotic, Vision Control Systems' technology lets you "use your head" to eye-track the cursor around the screen while keeping your hands free for other tasks like playing a MIDI controller (Figure 18.2*b*). The VCS system uses a miniature camera with holographic optics. Other head control systems are available, like the Prentke Romich Headmaster and the EVAS FreeWheel II. IntelliKeys from Rehab Designs is a hardware tray which will connect to a computer's keyboard port. IntelliKeys uses a series of visual overlays for a flexible system that could easily be customized for music entry.

Glove controllers already exist for virtual reality environments; someone will soon figure out a way to program an entry system that is sensitive to hand gestures. Just extend the mouse gestures of Nightingale notation entry to a glove that senses your hand movements, and you've got it! Sketch the note shape in the air with your hand and up it pops on the screen.

Music Optical Character Recognition

Check elsewhere in this text for information about scanners (Module 15), TWAIN drivers (Module 15), TIFF graphics (Module 14), and NIFF music notation files (Module 17).

Arthur Mendel wanted optical character recognition for music way back in 1965. Optical character recognition for text on a personal computer has become fairly sophisticated. Slip a document into a scanner or receive a document image on your fax modem, and OCR software can translate the text into ASCII codes—including styles and tabs in some cases—and drop it directly into your word processor. Music Optical Character Recognition (MOCR) keeps getting better, but still has a way to go. We are talking about a very complex task for a computer when we ask it to read the spatial layout of music notation, with all its nuances, on a score page, and translate all the graphic symbols it recognizes into a perfectly notated score.

Here's how music MOCR works. You place a page of music on a flatbed scanner (usually TWAIN compatible) and scan it in at 200- to 300-dpi resolution. From the graphics or scanning software you are using, you save a graphic image as a TIFF file. Then you use a music MOCR software package that attempts to translate the TIFF graphic image into either standard MIDI codes, or proprietary codes for a specific notation software like Score, or Nightingale, or standard NIFF codes for a music notation program like CERL's Lime. The music OCR software may offer some editing capabilities to let you clean up the graphic image and correct any errors in the translation that you see. You then load the SMF, NIFF, or proprietary notation codes into the appropriate notation software and perform the final editing of the music.

There are several MOCR software packages available for you to try. None of them will provide fast and accurate, automatic translation of printed music. MIDISCAN, for Windows, is designed to translate music images into either SMF files—most of the non-MIDI data on the music score page are thrown out, or into NIFF files which can contain full coding of many of the notation parameters on the printed page. MIDISCAN was originally developed for Windows, with a Macintosh version planned, and comes packaged with LIME music notation software, one of the few notation programs that can read NIFF files.

Another alternative is NOTESCAN from Musicware. This MOCR software is designed to accompany the Nightingale music notation package. The graphic TIFF image of the music score is processed by the NOTESCAN-to-Nightingale converter and then read by Nightingale. It is a Macintosh product. Because it is tailored for Nightingale, it makes every attempt to provide as much notation data as possible to the software. Other MOCR alternatives are ScorScan, developed by Nick Carter in England and designed to interface with the Score music notation package, and Moore Music's MUSICSCAN.

<table>
<tr><td>

Viewport
V

</td><td>

Summary

</td></tr>
</table>

We began this Viewport with an overview of music production software that includes titles that have either notation, sequencing, or digital audio editing as their main approach. These approaches are merging as companies combine capabilities. Table 16.1 is worth careful study as we explore the many music production software packages in this viewport and the ones that follow in Viewports VI and VII.

Uniqueness of Music Notation Software

Some might say that music notation software is to music what word processing is to words. Certainly, music notation software provides musicians with high-quality, printed notation—both scores and automatically extracted parts. Powerful editing and layout features save time, and MIDI playback realizes the sound of the music to help catch errors. Analogies can be drawn between much of this and what word processors do for writers, at least in terms of general function. However, there are at least two major differences that are rooted in a fundamental distinction between words and music.

Complexity. Musicians who have learned traditional notation have come to understand its logic (and sometimes its nonlogic) over many years of experience. We have developed an understanding of its lines, spaces, circles, special symbols, and layering effects. We often forget how graphically involved an orchestral score really is! Even an elementary piano solo is far more intricate than a simple string of words. Programmers who work to create rule-based notation programs know this very well. Music notation is among the most complicated symbol systems to represent in software on a computer.

It's very hard to create your first composition with technology—probably much harder than your first major writing assignment using a word processor. Part of this is because you are learning new software, but it is also because the tasks themselves are very complex, and good software needs to be written to support this complexity.

Sound. Word processors usually just create documents to be read; notation files are almost always expected to do much more, notably to reproduce sound. This expectation creates yet another level of complexity for the programmer. For example, not only must a slur marking be correctly represented graphically (placement, arch) but its effect on sound must be programmed (the attacks on successive notes under the slur must be softened while maintaining dynamics, pitch, duration, and timbre data). This is just one small example. Imagine the demands presented to a programmer and to the computer when an entire orchestral score is to be both visually *and* aurally represented at a standard acceptable to professional musicians! The most full-featured word processor can't touch this kind of challenge.

In Module 17, we explained how data structures that represent sound such as MIDI need to be linked by the software to visual elements to accomplish this objective. This is no small task. The MIDI protocol was developed with performance gestures, not sound from notation, in mind. Another difficulty is the lack of a standard file format for representing music visually, even though the NIFF universal notation format shows promise. This complicates the development of a standard for integrating notation with sound. Given these restrictions and complexities, it is to the enormous credit of software designers and programmers that we've come this far.

Broader Thinking

Assuming you want to notate your music with traditional symbols (not always an assumption one can make automatically about composers today), one major consideration is music context. Whether most of your work is for small chamber groups or for soloists with piano accompaniment, the circumstance will make a major difference in what software to consider. Flawless music notation may also not be necessary for every music context. Cost and learning time are yet other broad issues, as is the quality of music playback.

Another question that faces us is the trade-off between rules and freedom. Notation packages that are based on a rule structure save time, but sometimes force you into structures that are unacceptable and hard to change. Free-form programs allow great freedom to place symbols just where you want them, but they can force you to consume great amounts of time in doing so.

In our examples, we chose to go with a rule-based program that offers several options for larger ensembles and that has a number of advanced features. We also wanted a program with good MIDI sound playback. Your solution might be very different.

Working in a Systematic Order

Music software offers a number of common features that we detailed at length in Module 16. Perhaps more important than these features themselves is the order of execution. In word processing, graphics, and even in other music software, the order in which you do things may not be important. In notation software, however, order can matter. We suggest three stages of operation: note entry; careful editing; and printing. Within each of these stages, we provide a procedure that brings you from the rough layout of the score to the final printing.

Why this compulsion for order? It saves work time. Because music notation is a matrix of vertical and horizontal graphic elements, alignment is critical. If you change the attribute of a staff just before you print, enter lyrics before you create the notes that are linked with the words, or enter all the ties, dynamics, and articulations before entering all the notes, you will waste time. Most notation software can adjust to almost any change (some better than others), but it always takes precious time to reconfigure when major readjustments occur. Frustration can grow to the point of abandoning the entire enterprise. If you follow a systematic path of work in the three stages of development, music will be flowing out of your laser printer in record time.

MIDI, Note Entry, and Thinking in Sound

One of the features that attracts musicians to music notation software is the capability of entering music in a musical way: by performing it. This use of a MIDI device to enter music notation also celebrates the three important ingredients in each of our viewports: software, data, and hardware. All three come together to make machine-assisted note entry occur. You will be surprised when you first see music notation appear on a computer screen as a result of your playing on a MIDI keyboard.

The other important link between software, data, and hardware occurs when you direct staff systems to play certain timbres on your MIDI gear. Here, you can use the power of MIDI to realize a score aurally in ways never before possible. This is perhaps less dramatic for experienced composers and arrangers who already have a sense of what music structures assigned to various timbres will sound like through years of experience. But for younger composers, and certainly for children, this ability is really helpful in learning to think in sound.

Careful Editing

Most notation packages offer similar feature sets. Menus, palettes, and windows all offer similar basic services for note entry and basic editing. Creation and careful editing of certain music notation conventions, however, differ widely across software. Here are a few advanced features that you can expect to find only on select software (usually the more costly and sophisticated):

▶ Beaming between staves and across barlines

▶ Different staff designs, both in number of lines and in layout on the page

▶ Custom key and time signatures

▶ Linked measures in which content changes in one measure will automatically affect other measures

▶ A custom graphics designer, such as an object-oriented draw program, built in to create special graphics

▶ Search and replace

▶ Separate files for extracted parts

▶ File-exporting support for EPS and other formats

You may find that a careful study of the advanced features offered by the software is important in the ultimate decision to buy an expensive notation program, rather than starting with something you will soon outgrow. The time and effort to learn an advanced program from the start may well be the best choice for some people.

Printing, Fonts, and Files

In Module 17, we reviewed music fonts on personal computers, including a listing of some of the common fonts in use today. Bitmapped fonts for music notation are almost always used for screen displays; object-oriented outline fonts are used for high-quality printing.

Final Hardware Note

One last note about hardware: consider a large-screen display for notation work on large scores. With advances in processing speed provided by the PowerPC and Pentium chips, support for quick screen redrawing makes large screens a real asset for composers and arrangers.

Supplementary Readings

Brinkman, Alexander. *Pascal Programming for Music Research.* Chicago: University of Chicago Press, 1990.

Byrd, Donald. *Music Notation by Computer.* University of Michigan Dissertation. Ann Arbor: University Microfilms International, 1984.

Cope, David. *Experiments in Musical Intelligence.* Madison, Wis.: A-R Editions, 1996.

Cope, David. *New Music Notation.* Dubuque, Iowa: Kendall/Hunt Pub. Co., 1976.

Krammel, D. W., and Stanley Sadie (eds.). *Music Printing and Publishing.* New York: W. W. Norton, 1989.

Penfold, R. *Computers & Music* (2nd edition). London: Cimino Publishing Group, 1995.

Read, Gardner. *Music Notation: A Manual of Modern Practice* (2nd edition). London: Gollancz, 1974.

Read, Gardner. *20th-century Microtonal Notation.* New York: Greenwood Press, 1990.

Roads, Curtis (ed.). *Composers and the Computer.* Madison, Wis.: A-R Editions, 1985.

Rubin, David. *The Desktop Musician.* New York: Osborne, McGraw-Hill, 1995.

Selfridge-Field, Eleanor (ed.). *Beyond MIDI: The Handbook of Musical Codes.* Cambridge, Mass.: MIT Press, 1997.

Viewport VI

Music Sequencing and MIDI

We believe algorithmic composition is the beginning of a revolution in the musical use of computers. The potentialities for composers of recorded pieces should already be clear. Additional possibilities will shortly be put forward when computers become fast and cheap enough for improvisation.

—Max Mathews and L. Rosler in Von Foerster and Beauchamp's *Music by Computers* (1969)

Subliminal man (the real creative boss) gets along famously with material of such low definition that any self-respecting computer would have to reject it as unprogrammable.

—Roberto Gerhard in John Cage's *Notations* (1969)

. . . it will all eventually come together: interactive media, interactive composing, intelligent musical instruments, multimedia; listeners at home as performers, conductors, composers, improvisers, and participants; more ergonomic and sensitive performance devices; more expressive and powerful sound generators; more sophisticated, flexible, and creative software; and, of course, supersensitive extended-functionality improvements of traditional instruments for the concert hall.

—Joel Chadabe, *Electric Sound: The Past and Promise of Electronic Music* (1997)

Overview

In this viewport, we study music sequencing software as the third in our series of Fill-Your-Own applications. Like music notation software, music sequencing presents the musician with a bewildering array of choices. Using illustrations from a variety of software products and platforms, we review the common features of sequencers, and then touch on special features unique to some of the more sophisticated packages. We will also examine software for composition that does not use a *track* design in its user interface but implements, instead, an object-oriented approach to composition.

Sequencing software, more than any software we have studied thus far, demands an intimate relationship between software and hardware. The essential ingredient is MIDI. We continue to expand on our earlier discussion of MIDI and digital audio in Viewport III. In Module 21, the KISS (Keep It Short and Simple) MIDI System also returns from Viewport III as we study additional hardware options for MIDI. Module 22 expands further upon the KISS MIDI System, with additional hardware devices for enhancing music sequencing. For Module 20, the data module, we present a sample MIDI implementation chart and use this to continue to study MIDI data structures.

Specifically, in this viewport we will:

▶ Study a variety of music sequencing software, examining common and special features

▶ Position sequencing in historical perspective with regard to computer composition and electronic music

▶ Illustrate the common features of sequencers using MIDI and digital audio

▶ Explore the close relationship between MIDI hardware and music sequencers

▶ Revisit MIDI data structures using a generic MIDI implementation chart to explore advanced concepts related to MIDI control and system messages, as well as MIDI and SMPTE time codes

▶ Explore the requirements for a basic MIDI computer system (KISS MIDI System) with a MIDI interface, sound modules, and MIDI workstation

▶ Expand upon the KISS MIDI System to study effects generators, mixers, alternate controllers, patch bays and switch boxes, and SMPTE and multi-track recorders

HISTORICAL TIMELINE
The Technology of Music Sequencing

1700s	Music boxes code music sequences on cylinders with pins
	Mozart composes three pieces for mechanical barrel organs: K.594, K.608, and K.616
1800s	Beethoven composes *Wellington's Victory* overture for Maelzel's mechanical orchestra run by air pressure
1850s	Player pianos perform coded-music sequences from paper rolls with punched holes
1860s	Court rules that music boxes illegally use copyrighted music
1870s	Edison invents the phonograph
1890s	William Duddell invents one of the first electronic music instruments based on alterations in current from arc lamps (Singing Arc)
	Vlademar Poulsen invents an early magnetic tape recorder with sounds from a telephone recorded onto steel wire (Telegraphone)
	Edison sets up the first motion picture studio
1910s	Burstyn makes an electronic oscillator
1920s	Leon Theremin invents the Theremin, with vacuum tube oscillators controlled by proximity of hands to two antennas for frequency and amplitude

	Martenot develops the Ondes Martenot (Ondioline) as a solo electronic performing instrument, with a ribbon-like keyboard controlled with a thimble and capable of microtonal effects, glissandi, and vibrato
	Givelet and Coupleux create one of the earliest programmable analog synthesizers, with four oscillators controlled by punched paper rolls as a "pipeless organ"
	Fritz Pfleumer develops the process of magnetic coating on paper, then on plastic tape, for audio recording
1930s	Friedrich Trautwein invents the Trautonium, which uses filters (subtractive synthesis) to produce timbres from the sawtooth wave of neon oscillators
	Early electronic pianos appear, using electrostatic pickups (Miessner 88-note piano) and magnetic microphones (neo-Bechstein-Flügel piano) to detect vibration of strings
	Early electronic organs appear using electromagnetically activated reeds (Wurlitzer), oscillators (Hammond, Allen, Baldwin, and Vierling), and photoelectric sound generation (Velte and Rangertone)
	AEG Magnetophone (German) is one of the first magnetic tape recorders
	The Philips-Miller tape recorder is a precursor of optical disc recordings, using a chisel device to cut patterns into plastic tape to be read by use of a light-sensing scanner
	Standard pitch is set to A = 440 cps at the International Conference on Pitch in London
1940s	Percy Grainger and Burnett Cross build Free Music, one of the first American made synthesizers, with eight synchronized oscillators
	Illinois Automatic Computer (ILLIAC) is constructed at the University of Illinois, based on von Neumann's IAC computer built at Princeton
	First long-playing (LP) phonograph records appear
1950s	Fender introduces first solid-body electric guitar, the Telecaster or Broadcaster
	Olson and Belar design the Columbia-Princeton RCA Synthesizer, which uses punch cards to control tone and noise generators and processes synthesized sound through microphone inputs
	Hiller and Isaacson create the first computer-composed music, *Illiac Suite,* on the ILLIAC mainframe computer
	First successful commercial tape recorders introduced
1960s	Don Buchla designs a voltage-controlled analog synthesizer with the first electronic sequencer for Subotnick and Sender
	Robert Moog's analog synthesizer becomes the first popular commercial synthesizer; it has modular voltage-controlled design and is programmed with equal-tempered keyboard and patch boards
	Switched on Bach by Wendy Carlos, using a Moog, and *Silver Apples of the Moon* by Morton Subotnick, using a Buchla, create the first public awareness of electronic synthesizers
	R. M. Dolby develops the Dolby recording process, greatly reducing noise in tape recording
	Philips introduces first playback and recording cassette recorder
	The Society of Motion Picture and Television Engineers (SMPTE) creates a standard time code for synchronizing audio and video recording devices
1970s	EMS Synthi 100 is the first synthesizer to include a computer; it has two keyboards, two patch boards, oscilloscope, digital sequencer, and pitch-to-voltage converter
	ARP 2600 and the EMS Putney use the modular voltage controlled concept to create small, low-cost synthesizers ideal for music education
	Minimoog synthesizer becomes a commercial classic that sets a standard with its pitch-bend and modulation wheels to the left of the keyboard

	The Prophet, developed by Sequential Circuits, is the first programmable analog synthesizer that can remember patches and sequences and that can program polyphonic voices
	Synclavier and Fairlight are introduced as the first digital computer music workstations with software, digital and FM synthesis, polyphonic voices, and real-time sequencers
	Max Mathews develops a violin synthesizer where the signal from each string can be modified by filters
	Yamaha uses piezoelectric pickups to create electric pianos, CP70 and 80, that sound like an acoustic grand piano
	Bernardi and Noble develop Lyricon, the first electronic wind controller, with clarinet style keys and transducers to convert breath and lip pressure
	Linn Electronics LMI Drum Computer is introduced as the first electronic drum machine
	Roland MC-8 MicroComposer is the first digital sequencer controlled by a microprocessor
1980s	First music sequencing software for Apple II PCs appears: Micro Music's Music Composer using four-voice digital synthesis, and ALF software using three-voice analog synthesis
	Casio introduces portable home electronic keyboards
	The Music Instrument Digital Interface (MIDI) is established as an industry standard for communicating between electronic music devices
	Roland (MPU401) and Passport Design introduce the first PC MIDI interfaces
	The Prophet 600 from Sequential Circuits and the Jupiter 6 from Roland are two of the first MIDI instruments
	First pure MIDI guitar controllers appear: SynthAxe and Yamaha's G10 controller
	The Yamaha DX-7 MIDI keyboard/synthesizer is introduced, using Chowning's FM synthesis techniques
1985	The Casio CA-101 is produced: a low-cost, eight-voice polyphonic MIDI keyboard/synthesizer producing its distinctive sound by phase-angle distortion
	LA Piano Services and Yamaha develop kits to convert an acoustic piano to a MIDI controller, using touch-sensitive switches and optical sensors
	IBM produces its Music Feature Card based on the Yamaha FB-01 MIDI synthesizer with eight voices
	The first programmable rhythm machine appears as the Roland DR-55 (Boss Dr. Rhythm)
	First commercial MIDI wind controller (Yamaha WX-7) is developed in consultation with Sal Gallina, Lyricon artist
	MIDI File Standard with three data formats and MIDI Time Code (MTC) are adopted as part of the MIDI standard
	Professional Composer and Performer (Mark of the Unicorn) appear as the first serious PC notation and MIDI sequencing software using a graphic editing system
	Digital Audio Tape (DAT) cassette recorders are introduced
1990s	Vision sequencer software (Opcode) links patch-name information to patch libraries
	Sequencing software for the PC now integrates digital audio with MIDI sequencing in high-end software like Studio Vision, Logic, and Digital Performer
1995	Software for translating digital sound samples to MIDI and back is commercially available
	Digital audio tracks become commonplace in even low-end sequencing software
	Pitch-to-MIDI translation is now a software feature for sequencers and music notation
	Virtual PC music generation appears with software like the Roland Virtual PC and QuickTime MIDI sound generation using the Roland GS library of sound samples

	MIDI music gains in popularity as Web sites find the small file sizes easy to deliver over the Internet
	Hyperinstruments interacting with unique software environments like Opcode's MAX create exciting new possibilities for interactive composing and performance; Tod Machover's *Brain Opera* and Gary Lee Nelson's MIDI horn performances are examples
2000	Sequencers, digital audio editors, and patch editors and librarians merge into integrated software solutions—even with basic notation capabilites—where multitracks of MIDI sequences, digital audio tracks, and instrument samples can be edited and manipulated simultaneously

THE PEOPLE

Pierre Boulez working with an assistant
(Photo by Philippe Gontier)

REAL-WORLD PROFILE: PIERRE BOULEZ

Role: Composer, performer, conductor, and director of the Institut de Recherche et Coordination Acoustique/Musique (IRCAM) in Paris

A celebrated composer and conductor, Maestro Boulez maintains an impressive concert schedule while directing one of the world's most famous research centers for music technology, the Institute de Recherche et Coordination Acoustique/Musique (IRCAM) in Paris, France. Boulez has always been a proponent of new music as a conductor. He is generally considered one of the most musical interpreters of new music and is in high demand as a guest conductor for the world's most noted symphony orchestras. His appointment in 1974 as director of IRCAM has allowed him to continue his interest in electronic music using synthesizers and computers. He is most interested in the interaction between live performance and digital technology and imagines a day when concert music will achieve a mix of these two performance resources.

Interview: After a rehearsal with the Chicago Symphony Orchestra in December, 1992 (updated 1997).

What are you doing now with technology and music? I am doing work where the instrument sounds will be transformed or used to trigger things such as automatic scores played by the computer. The major breakthrough was when we were able to use technology in concert situations—when there were no more tapes or recordings. When the technology was advanced enough, fast enough, to allow things to happen instantly with performers, triggered by performers. For instance, we now have *score following:* when the performer is playing, the triggering is done automatically, following the main score, so the performer is absolutely free to add dimensions like aleatoric demands. We can decide that if the sound is longer than four seconds, for example, the program will trigger a sound, but if it is shorter than four seconds, the score will not be performed. This allows us to introduce performance gestures that I find so important in music. Also, in some of the works, not necessarily of mine but of younger composers, they take into consideration some aspect of the playing. For instance, using the MIDI system, one velocity level will trigger one kind of score, whereas another level of velocity will trigger another score. I want to work much more in this direction. If the performer plays slowly, this might trigger a set of micro-intervals. If the performer plays quicker, the score will define bigger intervals. So you see the future of the use of the computer in music is in this kind of interaction between the performer and the machine. The technology responds to the particular playing style of the performer.

How did you become interested in computers and music technology? In the early 1950s, I began working with technology. I was discouraged at first because the technology at that time was so primitive. It did not correspond to my own ideas about music composition. The first time I saw something that put me on the right track was when the Siemens people in Munich built a studio and they were beginning to use automation and automatic devices. This must have been around 1961 or '62. I got more interested in this work because it was less mechanical. I felt that the mechanical devices should be abandoned for something that would work more quickly. Then when I met Max Mathews at the Bell Labs when I was in New York in 1970–71 I thought: now here is the future. When I was asked to come back to France, I said that I would like to establish an institution that would bring together musicians and technicians to study these problems. I wanted to have the work done not in a corner somewhere, but as the central focus of the institution. I was lucky to meet the President of France, Georges Pompidou, who decided to build a center for contemporary art and who offered me the opportunity to be a part of it. So I said to him: "If you want me to come back, I would like to have this institute for research." And so it came to be. When I put together IRCAM, of course I expected the computer to develop, but I had no idea it would be so dramatic. Even the top scientists who advised me at the time were not thinking in terms of what computers can do today. Right from the start, I pushed IRCAM toward the concept of direct interaction between musicians and technology in concert situations. I insisted that we define our artistic goals as a function of the concert situation. We should use the achievements of technology progressively as they develop. And that is what happened.

What computers do you use? We use Macintosh and NeXT machines. *Répons*—my composition for traditional and electronic instruments—was first conceived with the help of the 4X computer invented by an Italian engineer and scientist. Now, ten or fifteen years later, after much research by our technicians, we decided that the NeXT, equipped with our own

software, is more appropriate for our thinking. It is especially good for programming. Software now is much more important than the hardware. With the 4X, we needed to invent everything—hardware and software. Now we concentrate on the software and take the hardware more and more from commercial sources.

The one music device you find you use most often? There is really a wide variety. We use sampling machines a great deal. You know, you have two points of view that are opposed to one another. You have the purist who thinks that sound must be synthesized right from the very beginning, and then there are those who are more practical, who say: if we have sampling why not use sampling. It's easier and quicker, and the results are there anyway. I think those two points of view are coming closer. You cannot be a purist, but on the other side one cannot be too practical.

Is there one thing that you would hope people will remember about your work with computers and technology? For me, I want the computer to respond to my musical ideas, and I think that the young composers today hold exactly the same view. The problem that preoccupies them is this: If we have written for a machine or a particular technology like the 4X, will our work be possible to perform later if this machine has disappeared? This is exactly the problem that is our concern. New machines should include all the possibilities of the old machine, and others as well. Old works should be transferred, and this is one of the tasks for which we have people working at IRCAM. We have specialists that transfer works from ten years ago to new machines, like from the 4X to the NeXT. And it works. We now perform *Répons* with the NeXT machine and it works very well. It actually sounds better.

If you could change one thing about how computers are used, what would it be? In general, I like people to work with musical ideas, not computer ideas; that is the main thing. Sometimes the dialog between scientists and musicians is difficult because scientists are interested in some parts of the computer and computer language that are really not very interesting to musicians. They need to understand that they must look for something that makes a musical result and not something that is just technical. This dialog, if initiated early enough, is very productive.

Do you have any predictions for the future in terms of how technology will develop? Since people already work at home with increasingly sophisticated equipment, it seems to me that the important issue will be *how* musicians can work amongst themselves in this context and what their relationship will be with musical institutions such as IRCAM. Therefore, the future lies in networks between individuals and institutions. It is very difficult right now because every center thinks it is the best. There is some jealousy. For me, I feel we need to cooperate. This is how it is in the scientific world. I have seen this working, for instance, between MIT and Stanford. I think for the future of our centers of music technology, it will be necessary to work together. We use a word in France, "synergy." In order to have synergy you have to have a group big enough to achieve something. We can distribute the work to smaller centers and this synergy will be global and not isolated.

One word of advice you have for musicians interested in computers? I would tell them to not to worry too much about technology, because the technology is accessible now. I would make a very trivial comparison: if you want to drive a car and you think that you need to know all the parts of the motor, you will never drive! It is the same with music technology. You must know something about how the programs work, but you may not need to know every detail. In music for instance, if you are a composer and you are writing for violin, you know that there are four strings, you know that there are positions, you know what the sound is—you must know how it works. But you need not know how to play a violin or an oboe; otherwise, no composer would compose for an orchestra. It is exactly the same with technology. You must be aware of the mechanism, how it functions, how it works, what is the best way to approach it, but you do not need to be a technician. If something is broken you can always consult an expert who can help you with the pure technology part.

That's wonderful advice for a person new to technology; musicians get turned off to technology without realizing the richness of the possibilities. Yes, you know we have sessions with composers who say to us, "I was very weak in mathematics!" We say: don't even think of that. Think about the sound! You know, when someone says to me that technology dehumanizes the arts, I ask them, "Do you really think a pipe organ is very human?" If you look at the mechanism of all of it, how absurd. All instruments are artifacts, are unnatural. Everything is unnatural. The music depends on the musician. This is why I want so much to introduce the computer into the concert situation, where the performer can tell the computer what to do.

<table>
<tr><td>

Module

19
</td><td>

Software for Music Sequencing
</td></tr>
</table>

In Viewport V, we reviewed software, data structures, and hardware that addressed the graphic *representation* of sound. In this viewport, we turn to music production software that actually *creates* the sound—to the very heart of music and technology. We noted the overlap between notation software and sequencing by showing how notation packages often use sequencer-like techniques for data entry and display. We now turn to software that is primarily designed to organize sound for performance, both MIDI sound and digital audio. Many software titles in this module also include some kind of notation capabilities such as those we have reviewed before. However, the real strength of sequencing software lies in the integration of MIDI and digital audio to create sound, and in the ability to edit both kinds of data.

This would be an excellent time to review Table 16.1 in Module 16. The second block of software titles is of interest here. Notice how so many of the titles merge notation, sequencing, and digital audio sampling into one program. Figure 19.1 is a screen from Digital Orchestrator Pro, the more advanced version of software from the family of Voyetra sequencers. This screen looks extremely complicated, but we will soon see how the windows represent an approach to music production that stresses integration. You will quickly learn to make sense of each window and will find that it is not as confusing as you first might think.

A music sequencer can be defined as a device that automates the playback and recording of sounds in a linear or sequential fashion.

A Sense of History

The topic of digital audio will continue to be developed in Viewport VII.

Have you ever watched a player piano work? If so, you probably noticed a paper piano roll with holes that moved across a metal cylinder. The holes are triggers that control which notes to play and how loud to play them. Even the keys and the pedals of the piano move appropriately, controlled by the paper roll.

The player piano and the principle that makes it work date back hundreds of years and provide an example of an early music sequencer. People have always been intrigued by machines that have the software and hardware to make music on their own. The tape recorder and the phonograph developed in the twentieth century as devices important in the recreation

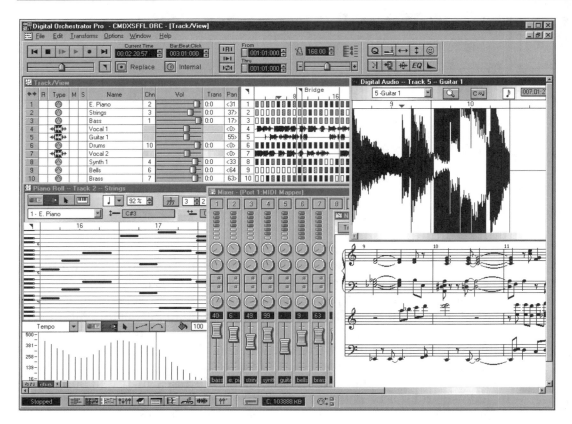

Figure 19.1
Digital Orchestrator Pro
(Voyetra Technologies
[Windows])

Be sure to read Modules 10
and 20 to fully understand
how MIDI works.

of sound were not unlike the music boxes and player pianos of years gone by. Today's compact disc players, computers, and digital music instruments, and the software to run them, will provide the twenty-first century with exciting expressive tools for creating and recording musical experiences.

This module begins with basic concepts that establish what sequencing is and how software is designed to support it. We review both basic and more advanced sequencing features, and include a special section on digital audio sampling and its integration. We conclude this module by looking at alternatives to track-based sequencing software.

Basic Design of Sequencing Software

What Does Sequencing Software Do? One answer is "record and process music data"; a more precise answer is "record and process MIDI and digital audio data." MIDI is a kind of digital language that describes music performance. It uses numerical codes to tell some *other device* to turn on a sound, play it at a certain loudness level and with certain effects, and then turn it off. Digital audio data, on the other hand, represent the sounds themselves.

Sequencing software acts as a tool for capturing and working with MIDI and digital audio data, usually for the purposes of composition or arranging. This software lets you record multiple layers of information, much as you might record multiple layers of sound on an audio tape to construct a piece of music.

HISTORICAL PERSPECTIVE

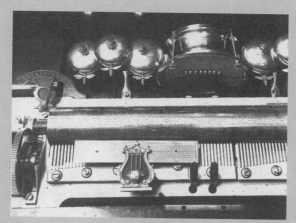

Music box sequencing mechanism (1890s) using pins on a cylinder
(Courtesy of the Smithsonian Institution)

Music sequencing machines are actually quite old. The timeline for this viewport begins in the eighteenth century with early music boxes and with music composed by Mozart for barrel organ. The paper piano rolls that followed were created by artists who understood patterns in music and their complexity in time. In 1804, an instrument called the Panharmonium was designed by Maelzel. It was driven by air pressure and was intended to reproduce the timbres of traditional instruments. Beethoven wrote the *Battle of Vittoira* for this device, but it was never performed because of technical problems. The calliope was developed by Boch and Wacher in 1895, using a metal disk with punched holes to represent music.

The beginning of the twentieth century saw the creation of a number of early, electronic instruments played by sequencers of some kind. In the 1920s, Givelet and Coupleux's Pipeless Organ was one of the first programmable analog music synthesizers. At the same time, Seeburg, Wurlitzer, and others were building the first electronic jukeboxes.

The 1950s saw experiments with some of the first computer systems, like the ILLIAC and the RCA Mark II Synthesizer. Music was created on these devices with the help of codes punched on cards or paper tape.

In the next decade, the invention of the transistor helped Buchla in his creation of a transistor-based analog synthesizer with the first built-in electronic sequencer. Moog created a synthesizer that became a popular hit, aided by the success of a set of sequenced renditions of Bach's music by Wendy Carlos. This growth in small keyboard systems continued into the 1970s with the classic Prophet analog synthesizer and the Fairlight and Synclavier devices that featured real-time sequencing. The first drum machine was created by the Linn company, and Roland produced the first digital sequencing device controlled by a microprocessor.

Of course the real boon for sequencing came in the 1980s with the implementation of the MIDI protocol together with the growth of personal computers. Keyboards like the Roland Jupiter 6 and

Paper-tape sequencing (1950s) with the RCA Electronic Music Synthesizer
(Courtesy of the David Sarnoff Research Center)

The music studio of Wendy Carlos (1960s) with Moog synthesizer
(Photo courtesy of Robert Moog)

On the computer side, the 1980s saw a growth in both Wintel and Macintosh music-related products. IBM produced its Music Feature Card, a sound card that allowed some software control of sound. Mark of the Unicorn's Performer software for the Macintosh was released and became the first professional software-based sequencing package on a PC. Today, such software is plentiful, and it is the focus of this module.

The MIDI protocol continues to be refined as the data structure of choice for sequencing. However, new approaches to combining digital audio with MIDI have emerged. Sequencing technology is pervasive now in all phases of the music enterprise, particularly in the popular music recording and concert scene. Sound tracks for movies and for many multimedia products rely heavily on sequencing. Composers and conductors such as our featured musician, Pierre Boulez, are experimenting with interesting combinations in live performance using analog instruments with MIDI sequences driving digital equipment. Sequencing will continue to play a role in the future development of music, just as it has in the past.

the Yamaha DX7 were among the first instruments to include MIDI. Hundreds of keyboard models have since followed suit, many having sequencers built into the hardware much like the Buchla. This tradition continues today, with most MIDI keyboards including sequencers as part of their feature set.

To better understand the difference between MIDI and digital audio data, see Module 17.

Take a look at Figure 19.2. This is our KISS (Keep It Short and Simple) music workstation in its most basic form. Notice that the computer is linked to a MIDI interface that is, in turn, linked to a MIDI device. We will discuss this hardware in detail in Modules 21 and 22.

Pretend that you are working with this KISS hardware with some sequencing software. You have a microphone linked to your computer. You tell the software to record and then move to the keyboard and play a passage using the bassoon timbre. You begin the passage softly in the low register and then end in a long crescendo with several notes played in a higher register. You play a ritard at the end for a special effect. Returning to your computer, you stop the recording process, "rewind," and listen to what you played. The MIDI workstation plays back the passage exactly the way you played it, with all the subtleties of phrasing and dynamics.

Next, you ask your software to record on a different *track* or layer. You return to your keyboard and add another line of percussion sounds while listening to your first passage played back to you by the same MIDI workstation. When finished, you "rewind" again and listen to the whole piece. You also ask your software to add a touch of rubato in the middle of the passage. You like what you hear.

Now, you rewind and add a third track by singing into a microphone. You sing a passage that goes along with your percussion and bassoon sounds. After listening to your voice, you decide to add a little reverb effect to it.

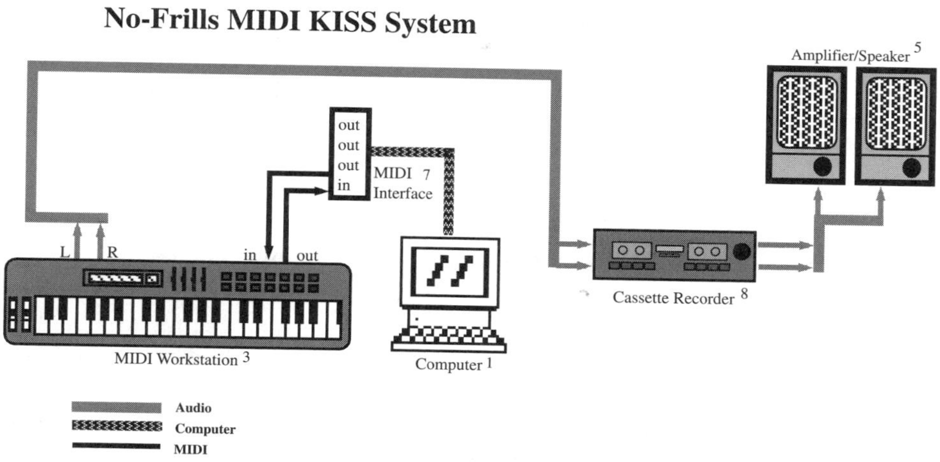

No-Frills MIDI KISS System

Figure 19.2
No-frills MIDI KISS system

When you are finished, you have two tracks of MIDI data and one track of digital audio. In a nutshell, this is what sequencing software accomplishes.

Sounds Like an Expensive Tape Deck! Sequencing programs do resemble the function of analog tape decks, but there are powerful differences. Take a moment to reread what you just did. What is actually happening here? During your playing, MIDI and digital audio data flowed into the RAM of the computer with the aid of the sequencing software. On command, this data flowed *back* to the MIDI device and speaker of your computer to perform the music.

Here is where it gets exciting. These MIDI instructions and audio data can be flexibly altered in an instant. You took advantage of this by asking your sequencing software to add a little rubato in the middle and edit the volume of the digital audio. Try doing that with an analog tape!

You can also ask the software to play back the data in a different key and in a different tempo. You can edit errors by simply changing values. All this flexibility is possible because the MIDI and audio data are just a set of numbers that describe a performance.

Besides this flexibility, several layers of MIDI and digital audio data can be recorded. Even the most inexpensive software sequencers can record up to 32 layers of MIDI sound and 8 layers of audio. Many packages can support several times this number depending on the computer and memory. You can move data back and forth between tracks. The same feat can be done with a multitrack analog tape recorder, but the sound will become progressively worse as it gets bounced from one track to another (like making photocopies of photocopies). MIDI and audio data are always fresh, no matter how much you process them.

Can't You Do the Same Thing with Notation Software? You *can* do the same with notation software, but only in a very limited way. In Module 16 we pointed out that real-time data entry is supported by nearly all notation software packages. The goal of the software is to create a notated score, not to create a *performance* of the music. Herein lies the difference between the two types of software. Notation packages contain sequencing capabilities, but only as tools for entering notation; few other features are offered to enhance and process the MIDI codes. If your primary focus as a musician is to create a performance, sequencing rather than notation software is what you want.

How Does Timing Work? Software sequencers constantly run a clock in the background during recording and playback of data. This clock keeps track of measures, beats, and fractions of beats, often referred to as *ticks*. The number of ticks per defined beat varies depending on the software, ranging from 96 to a resolution as high as 1,024. As data arrive at the sequencer, rhythm is coded against an invisible time grid represented by the tick resolution. This allows the sequencer to be extremely sensitive to nuances in performance tempo. Generally, the higher the resolution, the more accurate the sequencer is in coding rhythmic performance. However, this may not always be the case, because the speed and workload of the computer during sequencing are limiting factors.

The concept of *quantization* is also critical for understanding how sequencers work: Sequencers can be asked to adjust time values to make notes conform to standard grid alignments. Synchronization between audio and MIDI is possible; in fact some advanced programs allow the transformation of audio into MIDI data. This can be useful if you intend to export the file to a notation package for printing, or to fine-tune a section to make it sound tighter rhythmically. Quantization options are generally much more sophisticated in sequencing than in notation packages, as you will soon see.

Timing and MIDI data are discussed in depth in Module 21.

Important Terminology. There are three important concepts that you need to understand:

▶ *track*

▶ *patch* (sometimes called *program* or *instrument*)

▶ *channel*

If you understand these terms, you will understand how sequencers work.

Figure 19.3 displays a portion of the track display window from a typical sequencer that you might use to enter music. Note that five tracks are being used and that five different channels are assigned to each. There is a separate patch for each one.

Track. A track is a convenient way for the software to visually and internally represent a location for an entered line of music that has channel(s) and program(s) specified. Think of tracks as a linear sequence of MIDI or digital audio code that gets created as you play a musical line in time. For example, if you were creating a vocal solo accompanied by a piano, the vocal line might be entered as a digital audio track and the piano line entered as a MIDI track. Usually a piece of music will be created by adding

	Name	✔	Source	Key+	Vel+	Time+		Port	Chn	Bank	Patch	Vol	Pan	Size
1	dr	✔	⊙ MIDI	0	0		0	⊙ 1-<c	10	---	Acoustic Bass	127	64	228
2	bass	✔		0	0		0	⊙ 1-<c	2	---	Fretless Bass	126	63	72
3	piano	✔		0	0		0	⊙ 1-<c	1	---	Bright Acoustic	109	80	392
4	organ#1	✔		0	-15		0	⊙ 1-<c	3	---	Percussive Org	70	5	45
5	organ#2	✔		0	0		0	⊙ 1-<c	5	---	Rock Organ	70	20	74

Figure 19.3
Example of track, program, and channel using MasterTracks Pro (G-VOX Entertainment [Mac/Windows])

several tracks on top of each other. Sequencing software provides windows that let you edit these tracks and manipulate them. Portions of a single track can be moved around and defined in different ways by sequencing programs.

Software tracks can contain a large amount of information. Polyphonic textures created by a pianist, for example, can all be recorded on one track if desired. In some sequencing programs, multiple channels and their respective patches can even be included on a *single* track. For example, you might want to add a flute part to the bassoon melody by doubling an octave higher. Rather than create another track for the flute, it might be more sensible to add the flute line to the first track because it is playing the same music.

Patch. A patch is the sequencing term for an individual timbre. Most MIDI devices have a wide assortment of preset patches or timbres that can be addressed by MIDI. You used the bassoon patch setting in your work. The MIDI workstation sends the MIDI code to the computer with a certain patch number, and this number is used again when the computer sends the data back. MIDI supports up to 128 different programs or patches at one time. The concept of "patches" does not apply to digital audio recordings (which are unique recordings of actual sounds).

Channel. The MIDI language codes every note with a channel number, a kind of destination label like a channel on a TV. MIDI devices can be set to listen for notes on a specified channel. In this way, the sequencing software can send streams of notes to particular synthesizers or sound modules, for example. Again, this is not applicable to digital audio.

An important point to remember is that each unique patch *must* be carried on a unique channel. This means that for organ and drums to sound simultaneously it will require two different channels: one serving the organ and one for the drums.

One MIDI cable can send data to as many as 16 different channels simultaneously. If more channels are required, a second MIDI interface may be needed to bring the number up to 32 channels. Most sequencing software packages support 32 channels, more than adequate for most beginning and intermediate needs.

What Does One Actually Edit? In their early days, sequencers offered musicians a display window with numbers representing MIDI data, and a window that graphically provided a proportional view of note events much

Additional patches can be accessed from various *banks* of sounds, 128 sounds per bank.

See Module 20 for more on channels.

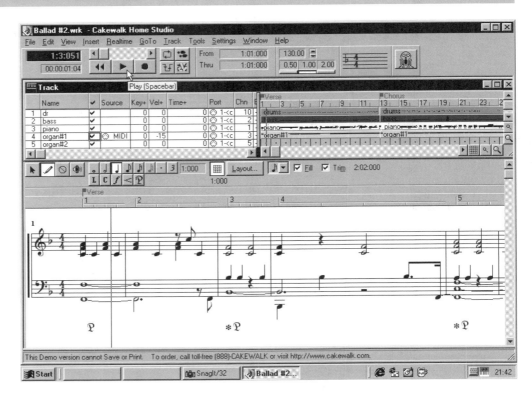

Figure 19.4
Home Studio
(Cakewalk Music Software
[Windows])

If a musician needs more
than 32 channels of MIDI
information at one time,
advanced hardware solu-
tions are necessary. Some
of these are described later
in Modules 21 and 22.

like the piano rolls of the nineteenth century. A simple overview window
that showed which measures had MIDI data in them was also common.

These features continue today, but many new views have been added.
For example, the graphic approach has been extended to include icons for
dynamics, tempo, and special effects. Traditional notation is often
included, although the options may be crude compared to what you
would find in notation software. Digital audio is now a standard part of
material to be edited and has its own waveform view, as can be seen in
Figure 19.1.

Another interesting addition has been a "patterns" or "chunks" view.
Appearing first in European software like Steinberg's Cubase and Emagic's
Logic, this top-down approach to manipulating larger units of data can be a
very natural and musical way to move MIDI and audio data around in a
sequencer. Once a set of MIDI or audio events have been recorded, you can
manipulate a graphic representing the entire set of events, rather than deal
with lower-level entities like notes, MIDI effects, and single waveforms.
Figure 19.4 displays a view of Cakewalk's Home Studio. Notice to the right
of the track descriptions there are small graphics that represent the contents of the tracks which are ready to be edited if needed. You will see several examples of these display options as we explore the features of
sequencing software.

We will now turn to the basics of using sequencers with MIDI data. Following this, we will summarize the basics of digital audio entry and manipulation.

Basics of Using Sequencers with MIDI Data

Software activity: "Sequencing a Music Composition with Music-shop, Master Tracks, Cakewalk's Home Studio, or Vision"

Sequencing Setup. The first thing you need to do is to prepare software for recording the MIDI data. To do this, you must familiarize yourself with the basic *transport* buttons that allow movement from place to place in the recording. You will also need to learn how to set the program settings, channels, and tracks, to choose recording options, and to check the hardware and software interface options.

Transport Buttons. Figure 19.5 provides an illustration of how you might begin to work with a sequencer. Notice that there are stop, play, record, and pause buttons. There is also a button for moving incrementally backwards or forwards in the sequence, much as in a CD or videotape controller. The program displays a timing window that keeps track of the measure, beat, and clock (subdivision of the beat, or *ticks*).

Channels and Patches within Tracks. As we learned earlier, you need to assign channel and patch settings to the instruments within tracks. We have opened a ballad called "Home Again" in Figure 19.5. It requires tracks, each dedicated to different patches. We have assigned different channels as well. Musicshop assigns program values by clicking on the little trumpet icon on the extreme left border of the main screen.

Recording Options. Next comes a series of options to control the recording. Nearly all sequencing software offers these options as standard features, although the way they are implemented will probably be different. Refer to Figure 19.5 and to the dialog boxes in Figure 19.6.

▶ *Tempo.* You will want to think of a comfortable tempo for recording the ballad. You might consider setting a slower tempo than you plan to use during

Figure 19.5
Basic sequencer operation in Musicshop (Opcode Systems [Mac/Windows])

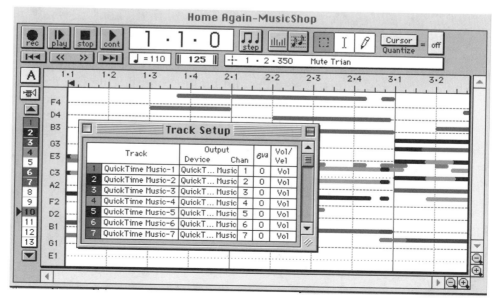

the final performance, because tempo can instantly be changed without altering other variables. In Figure 19.5, tempo is initially set directly on the main screen just under the timing display. We have chosen a quarter note equal to 110 beats per minute in this example.

▶ *Countoff, metronome off/on, auto rewind.*   Many of these options control important recording features. The countoff option plays a measure of time before recording, while the metronome can be turned off and on. The auto rewind option returns the sequence to the beginning automatically when you stop recording. You may find that you will use all of these features in your work.

▶ *Sync clock.*   You can set your sequencer to listen to the clock inside itself in order to manage all the timing of events. If you choose external synchronization, the program will listen for a clock outside the computer. This might be useful if at some point you want to have a drum machine, video device, or other machines control the sequencer software. It is often best to have the sequencer's own clock be the conductor for the music.

See MIDI THRU in Modules 11 and 20.

▶ *THRU.*   Most MIDI workstations have an option in their hardware utility set labeled *Local* or *Local Control.* You may discover that your workstation works better with the computer-based sequencing software if you set this to *Local Control Off.* This lets the computer take complete charge of the workstation during playback. The only problem is that you can't hear the sounds of the workstation while playing it! To remove this problem, most sequencers include a *THRU* option. You may want to have this selected so you can hear the workstation "thru" the computer. The software will simply send the MIDI data back to the workstation.

▶ *Looping.*   Most sequencers allow for the looping or repeated playing of a designated passage. If we want to have a percussion part repeat in our ballad, we simply enter a pattern once from the computer by using the drum set patches, then indicate that we wanted the track to repeat as a loop.

▶ *Metric setting and tempo control.*   Look now at Figure 19.6. It displays a set of dialog boxes taken from both MusicTracks and Musicshop to illustrate a number of other important recording options. The Change Conductor box from MasterTracks (*a*) demonstrates two options important for sequencers: metric settings and tempo control. One can enter the meter and specify the unit of basic beat. For the ballad, we will use the standard 4/4 time, with the quarter note as the unit of measure. The tempo control can be used after the music is entered to change the speed of playback.

▶ *Metronome settings.*   The Metronome Sound dialog box from Musicshop (*c*) displays common settings for the *click track* that can accompany sequencers. We decided to have the click track play only during recording, not during playback. Also, we elected to have the click come from the MIDI sounds. We assigned a specific pitch, and the pitch's velocity and duration.

▶ *Filtering MIDI during recording.*   Next we have the Record Filter dialog box from MasterTracks (*b*). Here, a musician can decide to filter out any MIDI

Change Conductor

From Measure **1** to 127

☐ Set Meter to 4/4 and Beat to ♩ ▲▼

○ Set all Tempos to 110

● Change to 100 % of current values

○ Change smoothly from 110 to 110

○ Change smoothly from 100 % to 100 %

○ Add 0 to all values

☐ Limit low values to 10

☐ Limit high values to 300

[Cancel]   [OK]

(a)

Record Filter

Select type of data to be recorded

☑ Notes   ☑ Controllers
☑ Pitch Bend   ☑ Modulation
☑ Channel Pressure ☑ Program Change
☑ Polyphonic Key Pressure

☐ Only on channel **1**

☐ Quantize to ♪ ▲▼ 60   ☐ Tuplet 3 : 2

Include notes up to 35 % ahead of the beat.

[Cancel]   [OK]

(b)

Metronome Sound

○ Internal Click
● MIDI Note:

	Channel	Note	Velocity	Duration
Accented:	1 : Quick...Music-1	E4	64	80
Unaccented:	1 : Quick...Music-1	C#1	64	80

☐ Click in Play
☑ Click in Record   [Cancel]   [OK]

(c)

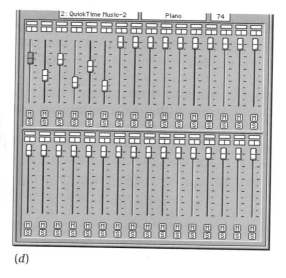

(d)

Figure 19.6
Recording options dialog boxes in MasterTracks and Musicshop

data that are not desired, such as pitch-wheel data. One may also set the program to quantize notes coming in. This would be useful if someone wanted to record passages in very strict rhythm for use in creating a standard MIDI file for a notation package. Otherwise, it is best to use the sequencer to capture the subtle rhythmic feel. A compromise can be struck by specifying a percentage limit on notes played ahead of the beat—a nice touch.

▶ *Mixer settings.* Finally, we come to the mixer dialog box from Musicshop (*d*). This is a setting for controlling the volume of tracks as you listen to what you have recorded. You will see many of these "virtual" mixers in both sequencing and sampling software.

Inputting Sequencing Codes. Now comes one of the most exciting parts of using sequencing software: recording the data. You have two approaches to consider: real-time and step-time. Real-time is by far the most common approach because sequencing software is optimized to work best using this approach. However, there are times when step-time is helpful.

Real-time input. Figures 19.7 and 19.8 capture moments in time as music is entered in real-time using MasterTracks and Musicshop. As we work through the following steps, refer to these figures and, if you can, practice some of this on a computer with sequencing software as you read.

We covered real-time and step-time entry for notation software in Module 16.

▶ *Step 1.* Begin by thinking through your music. What line has the greatest continuity and would therefore be good to start with? It might be good to put the drum line in first because that would set up the proper feel for the rest of the work. However, if your music doesn't use a continuous drum line, you may want to choose something else. Remember that you can also record portions of a piece and add measures later.

▶ *Step 2.* Practice before recording. Sequencers are quite flexible pieces of software, but they cannot be expected to solve every performance problem. You need to practice until you feel quite comfortable with the music, knowing that you can fix some problems in the editing phase. One important tip: sequencing software records all the nuances that you perform, including rubatos, phrasing, articulations, and dynamics. Try to include as much of this in your playing early in the recording; you can always "edit out" unwanted aspects of your performance but it is more difficult to "put in" missing elements! This is the major difference in approach between real-time entry in a sequencer and in a notation package. The emphasis here is on capturing as much of the performance data as possible.

Drums usually go in Track 10 in most sequencers that use General MIDI.

▶ *Step 3.* Double-check all the settings. Decide if you are comfortable with how the metronome is set. Practice a little with the metronome to be sure.

▶ *Step 4.* Now, record. In Figure 19.7, we have just recorded the drum track. Notice the dot in the Rec column for Track 6. You can click here to tell the program that what is about to be played should be recorded.

▶ *Step 5.* Listen to the track, and perform it again if necessary. Once the data are entered, you can simply rewind, then listen by clicking on the Play button. A wise safety procedure is to "deselect" the Record button to turn it off while listening. You can replace the data simply by recording over them if you don't like what you hear. Some sequencing software will allow you to *overdub* and *merge* as well. *Overdubbing* is recording new material onto the same track without erasing what is there. *Merging* is blending two previously created tracks together. Merging is often reversible later, but overdubbing may not be.

Sequencing software isn't designed to substitute for poor musicianship!

▶ *Step 6.* Add a new track. Now you can turn off the metronome, if you want, and add a second track, repeating the process until all the lines are recorded.

Step-time editing. Step-time entry is accomplished in different ways by sequencers, but the concept is the same. You can draw in pitches and dura-

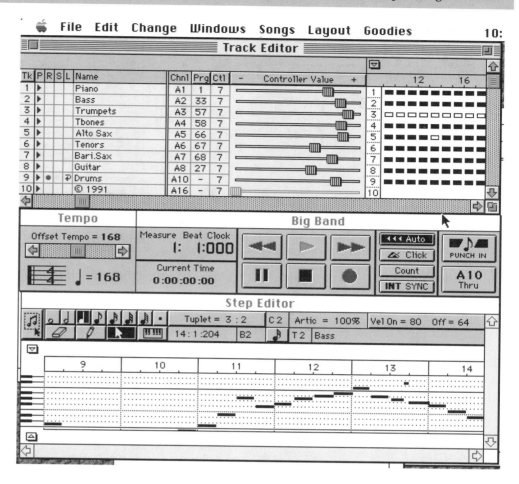

Figure 19.7
Recording in real-time and
with step editing using
MasterTracks

A hardware tip: You should
hear each track play its
assigned patch (timbre). If
not, check the workstation
to be sure it's in *multi* or
poly mode (Mode 3). See
Module 20.

tions with a pencil tool or some other pointer device, or you can use the
MIDI keyboard to determine a pitch level while you use your mouse to
choose a duration value. The latter approach is often called *MIDI step entry*.

Look at the right side of the Track Editor window in Figure 19.7. Filled-
in rectangles representing measures indicate that MIDI data are inside;
empty rectangles tell you that nothing is inside. Double-click on one of
these rectangles, and that measure appears in the Step Editor window
below. This view is a detailed "piano-roll" view commonly found in
sequencer packages. It is in this window that you can make changes to the
drum sequence that has just entered.

Study the Step Editor window carefully. If a musician wanted to add
some other drum sounds to a sequence, he or she could first choose a value
from the palette of notes and then use the pencil tool to add, or draw, the
value. This technique does not use the MIDI workstation for entry at all.
However, if the little piano icon is clicked, the keyboard can be used to enter
pitch values, and then the mouse used to choose durations. An eraser tool is
provided to fix errors in entry, and the user can also set velocity (loudness)
values and articulation values to make staccato and legato effects. Certain
pitches or pitch strings can be sent to different tracks and channels.

Step-time entry in sequencing packages is often used to notate particu-

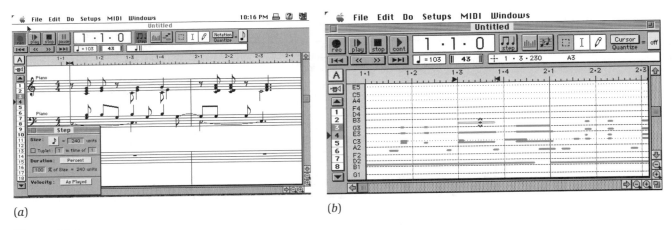

(a)   (b)

Figure 19.8
Step editing with traditional notation and piano roll using Musicshop

A sequencer that allows a duration step value different from the rhythmic value of the note you want to enter will give you more accurate notation from the start.

larly difficult rhythmic sequences for which real-time performance is a problem. For instance, you might consider step entry for passages that require tuplets. Tuplets are needed when a certain number of notes (usually an odd number) must be played in the space of a specified rhythmic division (usually even): for instance, three notes in the space of two eighth notes. This would be a 3:2 designation or *three against two*. Another possibility might be 5:4 (five sixteenth notes in the space of four). MasterTracks and other programs allow tuplet groupings to be created in step time.

Figure 19.8 displays how step editing can be accomplished in Musicshop by using traditional notation (*a*) and piano-roll views (*b*). Here, you can use the MIDI workstation to set pitch levels and the mouse to choose rhythmic unit, duration, and velocity using the dialog box. Tuplet groupings are possible in this program as well.

By the way, there is a third way to enter music into a sequencer: by importing a standard MIDI file (SMF). Someone could send you an SMF file on diskette or via the Internet. You might also decide to import an SMF from another application, like Band-in-a-Box, for one of your performance pieces.

Editing Sequences. In a relatively short time, you have entered many measures of music and it sounds pretty good. You also realize that a few sections need more work. There may be errors in pitch and rhythm here and there. You also might notice that a few passages are a little "off" rhythmically and need a tighter rhythmic feel. Finally, you would very much like to add a few aesthetic improvements such as changes in overall dynamic balance, variations in tempo, and special touches like pitch bend and a sustained pedal effect. You might want to change the key of the entire piece to make the range more comfortable for one of the singers working with you.

In this section, we will illustrate some simple but powerful editing features that are basic to sequencing packages. We continue to use Musicshop and will add another program, PowerTracks Pro Audio, to offer another perspective.

Views for editing. We have seen a number of ways in which sequencers provide views of the music. In addition to the Track Setup window, we have

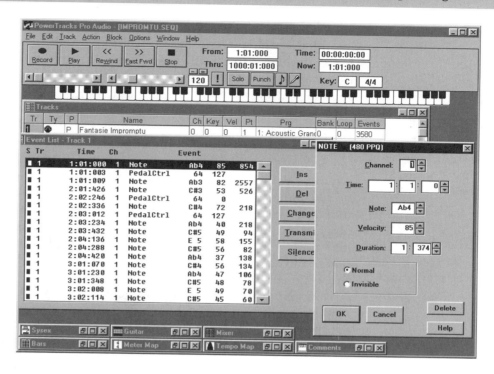

Figure 19.9
Event list using Power-Tracks
(PG Music [Windows])

seen graphic blocks, "piano roll" (Figure 19.7), and traditional notation (Figure 19.8). These are, by far, the most common in sequencing programs. There are at least three other views that you haven't seen yet and which have an important role to play in editing: event list, controller window, and section.

Event list. Figure 19.9 shows an important feature from the PowerTracks Pro Audio software: an event list. This is just what it sounds like, a listing of each MIDI event as numbers, and in the order of their input to the computer in the MIDI data stream. Here we have opened the list for Track 1.

Reading from left to right, we find:

▶ The track number

▶ The time of the onset of the event in measures, beats, and ticks

▶ The channel number

▶ The kind of event, and

▶ Parameters (e.g., note event, note name, velocity, or aftertouch value).

These values are all subject to editing, as seen in the box at the right of the figure. You can change a value or insert a new event such as a patch change.

Event lists offer an important window on the basic level of MIDI data. This is often important for precise control of performance data. More advanced software may include viewing filters that help screen out certain kinds of MIDI events to make event lists easier to use.

Controller data are described in detail in Module 20.

Controller window. Figure 19.10 shows two views that are different from anything we have seen. The first of these, midway down in the top window, has a number of vertical lines. This is Musicshop's graphical view of controller data. Controller data are special MIDI messages that provide values such as individual note velocity, duration, and patch change. Other values supported here include pitch bend, modulation wheel, pan settings, and sustain pedal. We shall return to this view in a moment when we speak about specialized editing of music expression.

Sections. The other view that Figure 19.10 reveals is the arrangement window at the bottom. We have been experimenting with adding sections, or *subsequences*, to the ballad. The arrangement window displays an *A* section and a *B* section. These sections can be easily moved around in the window, edited, and played by themselves. You can also use this subsequence idea to develop a set of tunes for your gig work at a club or for other settings. You can even place blank space between the performance of these subsections.

Correcting Errors. Sequencing software offers a number of ways to correct errors. We have seen one way to correct pitches by viewing the event list, but there are other ways using the "piano roll" view. The bottom portion of Figure 19.8 displayed how you can alter both the pitch and the duration value with the editing tools in Musicshop. The figure shows the pitch value A3 being moved. Similar possibilities exist for left-to-right manipulation.

Cutting, copying, and pasting are all supported by sequencing software. Keep in mind that most packages treat cutting and deletion as two different concepts. If you want to eliminate the first two measures of a composition and have the sequence automatically shift to the left, for example, you probably need to use the delete option. Cutting may only remove the notes and leave the measures. Also, some sequencing software expects you to indicate whether to shift music backwards in time following a deleted section. Many programs support Clear or Erase options. These differ from cutting because the material is not placed in clipboard memory for later retrieval but is simply eliminated from the score. Finally, if you copy and paste, be sure that the target track setup is similar to the one you are copying from; otherwise the software may refuse to paste the material.

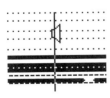

The Punch option is a neat way to record a single measure or other small section in real-time. You begin by identifying the spot you'd like to change. You then start playing a few measures before it. When the section arrives, you play the correct version in real-time and the computer automatically knows to *punch in* the new material, or insert it in the proper spot while overriding the offending data.

Sometimes it's hard to pick out the offending errors in a complicated texture while listening. Musicshop provides an impressive *scrub* feature. Notice the little vertical line and the speaker icon in the margin below the punch icon? That's created by clicking on top of the measure while holding down one of the keyboard keys. Pulling this icon forwards (or backwards!) plays the notes underneath. This is an elegant option for "proofhearing" your music.

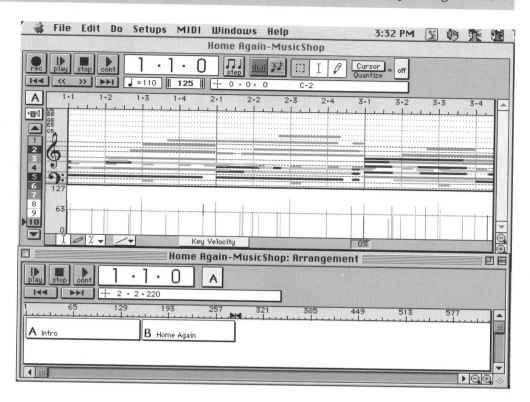

Figure 19.10
Controller and arrangement views in Musicshop

Quantizing. Quantization is a powerful option for tightening up your rhythmic performance, but it also can destroy the human feeling of the music if not used with care. Remember that no musician plays perfectly in time with the underlying "beat." To do so would be completely unmusical! The give-and-take of musical expression is the beauty of the musical experience. However, there are many occasions when real-time note entry will require some adjusting, and quantization is necessary for this. Also, quantization is essential if you want to prepare a file for export to a notation package. Nearly all sequencing packages offer some form of quantizing.

Perhaps you are wondering how quantization works if your composition contains both digital audio and MIDI information. Some of the more advanced titles such as Steinberg's Cubase VST and Score can, in fact, link audio to MIDI.

Attack and duration. Nearly all packages offer adjustment of both attack and duration: the beginning and end of notes. Figure 19.11 displays both unquantized (*a*) and quantized (*b*) versions of the third measure of the ballad tune. Notice in the quantized version how the software has taken its best guess as to how to place the beginnings and endings of the pitches. Quarternote quantization was chosen here but other values are possible, with ranges in Musicshop running from a dotted whole to a sixty-fourth note. Triplet divisions are also supported. Musicshop also offers a "nondestructive" kind of quantization in which you can first hear what the effect is before saving a fully quantized passage.

Percentage adjustments. PowerTracks offers a percentage factor in quan-

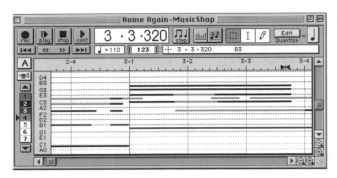

(*a*) Unquantized

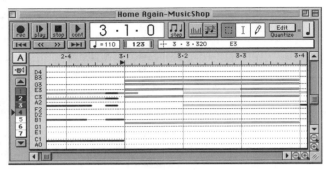

(*b*) Quantized

Figure 19.11
Comparisons in Musicshop

tizing to help retain a human feel. For instance, if you decided to quantize to the nearest eighth note but still retain some inexactness to give a sense of human quality, you might choose an offset factor of 50 percent. This would mean that the notes would be shifted toward the closest eighth note, but by only half the distance.

Other programs offer a criterion setting for making quantizing decisions. If this were set to, say, 33 percent, notes whose attacks fall 33 percent or less after the beat would be set back, but those attacks over 33 percent would be sent forward; this works for attacks before the beat as well. This feature helps to make better corrections if you consistently play behind or ahead of the beat.

Special Touches. There are many editorial capabilities that make both global and local changes to MIDI data that make the sequence sound especially musical. Here are a few of the most common, beginning with local changes.

Controller data. Look back at the vertical lines in Figure 19.10 to find the graphic display of controller data in Musicshop. The data illustrated in the figure are key velocities, or loudness. Notice that there are lines of different length representing the loudness of each note at the onset of each track. If a musician were interested in changing these velocities, the options in this graphic window could be used to do so.

Figure 19.12 displays the pop-up options for this graphic view. The large box at the bottom contains some of the MIDI messages that can be edited. The smaller box on the top left provides options for shapes of curves; the box to the top right offers options for amount of change. For example, you could change the key velocity of a range of measures to create a crescendo. But rather than using the Straight tool, which would produce an exactly even crescendo, one might choose the % Scale option, which keeps the naturally accented notes in proportion as the crescendo develops. This might create a much more musical result. Figure 19.13 demonstrates this in three steps. The options provided by these combinations will keep you busy for weeks. You might never get around to creating another sequence!

Mixing. Overall dynamic options are offered by a number of sequencing packages. Look back at Figure 19.7 displaying the MasterTracks software

Other programs offer control of continuous MIDI data with dialog boxes that designate regions.

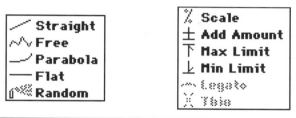

Figure 19.12
Options for editing controller data using Musicshop

and you can see a mixer just to the right of the track data. These "virtual faders" control the loudness of each track and help to create a musical product. Figure 19.1 of Digital Orchestrator Pro contained a much more advanced example of a virtual mixer with pan settings and other controls. (This graphic should look much less mysterious to you now!)

Transposition. All software sequencers offer some kind of transposition. PowerTracks approaches transposition most directly by including a column in the Tracks window for adjusting pitches by semitones. Other programs use a simple dialog box. Most sequencers allow for tracks such as those reserved for drum sounds to be isolated from transposition in order to preserve the integrity of nonpitched instruments.

Saving and Performing Sequences. After fine-tuning your music, you are ready to save it for your gig on Saturday night. At this point you have the option of saving this work as a standard MIDI file or in the format of the application you are using. You will likely choose the latter because you have your own equipment and software. There will be times, however, that you will want to save your work as a standard MIDI file (SMF) and share it with others who do not have the same computer or software.

Most software sequencers allow for saving two kinds of SMFs: Type 0 puts all the data into one track; Type 1 saves multiple tracks. You will probably want to save your SMF as a Type-1 file so that the person getting the file can manipulate the tracks. However, you will have to be sure that your friend's sequencer can import Type-1 files.

There is another important use for these standard files: input for music notation software. A musician could use the notation options found in software like Musicshop and PowerTracks Pro Audio, but also might prefer the benefits of more sophisticated notation programs. If your sequencer doesn't save files in the specialized format read by a particular notation program,

Refer to Module 16 dealing with notation software and Module 17 where MIDI file formats are mentioned.

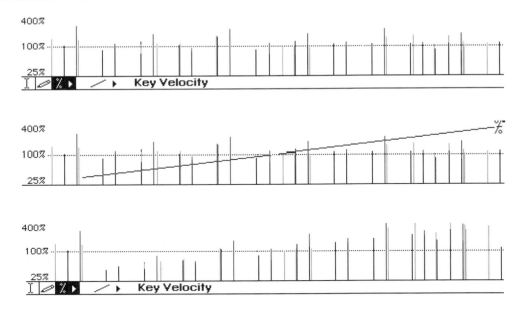

Figure 19.13
Editing continuous controller MIDI data using Musicshop

you can export the music as a standard MIDI file format and import them into your notation program. Follow these steps:

▶ Make a duplicate sequencer file

▶ Rigorously quantize all the parts in the new file to remove subtleties of timing

▶ Save it as a Type 1 SMF to allow for separate staves

▶ Open this file in your favorite notation software for further editing

If your file contains digital audio information that you wish to represent in notation, you must use a sequencing program that supports digital-sound-to-MIDI conversion. The more advanced titles do this, including Studio Vision Pro and Cakewalk Pro Audio.

Performance options. You might be tempted to record your arrangement on analog or digital tape and use this during performance as a backup for your work. That may not be a good idea. You will lose all the wonderful digital features that can be exploited during live performance. For instance, by using the computer technology to play back your work live, you can:

▶ Alter the tempo or key

▶ Mute a line, such as the melody, to allow for improvisation

▶ Reassign a track to new channels and programs

▶ Quickly create new arrangements with different loops for drum parts, or new sections such as introductions and endings

▶ Instantly pause the music or start the music in a new location within the sequence

This last feature is made possible by a technique called *chasing* that automatically scans backwards in the tracks of a sequence to find what controllers need to be read to make the music sound correct. Although advanced sequencing software offers sophisticated options for chasing, most basic titles offer some form of this feature.

Special Problems with MIDI Sequencers. Some words about potential problems musicians might encounter with standard MIDI files and MIDI in general are important.

Meta-events. The standard MIDI format (Version 1) contains provisions for what are known as *meta-events.* These are important visual specifications such as time and key signatures, tempo and tempo changes, instrument names, text and lyrics, markers, and cue points. A sequencer like Musicshop or Cubase will probably support these in their own way. As long as you stay with the same sequencer software, all is well.

The problem is that when you save your sequences as standard MIDI files in order to share them with someone who uses different sequencing software, not all these events are saved. To complicate matters further, even if these events are saved, not all of them may be *read* by the new sequencer. Not all notation software packages read them either, so this can be a concern when moving to music printing. You need to experiment to see what does and does not work, and you must be prepared to do some extra editing.

Rests and loops. After you have used MIDI files for a while, you will notice that there are no rests. MIDI format makes no provision for rests as defined objects, choosing instead to let the note-on and note-off data define silences in the music. When a MIDI file is read into a notation program, rests are assumed between note-off and note-on data and are supplied as needed. This works reasonably well, but if you are working directly with MIDI data in a sequencer, the absence of rest data can be confusing. If subtle or not-so-subtle changes in time are needed for MIDI data in a track, you will need to use the options for sliding or shifting MIDI data from one point to another.

Also, using a lot of looping in MIDI sequences can cause problems when exporting to a music notation program. Standard MIDI files have trouble communicating the presence of a loop to notation software; cutting and pasting may be necessary to correct this problem.

Cross-platform issues. Finally, you need to be aware of a few problems in moving MIDI files between Mac and Windows environments.

Windows to Mac. Most Windows sequencers will save standard MIDI files with the *.mid* extension added to the name. You can take the diskette on which a file is saved and insert it into a Macintosh. Macintoshes will read this Windows-formatted diskette and let you copy the file to the Mac's hard disk. Unfortunately, a Mac sequencer will probably not recognize the .mid file automatically. That's because there is a setting inside the file called *type* that needs to be set to the word *Midi* before the sequencer will recognize it as a standard MIDI file. You might use a file utility program like File Buddy in order to accomplish this simple change.

Mac to Windows. This one is easy. Again, Macintosh computers can recognize *and* format Windows diskettes, so the best plan here is to save stan-

Check out Module 6 on communications software for similar problems with files downloaded from the Internet.

Check out file naming issues in Module 5 in Viewport 2.

Be sure to read about Wintel soundcards and Mac and Wintel MIDI issues in Module 21.

More on drivers in the hardware modules. Be sure to check with your computer's manuals and your software for the latest information on how to manage MIDI data flow.

dard MIDI files on Windows-formatted diskettes. If you are using a version of the Windows operating system before Windows 95 or 98, a few additional concerns are worth noting. A Windows sequencer may not recognize MIDI files unless the *.mid* extension is part of the name. Also, the name of the file before the extension must be eight characters or fewer, and there must be no spaces in the title.

Setting Up and Controlling MIDI Data Flow. We have covered the basics of navigating around a computer sequencer. Regardless of which computer is in use, what MIDI workstation or interface is chosen, or what software is employed, you will need to understand how the pieces fit together. A critical piece is getting the computer and the sequencing software to talk with the MIDI hardware. Here are a few guidelines for both Windows and Macintosh computers that may help with installing software that uses MIDI.

MIDI data flow in your computer. The most common way to connect an external device to a Wintel computer is through a simple cable extension to the soundcard that comes with all multimedia Wintel machines. Nearly all soundcards for Wintel computers comply with hardware standards that allow for these connections.

The Windows operating environment helps to standardize how your software, the soundcard, and your connected MIDI hardware work with each other. When a hardware company creates a soundcard or any other kind of card for a Windows machine, it must provide a small software program that links it to the Windows environment. These software programs are called *drivers.* Because you are likely to install more than one card, Windows helps keep track of these drivers and helps with possible conflicts that might occur.

This works from the software side, too. Software authors, knowing that Windows is the operating environment that will serve as host for their work, write their code with this in mind. When you install a software sequencer, the installation procedure will ask you to identify which hardware drivers to use; otherwise, it automatically chooses a set of drivers for you. Windows helps with this linkage. Most software programs will work with most MIDI interface cards because each has been designed to work within the multimedia standards of the operating environment.

The most common way to connect MIDI hardware to a Macintosh computer is through the Mac's two standard serial or USB ports. A special MIDI interface is often required to connect an external MIDI device to a Mac; however, some devices provide a simple serial cable option. You will want a separate MIDI interface, however, if your performance requirements become more complex. Macintosh computers require driver software programs similar to those in Windows, and designers must write such routines for their products to work with these ports. Several years ago, Apple developed a standardized software solution that replaced much of what is needed in separate software drivers. This system software, known as the Apple MIDI Manager, serves as a kind of traffic cop for incoming and outgoing MIDI data, even for more than one MIDI application at a time. If software companies choose to use the Apple MIDI Manager in place of, or in addition to, their

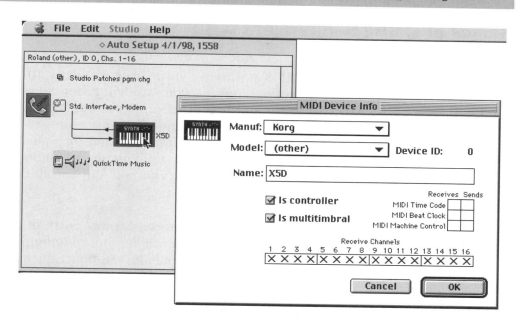

Figure 19.14
A setup from the Open
MIDI System

Closely related to the functions of OMS are programs designed to organize and edit sounds contained in multiple MIDI devices. See Module 23 for information on librarians and sound editors.

Another option for MIDI management for Macintosh computers is Mark of the Unicorn's FreeMIDI system.

own drivers, there is less worry about timing problems. The system software handles the MIDI network. Another important advantage to Apple MIDI Manager is that MIDI data can be routed among applications *internally* without need for clumsy MIDI cabling or file transfers.

In recent years, the music software industry has moved to adopt a more advanced MIDI management system developed by Opcode Systems, The Open MIDI System (OMS), for both Macintosh and Wintel computers. OMS goes further than Apple MIDI Manager by helping to keep track of the MIDI devices connected to the computer. OMS is actually a flexible database of connections and device characteristics that can be used to greatly simplify studio management as well as MIDI data flow. Information might include how the separate devices are physically connected, what kind of MIDI interface is used, what brand names of sound devices are owned, and what channels are set on which gear. OMS can document your use of MIDI patches and MIDI *cableized* interfaces such as those described in Module 21 and 22.

You can define your setup just once, and then it is recorded for future use by OMS-compliant software. OMS is intelligent about figuring out what you have connected. This saves enormous time, particularly in complex studio setups that include many sound modules, keyboards, and controllers. Another important feature is the ability of OMS to save more than one setup. If you use a portable computer as you travel between your equipment setup at a remote performance site and your own home, you can keep two separate sets of data that can be used by the same set of MIDI files.

A simple example of an OMS setup is displayed in Figure 19.14. Notice that we have two sound sources identified, the internal QuickTime musical instruments and a Korg keyboard synthesizer that is external.

Basics of Using Sequencers with Digital Audio Data

Up to this point, we have been concentrating on the MIDI side of sequencers. In this section we will review some of the features that exist for the entry and treatment of digital audio information, focusing on the entry, mixing and editing, and effects processing of sound in sequencing programs. Keep in mind that the entry and manipulation of digital sound has much in common with the sampling, digital audio editing, and sound shaping ideas that we present in Viewport VII. You should continue your reading about digital sound in those pages.

Basic Entry and Data Representation. Entry of digital audio information into your sequencer can occur by simply importing an audio file already created or by recording sounds in real-time, much like real-time entry with MIDI data. This second approach is by far the most common and is accomplished using the microphone and sound capturing hardware that is part of both Macintosh and Wintel machines. The microphones that come with computers will work satisfactorily for most real-time recording, but you may want better quality microphones as your needs become more demanding.

As we will learn in the Viewport VII, the digital audio information is recorded directly to your hard disk. The number of tracks you can record for a project depends on the computer you are using. Both PowerPC Macintosh and Pentium Wintel computers manufactured in the last two years can easily support 8 to 16 tracks of digital audio sound or more with the standard audio hardware. Large amounts of hard disk space are a must, especially if you are recording works that last longer than a few minutes.

Representation of digital audio by most sequencers is integrated right into the track window displays. Return to Figure 19.1, the Digital Orchestrator Pro program that opened this module. Notice that the track window contains a mixture of boxes and small waveforms. The boxes represent MIDI data, and the waveforms indicate digital audio tracks. This is a common approach. Figure 19.15 displays a view from Cakewalk Pro Audio and gives another view of the "clips" of audio that the program can record. Notice the use of waveform icons in the track window and the audio reference in the Port column. MIDI data are represented in a different way.

Cakewalk programs call these audio segments "clips" and provide a number of ways to copy the clips to other tracks. A clip can be linked to its parent as well, so that changes in the original will alter the clone. Sequencers take very different approaches to how they structure and organize these clips. For example, the Cubase family of sequencers use a more complicated structure of "parts," "segments," and "events." This allows for greater flexibility in editing, but also requires more work to understand.

Editing and Mixing. Double-clicking on any audio "clip" or "part" in a track window will almost always lead you to an expanded waveform representation of the recording. This provides a visual aid in performing some standard waveform editing. Figure 19.16 provides a view of an editing win-

Module 23 shows you how to create a complete virtual sequencer for both MIDI and digital audio.

Digital audio software allows the creation of "virtual" tracks as opposed to the real tracks that you might see represented visually. These virtual tracks hold versions of your editing, allowing you to compare different approaches to the sonic experience until you decide on the one you want.

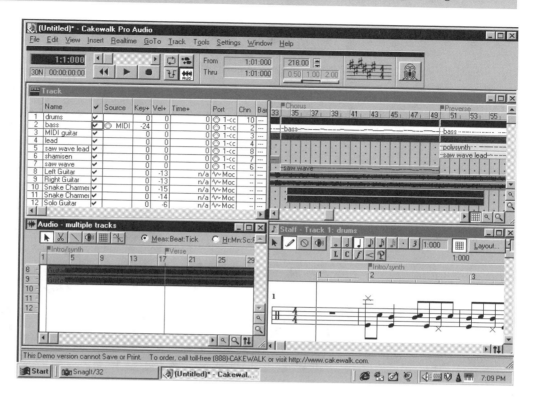

Figure 19.15
Track view in Cakewalk's
Pro Audio
(Cakewalk Music Soft-
ware [Windows])

dow from PowerTracks Audio Pro. Windows such as these allow you to snip off unwanted entrance and exit sounds from the audio waveform. Loudness can be scaled and some programs will provide fade-ins and fade-outs at this basic level.

An important point to remember with digital audio is that the number of recorded tracks that your music system supports is not necessarily the same as the number of tracks that can actually be produced at the same time. Your computer and its sound hardware might be designed to produce fewer tracks then you have, so some "mixdown" of tracks may be necessary. The Cubase family of sequencers offer powerful virtual mixers, as do other more advanced digital audio sequencer packages.

Effects Processing. In years past, it was enough just to have some kind of digital audio recording capability in music sequencing programs. Now, competition between manufacturers has caused a trend for more powerful features such as digital signal processing (DSP) effects. This is possible because computers and sound hardware have improved to a point where DSP can now be included as part of a music sequencer's options instead of being included only in separate programs. We will have much more to say about DSP in Viewport VII. At this point, take a look at the menu options available for effects processing in Cakewalk's Pro Audio (*a*) and PG Music's Power-Tracks Pro Audio (*b*) that are displayed in Figure 19.17. Common options include quantize, transpose, slide, equalizing, reverb, chorusing, flanging, time/pitch change, remove silence, and echo effects.

More on audio DSPs in
Viewport VII.

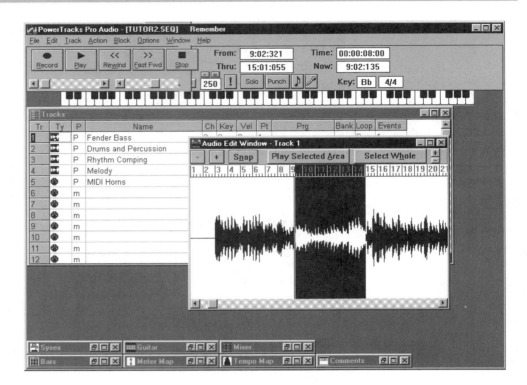

Figure 19.16
Edit view of an audio event in PowerTracks Pro Audio

Some of these effects can actually be done in real-time, that is, you can alter the effect during playback. Others require the processing to be done separately from playback. Software-based effects processing such as those described here and in Viewport VII may soon replace hardware devices designed to accomplish the same thing.

One other point about effects processing in these sequencing programs that you should note: many of the midrange and advanced packages sub-

Figure 19.17
Effects Processing Menus

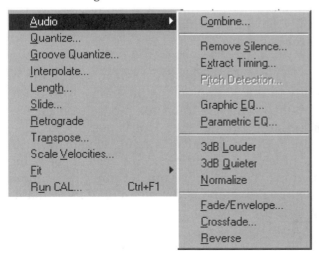

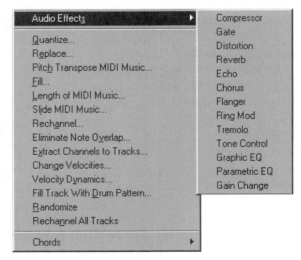

(a) From Cakewalk's Pro Audio   (b) From PG Music's PowerTracks Pro Audio

scribe to some type of "plug-in" architecture. This means that other companies can create special-effect plug-in modules for a sequencer. For example, Microsoft's DirectX protocols are supported by Cakewalk and Opcode, which means that their sequencers can take advantage of a whole set of third party products especially designed to process audio.

Advanced Topics

Acomplete description of the advanced features of sequencing software could easily occupy an entire volume. Here we will selectively examine some additional features of sequencing software in order to give you a sense of what lies beyond the first levels of use. We organize these features in three categories: viewing and setup; input and editing; and timing and notation.

Viewing and Setup. Professional titles offer more than just three or four ways to view the results of MIDI recording. Mark of the Unicorn's Performer family, for example, has a long tradition of offering numerous views depending on various needs: event list, overview, graphic, notation, and a pattern window. Marker, controller, velocity, sequence, song, and conductor windows also can be accessed. Such variety of choices makes the program flexible to use in a variety of situations including music education settings and performance research.

Emagic's Logic offers a number of traditional views and a few new approaches as well. Figure 19.18 displays Transport, Event List, Score, Matrix Edit ("piano roll"), and Hyper Edit (continuous controller) windows that we have seen before; however, note the interesting Arrange window that shows the musician an overview of the sequence. Similar to the track sheet in other programs, the Arrange window uses icons to represent instruments in each track. Notice the Folder in Track 3 that contains percussion data. Folders are used to create separate sequences within the larger arrangement—a nesting design much like that of the computer's GUI operating system. Here, separate percussion tracks are logically organized within one folder. The company's more advanced product, Logic Audio, uses these same features and includes audio segments as part of the hierarchy.

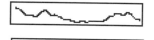

Across from the instrument and folder icons, note the rectangular blocks keyed to measure numbers to indicate lines of MIDI data. These are called *objects* in Logic's nomenclature; we have chosen the acoustic bass object between measures 5 and 13. Most of the windows in the figure are based on this object. Many of the advanced sequencers have begun to add this object-oriented, hierarchical approach. For instance, Opcode's Vision and Studio Vision can create similar objects as phrase boxes that pictorially represent the phrase itself. Several are illustrated in the margin here. This approach has embraced digital audio segments, as we have seen already.

The Environment window in Logic is another new view. Here, icons represent the flow of MIDI data in the studio setup that is being used. Connections can be established between MIDI devices and special effects, all supported inside the software.

Two last points about Logic's treatment of windows. If the musician

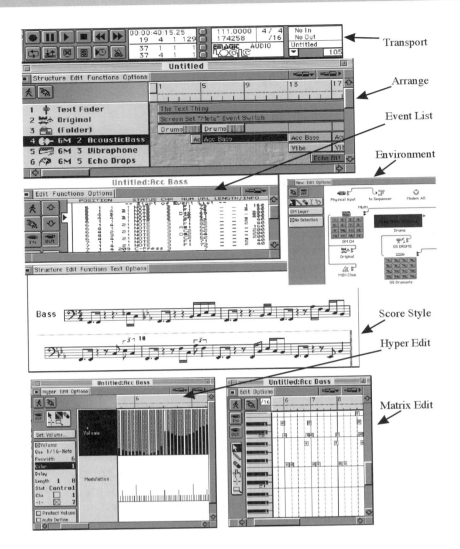

Figure 19.18
Multiple views of MIDI
recording using Logic
(Emagic [Mac/Windows])

puts Logic in the play mode, *all* the windows displayed will scroll, not just the active one. This provides a simultaneous view of the MIDI data on many levels. Finally, rather than putting all menu items in a set of main menus, each window has its own set of menus associated with its particular function.

Machine control. Professional musicians are busy people on stage. If heavy use is made of a computer-based sequencer, turning on and off settings on a computer can be very distracting. Some software offers operation of sequencer functions by remote control from a MIDI keyboard. Functions are simply mapped to a particular MIDI keystroke combination. Figure 19.19*a* displays a dialog box that sets up this remote-control arrangement from Master Tracks Pro. Notice how step-time procedures can be controlled as well.

A kind of machine control more appropriate for the studio is displayed in Figure 19.19*b*. This window from the Performer software package represents

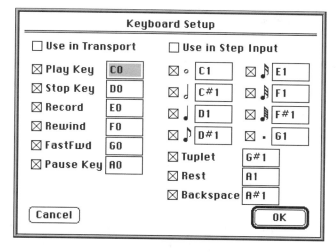

(*a*) Master Tracks Pro

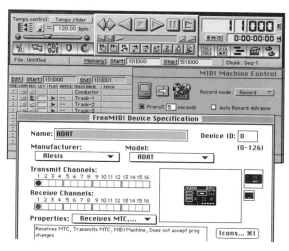

(*b*) Performer (Mark of the Unicorn [Mac])

Figure 19.19
Machine Control options

the software's ability to control external tape decks that comply with MIDI Machine Control (MMC). The software can determine a particular measure and beat location and communicate it to the attached tape deck. This is also a good example of the continuing development of MIDI as a communications protocol for all sorts of performance and recording applications.

Expanding channel options. In the basic sequencers just reviewed, you were able to add more than one channel per track. But how about other options? It's possible with advanced software to record multiple tracks *at the same time,* supporting special guitar sequencing or perhaps a jam session where multiple instruments are laying down tracks for possible use later.

One of the most important benefits of advanced sequencing software is the ability to employ more than 32 MIDI channels. To a beginner, this may seem like overkill. Why so many channels? The fact is that more and more equipment is being controlled by MIDI. In addition to the powerful multi-timbral workstations, professionals are beginning to use MIDI-controlled audio and special effects devices, routers, light controllers, and digital tape decks. In order to meet this need, special MIDI networking hardware is needed to support more than 32 channels. These options must also be supported in software.

Virtual instruments and faders. As musicians become more comfortable with multiple MIDI devices working together, some efficient way of harnessing the power for multiple combinations of instruments and special effects is a natural need for advanced software. Let's say you are disappointed with the brass program setting on your keyboard synthesizer and find that if you add your sound module's brass timbre to the mix with special volume settings, the sound is greatly improved. How do you use your sequencing software to accomplish this? You might simply send the same track to both devices, with the proper settings. This would work, but you would have to make all these settings each time you wanted this special combination. What if you discovered that six or seven sound combinations

Modules 21 and 22 present various options for expanding MIDI interfaces.

Module 21 provides a good discussion on MIDI controllers and control data.

Look ahead to the treatment of SysEx data in Module 20 and sound synthesis options in Module 23.

Making changes in music in real time is like using advanced graphics programs that let you change the brightness, contrast, or focus of a scanned image before saving it.

Shifting time is one of the features suggested earlier to help remove and add rests to a sequence.

will be used all the time? You would spend most of your day pushing the same buttons over and over—not what professional computer musicians should do.

The ability of advanced software to create *virtual instruments* solves this problem. A virtual instrument is simply a preassigned instrumental combination that the software remembers and returns to the musician with the click of a button. This can also be accomplished by use of MIDI management software such as OMS.

Closely related to virtual instruments are customized fader controls for MIDI effects. You might have used simple faders in your beginning software experiences to control the volume of tracks, but more sophisticated ones that permit controlling effects for more than one instrument can be found in advanced sequencers.

System exclusive. Finally, in terms of setup, advanced sequencers support the sending and receiving of system exclusive (SysEx) MIDI data. Each manufacturer of MIDI gear assigns special codes that permit very precise control of the internal functions of the device. One might find the ability to send system exclusive data to a particular MIDI device very helpful if a MIDI file was needed to help configure a workstation's setting for a particular program (timbre) within a sequence. Programming instrument and sound samples for MIDI devices are topics in Viewport VII.

Advanced Sequencing Options for Input and Editing. Not only are setup and viewing options extended in advanced sequencing software, but so are input and editing capabilities. One especially powerful option is editing music while it is playing. The Cubase family, for example, allows quantization to occur during playback, so the musician can hear the effect of various options. These programs also allow experimentation with blocks of MIDI data. For example, you could take one of the blocks in one track, move it to another track, and listen to the effect created by a different instrument or patch on that channel. Blocks can be lengthened and shortened in time—all this while the music continues to play.

Scaling and shifting time. Subtle timing options are available in advanced programs. For example, dialog boxes provide options for compressing or expanding the tempo of passages, or shifting events slightly ahead or back. Scaling time is a process similar to augmentation and diminution of note values in notation software (see Module 16). In notation software, all timing events are either expanded or contracted by a ratio. Scaling does the same thing but within a specified time. All proportions are the same, but the events fit into a defined time frame. This has obvious applications in working with film, live drama, or radio and television.

Shifting or sliding music is just what it implies: moving all events slightly back or forward in time. You can do this with or without quantization. Most programs allow you to slide either all events or just the MIDI note values. Scaling and shifting music in sequencers can be accomplished with both MIDI and digital audio data.

Noncontinuous selection. A powerful feature for MIDI data is the ability

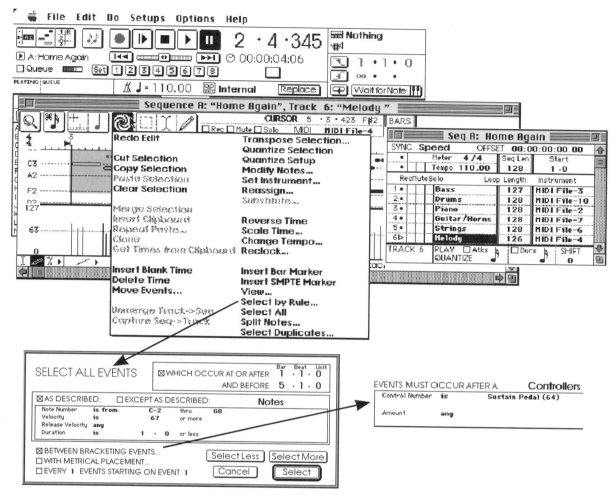

Figure 19.20
Selecting noncontinuous
MIDI data using Vision
(Opcode Systems [Mac/Windows])

to support noncontinuous selection. Suppose a musician wanted to select a series of specified pitches that occurred quite fast, loud, and only when the sustain pedal controller was engaged. This combination of MIDI events might occur throughout a lengthy sequence, and the performer would want to select them for editing purposes without having to tediously find every single occurrence.

Figure 19.20 displays how this might be done using a version of Vision. You would first choose the desired track from the track sheet window, *Seq A: Home Again* in our example. This would reveal a graphics view for this track. We have chosen Track 6, Melody, in this example, and it is in the center of our display. We have chosen to click on the Mogrify button in the horizontal bar of icons at the top of the window, and this powerful option has revealed a context-sensitive menu beneath it. Choosing the Selection by Rule option, you can then specify increasingly more complex criteria for creating noncontinuous selection. In our example, we have opted to indicate the note range, loudness (velocity), duration, and the sustained pedal controller.

Systematic remapping of notes. Some advanced software, such as Performer and Digital Performer, provides inversion, retrograde, and retrograde inversion of selected pitches. This allows for experimentation with compositional ideas within the sequencer. Remapping of notes in other ways is also possible.

Algorithmic composition. A few sequencing packages like those in the Vision and Cubase families offer some automatic composition features. Music ideas entered into these built-in routines come out in a number of possible permutations based on settings that you specify. If something you like is created, you can capture its MIDI data and use it as part of your creative work. We will discuss this topic further at the close of this module.

Advanced quantization. In an effort to find a compromise between rhythmic accuracy and human feel, software designers have created a number of options. Some of these involve how the music is recorded and marked with a pulse; other use special software solutions to preserve the musical feeling. Software solutions include a *humanize* option that quantizes in a random fashion to simulate real playing and a *groove* quantize choice that creates a certain musical style. Figure 19.21 shows a powerful example of this option found in the Performer family. Notice the choice of styles and the sliders, which vary the effect of quantization for duration, velocity, and timing.

Built-in language. At least one sequencer, Cakewalk's Pro Audio, contains a set of language commands that can build custom functions. The Cakewalk Application Language (CAL) allows musicians to build functions that automate the construction of certain chords above selected notes or perform splits of notes in MIDI tracks. Some functions are already provided as examples.

Synchronization. One of the great differences between beginning and intermediate levels and advanced software sequencers is how synchronization to external sources is handled. All the advanced packages reviewed here offer flexible ways to control the flow of MIDI data.

Advanced synchronization is explained in Module 22.

Figure 19.21
Groove quantization using Performer
(Mark of the Unicorn [Mac])

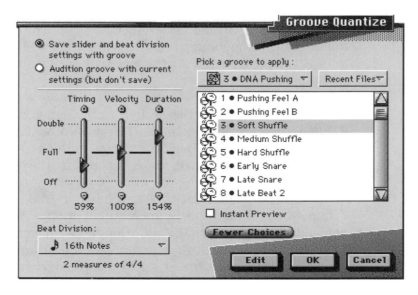

Alternatives to Track-Based Sequencers

Going Trackless. Not all sequencers use the track-based metaphor. One product that supports a trackless approach to MIDI sequencing is Mark of the Unicorn's FreeStyle (see Figure 19.22). Notice that all the MIDI events are displayed together in a unified window, like the view we highlighted in Musicshop in Figure 19.8. However, unlike Musicshop and the other programs described thus far in this module, FreeStyle does not organize its data entry into discrete tracks. The program has many structures for instrument groups, called ensembles, already defined for you and features percussion backgrounds already created. A tempo sensing feature is also unique. Notice the use of other features we have presented in this module, including the

Figure 19.22
FreeStyle
(Mark of the Unicorn
[Mac/Windows])

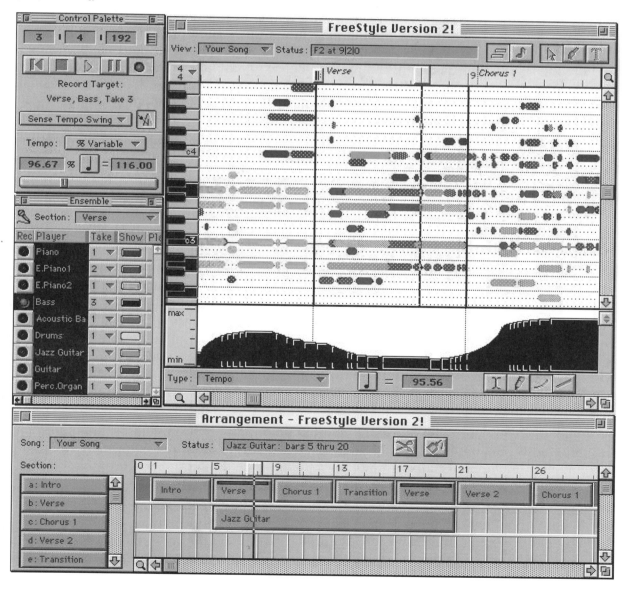

use of arrangement blocks (this time for multiple instrument parts) and the graphic editing of controller data such as tempo and loudness.

FreeStyle retains some of the expected features of a midrange sequencer but takes a different approach to organization. It is especially useful for the quick constructing of music that has standard instrumentation and formal properties.

Object-Oriented Programming (OOP) Environments for Composition. Up to now, we have concentrated on software that uses MIDI data represented either by traditional notation symbols (CAI programs in Module 8 and notation packages in Module 17) or by numeric descriptions and graphics within vertical tracks (sequencers in this module). These are, by far, the most common applications. Another way to control MIDI codes is by using graphic objects in a more open, free-form system that provides unlimited interaction and interconnection between music objects.

We have actually seen an example of this already in Module 16 when we were discussing alternate forms of music representation for notation. Another example is included here as Figure 19.23; it demonstrates how a music passage is entered in Opcode's Max, altered by a prescribed delay, and then played. This graphic representation can itself be made into a small object and used in a larger context to form a composition of many objects like itself. In addition to MIDI events, Max can also use digital audio files and link to other multimedia extensions.

Max, designed as an object-oriented programming environment for MIDI, is particularly attractive to contemporary composers. One reason for this is that it frees composers to think in sound not by using linear tracks as the organizing structure but by using graphic representations of musical

Refer ahead to Module 28 for more information on OOP. Also check out Gary Lee Nelson's use of Max with his MIDI horn in Module 22!

Figure 19.23
An object created by use of Max
(Opcode Systems [Mac])

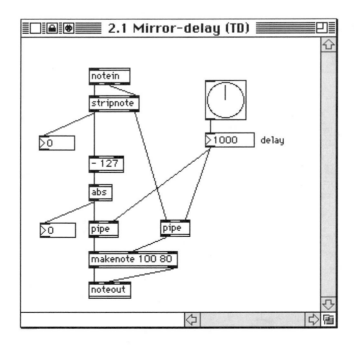

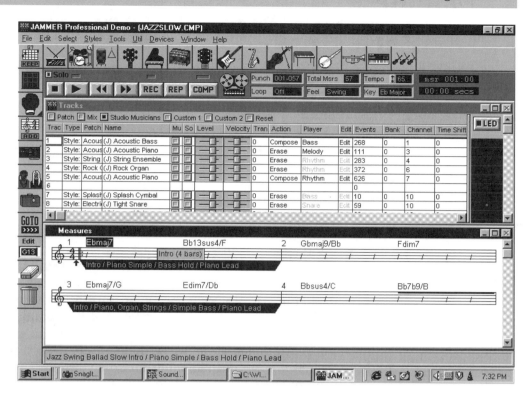

Figure 19.24
The Jammer
Professional
(Soundtrek [Windows])

events arranged in whatever space makes sense. Some sequencing packages, like the Cubase and Logic families, incorporate limited kinds of objects within a traditional track, but none approach the programmatic flexibility of a program like Max.

Algorithmic Composing. Algorithmic composing (using mathematical formulae to create musical material) is a feature found in certain sequencers such as those from the Vision and Cubase families. There are also separate programs that are designed to automatically create music. The composer specifies certain parameters and then awaits the result. Rarely do these products create a finished composition; rather, they return material that might be interesting for the composer to use as a basis for further compositional work.

Figure 19.24 is taken from a program called The Jammer Professional. The program creates different music options based on the structure that is established in the lower window.

A Long Journey. These alternatives to track-based sequencing add still more options for music making. There is a great deal here for you to think about and plenty of room for you to grow as a performance musician using technology. Modules 20, 21, and 22 will build on this solid introduction to sequencing software by completing our explanations of MIDI and digital audio data structures and the hardware that can take advantage of them.

David Cope discusses his experiments with EMI and his use of algorithmic composing in his interview for Viewport IV.

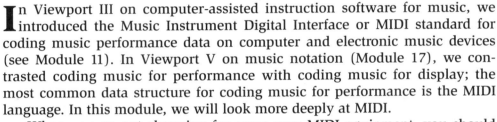

Module 20   MIDI Data Structures Revisited

In Viewport III on computer-assisted instruction software for music, we introduced the Music Instrument Digital Interface or MIDI standard for coding music performance data on computer and electronic music devices (see Module 11). In Viewport V on music notation (Module 17), we contrasted coding music for performance with coding music for display; the most common data structure for coding music for performance is the MIDI language. In this module, we will look more deeply at MIDI.

When you go out shopping for some new MIDI equipment, you should ask to see the manuals that go with the various MIDI devices, be they keyboards, sound modules, guitar controllers, or the like. You will notice in these manuals a mysterious chart of codes called the MIDI *implementation chart*. At first glance, it looks like the list of ingredients on breakfast cereal boxes. Who wants to read the fine print? Who needs to? It is important for you to learn to decipher implementation charts, because they give you a comprehensive view of all the capabilities of the MIDI device. The chart, like the fine print on the cereal box, lists all the essential ingredients in one place.

To help explain the next level of MIDI data structures, we have created a model of a plain vanilla MIDI keyboard synthesizer. We'll call this device the Vanilla-1. If you can learn to decipher its implementation chart, then you can easily learn to cope with charts from more sophisticated MIDI instruments. We will use the MIDI implementation chart of the Vanilla-1 synthesizer as a guide to review the basic functions of MIDI covered in Module 11, and then we will examine more advanced topics including:

Be sure to read the discussion of music sequencers in Module 19.

▶ Pressure and Pitch-Bend messages

▶ Mode messages

▶ Controller messages (Control Changes and Channel Mode messages)

▶ System messages, especially the System Exclusive (SysEx) message

▶ MIDI timing and SMPTE

▶ General MIDI

▶ Variations on General MIDI for multimedia and the Internet

▶ MIDI and digital audio détente

Remember that MIDI messages are grouped into the following categories:

▶ Channel messages: These messages are publicly broadcast to all MIDI devices tuned to a selected channel and include *Channel Voice* messages and *Channel Mode* messages.

▶ System messages: These messages are publicly broadcast over the MIDI network to all devices on all channels and include *System Real-Time*, *System Common*, and *System Exclusive* messages.

For the basics of MIDI, review Module 11.

A SPECIAL NOTE ON MIDI CHANNELS

Every MIDI channel message contains as part of its coding a number that selects the channel for broadcasting that message. The format for this code is often shown as a number with an *n* after it; for example, the code for a Note On message is *9n*. The *n* is replaced with one of the MIDI channel numbers 0-15, for the 16 possible MIDI channels. Therefore a Note On message sent to channel 1 would be *90*, to channel 2, *91*, and on the highest channel, channel 16, *9F*. Why *F*, you ask? MIDI codes are stated in base 16 (hexadecimal) numbers instead of the usual base 10 or decimal values. In base 16 you count from 0 to F, that's 0, 1, 2, . . . 9, A, B, C, D, E, F, enabling you to count to 16 with single characters.

MIDI Implementation Charts

We have created in Table 20.1 a MIDI implementation chart for our music synthesizer, the Vanilla-1. The synthesizer's sounds are all digital, so in this respect it is a sample player. It has a built-in sequencer with the capability of storing up to ten sequences in its memory. The keyboard has a five-octave range.

The chart has four columns. The first column lists basic MIDI functions. The second and third columns tell you which functions are implemented on this device: × = not implemented; and o = yes, or implemented. The second column indicates that these messages are transmitted or sent by the synthesizer; the third column indicates whether or not the synthesizer recognizes these message when they are sent by some other device.

Distinctions between synthesizers, samplers, sample players, and other MIDI devices were first presented in Module 12 and Table 12.2.

Don't feel bad if you have to think a second time about transmitting and receiving MIDI messages, as it is easy to get confused. Put yourself in the place of the MIDI device to keep these terms straight. *Transmitted* indicates the MIDI messages you will send out to other MIDI devices, like a computer or a sound module. *Received*, or *Recognized* (as it is labeled in the implementation chart), pertains to incoming MIDI data; for example, the MIDI codes a computer running sequencing software could send to you, the Vanilla-1.

The fourth column contains additional *remarks*. In the following pages, we will discuss the functions of the chart in more detail.

Basic MIDI Messages

Having gained some MIDI savvy in Module 11, you should be able to understand some of the functions on the implementation chart: Basic Channel, Note Number, Velocity, and Program Change. Find each of these functions in the chart.

Under the Basic Channel function, the chart tells you that this synthesizer can transmit and recognize all 16 channels available for MIDI data. The default row dates from early MIDI devices that would automatically default to one channel, e.g., Channel 1. *Memorized* in the remarks column indicates that this device remembers what channel you last set it to, and it will use that as the setting when you next turn it on. The Change row indicates the range of channels that can be set from the keyboard, i.e., all 16.

The Note Number data tell us that the Vanilla-1 has a five-octave keyboard that can transmit MIDI pitch values in the range of 36 to 96, or 60 notes in all. However, the synthesizer can recognize all 128 pitch values $(0 \sim 127)$ from another MIDI device (e.g., a personal computer running a sequencer program). The remarks column also tells us that the Vanilla-1's internal sequencer will transmit all 128 notes even though its keyboard has a more restricted range. The row marked *True Voice* gives you the overall range of $0 \sim 127$ that the instrument can recognize from pitch data coming from other devices (the "*****" indicates that this parameter is meaningless for transmitting MIDI pitch data).

Velocity data deal with how fast the key goes from its up to its down position, an indicator of the intensity or dynamics of the note. The chart indicates that both the Note On and Note Off messages can contain velocity data. But the Vanilla-1 does not recognize or transmit velocity for the Note Off message, hence the *x* in both columns. Notice the *o 9n V = 1 ~ 127* in the Note On row. This means that the device will transmit and recognize velocity data (*o*) with a range of values from 1 to 127 using the MIDI Note On code *9n*. As we discussed above, the *n* is the channel number over which the Note On is transmitted. The remark indicates that the Vanilla-1's internal sequencer also transmits the full range of values, 1 to 127.

The Program Change function, discussed in Module 11 and in Module 19, is also sometimes known as *patch, instrument, program,* or *timbre.* This indicates the number of internal sounds that the synthesizer has built in; because the Vanilla-1 is a digital synthesizer, this tells you how many internal sound samples the device has in its ROM. This synthesizer can recognize and transmit the full range of 128 program changes or instruments, and the actual number of sound samples it contains is also 128 $(0 \sim 127)$.

Pressure and Pitch-Bend Messages

Now to introduce some new features of MIDI: Pressure and Pitch Bend. Pressure is also known as *aftertouch.* Turning to our chart, the first row for Pressure is *Poly Key,* or Polyphonic Key Pressure. Polyphonic Pressure is a data value $(0 \sim 127)$ representing the pressure on a key *after* the key is down, and it is available for *every key* on the keyboard. It allows you to create special expressive effects, like momentary dynamic or timbre changes, that were

Table 20.1 VANILLA-1 MIDI Implementation Chart

Function		Transmitted	Recognized	Remarks
Basic Channel	Default	1 ~ 16	1 ~ 16	Memorized
	Change	1 ~ 16	1 ~ 16	
Mode	Default	x	3	
	Messages	x	1, 3	
	Altered	******		
Note Number		36 ~ 96	0 ~ 127	Sequencer transmits 0 to 127
	True Voice	******	0 ~ 127	
Velocity	Note On	o 9n, V = 1 ~ 127	o 9n, V = 1 ~ 127	Sequencer transmits 1 to 127
	Note Off	x	x	
Pressure	Poly Key	x	x	
	Channel	o	o	
Pitch Bend		o	o 0 ~ 12 semitones	7-bit resolution
Control Change	0, 32	x	o	Bank switch (MSB + LSB)
	1	o	o	Modulation wheel[3]
	2	o	o	Breath control
	4	o	o	Foot controller
	5	o	o	Portamento time[1]
	6, 38	o	o	Slider data entry (MSB + LSB)
	7	o	o	Volume[1,3]
	10	o	o	Pan[3]
	11	o	o	Expression[1,3]
	64	o	o	Sustain switch (on or off)[3]
	65	o	o	Portamento switch (on or off)
	0—101	o	o	Send and Rec'v Seq. Data only
	121	x	o	Reset all controllers[3]
	123	x	o	All Notes Off[3]
Program Change		o ~ 127	o 0 ~ 127	
	Actual No.	******	o 0 ~ 127	
System Exclusive		o	o	2
System Common	:Song pos.	o	o	10 song locations available in sequencer
	:Song sel.	o 0 ~ 9	o 0 ~ 9	
	:Tune	x	x	
System Realtime	:Clock	o	o	
	:Commands	o	o	
Aux Messages	:Local ON/OFF	x	o	
	:All notes off	x	o	
	:Active sensing	o	o	
	:Reset	x	x	

Notes: [1]Receive if switch is on. [2]System exclusive details are not given in this table; they are given elsewhere in the equipment's manual. [3]General MIDI performance requirement.

Mode 1: Omni On, Poly	Mode 2: Omni On, Mono	o: Yes	
Mode 3: Omni Off, Poly	Mode 4: Omni Off, Mono	x: No	

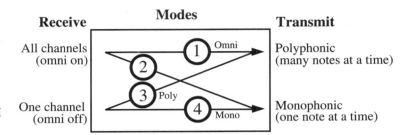

Figure 20.1
Four combinations of MIDI channel mode messages

linked to your finger pressure on a key while it was down and sustaining. Generally, these effects are only available on high-end synthesizers, because they are more expensive to implement. These expressive techniques are not possible on a controller with channel pressure only, like the Vanilla-1.

The second row under the Pressure function is Channel Pressure. The Vanilla-1 both transmits and recognizes Channel Pressure. This is a value from 0 to 127 that tells you the *average* pressure on all keys on the MIDI device. Most MIDI controllers provide this function. The Channel Pressure value would let you capture and manipulate the overall dynamic information for the performance of any MIDI instrument.

Immediately below the Pressure row is the Pitch-Bend function. Pitch Bend indicates to what extent you can momentarily modify the pitch of a note above or below its normal setting. According to the chart, the pitch-bend range is ±12 semitones; the remark about 7-bit resolution means you have 128 values to work with. Pitch bend lets you add special effects with subtle pitch changes like those used in jazz, rock, and pop styles. The Vanilla-1 both transmits and recognizes Pitch-Bend messages.

Mode Messages

We have skipped two functions, Mode and Control Change. Let's try to understand these more complex functions.

Look at the Default row under the Mode category. It indicates that when the Vanilla-1 is turned on, it does not transmit mode data and the default setting is Mode 3. While the synthesizer is operating, it does not transmit any Mode messages but will recognize Modes 1 and 3.

The MIDI standard offers four possible channel mode messages: *Omni Mode On, Omni Mode Off, Mono On,* and *Poly On.* Figure 20.1 illustrates the various mode combinations.

Mode 1 (Omni On/Poly) is the "goof-proof" setting, and some devices, especially older ones, defaulted to this mode. Everything on every channel gets performed by a device. For a simple music CAI setup like those discussed in Viewport III, this mode works well. If a musician uses some of the older MIDI devices, the device's default setting is to Mode 1.

Mode 2 (Omni On/Mono) is rarely used, and some devices, like our Vanilla-1, may not recognize it. One possible application of Mode 2 might be in a very simple MIDI network. One synthesizer would be controlling another and both running all the time on all notes without your having to worry about channel assignments.

Mode 3 (Omni Off/Poly) is known as the *Poly* mode and is the one frequently used as the default setting on MIDI devices; our Vanilla-1 defaults to Mode 3. In this mode each channel contains specific polyphonic performance data—what you want when working with sequencers. Omni Off indicates that performance data are being sent to specific channels and are not being broadcast on all channels at once. This is the mode you will likely find as the default setting on most new MIDI keyboards and other devices you work with.

Mode 4 (Omni off/mono) is known as the *mono* mode, and like Mode 2 is less frequently used. In this mode, each monophonic line can be assigned to a single monophonic voice of the synthesizer. For example with a woodwind quintet, starting with the base channel 1, the flute line could be assigned to 1, clarinet to 2, oboe to 3, horn to 4, and bassoon to channel 5. The same arrangement works effectively with a hexaphonic guitar controller where each of the six strings are assigned to a different MIDI channel, 1 through 6; "hammer on" percussive effects can be performed on the guitar controller with this setup.

Controller Messages and Things

Controllers are supported and represented in sequencing software as shown in Module 19.

Controllers. Controllers and controller messages are very important to creative work with MIDI devices. The first obvious thing you see when you look at a synthesizer keyboard is the keys; you can easily think in terms of notes on and notes off. But, the expressive control so important to creating music is in the *controller messages* that the MIDI language provides. Among the standard controllers available on MIDI devices are modulation wheels for vibrato; foot controllers that can be used for many different special effects including dynamics; breath controllers from wind devices; volume controllers and their more subtle counterparts, expression controllers; pan controllers for stereo balance; and various switches for turning effects like sustain and portamento on and off.

The MIDI data structure provides for a large set of controller devices, all under the Control Change messages; you can locate these on the MIDI implementation chart in Table 20.1. There are 128 numbers for controllers in the MIDI data structure. Along each MIDI channel, up to 128 controllers can be talking to one another, like mini-channels that exist within each channel. MIDI devices on the same channel can listen in on any controller's number and pick up on the messages.

If you have another synthesizer networked as a slave to the Vanilla-1 and both have a modulation wheel with controller number 1, then the Vanilla-1's modulation wheel that is sending the data will control the slave wheel on the other synthesizer. Similar controller numbers talk to each other. If the numbers for the controller functions do not match up, you can get interesting but unpredictable effects, but most MIDI devices let you assign controller numbers. You could map the Breath Controller (2) of a wind controller to the Expression Controller (11) of the Vanilla-1 synthesizer and produce dynamic changes while sustaining a note. Likewise, the Foot Controller (4) of the Vanilla-1 could be mapped to the modulation wheel (1) on another device to control vibrato.

Table 20.2. Controller Assignments in MIDI for the Control Change Function in Table 20.1	
Controller Types	**MIDI Number Range**
Continuous controllers (MSB)	0–31
Continuous controllers (LSB)	32–63
Switch controllers	64–95
Data increment controllers and others	96–101
Other miscellaneous controllers	102–119
Channel mode messages	120–127

If you need to review bytes, check back to Module 7.

Table 20.2 provides an overview of the 128 controller numbers and how they are grouped. Continuous controllers are ones that send a stream of numbers over a range of, typically, 0 to 127; here we have modulation wheels, breath controllers, foot controllers, and the like. These exist as a parallel set of values, 0–31 and 32–63, labeled as *MSB* (Most Significant Byte) and *LSB* (Least Significant Byte). By combining these you can increase the range to 0 to 16,368 values.

Examine the row for the Control Change function in the Vanilla-1 MIDI implementation chart. Notice that the first nine controllers are all continuous controllers; their controller numbers are below 64. Controllers 64 and 65 are switches that turn on or off the sustain and portamento effects.

The chart also tells us that the built-in sequencer will recognize and transmit any controller messages in the range of 0 to 101: it cannot perform all the controller effects but will at least record them and transmit them on to other devices that perhaps can perform them via the device's MIDI

Table 20.3. Continuous and Switch Controller Codes Used by the VANILLA-1 in Table 20.1		
Controller number(s)	**Resolution**	**Function**
0, 32	high	Back switch
1	low	Modulation wheel
2	low	Breath Controller
4	low	Foot Controller
5	low	Portamento time
6, 38	high	Slider data entry
7	low	Volume
10	low	Pan
11	low	Expression
64	on or off	Sustain switch
65	on or off	Portamento switch

THRU port. The continuous controllers are worth further inspection; a summary of the continuous and switch controllers for the Vanilla-1 is shown in Table 20.3.

This set of controllers is fairly typical. Others exist, but tend to be idiosyncratic to certain devices and manufacturers. Table 20.3 shows two controllers, Bank Switch and Slider Data Entry, to be high-resolution controllers and to use a pair of bytes from the LSB and MSB groups that generate values up to 16,368. All the other controllers are low resolution and generate values in the range of 0 to 127.

This is a good time to discuss how some of these controllers are used. First, there are two continuous controllers that are used for operational control, the Bank Switch and Slider Data Entry controllers. The Bank Switch controller (0 and 32) is used to switch between different sets of program changes or instruments. For example, a MIDI sound module may have several banks of 128 instruments each: one for General MIDI sounds; one that matches the older DX-7 sounds or the Roland CM32-L; additional banks of patches that are unique to the sound module; and, possibly, even one that you can program with your own instrument sounds. The Slider Data Entry controller (6 and 38) represents a physical slider on the synthesizer keyboard that can be used to enter different data values manually into the synthesizer.

Second, there is a set of continuous controllers that permits special music effects. The Modulation Wheel provides control over vibrato. Portamento Time lets you set up a pitch slide or glissando and control the time between its starting and ending pitch; note that the implementation chart (Table 20.1) has a footnote indicating that the Portamento Switch (controller 65) must be on for this to work.

Third, there are three continuous controllers that provide dynamic and loudness effects: Volume (7), Pan (10), and Expression (11). Volume lets you control overall loudness levels and fade-like dynamics. Expression is best for crescendos and diminuendos. Pan controls the balance of loudness between left to right in a stereo sound field.

Last, we have the Breath (2) and Foot (4) controllers. Breath provides a range of MIDI values that come typically from a wind-controller device that can detect the movement of air. The Foot controller detects the movement of the foot on a pedal attached to the MIDI device.

Channel Mode Messages. That covers most of the capabilities of our Vanilla-1 synthesizer and its Control Change functions. There is one subset of the Control Change numbers, 120–127, in Table 20.2 labeled as Channel Mode Messages. Table 20.4 shows the Channel Mode messages and their Control Change numbers.

Numbers 124 to 127 should look very familiar to you; they are the messages used to create the four modes (e.g., Omni, Poly, etc.) discussed earlier.

Look back at the implementation chart in Table 20.1. The functions in the bottom row are labeled *Aux Messages. Local On/Off,* and *All Notes Off* represent the control change numbers 122 and 123 in Table 20.4. The channel mode All Notes Off command (123) is handy because MIDI devices

Table 20.4. Channel Mode Messages (Controller Number Range 120–127 Shown in Table 20.2)	
Controller Change Number	**Channel Mode Message**
120	All sound off
121	Reset all controllers
122	Local control on/off
123	All notes off
124	Omni mode on
125	Omni mode off
126	Mono mode on
127	Poly mode off

sometimes get stuck in play mode, and this command tells them all to shut off. The Vanilla-1 synthesizer will recognize but not transmit the All Notes Off message.

The Local On/Off message (122) controls whether a MIDI device will respond to the MIDI messages actually generated by its own device. This lets you disable the keyboard and controllers on a MIDI device. The Reset All Controllers message (121) will put all controllers in their normal default state. This message, along with All Notes Off, should be used at the end of a sequence as a common courtesy to clear the devices for the next MIDI file to be performed.

System Messages and SysEx

We have covered all of the implementation chart in Table 20.1 except the System messages: System Exclusive, System Common, and System Real-Time. Remember, the System messages, unlike the Channel messages, get broadcast to all MIDI devices on a network be they drum machines, effects generators, keyboards, sound modules, or tape recorders.

System Common Messages. System Common messages are used when the MIDI device has built-in sequencing; the Common messages let you select sequencer "songs," select play and recording position within "songs," and synchronize other MIDI devices with the sequencer. Looking at the chart in Table 20.1, the row marked *System Common*, you can see that the Vanilla-1 has a sequencer that can store up to 10 songs. Furthermore, the device will both transmit and recognize the Song Position message and the Song Select message for up to 10 songs (0–9).

The Common messages give you two ways to control sequencing: by absolute number of beats and by relative time. The Position message lets you locate any place within a song in sixteenth-note beats from the beginning of the song. The MTC or MIDI Time Code provides absolute time addressing through quarter-time codes sent 120 times per second. We will return to song position pointers (SPPs) and MTC later.

There are a few extraneous messages in the system common category, including the Tune Request for tuning analog oscillators in analog synthesizers (you won't find many of these any more). So it is with the Vanilla-1. You will note in the chart that the synthesizer has *x* marked in the columns for Transmitted and Recognized for Tune. The EOX or End Of Exclusive Message is also in this category; we'll talk about this when we discuss System Exclusive messages.

System Real-Time Messages. Like the Common messages, Real-Time messages primarily control sequencing and synchronizing MIDI devices over the MIDI network. Look at the row labeled System Real-Time in the implementation chart (Table 20.1). It tells us that the Vanilla-1 synthesizer can transmit and recognize the Real-Time Clock and Command messages. The commands are similar to tape recorder controls: start, stop, and continue playing a sequencer song. The Clock message is tied to the beat; the MIDI device sends out 24 pulses per beat, the beat being adjustable by the tempo.

Like the Common messages, the Real-Time messages also contain a few extraneous ones: Active Sensing and System Reset. Look at Table 20.1 under Aux Messages. The Vanilla-1 has Active Sensing but the Reset is not available (note the × in the Transmitted and Recognized columns). With the Vanilla's Active Sensing messages, if any of the cables to the device are accidentally unplugged, the Vanilla will automatically turn off all notes. Otherwise, if a cable gets unplugged, all of the notes would get stuck on! The Reset command, if it were available on the Vanilla-1, would set all the MIDI parameters in an instrument back to its default mode.

SysEx Messages: "Can we have a little privacy, please!" The System Exclusive or SysEx message is one of the most powerful facilities built into the MIDI language. All the MIDI messages we have discussed so far are public messages. The Channel commands are public to everyone on a single MIDI network channel; the System commands are public to everyone on every channel. The one exception is the System Exclusive message; it lets you send an exclusive message to one device only, "in private." Moreover, the exclusive message may be unique to one manufacturer's MIDI product: a Yamaha wind controller may have its own private SysEx commands that are different from those of a Roland synthesizer, and different still from those of an Ensoniq sound module. Looking at the implementation chart for the Vanilla-1, you can see that it does transmit and recognize SysEx commands; the footnote tells you that you would have to look elsewhere in the document to find out what those exclusive messages are and how they are coded.

Let's take a quick look at a simplified format for a SysEx command. This will help you understand how they work.

SysEx message	Manufacturer's ID	Model ID	Data string	EOX message

The SysEx message is like sending private mail to a MIDI device. The first part of the message is the MIDI code that lets everyone on the network

Nostalgia prevails and the older analog sounds like those from Arps and Moogs have found their way back into MIDI instruments as digitized sound samples of the vintage electronic instruments.

Extensions to General MIDI like Roland GS and Yamaha XG use SysEx data strings for implementing the new MIDI codes.

know that a SysEx message is coming. The next two parts of the message identify the manufacturer of the MIDI device and the type of instrument the message is for. Every manufacturer of MIDI instruments has a unique ID, and they, in turn, assign IDs to their different MIDI products. Sending a SysEx message to a Yamaha TG100 sound module, for example, uses Yamaha's ID of 67 and the TG100's ID of 39. For sending to a Roland CM-32L sound module, Roland's ID is 65 and the CM-32L's ID is 22.

At this point in the message, given the various IDs provided, there is no doubt to whom this SysEx message is addressed. In between the IDs and the EOX message (this marks the end of the SysEx message) is a *data string* of an unlimited number of codes. This string can contain anything that the receiving MIDI device is designed to understand.

Let's talk about what typically goes in the data string sent to MIDI devices. SysEx data strings generally are used to send *bulk dumps* or *real-time controls* between MIDI devices. Take the case of transferring bulk dumps between a synthesizer and a computer. Bulk dumps can transfer all of the synthesizer's sound patches to the computer, all of the settings of its controllers and other parameters, and, if it is a sampling synthesizer, any of the sound samples. This lets you sort through sound patches, capture the synthesizer's settings for performing, and edit and create new sound samples.

The other feature that SysEx data strings can give you is real-time control of the synthesizer from the computer. A true virtuoso of the MIDI keys knows how to pull from a MIDI device every electronic nuance by using the SysEx messages to gain real-time control over every accessible parameter, be it a slider, buttons, aftertouch, pitch bend, etc. Just about anything is possible with skillful programming of SysEx real-time messages.

As greater use is being made of the System Exclusive messages for dumps and real-time control, certain standards are emerging. For one, there are Universal System Exclusive messages. These are messages that are used consistently across manufacturers for controlling bulk dumps and real-time control. One particular Universal SysEx message that we will touch on in a moment is the SysEx command to enable the General MIDI standard. Other standards are the Sample Dump Standard (SDS) and the Downloadable Sounds Specification (DLS) for General MIDI. These attempt to standardize the formatting of sample data being exchanged between MIDI instruments.

Would you believe we have made it through the entire MIDI implementation chart for the Vanilla-1? We hope you have overcome some of the fear you might have had about reading the small print in these MIDI charts and that the next time you go shopping for new MIDI devices you will jump right in and scan the implementation chart with confidence. The next time the salesperson at the local music shop tries to sell you a new MIDI instrument, show them you are a MIDI expert: Ask to see the MIDI implementation chart!

There are a few other issues related to MIDI data structures we'd like you to know about before we leave this module. Those issues are timing and synchronization in MIDI, more details related to the General MIDI standard and extensions for General MIDI, and the merger of MIDI and digital audio data structures.

More on General MIDI, DLS, GS, and XG later in this module.

MIDI Timing, SMPTE, and Other Timing Variations

The data structures we've studied so far in relation to MIDI have been, for the most part, static ones. We've examined the messages that MIDI uses to communicate performance data among devices on a MIDI network. But, as you well know, music is the unfolding of sound events over time. Computers need to talk to synthesizers, drum machines, sound modules, wind controllers, tape recorders, and mixers; the flow of MIDI messages among all of these devices must be accurately synchronized. Let's take a brief look at the data structures that MIDI and audio and video devices use to maintain synchrony.

Who's Conducting This Group? Think of all of the things you do with MIDI devices that require the software and the MIDI devices to always know where they are in time. The list would include multitrack recording; adding music to video productions; performing live with MIDI instruments; producing multimedia presentations with audio, digital, and analog video, graphic stills, and MIDI music events.

Have you ever seen a movie showing how they put music to film in the old days? They would assemble the orchestra with a conductor. Behind the orchestra would be a large screen for the conductor to view the movie. Then the orchestra would perform the score as the conductor kept the music synchronized with the film using his or her eye and ear as guides. Who in a MIDI network is the conductor? And how do all the components communicate and stay together?

Something must serve the role of the master timing device from which all other devices (the *slave* devices, as they are called) keep in time. Figure 20.2 shows three MIDI networks, each with a different conductor. Figure 20.2*a* shows a MIDI network with a drum machine, a synthesizer, and a sound module. Note that the drum machine is the master whose internal clock generates the beat for the other two MIDI instruments; the synthesizer and sound module are set to receive the timing beat from the external drum machine. This is a typical setup for any stand-alone MIDI configuration without a computer, one that is commonly used for live performance.

Now look at Figure 20.2*b*. In this network, a computer system is the master device; it is providing the beat for synchronizing the other devices on the network. This is a typical configuration for using a computer in a MIDI network for music sequencing or notation activities.

Figure 20.2*c* adds a very different twist to the setup. A digital recorder (ADAT, DAT, MiniDisc, or hard disk recorder) is included in the network. Notice that the tape recorder is the master device. The computer and all of the MIDI instruments are synchronized to the tape recorder with a very interesting configuration. This is one way in which you would do multitrack recording with a MIDI setup.

You can also purchase more sophisticated MIDI interfaces that provide the timing codes like those from Opcode, MidiMan, or Mark of the Unicorn, or purchase various hardware synchronizers such as Mark of the Unicorn's

How digital recorders provide SMPTE time codes will be covered in more detail in Module 22 of this viewport.

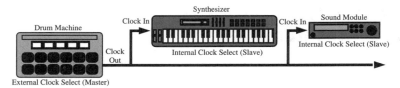

(*a*) A drum machine as the master timing

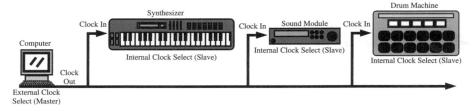

(*b*) A computer as the master device

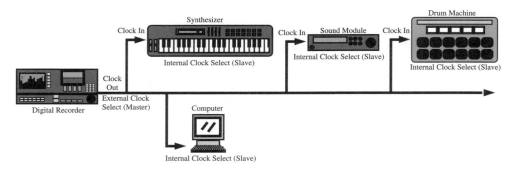

Figure 20.2
MIDI networks showing
master-slave timing

(*c*) Synchronizing a MIDI network to a digital recorder

Digital Timepiece or MidiMan's Synchman Pro. There are a host of devices that will serve as the conductor for your MIDI network. Now that we know who is conducting the MIDI network, we can turn our attention to the techniques used to keep everyone together in time.

Keeping the Tape Time. We can begin with the analog world of tape and video recording: non-MIDI devices. How are events synchronized in the music recording and video world? We will first touch on two timing techniques: FSK (frequency shift keying) code and SMPTE (Society for Motion Picture and Television Engineers, pronounced "simpty") code. Then we will briefly note some other alternatives such as ADAT clock sync, word clock sync, and Pro Tool Superclock sync.

Frequency shift keying or FSK coding. FSK timing is the simplest of the systems for coding time on audio recordings. An alternating pattern of two tones (e.g., 1 KHz and 3 KHz) is recorded on one of the tracks of a multitrack recording throughout the tape. This is like having someone record "1 and 2 and 1 and 2 and 1 and 2 . . ." on a track of the tape. When you add music to the other tracks, you listen to the FSK coded track to keep the beat. There are electronic devices that can listen to the FSK coded track and automatically synchronize events for recording and performing.

There are several different types of SMPTE timing used in the video and audio recording industry. Our discussion here is based on the more common format for MIDI environments called either the "30 nondrop" format or the LTC (Longitudinal Time Code) format.

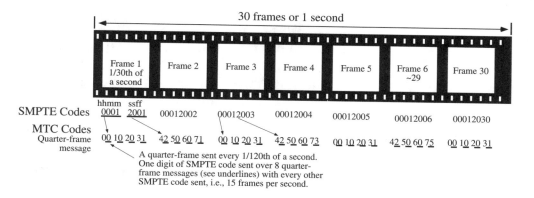

Figure 20.3

The data structure for SMPTE and MTC codes mapped on 30 frames of a film

Society for Motion Picture and Television Engineers or *SMPTE coding.* The NASA space program in the 1960s developed a special coding system for recording telemetry data that was adopted by the Society for Motion Picture and Television Engineers as their standard timing system for film, video, and television. This is known as SMPTE time coding. It is much more sophisticated than FSK coding and much more accurate. Because film is structured as a series of still frames, the SMPTE time code provides an absolute time address for each frame. In some cases, even time codes within a frame, called *subframes* or *quarter-frames,* are available. Everything is measured in terms of number of frames per second (fps): American television and video tape use 30 fps, and motion picture film uses 24 fps.

Frames are coded as hours, minutes, seconds, and frames (hhmmssff) in eight-digit numeric values. For example, 01302015, would locate a frame 1 hour, 30 minutes, 20 seconds, and 15 frames into the film. Instead of the "1 and 2 and 1 and 2 . . ." pattern of FSK codes, SMPTE lays down a pattern of absolute references "00000000 00000001 00000002 . . . 01302015," and so on, one for each frame. SMPTE coding can also show a subframe with a 10-digit number; there are 80 subframes (b) per frame (hhmmssffbb). Another variation is the quarter-frame (q) system where there are four units of time per frame (hhmmssffqq). We will see this as part of the MIDI Time Code in a moment.

Because of the pervasiveness of SMPTE time codes in the recording industry, SMPTE has become a common data structure for synchronizing audio as well as video recordings. SMPTE boxes of different varieties are available for placing timing codes on video and audio recording. Special SMPTE generators create these timing patterns on tape with a technique known as *striping,* or prerecording SMPTE codes. SMPTE codes for video are directly coded into the video signal data on each frame, and codes for audio are recorded onto an inaudible track of the tape. With newer technology like that in ADAT, DAT, or hard disk digital recorders, or the synchronizer hardware from Opcode, MidiMan, or Mark of the Unicorn, SMPTE codes are automatically generated in the digital signals being sent between these devices and striping of an audio track is not necessary (essentially freeing up a track from time codes).

Some MIDI devices generate more beats per quarter note, like 48 or 96 pulses-per-quarter or ppq rates.

MTC was discussed earlier in this Viewport.

Keeping the MIDI Time. We have examined timing structures for video and audio tape. What about MIDI? You will remember from our discussion of the Vanilla-1 implementation chart that we talked about certain system messages that controlled song selection, position, and the MIDI clock.

There are three systems within the current MIDI language for sequencing and synchronizing events over time:

MIDI Sync (Timing Clock)	System Real-Time Message
Song Position Pointers (SPP)	System Common Message
MIDI Time Code (MTC)	System Common Message

MIDI Sync and Song Position Pointers were in the initial 1983 MIDI standard specification; MIDI Time Code was added in the 1987 revision of the MIDI standard to deal directly with the need to work in SMPTE environments for recording. It's best to think of MIDI Sync and Song Position Pointers in a familiar music context. MIDI *Sync* is the musician's metronome beating away at 24 pulses per quarter note or 24 ppq. Tempo changes can speed up or slow down the rate, but there is always the same number of pulses per quarter note. The 24 ppqs timing clock keeps all the MIDI instruments in sync with the same beat—their electronic "feet" all tapping together.

The next problem is getting the instruments always to start in the same place, or, if we need to jump around while rehearsing, having a way to communicate where we are starting. The Song Position Pointer or SPP is MIDI's equivalent to the measure numbers in the score. Just as we can say "start at measure 21," MIDI can say "set the SPP to 500 beats from the beginning" or "go set the SSP back to beat 201." Look back in this module to our discussion of MIDI System Common messages, where we also discussed the Stop, Start, and Continue messages. The Start message sets the SPP to 0; the Stop message does not change the SPP, it stays right where the beat stopped; and the Continue message resumes playing at the current SPP.

What about the newer MIDI Time Code or MTC? The MTC data structure is like the SMPTE code in that it provides an absolute reference; frames are coded with an absolute time value. MTC also captures the relative nature of MIDI sync or FSK coding by providing a constant pulse for maintaining synchrony among instruments.

The MTC quarter-time codes provide an absolute address in eight digits, just like the SMPTE code (hhmmssff); however, this address is provided every two frames. Within each frame there are four quarter-frame messages. The frame rate, like SMPTE, is 30 frames per second. So you get an absolute frame address every other frame, or 15 times per second. But you also get a pulse provided by the quarter-time messages, four times per frame or 120 times per second (that's 4×30 fps).

A concern in a MIDI environment is overloading the MIDI network with too many data. Using SMPTE coding directly would use up about 10 percent of the traffic flow in a MIDI network. The MTC quarter-frame compromise coding, distributing absolute addresses across two frames of data in eight quarter-frame messages, reduces the network load to about 8 percent.

You now see that any MIDI device, including the computer, can be the "conductor" or master timing device on the network. This "conductor" can keep the beat through relative MIDI Sync and Song Pointers, or through absolute MIDI Time Codes that number frames 15 times per second. Should you want to work with audio tape or videotape, then that device becomes the "conductor" for your network. Using FSK or, more likely, SMPTE codes, both the relative beat and absolute time references can be translated into MIDI SPP and MTC codes, and back into SMPTE codes. Hardware synchronizers, and the more sophisticated MIDI interfaces, can perform SMPTE and MTC conversions automatically so that ADATs, videotape devices, and MIDI devices in your MIDI network all tap their electronic feet in perfect time.

Variations on Time: ADAT, Word Clock, and Pro Tools Sync. Other timing systems have emerged from the need for keeping recording hardware and MIDI devices synchronized. ADAT clock, Word Clock, and SuperClock are additional techniques for synchronizing MIDI and recording devices. Each time code evolved from the need to communicate between unique audio, MIDI, or recording hardware. The ADAT time sync is designed for digital tape decks like the Alesis DAT recorder (hence the acronym ADAT), because the ADAT recorder is the master synchronizer for the network of MIDI, computer, and recording devices. Most high-end MIDI workstations, effects processors, mixers, and the like have the ability to synchronize using ADAT clock sync, even more so than SMPTE time sync. The Word Clock code is a timing code especially designed for digital sampling or sampler devices to synchronize with each other; the timing is essentially the sampling rate being used for capturing or generating the digital audio. And SuperClock is a timing system unique to Digidesign's Pro Tools and digital audio hardware.

It is not uncommon, in a sophisticated computer music studio, to have to deal with several of these timing systems. As we will discuss in Module 22, there are various hardware devices that can translate between these different time codes and keep them all synchronized together. Examples include the Mark of the Unicorn MIDI Timepiece and the Opcode Studio series of MIDI interfaces.

There are also MMC or MIDI Machine Control codes that can be used to send control signals between devices in a MIDI network to perform such functions as starting, stopping, and rewinding a MIDI controlled recorder, for example.

General MIDI Issues

In Module 11, we pointed out the significance of the addition of General MIDI (GM) specifications to the MIDI standards. After our discussion of the MIDI implementation chart and a more in-depth look at the MIDI language, you are in a better position to appreciate the importance of General MIDI. Consider the chaos that surfaced as manufacturers of MIDI instruments assigned different values to MIDI codes to suit the idiosyncrasies of their instruments. The values for Program Change codes representing different instrument timbres or patches were different. Percussion sounds were assigned to different keyboard keys. Controllers like modulation, breath control, and portamento were assigned different values. The Timing Code varied from 24 pulses per quarter note to 96 or more. The instruments defaulted to

Table 20.5. General MIDI Channels.	
Channel	**Part**
1	Piano
2	Bass
3	Chord
4	Melody
5	Sub Chord
6	Sub Melody
7	Lower Part
8	Harmony Part
9	Melodic Part
10	Rhythm (Drum)

General MIDI is even more important as multimedia environments like QuickTime movies implement MIDI sound and as MIDI sequences are distributed widely across the Internet.

different settings, some to Mode 3 and others Mode 1. Do you see the problem? It made it very difficult to prepare a MIDI score with one network configuration and expect it to work on another. With the rapidly expanding consumer market using MIDI instruments, plug-and-play capability regardless of the instrument manufacturer was critical.

Enter the GM standard. General MIDI defines a set of minimum standards among MIDI devices. There is a MIDI code under the Universal System Exclusive messages that can be used to turn GM settings on and off. The GM instrument should provide at least the following:

▶ *Sound set* provides the standard set of 16 instrument groups defined with 128 patches or program changes within those groups, and the defined key set for percussion instruments (see Tables 20.6 and 20.7).

▶ *Voices* perform 24 notes simultaneously, or 16 notes and eight percussion sounds.

▶ *Channels* provide the full 16 channels, with 10 reserved for percussion sounds (see Table 20.5).

▶ *Channel messages* provide for velocity sensitivity and channel and polyphonic key pressure, and provide pitch bend with at least a ±2 semitone range.

▶ *Controllers* provide modulation control (1), volume (7), pan (10), expression (11), sustain (64), reset all controllers (121), and all notes off (123).

Table 20.5 shows the suggested channel assignment with the critical Channel 10 reserved for percussion or rhythm.

Table 20.6 shows the 16 instrument groups established for General MIDI. Within each group are eight patches or instruments for program changes, providing a total set of 128 instruments. Each manufacturer is to match their instruments as closely as possible to these groups. There will of course be some variation in sound, because different synthesizers and sound modules use different samples and different sound generation tech-

Table 20.6. General MIDI Instruments.

Program Change #	Instrument Group	Instrument	Program Change #	Instrument Group	Instrument
1	Piano	Acoustic Grand Piano	65	Reed	Soprano Sax
2		Bright Acoustic Piano	66		Alto Sax
3		Electric Grand Piano	67		Tenor Sax
4		Honky-tonk Piano	68		Baritone Sax
5		Electric Piano 1	69		Oboe
6		Electric Piano 2	70		English Horn
7		Harpsichord	71		Bassoon
8		Clavi	72		Clarinet
9	Chromatic	Celesta	73	Pipe	Piccolo
10	Percussion	Glockenspiel	74		Flute
11		Music Box	75		Recorder
12		Vibraphone	76		Pan Flute
13		Marimba	77		Blown Bottle
14		Xylophone	78		Shakuhachi
15		Tubular Bells	79		Whistle
16		Dulcimer	80		Ocarina
17	Organ	Drawbar Organ	81	Synth Lead	Lead 1 (square)
18		Percussive Organ	82		Lead 2 (sawtooth)
19		Rock Organ	83		Lead 3 (calliope)
20		Church Organ	84		Lead 4 (chiff)
21		Reed Organ	85		Lead 5 (charang)
22		Accordion	86		Lead 6 (voice)
23		Harmonica	87		Lead 7 (fifths)
24		Tango Accordion	88		Lead 8 (bass + lead)
25	Guitar	Acoustic Guitar (nylon)	89	Synth Pad	Pad 1 (new age)
26		Acoustic Guitar (steel)	90		Pad 2 (warm)
27		Electric Guitar (jazz)	91		Pad 3 (polysynth)
28		Electric Guitar (clean)	92		Pad 4 (choir)
29		Electric Guitar (muted)	93		Pad 5 (bowed)
30		Overdriven Guitar	94		Pad 6 (metallic)
31		Distortion Guitar	95		Pad 7 (halo)
32		Guitar Harmonics	96		Pad 8 (sweep)
33	Bass	Acoustic Bass	97	Synth Effects	FX 1 (rain)
34		Electric Bass (finger)	98		FX 2 (soundtrack)
35		Electric Bass (pick)	99		FX 3 (crystal)
36		Fretless Bass	100		FX 4 (atmosphere)
37		Slap Bass 1	101		FX 5 (brightness)
38		Slap Bass 2	102		FX 6 (goblins)
39		Synth Bass 1	103		FX 7 (echoes)
40		Synth Bass 2	104		FX 8 (sci-fi)
41	Solo Strings	Violin	105	Ethnic	Sitar
42		Viola	106		Banjo
43		Cello	107		Shamisen
44		Contrabass	108		Koto
45		Tremolo Strings	109		Kalimba
46		Pizzicato Strings	110		Bag Pipe

Table 20.6. General MIDI Instruments (continued)

Program Change #	Instrument Group #	Instrument	Program Change #	Instrument Group	Instrument
47		Orchestral Harp	111		Fiddle
48		Timpani	112		Shanai
49	Ensemble	String Ensemble 1	113	Percussive	Tinkle Bell
50		String Ensemble 2	114		Agogo
51		SynthStrings 1	115		Steel Drums
52		SynthStrings 2	116		Woodblock
53		Choir Aahs	117		Taiko Drum
54		Voice Oohs	118		Melodic Tom
55		Synth Voice	119		Synth Drum
56		Orchestra Hit	120		Reverse Cymbal
57	Brass	Trumpet	121	Sound Effects	Guitar Fret Noise
58		Trombone	122		Breath Noise
59		Tuba	123		Seashore
60		Muted Trumpet	124		Bird Tweet
61		French Horn	125		Telephone Ring
62		Brass Section	126		Helicopter
63		SynthBrass 1	127		Applause
64		SynthBrass 2	128		Gunshot

niques, but basically a clarinet will sound like a clarinet, and a shakuhachi like a shakuhachi.

Table 20.7 gives you a list of how percussion sounds are mapped onto the keys of the keyboard (MIDI notes 35–81) in the GM specifications. These sounds are also consistent across all General MIDI devices.

General MIDI will be more important to you as you increase your interest in, and use of, MIDI instruments for CAI, composing, performing, and arranging. This is even more critical when you want to share your MIDI sequences over the Internet so that any person, no matter where in the world or what computer or synthesizer used, will be able to play your MIDI sequence. When you look at the MIDI implementation charts and the rest of the technical manuals for an instrument, be sure to always look for whether the instrument is "General MIDI compatible."

Variations on General MIDI for Multimedia and the Internet

What do GS, XP, QuickTime, Beatnik, SoundFont, DLS, and XMIDI have in common? They are all variations on techniques to extend the capabilities of MIDI, especially General MIDI. The General MIDI (GM) standard has been widely adopted for incorporating sounds in all forms of multimedia and for distributing music sequences over the Internet. For multimedia, especially with CD-ROM, and the Internet, a platform-independent format for distributing small, compact music files is crucial. MIDI is the format of choice when it comes to the size of the files, but the quality and diversity of its palette of

Table 20.7. General MIDI Keys for Percussion

Key #	Instrument	Key #	Instrument
35	Acoustic Bass Drum	59	Ride Cymbal 2
36	Bass Drum 1	60	Hi Bongo
37	Side Stick	61	Low Bongo
38	Acoustic Snare	62	Mute Hi Conga
39	Hand Clap	63	Open Hi Conga
40	Electric Snare	64	Low Conga
41	Low Floor Tom	65	High Timbale
42	Closed Hi Hat	66	Low Timbale
43	High Floor Tom	67	High Agogo
44	Pedal Hi-Hat	68	Low Agogo
45	Low Tom	69	Cabasa
46	Open Hi-Hat	70	Maracas
47	Low-Mid Tom	71	Short Whistle
48	Hi Mid Tom	72	Long Whistle
49	Crash Cymbal 1	73	Short Guiro
50	High Tom	74	Long Guiro
51	Ride Cymbal 1	75	Claves
52	Chinese Cymbal	76	Hi Wood Block
53	Ride Bell	77	Low Wood Block
54	Tambourine	78	Mute Cuica
55	Splash Cymbal	79	Open Cuica
56	Cowbell	80	Mute Triangle
57	Crash Cymbal 2	81	Open Triangle
58	Vibraslap		

timbres is small, restricted to the basic bank of 128 GM sounds.

Musicians and engineers have been experimenting with various ways to extend MIDI's capabilities and overcome its deficiencies. Expanding the palette of 128 instrument sounds would do much to enhance music performed from a GM music sequence. Adding the ability to edit instrument sounds or to synthesize new instruments would also expand the palette of timbres available to a composer working in GM sound. To further increase control over the interpretive and environmental aspects of music performance, effects processing with such features as reverb, chorus, filtering, and the like would be a highly desirable capability. Let's take a quick tour of some experiments with the General MIDI format.

The first extension to the GM standard is the *GS format* developed by Roland for their Sound Canvas MIDI technology. The GS format adds additional instruments to the 128 GM sounds and provides MIDI functions for features such as tone editing, chorus, and reverb. The GS extensions are implemented by combining the bank select switch (see Table 20.3) with program changes and SysEx data coded to the Roland unique instrument ID for Sound Canvas instruments.

Following the same strategy as Roland, Yamaha developed its own proprietary *XG format* as an extension to the GM format. An XG-compatible

QuickTime is discussed in several places in Viewport XIII along with multimedia software, authoring, and digital video file formats.

Music MOD files are also discussed in Module 24 with other music file formats.

XMIDI was developed by Digital Design and Development as a system that extended the hardware as well as the coding capabilities of MIDI to provide greater bandwidth and extensibility to the current MIDI specifications. XMIDI was officially considered in 1995 by the MIDI Manufacturers Association (MMA) but has not been adopted as an industry standard.

sound device has a greatly extended range of instrument banks (a minimum of 480 instruments or more), and the ability to:

▶ Alter instrument sounds for brightness, harmonic content, attack-release times, and the like

▶ Produce a wide range of sonic effects from chorus and reverb to many others

▶ Have external music performance mixed with MIDI output (the "karaoke effect")

Like the Roland GS format, XG is implemented by using the bank select switch, program changes, and SysEx data.

GS or XG sound files will play adequately on any GM instrument, but the performance will be greatly enhanced if they are performed on the appropriate GS or XG MIDI instrument. The Yamaha Web plug-in, MID-Plug, is a software MIDI XG virtual synthesizer that will play MIDI XG sequences.

Apple's QuickTime and Headspace's Beatnik are both variations on the General MIDI format that seek to expand software flexibility. MIDI was added to *QuickTime* to enhance the multipurpose nature of its software audiovisual delivery. MIDI files imported into QuickTime are recoded into special QuickTime MIDI codes that are encapsulated and compressed with QuickTime's video, sound, text, and graphics, permitting an excellent, self-contained multimedia environment. When performed, the MIDI sounds can be generated with the Roland GS sound engine software installed with QuickTime on either a Macintosh or Windows computer, or they can output to any GM or Roland GS MIDI hardware sound device. With QuickTime 3.0, the full 128 instruments and some extensions to the Roland GS format are available.

Beatnik, SoundFonts, and DLS files are all conceptually similar to a music file format that has been popular on electronic bulletin boards and the Internet for many years, MOD files. MOD files are a combination of unique, non-MIDI codes for pitch and duration, packaged with waveform samples as instruments to use in performing those music codes.

Headspace's *Beatnik* is a music file format created for delivering high-quality music and sound over the Internet and the Web. It combines General MIDI codes with the use of custom samples, encapsulated in an encrypted file format that also includes copyright information. Instead of depending on additional hardware instrument samples and effects as the GS and XG formats do, Beatnik uses self-enclosed instrument samples for the MIDI performance.

The *SoundFont* format developed by E-mu Systems and Creative Labs is similar in design to Beatnik. The primary difference is that SoundFonts are digital sound samples designed to be played on Creative Labs SoundBlaster cards. GM MIDI codes are used to create the music, and SoundFont files store the sampled waveforms you want to use with the performance.

MIDI DLS Standards. The MMA (MIDI Manufacturers Association) officially endorsed a new standard in 1997 in order to respond to the need for downloading instrument sounds along with GM music codes to provide more consistent control over the timbres and effects used in a MIDI sequence. This is the same need which Beatnik and SoundFont respond to as software solutions, and Roland GS and Yamaha XG respond to as hardware solutions.

The MMA *DownLoadable Sounds* or DLS format provides an industry-wide standard for adding digital sound data and "articulation parameters" to General MIDI sequences. The articulation parameters include features such as envelope and looping data that can be used by a digital oscillator and a digital controlled amplifier in constructing a digital instrument sound. In fact, one file of digital sound data can be used with several sets of articulation parameters to generate several melodic instruments or drum kits. Using a unique set of coding through bank select, program changes, and SysEx MIDI codes, any DLS-compatible sound device, realized either through hardware or software, will be able to play GM music or sound sequences with DLS extensions, sound data, and effects attributes.

MIDI and Digital Audio Détente

Table 20.8 presents a summary of the attributes of both MIDI and digital audio data structures.

We need both data structures in our music workstation: MIDI's ability to capture performance event data and the sonic realism of digital audio. In the past we may have thought in terms of working with MIDI or working with digital audio as two separate environments; indeed, the software has reinforced this distinction. That is no longer valid. MIDI is part of the same all-digital world that uses its data structures to manipulate and control the sonic realism of digital audio.

In Module 19, we presented an integrated environment for working simultaneously with channels of MIDI and digital audio data: sequencing software that permits capturing and editing tracks of both MIDI and digital

Table 20.8. A Comparison of MIDI and Digital Audio Data Structures.

MIDI	Digital Audio
Performance or event data	Sampled sound data
Sound quality dependent on external sources	Sound quality inherent in sampled data
Flexible data structure	Inflexible data structure
Parts can be separated from the whole	Parts cannot be separated from the whole
Small storage demands	Large storage demands
Reproduction dependent on external sound source	Reproduction dependent upon sampling hardware
Less than perfect reproduction of performance nuance	Perfect reproduction of performance nuance
Best suited for extended music performance	Best suited for short excerpts except where storage is not an issue (e.g., CD- or DVD-ROM)

Software for integrating MIDI with digital audio can be studied in Module 19, and digital file formats can be studied in Viewport VII.

audio data. You can even quantize or synchronize rhythmic events between the digital and MIDI domains.

The synthesizers and sound modules that MIDI needs for sound generation are digital devices. Because of this integration, sequencing and editing software has evolved environments where the two data structures can coexist. And, more importantly, these integrated environments provide the ability to synchronize data from both structures to produce music that uses MIDI's event structures and digital audio's sonic structures where each is best suited. The extensions to MIDI that we explored above, such as Sound-Fonts, Beatnik, and DLS, point the way to the next evolution in music computing when the current file formats (WAVs, AIFFs, RAs, SMFs, and MIDs) are replaced by new ones that easily permit storage and modification of MIDI and digital audio events within the same file structure.

At this point you should have a thorough understanding of MIDI data structures. Uniting digital sound data to capture the unique sounds of traditional or new music instruments along with the MIDI codes that produce the music is a powerful combination. The sampled sound data of digital audio and the music event data of MIDI are finding a common ground so that musicians can work interactively and simultaneously within both structures.

Module 21

MIDI Hardware: The MIDI KISS System

A moment taken to review MIDI hardware first presented in Module 12 might be helpful before jumping into these more advanced MIDI hardware topics.

In this module we return to the topic of MIDI hardware begun in Viewport III. In Module 12 our hardware concerns were limited to MIDI equipment needed to set up simple CAI workstations with MIDI sound generation and MIDI input from a keyboard. With the use of sequencers for performing and composing music, we face a host of new issues related to MIDI hardware. Below is the familiar IPOS universal systems model (Figure 21.1) expanded from the one shown in Module 12. The model illustrates the MIDI devices for input and output, as well as for modification of music data, that we will be discussing in this module and Module 22.

Notice the variety of controllers for inputting data; we mentioned these briefly in Module 12. Some audio gear has been added: tape, DAT, MiniDisc, and hard disk recorders, and a microphone for capturing live performance. On the output side of the IPOS model, we show a variety of MIDI instruments including sound modules, drum machines, synthesizers, and MIDI workstations. Tape, DAT, MiniDisc, and hard disk recorders are included on the output side as well as audio amplifiers, speakers, and headphones.

A new box is added to the diagram. *Modifiers* are devices that are used to alter or modify sound in some way. We will look at effects generators and mixers in this category. The lower box shows a variety of MIDI interfacing devices from the simple MIDI interface to patch bays, THRU boxes, and SMPTE-to-MIDI converters.

There are a lot of things to cover here. The topics have been divided across this module and Module 22 so that you can pace your study. We will discuss the various MIDI devices shown in the IPOS model with a view to creating simple computer music systems for a variety of applications.

KISS Music Systems

We introduced the first "Keep It Short and Simple" or KISS music system in Module 12. Here is a list of the KISS music systems as they evolve throughout the textbook:

▶ Music CAI KISS System (Figure 12.12)

▶ No-Frills MIDI KISS System (Figure 19.2)

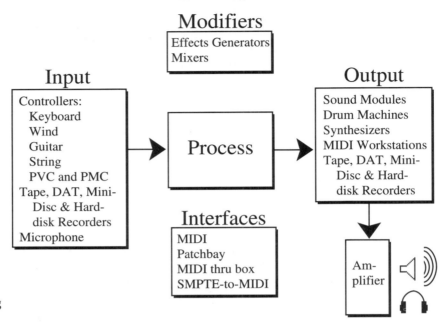

Figure 21.1
The IPOS model showing MIDI devices for performing and composing

▶ MIDI KISS System (Figure 21.2)

▶ Enhanced MIDI KISS System (Figure 22.1)

▶ SMPTE MIDI KISS System (Figure 22.11)

▶ Digital Audio KISS System (Figure 26.2)

If you need to review the basics of MIDI, go back and look at Modules 11 and 20 again.

Software activity: "Designing Your Own MIDI Studio"

The Music CAI KISS System (Module 12) presented essential hardware for doing music instruction in a classroom for music computer-assisted instruction and multimedia software. In Module 19, the No-Frills MIDI KISS System presented the essential hardware needed to do the most basic MIDI operations. In Figure 21.2 we will begin to add a few new features to the KISS system to expand the system for music sequencing activities. We will then show you in Module 22 how a musician could enhance the MIDI system to add more features and controls. We will also show you how SMPTE timing control from an ADAT or other multitrack recorder or a videotape could be added to the system. And, finally, in Module 26, we reconfigure the KISS system for digital sound recording and editing. In each case, we have tried to keep the system very simple with just the essentials to do each task. Ultimately, you will pick and choose from each of these models to create the perfect computer music system, given your needs and budget.

MIDI KISS System

The MIDI KISS System gives you a beginning MIDI setup for working with a computer music sequencer. You can compose or arrange music with this system. You can perform with this system. And, you can record your perfor-

MIDI KISS System

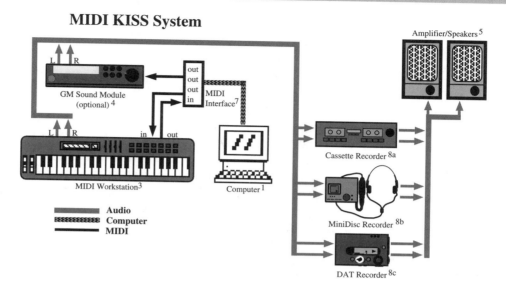

Figure 21.2
MIDI KISS System

MIDI interfaces were
covered in Module 12 and
computer systems in
Module 8.

mance in stereo on either analog tape or digital media.

Don't misunderstand the use of the term *beginning* here. This is an initial set of MIDI hardware that will let you create very effective, professional music productions. This system will also serve as an excellent foundation for future expansion when you add options to increase your ability to control sound events.

We will discuss each of the components of this system in turn (see Figure 21.2). Note that there are three kinds of data flowing among the hardware components: MIDI data are represented by the black lines, computer data by the dashed lines, and audio sound by the gray lines. Take note of the numeric superscripts on the labels for the various components; we will refer to these in the discussion.

Computers and MIDI Interfaces

The term "workstation"
is used here as a generic
term to refer to any
MIDI instrument where
a keyboard controller is
combined with a syn-
thesizer, sample player,
effects processors, alternative controllers, and
other features into one
hardware package.

The first and most important components in this MIDI system are the computer and the sequencer software used on the computer (see Module 19). The KISS strategy is to place most of the power and flexibility with the computer and its software. By letting the computer and its sequencer software take the pivotal role in this MIDI system you gain:

▶ Multitrack editing and recording directly from the software

▶ Major amounts of storage space, in RAM and on disk, that can easily be expanded

▶ Unlimited flexibility: if you want to do something else, just change the software

The computer for KISS (number 1 in Figure 21.2) can be any personal computer; at this level the computer doesn't have to be the fastest "kid on the block" to work effectively for you. Adequate amounts of RAM and a good-sized hard drive of several gigabytes or more are the more important concerns.

Depending on your computer system, you can purchase a MIDI interface that is a bus-extended card that plugs inside your PC, one that is built into your PC sound card, or one that resides outside in a small box connected to the serial port of your computer. The MIDI interface in the KISS diagram (number 7 in Figure 21.2) is an external box connected to the PC via the serial port. The MIDI interface is a simple MIDI box with one MIDI IN and three MIDI OUT jacks. The MIDI workstation is connected with a MIDI cable to the IN of the interface; two of the three OUTs are connected back to the MIDI workstation (3) and the GM (General MIDI) sound module (4). The layout of this MIDI network is a *star network*, with each OUT radiating from the MIDI interface as the center point in a star. That's all there is to it.

MIDI Workstations

Back in Module 12, we first presented a classification of the common types of MIDI instruments. Review the list for a moment, noting the differences in each category. One new item, *effects processors*, has been added to the list (see Table 21.1).

Pick up a MIDI magazine like *Electronic Musician* or *Keyboard* and scan the ads and the reviews. You will find that the devices in Table 21.1 are combined by manufacturers of MIDI instruments in many ways and with many different labels: sampling keyboards, keyboard synthesizers, synthesizers with drum machines and sequencers built in, and MIDI *workstations*. Buying MIDI equipment is like trying to buy a basic car with standard transmission and no air, radio, or electric windows and door locks. You just don't find them easily. What you do find are MIDI instruments with extras added on, packaged in different ways, and with a variety of names invented to give them market appeal.

For our MIDI KISS studio we have chosen to focus on a MIDI *workstation* as the central instrument for the system. There are different commercial

Table 21.1. Common Types of MIDI Instruments.	
MIDI Device	**Function**
Controllers (Keyboard, Wind, Drum, . . .)	Translate performance actions
Synthesizers	Modify and manipulate sounds, analog and digital
Samplers	Record and play back digital representations of sounds
Sample Players	Play back digital representations of sounds
Tone Generators	Generate sound with analog or digital oscillators
Effects Processors or DSP effects	Modify sound with effects like reverb, echo, flanging, pan, etc.
Drum Machines	Sequencing of percussion sounds
Sequencers (hardware)	Record and manipulate sequences of MIDI or digital performance data

uses of this term. We are using *workstation* as a generic term to refer to any MIDI instrument where several of the devices in Table 21.1 are combined with a keyboard controller into one hardware package.

Our generic MIDI workstation has some, if not all of the following features (those features in italics are not critical):

► Keyboard controller

► Alternative controllers such as pitch and modulation wheels, sliders, and foot pedals

► General MIDI sample player and *real-time sampler*

► Synthesizer

► *Sequencer*

► Drum kit

► DSP Effects

► Digital expansion for *storage* or connecting to other computers or digital devices

Some might call a MIDI instrument with these features a MIDI keyboard, a MIDI keyboard synthesizer, or a MIDI or music workstation. The difference is often the price or target audience for the product. MIDI instruments tend to fall into entry-level and professional categories in terms of quality and features. Instruments that are commercially labeled as workstations fall into the professional category. Don't let this fool you, however. If you shop smart and look only for the features you need, you may find an entry-level MIDI keyboard that is really a budget MIDI workstation in disguise.

Which features of a workstation do you need for a MIDI KISS system? You need the keyboard, alternative controllers, synthesizer, drum kit, and effects processor. You can forget the sequencer. And, if the digital expansion is merely some form of disk storage, you can forgot that as well. You can do real-time capture of digital audio with a PC sound card in your computer. In fact, if you can find a workstation with only the most needed features, all the better. (Does a musician playing a gig at the North Pole need air conditioning?) Who needs a dedicated floppy disk and a hardware sequencer when you have a computer with lots of RAM, a hard drive, and sequencing software along with MIDI librarians and editors?

We've put together a comparative chart in Table 21.2 showing the features you find when you move up in price from the entry end of the workstation products to professional equipment. The chart shows the features you typically find in workstations in three categories: Entry ($500 or less); Budget Pro (around $1,000); and Midrange Pro ($2,000 or more). Pricing is just a relative benchmark; one may well find these much cheaper. Features shown in each category are continuously changing. Advanced features in this chart may well move down into the lower categories as companies provide more features for the same dollars in cost.

Among the many companies making MIDI workstations are Alesis, Casio,

Table 21.2. A Comparative Chart for MIDI Workstations.

Components	Entry	Budget Pro	Midrange Pro
Keyboard	61 full-sized, unweighted keys; velocity sensing	61 full-sized, weighted or semi-weighted keys; velocity/aftertouch	76 or 88 full-sized, weighted or semi-weighted keys; velocity/aftertouch
Alternative controllers	Pitch bend and mod wheel; drum pads	Multiple sliders, pitch bend and mod wheels, and footpedals	Multiple buttons, sliders, wheels, foot pedals, breath control, pressure strips
MIDI (notes/timbres)[a]	GM[d]; ~32/16[b]	GM, GS, XG[d]; 64/16	48 ~ 64/32
Sound Generation	Digital samples	Digital samples; some with shaping and modeling[e]	Digital samples with more sophisticated shaping and modeling[e]
Sample Player (ROM or RAM)	~128 ROM samples	ROM and RAM samples; 8 to 16 MB of sounds	16 ~ 128 mb of sample ROM and RAM memory for sounds
Real-time Sampler	No	No	Yes
Synthesis	No	Some use of filters, envelope, layering, modeling, etc.[c]	More sophisticated digital shaping, and modeling[c]
Digital Effects	Reverb, chorus, harmony	1 or 2 DSPs for full range of effects[c]	More DSPs for independent effects processing[c]
Drum Kits and Sounds	5 ~ 10 kits	Up to ~200 drum sounds including GM kits	And more drum sounds including GM kits
Sequencer	5-track	Generally no	32-track
Digital Expansion	ROM cartridges	MIDI, PCMCIA cards, floppy disk, PC ports	MIDI, PCMCIA cards, floppy disk, PC and SCSI ports; ADAT and S/PDIF and AES/EBU digital ports
Typical Units	Yamaha PSR 330; Casio CTK-650; Kawai 150	Roland XP-10; Korg X5D; Alesis Q6	Roland XP-80; Korg Z1; Kurzweil K2500; Alesis Q8
Costs	Under $500[g]	Around $1000	$2000 or more

Notes: [a]notes/timbres refers to maximum polyphonic notes/maximum timbres played at one time; [b]the ~ sign indicates an approximate value; [c]reverb, echo, chorus, flanging, phasing, pitch shifting, delay, distortion, enhancers, pan, etc.; [d]GM is General MIDI, GS is Roland GM extended, XG is Yamaha GM extended MIDI; [e]digital shaping includes Korg AI2, Kurzweil VAST, and Alesis QS Composite Synthesis as examples; [f]physical modeling includes Yamaha/Stanford VA synthesis/waveguides, Roland COSM, and Korg Prophesy as examples; [g]pricing is intended as relative benchmarks.

E-Mu, Ensoniq, Kawai, Korg, Kurzweil, Roland, and Yamaha. We have indicated a few instruments in each category as examples. We will discuss the features of each and then let you decide which category best fits your needs.

Keyboard. A keyboard controller in a workstation suitable for the KISS system needs to have full-sized, velocity-sensing keys. All the workstations in Table 21.2 offer at least 61 keys or five octaves with these characteristics. As you get into the budget and midrange-professional workstations, you will also find channel-aftertouch key pressure that can be used to program expressive effects while notes are sustaining. Weighted or semi-weighted key action and polyphonic aftertouch are found in the more expensive units.

Module 20 discussed channel and polyphonic aftertouch.

Alternative Controllers. Expressive effects are critical to computer music activities. Controller wheels, sliders, and foot pedals generate many of the controller change messages we identified in the MIDI implementation chart in Module 20. These messages can be used to create dynamic changes, tempo changes, timbral shifts, portamento effects, and the like.

Look across the *alternative controllers* row in Table 21.2. As you move up in sophistication and cost, the workstations offer a greater variety of controller wheels, sliders, and foot switches and pedals. The midrange-pro systems even offer various programmable MIDI buttons, pressure sensitive strips, and an input for breath controllers.

You would want a workstation with at least one wheel and an input for a foot pedal; two wheels for pitch bend and modulation or vibrato control would be ideal. The Yamaha (shown in Figure 21.3a), Casio, and Kawai entry workstations all have some assortment of a pitch-bend wheel, a modulation wheel, and at least a foot switch control that can act as a sustain or damper pedal. The Yamaha and Casio even have small pads for playing rhythm patterns.

General MIDI becomes less important the higher you get in the professional world of MIDI synthesizers

As you move up to the budget- and midlevel-pro workstations, you get more controller options. The Alesis Q6 shown in Figure 21.3b, for example, has two pedal inputs, pitch and modulation wheels, and a slider control. For the midrange-pro workstation, the Korg Z1 (Figure 21.3c) comes loaded with pitch-bend and modulation wheels; various control knobs and switches for filters, amplitude, and portamento; an X-Y touch pad that provides a grid for programming MIDI controller messages in real time; and inputs for up to four foot pedals. As you can see, the particular combination of sliders, wheels, and foot controls is idiosyncratic to the manufacturer, and some of the higher-end workstations provide rather unique controller devices of their own design.

MIDI. Of course, we would not want a workstation without MIDI—really without General MIDI. Be aware that many entry-level, inexpensive keyboards have many features but do not have MIDI IN and OUT. The inexpensive Casio CTK-650 and Yamaha PSR 330 models, for example, do have MIDI IN and OUT, as do all of the workstations in Table 21.2. All of the MIDI workstations in the table also have either General MIDI (GM) or an extended GM set.

Another issue in selecting a workstation is the number of notes it can

(*a*) The Yamaha PSR 230 for the entry level

(*b*) the Alesis Q26 for the budget-pro level

Figure 21.3
An example of three levels of
MIDI workstations
(Courtesy of Yamaha Corporation, Japan and Yamaha Corporation of America; Alesis Corporation; and Korg USA, Inc.)

(*c*) a Korg Z1 for the midrange-pro level.

play at one time (its *polyphony*, in MIDI terms) and the number of different sounds or timbres it can produce simultaneously (its *multitimbrality*). The more notes and timbres the better. Examining the MIDI row in Table 21.2, you can see that all the workstations can produce 16 timbres, and the number of polyphonic voices ranges between 32 and 64. The General MIDI polyphony standard is for 16 voices for melodic information and 8 for percussion, for a total of 24-note polyphony; the GM multitimbral standard is 16 unique timbres playing simultaneously. The 24/16 GM standard has influenced the design of entry-level MIDI workstations; many offer this configuration or better as standard. Even the Yamaha PSR 330 offers 31 polyphonic voices and 16 simultaneous timbres.

The MIDI KISS System is designed around the computer and multitrack sequencing *software*—as we noted before, the software replaces the need for

Layering of sounds can reduce the usable polyphony of a MIDI instrument.

Physical modeling was first discussed in Module 10, and wave shaping was discussed in Module 11.

a multitrack tape recorder. A multitimbral MIDI workstation with as many simultaneous timbres as possible is critical to this design. You will want to be able to assign unique timbres to the various channels or tracks in your sequencer, and, to do that, you will need a MIDI multitimbral workstation.

Be aware that, depending on the design of the MIDI instrument, the number of polyphonic voices can be used up rapidly. The polyphony of the instrument, remember, is essentially the number of notes or sounds of any kind it can make simultaneously. To create complex timbres in a MIDI instrument, the manufacturers often use a concept known as *layering*. Layering means that more complex timbres are created by combining several of the preset timbres of the instrument. If you have 32 polyphonic voices, that means that 32 notes can be sounding at once. If the timbre you've chosen requires four layers (i.e., four timbres), then you have effectively reduced the number of notes you can play at once by a factor of four. This means that you can play eight simultaneous notes (8×4 layers or waveforms = 32 simultaneous sounds).

MIDI instruments that use digital sampling to create timbres eliminate this problem, in part. Each sample in ROM is a single timbre without layering; however, should a synthesizer permit layering with digital samples to create new sounds, you will still need to be aware that the layering of sounds will reduce the usable number of polyphonic voices of the instrument.

Sound Generation, Sample Playing, and Real-Time Sampling. Given the various MIDI devices listed in Table 21.1, most workstations can be classified by definition as *sample players*. This means that the workstations use some form of digital sound production with digital samples stored in ROM or a battery-supported RAM that retains the information even when power is turned off. Should the workstation also provide the means for recording samples in real time, then it would be classed as a *sampler* (see Table 21.1). Real-time sampling usually is a feature on only the more expensive midrange-pro workstations.

Sound generation. Workstations have all shifted to some form of digital sound production through various combinations of waveforms, samples, and digital oscillators. At the entry level, the sound generation tends to be simple digital waveforms or PCM (Pulse Code Modulation) as it is sometimes called. At the budget-pro and midlevel-pro levels, techniques like Korg's AI2 (Advanced Integrated sample synthesis), Yamaha's AWM (Advanced Wave Memory), Kurzweil's VAST (Variable Architecture Synthesis Technology), and Alesis's QS Composite Synthesis offer more complex digital sound generation where algorithms are used to *shape* the digital waveform through various combinations of digital-controlled amplifiers and digital-controlled filters. The more expensive the workstation, the greater the flexibility in *shaping* the sounds to create new or more realistic instruments. *Physical modeling* is an alternative to digital sampling just as FM synthesis was in the past.

Sample playing. Today, most workstations are also sample players. Again, this means that sounds are generated by playing any one of many instrument samples stored in the ROM or RAM of the MIDI workstation.

Remember, once you leave the basic set of General MIDI sounds, your music sequence becomes dependent on the brand of MIDI workstation and the synthesis engine you used to create your sounds. If you synthesize some wonderful sounds with your Korg Z1, then that sequence will need to be played from the Korg Z1. The MIDI DLS file format for downloadable samples (discussed in Module 20) may help in exporting some sound samples, but not all.

Examine the row labeled *Sample Player* in Table 21.2. Notice that the typical entry-level workstation has samples stored in ROM, usually the required 128 General MIDI instruments and drum kits. The entry-level Yamaha PSR 330 has 126 instrument voices as well as the 128 General MIDI sounds in ROM. With the budget- and midrange-pro systems, however, there are large sets of samples provided in ROM, including the requisite 128 General MIDI instruments, as well as samples stored in RAM. In fact, the amount of space provided for RAM samples is so voluminous that specifications for these workstations have shifted from listing how many instrument sounds they have to how much ROM and RAM memory is provided. The Alesis Q6 workstation comes with 8 megabytes, the Alesis QS7 and QS8 have 16 megabytes of sample storage on board, and the Kurzweil 2500 can provide up to 28 megabytes of sounds.

The presence of RAM sample storage means that you can edit and create your own samples on your computer through software. You can then download the samples to the workstation either through the MIDI connection, or a computer serial, parallel, or SCSI connection, or you can place them on a PCMCIA memory card. This is a powerful feature that makes the argument for investing in a budget-pro workstation that includes a computer port—a feature you are not likely to find with an entry-level workstation.

The number of ROM samples (also called patches, presets, programs, instruments, voices, or timbres) increases as you move up in the quality of the workstation. The entry workstations typically have the minimum 128 General MIDI samples, with the budget- and midrange-pro-level workstations adding many, many more. The ROM samples are grouped in banks that you can selectively choose with the MIDI bank select option. This usually happens transparently: working in your sequencing software, you pick and choose instruments from those displayed in its menus and tables. If your sequencing software doesn't have the built-in listings of instruments for a given MIDI workstation, then you will need to enter the names by hand. Some MIDI workstations also provide slots for additional ROM or RAM samples to be added, like the cartridges that can be plugged into the Yamaha PSR 330, or the PCMCIA or flash memory cards that can be used with the Alesis models, the Kurzweil 2500, or the Korg Z1.

Synthesis and Digital Effects. To be classed as a synthesizer, an electronic musical instrument must provide the means for generating new sounds. The ability to simply play back sampled sounds does not make a synthesizer; that is the function of a sample player. When you can take those sound samples and manipulate and use them to build new and unique sounds, you have a music synthesizer.

In Table 21.2, the row labeled *Synthesizer* indicates that most entry-level workstations are no more than basic sample players with no synthesis capability. However, budget and midrange-pro workstations offer various functions that qualify them as music synthesizers through either digital processing, shaping, digital effects, or modeling.

Shaping instrument sounds. In Module 10, we noted three synthesis techniques: additive; subtractive; and distortive. Sample-based synthesizers

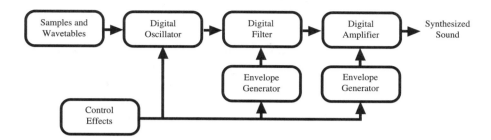

Figure 21.4
The synthesizer chain of
events

Remember our discussion
of layering in our discussion of MIDI's multitim-
bral capabilities.

can use any combination of these techniques. What this means is that complex waveforms (the samples) can be filtered (subtracting out sounds) to
produce new sounds; several waveforms can be layered (adding sounds) to
create new sounds; or waveforms can be enhanced through various modulation controls or digital signal processing effects (distorted).

Figure 21.4 shows a simplified diagram of the chain of events that produce a synthesized sound. The primary components of every synthesis
chain are the oscillator, the filter, the amplifier, and digital effect processors.
Because we are dealing with digital synthesizers, all of these components
are digital, designed to process sounds as streams of numbers. Let's follow
sound as it makes its way through this chain and emerges synthesized.

The food that feeds the *digital controlled oscillator* (DCO) in the chain is
the samples stored in ROM and RAM of the workstation. Samples can be
combined or layered, and other events, such as noise, can be added to the
mix. The sounds from the DCO are then passed onto the filters (DCFs). This
is subtractive synthesis, so the filter can be programmed to selectively
remove certain harmonics from the DCO's sound. Which harmonics are sub-
tracted from the DCO's sound, and when, are controlled by the filter's envelope generator. The sound is then passed on in the chain to the digital
amplifier (DCA). The amplifier is controlled by another envelope generator
that can be programmed to change the amplitude of the sound from its
onset or attack through to its release.

Digital effects. At the end of the chain comes some digital effect processing that can alter the sound by adding reverb, harmonizing, panning, distortion, pitch shifting, and a host of other effects (see the *Digital Effects* row in
Table 21.2). The effects are typically generated by digital signal processing
(DSP) chips that are optimized for processing large amounts of digital sound
data. The greater the number of independent DSP chips, the greater the
range of effects that can be imposed on the sound at one time. (More on
DSPs in Viewport VII.)

Synthesis controls. There is an additional level of control that can be programmed to alter the pitch of the oscillator, the envelope of the filter, the
envelope of the amplifier, or the effects processor. Control messages emanating from MIDI pitch-bend or modulator wheels, foot pedals, sliders, breath
controllers, and the like can all be programmed to alter the patterns of any
of these functions.

The programming of the chain of events is also handled through algorithms or patches either predefined in the instrument or programmed by the

user. The number of algorithms available, and the number that can be used simultaneously, is a measure of the programming capabilities of the synthesizer. Each algorithm or patch will have a number of parameters that can be programmed either through panel controls on the workstation or through software patch editors on the computer.

To review then, here are some things to consider when evaluating the synthesis capability of a digital synthesizer:

▶ Layering and the number of layers per voice

▶ Filtering and the number of filters per voice

▶ Amplitude envelope per voice

▶ Digital effects processing and the number of effects that can be used simultaneously

▶ Programmability of algorithms or patches, the number available, and the number that can be used simultaneously

More on physical modeling in Module 10 and Module 23.

No synthesis options are available at the entry workstation level, but some basic digital effects like reverb and chorus are found (see the Synthesizer row in Table 21.2). Budget and midrange-pro workstations and their synthesis engines are often quite similar. The Alesis QS synthesis engine, for example, is available on their full range of workstations. What changes is the number of "programs" and "mixes" and the amount of waveform memory that comes with the workstation, and whether additional PCM-CIA slots above the one included with the budget-pro Alesis QS6 are provided.

The more expensive MIDI workstations, however, are often leading-edge systems developed to showcase the newest and most acoustically stunning sound-generation technology. The Korg AI² synthesis engine is used on many of its keyboards, including the budget-pro X5D. But the Korg Z1 and Trinity workstations (both midrange-pro) use a new synthesis engine called MOSS or Multi-Oscillator Synthesis System with a wide array of algorithmic programming control and DSP synthesis options. As you move up from the budget-pro Roland XP-10 to the midrange-pro XP-80, you are likewise getting more synthesis power for your dollar. The XP-10 has 28-voice polyphony and 594 sounds; the XP-80 has 64-voice polyphony with 8 megabytes of internal waveform memory, a custom RISC processor chip just like those found in PowerPC computers, and 40 digital effects and 3 independent effects processors.

Physical modeling. Not all sound engines are sampling engines. The older FM synthesis made popular in the 1980s by Yamaha was not a sampling technique. A new sound engine being explored by Roland, Yamaha, and Korg, among others, is physical-modeling synthesis.

Rather than capturing a bitmapped image of a sound and shaping it with various synthesis techniques, modeling attempts to simulate the acoustic properties of a sound through mathematical formulas. A model is a simulation that enables a computer to physically recreate the acoustical behavior of a vibrating body and then alter that model by altering the mathematical formula. No image of the sound is stored in the computer, only the model of its acoustical vibrating behavior. So, instead of using eighty eight unique samples to create a Bösendorfer grand piano, one model could be created that simulates the acoustical behavior of a key striking on the Bösendorfer grand, and then the model could be adjusted to fit the changing acoustical traits of each key as you move up the eighty eight keys of the piano. It is only with the newer computer CPUs, and their fast processor speeds, that physical modeling is possible either in a computer or in a MIDI workstation.

Drum Kits and Sounds. Did you notice that we do not have a drum machine in our KISS system? There is a good reason for that omission. Most workstations come with a full repertoire of drum sounds, eliminating the need for a separate drum machine. All workstations come with a large number of drum samples (see Table 21.2). The entry-level unit typically has 25 to 50 samples, and some entry-level workstations, e.g., the Yamaha and Casio, even come with small drum pad controllers. As we move up to the pro-level, workstations offer hundreds of different drum samples to work with. The real challenge becomes keeping track of all of them in your sequencing software.

Sequencer. A built-in sequencer in a workstation is a nice feature if you use the instrument for solo performing. But for a computer MIDI system, it is superfluous. You have to purchase a midrange professional workstation to get 32-track sequencing. The entry-level units have a simple, 5-track sequencer that will record one sequence with a melody, a harmony, and a rhythm track. There are many budget-pro workstations that, conveniently, for our purposes, do not have a sequencer.

Should you still feel the need for a hardware sequencer, consider the number of tracks it provides (typically 32) and the amount of memory available for storing MIDI events. Remember: MIDI controllers can generate lots of MIDI event data that will very quickly fill up a sequencer's memory.

Digital Expansion. As in the case of a hardware sequencer, there is little need for disk drive storage built into a MIDI workstation when you have a computer as part of your MIDI KISS Music System. You will typically find disk drives on workstations with 32-track sequencers and on those with lots of RAM storage for digital samples. The disk drive is provided as an option for saving and retrieving samples, sequences, and patches when a computer is not available.

There are other digital expansion options besides disk drives that are a bit more attractive. PCMCIA cards (PC cards) and flash memory cards are replacing floppy disk drives on MIDI workstations. PC cards can make it easy to edit patches and samples with your editor/librarian software, provided you have a PC card slot on your computer. They are usually provided along with laptop computers; external PC card slots can be purchased for desktop computers. After saving onto the PC card, you can then pop the PC card back into the MIDI workstation when you are ready to perform. As

Roland uses physical modeling with their COSM technology and their VG-8 Virtual Guitar System; Korg uses modeling synthesis with their Prophesy synthesizer (included in the Trinity workstation along with the MOSS synthesis); and Yamaha uses their SVA Physical Modeling Synthesis with their VL70 tone module and their AN1x Analogue Physical Modeling Synthesizer. The Yamaha modeling synthesis is licensed from Stanford University and the CCRMA research center, where the sound models were developed as "waveguides." This is the same research center where Yamaha licensed its FM synthesis not so many years ago.

PCMCIA or PC cards; SCSI, parallel and serial; and USB interfaces were first presented in Module 8.

Digital I/O on a MIDI workstation is a boon to computer-based digital editing and production of music CD and DVD audio! If the terms digital I/O, Firewire, S/PDIF, and AES/EBU have left you baffled, you can look ahead to Module 26 for some help.

with the floppy disk drive, however, you don't really need to pay for this feature if your MIDI workstation is usually connected to your computer. PC cards can hold 4 to 16 megabytes of samples, patches, and sequences.

The digital expansion options that you really want to look for are those that improve the connection between your MIDI workstation and your computer. Using MIDI to swap samples and patches between your MIDI workstation and computer is very slow. A serial, parallel, SCSI, USB, or Firewire computer port in your workstation gives you a nice, fast way to communicate with your PC for uploading and downloading patches and samples.

Things can get really exciting if a MIDI workstation has a digital audio port. The feature is available on midrange-pro workstations, but will likely filter down to the budget-pro level. The Alesis Q8, the Kurzweil 2500, and the Korg Z1, for example, either come with, or have an installed option for, digital audio ports. Digital audio input/output ports will let you make direct digital connections between your MiniDisc or ADAT or DAT tape decks, your PC sound cards, and a digital mixer with S/PDIF or AES/EBU connections.

Why is this useful? Let's say you are trying to burn a CD of a terrific composition you created with your software sequencer (e.g., Cakewalk's Pro Audio). You've laid down both MIDI tracks and digital audio tracks of live performance. To turn the MIDI tracks into digital audio tracks, you will have to play the MIDI tracks on your synthesizer and then capture them as digital audio tracks back in your sequencer. You need, in other words, to convert all the MIDI tracks in your composition to digital audio tracks so you can create a complete digital audio performance for the CD-ROM.

Many synthesizers only offer analog audio output. To record its sounds onto a CD, you will need to digitize the audio through a digital audio card of some type. You are, in fact, going from the digital MIDI codes, to the digital sounds in your MIDI synthesizer, to the analog audio output of your synth, and then back to digital when your computer's digital audio or sound card reconverts the analog sound back to digital audio. The digital audio gets imported into your sequencer now as a digital track.

If, on the other hand, your synthesizer and sound card has digital I/O, you don't have to return to the analog world for audio. You will go from the digital MIDI codes on your computer to the digital sounds in your MIDI synthesizer, and then you exchange the digital audio between the digital I/O port on your synthesizer and your digital audio card. The digital audio gets added as a digital track directly into your sequencer. Everything stays digital and clean!

Subjective Factors. We have considered the important hardware features of MIDI workstations. You can read, measure, and count the facts on specification sheets but, as every musician knows, ultimately the decision depends on the subjective factors of how it feels and sounds. Briefly let's touch on a few of these:

▶ Keyboard feel

▶ Controller feel (wheels, sliders, and pedals)

▶ Quality of the sound

▶ Layout and user interface for the workstation controls

To check out these factors you need to play the instrument, working the keys and the controllers. Listen carefully to the sounds; flip through the preset instruments and listen to the quality of the winds, strings, percussion, and so on. Your ear is the best test. Can you easily figure out how to do simple operations from the keyboard like access factory presets? How well human engineered are the controls? Ask to see a manual. Try programming the workstation directly from its own panels and control buttons and sliders. Is it confusing or easy to program? If students are going to be using this keyboard in a music lab, the user interface is a crucial feature. The easier it is to program, the less time you will spend as the instructor, answering questions and writing your own tutorials. Should all these tests leave you feeling less than satisfied with a particular brand of workstation, keep looking.

In Conclusion. You can see that picking a workstation is not easy. There are lots of things to take into consideration. The philosophy behind the design of the MIDI KISS system was to find a workstation that had the critical components needed for the smallest number of dollars. We were thinking in terms of a "poor person's approach" to a computer music system.

Your first choice should be to carefully consider an entry-level workstation under $500 that has good key action, good sampled sound, one or two controller wheels, and a foot pedal input. Then, if you really feel you need the samples, synthesis, and digital effects provided by the budget-pro workstations, start moving up. There's a good chance you will not need to go any higher. Only consider putting the dollars down for a midrange-pro workstation if you truly feel your music creativity has outgrown the capabilities of your budget-pro system and you like what you hear and read about the higher-end MIDI workstations.

Sound Modules: General MIDI and More

We discussed sound modules (also called tone generators when used with FM or modeling synthesis) back in Module 12. Remember the WolfieBox?

Did you notice that we had a General MIDI (GM) sound module in the MIDI KISS design shown in Figure 21.2 (Item 4)? A sound module is just the sample player, and perhaps the synthesis engine, with lots of samples. It will greatly increase the number of sound samples and drum kits available for sequencing activities. Furthermore, many sound modules also have effects processors—another feature that will enhance a low-budget workstation.

Most of the MIDI workstations we've looked at in this module have a sound-module-only version. The Roland Sound Canvas or GS sound modules offer the same engine you will find in the Roland GS workstations. The Korg X5DR sound module has most of the same 64-voice polyphony, 8-megabyte ROM of sound and drum samples, and digital effects as the X5D workstation. The Alesis QSR synthesizer module is the same synthesis engine as the Alesis Q7 and Q8 workstations including the PCMCIA card, the serial computer port, and the digital I/O ports. Did you entertain the thought earlier when reading about the Yamaha physical modeling synthesis that it would be really neat to experiment with those sounds? You can do that by adding the VL70 tone generator module rather than the full keyboard workstation to your computer music system. All of these systems are significantly less expensive, some half the price of the related workstation!

Do you catch our drift? Buy a solid budget-pro MIDI workstation (or even an entry-level system if that works for you) and then enhance your system by adding a variety of sound modules. You only need one keyboard controller. You only need a few pitch and mod wheels and pedal controllers. All of these come with the entry-level and budget-pro workstations. Expand your repertoire of sounds and synthesis engines with more economical MIDI sound modules and greatly increase the flexibility of your computer MIDI system.

Recorders and Other Audio Gear

You've finished sequencing your first computer-generated composition and now you're ready to record the final production. Our MIDI KISS music system has some options for audio gear. First, a pair of amplified speakers. Then, take your choice of budget-minded recording systems: a cassette tape recorder (item 8a in Figure 21.2); a portable MiniDisc recorder (item 8b); or a portable DAT recorder (item 8c). No mixer is included in our most basic MIDI design; the audio is going directly into the recorder.

In order to connect both the MIDI workstation (item 3) and the General MIDI module (item 4) to a recorder, you will need to use a Y-splitter for the left- and right-channel audio coming into the audio input of the recorder. In Module 22 we will look at the addition of an audio mixer to solve this problem and allow for more audio equipment to be patched into the recorder. We will also discuss multitrack recording in that module.

MiniDisc, DAT, ADAT, and various hard disk recorders are discussed in more depth in Module 26.

A simple stereo recording is all that is required with the current KISS music system because the multitracking is done by the sequencing software. We have 16 channels to work with and our workstation and sound module are both 16-channel multitimbral, so we can program 16 unique tracks of instrument sounds with our sequencer and then record them in stereo onto our choice of recording device.

Choose any one of these three recorder options. You can start with as little as a $100 for a traditional analog cassette tape recorder. If you want to be able to easily share your arrangements and compositions with family and friends, nothing beats an audio cassette recording. A CD audio disc is certainly another option here, but that takes additional hardware (see Module 26).

Add another hundred dollars or so and you can move up to one of the portable MiniDisc recorders. Or move up another notch in the budget: add a digital audio tape or DAT recorder to your computer music system. The advantage of either the MiniDisc laser technology or the DAT digital tape technology is the exceptional high quality of the recording. If you connect either of these digital recording options directly to the digital I/O ports on your PC sound card or your MIDI workstation, you will be working completely in the digital realm with no loss of sound fidelity by going to analog. Although MiniDiscs use a form of digital compression where some fidelity is lost, the quality is still far superior to analog tape recordings. The digital recording option is the one to choose if you need professional quality recordings for performance, CD audio production, or sharing with other musicians who have similar recording technology.

<table>
<tr><td>Module
22</td><td>MIDI Hardware: Enhancing the
MIDI KISS System</td></tr>
</table>

After you have set up a basic MIDI KISS system like the one in Module 21 for your composing or arranging work, it is not uncommon, after a few months of experience, to start asking questions about how to expand its MIDI capabilities. You might ask about adding other controllers—like drum and guitar controllers—to your system. You might be anxious to do more with mixing sounds from the various MIDI devices, including some live voice and performance recordings. You might see advertisements in the magazines about MIDI effects processors and decide that the effects processor in your MIDI workstation is not flexible or powerful enough for you.

Figure 22.1 shows how the MIDI KISS system can be enhanced to offer some of these new and expanded features. Our discussions will focus on the new components added to the expanded system: MIDI controllers, mixers, and effects processors. In order to add more devices to a MIDI network, we also need to examine ways to expand the connections to your MIDI interface through patchbays and MIDI THRU boxes. MIDI controllers will receive major attention in this section; the performance features offered by wind, percussion, voice, and string, as well as keyboard, controllers provide a wonderful creative boon to any MIDI music system.

MIDI Boxes: THRUs, Switches, Mergers, and Patch Bays

Have you ever had to wire up a stereo or video system? If you have, you are probably familiar with the wiring spaghetti that you have to contend with as the number of units expands: jacks and plugs, ins and outs, lefts and rights, phone and phono jacks; and Y-jacks and splitters. As you expand a MIDI network, you can just as easily get into a confusing maze of wiring possibilities and difficulties. Let us introduce you briefly to some of the adapter boxes used in MIDI networks.

MIDI THRU Boxes. Figure 22.2 shows two ways we could have wired the MIDI interface for the KISS system in order to create a star network—the best network configuration. With a one-IN and three-OUT MIDI interface, you can easily create a star network. However, many MIDI interfaces are only one IN and one OUT; or you may want to expand beyond three OUTs.

Expanded MIDI KISS System

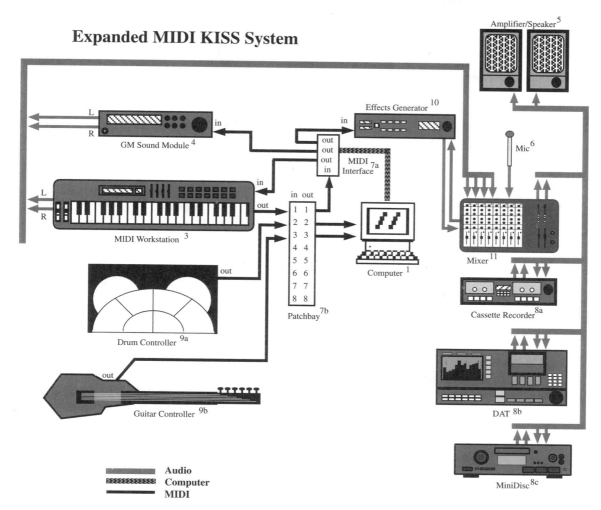

Figure 22.1
The enhanced MIDI KISS
music system

Enter the MIDI THRU box. The MIDI interface connection on the right of the computer shows how a MIDI THRU box expands a single MIDI out to three MIDI THRUs. This is the same as three MIDI OUTs in the interface to the left. The MIDI codes being transmitted are duplicated across the three MIDI outs. So, if you need more MIDI OUTs or THRUs, use a MIDI THRU box.

MIDI Switch Boxes. What if you need more MIDI INs? Looking back at Figure 22.1 for our Enhanced MIDI KISS system, you can see that we added drum and guitar controllers. Our interface has only one MIDI IN. For this problem there are at least three solutions (see Figure 22.3). We will look at using MIDI switch and merger boxes and at the solution we used in our expanded KISS system, the MIDI patchbay.

Figure 22.3*a* shows how a pair of MIDI switch boxes might let us connect three controllers to the KISS system. A switch box lets you choose between one of two MIDI signals with a mechanical switch; by pairing up

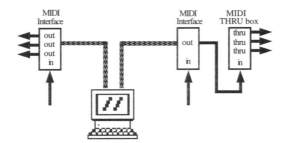

Figure 22.2
Increasing OUTs in a
MIDI network

two switch boxes we can have three controller options. The diagram shows the guitar controller switched as the current MIDI input device. This is probably the cheapest solution, but the least elegant. As we add more input controllers, the switch boxes become cumbersome.

MIDI Merger Boxes. Figure 22.3*b* shows another way to solve the problem of adding more MIDI INs for controllers. Bear in mind that we are combining MIDI data from two or more MIDI controllers: timing is very critical. You cannot simply split a MIDI cable with a Y-adapter as you can an audio or video signal. The MIDI merger box combines the MIDI data from the various controllers. For this reason, the merger box has a memory buffer. This gives the merger box a place to hold data from one device while it is processing data from another; when there is a lull in the data transmission, the merger box then transmits the data in its memory buffer.

You can see that MIDI merger boxes are more complex than switches, and also more expensive. Also consider that the memory buffer has finite space; too much MIDI activity from competing controllers can easily overwhelm the box and MIDI data will be lost.

MIDI Patchbays. Now we arrive at the third solution, and the one we chose to use in the Enhanced KISS system (see item 7b in Figure 22.1). The MIDI patchbay, in its simplest form, is a bank of MIDI switches. Notice that

Figure 22.3
Three methods for
increasing MIDI INs in a
network

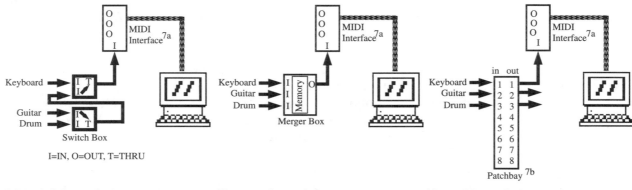

(*a*) Switch box solution   (*b*) Merge box solution   (*c*) Patchbay solution

The more sophisticated MIDI interfaces with 32 channels or more are sometimes called "hybrid" MIDI interfaces because they combine many different features into one box, or "synch boxes" because they offer conversion for many different timing systems for synchronizing MIDI data.

the MIDI patchbay in Figure 22.3c has eight INs and eight OUTs. We are using the patchbay in the KISS system to simply let us patch between one of three input controllers; the guitar controller is patched to the computer interface IN.

The logical question to ask next is: "Why not just use the switch box solution?" There are several reasons why the patchbay is a better choice. First, you can patch among many MIDI devices, both INs and OUTs; if you connected every MIDI IN and OUT of every device in your system, then the patchbay would let you quickly reconfigure your entire system. This is especially useful when you have many MIDI devices.

The second reason is that many patchbays let you store presets, and some are MIDI programmable. With presets you can create different setups and quickly change between them during a performance. With a MIDI-programmable patchbay, you can store the preset patch configuration as part of your MIDI sequencer data. Patchbay changes can be completely automated throughout a sequencer performance, and virtual software patchbays can make it easier to manage the hardware.

Beyond 32 Channels. The MIDI specification allows for 16 channels of MIDI data. When we reviewed MIDI sequencing software, you saw that many sequencing packages—especially professional-level sequencers—go far beyond the 16-channel limit to produce as many channels as the hardware will allow. To go beyond the initial 16 channels, you add multiple MIDI interfaces, or you can use one of the more sophisticated MIDI interfaces.

MIDI interfaces by Opcode and Mark of the Unicorn (MOTU), for example, use advanced computer switching and control to provide from 96 to 512 channels. Each set of 16 channels of IN and OUT MIDI data is sometimes referred to as a *cable,* and these more advanced MIDI interfaces are multi-cable routers of MIDI data. The Opcode Studio 5LX interface, for example, has 16 cables or 256 channels (16×16). The Studio 5 also serves as a MIDI patchbay and SMTPE synchronizer (more on that topic later in the module). MOTU's MIDI Express XT has 128 channels or 8 cables. Remember that anything beyond 16 channels or one cable is not standard MIDI. You must carefully match the *cableized* hardware interface to the software. That is why Mark of the Unicorn builds the MIDI Time Express and Opcode builds the Studio 5; both companies specialize in professional-level sequencers.

Controllers were first introduced in Module 12.

Your Choice. Which MIDI networking devices you choose—switch box, merger box, patchbay, or high-end multi-channeled MIDI interface—depends on your performance needs and how much you are prepared to spend. If you simply need to select between two MIDI controllers and only use one at a time, get a switch box. If you need to perform on both at the same time or to alternate quickly between them, consider a merger box. Just make sure your performance demands don't overwhelm the memory of the box. For a good general solution, an inexpensive patchbay is a good choice and a flexible one at that. For more professional needs, then look to the multi-channeled MIDI controllers like those from MOTU and Opcode.

MIDI Controllers: Expanding Your Performance Options

The basic MIDI KISS system for sequencing introduced in Module 21 has one input for performance data: a music keyboard controller built into the MIDI workstation. There are many other alternatives for translating performance gestures into MIDI data. In this section we will touch on a variety of MIDI controllers for drum, wind, string, and voice, and a sampling of the more unusual options.

As we noted in Module 12, a MIDI controller is any device that translates music performance actions into MIDI data. These actions can include fingers pressing down keys; sticks hitting a drum head; bowing, strumming, or plucking strings; air and lip pressure; pressing on a pedal; and possibilities we haven't even thought of yet. MIDI devices translate performance data into an unbiased code; the computer does not know whether the MIDI note data originated from a drum pad or a violin.

In the discussion in Module 12 we made a distinction between two types of MIDI controller design: acoustic or synthetic. To review briefly, standard traditional music instruments can be turned into *acoustic* MIDI controllers by equipping them with sensors that translate analog actions or vibrations into digital MIDI data. *Synthetic* MIDI controllers are designed from scratch as electronic performance instruments. They are constructed to simulate acoustic instruments or to create new and unique instruments that optimize the electronic translation of performance actions to MIDI.

The quality of a controller's performance is effected by two functions: *tracking error* and *tracking delay. Tracking error* measures the accuracy with which a controller translates the performed pitch or action. *Tracking delay* measures the time it takes the controller to determine what note is being played. When you strum a guitar, generating sympathetic vibrations from other strings and incidental noises, tracking error is going to increase. When a controller is trying to translate a flute sound or a human voice into MIDI data, there is going to be tracking delay. This means that the MIDI note data will occur later than the human performance. Generally speaking, the more complex the acoustic vibration that needs to be translated into MIDI data, the greater the likelihood of error in translation.

Our Enhanced MIDI KISS system shown in Figure 22.1 has a keyboard controller (item 3), and a drum controller and a guitar controller (items 9a and 9b) have been added. Keyboard controllers were discussed in Module 12, so we will pass over those and move on to the others.

Drum Controllers. As with keyboards, there is a wide variety of MIDI drum controllers. The translation mechanism used in a drum controller is a *trigger-to-MIDI* converter. An electronic trigger device picks up a vibration from the drum and creates a voltage that is converted into MIDI Note On/Off data. Usually the drum controller detects only the Note On and sends an immediate Note Off to simulate the tap of a drum stick. Some drum controllers provide a control that will vary the time between the Note On and Off data. Velocity and aftertouch data can also be provided

Figure 22.4
E-mu Systems, Inc., KAT line of MIDI percussion controllers: from the top down, the malletKAT, trapKAT, then the classic drumKAT on the right and the DK10 on the left
(Courtesy of E-mu Systems, Inc.)

from the intensity or amplitude of the voltage created by the impact of the drum stick.

Acoustic drum controllers are made that attach to the head or the shell of the drum. Vibrations in the drum head set off the trigger-to-MIDI converter that subsequently generates the MIDI data.

Synthetic drum controllers are usually called MIDI *drum pads*. They use a rubber pad much like any drum practice pad; the trigger mechanism is placed under the rubber pad. More sophisticated pads have separate sensors for distinctive areas like the center, edge, and rim, each generating MIDI data.

Drum pads come in different shapes and number of pads in a set. The classic drumKAT, for example, shown in Figure 22.4, has 10 pads arranged to look like mouse ears. The Roland SPD-11 drum controller provides eight square pads in two rows of four. It also provides 255 onboard sound samples and an effects processor so the device can be played without a connection to a MIDI sound module. There are also mallet drum controllers like the malletKAT (Figure 22.4) that provide a keyboard-like arrangement of pads. Each pad, and locations within a pad, can be assigned to different notes or to different MIDI channels. Yes, it is possible to program your drum pad to play the kazoo part in your new arrangement!

Guitar and String Controllers. Electric versions of most string instruments have been around since the 1930s: violins, basses, cellos, and most notably, guitars. While there have been MIDI versions of most of the electric string instruments—for example, the Zeta Music Systems MIDI violin—the MIDI guitar is the most widely used.

The mechanisms for translating guitar performance into MIDI data apply to any of the other string instruments. Unique synthetic guitar controllers include the SynthAxe, the Casio MG-500, the Yamaha G10, and the StarrLabs Ztar Guitar. The Ztar synthetic controller, for example, has a six-string by twenty-four-fret, stringless or touch-sensitive fingerboard that decodes finger pressure into MIDI codes. Other controllers modify a standard electric or

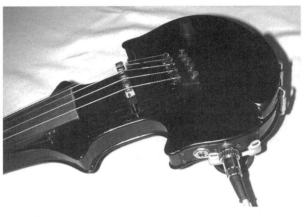

(a)

(b)

Figure 22.5
Two views of the Zeta Jazz electronic violin. (Courtesy of David B. Williams)

acoustic guitar to add MIDI capability and fall loosely into the category of acoustic controllers.

MIDI conversion from guitars is not a trivial engineering problem, and tracking error, especially, can be difficult. Three techniques have been used alone or in combination to adapt a guitar to MIDI control:

▶ Special audio pickups called *hexaphonic* pickups can be placed under each string near the bridge to determine pitch and velocity data

▶ Frets can be wired to act as switches when they make contact with the guitar strings

▶ Pitch-to-voltage converters or PVCs can be connected to each of the guitar strings to translate the individual string vibrations into MIDI data

The older Roland GR-700 used hexaphonic pickups, as does the newer GK-2A MIDI converter pickup, which can be mounted onto almost any acoustic and electronic guitar. The GK-2A can be combined with the Roland GR-30 guitar synthesizer, for example, or almost any pitch-to-MIDI converter. Or, you can also take the GK-2A pickup and attach it to your acoustic guitar and use the physical modeling synthesis (discussed in Module 21) of the Roland VG-8 guitar system to model both new and classic guitar sounds (or nonguitar sounds for that matter) from the vibrations of your acoustic guitar. Remember, once you have a MIDI signal, your can connect to any MIDI sound module or synthesizer.

The Peavey Cyberbass 5 uses contact sensing frets for fast and accurate MIDI conversion. The Zeta MIDI controller uses pitch-to-MIDI conversion from the Zeta electric violin, viola, or cello instrument or, with the Zeta RetroPak, from any acoustic violin, viola, or cello (see Figure 22.5). The MIDI controller can then be connected to Zeta's Synthony synthesizer. And, if you just want to simulate strumming or finger-picking effects with your MIDI keyboard harmony, you can use the Oberheim Strummer or the Charlie Lab Digitar. Hold down a chord on the MIDI keyboard while you strum away on one of these small guitar simulators. They automatically remap the keyboard chords into guitar voicings.

Pitch-to-Voltage (PVCs) and Pitch-to-MIDI Converters (PMCs). Before we look at wind controllers, we need to look at what are called *pitch-to-voltage converters, pitch trackers, pitch extractors,* or, when applied to MIDI, *pitch-to-MIDI converters.* Let's just call them PVCs or PMCs for short. These devices are critical to wind, voice, and string controllers such as the guitar controllers discussed above. If you want to sing into a computer, you will need a PVC device.

PVC devices are difficult to build and often suffer from tracking error and delay. Translating complex analog sounds from human voice and wind instruments into a MIDI pitch value is not a trivial task. The name *PVC* implies that it translates a pitch into a voltage; however, this is somewhat of a misnomer. What it really does is translate a complex acoustic sound vibration—like a tone from a singing voice or a vibrating string—into a voltage that represents its best guess as to its pitch. The device is mechanically attempting to make a human decision in a nonhuman way.

How does a PVC make its best guess as to the pitch? One technique is to electronically strip off or filter out all of the harmonics from the complex sound and find the fundamental frequency. The device can then decide what voltage to assign the frequency or, in the case of PMCs, which MIDI note to assign the frequency. PVCs and PMCs can best handle monophonic or melodic solo lines.

Because of the difficulty in designing effective PVC and PMC devices, they have met with mixed commercial success. But, having said that, they keep getting better. The IVL Pitchrider was one of the first commercial pitch-to-MIDI controllers developed in 1985. It was originally designed as a training device for teaching sight singing and intonation. The Pitchrider transmitted Note On-Off data, pitch bend, velocity, and aftertouch. The controller also came in a six-channel version that could be used as a string controller, with each string assigned to a different channel. The Pitchrider is no longer produced. The PMC technology developed by IVL Technologies, however, is still used in their current products for karaoke electronics, digital harmonizers, the SmartMusic system (formerly called Vivace) for Coda Music Technology, and a variety of MIDI devices for other companies like DigiTech.

Another unique experiment was a voice controller called the Synchrovoice Midivox. The device fastened to your neck like a big dog collar. To avoid the deficiencies in the PMC system for voice-to-MIDI translation, it sent a 5-MHz radio signal through the neck to measure vocal cord vibrations. Designed originally for medical monitoring, this synthetic voice controller avoided the need for microphone pickups or Fourier analysis in order to obtain a fast pitch-to-MIDI conversion.

Several PMC devices are being incorporated into music education and music performance systems. One of most exciting is the Coda Music Technology SmartMusic system that uses PMC technology to track solo performances and synchronize prerecorded accompaniments to the soloist— what Coda calls "intelligent accompaniment." "Amadeus al fine" is a

LINK

Review pitch, frequency, and harmonic spectra in Module 10 if you need to brush up on these concepts.

hardware pitch-to-MIDI device being packaged by Pyware with its software for basic music skills, but it can be used with any software that accepts MIDI input.

The Roland G-10 guitar pitch-to-MIDI converter can be used with other music input devices for some PMC applications. Take the Yamaha Silent Brass system, for example. A microphone-equipped horn mute fits in the bell of the brass instrument to greatly reduce the natural sound output of the brass instrument. A control module then processes the special mute's audio signal so that it can be heard with headphones by the student playing. To turn the mute into a PMC system, the headphone audio can be connected to something like the Roland G-10 guitar-to-MIDI converter (because it is really a pitch-to-MIDI converter) to create an instant brass-to-MIDI interface. The Silent Brass audio could be also be connected to the Amadeus hardware to accomplish the pitch-to-MIDI conversion.

These days, computers are fast enough that pitch-to-MIDI conversion can be done in software with just a microphone input to the computer. Wildcat Canyon Software's AutoScore converts sound input to a PC sound card into MIDI codes and notation. Sing or play your favorite instrument to input your music notation or sequence. Cakewalk's Pro Audio sequencing software has PMC built into the sequencing package. Musicware's Music-Lab music training software has exercises for students to sing their response with PMC software used to convert the vibrations of the voice into music codes. And, much of the PMC operation with Coda's SmartMusic system is now done in software rather than the original hardware IVL PMC device.

Wind Controllers. Designers of wind controllers face the challenge of varying key and fingering layouts for acoustic wind instruments, both brass and woodwind. Acoustic wind controllers simply use PVC or PMC devices to convert these instruments into MIDI controllers. A PMC/PVC device is attached to the wind instrument so that it picks up its vibrations and then translates the acoustic sounds into MIDI data. The success of the PMC translation depends upon the instrument; this approach inherits all of the tracking and delay problems associated with pitch-to-voltage conversion.

Synthetic wind controllers come in woodwind and brass varieties. However, few of them have the feel of their acoustic counterparts. The pre-MIDI Lyricon (1972) was one of the first wind controllers for a synthesizer. It was based on a clarinet key layout, and its signals came from a combination of electronic switches for the keys and transducers to pick up breath and lip pressure changes. The Yamaha WX-7 wind controller introduced in 1987 provided a MIDI Lyricon-like controller with lip- and breath-sensing control. The key layout, however, was modeled on the saxophone or, optionally, the recorder. It was replaced by the WX-11 and then the more current WX-5 wind controller (Figure 22.6a). The EWI (Electronic Wind Instrument) and the EVI (Electronic Value Instrument) were developed from the Steiner Phone, a device created by Nyle Steiner in the late 1970s (see Figure 22.6b). Akai markets MIDI versions of the instruments. Touch-sensitive plates rather than moving key switches are used to simulate a trumpet (EVI) and a clarinet or saxophone (EWI) fingering.

The use of pitch-to-MIDI conversion is very important to music CAI applications, as was noted in Viewport III.

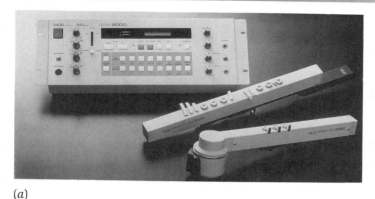

(a)

(b)

Figure 22.6
(a)The Akai EVI and EWI1000 brass and wind controllers, and (b) the Yamaha WX-5 wind controller
(Courtesy of Akai Musical Instrument Corporation and of Yamaha Corporation, Japan, and Yamaha Corporation of America)

Mind-Expanding MIDI Controllers. All the controllers we've covered so far have conformed to traditional musical instruments, and as you have seen, there is no limit to modifying these instruments for use as MIDI controllers. There are even MIDI accordians! However, don't let convention stand in your way. Almost anything that moves can be converted to a MIDI controller. We will now take a look at some of the more mind-expanding controllers that musicians have created and used to open up new modes of musical expression.

The pioneers experimenting. The Theremin was invented by the Russian inventor Leon Theremin in the 1920s and used the interaction of the performer's hands with two radio antennas to change frequency and amplitude. Its glissandi sounds became familiar as sound effects that accented many a sci-fi movie; the movie *The Day the Earth Stood Still* (1951) used a bass and violin Theremin. Robert Moog, who built Theremins to pay his way through school, produces a MIDI version called the Ethervox MIDI Theremin. Moog, of course, is one of the pioneers of the voltage-controlled synthesizers of the 1960s, along with Donald Buchla. Buchla's more recent experimentation has created the Lightning and Thunder MIDI controllers. The Thunder uses pressure- and position-sensitive strips to control MIDI parameters like tempo and dynamics. Max Mathews, another pioneer in music synthesis, designed the Radio Baton, a three-dimensional MIDI controller. Mathews lets the computer play the notes while the performer uses the Radio Baton to control tempo, volume, articulation, and timbre.

Creating new horns and guitars. Gary Lee Nelson, working with the music engineer John Talbert, has created his personal digital wind instrument, the MIDI Horn. This device has a four-note key system based on a tuba, because Nelson was originally a tuba player. One set of four keys controls MIDI pitch while another set of three keys controls the device's eight-octave range. There is a breath transducer that reacts to air flow and an array of two joysticks and eight buttons on the bottom of the horn that,

LINK

Check out the interview with Max Mathews in Viewport 7 and a view of his Radio Baton.

(*a*)   (*b*)

Figure 22.7
On the left (*a*) is Roy "Future Man" Wooten (from Béla Fleck and the Flecktones) with his custom Synthaxe-Drumitar (Photo © 1990 Jon Sievert) On the right (*b*) is the commercial version of Roy's instrument, the ZenDrum (Photo by Gina Boger-Haney © 1995, courtesy of Zendrum Corporation)

Check out Max software in Module 19 of this Viewport.

through the use of software like Opcode's Max, can be programmed for all sorts of MIDI sonorities and controller effects. Nelson's real-time interactive performance with the MIDI Horn uses "hyperinstruments." A hyperinstrument consists of a computer, a set of digital synthesizers, a performance interface, and software for linking them all together.

Roy "Future Man" Wooten plays with Béla Fleck and the Flecktones using a custom-built MIDI controller shown in Figure 22.7*a*, the SynthAxe-Drumitar. The original casing for the instrument was the British MIDI SynthAxe, but the internal circuitry was completely redesigned by the engineer Chris deHaas, and Richard Battaglia, the sound engineer for the Flecktones, added special sensors to the exterior. Richard mounted clusters of small discs with drum triggers and mounted additional clusters of small plastic discs with force-sensing resistors (FSRs) that look like bubbles on the body of the SynthAxe. The drum triggers can be tapped with the fingers like small drum pads. The FSRs replace the conventional wheel-type controllers on MIDI devices by creating voltages that match the pressure which Roy is applying to the plastic bubbles with his finger. Chris deHaas's internal circuitry then converts the voltage into MIDI data. The instrument is designed to handle up to 127 pads, with each pad being assigned to its own MIDI Note and MIDI Channel.

The end result is a keyboard of miniature drum pads and FSR pads, all sending MIDI data to the samplers and synthesizers which Roy Wooten uses in performance. Roy is trying to expand upon what he feels is a natural lineage between the drum and the piano keyboard as percussion instruments. He sees his unique MIDI controller as using technology to create "sound clusters" that can be performed with the range and virtuosity possible on a piano keyboard. Figure 22.7*b* shows a commercial version of "Future Man's" MIDI instrument, the Zendrum.

Sweat, body movement, and brain wave controllers! If the MIDI controllers so far sound a bit tame to you then consider some of these more bizarre applications. The Amsterdam STEIM (Studio for Electro Instrumen-

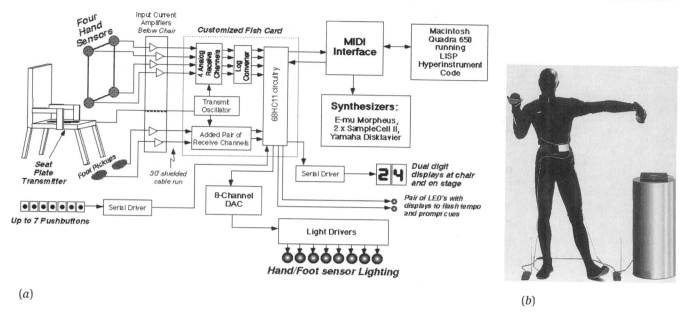

(a)

(b)

Figure 22.8

(a) A diagram of Tod Machover's MIDI Sensor Chair and (b) Yamaha's Miburi MIDI suit. (Diagram courtesy of MIT Press and taken from "Musical Applications of Electronic Field Sensing," by Joseph A. Paradiso and Neil Gershenfeld, *Computer Music Journal*, 21(2), 1997, pp. 69–89; Miburi courtesy of Yamaha Corporation of America)

tal Music) research group exists just to experiment with the construction and design of new and innovative electronic instruments. As the STEIM Web page indicates, "STEIM develops new instruments and software which…have to be sensitive to the slightest human movement because they function as an extension of the individual's physical and mental communicative qualities. These sometimes microscopic movements—often wrongly interpreted as human imprecision—contain essential musical information that an instrument should recognize and transfer."

Ray Edgar's Sweatstick is one such instrument developed from the STEIM SensorLab hardware and software toolkit. The stick bends in the middle, sending MIDI controller data from the physical bending as well as from sliding and twisting the two hand grips. The "sweat" term comes from the exercise necessary to physically play this MIDI controller.

Tod Machover designed The Sensor Chair in the fall of 1994 for a new mini-opera entitled *Media/Medium,* and the device was later used in his *Brain Opera* performances at Lincoln Center. The Sensor Chair is another example of a hyperinstrument. The person seated in the chair becomes an extension of numerous antennas placed in and around the chair (see Figure 22.8a). The strength of the signals picked up by the antennas is determined by the capacitance between the performer's body and any one of the antennae. Through a voltage-to-MIDI conversion, movements of the arms and upper body are turned into musical sounds and gestures.

For a commercial product that provides MIDI sensing of body movement, there is the Yamaha Miburi shown in Figure 22.8b. The Miburi MIDI suit provides sensors for shoulder and elbow movement, wrist movement, toe and heel impact, and grip units with various keys and controllers. The belt unit controls the programming of the various sensors and the MIDI signals can either be sent wireless or with a cable to the independent sound unit. Just think what Fred Astaire and Ginger Rogers could have done with this outfit!

And there's more. Michael Waisnez's MIDI gloves have mercury and contract switches that translate finger patterns and hand gestures; Mark Coniglio's MidiDancer translates body movements into MIDI data that control expressive music properties, stage lighting, and videodisc as well; and Ben Knapp and Hugh Lusted's Biomuse translates galvanic skin response, muscle and eye movements, and brain waves into MIDI data as a creative tool for the disabled. The commercial products Soundbeams and Synth-A-Beam can be used to program MIDI effects from intersecting light and sounds. Soundbeam is a distance-to-voltage-to-MIDI device that converts physical movements into sound by using information derived from interruptions of a stream of ultrasonic pulses.

With all these innovative ways to produce MIDI music, can't you see yourself hooking up a Miburi or a Sweatstick to your computer, running a sequencing program like Opcode's Max, and sending all kinds of wild MIDI data as you dance around your own studio? A MIDI trip to the MAX!

Coping with Audio Inputs and Mixers

What do you do when you want to:

▶ record more than two audio inputs into the L and R stereo inputs provided with your tape recorder?

▶ adjust the volume of one sound source or channel so that it is louder than another?

▶ adjust the balance between the stereo channels?

▶ add live performance to your MIDI *production?*

The solution is to add an audio mixer to your MIDI music system. A mixer gives you professional-level control over the audio signals or channels in your music-sequencing activity.

In the No-Frills and basic MIDI KISS systems (refer back to Figures 19.1 and 21.2, respectively), we have the stereo audio channels from the MIDI workstation (3) and the MIDI sound module (4) connected to the left (L) and right (R) stereo inputs of the cassette tape recorder (8) (or to the Mini-Disc or DAT recorders, if available). A cheap solution is to use two audio Y-splitters for the L and R inputs of the recorder to combine the two L inputs and the two R inputs into one L and R signal. Another would be to find a recorder with more than one input channel. In our Enhanced MIDI KISS system (Figure 22.1), we use an audio mixer as an alternative and preferred solution. Let's take a moment to discuss the technical aspects of this setup and the general features of audio mixers. We will include in our discussion basic features found in most audio mixers.

Figure 22.9*a* focuses on four components from the enhanced KISS system: mixer (11), effects generator (10), microphone (6), and cassette tape recorder (8*a*). A MiniDisc (8*c*) or DAT (8*b*) recorder can easily be substituted here for a cassette recorder. The gray lines between the components

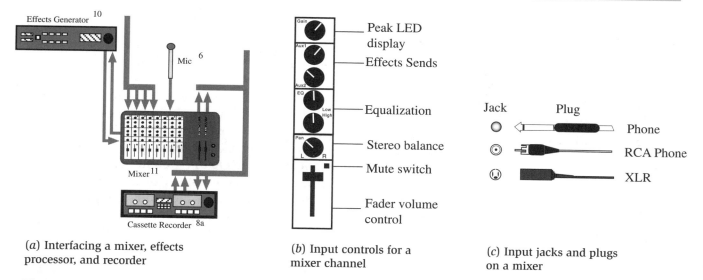

(*a*) Interfacing a mixer, effects processor, and recorder

(*b*) Input controls for a mixer channel

(*c*) Input jacks and plugs on a mixer

Figure 22.9
Audio mixing with the enhanced MIDI KISS system

represent audio connections. As you can see, everything passes through the mixer (11). The mixer in the KISS system is an 8×2 mixer; this means that it has eight input channels and two output channels. Each channel is monophonic, so the left stereo signal of the MIDI workstation (3) goes to the first channel and the right stereo signal to the second channel. The left stereo signal from the General MIDI sound module (4) goes to the third channel and the right stereo signal to the fourth channel. That leaves four channels available for other inputs. In the illustration, the microphone (6) is connected to one of the channels.

The mixer has two outputs, representing the stereo left and right of the output signal going to the recorder. Mixers come in all sorts of configurations besides the 8×2 shown here: 12, 14, or 16×2; 24 or 32×4; 16×4×2, and so on with infinite variety. A configuration like 16×4×2 is one in which the mixer will let you output either a group of four channels (e.g., to a multitrack recorder) or a group of two channels. When estimating how many input channels you will need in a mixer, you should count the number of MIDI sound devices, of microphone channels needed for live performance, of channels for audio from your computer, and of any additional channels you might need for special effects.

Notice in Figure 22.9*a* that there are separate audio channels connecting the effects generator (10) to the mixer (11). Mixers usually provide separate channels and controls for adding or mixing effects into the audio stream. Many mixers label the effects channels as *aux* or auxiliary channels. The mixer in our chart has a common configuration of two effect sends (aux 1 and 2) and two effect receives; only one send and receive is connected in the diagram.

Mixer Input Controls. Figure 22.19*b* shows the detailed controls available on the 8×2 mixer. Remember, each channel of sound in a mixer can be manipulated by a unique set of controls. The KISS mixer has eight monophonic input channels.

Pots are the round control knobs, *faders* the sliding controls, and *switches* the on/off controls on a mixer.

When no effects have been mixed with an audio signal, it is a *dry* signal; the signal becomes *wet* as effects are added.

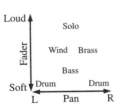

Three types of input connections are typically provided with a mixer. Some combination of these connectors will be provided for each channel of the mixer. Figure 22.9c shows the three common audio connectors: the *phone* and *phono* audio jack and plug; RCA phono jack and plug connectors common in consumer audio; and the special XLR connector used for professional audio. Most of your MIDI sound equipment, tape recorders, and amplifiers use phono and phone plugs and jacks. Semiprofessional microphones typically use phone jacks. Professional microphones almost invariably use XLR connections. Some mixers may provide phone and phono jacks for each input channel but provide XLR microphone connections for only a few of the channels. XLR connectors are superior because they provide the highest quality of electrical connectivity and grounding, thus minimizing the likelihood of hum and static due to poor connections.

We'll walk down the face of the control panel shown in Fig 22.9b and discuss each control feature.

At the top of the control panel, find the control knob or *pot* (short for *potentiometer*) labeled *gain* with the *peak* LED display in the upper right-hand corner. This pot lets you control the overall intensity of the signal coming into the mixer. The LED light comes on when the intensity of the input signal exceeds the *peak* level: the point at which audio distortion will occur.

The next pair of pots are labeled *Aux 1* and *Aux 2*. These let you connect up to two effects processors to the mixer, allowing you to add reverb, echo, flanging, and other electronic processing to your audio signal. The Aux 1 and 2 pots give you control over how much of a given effect is added to the signal on this channel. For example, should you have reverb programmed in an effects processor connected to Aux 1, the more you rotate the Aux 1 knob clockwise the more reverb would be added to the audio on this channel.

Next we have the equalization or EQ pots. Equalization lets you boost, reduce, or eliminate certain frequencies of the audio channel by selective filtering. Our KISS mixer uses the simplest EQ, with only a high and low filter control similar to the treble (removing or adding high frequencies) and bass (removing or adding low frequencies) adjustments on a car radio. The EQ controls on mixers can get very complex, with tunable filters that let you precisely control the range of frequencies that are filtered out of an audio signal.

Volume Faders and Pan Pots. Following the EQ pots is the *pan* pot. The pan pot lets you control the location of the audio signal within the left-to-right balance of the stereo output. The bottom panel control is the volume *fader*, which lets you control how much of the audio signal from this channel you want to mix into the output stereo signal from the mixer. You will also note a *mute* switch, which will toggle the audio from this channel on or off.

Study the chart in the margin. Part of the art of mixing involves the practiced placement of your music channels into audio space. Audio space is manipulated by faders that control the volume of each audio channel and pan pots that control the left-to-right proximity of each channel. The chart shows six channels of solo, wind, brass, and bass, and two drum channels.

The perceived location of each of these channels is created by the interaction of the fader and pan controls.

Mixer Output Controls. Now we will examine the output side of the mixer. Because this is an 8×2 mixer, it features a set of faders and pots to control the final stereo output signals for the left and right channels. You will see a pair of faders under the output audio in Figure 22.9*a*. To let you view the output signal, mixers provide either a *VU meter* or an *LED ladder* for each output channel. The VU meter is an analog dial that shows the strength of the output signal; the LED ladder gives you a row or ladder of small LED lights indicating the strength of the signal. There are also two pots in the lower right-hand corner of the mixer. These control the overall volume of the effects send and receive for the mixer. Some mixers may also provide a headphone output and a control-room output with separate control pots for monitoring the final output mix.

Programmable Mixers. The KISS mixer is a manual mixer; everything must be set by hand. To recreate the performance of a composition created with a sequencer, you will have to reset all of the mixing controls manually.

There are two types of programmable mixers. The first has memory capabilities built in so that a group of settings for switches, pots, faders, and so forth can be saved to memory and retrieved for later use. These groups are called "snapshots." You can use MIDI program-change messages to select the snapshot that has been saved in the mixer's programmable memory, automating the process. The second type of programmable mixer permits full control over all of the features in real time. MIDI program, controller, and SysEx messages are used to alter the mixer's control parameters. With either type of mixer, your mixing controls can be stored as MIDI messages within your computer sequencing software. Some mixers may even offer a built-in MIDI sequencer that plays standard MIDI files, letting you record the custom MIDI messages in real time for various fader, pot, and other controls.

Digital Mixers. As you have seen throughout the textbook, so much of the audio process is going digital. In a digital world, analog mixers get to be a drag: you have to convert digital audio into analog just to mix the signal with other analog sound sources, and then back to digital again in order to work on the signal from your computer. A digital mixer, on the other hand, lets you stay entirely in the digital world with 24-bit resolution of your audio signal. Digital mixers are more expensive than analog, but, as with everything else in technology, the price keeps coming down to the realm of the small music studio budget.

There are some other advantages to digital mixers over the traditional analog mixers. These mixers usually have DSP chips built in to provide effects processing for every channel of the mix. EQ and dynamics processing can also be applied to every channel, with extremely precise control. Got an offending bit of audio noise in your recording? You can precisely tune the digital EQ to eliminate the offending frequencies of the sound.

(*a*) Mackie 12×2 channel mixer

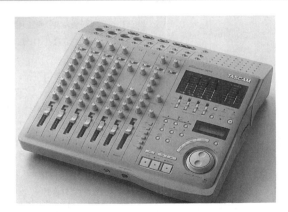

(*b*) Tascam 8-channel Portastudio with digital-MiniDisc-recording built in

Figure 22.10
Examples of a mixer and a mixer/recorder combo (Mixer photo courtesy of Mackie Designs; Portastudio reprinted with permission from TEAC America)

Just as with programmable analog mixers, you can save snapshots of all the settings on a digital mixer or save real-time changes of faders and pots for future use. For example, if you want to have different setups for several performance pieces you are doing or for different ensembles you are recording, you can create a library of snapshots that can be recalled and applied with one flick of the finger. Digital mixers also offer graphic display of sound data, another useful capability.

Mixers Meet Recorders. What happens when you cross a mixer with a recording device? A portable studio or recording workstation emerges. The first "portastudios" were typically 4-track cassette tape recorders integrated into the same box with a 4- or 8-channel mixer. The portastudios now offer MiniDisc, DAT, ADAT, and hard disk recording for a variety of options, some completely digital. The portastudio or recording-workstation combination gives a musician multitrack recording, mixing, equalization, and effects processing all bundled in one convenient package. Figure 22.10*b* shows one of the Tascam digital portastudios that uses MiniDisc recording technology.

Details on MiniDisc, DAT, ADAT, and hard disk recorders are covered in Module 26.

Cost Factors in Selecting a Mixer. For around a few hundred dollars you can purchase a mixer with features similar to those of the KISS Mixer. Here are some of the features found as you move up to more expensive mixers:

▶ An increase in the number of input and output channels and in sophistication as to how these channels can be grouped

▶ The addition of more effects send and receive channels

▶ Increased sophistication in equalization controls

▶ Professional-level XLR mic connections and amplification

▶ Increased quality and sophistication in the design and construction of switches, pots, faders, and displays

▶ MIDI programmability

▶ Digital mixing, effects, and recording options

Table 22.1. Effects and Signal Processing Techniques

Chorus	Duplication of a sound into many parallel voices with random delays and amplitudes added to simulate the imperfections of a chorus of human voices. Chorus adds fullness to the sound by making one instrument sound like many.
Clipping or Rectification	Two distortion techniques that affect the two phases of a sound's oscillation. Clipping cuts or "clips" the tops and bottoms of each oscillation of a sound; rectification flattens one-half of the oscillation's cycle or switches one-half of the cycle to the opposite polarity. Both of these produce a strong octave effect.
Compression and Expansion	These are effects for altering the dynamic range of a sound. A *compressor* keeps a sound from exceeding a certain threshold of amplitude; an *expander* increases a sound's dynamic range.
Echo or Delay	Simulation of an echo, where the sound is repeated many times, each time at a lesser intensity. A touch of echo will help sustain a sound that fades too quickly.
Equalization (EQ)	Removing or filtering selected frequencies from the harmonic spectrum of a sound. *Graphic equalizers* provide frequency bands (e.g., 10 or more) that can be program controlled; *parametric equalizers* prove a set of controls or parameters that let you tune the desired EQ effect.
Flanging	Duplication of a sound source like chorusing, but in sequence rather than in parallel; as the sound is duplicated at rapidly decreasing delay times, it is mixed back in with the original sound. This adds futuristic effects to voices and sounds.
Harmonizing	Generation of notes at various intervals with the notes being played to create parallel harmony; creating musically effective intervals electronically is a challenge.
Noise Gating	When the sounds reaches a certain noise threshold, the gate will turn the output of the sound off.
Phasing	Simulating a forward and backward alternation in sound by duplicating the sound source and repeating the sound at two different amplitudes, similar to a Doppler effect.
Panning	Alternating the location of a sound in stereo audio space between the left and right sound position.
Reverb	Simulation of the decay caused by sound reflecting off of walls in acoustic space (e.g., concert halls, gyms, churches, rooms, and out-of-doors). Can effectively be used to add depth to the sound. One of the most commonly used effects.
Resonator and Wah	A filter with a boost in frequency in a narrow range is a resonator; when the center frequency of the resonator moves up and down by use of a pedal or other controller, an effect is created that mimics the human vocal sound of "wah" or a trumpet player using a mute.

Some of the manufacturers of mixers include Alesis, Behringer, Korg, Mackie, MidiMan, Oram, Peavey, Ramsa, Roland, Soundcraft, Summit, Tascam, Topaz, and Yamaha. They come in tabletop and rack-mounted designs. You will be spending lots of time at the controls of your mixer, so don't purchase a mixer without first having an opportunity to try it out.

Effects and Signal Processors

Another component to be added to our enhanced MIDI KISS system is a MIDI effects generator (see item 10 in Figures 22.1 and 22.9a). Effects processors let you augment, enhance, and spice up your sound source by

More and more, effects processing is moving to software that takes advantage either of the fast processor speed of present-day computers or of special DSP chips added to the computer or the sound cards. Software plug-ins can be found on the Internet or purchased that add an incredible array of effects editing power to your digital audio software.

adding reverberation, echo, flanging, and many other electronic audio effects. Effects processors are, in fact, signal processors. Sometimes the terms *effects* and *signal processing* are used interchangeably. With DSP or digital signal processing chips readily available, you will find digital effects processing embedded in most any audio and MIDI equipment, including MIDI synthesizers and workstations, MIDI sound modules, guitar and drum synthesizers, mixers, and recorders, as well as stand-alone effects processors.

We mentioned effects processing briefly in the discussion of MIDI workstations in Module 21. Entry-level MIDI workstations typically provide only a few effects like reverb and chorus, with the more expensive workstations providing a wide variety of signal processing options. Table 21.1 shows the effects processing options for various MIDI workstations. Stand-alone hardware for audio effects processing, as shown in the enhanced MIDI KISS system, continues to be available; examples include the Alesis Quadraverb and Midiverb effects processors and the Zoom Studio Multi-Effects Processor, as well as more specialized units such as the Eventide Ultra-Harmonizer and the DigitTech Vocalist Workstation. With the latest generation of computers with very fast CPUs and lots of RAM, audio signal processing is also showing up as software options in sequencers (see Module 19) and digital audio editors (see Module 23). Just as graphics software like Adobe's Photoshop provides a host of graphic processing filters and special effects that can be applied to visual images, music sequencers and sound editing software like Studio Vision or Sound Forge provide a host of signal processing effects that can be applied to sound directly in software.

No matter whether you use hardware or software DSPs, the key is in understanding the different kinds of effects available and the labels used to describe them. We can classify effects into the following basic groups, allowing for some overlap:

► Amplitude-based or sound enhancing effects: examples include amplitude control, tremolo, panning, compression and expansion, envelope or ADSR manipulation, limiting, and noise gating

► Distortion effects: examples include clipping, limiting, and rectification

► Frequency-altering or filtering effects: examples include equalization, resonator, various wah effects, vibrato, ring modulation, Karaoke, stereoize, and phase shifting

► Time-altering effects: examples include reverb, echo, vibrato, flanging, and chorus

► Specialized effects: examples include harmonizing, vocalizing, ring modulation, octave division, and Leslie speaker rotation.

Table 22.1 gives you a sampling of effects with their descriptions. These are not concepts easily understood by reading. Get your hands on a mixer, MIDI workstation, or effects processor and experiment with applying these various signal processing effects to a sound source of your own.

Figure 22.9*a* and the full diagram in Figure 22.1 show how an effects generator might be added to the enhanced KISS system and its relation to the mixer and recorder. As we explained in the previous section on mixers, audio mixers have *aux* or auxiliary channels devoted to effects send and receive, many with a monophonic send channel and stereo receive channels. The reason for this is that electronic effects like panning can simulate stereo effects by manipulating the left and right dimensions of stereo space, so what you send to an effects processor as a mono channel may come back as a processed stereo signal.

How is an effects processor programmed? Either through factory presets or user-defined snapshots of the effects settings, or through direct programmable control of the processor's features. Effects processors use programmable algorithms that manipulate the digital sound data as they pass through the device. An algorithm might add a little reverb or mix in some delay, a bit of phase shifting, or some selective equalization to the digitized signal. The sophistication of an effects processor can be determined by the number of simultaneous algorithms possible and the repertoire of effects within the device.

Let's look at two examples of stand-alone effects processors to illustrate the capabilities of a budget processor and a more expensive alternative. The Zoom Studio 1204 multi-effects processor is an inexpensive unit that offers 512 factory-preset algorithms with thirty-two basic effects and memory to store up to 100 of your own algorithms. Its effects repertoire includes various reverbs, tremolo, flanger, pitch shifter, delay, and echo. The device can be controlled by external MIDI signals. The Alesis Quadraverb 2, on the other hand, is a more expensive effects processor. It features fifty effects algorithms—including equalization, tremolo, overdrive, delay, chorus, flange, phaser, halls, plates, rooms, and the like—which are the building blocks for 100 preset and 200 user programs. Advanced programs for stereo sampling, rotating speaker, surround sound encoding, Doppler effects, and triggered pan are also provided. Up to eight different multi-effects can be created at one time, and the programming capabilities let you route your signal through almost any combination of effects in any order.

Both the Zoom and the Quadraverb effect processors are digital processors and offer 18-bit digital processing that converts your analog input sound signal into digital for the signal processing, and then back to analog for the sound output. The Alesis also provides digital I/O for direct interface to ADAT ports on workstations, digital mixers, or digital recorders.

Like mixing, effects processing is an art form. Look, hear, and feel are critical in selecting an effects processor. With the algorithmic programming power of the multi-effects units, incredibly creative special effects can be designed for electronic music processing.

Adding SMPTE and Multitrack Recording to the MIDI KISS System

There are two other topics we need to touch on briefly: multitrack recording and SMPTE synchronization; you will see these topics just about every time you pick up a MIDI magazine. They represent additional alternatives for our KISS music system. However, as with the other KISS music

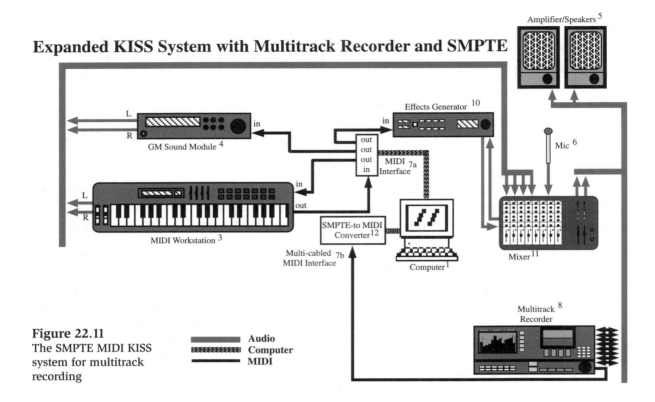

Expanded KISS System with Multitrack Recorder and SMPTE

Figure 22.11
The SMPTE MIDI KISS system for multitrack recording

SMPTE and MTC are explained in Module 20; see especially Figure 20.2.

models we've provided, we will give you the Keep-It-Short-and-Simple version of SMPTE and multitrack recording, knowing you can go way beyond what we discuss here in complexity.

Figure 22.11 shows the KISS system with a multitrack digital recorder—replacing the two-track recorder in the MIDI KISS system (8), and a multi-cabled, or hybrid MIDI interface (7b) with SMPTE-to-MIDI conversion (12) built in.

SMPTE-to-MIDI Conversion. Earlier in this module, we discussed expanding a MIDI network with THRU and merger boxes as well as patchbays. We also discussed expanded or hybrid MIDI interfaces where multiple *cables* of 16 channels each are self-contained in one box. These multi-cabled MIDI interfaces usually provide timing synchronization and conversion as well, especially the SMPTE conversion we need for the KISS setup presented in Figure 22.11. The Opcode and Mark of the Unicorn multi-cabled MIDI interfaces are very suitable for this application. In fact, this type of MIDI interface could serve all of the MIDI devices in the KISS network, including the devices now served by the basic MIDI interface (7a).

In Module 20, we discussed SMPTE and MIDI time codes (MTCs). A key point was that, in order to have everything within your MIDI network synchronized in time, something has to serve as the conductor generating the master time clock; all other devices in the network are slaved to this master time unit. In the MIDI KISS system shown in Figure 22.11, the multitrack

Other timing systems besides SMPTE are discussed in Module 20, including FSK, MTC or MIDI time codes, ADAT sync, word clock sync, and Pro Tools superclock sync; any of these could be used in place of SMPTE as the synchronizer for a MIDI network.

recorder is generating the master time clock as SMPTE time codes. The time codes could come from one of the tracks of the tape itself, or the multitrack recorder could have the capability of generating SMPTE time codes directly. The multi-cable MIDI interface with synchronization capabilities converts the SMPTE time codes to MIDI Time Codes that the computer's sequencing software can understand, and serves to keep everything within the sequencer time locked to the SMPTE multitrack recorder.

Multitrack Recording. You do not really need a multitrack recorder to do most of your MIDI sequencing and performing activities. The computer software sequencer provides a virtual recording environment; in combination with an eight- to 16-channel mixer and a basic, two-track recorder, you will have all the flexibility that you need.

Then why show a multitrack recorder (8) as an extension to the KISS system? A multitrack digital recorder provides more than the two tracks on a stereo cassette, MiniDisc, or DAT recorder. Typically, a multitrack recorder can offer anywhere from four to 32 simultaneous tracks for recording different audio signals. A timing code like SMPTE is frequently *stripped* on one track of the tape from beginning to end and used to synchronize the recording of all the other tracks. Digital multitrack units like the Alesis ADAT, Tascam DA-88, or the professional multitrack versions of the Sony MiniDisc easily provide 8 tracks of digital audio. These units, though more expensive than their multitrack analog tape counterparts, provide random access to any place in the recording, exceptional CD sound quality, and a lot of recording time.

Here are a few legitimate cases for using a multitrack recorder:

In Module 26, Mini-Disc, DAT, MDM and ADAT, and hard disk recorders are compared and discussed.

▶ Insufficient polyphony on your MIDI devices, or the need to use more than the 16 channels available to you within the MIDI network

▶ Need to record traditional instruments and voice against MIDI recorded tracks

▶ Need for more mixing and recording options than you can get with just a mixer, especially if you are using lots of signal-processing effects

▶ Ability to record in the newer multitrack audio formats like Surround Sound or the AC-3 Dolby Digital 5.1-channel sound

Hardware or Software Views of the KISS MIDI System?

At this point in the evolution of the KISS music systems, we have studied a large number of hardware devices, from the computer itself to various MIDI controllers and sound generators, to mixers and audio recorders. In Viewport VII we focus on sound digital audio, sampling, and other alternatives to the KISS music system. Fast computers with lots of memory make it increasingly easier to create music while staying entirely within the digital domain. It is possible to replace much of the traditional external hardware like mixers, effects processors, tape recorders, and the like, with software solutions. Virtual mixers, patchbays, multitrack sequencing, signal processing, and digital editing are commercially available and will continue to become more sophisticated and musician friendly. Once a music event from the analog world is digitized and captured in the computer, it may never have to leave the digital realm again, all the way to the creation of a CD or DVD disc. Your selection will come from choosing between the various options presented here to find a best-fit computer music studio that meets your needs as a musician.

Viewport VI | Summary

Our interest in music sequencing with MIDI and digital audio is part of a long tradition in Western culture of musicians using technology as an aid to composition and performance. Player pianos of the eighteenth and nineteenth centuries have given way to today's enormous variety of software, computers, and MIDI hardware. This technology is used by musicians engaged in all styles of music, not just by popular rock stars. Examples include our distinguished conductor and composer Pierre Boulez, who works with sequencing and MIDI technology in live concert performance (see the introduction to this viewport); Henry Panion arranging for Stevie Wonder (Viewport V); Roy "Future Man" Wooten playing his SynthAxe/Drumitar with Béla Fleck and the Flecktones; large numbers of composers and arrangers working in film and television; and club performers.

Musicianship First

This brings us to an important topic as we conclude this viewport on sequencing: musicianship. In the very early pages of this book, we made the point that bad music can certainly be made with technology. We have described some very sophisticated technology for making music, but none of it makes good music by itself. Good music comes from good musicians with interesting musical ideas. If the music sounds sterile, synthetic, or just plain boring, the fault is most often with the people making it, not the technology. Today's technology provides wonderful tools, but they must be used by good musicians. If you become a success with your sequenced music, it will be largely because of you, not because of your computer or MIDI workstation.

Importance of the Systems Approach

As in other viewports, we have presented information about the software, data structures, and hardware of music sequencing. Perhaps there is no other viewport topic in this book where the combination of these components is so important. In order for you to find solutions to grow as a musician using MIDI and digital audio sequencing, you need to know as much as possible about MIDI and digital audio as data structures and the hardware that supports them. The computer and its software are not the major focal points, but rather the complete music technology system.

For example, consider the concepts of *patch, track,* and *channel* that began the software module. Your use of these concepts in software is made far easier if you understand how these ideas work in the MIDI language. If the sounds emanating from your workstation are not right, you also need to understand how the hardware works in order to find the root of the problem. This is why the systems approach is so important.

Getting Started

We have provided you with enough knowledge to make some initial decisions about basic sequencing, and we have added a fair amount of information for some advanced work. Let's review some of what's been learned.

Software. Programs like Musicshop and PowerTracks have plenty of power to record and play back MIDI data for your basic work. These programs provide a set of simulated transport buttons similar to those on your other audio equipment. You can easily record and edit performances by organizing layers of MIDI and digital audio like the melody and accompaniment in tracks. You can assign the proper program and channel assignments so the hardware makes correct sounds. You have a number of recording options, too, including the ability to change tempo, loop and bounce tracks, filter incoming MIDI data, and process digital audio sounds. You can record the music in real time and by step, just as in notation software. If you don't like the result, you can record your performance data again until they are acceptable.

Editing sequences can be done in a variety of *views*, including traditional notation, that represent the MIDI data. Some software even offers a list that lets you edit individual events. Quantizing is easily accomplished, and sequencing software offers "humanizing" options that preserve some of the musical feel while still tightening up the performance. Editing continuous controller data is possible for adding special effects, as is mixing volumes of tracks and transposing.

Performance is a joy. You can call up files for performance at any time and play along with your wind controller or any other controller. You can make tempo and key changes quickly and can mute certain parts easily. Files can be saved in their native application format or as standard MIDI and audio files to be shared with others.

One other tip might be useful in choosing software. Companies often produce software titles in families ranging from simpler to more complex. Moving to a more advanced title created by the same company is easier than learning an entirely new program, because the interface is well known.

Data. You now have a much richer understanding of MIDI data structures, and have found that this understanding is vital for using software and hardware. MIDI consists of channel and system messages. Channel messages are used to control the various devices in a setup. A device can be set to respond only to "Channel 2" messages, for example. System messages are "broadcast" to all the devices on the system, and include timing codes to synchronize the workings of the various components. System exclusive (SysEx) messages include special information installed by individual manufacturers to control their specific equipment.

You've learned the difference between transmitting data (sending MIDI information out) and receiving or responding to it (being able to recognize incoming MIDI information). You've learned how MIDI information includes the specific patch (or instrument sound) that should perform a particular part, as well as all of the musical effects that go into making the sound.

You have also learned about extensions to the MIDI standard and about new ideas spurred by the growth of music on the Internet. We presented information about the QuickTime system extensions and the growing trend to merge MIDI data with digital audio.

Hardware. You can meet all the basic hardware needs with a simple MIDI interface connected to one serial, parallel, or USB port and then to your MIDI gear. The MIDI interface will have, as a minimum, one IN and one OUT port. During recording at home, you can have a MIDI keyboard connected to the IN and OUT ports. During performance at another location, you can add a wind controller as the IN device and control the whole system with it if you want. If your interface has a second OUT port, you can connect that to a sound module for more options.

The MIDI setup necessary for you to accomplish your goals can be very basic. We have tried to summarize the major options, and our guess is that you would be best served by a workstation midrange in price and capabilities. You will probably want a touch-sensitive keyboard, polyphonic multitimbral capability, and some kind of drum kit. Other features that are likely to come with your workstation will be an effects processor, pedal and wheel controllers, and a hardware sequencer. The last two items are not really necessary, but you will probably get them as part of your workstation whether you want them or not. Finally, you may decide to look for a workstation that supports General MIDI. General MIDI support will make your software easier to use because you can take advantage of the standardized program numbers.

In Module 22, we extended the workstation to a much more advanced KISS system by adding additional controllers, a mixer, and recording gear. To round out your setup, you will probably want to invest in some good sound-amplification equipment and speakers. An analog or DAT deck, MiniDisc, or hard-disk recorder would be handy for recording if your budget allows.

Moving On

You will get better at sequencing and will need more than what basic software and hardware can offer. Your situation may change from rather simple, one-person performance settings to far more challenging concert work with larger numbers of people. Perhaps you will become involved with advanced studio work for film and television.

Here are just a few of the more important advanced features that cut across software, hardware, and data:

▶ Additional ways to view MIDI data, including newer object-oriented approaches that make moving MIDI data easier

▶ Hundreds of tracks and channels possible, with sophisticated MIDI interfaces, switchers, mergers, and patchbays

▶ Custom virtual faders, tracks, and instruments that control special effects and complex combinations of MIDI devices

▶ Sophisticated editing features, including quantizing, filtering, scaling, and remapping of MIDI data

▶ Algorithmic composition both within a sequencing package and as an alternative approach to sequencing software

▶ Support for SMPTE to MIDI synchronization in software as well as support for other timing systems, and support for their role in more sophisticated hardware designs

▶ Support for System Exclusive messages for refining the communication with MIDI hardware

▶ Development of new MIDI controllers and their support in software

▶ Support for controlling the flow of MIDI data within and outside computers, including OMS for Macintosh computers and Windows machines

Room for Improvement

Despite the amazing growth in sophistication of sequencing technology, there still is work to be done. Software needs to be made more intuitive for the musician, especially for complicated channel, track, and program assignments. Drag-and-drop techniques are needed, as are better support for electronic copying and pasting of music data. Better links between MIDI and digital audio are needed.

MIDI hardware devices remain complicated, and implementation of sound synthesis, sampling, effects processing—and even their general operation—are all very different from device to device. Cabling schemes for MIDI and audio, even with intermediate-level equipment, can become very complex and time-consuming. Software solutions for this are not entirely satisfactory.

Perhaps the most important changes needed are with the implementation of MIDI by manufacturers, and with MIDI itself. We have noted the problems in transferring standard MIDI files among applications because of the nonstandard way manufacturers support meta-events (time signature and key changes, instrument assignments, and so on). Of course, these devices vary greatly in their physical implementation of MIDI, and this can cause confusion for musicians who do not understand complicated MIDI charts.

The protocol itself needs further attention. We have noted the need to support certain requirements for music printing programs, because many musicians use MIDI for sound *and* help with visual representation. The

NIFF notation exchange format shows promise. Another important issue relates purely to sound: MIDI speed restraints. As MIDI devices increase in number on a network and as messages become more complex, MIDI can choke, and important information can be lost. Finally, improvement in MIDI's support for subtlety in music expression continues to be needed.

You will probably not run into these problems immediately, but somewhere down the line you will. Sequencing technology provides musicians with much to learn and much to look forward to.

Supplementary Readings

Anderton, Craig. *MIDI for Musicians.* New York: Amsco, 1986.

Bowen, Jeff. *Becoming a Computer Musician.* Indianapolis: Sams Publishing, 1994.

Heywood, Brian, and Roger Evan. *The PC Music Handbook.* Kent (England): PC Publishing, 1991.

Hill, Brad. *Going Digital.* New York: Schirmer Books, 1998.

Jungleib, Stanley. *General MIDI.* Madison, Wis.: A-R Editions, 1995.

Muro, Don. *Sequencing Basics.* Miami: Warner Brothers Publications, 1998.

Rona, Jeff. *The MIDI Companion.* Winona, Minn.: Hal Leonard, 1994.

Rothstein, Joseph. *MIDI: A Comprehensive Introduction* (2nd edition). Madison, Wis.: A-R Editions, 1995.

Rumsey, Francis. *Sound and Recording: An Introduction* (2nd edition). Oxford; Boston: Focal Press, 1994.

Trubitt, David (ed.). *Making Music with Your Computer.* Milwaukee: Hal Leonard Publishing, 1993.

Whitmore, Lee. *MIDI Basics.* Miami: Warner Brothers Publications, 1998.

Yavelow, Christopher. *MacWorld Music & Sound Bible.* San Mateo: IDG Books Worldwide, 1992.

Young, Rob. *The Midi Files.* Englewood-Cliffs, N.J.: Prentice Hall Computer Books, 1996.

Viewport VII

Creating Sounds and Music with Digital Audio

By looking for the structure in signals, how they were generated, we go beyond the surface appearance of bits and discover the building blocks out of which image, sound, or text came. This is one of the most important facts of digital life.

—Nicholas Negroponte, *Being Digital* (1995)

Frankly, I think that electrical engineers and other audio gurus have made great advances in terms of what machines can do, and what really hasn't changed a lot in the past couple of decades is the creative output. The music itself is evolving, but the way it is recorded and the way it's presented to the consumer really hasn't budged since the 1950s. . . . What we really need is . . . some individual to . . . demonstrate what can be done creatively—how to use all this great technology in a more creative, artistic way.

—Ken Pohlmann, digital recording guru, "The Crystal Ball,"
Mix magazine (20th Anniversary Issue, 1997)

I think the next big change will be that the music-only album is pretty much dead, and what we'll see change in the next five years will be that most things will come out on some music-plus format; in other words, music with multimedia, music with graphics, music with video. . . . If the DVD takes hold you're going to see a lot more movement in the direction of presenting music in a different context.

—Toby Mountain, master recording engineer, "The Crystal Ball,"
Mix magazine (20th Anniversary Issue, 1997)

Overview

It's all going digital! That is the important message to this final viewport in our series of Fill-Your-Own applications for musicians. We turn our attention to software for manipulating digital sound, a technology that is pervasive throughout the music industry from CD audio laser discs to digital sampling keyboards. We will explore software that captures, creates, and edits digital representations of sound by focusing on those titles that emphasize the recording of digital audio tracks and manipulating those tracks with digital sound processing (DSP) techniques. We will summarize the common and special features of software for helping to create and store sound within MIDI devices such as synthesizers and sample players. As in previous viewports, we will illustrate the important features of each of these applications through commercial software on both Macintosh and Wintel platforms.

In the data module, we will revisit the initial discussions of digital audio and sampling from Viewport III in greater depth. The issue here is optimizing audio quality, and we will study such topics as Nyquist frequencies, signal-to-noise ratios, aliasing, filters, oversampling, and Dolby Digital 5.1 channel sound. File formats and compression techniques for digital audio data will also be discussed. In the hardware module we will create a new KISS music system where all sound processing is digital under software control. We will examine options for adding digital audio boards, multitrack digital audio hardware, direct-to-disk recording, and various digital tape and disc recorders.

In this viewport we will:

▶ Study a variety of software solutions for computer-based digital sound and review both standard and advanced features

▶ Explore the history of music synthesis, sound sampling, and digital audio

▶ Summarize the features of software that help create, edit, and store sounds within a MIDI device

▶ Revisit sampling data structures to review issues that affect audio quality

▶ Study the importance and design of digital-signal processor (DSP) chips for audio

▶ Create a totally digital KISS music system with multitrack digital I/O and with all sound processing under software control

▶ Study the hardware available for digital sound boards, multitrack digital audio processing, direct-to-disk recording, and digital tape and disc recorders

HISTORICAL TIMELINE
The Technology of Sound Synthesis

1700s	Sauveau proposes the overtone series in his *Système Général Des Intervalles des Sons*
1800s	Fourier formulates the theorem that any periodic motion can be represented as a sum of harmonically related sine waves
	Helmholtz uses hollow glass spheres to analyze the harmonics in a complex wave following Fourier's theorem
1860s	Helmholtz authors *On the Sensations of Tone*, which stands as a landmark publication on acoustics
1900s	Thaddeus Cahill's Telharmonium is the first additive synthesizer, using huge rotors (200 tons of dynamos) to mix harmonics that create various timbres
1910s	Lee de Forest builds an electronic oscillator based on his triode vacuum tube, which serves as the basis of early electronic instruments
1920s	Harry Nyquist publishes his sampling theorem, the basis for all digital storage and communication systems
1940s	Homer Dudley's Vocoder, invented at Bell Labs, is one of the earliest examples of speech synthesis
	Dennis Gabor proposes granular synthesis, sounds made up of "grains," the shortest sounds that could be discriminated by the ear
1950s	Earliest experiments in digital synthesis carried out by Max Mathews and others at Bell Telephone Laboratories

	Mathews designs the first digital-music computer, using an IBM 704 computer with a digital-to-analog converter, filter, and amplifier
	James Beauchamp designs early electronic voltage-controlled tone generators at the University of Illinois
1960s	Voltage-controlled sound appears; music synthesis is created with voltages controlling sound parameters
	Robert Moog presents a key paper, "Voltage Controlled Electronic Music Modules," at the 16th Annual Convention of the Audio Engineering Society
	Max Mathews authors classic paper on theory of digital music synthesis, "The Technology of Computer Music"
	Manfred Schroeder authors first paper on algorithms for digital reverberation
	John Chowning creates FM synthesis by modulating the frequency of one oscillator by another (later used in first Yamaha synthesizers)
	Jean-Claude Risset first to use wave shaping or nonlinear distortion in music synthesis (later used in the Casio CZ-series synthesizers)
	The Mellotron offers an early form of a sampling keyboard using magnetic-taped sounds linked to a keyboard
1970s	First example of minicomputer synthesis produced by Barry Vercoe in his implementation of Mathews MUSIC 4 on a PDP computer
	Allen Organ introduces the first digital organ, based on Philips digital tone generators with sampled recordings of selected acoustic pipes
	Formant wave function (FOF) synthesis is developed by Xavier Rodet as part of IRCAM's CHANT project exploring the realistic synthesis of the human voice
	James Moorer produces unique computer-generated 3-D analyses of music waveforms
	Harry Mendell designs the Melodian sampling synthesizer used by Stevie Wonder
	Alonso, Jones, and Appleton develop the Synclavier, a stand-alone music workstation using FM and digital synthesis
	Fairlight Computer Music Instrument (CMI) is introduced as a digital-sampling music workstation with software, eight simultaneous voices, real-time sequencers, and the Music Composition Language (CML)
	First digital music introduced for Apple II (MMI DAC Board) and Commodore PET, based on "Techniques for Computer Performance of Music" by Hal Chamberlin (BYTE, September, 1977)
	First commercial digital tape recorders appear
1980s	First digital editing software for PCs appears (MMI Envelope Construction and Mountain Music Systems)
	AlphaSyntauri introduces the first sophisticated digital system for a PC
	Ensoniq sound chip (Q-chip) is one of the first sophisticated music synthesizers on a chip used in the Mirage sampling keyboard and the Apple IIGS computer
	Raymond Kurzweil creates a high-end sampling keyboard using artificial intelligence to produce authentic instrument sounds
	The first mass-market sampling keyboards are produced by E-mu Systems
	The first sampling drum machine appears as the SP12 from E-mu Systems, followed by the Casio RZI
	Martin Prevel's Melocaptor is one of the first PC-based pitch extractors and sight-singing teaching devices; Prevel went on to start AdLib to build PC sound cards
	Introduction of CD optical storage
1985	First 8- and 16-bit sampling cards for PCs available: Ensoniq, Proteus, Digidesign, and others

	Commodore Amiga PC, a high-quality digital-sampling and high-resolution graphics computer, is introduced
	The NeXT computer is announced, with DSP chips for professional-quality digital synthesis
	The Digidesign Sound System offers the first 16-bit direct-to-disk sampling for PCs
1990s	The first direct-to-disk recording system for the PC is introduced as the the IMS Dyaxis
	Integrated sequencer-and-sampling software appears for the PC: Digital Performer, Studio Vision, Cubase, and others
1995	Opcode's Studio Vision software permits software translation from digital audio to MIDI and back to digital audio
	Introduction of DVD optical storage for home video
	Multitrack digital audio I/O hardware like the Layla and the Korg 1212I/O cards make possible the first home digital audio workstations
	Writeable CD discs become common hardware in computer workstations
	RealAudio, developed by Rob Glaser and RealNetworks, Inc., provides an efficient compression format and streaming audio for distributing stereo music with comparatively small file sizes over the Internet
	The upper limit of resolution for digital audio jumps to a 24-bit sample size and a 96-KHz sampling rate
2000	Specialized music and audio hardware disappear to be replaced by software solutions for such items as mixers, effects generators, and sound cards; every computer workstation can be easily transformed into a software-based digital audio workstation with multiple tracks of digital input and output
	DVD playable and recordable discs become the de facto industry standard for laser strorage, and the cost of DVD technology becomes cheap enough to replace audio and videotape technologies for recording and distribution

THE PEOPLE

REAL-WORLD PROFILE #1:   DR. MAX MATHEWS

Role: Researcher at the CCRMA music research lab at Stanford University; professor, writer, and inventor of new music instruments

Dr. Mathews is one of the most distinguished scientists of sound engineering and music instrument design today and is often referred to as "the Father of Digital Music." After his training in electrical engineering, he joined Bell Labs in 1955 and developed some of the first computer composition software, MUSIC and GROOVE. He has written many significant books and articles on computer music, including the books *The Technology of Computer Music* and *Current Directions in Computer Music Research*, co-authored with John Pierce. His recent research links real-time conducting gestures with

Max Mathews playing his radio drum
(Photo by Patte Wood)

electronic instruments, and he has collaborated with Boulez and others on this topic. The MIDI Radio Baton and his Conductor expressive sequencer are his current work at Stanford University.

Interview:

What do you do? I am an engineer (and an amateur violinist) who invents new musical instruments, instruments that involve the computer. While at Bell Labs we created the MUSIC and GROOVE computer-aided composition software to program the digital computer music systems I designed. Most recently I invented the Radio Baton, a MIDI instrument, and an "expressive sequencer" called *Conductor*. The only instrument I created that didn't use a computer was an electronic violin.

How did you become interested in computers and music technology? My career started at Bell Labs in the late 1950s. We were using computers to simulate telephones with digital-to-analog and analog-to-digital synthesis of speech. I did the practical part of building digital circuits and connecting them to computers. This was very successful for telephony research. But a wonderful by-product was that all I needed to do was write a software program and this equipment could play music. Since we had the sampling theorem, we knew that this was a perfectly general source of sound and had the potential for making any sound and any music that the human ear can hear.

Bell Labs must have been a very creative place to work in the late '50s? I was fortunate to be involved in what some call the Golden Age of Bell Labs. One of the strong points of Bell Labs is the interaction: people talk and listen and help each other.

What reflections do you have thinking back to these first experiments with digital music just 30 years ago, given how everything is digital sampling now? The most dramatic example of that is at Paris and IRCAM. When Boulez first set up IRCAM his intentions were that only a quarter of the emphasis would be on digital computer music; today it is very close to 100 percent.

What computers do you use? My main computer is the PC [Wintel]. Most of what I am doing now I can run on most any small computer: UNIX workstations, IBMs, and Apples. The languages that I use are more interesting. I write almost all my code in the C language in a DOS environment. UNIX is a bad environment for real-time work like music performance since it continuously interrupts all the processes for resource allocation.

Ways you use computers and music technology? I use computers primarily for programming and the development work that I do with computers and music instruments. I'm working on my Conductor program, which I call an "expressive sequencer." The sequence of notes to be played is in the computer's memory much like any other sequencer, but when you play it back the performance is controlled by the batons—my MIDI Radio batons—that the performer moves, wiggles, or beats time with. I think the expressive part is an important addition to the world of sequencers. This is the primary project I am working on at this time. When the phone rang for our interview, I was in the process of porting Conductor to a Macintosh, which is easy since it is written in C.

At a College Music Society Conference in San Diego, you mentioned a unique database project you were working on. Could you tell us about that? Yes, that is a music archive called the International Digital Archive of Electric Acoustic Music. We want to digitize the important taped music that only exists as a recording so it will be preserved, we think, indefinitely. The technology for this is pretty straightforward; the media that we are currently planning to put the digitized information on is recordable CD-ROM. The reason we think that this will be a much more secure and long-lived way of storing the information is not that the CD-ROMs have an infinite life, but the fact that you can use error-correcting codes and recopy the information exactly as many times as you want. I think there's no question that this is the form of preserving archives for the future.

The one most used music device connected to your computer? I've used a variety of synthesizers, but the ones I enjoy the most now are the E-mu synthesizers. I think, however, that there is a big step ahead that will happen shortly. The sound sources or sample files will be stored on the computer disks or in memory rather than on the synthesizers. This will be very important because one can store so much more sound in a computer sound file and because it is easier to record your own sounds from there. This may not sound like much of a technical change, but I think actually it will be a musical revolution. There will be more flexibility in the realm of what sounds a performer or composer can draw upon: recordings of live instrumentalists, a particular passage, concrete sounds, purely synthesized sounds that can all be put into disk form. All the transformations of samples that are done currently on synthesizers can be done on sound files, and probably a lot more. All the hardware for this is available now; we are just waiting for the software to catch up.

The one most significant change 10 years from now? Certainly real-time performance with computers is going to be the biggest thing. Music is all going to be made live.

One word of advice you have for musicians interested in computers? Get as strong a background as you are capable of in computer technology so that you are comfortable with computers.

Down to the programming level? No, I wouldn't say that. There are many people who can use the commercial applications. That is a very useful way for them to use computers, and it will get more so as more applications are developed. I can't even say that composers ought to learn programming; I think it does open big possibilities for innovations to anyone that can do it.

Libby Larsen in rehearsal
(Courtesy of Libby Larsen)

REAL-WORLD PROFILE #2:   LIBBY LARSEN

Role: Composer and teacher of music composition

Dr. Larsen is a freelance composer based in Minneapolis. She is well-known for her compositions, which integrate electronic technology into the traditional repertoire of the concert hall and stage. Her orchestral piece *Ghost of an Old Ceremony* and her chamber orchestra piece *Schönberg, Schenker, and Schillinger*, illustrate how she uses an Emax digital sampler to expand the traditional sound lexicon of the orchestra. Her works include chamber pieces, symphonies, choral works, and opera. She has

received commissions from the Los Angeles Chamber Orchestra, the Minnesota Orchestra, the St. Louis Symphony, and the American Composers Orchestra. Libby uses her Macintosh for word processing, orchestration, postcompositional notation of her scores, and experimentation and design of new digital timbres. She still feels that the music keyboard, with lots of manuscript paper and pencils, best facilitates her creative process when composing.

Interview

What do you do? I am a composer, a composer who works within the traditional bounds of the concert hall and stage through symphonies, opera, and choral works, as well as chamber and recital music. My compositions can be programmed alongside the traditional classic repertoire; the uniqueness I contribute is creating new instruments, new digitally sampled sounds beyond the traditional lexicon of music sound, and combining this new sound with traditional sounds.

I especially like to work with mass-market digital instruments like the Emax II keyboard sampler. To create new sounds I can either build new digital samples from scratch, or I can take a micro-element of an existing sound and use it as the basis for a new sound. In one of my orchestral pieces, *Ghost of an Old Ceremony*, which has a major sampler part in it, all the sound is created sound. For example, one of the banks in the Emax sampler was programmed with sounds made from two pieces of glass clinking together. We looked into the glass-clinking waveforms and found a beautiful ostinato. There were wonderful details in that sound that could be amplified and isolated to create music.

How did you become interested in computers and music technology? In 1972 I had a teaching assistantship in acoustics with the physics department at the University of Minnesota. I soon discovered the School of Music's electronic music studio with its original Buchla synthesizer, two reel-to-reel tape decks, and a good supply of splicing tape and razor blades. I was truly interested in sound, the properties of sound, and the composers who were looking at sound for its potential in our culture beyond what we knew as the traditional instruments at that time (e.g., Varèse, Cowell, Schaeffer, and Cage). I saw the use of electronic instruments as one of the tidal waves of the future. I wanted to compose for the concert hall and bide my time and wait until those who were really interested in the technology of it had developed these instruments. That took about ten years to happen; ten very fast years! When the Emax II sampler became available, I received a Bush fellowship to study with Morton Subotnick. Subotnick is always on the cutting edge of what is possible in music technology. Since then all of my works have been influenced by what's possible to do with sampled sound.

What computers do you use? I work strictly on Macintosh.

Ways you use computers and music technology? Postcompositional tool for notation and an orchestrating tool; construction of new digital sounds with my MIDI Emax sampler; and word processing. I do my sketches with Finale and then work with a Finale expert to prepare the score for publication. I never rely on the computer to listen to my music. I insist on being able to hear everything I compose in my head, fully mixed.

If you could change one thing about how computers are used, what it would be? Composers need to be in direct contact with the engineers who design music software and hardware. With a strong dialog between composer and engineer, I think we can find better ways for the computer to access realistic acoustic sounds in playback, and address what I call the "physicality" factors in using a computer for composing. We need better natural acoustic sound samples to work with and we need tools that simulate for us such things as ensemble balance, dynamics, and room acoustics. We also need computer tools that don't physically get in the way of the creative process, simulating more closely what a composer does when sketching by hand on manuscript paper. Whether we realize it or not, the use of the whole body is actually part of the composer's skill.

I find that the computer screen (I have a two-page screen), the computer keyboard, and the MIDI keyboard limit an inherent physicality that is a part of composition: they create a delay between my thoughts, the keyboard, and the manuscript page. The thinking that goes on within that motion-time

of playing a gesture on the keyboard and writing the notation on the page is infinite and it is important that the computer not get in the way of this. The size of the screen, too, limits a composer's perception of music moving through time. That's why I use Finale as a postcompositional tool after I have done my sketches by hand on paper.

Let me give you an example. There is a curious phenomenon I see when I work with beginning students of composition. Range and balance are severely limited when students first work at the computer. When they begin to write for strings, they need to quickly move above the staff, use doublings, shift clefs, and so on. But, the notation software provides too small a space for this to happen easily; the default space between the staves is too small. Students don't know how to work around this. We really need premade software templates to help them around the "physical" constraints which the software is placing on their creative efforts.

The one most significant change 10 years from now? You know, I think that societies evolve the musical instruments they need. What has happened since 1950 is a whole new evolution of electric guitars, synthesizers, recording studios, and digital representation of sound. I suspect that the symphony orchestra, perhaps by the middle of the next century—those orchestras that are current with their own evolution—will have an electronic section of some kind. It may be a mixing board, it may be a grouping of speakers, it may a grouping of keyboards and computers. The orchestra over the last 500 years has simply added groups of instruments that have evolved with the century; orchestral music and its ensembles will evolve, as well, to include the current electronic technology.

One word of advice you have for musicians interested in computers? If you want to be a composer, get any kind of job you can with a sound studio. Do anything you can to be around commercial studios, much as I did as a graduate assistant at the University of Minnesota. You need to be around the studios where all the research and development of new instruments are taking place.

Module 23

Software for Capturing, Editing, and Organizing Digital Sounds

In Viewport VI, we studied MIDI as a way to create music. We used software on a computer, together with MIDI instruments, to generate sound. We did the same thing in Viewport V when we viewed, printed, and listened to music rendered by music notation software. In Viewport III, we used digitized sound in CAI software, as well as excerpts from audio CDs and MIDI instruments, as we explored resources for teaching music. In each of these cases, the sounds were already made. They were either provided with the software or produced by devices like CD players, DVD players, and MIDI sound modules or keyboard synthesizers.

Remember that the term "digital audio" refers to sound that is represented by a series of numbers. The numbers represent complex analog sounds that our ear and brain perceive as they unfold in time. Hardware converters (analog-to-digital and digital-to-analog) are used to record, store, process, and play back digital audio. The quality of this sound is dependent on both the sampling rate and the resolution of the digital recording.

Review Modules 10 and 11 for information on acoustics and digital audio. You can look ahead to Modules 24 and 26 for more advanced digital audio topics as well.

We have discussed capturing digital audio, also referred to as "sampling" sound. But a closely related concept that we have not presented yet is "sound design." Sound design refers to those procedures that result in the shaping or "sculpting" of sound for a special need or effect after the initial sample has been obtained. Because sound is captured in digital form, the numbers can be easily altered to change any of the dimensions of sound such as envelope, frequency, harmonic spectrum, and so on.

In this module, we turn our attention to software that allows musicians to actually create, edit, and organize their own sounds and to "design" sounds. We will stress the importance of understanding digital audio techniques in today's music culture. A set of tasks will be defined and we will sort out how each task might be solved with different kinds of digital audio software.

Why Digital Sounds?

Digital audio is the most pervasive method used today to represent sound and music. The sound effects that you hear at the basketball game and the sound bites that come over the radio are all digitally recorded, shaped, and played back. The sounds that come from your multimedia software are all digitally recorded and edited. Even broadcast television is using digital resources more and more. Soon, all televised sound and visual images will come to our homes in digital form.

Perhaps the most important use of digital audio for musicians is rooted in the commercial sales of recordings. Full-length music albums in all styles of music are frequently recorded digitally, either directly to special hard disk systems as we explain in Module 26 or to digital tape. These recordings are edited and processed digitally and then finally transferred to compact discs in digital form, ready for the consumer's CD or DVD player. It's quite likely that the disc you buy at your favorite music store has been entirely produced with digital audio techniques.

Here are a few key reasons for the enormous interest in digital audio today:

▶ *Flexibility.* Digital information can be easily edited and processed.

▶ *Convenience.* Access to any point in a digital recording is instantaneous.

▶ *Clarity.* The quality of digital sound can exceed the limits of human hearing.

▶ *Longevity.* Digital recordings have an extremely long life span.

▶ *Affordability.* Today's computers come with digital audio hardware and software.

Common Tasks Using Digital Audio and Sound Design

See Module 12 for a review of the distinctions between sample players, samplers, synthesizers, and so on. You will see with the KISS digital audio system presented in Module 26 that you can also do all of this inside the computer itself with multichannel digital audio hardware.

In order to give you an overall understanding of digital audio, how you might capture, edit, organize, and design digital sounds and music for your professional work, we will describe four tasks that you could easily do yourself with a modest amount of hardware and software. Each task is taken from work done every day by hundreds of people in music performance and recording, sound engineering, multimedia development, and education. We will guide you through the kinds of software that might be appropriate for each task we describe. If you study this material closely, you will emerge with an excellent understanding of what can be accomplished with digital sound using only modest resources.

In order to give the tasks a sense of continuity, we will assume that you have been hired by a theater company to supply sound for a play being produced. As sound engineer, you are expected to create, edit, and organize the audio necessary for all aspects of the production.

We will assume that you own some basic equipment for these tasks. You have a PC with at least 64 megabytes of memory, a 6-gigabyte hard drive, a CD or DVD player, and a removable disk drive for extra storage.

You also own two MIDI devices to help accomplish this work. The first is a keyboard sampler such as E-mu's E-Synth or EIV in the tradition of the old Emulator and Mirage keyboards. This device should accept sample data directly into its SCSI or MIDI ports from a computer, or through the digital I/O ports provided with high-end samplers and synthesizers. It should also

HISTORICAL PERSPECTIVE

We are all familiar with the sounds of traditional musical instruments such as those in the brass, woodwind, string, and percussion families. These sounds are produced naturally by vibrating materials of one form or another and are most often played without any form of electricity or sound amplification. We have come to appreciate the wonderful sounds they produce. But what of sounds that come from electronic sources? It may be tempting to assume that such sounds are quite recent. After all, devices like computers, MIDI-equipped keyboards, and DVD players have come to us in just the last few years. Actually, experiments with electronically produced sound and the use of such sounds for aesthetic purposes can be traced to the late nineteenth century.

Early Sound Synthesis

Building on the work of Joseph Sauveau a century before, during the 1800s Jean Fourier and Hermann von Helmholtz studied overtones and complex waveforms. These individuals were interested in the physics of sound, especially as it applied to

musical instruments. They dealt with a basic principle of sound construction, the harmonic series, which was at the heart of Thaddeus Cahill's construction of the Telharmonium in 1906. Cahill used electric dynamos running at different rates of speed, producing sine waves. These waves were synchronized and fed into telephone lines so people could hear complex waveforms produced at the other end of the line. He found that if he could vary these generators just right, he could produce reasonable representations of

Dynamos and wires for Cahill's Telharmonium and a view of two performers at the keyboard in the upper right-hand corner
(From "New Music for an Old World" by R. Baker, McClure's Magazine, 1906)

common complex waveforms. An organ keyboard and foot pedal were used to manage pitch and volume. For a monthly fee, subscribers could choose to hear the music over their phone lines!

Although the experiment failed as a commercial venture, Cahill demonstrated effective electronic control over timbre. In fact, in 1929, Laurens Hammond used a similar but vastly more efficient system in his now famous Hammond organ. Other interesting experiments with electronic performance instruments followed from 1930 to 1950, using some form of either additive or subtractive synthesis to create sound by altering harmonics and amplitude.

Electronic Music Studios

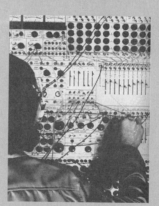

Modules and patch cords on a Buchla installation
(Reproduced by permission of Don Buchla)

In the early 1950s, more complex solutions were built in electronic music studios like the NWDR in Cologne, the RTF in Paris, and the RAI in Milan. Studios in the United States were typically formed at universities, such as Illinois and Columbia-Princeton. Important composers who worked in such studios included Babbitt, Davidovsky, Hiller, Luening, Maderna, Stockhausen, Ussachevsky, and Varèse. Edgar Varèse's *Poeme Electronique* (1958), Stockhausen's *Kontakte* (1959-60), and John Cage's *Fontana Mix* (1956–1958) came out of these studios. Important new techniques were established that have now become standard fare for sound synthesis. Instead of crude generators to produce sound, these studios used specially designed oscillators, filters, and ring modulators to create effects. To capture and further treat sounds, tape recorders were used and special techniques, such as playing sounds backwards or creating tape loops, were developed.

The Voltage-Controlled Music Synthesizer

The voltage-controlled music synthesizer became the staple of analog sound synthesis during the 1960s and 1970s. Most notable were the Moog and Buchla synthesizers. These devices were self-contained integrated systems designed to create synthesized sound. Most had music keyboards and were programmable by use of knobs, switches, and patch cords to connect internal components. Building on the concepts developed in the big electronic studios of the day, the voltage-controlled synthesizer became a popular instrument for smaller studios and school settings. These instruments were the forerunners of today's digital synthesizer. A typical voltage-controlled music synthesizer, like the Buchla pictured earlier, would have a voltage-controlled oscillator (VCO) as a sound source controlled by other voltage-controlled devices like amplifiers (VCAs), filters (VCFs), and envelope generators. The sound could then be processed and mixed with effects like reverberation, filtering, and equalization. The final sound could be part of a live performance or, more typically, saved to analog tape for use in a composition. Morton Subotnick used the Buchla for his famous *Silver Apples of the Moon* (1967), and Wendy Carlos used the Moog to create the first popular electronic recording, *Switched-On Bach* (1968). These instruments were joined by ones produced by other companies like Arp (with their classic Arp 2600 voltage-controlled system), Korg, Oberheim, Roland, and Sequential Circuits (with their classic Prophet-5 synthesizer).

Digital Synthesis: A New Era

At the same time that the famous electronic music studios were being formed in the 1950s, others were working on an entirely different approach to creating and manipulating sound. Max Mathews, musician and engineer, was conducting experiments at Bell Labs using computers to convert analog speech to digital representation and back again in order to study telephone communications. He found this sound sampling technology also worked well for generating music waveforms and composing music. The reasoning went something like this: instead of using analog oscillators and envelope generators to produce sounds electronically and then manipulate them still further with filters and mixers, why not use a computer to sample or create basic analog waveforms digitally, and then manipulate the numbers for the desired effect? Mathews and others created computer programs designed to do just this. Music software programs like Mathews' MUSIC IV and GROOVE are examples of this kind of computer-music application. Subroutines in this software replicated some of the basic analog processes like those used in Moog and Buchla synthesizers. Such an approach had an immediate appeal over analog synthesis. More control could be exercised over pitch materials, and sampling allowed a faithful representation of many complex waveforms. The immediate access to sounds and their editing was also seen as an improvement, eliminating some of the cumbersome physical problems of analog tape. Risset composed *Mutations I* (1969) using MUSIC V at Bell Labs. Vercoe composed *Synthesism* in the same year at the Princeton University lab using MUSIC 360, a programming language that ran much faster than older digital composition programs. Throughout the 1960s and 1970s, digital electronic music was only possible at larger studios with ample resources. Digital encoding of high-quality sound placed huge demands on storage space and required large, expensive computers for processing. For this reason, both analog and digital systems coexisted until the technology improved.

Fairlight Computer Musical Instrument in the Luther College music lab
(Photography by Julie Strom)

Digital Synthesizers Come of Age

The technology did improve, and more modular instruments were built. Through the 1970s and 1980s, storage became more affordable and chip design put more powerful electronic circuitry into smaller and cheaper packages. Two basic types of digital synthesizers emerged to carry on the tradition begun by the voltage-controlled devices. Digital samplers were designed to be used as a major platform for sound sampling. Once sampled, the sounds could then be used in many creative ways. The other type was manufactured with many preset waveforms digitally encoded and was designed to be used as the basis for sound synthesis. These instruments also added their own special techniques such as FM and waveshaping synthesis. Today we call these *synthesizers*. The Synclavier and Fairlight systems designed in the 1970s were

Yamaha DX7 keyboard synthesizer
(Courtesy of Yamaha Corporation, Japan, and Yamaha Corporation of America)

some of the first commercial sampler workstations. They contained powerful programmable digital technology, including sampling capabilities and waveform editing. These devices also broke new ground by having real-time capabilities. Musicians could experiment with changes in synthesis design and hear the results of these changes immediately. Certain models could be used in performance situations as well as studios. Jon Appleton's *Georganna's Farewell* was written for an early version of the Synclavier; the Fairlight is still actively used in many major motion picture and recording studios.

Both the Synclavier and the Fairlight were priced beyond the reach of most musicians. The early 1980s saw the development of two affordable keyboards that placed emphasis on sound sampling, the E-mu Emulator and the Ensoniq Mirage. These devices did not have the computer-music capabilities of Synclaviers and Fairlights but did have a MIDI sequencer and excellent sampling technology. To this day, the sampler keyboard offers the musician a very powerful device for sound creation. This type of keyboard sampler (like the Emax) is used by composers like Libby Larsen (see the interview that begins this module) for concert music and by many artists performing and composing popular music. Digital synthesizers also continued to develop. The Yamaha DX7 was most popular in the mid-1980s, offering a digital approach to FM-sound synthesis; also very popular was the Casio CZ-series, offering phase-distortion synthesis. As costs fell and MIDI became more pervasive, other digital synthesizers continued to be marketed. Most now use digital samples of instrumental timbres as the basis for sound synthesis. The designs and metaphors used in hardware and software available today for music sampling and synthesis reflect the evolution from the electronic studios of the 1950s, the voltage-controlled techniques of the 1960s, the first computer-generated music and digital sampling in the 1950s and 1960s, and the first commercial workstations for music in the 1970s.

E-Mu Emax keyboard sampler
(Courtesy of E-Mu Systems, Inc.)

be capable of recording live sound from a microphone. The second device is a sound module synthesizer such as Korg's NS5R that has several preset orchestral timbres and sound effects built in. This second unit is similar to devices in the tradition of the Yamaha TX81Z, but much more recent. The preset sounds are based on digital samples of traditional instruments, and the synthesizer is capable of creating unique sounds by changing settings.

Table 23.1 Tasks Using Software for Creating, Editing, and Organizing Sound

Task Description	Types of Computer Software	Sound Source
1. Extended speech added to music	Multitrack, direct-to-disk recording	Computer
2. Live vocal mixed with taped music	Multitrack, direct-to-disk recording: synchronized to digital movie	Computer advanced features
3. Excerpts from audio CDs	CD to hard disk transfer	Computer
4. Newly designed sounds	Sound synthesis	Computer, keyboard sampler, and sound module synthesizer

This sound module synthesizer is a rack-mounted unit and, of course, has no keyboard.

Both of your MIDI units are connected to your computer with a standard MIDI interface and cables. Your only software for creating, organizing, and editing sound is what came with the computer's operating system, but you do have a budget to buy a few more software titles. You're also able to borrow some additional hardware from other sources.

Let's now take a closer look at the tasks. You have met with the director of the play and have been given your orders. Table 23.1 offers a brief description of the kind of work you must do and the resources needed. The first three tasks are largely computer based, with digital audio editing software. These are the most common tasks in digital sound work. The last task uses a sampling device together with the computer.

The Tasks. The first three tasks require you to digitize or capture segments of sound directly to disk. In Task 1, passages of digitized speech must be combined with some simple background music from an audio tape. The speech needs to be treated with a few special effects and blended in interesting ways with the music.

Task 2 is similar, but requires far more from the software. The director wants you to record a *voice-over* with a singer and a prerecorded analog tape. This doesn't seem too complicated until you learn that the soloist is to be the mayor of your town, accompanied by a recording of his daughter's school orchestra! The director points out that you may need to *process* the file in order to make it sound acceptable (the mayor has not provided a very good recording). Sections may need to be moved around, filtering techniques applied, and some timings and pitches changed. What makes it even more demanding is that the sound file must be synchronized with a digital movie!

Task 3 calls for several extended *cuts* from standard audio CDs. The director has given you these resources, and the excerpts must be isolated and transferred to disk for immediate playback.

Finally, you've been asked to produce some chilling, echoing laughter effects. You have nothing appropriate to work from on your synthesizer, so Task 4 requires you to create a totally new sound using your sampler and computer.

ASIDE

Copyright, of course, would be a concern here, when one borrows music from a commercial CD.

Preparing for Computer-Based Digital Audio Editing

Make sure your PC's audio system is a full-duplex system permitting you to play music and capture music at the same time. Laptops, especially, are often only half-duplex audio.

For the first three tasks, you will use the computer to do the sampling work. Although most computers today come ready to do this from the factory, some tips for preparing your computer to manage incoming sound are in order. You will need to check a few settings in your system software to be sure that the computer understands that sound will be coming in. This is similar to what needed to be done before we could use MIDI input.

Wintel Machines. In Viewport VI, Module 19, we explained how the multimedia standards allow manufacturers to supply driver software for the Windows system to help with the flow of MIDI data using the sound card. This is also the case for managing digital audio. In fact, sequencer software that incorporates both MIDI and digital sound uses these drivers as well.

To prepare your computer for sound input, you might also check the settings for sound management that can be found in software supplied by the manufacturer of your sound card. Figure 23.1 is a sample of one such program. Your particular Wintel computer may have a different program.

Reading from left to right in Figure 23.1a, we have three volume controls for overall sound (including treble and bass), a control for the internal wavetable sound, MIDI, CD, line-in audio, and microphone. These last three settings will be important when you use the card to sample sound from the CD, an external device like a tape deck, and live voice. Notice the small buttons under the icons. The one to the right in each set controls whether sound is sent to the board. The one to the left passes sound through to the speakers so you can hear what you are recording. The visual display to the right monitors the sound being recorded. Figure 23.1b is a recording settings dialog box that is part of this same software. These direct sounds to one channel or the other. An important setting in this window is the gain control level, which boosts volume level during recording. You will probably want to boost the gain and also select the Automatic Gain Control (AGC) to get the best results when you digitize speech.

It may be that your application software will have commands that duplicate these settings from the sound card manufacturer. Check both possibilities as you work with digital sound on Wintel computers.

Figure 23.1
Creative Mixer
(Creative Labs [Windows])

Macintosh Machines. Similar system software exists for Macintosh computers. In Viewport VI, we discussed the Apple MIDI Manager and Opcode's

(*a*) Master mixing control

(*b*) Recording settings

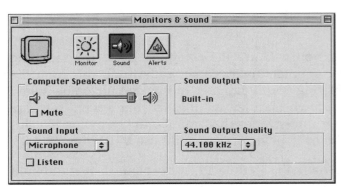

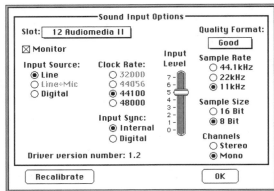

(a) Monitors and sound options

(b) Digidesign sound options for Audiomedia III card

Figure 23.2
Sound management
within the Macintosh

OMS, which act as system management software for MIDI. Apple also provides system-level software called the Sound Manager, which is similar in function to the mixer application for Wintel machines, for working with digital sound. The Sound Manager supports 16-bit stereo sound at 44 KHz and also works as a system extension to support other manufacturers' sound cards such as Digidesign's Audiomedia II and III. Links between the audio CD, the speaker ports, and internal circuitry are also handed by the Sound Manager.

Figure 23.2 displays important elements of this extension. If you use the built-in sound capabilities of your Mac, you will want to choose the Monitors and Sound control panel and select sound (a). Here you can set options for sound in and out. If you have a special sound card installed such as an Audiomedia card, the system probably will detect the presence of the sound driver that was installed when you added your card. For our example here, we have installed an Audiomedia card, and its Options box appears as Figure 23.2b. Note the many options that the special card offers, including direct digital input from a digital audio tape or other digital source.

Multitrack Recording and Sound Editing: Tasks 1–3

Now that the computer is ready to sample sound, you need software to complete Tasks 1 and 2. Recall that for Task 1, you need to sample some simple background music and then add speech. This will require only basic-level software with standard features. Task 2 also requires sampling two tracks of sound, one for the recording of the school orchestra and the other for the mayor's vocal performance. For this task you need some fairly sophisticated capabilities because of the need to process the sound to enhance its quality and perhaps to cover errors in the performance. You also need to coordinate the music with a digital movie.

We have carefully reviewed a number of Macintosh and Windows software titles for you and have indentified two feature sets: basic and advanced (see Table 16.1 in Module 16). Table 23.2 outlines the differences between these different levels of capabilities. As with other software module tables in

Table 23.2 Basic and Advanced Features of Sampling Software

Basic Features	Advanced Features
Entry and Display	
Windows for waveforms with zoom options	Pre-allocation of contiguous disk space
Controls for playback and record	Multiple views of wave data
Record level meters	Scrubbing
Basic format settings for rate, resolution, and mode (stereo, mono)	Fast Fourier Transform (FFT) displays and other views for spectral analysis
Ability to import standard sound files	
Minimum of two tracks, often more	
Editing	
Cut/copy/paste	Nondestructive editing (playlist)
Crop or trim	Time compression and expansion
Add silence	Graphic and parametric equalization
Offset or sliding of tracks	Filtering (low-pass, high-pass, noise)
Reversing wave (play backwards)	Envelope (amplitude and pitch)
Amplify	Normalize
Pitch change	Reverberation
Echo	Delay (one echo cycle)
Swap channels	Pencil editing and other assists for loop construction
Pan	Ability to hear changes in real time
Fade in and out	Add-on modules
Saving and Playback	
Mix (merge)	Advanced synchronization (MIDI and SMPTE)
Conversion of rates, resolution, and mode	Support for digital movies
Support of basic sound formats	Support for downloading to samplers
	Support for many file formats

Software activity: "Creating and Editing Music on Your Computer with SoundEdit 16, Peak LE, or Sound Forge XP"

this book, we organize the features into input (entry and display), editing, saving, and playback features. This is a rough guide. The more advanced features are contained in more expensive software designed for professional use, although some of these more advanced features may be found in all the available products.

For the examples that follow, we have selected six products: BIAS's Peak LE, Macromedia's SoundEdit 16, Sonic Foundry's Sound Forge, Digidesign's Sound Designer II, SEK'D's Samplitude Studio, and Steinberg's WaveLab. Each of these programs is designed to capture and edit digital audio up to the limits of available disk space. Sound Forge, Sound Designer II, Samplitude Studio, and WaveLab support most of the basic and advanced features, while the other titles offer somewhat fewer capabilties. You will find any one of these products quite useful for most of the work with these tasks.

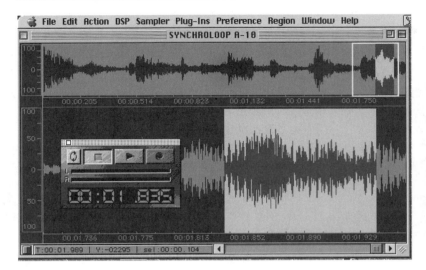

(a) Main recording window

(b) Record settings and monitor

Figure 23.3
Peak LE
(BIAS [Mac])

You may want to review information about sound format, rate, and size in Module 11 and more advanced ideas in Module 24.

Task 1: Basic Features with Music and Speech. Let's begin with entry and display features found in Peak; these are quite typical of most recording software. Figure 23.3 provides a view of the main recording window (a) and the dialog box for setting options for recording (b). Note the transport palette for controlling playback and recording. The window at the top shows an overview of the recording, and the window at the bottom displays an expanded view. You can zoom in on a very close view of the *waveform*. Waveform is a term that we will use throughout the module to refer to the visual representation of digital audio in a track.

Peak can record sounds from a microphone or import sounds from an audio CD. In the record dialog box (b), you can set the usual options for sound format, sample size, and rate. For speech sounds, you might want to choose mono, 22 KHz, and 8 bits to conserve space because speech does not require the full audio spectrum for most sounds. If you were recording music, however, mono or stereo formats at the highest rate and resolution are recommended for the best results. We have chosen those options here.

Note the handy reference for the amount of space that is available for your recording and the level meters that allow you to judge the strength of the incoming signal. If the signal is too loud, clipping will occur and distortion will result. This is particularly harsh in digital recording and must be avoided at all costs. Some of the more advanced software actually includes graphic indicators to mark the occurrence of clipping.

In addition to capturing live sound, nearly all audio software supports importing sound from another sound file. You can also record directly into the computer from an analog sound source like a tape recorder or the analog output from a synthesizer. These options might be handy if you have some nice effects from your keyboard sampler that you would like to add to the computer project.

Editing. You can accomplish many basic editing tasks with this software. You can easily cut, paste, and copy sounds and silences. Observe the two

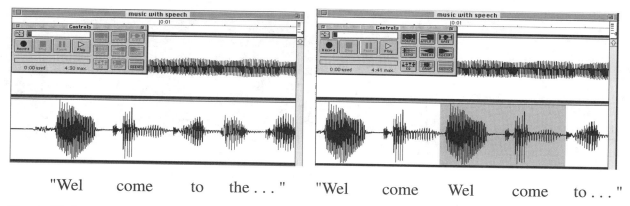

"Wel   come   to   the . . . "   "Wel   come   Wel   come   to . . . "

Figure 23.4
Cutting and pasting audio events using SoundEdit 16 (Macromedia [Mac])

Module 24 explains how to understand amplitude envelopes like those in Figures 23.4 and 23.5.

Some of these digital-signal processing (DSP) techniques were first presented in Module 19 when we were covering digital sound in sequencers. These will be discussed in more depth in Modules 24 and 25.

screens in Figure 23.4. Your work has begun on the speech track using SoundEdit 16. In the first screen to the left, we show the beginning of the phrase "Welcome to the beginning of Act II." Notice how the waveforms correspond with the syllables of the words. This works with music as well, with major accents and subordinate pulses identified with specific waveforms. It doesn't take long to learn to read how the software represents the sound visually. This makes editing easier.

The right screen shows how you can copy and paste in another "Welcome" right after the first. You also can crop or trim out the beginning silences. The Play button lets you check what you have selected with the mouse, and the zoom features let you isolate an exact beginning and ending point. It would also be easy to add a word here and there or perhaps change a few sentences around. It is so easy, in fact, that it raises legal and ethical questions about digital technology!

Other editing features are more dramatic. Figure 23.5 includes dialog boxes from Peak LE and SoundEdit 16 that support some of the common editing functions. You may want to add some gain to make certain words or phases louder or softer. This can be done with the gain and gain envelope controls (*a*) and (*b*). Two other important features are fading (*c*) and adding silence (*d*). You can fade your speech or music in or out, designating a region and establishing a magnitude of fade. It's also easy to add some silence. Finally, you can raise or lower part or all of the speech's pitch quite easily (*e*).

The other figures (*f*) and (*g*) display how these and other effects might look as you work. Screen (*f*) is the original and screen (*g*) is the edited version. Notice that you can amplify the top track (music), then fade it down as the speech enters. You can move the speech line over and add echo effects to the voice. Finally, you might raise the second "Welcome" a half step in pitch for added emphasis.

Another basic editing feature is the ability to reverse the waveform so that the original is played backwards. Some software includes an option for inverting the waveform. Waveforms can be switched from one channel or track to another, and the signal can be panned as well.

One last point: all these actions may be final in nature, or what is often referred to as "destructive" editing. This means that saving the file causes

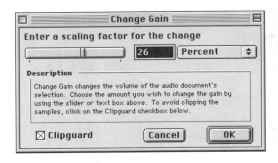

(a) Gain

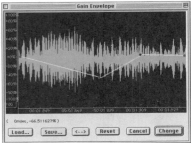

(b) Gain Envelope

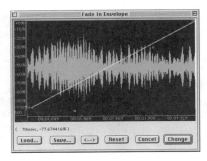

(c) Fade

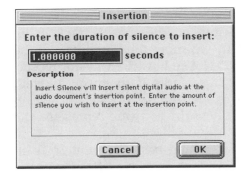

(d) Adding silence

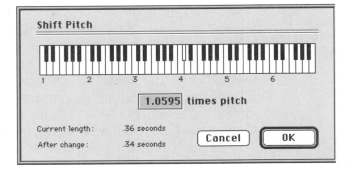

(e) Pitch shift

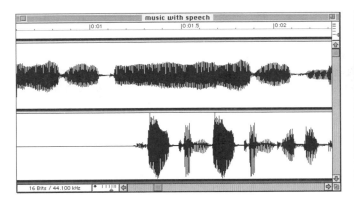

(f) Original version

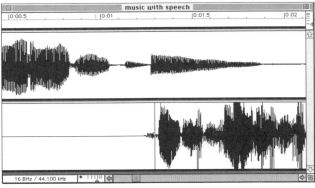

(g) Edited version

Figure 23.5
Other editing possibilities using Peak LE and SoundEdit 16: (a–d) Peak LE, (e–g) SoundEdit 16

the original data to be altered completely and finally. For this reason, you might want to keep several backups of work along the way.

Saving and playback. Options for saving and playback with basic software are straightforward. Most packages allow for many more than two tracks of digital data, but these tracks generally must be merged or mixed down into two for stereo playback. Unlike the case with conventional analog tape, you can merge as many tracks together as you wish without any degradation in sound quality.

Most software provides the ability to create a smaller-sized file after all the editing is finished. Conversions of this sort are accomplished by going from 44-KHz to 22-KHz or from 16-bit to 8- bit sound. Each of these conversion options saves disk space and may not change the sound significantly for certain applications. Most software saves files in the standard formats presented in Module 24.

Task 2: Advanced Features with Voice and Accompaniment. Task 2 is a bit more involved. The requirement is to sample an audio tape of a school orchestra that will form the accompaniment to a solo voice performance by the mayor. Once this is accomplished, the music must be added to the sound track of a digital movie. Both the voice performance and the tape will need to be edited for quality.

Entry and display. More advanced software offers a number of ways to view data. Figure 23.6 displays the scrubbing and pencil tools for careful editing in Sound Designer II. The scrubbing tool will allow you to listen to a portion of the waveform to hear exactly what is being viewed. We saw this in Viewport VI as an option for working with sequencing files as well. The window to the right shows a much more detailed view of the exact area being played. We are about to use the pencil tool to do some careful shaping of the waveform. This kind of detailed work is necessary for preparing loops for samplers as well as for careful editing in longer sound files.

Advanced editing. One of the most important features of more advanced digital audio software is the support of nondestructive editing. (It's called nondestructive editing because the original data are not fundamentally changed.) You will find this most helpful as you are working with the mayor's voice track. It is likely that the mayor will not sing through all the music correctly at any one time. If the recording session is like most, the singer will do several *takes*. You will record these each time and have several tracks of data to then *postproduce* after the singer has left

Figure 23.6
Specialized views of digital waveforms using Sound Designer II
(Macromedia, Inc. [Mac])

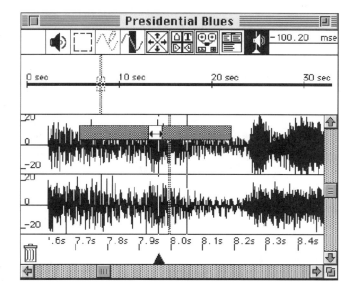
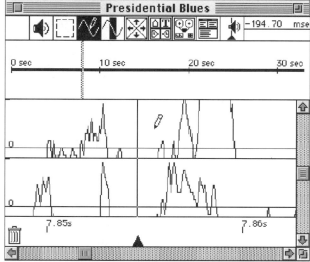

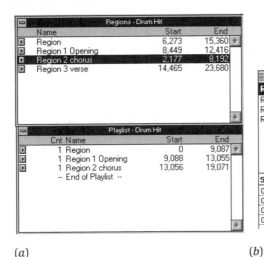

(a)

(b)

Figure 23.7
Playlists in nondestructive editing using Sound Forge (a) and Sound Designer II (b) (Sonic Foundry [Windows]; and Sound Designer II [Mac])

With virtual tracks you can preview several versions of the same track so that you can try out new effects and edits without destroying the original version. Much of today's hard disk recording software use this nondestructive approach.

See Module 24 for an explanation of various audio compression schemes.

the recording session. A *playlist* is a road map to these various virtual tracks so that the sections can be combined in a final edit or various clips can be "bounced" to a new virtual track to make the final version. Figure 23.7 provides examples of playlists from Sound Forge (a) and Sound Designer II (b). Notice that regions are defined and then ordered. Sound Designer offers different types of transitions between these regions.

It's likely that you will need to adjust the clock times of the two tracks in order to synchronize with the digital audio when it is added later. Advanced audio features offer powerful compression and expansion of musical material without changing fundamental pitch! Using the digital information in an intelligent way, the software is capable of adding and deleting samples within regions. Perhaps you might wish to extend the mayor's phrasing a little, or make a ritard in a certain spot. Figure 23.8a displays a dialog box in Sound Forge that allows these manipulations. Note the Preview button that allows you to hear what the data sound like after extension or compression.

The tape of the school orchestra is likely to have a good deal of hiss and background noise. This poor sound quality can be edited out of the mix by use of advanced software. Filtering as graphic and parametric equalization are standard fare. Figures 23.8b and c show settings for these options. Equalization allows you to highlight certain frequencies and not others; you probably have some sort of equalizer in your home stereo system. Here, it's part of the software.

Recall that envelopes refer to the shaping of the attack, decay, sustain, and release of a single or complex waveform in time (see Module 10). Sampling and editing software can help to do this digitally. Again, a region is chosen and the envelope can be adjusted for just that selection. Figure 23.8d displays a way to do this. You may need to use this in spots to control balance or to add a special effect.

Finally, we will mention a few other advanced editing possibilities that you might find useful:

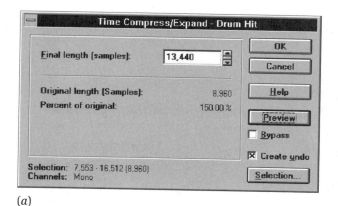

(a)

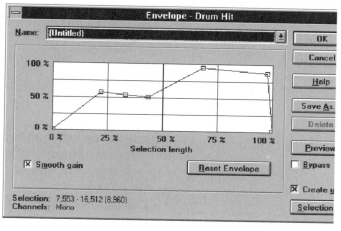

(b)

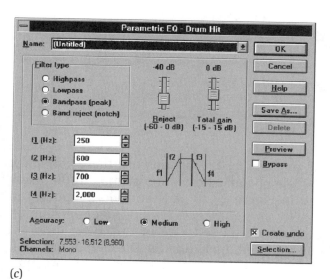

(c)

(d)

Figure 23.8
Advanced editing features using Sound Forge

▶ *Normalization.* This option amplifies sound to the maximum without causing distortion. The software studies the full spectrum of the region selected and adjusts everything in context.

▶ *Reverberation.* This feature adds subtle decay to the releases of sounds to produce a natural echo-like effect. The software simulates what the music might sound like in a particular kind of room.

▶ *Delay.* This is a special kind of echo that creates only one recurrence of the sound. The intensity and length of the echo can be set through software.

▶ *Pencil editing.* This feature allows the careful editing of sounds, especially if you are creating a loop that will be sent to a keyboard sampler. Advanced software features provides special transitions for loops so that they sound acceptable.

Figures 23.9 and 23.10 provide views of two more advanced editing programs, Samplitude Studio and WaveLab. These offer many of the more pow-

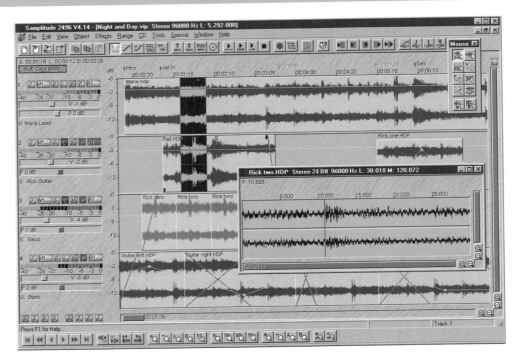

Figure 23.9
Samplitude Studio
(SEK'D [Windows])

erful features listed above and in Table 23.2. Programs like these will allow this kind of editing. Notice the use of sophisticated crossfading in the many support tracks of stereo sound in Figure 23.10 and the echo treatments in Figure 23.9.

One additional point about advanced software of this type: different plug-in architectures are often supported, including for Direct-X (Microsoft), VST (Cubase), and Premiere (Adobe). This means that even if the programs themselves do not contain an advanced feature that you want, it may be available by way of DSP plug-ins like BIAS's SFX Machine or Arboretum's Hyperprism.

Other powerful software packages for Wintel machines include the family of software from Innovative called SAW and the Cool Edit program from Syntrillium.

Saving and playback. Options for saving are much more plentiful with higher-end audio software. In addition to a greater variety of supported file formats and the ability to download files to samplers, advanced audio software will enable you either to add music to digital movies as sound tracks or to synchronize it in other ways using SMPTE. Figure 23.11 displays one approach, taken by SoundEdit 16. This software allows you to open a digital movie and edit the original sound track or add a new one. Notice that the various frames of the movie are displayed above the waveforms. You can set cue points in the movie that match sound tracks displayed below the movie. Dialog boxes, such as the one included here, help make this process easier. Once you have sampled and edited the sound track of the mayor and the accompanying orchestra, you can add it to the digital movie and further process the sound track.

More on SMPTE and time codes in Modules 20 and 22.

Figure 23.10
WaveLab
(Steinberg [Windows])

A word of caution for either you or your show's director: make sure that copyright and licensing agreements are in place for any digitized audio or video tracks that are legally owned by others.

Software Activity: "Recording and Editing a Music Clip from an Audio CD Using MoviePlayer"

This should be enough information for you to be able to complete Tasks 1 and 2. These direct-to-disk applications represent the major types of digital audio editing software for musicians.

Task 3: Extracting Excerpts from an Audio CD. Task 3 involves the extraction of excerpts from a number of audio CDs. When the director handed you the CDs with the music he had selected, your original plan might have been to play these excerpts directly from a CD player during the performance. Of course this might work, but it would be very awkward to do and be prone to error. There is a much better way to work. Each excerpt could be recorded directly into a digital sound file suitable for playback by a computer. Note that this really is not sampling, but more like transferring digital information from one medium to another.

Accomplishing this using the software that comes with your sound card on a Wintel machine is a snap. Figure 23.12 displays software that came with one of our Wintel machines. Notice that the CD Sync button is selected. When you find the selection you wish to record on the CD, you simply hit the Start button and the software starts the CD. You wait until the excerpt is over and then stop the recording and save the file.

Accomplishing the same thing on a Macintosh is just as simple. Using the QuickTime movie utility MoviePlayer, you can open any track of an audio CD just like a file, specify the area of the track to extract, and then ask that a file be made. Figure 23.13 shows this procedure, reading from left to right. MoviePlayer is widely distributed and is available from Apple's Internet site.

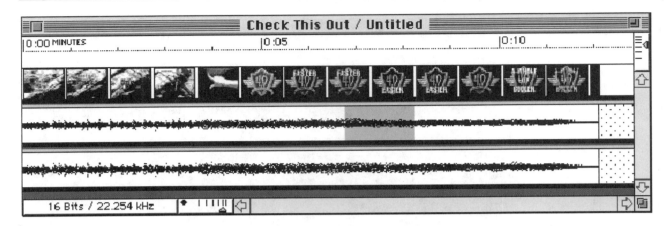

Figure 23.11
Synchronizing
sound files with
movies using
SoundEdit 16

The ability to capture audio from a CD is also built into almost all sound programs such as those reviewed here. Even sequencer packages reviewed in Viewport VI can do this.

Adding MIDI to Digital Audio Software

In Viewport VIII we will learn about other multimedia programs that support digital sound editing with movies.

Before turning to Task 4, we need to remind you again of the relationship between the worlds of digital and MIDI sound. In Viewport VI, we dealt extensively with MIDI sequencers that have begun to add the capability to work with digital audio tracks as well. This marriage can work the other way: Certain sound-editing programs can add MIDI capability, although as Table 16.1 shows, this is rare.

BIAS's DECK II is an example of a multitrack digital audio program that can import MIDI files but cannot create them from scratch. Figure 23.14 presents a few of DECK II's windows and menus. Start first by studying the set of windows in the upper left. To help you see how this works, we imported the accompaniment to the pop ballad "Yesterday" into the MIDI window and

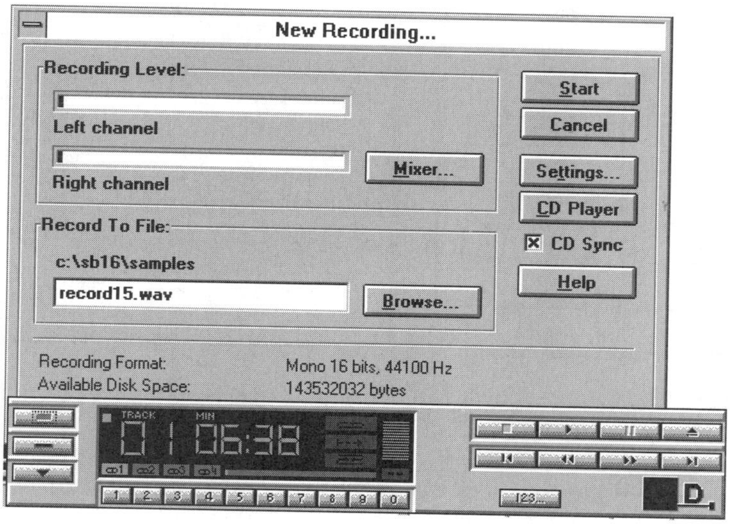

Figure 23.12
Capturing digital audio from CD using Wavestudio
(Creative Labs [Windows])

QuickTime was developed by Apple Computer as a digital video technology to support the kind of movie production that was used in Task 3; you learned about it in Viewport III and in Module 20 of Viewport VI. We will use QuickTime technology when we address multimedia in Viewport VIII.

started the sequencer playing. Next, we began singing into the microphone and recorded digital audio data onto Track 1. DECK II supports several initial tracks, depending on the computer, and two final tracks for output. Notice the little "lighted" buttons along the side that act as a sound level meter. Once the performance is recorded, we hit the Return button, sat back, and listened to the marriage of two very different worlds.

The Tracks window in Figure 23.14 displays the digital data ready to be shaped and edited. A big part of editing both here and in other digital/MIDI sequencers is *bouncing*. Bouncing is the process of submixing sections of multiple tracks together to form a final version. With a playlist to keep track of the movements, the software can use many combinations to create the final version without any loss in audio quality. Some of the mixing commands are displayed in the big menu list to the right. DECK II supports automated mixing, which means that it remembers the mixing commands that the performer or engineer makes the first time through. This simulates expensive studio equipment right in the computer.

Notice that the software supports a number of *crossfades*. Crossfades are ways to blend the end of one line of waveform data with another without an obvious blip in sound. We saw this technique displayed in Figure 23.10. Another feature of DECK II worth noting is the Compact Session command, which compresses previously recorded tracks to save disk space.

Newly Designed Sound: Task 4 Now you are ready to tackle the last requirement: Task 4, a newly designed sound effect. This is where your sampler and computer can really shine. You need "a special kind of sinister laugh with a sense of depth"; at least, that's what the director wants. You begin to experiment with your sampler and its built-in sounds. No luck. You can find plenty of laugh sounds to treat, but nothing seems to work.

Software to the rescue! Computers are digital powerhouses when it comes to sculpting sound and can often go far beyond the ability of many samplers.

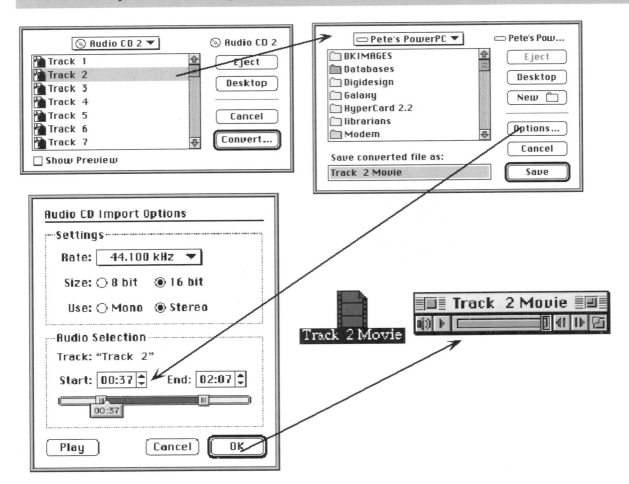

Figure 23.13
Capturing digital audio from CD using MoviePlayer (Apple Computer [Mac/Windows])

A good example of a program that accomplishes this is Digidesign's TurboSynth. We will use this software to create the sound we want, then transfer it to the sampler for use in the play.

What's Being Stored and Edited? Before we do this, let's examine the typical way that sound creating works with electronic equipment. Take a look at Figure 23.15. This basic *signal path,* showing how a patch was created, is a typical way most synthesizers and samplers work today. The path goes something like this:

▶ *Generation.* Sound is generated from an internal source. This could be a basic waveform like a sine or square wave or, in present-day synthesis, it could be a sampled sound from an acoustic instrument that is "stored" inside a microchip. In the case of a sampler device, it is likely that this basic sound is a digital waveform you might put in yourself with your own microphone, or perhaps it is from another digital source like your computer. This initial sound source might also be formed out of a combination of sources by use of the various methods of sound synthesis noted in Module 10: additive, subtractive, distortive (e.g., FM), wave synthesis, or physical modeling.

ASIDE

This might be a good time to read or reread the historical perspective in this module on the development of devices for sound synthesis.

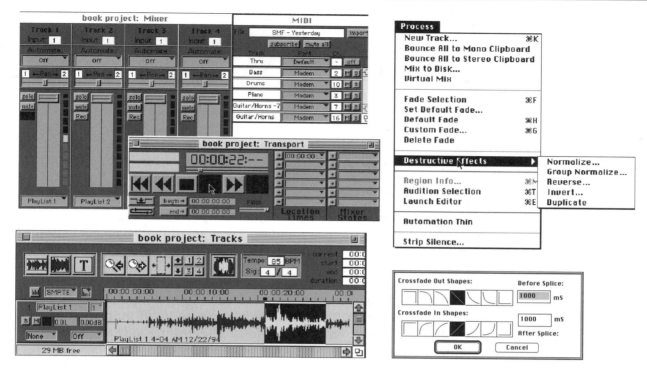

Figure 23.14
Digital audio recording
with MIDI using DECK II
(BIAS [Mac])

▶ *Control.* This sound is controlled by some source (keyboard or other triggering device) so that it can be initiated and perhaps altered over time (i.e., envelope shaping: attack, decay, sustain, release).

▶ *Processing.* Concurrently, the sound can be processed in other ways. These might include filtering of frequencies, reverb (echo), panning (moving sounds from one stereo channel to another), and frequency modulation (vibrato). With MIDI devices, the sound can also be affected by MIDI controllers like the pedal or pitch wheel, but these are more related to real-time performance than to the structure of the sound itself.

The Turbosynth software is designed for musicians who wish to build sounds in the style of the synthesis techniques pictured in Figure 23.15. Instead of using a sampler or synthesizer to do this work, the steps outlined above are accomplished in software. Using your computer in this manner, you can create a sound file that can be transferred to your sampler for storage, performance, or even more editing within the sampler if needed. In this case, the computer is not actually performing the sound (although it could if needed) but is shaping the sound structurally. Again, it is possible to do this with the controls and LCD window on your hardware sequencer, but it is far more difficult and time consuming.

Creating the Sound. Figure 23.16 displays the design of a sound called *Dick's Laugh*. The center window (*a*) displays icons that represent the building blocks for the sound. The smaller windows around the outside show the pieces of the puzzle. Take a close look at the three columns of icons to the

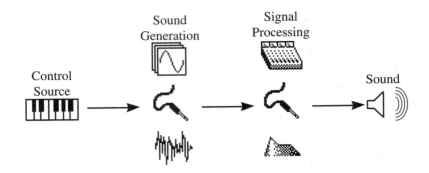

Figure 23.15
Signal path for constructing a patch

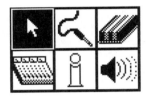

left of the center window (*a*). These contain tools and modules that represent the building blocks of a complex sound. These building blocks are placed in the open space to the right and connected to form a signal path that produces an output (notice the audio plug at the bottom of the flowchart that indicates output).

The Mixer tool accepts as many as 32 sound inputs but sends only one stereo output to the plug (our example happens to be in mono). The patch cord, speaker, and eraser tools are obvious. The lowercase letter *i* represents an information tool for the entire sound. It displays data about memory. TurboSynth uses RAM as the space for sound construction, and you might use the 64 megabytes of RAM in your computer to good advantage. The remaining icons represent modules that either produce or alter sound.

Let's trace the design of *Dick's Laugh* while briefly describing some of these modules. We begin with sound generation of some sort. In this case, there are three possible modules to use; they can be seen in the third row of Figure 23.16 and in the margin on the left. The sine wave module represents oscillator-like digital waveforms. Many waveforms are included as standard choices, but you can also draw your own or import them from a database of earlier work.

The next module to the right is the sample option. You can import your own sound file as a building block. Using the recording capabilities of your sampler, for instance, you could use a microphone to record a sound directly into the MIDI device and then transport it over to the computer for processing in TurboSynth. You can also use the same microphone to sample directly into the computer if you have an audio card such as the Audiomedia III. This is, in fact, what we have done here. Note the box in the upper right that is produced by TurboSynth when we double-click on the sample module (Figure 23.16*b*). It represents the complex waveform that we have recorded as the basis for the laugh—two evil sounding "ha-has." This module, like others in this program, has a number of tools of its own, including ones to accomplish looping, crossfades, scaling, and other advanced digital audio techniques. The third module for creating sound is the noise option.

If you look carefully at the center window, you will see that we actually have three separate samples that follow a path directly to the mixer and to the output. We have copied a sampled laugh two times to form these three signal paths. Each sample has a different treatment.

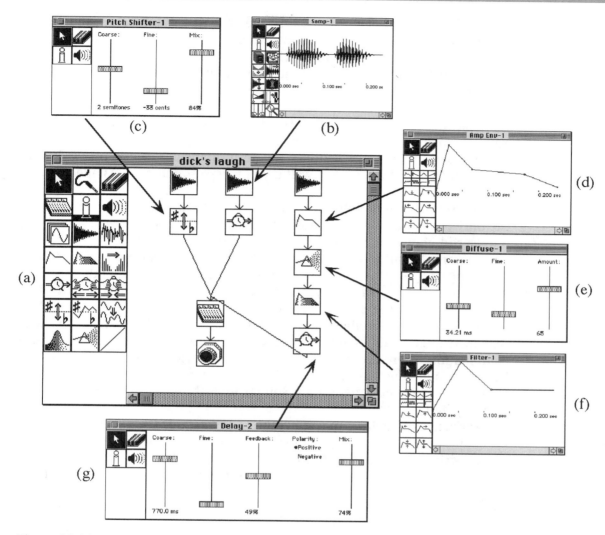

Figure 23.16
TurboSynth SE
(Digidesign, Inc. [Mac])

Refer ahead to Module 26 for information on the DSP chip.

The one in the upper left is patched to the Pitch Shifter module (Figure 23.16*c*). This module shifts the pitch of the sample, acting like a sound controller. In this case, we have found that a shift upwards by two semitones is effective, together with a mixing of the original with the shifted sound. This quality is sent directly to the mixer, and this laugh is over quickly.

Now look at the signal path to the extreme right. This one is the most complex. It first goes through the Amplifier Envelope module (Figure 23.16*d*), which varies the volume of the sample over time. It acts like the voltage-controlled amplifier (VCA) in analog synthesizers. Next, the signal gets treated by the Diffuse Module (*e*). This is a special feature of TurboSynth that uses the DSP chip either within the computer or on its special sound card, or a plug-in that performs the DSP function in software. This option "smears" the sound over time, making it possible to create reverberation effects. Next it goes though the low-pass filter module (*f*) to rid it of high frequencies. Finally it is processed by the Delay module (*g*) that gives the sound an echo effect. In this case the delay is set quite slow. Finally, the middle signal path is left untreated, except for some delay. This delay is set slightly faster than the one on the right.

What results is a fascinating melange of laughs, some happening immediately while others fade out over time. The sound quality of each set of laughs is very different, and the total effect is indeed a "special kind of sinister laugh with a sense of depth." The director of your show should be happy. You can save the file in a format that your sampler understands and then download the file to the sampler for performance. You can also ask your computer to play the sound as well if you have a sound card installed.

Other Approaches to Software-Based Sound Synthesis. TurboSynth is not the only choice for software-based sound synthesis. Seer Systems's Reality is a powerful choice for the Wintel platform. It is a real-time software synthesis program that allows you to construct sounds and hear them immediately. The program does not require a special sound card, although the more advanced sound cards for your Wintel machine will produce the best results. A technique called "modal" synthesis is supported as well. This approach to sound synthesis uses a metaphor more closely associated with real instruments. Eight frequencies are used to create an almost endless combination of vibrating parts to create sound. This approach is similar to "physical modeling" synthesis, which is presented in Modules 10 and 21. Other aspects of the program are similar to Turbosynth in terms of control, filtering, and effects.

Another approach to sound synthesis is Csound. Csound is a programming language for sound synthesis and score construction that began its life as the MUSIC code in the Bell Labs in the late 1950s and was later developed by Barry Vercoe at MIT. Using a modular structure, the programming language allows the construction of sounds by use of small programs in combination. In this way, it is similar to Max, which we described in Module 19. The idea is to build virtual instruments and link them together to create a score. Csound began as a Unix-based program and runs most often on Unix machines such as workstations by Sun and Silicon Graphics. There are efforts now to translate the programming environment to Wintel and Macintosh machines, and there are conversion programs that convert MIDI files to Csound resources. There are no complete commercial products based on Csound, but there are many Windows and Macintosh freeware and shareware products available from computer music studios that support some Csound programming.

See Max Mathews' MUSIC code discussed in Module 17.

Concluding Ideas

A few final thoughts are in order as you finish reading this introduction to sound creation and editing.

Storing and Editing Sounds from MIDI Equipment: Librarians and Patch Editors. If your work involves the use of sounds from MIDI devices such as keyboard synthesizers, you might find software librarians and patch editors useful in organizing and editing tasks. Librarian software keeps track of all the sounds from your MIDI gear that are available to you. Much like the OMS management software we noted earlier, librarians can be very useful in helping you find just the right sound for sound effects or for use in a sequenced composition such as we described in Viewport VI. Librarian software can transfer the parameters of sounds from your MIDI gear to the computer and back again by way of your MIDI interface, allowing you to store several different sets of sound in your computer. This transfer uses the MIDI System Exclusive (SysEx) message that we described in Modules 11 and 20.

Patch editing software (often combined with librarian software as part of the same product) allows you to use the computer to actually edit the sounds in your synthesizer. Using the same approach that we diagrammed in Figure 23.15, the software lets you manipulate the options provided by your synthesizer to alter the sounds. You could use your synthesizer itself to do this, but it is so much easier to use the computer screen to accomplish these tasks. As with librarians, patch editors use MIDI SysEx messages and must be written especially for a particular MIDI device. Remember that both librarians and patch editors allow the computer to manipulate MIDI-based information *about* the sound, not the actual sound waveform itself. Good examples of librarian and patch editing software are Midi Quest from Sound Quest (Mac/Windows) and Galaxy Plus Editors from Opcode Systems (Mac/Windows).

More on hard disc recorders in Module 26

Capturing Digital Audio without a PC or without MIDI Gear. We stressed the role of a personal computer as part of our solutions to digital sound sampling tasks. What about doing all this work without a computer or without these MIDI devices? Is this possible?

Actually, yes. It is possible to purchase dedicated audio recording devices that do not use a personal computer at all, but use their own hard drives and built-in software. These direct-to-disk solutions, such as the Korg D8 or the Roland 840 and 880 hard disk recorders, are closer in spirit to the equipment used by major recording companies such as Telarc, Philips, or Deutsche Grammophon (see Module 26).

In a similar vein, there are sampling cards such as Digidesign's Sample Cell series that fit right into your computer and are designed to replicate the function of external samplers. These cards can maintain several digitized sounds and can be played by external keyboards or other MIDI devices, turning the computer into a high-quality sample instrument. Again, this is a neat option for certain settings, but you can probably accomplish your tasks more quickly and economically by using your MIDI equipment together with your computer. Be sure to keep these options in mind as you study the KISS digital audio model that we present in the coming modules.

Digital audio and sampling was first discussed in Module 10.

Two important music data structures have been emphasized throughout this book: The MIDI data structure is the primary way we represent music event data in a computer; digital audio sampling is the way we represent music sound data. We concluded Module 20 with a discussion of how MIDI event structures are merging with digital sound structures to provide the musician with the best of both worlds. In this module, we will revisit the topic of digital audio and sampling. We will go into greater depth on the technical aspects of digital sampling and review the different structures of sound file formats and compression techniques.

Digital Sampling: Nyquist and S/N Ratios

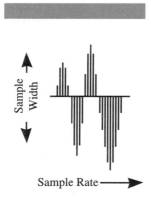

Figure 24.1 first appeared in Module 10. It diagrams the stages in digitizing analog sound vibrations. To briefly review, the analog sound (e.g., the human voice) is digitized (converted to numeric values) by an analog-to-digital converter (ADC). To recreate the sound as analog vibrations, the series of numeric values (shown here as binary 1s and 0s) is changed back into an analog signal by a digital-to-analog converter (DAC).

Optimizing the Quality of Digital Audio. The goal in terms of quality digital audio and sound sampling is to match output to input. The quality of digital audio produced from a device like a computer must be equal to or better than the original analog audio that was digitized.

Examine the chart in the margin to the left. As analog sound is converted to digital numeric values through an analog-to-digital converter

Figure 24.1
The process of digitizing sound

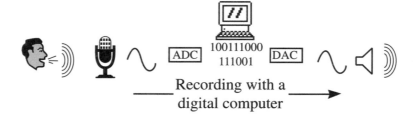

(ADC), there are two fundamental variables that affect the quality of the digital sampling process. The *sampling rate* is the number of samples of the analog sound signal the computer captures in an interval of time. Typically the sampling rate is something like 11,000 (11 KHz), 22,000 (22 KHz), 44,000 (44 KHz), or 48,000 (48 KHz) samples per second. The faster the rate, the more realistic the digital sample will sound when it is played back. Also, the faster the rate, the more memory is needed to represent the sampled sound; at 44 KHz that is 44,000 bytes of data per second. Sampling rate is indicated by the *x*-axis, or time, in the chart in the margin.

The *sampling width* or *quantization* reflects the resolution of the digital sample. The width represents the size of the numeric values used for each sample point that goes to make up the digital sound sample, e.g., 8, 12, 16, or 24 bits per sample. The width of a sound sample is represented by the *y*-axis, or height, in the chart.

Given the relationship of rate to width, there are two rules related to digital sampling that are important in furthering your understanding of digital audio:

▶ The usable frequency range of a sampled sound (*S*) is from 0 up to one-half the sampling rate (*S*/2).

▶ The dynamic range of a sampled sound or its signal-to-noise ratio (*S/N*) can be determined by multiplying the sampling width (*W*) times 6 decibels (6 × *W* decibels).

Need a quick brush up on music acoustics? Refer to Module 10.

The first concept was proposed by Harry Nyquist in a paper on telegraph transmission back in 1928. In fact, the *S*/2 ratio is also known as the Nyquist frequency. When Max Mathews and others began experimenting with digital audio in the late 1950s, Nyquist's concept became critical in the design of digital audio techniques.

Frequency range. The Nyquist theorem helps to determine the affect of sampling rate on the quality of the digital audio. Figure 24.2 shows a continuum of frequencies beginning with the lowest sound the human ear can detect, 20 cycles per second or 20 Hz. The highest note (C8) on the piano is shown at 4,200 Hz or 4.2 KHz. The upper limit of human hearing is 20 KHz. Bear in mind that even though the highest note on the piano at 4.2 KHz is a long way from the 20-KHz limit of the ear, we must take into account the frequencies of all of the harmonics of an instrument's harmonic

Figure 24.2
A comparison of frequencies in relation to the Nyquist frequency

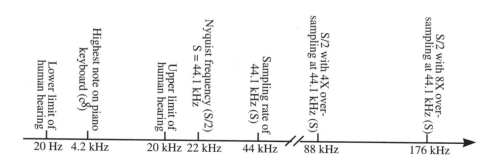

spectrum. The eighth harmonic of a 4.2-KHz tone would be 33.6 KHz (8 × 4.2 KHz), well beyond the range of the human ear.

What Nyquist's theorem says is that the rate we use for sampling audio must be twice as high as the usable frequency we need. So if we want a sample rate that will be at or above the upper range of the human ear, then the sampling rate needs to be twice as high, or 40 KHz (2 × 20 KHz). In practice, the frequency range is "up to a little less" than one-half the sampling rate. For this reason, a common sampling rate used in the industry is 44 KHz (technically, 44.1 KHz) with a usable Nyquist frequency of 22 KHz, 2 KHz above the upper limit of the human ear. This is what is shown in Figure 24.2. Sampling rates of 48 KHz and even 96 KHz are also being used on commercial CD audio and DVD audio recordings.

The audio card or component built into most of the computer systems can sample a full range from 11 KHz to 44 KHz, and even higher. Using a sampling rate of 22 KHz, the Nyquist frequency will only be 11 KHz ($S/2$); the computer will not be able to reproduce the full range of frequencies that the human ear can detect. With a sampling rate of 44 KHz, however, the Nyquist frequency will be increased to 22 KHz. In terms of our goal of having the output of a digital audio system equal to or better than the input, you can see that sampling rates less that 44 KHz will give us less than the optimum quality we seek. Having said that, a 22-KHz sampling rate is quite adequate for spoken voice; a 44- to 48-KHz sampling rate is needed for good quality digitizing of music.

The dynamic range or signal-to-noise ratio. The second rule helps us determine the effect of sampling width on the quality of the digital audio process. This concept says that the usable dynamic range of the sampling process is a function of the sampling width; this is similar to what is known as the signal-to-noise (S/N) ratio. Common sense should tell you that the greater the number of digits you use in measuring something (i.e., the numeric width), the more accurate the measurement. With any measurement, you have to round off the value at some point, and, the greater the size or width of the value, the less likely any errors due to rounding will have a noticeable effect. Thus, the larger the S/N ratio in digital sampling, the less likely rounding errors will be detectable by the human ear when the digital sample is recreated.

The rule also says that, in calculating the signal-to-noise ratio, for each bit added to the value used for measuring a sample, the dynamic range is improved by 6 dB. The table in the margin shows how the S/N ratio increases as the size of the value representing each sample increases.

Let's do a quick comparison of some traditional audio equipment you might have around to see how this equipment compares with the digital standards we've been discussing. A quick glance at the specification sheets for this equipment shows that your CD audio player has a frequency response of 20 KHz and an S/N ratio of 94 dB. The digital audio board in your computer is a 24-bit/48-KHz sampling device. You can see that with a 24-bit/48-KHz computer sampling system, the audio quality of the computer should match the audio quality of your CD player. Terrific!

Your old dual-cassette tape deck has an S/N ratio of around 75 dB and an

Width	S/N Ratio
1 bit	6 dB
8 bit	48 dB
12 bit	72 dB
16 bit	96 dB

upper frequency response of 15 KHz. This was somewhat better than sampling with some of the older sampling cards for PC computers, but less than the quality of the newest digital audio technology in most computers. When you look up the specs on your 1960s vintage reel-to-reel tape deck, however, you find that the *S/N* ratio of the tape recorder was 55 dB and the frequency response was 15 KHz. The quality of 1960s audio recording was comparable to 8-bit audio sampling built into some of the earlier personal computers.

Going Higher: 24 Bits at 48 or 96 KHz. Sampling with 16 bits and 44.1 KHz seemed like the ideal upper limit for CD-quality digital audio. However, if you look at the specifications for high-end digital audio hardware these days, sampling rates are often 48 KHz or even 96 KHz. DVD audio uses 48 KHz as a minimum, with 96 KHz preferred. And, instead of 16 bits of sampling depth, we now have 24 bits of sampling precision.

Is there anything to gain by the increased sampling resolution? Believe it or not, there is a subtle but perceptible gain in audio quality. We can look to digital graphics for a parallel. You can create superb digital color images with 16-bit, 300-dpi scans of photos. But, when you place this image against a 32-bit, 600- or 1200-dpi scan, the eye appreciates the difference in the realism. Similarly with improvements in digital sampling; the trained ear can appreciate the difference in the smoothness, the clarity, and the realism of the resulting sound. Yes indeed, the ceiling for digital audio quality has moved up a few notches to 24-bit, 96-KHz resolution.

Digital Sampling: Aliasing, Filters, and Oversampling

In our quest for the best quality possible in reproducing an audio image from a digitized sound sample, there are a few more factors to consider besides sampling rate and width. In Figure 24.3, notice that we have added filters to the digitizing chain: one before the ADC and another after the DAC. The filters are added to eliminate aliasing and jaggies generated by the sampling process. Let's look at each of them.

Figure 24.3
Adding filters to the digitizing process

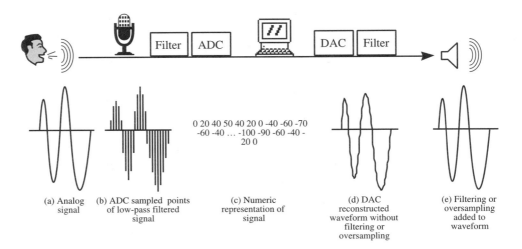

(a) Analog signal

(b) ADC sampled points of low-pass filtered signal

(c) Numeric representation of signal

(d) DAC reconstructed waveform without filtering or oversampling

(e) Filtering or oversampling added to waveform

Jaggies and Aliasing. Look at figure 24.3. The resulting audio signal from the DAC (*d*) prior to filtering is not equal to the initial audio signal (*a*). The audio signal output from the DAC has jaggies similar to those one gets when digitizing bitmapped graphic images. The jaggies are the result of unwanted harmonics added to the sample during the ADC phase (*b*).

There is another issue with sampling known as audio aliasing. Aliasing refers to unwanted sounds that are audible in the output from a DAC, sounds that add distortion and are masquerading—hence the word alias—for a frequency beyond the Nyquist frequency. Do you remember that the eighth harmonic for the piano tone of 4.2 KHz would be 33.6 KHz? Take another look at the chart in Figure 24.2 and you will see that with a 44-KHz sampling rate, the 33.6-KHz harmonic would be above the Nyquist frequency of 22 KHz. This sampling rate can't keep up with a 33.6-KHz sound. The data are undersampled and, systematically, samples are lost. With undersampling, the audio result that you hear will be frequencies below the Nyquist frequency of 22 KHz, dissonant and unwanted sounds that are aliases for sounds above the Nyquist point.

Filters. Different techniques are used for eliminating unwanted aliasing and to smooth the jaggies from digital audio. One alternative is the placement of what are known as low-pass or antialiasing filters before the ADC, and brickwall "anti-imaging" filters after the DAC, in the digital audio processing chain (see Figures 24.3*b* and 24.3*d*). A low-pass audio filter allows all frequencies below the threshold of the filter to pass; all frequencies above the filter's threshold are removed. A brickwall low-pass filter has a very sharp or rapid cutoff that allows very few frequencies beyond its threshold to pass. A brickwall filter set to 20 KHz (just below 22 KHz for a safe margin) will stop any frequency beyond a 22-KHz Nyquist frequency from being passed along; the higher frequencies figuratively run into a brick wall.

By use of a 20-KHz brickwall filter before the ADC (Figure 24.3*b*), sounds that could cause aliasing will be filtered out before they reach the ADC. The brickwall filter after the DAC smooths out the jaggies in the digital-to-analog process by removing any frequencies beyond the Nyquist frequency that may result from the sampling process itself.

It is also possible to perform the sampling process with a technique known as *oversampling*. It is common to see ads for MIDI devices, audio CD players, and hard-disc recorders that make claims, for example, such as "8x oversampling D/A converters." An oversampling filter increases the sampling rate by adding more samples between the ones obtained from the analog signal. In the case of 8x oversampling, seven interpolated samples are placed between each sample point by making an electronic best guess at the data in between.

What advantage is this? Look back at the continuum in Figure 24.2. Notice that we have indicated where the Nyquist frequency will fall with 4x and 8x oversampling. Oversampling electronically improves the sampling rate through digital signal processing. At 8x oversampling and a 176-KHz Nyquist frequency (22 KHz × 8), the high-frequency jaggies have been greatly reduced. So, instead of using brute force with a brickwall filter, over-

Have you noticed wagon wheels in Western movies that go backward? That is visual aliasing. The camera, at 24 frames per second, is undersampling the wagon wheel because it is spinning faster.

sampling filters simply move the Nyquist frequency way out of the range of human hearing to minimize distortion.

Low-Bit Solutions to Digitizing Quality

The sophisticated digital audio technology we have today has passed through several stages of development. Each stage represents a greater reliance on digital solutions to the analog-to-digital-to-analog chain and on more sophisticated signal processing made possible through integrated circuitry and DSP chips. The first stage in the evolution used ADCs and DACs with low-pass filtering of the analog signal before and after to clean up the process. The next stage introduced the use of oversampling filters directly on the digital data to boost the Nyquist frequency out of the way of aliasing problems. The latest stage in this evolution now attacks the design of the ADC and DAC components in the sampling chain and moves the conversion process almost entirely into the digital domain along with filtering.

We have emphasized that sampling width is critical when it comes to quality digital audio. The more bits we have to represent a sample, the better the dynamic range of the signal. Hence, if you have a choice, always pick 16- or even 20-bit ADCs and DACs over 8-bit ones.

But wait! What are the ads you see advertising 1-bit digital converters? This doesn't seem to fit the concept that "more bits is better." Low-bit digital converters are, in fact, a different concept in digitizing audio. Instead of capturing the amplitude of each sample over time and storing it as an 8- or 16-bit value, the new concept only uses two data points, 0 and 1, or one bit of data. The waveform is described by taking very fast (e.g., 11-megahertz as compared to 44-kilohertz) time samples and recording whether the wave is in a positive or a negative state. A string of all 1s (e.g., 1111111111) would indicate a high positive value, a string of all 0s (e.g., 0000000000) would indicate a high negative value, and a string of alternating 1s and 0s (e.g., 10101010101) would be zero value. Somewhere in between, patterns of alternating 1s and 0s are captured at very high speed and, when played back, recreate the analog waveform.

What advantage does this system have? The conversion process, when going from analog to digital and back to analog, is now a serial process. The sampled sound is a continuous series of 0 or 1 bits, known as a bitstream. Traditional amplitude conversion uses 8-bit or 16-bit parallel conversion to turn a binary value back into an analog voltage. The serial process greatly simplifies the process and, more importantly, places most of the conversion process in the digital domain. Combined with the digital techniques of oversampling for filtering, only a single bit has to be converted to analog. DSP chips make the computing-intensive operations for this process possible (see Module 26).

FFTs and Other Graphic Representations of Sound Samples

There are several ways you can view the data that represent a sampled sound. One way would be to examine the 8-bit or 16-bit numeric values

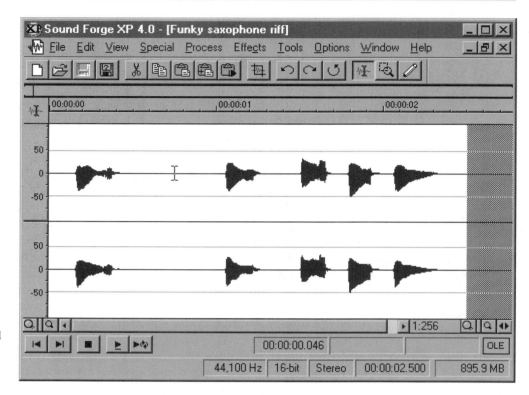

Figure 24.4
Waveform view of a sound waveform editor with Sound Forge XP
(Sonic Foundry [Windows])

Module 23 has more illustrations of digital waveform graphics.

Head back to Module 10, an acoustics primer, if you are having difficulty understanding harmonics and the like.

for each sample, either in binary, hexadecimal, or decimal form. Many software applications for capturing sounds give you the option of saving the numeric data and importing them to a spreadsheet. It is much easier, however, to view samples as graphic images. Figures 24.4 and 24.5 show two common graphic views of sampled sounds.

Figure 24.4 shows a plot of a stereo waveform with the left and right sound channels. The vertical or *y*-axis of the plot for each stereo channel represents amplitude; the horizontal or *x*-axis of the plot for each channel represents time. Where the plot hovers around zero (0) amplitude, this indicates the presence of background noise. Deviations from zero indicate the presence of sound signals captured by the sample. Digital audio software usually provides a waveform plot for editing the waveform: cutting, pasting, deleting, and applying effects to the sampled sound.

The waveform plot is convenient for editing a sound sample, but it doesn't give you much information about the components or harmonics that make up the timbre that you hear. A spectral view of a sound sample like the one shown in Figure 24.5 gives you information about a sound's harmonic structure. As we discussed in Module 10, any complex sound can be broken down into simple vibrations or sine waves that represent each harmonic present in the sound; this process is called spectral or harmonic analysis. To create the plot in Figure 24.5, a mathematical procedure was applied to the sample's data to derive the harmonic information shown in this plot. The procedure is call Fast Fourier Transform or FFT.

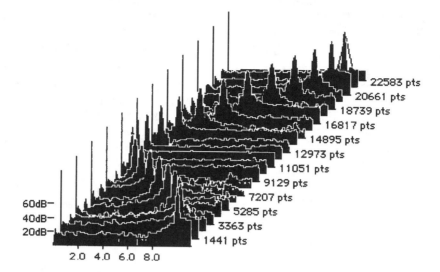

Figure 24.5
Spectral view of a sound sample produced by FFT with SoundEdit 16 (Macromedia [Mac])

The horizontal or *x*-axis again represents time. The *y*-axis (or height in this plot) still represents amplitude, but the spectral view shows the amplitude for a range of frequencies up to the Nyquist frequency (in this case, 22 KHz). The *z*-axis (the one moving backward at an angle) indicates the frequency intervals (labeled as points or pts in Figure 24.5) for the spectral analysis up to 22 KHz. The spectral view is important when you want to compare or alter waveforms as you vary harmonics to create a unique timbre; you can let your ear and eye be your guide.

Formats and Compression Techniques for Digital Audio Files

When you search the Internet for digital sound and music files, you will be excited to find so many offerings to download. Your excitement will diminish quickly when you notice all the different sound file types that Macintosh, Wintel, and other computer users employ in saving their music files. Table 24.1 shows you some of the more common sound and music file types that you will encounter, including those for proprietary sound hardware such as Digidesign Sound Designer and Sound Designer II files. The table begins with audio formats that are common to specific computer systems, followed by more universal formats which can be created or played on most common computers and are distributed widely over the Internet.

There are many software utilities available to translate sampled data files between formats and across platforms. You can take a WAV file created on a Wintel machine with a Sound Blaster card and convert it to a Mac SND or AIFF file; the WAV sound files also could be converted to AIFF files or AU and RealAudio file formats used over the Internet. Using sample-editor software such as SoundForge, CoolEdit, SoundEdit 16, SoundEffects, or ProTools, you can even create your own digital audio files at quality rates that range from low (mono, 8 bit, 11 KHz) to CD quality (stereo, 24

The Internet was discussed in Viewport II.

File Extension	Computer	Description
.snd	Mac	Mac system format for sampled sounds
.wav or .voc	Win	Windows and DOS system formats for sampled sounds
.aif or .aifc	Mac	Audio Interchange File Format (AIFF) for sampled sounds
.sd2	Mac or Win	Sound Designer II sample sound files (Digidesign)
.sds	any	MIDI Sample Dump Standard for sampled digital audio files
.mod	any	Unique format for MOD players (originated on Amiga)
.au	any	Sun Unix format used on the Internet
.mpg, .mp2	any	MPEG industry standard format used for DVD, Internet, etc.
.ra or .rm	any	Proprietary RealAudio format with high compression used on Internet

Table 24.1. Common Sound Formats for Digital Audio and MIDI Files.

Graphic files and compression were discussed in Module 14.

bit, 48 KHz). Let's look at some of the more common audio formats and the compression schemes they use to conserve space or bandwidth in storage and distribution.

Sound Compression. In the process of creating digital sound files on your computer, the space on your hard drive disappears rapidly! Five- to twenty-megabyte sound samples will quickly fill your hard drive, especially if you try to capture entire tracks of music from a CD. One solution to this dilemma is to begin exploring the use of compression techniques that would effectively reduce the size of the files of your audio samples. Of course another solution is to purchase a bigger hard drive or a removable disk storage device like Iomega's Jaz drive!

In the worlds of both sound and graphics data compression, there are two approaches: lossy and lossless. When a compression technique is said to be "lossy," that means that data are lost in the compression process that will not be replaced when the file is decompressed. A "lossless" compressed file, when decompressed, restores all the data back to its original form. Sound files that are compressed almost always use some form of a lossy technique. This means that audio quality suffers to some degree; whether you can hear the loss is the critical issue.

Just about any lossy compression will affect the perceived sound quality, depending on how discriminating an ear you have for sound. In most cases it is a judgment call between bandwidth (how big a file you can use) and audio quality (how good it sounds).

One lossy scheme to reduce the size of sampled sound files is downsampling. This is technically not considered compression. Bytes are systematically dropped from the sample, e.g., every other byte. However, eliminating every other byte cuts the sampling rate in half (and the Nyquist frequency, as well). When you sample something at 22 KHz and then drop the sampling rate to 11 KHz, you have downsampled the sound. This technique would cut the size of your audio file in half but greatly reduce the quality of the audio.

One of the simplest lossy compression schemes is to systematically drop bits from each sample. A 2:1 compression drops one bit from each sample. For example, with 8-bit samples, only 7 bits of each sample would be saved, dropping off the least significant bit. An 8:1 compression, with an 8-bit sample size, would leave only 1 bit per sample. The sampling rate is maintained, but the width or resolution is diminished. AU or μ-law files used on the Internet essentially compress 16-bit samples into 8 bits in this fashion to create mono, 8-bit, 11-KHz audio files.

Increasing Compression While Fooling the Ear. Information can be selectively eliminated from a soundwave through algorithmically reducing the sound sample size. What this means is that the computer software is intelligently eliminating samples rather than just dropping samples or bits. Most of the software formats in Table 24.1 use some form of Pulse Code Modulation (PCM) to convert analog sounds to digital strings of electrical pulses. ADPCM, or Adaptive Difference Pulse Code Modulation compression, converts the data into a more compact code by taking the difference between the values for each sample and then converting the binary value into pulse code. ADPCM is used on a variety of proprietary file compression formats. The VOC file format originally created by Creative Labs, for example, permits 2:1, 3:1, and 4:1 compression ratios using ADPCM, as do compression of WAV files and AIFC, a compressed version of AIFF files.

The MiniDisc and DCC tape systems are covered in Module 26.

The greatest sophistication in audio compression is apparent in two techniques developed by Sony and Phillips for their MiniDisc (MD) and Digital Compact Cassette (DCC) formats, respectively. MD is a laser-disc technology, and DCC is a digital-tape technology. (The DCC technology is no longer being produced.) The Sony compression technique is called ATRAC, for Adaptive TRansform Acoustic Coding; the Philips, PASC or Precision Adaptive Sub-band Coding. Both are lossy techniques and may be referred to as perceptual compression algorithms. Data are intelligently removed from the digital samples: sounds that the human ear is unable to hear (hence the term perceptual compression). If you are not going to hear it anyway, then you don't need to save it! Our hearing is more or less sensitive to sounds as they move across the range of hearing from 20 Hz to 20 KHz; and certain sounds, depending upon amplitude, tend to mask or cover up other sounds. Because this is a perceptual technique, the only way to determine its effectiveness is to listen to a recording using it and judge for yourself.

Audio Reserved for Your Computer Only. The first audio formats in Table 24.1 are all basically PCM coding schemes with varying degrees of compression available. VOC was the format developed by Creative Labs for its SoundBlaster PC cards, and WAV was the Microsoft version of PCM sound files design for use in the Windows operating system. Macintosh first used SND or system sound files for digital audio but then moved to a more sophisticated AIFF format first proposed by the music software and computer game company Electronic Arts. The AIFF format allows stereo and multiple channel sound coding and even mixing of MIDI codes with digital audio. Even though these audio file formats are associated with a specific platform, most software and Web browsers will play any of these formats regardless of the computer platform that created the file. The Sound Designer file format originated on the Macintosh computer, but now it is used also on Wintel machines.

MOD files were discussed in Module 20 along, with extensions to MIDI and GM MIDI.

You can use the RealAudio compression format without the streaming feature and the need for a RealAudio server; you create and save them just like any other sound format and still take advantage of the high compression ratio and small file size.

MPEG is critical in the design of DVD video and audio discs; check out Modules 12 and 25 for more on DVD.

Packaging Audio Files for the Internet. There are several universal file extensions that are used extensively over the Internet: .mod, .au, .ra, and .rm, the close cousin to RA files (see Table 24.1; we will discuss .mpg files in the next section).

MOD files have their origin with Amiga computers and electronic bulletin boards or BBSs. MOD audio files are created on digital audio and sequencing software called "Trackers" and played back on MOD software "Players." Music modules (or MODs) combine aspects of digitized audio clips with aspects of MIDI files to produce high-quality digital audio. A typical MOD is composed of a number of samples (generally one note for each instrument) and the musical score (referred to as "tracks" and "patterns") that tells the MOD player how to combine and distort these samples in order to produce a music composition or arrangement.

AU or μ-law (pronounced "mew-law") was the first audio file that most Web browsers automatically recognized and played. The μ-law format is a basic PCM format that originated as a compression coding for telephony. It provides 2:1 compression by packing 16-bit sound samples into 8 bits. The audio quality (mono, 8 bit, 11 KHz) is sufficient for sound effects and voice but not very satisfactory for music. Like many formats used on the Internet, the μ-law file format proliferated because it had been commonly used on Unix computers.

RealAudio (and RealMedia) is a proprietary audio and media format developed by RealNetworks that provides highly compressed, streaming audio over the Internet. "Streaming" means that the audio file is not completely downloaded to a computer desktop before it starts playing. After a small portion of the RealAudio file has been received, the computer begins to play the audio while it continues to download or stream more of the data from its source, the RealAudio server. RealAudio was designed for Internet radio broadcasts and requires a special RA player available without cost from RealNetworks. The format is an ideal one for distributing digital audio over the Internet for many music applications. In its original format alone, the RA format provided 16:1 compression of stereo audio. This permits compressing the full movement of a symphony or concerto down to 2 or 3 megabytes of data. The one downside to RealAudio is that, to play RA files, you need a fast Pentium or PowerPC computer and a minimum of a 28.8K modem connection.

Many other formats are surfacing to compete with RealAudio. Where RealAudio and the newer RealMedia were designed to bring radio and TV to the Internet, other proprietary high-compression audio formats are designed to bring commercial CD audio on demand over the Internet. This includes the ability to buy the latest track or entire album of your favorite artist and burn or record the album to your own CD-R recorder connected to your computer. You can see that high quality, high compression is critical to make this happen over the Internet. Some of the competitors in the CD-on-demand market are Liquid Audio, N2K's e_mod (encoded music on-line delivery) music, and the British Cerberus music on-line.

Bringing Movie Theatre Sound to Home and Desktop. Audio formats used extensively in motion pictures are making their way into the computing and the Internet mainstream: MPEG and AC-3. AC-3 and MPEG, just like MiniDisk and DCC players (see above), use perceptual coding compression. By using the power of computers and DSP chips, these systems can intelligently omit sounds that our ears are not likely to perceive, gaining considerable compression in the audio data while maintaining a high-quality sonic experience.

More on DSP chips in Modules 23 and 26.

MPEG or the Motion Picture Experts Group format is an international standard for coding both audio and video. MPEG in the past has required special hardware for encoding and decoding the audio and video data. However, with the present-day speed of computer processors, software-only solutions as well as inexpensive DSP chips for coding MPEG make the format much more accessible. MPEG may well replace some of the older formats, like WAV and AIFF, and certainly AU because of its poor quality, when more people own higher-powered, 200-MHz or better Pentium or PowerPC computers.

There are several versions of the MPEG standard beginning with MPEG-1, which offers low-end quality currently used for CD-ROM applications and games. MPEG-2 and MPEG-4 offer additional capabilities for home audio and video, multimedia, and Internet and networked-based applications. (MPEG-3 was short lived.) The audio portion of MPEG uses sophisticated, lossy algorithms optimized for digital audio that allow quite high compression rates (theoretically up to 22:1 but typically about 6:1). The average 3-minute song in WAV (16-bit, 44-khz, stereo) format is around 30–40 megabytes, but with the use of MPEG audio encoding the same file can be reduced to about 3 megabytes.

More will be said about MPEG video in Viewport IX when multimedia is discussed.

The audio specification for all versions of MPEG has three possible coding systems, or "layers" as they are called. Each layer offers greater compression, a parallel increase in the time delay required to decode it, and, most importantly, an increase in the quality of the audio with better file compression. The layers work pretty much the same whatever version of MPEG you're using, so be careful about not confusing the three layers with MPEG-1, MPEG-2, and MPEG-4. A file extension ".mp2" or ".mp3" denotes use of the MPEG audio layers 2 or 3, and not MPEG-2 or MPEG-3.

Another development in digital audio file formats is multichannel recording. The earliest experiments with stereo audio in the 1930s at Bell Labs used a three-channel format. The two-channel stereo that evolved commercially omitted the third channel because the phonograph record could only handle two channels or signals on two sides of the vinyl grooves in the record. Since the 1950s, however, films viewed in movie theatres had at least four channels of sound. One of the newest formats used in motion pictures is the Dolby Digital AC-3 format with 5.1 discrete channels of sound: front left and right, surround or back left and right, and center channel; a special effects or subwoofer channel provides the sixth, or .1, of the channels. This six-channel system of compressed AC-3 audio format is now available for consumer enjoyment through laser-disc, DVD disc, digital TV, and home theatre audio/video systems.

Surround sound, multichannel digital audio is also possible with computer generated digital audio. The MPEG-2 standard added the ability to code six channels of surround sound to the compression scheme, as well as providing as high as 96-KHz sampling rates and 24-bit sample sizes over multiple channels, similarly to AC-3. With the introduction of DVD-R recorders for computer workstations, professional level surround-sound digital audio is now a reality, using MPEG-2 file formats.

Data Structures for Laser Audio and Video

Hardware issues related to laser discs have been discussed in Module 12; there is more to follow in Modules 26 and 29.

Laser-disc players generate music, graphics, and video external to a computer, as do MIDI devices; the computer only serves as a controller directing the playback. Laser discs offer exceptional sound and video quality. They are ideally suited to CAI applications in music, provide an excellent storage medium for large volumes of data like digital audio tracks of music, and offer a vast resource for interactive multimedia applications where large amounts of storage are required for high-resolution sound and imagery. In this module, we will introduce you to some of the details of how data are formatted on CD audio, CD-ROM, DVD, and video laser discs.

There are many varieties of laser discs and laser-disc players. They range in application from commercial compact audio discs for music (known as CD audio or CD-DA), to the larger LaserVision videodiscs for film and video, to the newest DVD format for feature-length movies, to the Kodak PhotoCD discs that hold digital representations of 35-mm slides and photos. All of them figure prominently in music software and computer music applications, or will in the near future. And the life span of this medium is over 100 years, so these discs will be around for a long time to come! To begin, let's look at features common to all laser discs.

General Characteristics of Laser Discs

Optical laser discs store data that are encoded on the disc by minute pits configured to represent binary information. The information is read by a laser light beam that is shone against the reflective surface of the disc. The light beam is either reflected directly back when it strikes the flat surface or is dispersed when it strikes a bump caused by a pit. This pattern is graphically shown in Figure 25.1c.

Data on a laser disc are laid down starting at the inside of the disc and moving outward in a continuous spiral of tracks (see Figure 25.1a). The first data placed on the disc constitute the *lead-in area*, followed by the table of contents (TOC) information (Figure 25.1b). Then follows the actual program data (e.g., music, graphics, or video). The space left on the outer edge is the *lead-out area*; the lead-in and lead-out areas are used as cues by the laser player to identify the beginning and end of a disc.

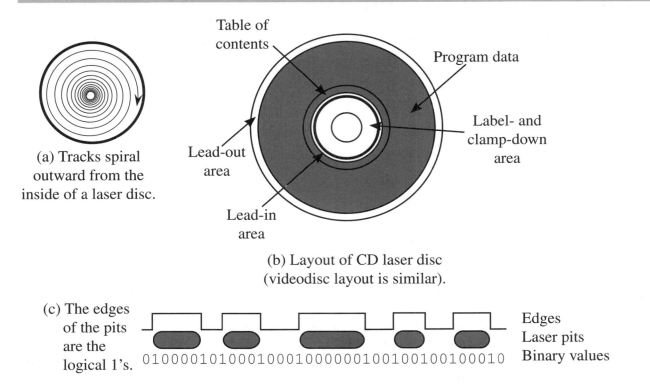

(a) Tracks spiral outward from the inside of a laser disc.

(b) Layout of CD laser disc (videodisc layout is similar).

(c) The edges of the pits are the logical 1's.

Figure 25.1
The layout and format of a laser disc with (*a*) spiral tracks, (*b*) program and table of contents areas, and (*c*) binary patterns of pits

The DVD format multiplies the amount of storage seven times from the CD disc by packing the pits more densely and using a shorter wavelength laser to read them back.

The type of data stored on these tracks varies depending upon which format (e.g., CD audio, CD-ROM, PhotoCD) is used. On a typical compact audio disc 4.75 inches in diameter, there are some two billion data pits across more than three miles, or 22,000 revolutions, of spiraling tracks.

Two general methods are used to format data on the tracks: constant linear velocity (CLV) and constant angular velocity (CAV). CD discs and extended play videodiscs use the CLV technique. With CLV discs, the speed at which the disc spins varies inversely with the location of data being read on the disc. As you see by studying the pattern of spiral tracks on the disc in Figure 25.1*a*, more data can be stored on the outer tracks than on the inner tracks. So, in order to read all data at the same speed, the disc spins faster when the inner tracks are being read then when the outer tracks are being read. Technology keeps finding ways to pack more and more laser data into the same-sized disc. On CAV formatted videodiscs, the disc always spins at the same speed no matter what track is being read. Each track is designed to hold the same amount of data. Phonograph recordings also use the CAV technique: the record always spins at a fixed speed, 33⅓ or 45 RPM.

The laser disc standards are denoted by *book colors,* first defined by Sony and Philips when the two companies created the digital audio disc back in the 1980s. CD audio is the *Red Book* standard, for example, and videodisc follows the *Blue Book* standard, and so on. Table 25.1 gives an overview of the more common laser-disc formats, all of which, except for the newest DVD format, evolved from the Sony-Philips Red Book standard. We will focus the discussion that follows on an examination of each of the formats shown in Table 25.1, concluding with the laser video format.

Table 25.1. Common Disc Formats for Laser Playback Media

Name	Book Code	Standard	Size	Comments
Compact Disc Digital Audio	CD-DA	Red	4.7	Music recordings
Compact Disc Read-Only Memory	CD-ROM or /XA	Yellow	4.7	Computer data
Photo Compact Disc	PhotoCD	Orange	4.7	Photo images on a disc
Video Compact Disc	VideoCD	White	4.7	MPEG-1 movies on CD
Digital Versatile Disc	DVD or DVD-ROM	DVD/UDF	4.7	MPEG-2 video/audio & data
LaserVision Videodisc	LV CAV or CLV	Blue	12	Film recordings

Compact Disc-Digital Audio Format (CD-DA)

CD audio and its application to music CAI was discussed in Module 9 and in Module 27 in relation to multimedia development.

First introduced in 1980, the Compact Disc-Digital Audio (CD-DA) format is the basis for most compact disc data structures. The format, though initially used for commercial audio production, was flexible enough to allow the medium to be extended and adapted for other applications.

The CD audio format permits 74 minutes and 33 seconds of recording on one side of the 4.75-inch laser disc. Rumor has it that 74 minutes was picked as the length of a compact audio disc because the well-known conductor of the Berlin Philharmonic, Herbert von Karajan, wanted to record Beethoven's Symphony No. 9 on one disc. Another version of this story is that the wife of Akio Morita, one of the founders of Sony, wanted her favorite piece of music, Beethoven's Ninth Symphony, recorded on the first compact disc.

Audio on a CD-DA disc is digitally sampled. The typical sampling rate is 44.1 KHz, and the quantizing resolution is 16 bits per sample. Remember from our discussions in Modules 11 and 24 that a 44-KHz sampling rate gives a usable upper frequency response of 22 KHz. Sampling rates for commercial digital recordings may now be as high as 96 KHz with 24 bits per sample.

The CD-DA Red Book format contains extensive information about the contents of the disc, considerable error checking information built into the data structure, and precise timing data for each frame. CD-DA discs use the CLV technique for storing data in tracks on the disc. Data are stored in *frames* that are then grouped into *blocks,* with a resolution of 75 blocks per second. You can access music by track numbers (0 to 99) or by relative times within a track. With the proper software, you can also access music by location in minutes (0 to 73), seconds (0 to 59), and blocks of time (0 to 74). A typical compact audio disc uses one-third of its space for audio program data and the remainder for timing, content information, and error checking data.

The data structure designed by Philips and Sony is very robust. Your CD player uses these data to produce a flawless playback performance, regardless of those fingerprints and few scratches that have accumulated on your disc. This wealth of data is also accessible by a computer for interactively stopping and starting the performance at any time within $\frac{1}{75}$ of a second, and it is an important feature used by CD-ROM multimedia software. As we now examine other CD formats, the Red Book audio format will serve as a point of reference. The other formats are all variations on the CD audio theme.

Compact Disc Read-Only Memory (CD-ROM)

CD-ROM discs are used for storing large amounts of data for computer systems, like text, numbers, and digital graphics and sound. The data structure for CD-ROM is defined by the Sony-Philips Yellow Book documentation. Data on CD-ROM discs can be formatted to conform to common computer operating systems like DOS, Windows, and Mac OS, or to an industry standard file structure like the *High Sierra* or ISO 9660 format. This makes it possible to read the CD-ROM data on any computer system.

Part of the information coded on a CD disc tells the CD player what disc standard is being used. Thus, if you are using a CD-ROM player designed for use with a computer system, it will probably play both CD-ROM discs and CD-DA (audio) discs. The computer reads the codes on the disc and switches to the correct format.

Reflect back on our discussion of CD-DA frames and blocks. Those areas that were used for audio data on CD-DA are used by CD-ROM for computer data. Each block becomes a data sector for storing computer information. The basic frame structure remains the same. Even the timing system is maintained. Data are accessed in terms of minutes, seconds, and blocks. The computer can read the sector of data in, say, the 20th block, which is 34 minutes and 10 seconds into the disc. Between 550 and 650 megabytes of data can be stored on a CD-ROM disc.

A newer format, CD-ROM/XA or CD-ROM eXtended, has the flexibility to use both audio and computer data in the same format. This format came about because of the need to access some of the features of a special interactive form of CD-ROM, called CD-I, from a computer workstation. The extended mode, or CD-ROM/XA, allows for interleaving audio and picture data with the computer data for applications such as multimedia CAI, where computer data, audio, and picture images need to be accessed quickly and simultaneously. This is a format designed for interactive multimedia productions on a personal computer.

Photo Compact Disc (PhotoCD)

The Kodak PhotoCD is another example of practical uses of the compact disc formats. Up to 100 film negatives or 35-mm slides can be stored on a PhotoCD and viewed with a stand-alone PhotoCD player on a TV screen, printed on a color printer, or accessed from your personal computer. While viewing an image on a PhotoCD player, you can zoom in and out and pan across all of the images on the disc.

The PhotoCD disc conforms to Orange Book specifications, which set down standards for compact discs that can be written on or recorded to. This means that there is the potential for adding other information, like music, MIDI codes, and motion video, to CDs using this format.

You have photo images put on a PhotoCD by a local commercial photo service, just as you would have film developed. You can keep adding images until it reaches its maximum of 100. The user of a PhotoCD cannot change its contents; this must be done on a special workstation used by commercial concerns licensed by Kodak.

PhotoCDs can also be played on CD-ROM players with the appropriate software. This provides a fast and low-cost method for producing high-resolution digital graphics for interactive multimedia CAI in music, eliminating the expensive and tedious process of scanning high resolution graphic images.

MPEG is an important industry standard for digital video and audio. More on MPEG-2 under the discussion of DVD below. For more information on video resolution, refer to Module 14.

Videodisc Formats

The videodisc medium was at one time trumpeted as the next big thing in home video. However, this 12-inch laser format has never really caught on. The DVD format has pretty much put the nail in the coffin for this format.

LV videodiscs follow the Blue Book standard. Videodiscs are 12 inches in diameter and can be recorded on both sides of the disc, and, unlike most CD discs, the video data are placed on the disc in analog form, not digital. Instead of coding data as binary numbers onto the disc, analog patterns are used.

Only a few computer-assisted instruction materials have been developed for music education that take advantage of the unique capabilities of the interactive videodisc format. Perhaps the DVD disc, as a natural successor to the popular CD disc, will generate more interest in the instructional applications in music for interactive audio and video from a fast, random-access laser medium.

Video Compact Disc (VideoCD)

Full-motion video is possible on CD laser discs with the VideoCD format. It uses the MPEG-1 standard to cram 70 minutes of movie time onto a CD! This format and the newer DVD format may well lead to the demise of the 12-inch videodisc format.

Digital Versatile Disc (DVD and DVD-ROM)

The newest kid on the laser disc block is the Digital Versatile Disc or DVD format, also called Digital Video Disc. Industry has sought a means to put a full, feature-length film on a 4.7-inch laser disc, and DVD has finally delivered using the same-sized platter as CD audio. Home video movie rentals are now available in DVD disc format as well as video tape. DVD players for home video viewing started shipping in quantity in 1997, as well as DVD-ROM players for personal computers.

Data	CD-ROM	Single-sided Single-layer	Single-sided Double-layer	Double-sided Double-layer
Computer storage	.65 GB (650 MB)	4.7 GB	8.5 GB	17 GB
Video	70 min	2.2 hrs	4.4 hrs	8.8 hrs
CD audio	1.25 hrs (75 min)	7.5 hrs	15 hrs	30 hrs
Music recordings	Beethoven's 9th Symphony	All 9 Beethoven Symphonies	Recording of the Wagner Opera Ring	Beatles and Grateful Dead Complete Anthologies

Table 25.2. DVD and DVD-ROM Storage Capacity

DVD and DVD-ROM players are made to be backwards compatible so you can play all of your CD audio, CD-ROM, and PhotoCD discs on the one player.

To hear the full effect of Dolby Digital you will need an amplifier or receiver that will handle AC-3 audio format and five or more speakers. You can also purchase an AC-3 decoder separately if you want to use DVD with an amplifier that is not set up for AC-3. DVD players, however, do come equipped with common stereo left and right channels for playing DVD video on standard high fidelity audio systems.

DVD is to video what the release of the CD audio in the early 1980s was to music. And, the DVD-ROM is to data what the CD-ROM was to data, but this time data storage on steroids! A DVD disc holds seven times more data than a CD; that's going from 650 MB of data to 4.7 GB of data, or 75 minutes of music to over 7 hours of CD-quality music, or 70 minutes of small-screen digital video to 133 minutes of full-screen, full-motion digital video of commercial quality.

It gets even better! DVD is designed so that two layers can be created on one side of the disc to double its capacity. You can have single-sided single-layer (SSSL) discs or single-sided double-layer (SSDL) discs. And there's more. The flip side can be recorded on as well to give you a double-layer double-sided (DSDL) disc which will, once again, double the capacity. Table 25.2 demonstrates the dramatic storage capacity of the DVD medium.

DVD Book Formats. DVD is a new format that developed from the MMCD (Multimedia Compact Disc) format developed by Sony and Philips and from the SD (Super Density) format proposed by Toshiba, Time Warner, and an alliance of many other manufacturers. Unlike the development of CD formats, DVD was designed to be a computer compatible standard from the start. At the heart of the DVD format is the Universal File System, a cross-platform, random-access file structure that can be supported by most computer operating systems. This means that all DVD media of any type will mount on your desktop, just as your other disc storage media will mount on your desktop, whether you are using Mac, Windows, Unix, or some other operating system.

There are five DVD Books, all formats using UDF: books for DVD-ROM, video, audio, and recordable and rewriteable formats. Some of the format standards are still in flux and being worked out by the industry, especially for DVD audio and the DVD recordable formats. Copy protection will remain a key issue for the complete commercial success of DVD.

MPEG-2 and AC-3: The Heart of the DVD Magic. The real power in the DVD format is more than just enormous storage capacity. It is DVD's ability

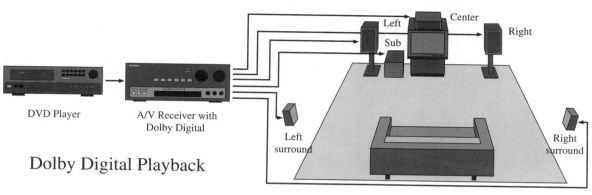

Dolby Digital Playback

Figure 25.2
The 5.1 (six) channels of
Dolby Digital audio in a
home theatre system.

DVD audio and other digital audio formats like
MPEG are discussed in
Module 24.

to deliver professional quality digital video and audio. The video format uses the MPEG-2 standard, which provides 60-frame-per-second video (commercial quality delivery speed) and full screen resolution of 780×480 pixels of 24-bit color. A DVD disc can hold 133 minutes of MPEG-2 video on a single layer, enough time for most feature-length films.

If the video is a knockout, so is the audio to accompany the video. The audio format is AC-3, or Dolby Digital, a descendent of Dolby Surround. Figure 25.2 illustrates the six channels (5.1, as they are defined) of Dolby Digital as they would be placed in a home theatre arrangement with a DVD player, an AC-3 amplifier, and six speakers. The five channels are the traditional stereo or front left and right, a center channel, and two rear or surround left and right channels. Then, for the sixth channel, or .1 of the 5.1 layout, there is a subwoofer speaker for "knockout" special effects.

<table>
<tr><td>

**Module
26**

</td><td>

Hardware for a Digital Audio Workstation

</td></tr>
</table>

Hardware for digitizing sound was first discussed in Module 12.

Digital Signal Processing or DSP can be done with a hardware chip, in software, or a combination of both

Viewport VII has taken you on a tour of software applications for digital audio processing and has discussed some of the important concepts behind digital sampling techniques. It is now time to look at the hardware options you should consider when upgrading to professional-level digital audio on your personal computer with the goal of building a digital audio workstation for your music creativity. Fortunately, the industry is moving in your favor. The quality of digital sampling by personal computers continues to improve. Consumer emphasis is on multimedia workstations, and that translates into a continued improvement in digital sound capabilities. Digital Signal Processing (DSP) chips, being used for everything from digital voice synthesis to modems, are also boosting the computer's power for processing digital sound and music.

Figure 26.1 brings back the familiar IPOS universal systems model. In this module we will take our KISS MIDI system designed in Modules 21 and 22 and add digital audio. We have developed a very strong case in Viewports VI and VII for the need to integrate MIDI and digital audio in any computer music system you design.

On the input side, we will discuss analog-to-digital converters (ADCs), high-performance hard disks, DAT and ADAT tape recorders, MiniDisc (MD) recorders, and CD and DVD laser disc recorders or rewriteables. On the output side, we will discuss digital-to-analog converters (DACs). Because hard disks, DATs, MDs, and CD or DVD recorders permit reading and writing of sound data, these devices appear on the output side of the model as well. For the process stage, the important component is the DSP or digital signal processing chip. DSP technology is what makes professional quality digital audio possible on a personal computer. Last, we will discuss a few interface technologies relevant to digital audio. SCSI and SMPTE are not new topics, but we will review their application to digital audio. Digital I/O interfaces, both S/PDIF and AES/EBU, are topics specific to audio applications, and Firewire and USB are new interfaces for audio and multimedia as well as for PCs in general.

KISS MIDI System Goes Digital

Before we jump into the devices shown in the IPOS model, let's return to the KISS music systems presented in Viewport VI. These KISS music

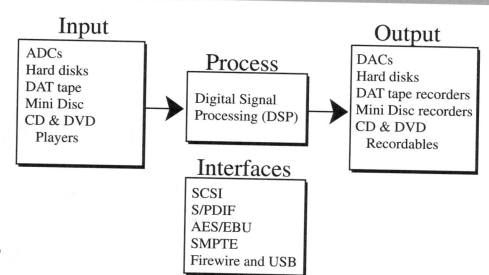

Figure 26.1
IPOS model for digital audio
and sampling hardware

Module 23 looks at Studio
Vision, Cakewalk, ProAudio, Cubase Audio, Digital
Performer, and other professional sequencing software where both MIDI and
digital audio tracks can be
recorded and manipulated.

workstations presented a MIDI-centric view of hardware configurations for sequencing and performing; we will now take a digital-centric view. With the powerful ability to bring almost all the elements of the audio recording process into the digital realm, and the likewise powerful ability to manipulate both MIDI events and digital audio data from within the same software application, we can build a computer workstation where we move as much as possible into the digital domain. Our goal is to get all audio in digital form and to relegate most, if not all, of the audio editing, mixing, signal processing, and recording to software.

For the Digital Audio KISS system shown in Figure 26.2, we have reworked the KISS design to maximize the use of digital software operations and to use components that can be added inside the computer itself. The computer in this KISS model would need to be a fast Pentium or PowerPC workstation with 64 megabytes of RAM or more. The components added into the computer workstation include:

▶ A MIDI interface (item 7) which may be integrated into the PC sound card or exist as a separate component

▶ A digital PC sound card (2) with General MIDI, and wavetable and/or physical modeling synthesis

▶ A multitrack digital audio I/O (input/output) system (13) capable of digitizing from 4 to 16 channels or more of analog audio with 16- to 24-bit resolution and a 48-KHz sampling rate

▶ A CD-RW or DVD-RAM drive (16) for reading and writing laser discs

▶ Removable disk storage (15)

▶ A high-speed, large-capacity AV hard drive (14) for direct-to-hard-disk recording

Digital Audio KISS System

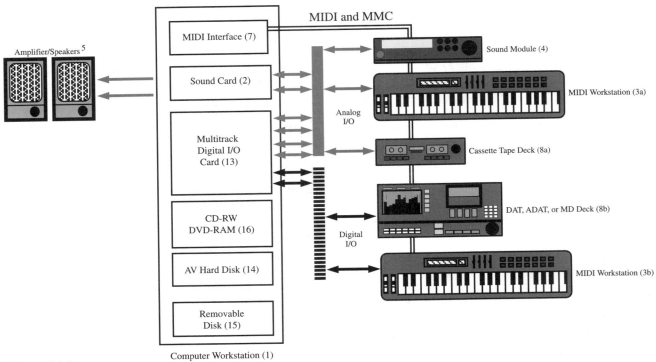

Figure 26.2
Digital Audio KISS System

Components added externally to the computer workstation may include:

▶ An array of MIDI workstations, modules, and controllers (4 and 3a) with analog sound output

▶ Analog recording gear like a cassette tape deck (8a)

▶ Multitrack digital tape recorder (e.g., DAT, ADAT, or MD deck) (8b) with digital I/O

▶ An array of MIDI workstations, modules, and controllers (3b) with digital I/O (3b)

The numbers for the items in the KISS models may appear out of order, but they fit logically with numbers used across all of the KISS diagrams in previous modules.

Items in the digital audio KISS system like the sound module (4), the cassette deck (5a), and a MIDI workstation with both analog and digital I/O are not really necessary for this all-digital system. For the most part, they are placed here to illustrate the variety of devices that could be attached to the system. The analog cassette deck is placed here because it is still the most common and portable way to distribute your music, even if it is just a copy of your latest album to send home to the folks!

Look again at Figure 26.2, paying particular attention to the routing of the audio, digital, and MIDI channels. With this system you have the ability to intermix live, MIDI-generated, and digital audio in all kinds of creative combinations. Everything, however, ends up in the digital domain for computer processing. All analog sound is routed to the digital I/O cards, where it is converted to high-resolution digital audio. Besides sounds from MIDI devices and tape recordings, this would also include live performance. Everything that is already in digital form stays that way: digital audio either from the DAT tape recorder or generated from MIDI devices that have a digital interface built in. Most external devices in the KISS system can be controlled with MIDI performance and event data, or with MIDI machine control (MMC) data.

A fast AV (audio/video) hard drive especially designed for processing media, 4 or more gigabytes in size, is used to store the digital sampling data generated by the system. Removable disk media, for example Iomega Jaz cartridges of 1 or 2 gigabytes, are provided for storage and backup of digital audio files. Two options are available for recording. The music can be recorded to digital audio tape (DAT, ADAT, or MiniDisc) by directly saving the digital codes onto tape or disc through the digital audio I/O connection. Or, the finished production can be recorded directly onto the CD-R or CD-RW drive (or a DVD-R or DVD–RAM drive, if available) to create a CD audio disc.

Notice: There is no hardware mixer in the digital KISS system; there are no external effects processors. Software like Deck II, Digital Performer, mxTrax, Cakewalk's Pro Audio, Studio Vision, and Pro Tools—all covered in Module 24—create virtual mixers, sequencers, and effects generators in concert with the multitrack digital I/O card and its array of digital signal processors (DSP) and extremely fast audio conversion hardware.

Superheroes: The DSP Chips

At the heart of recent advances in digital audio technology is something called *digital signal processing* and the chips, or integrated circuits, known as *DSP chips*.

Digital signal processing refers to computer processing and manipulation of bitmaps of graphic or sound images. Remember that digitized audio and graphics, when translated into computer data, are merely sequences of binary 1s and 0s. The computer couldn't care less whether the binary data are digital descriptions of a van Gogh painting, a Vivaldi concerto, or a Blues Traveler concert.

Changing the digitized painting from color to grayscale, inverting its colors, or rotating the image would require the computer to process a very large amount of digital data at one time. Likewise, if we wanted to equalize or filter the digitized concerto to remove some low-frequency noise in the recording, create the impression of a large concert hall with digital reverb, or convert a monophonic to a stereo recording, the computer would have to process a very large amount of data to perform the computation necessary to digitally create these effects.

Performing any of these operations on graphics or sound is *digital signal processing*, based on an algorithm that someone has programmed to instruct the computer in how to carry out these tasks. The reverb effect to simulate a concert hall is one example of a DSP algorithm.

Signal processing has been around for a while, but signal processing

Check out the discussion of digital signal processing in Module 22, where effects processors were discussed, as well as Modules 19 and 23.

using large amounts of graphic and sound data in a personal computer has not! Only recently, through the use of specially designed chips to carry out DSP algorithms, have personal computers been able to perform DSP tasks quickly and cost-effectively.

To review, a DSP chip is a very fast electronic circuit optimized to perform a complex algorithm or mathematical operation for manipulating large amounts of digital information. DSP chips may contain a fixed program (e.g., an algorithm for digital reverb or for physically modeling a musical instrument) or may be programmable so that they can perform several tasks. Firms like Motorola, Lucent Technologies, Texas Instruments, and Analog Devices make DSPs for use in fax, voice, graphic image, and audio applications. The power behind the new generation of video games making use of exceptional quality 3-D animation is the DSP chip; the multifaceted power in palmtop or personal digital assistant computers is the DSP chip. It is truly the superhero of computing power in the 1990s.

Digital Sound Cards

Now that you understand something about the DSP engine under the hood of digital audio, we will take a look at digital sound cards for PC workstations (Figure 26.2, item 2). In Module 12 we briefly examined options for digital audio. Most computers come with the basic capability to digitize and play back 16-bit stereo audio at a 44-KHz sampling rate with General MIDI sounds included. The internal digitizing circuitry and software of the Macintosh give you this facility; on the Wintel platform, you can obtain this capability through basic sound cards like the popular Creative Labs Sound Blaster.

As you begin to move up in the sophistication of the sound card for your PC, the sampling capabilities and options increase. Examples include the Creative Labs SoundBlaster AWE64 Gold, Diamond Multimedia Monster-Sound, Ensoniq Soundscape, or Orchid Technologies NuSound. You can add additional waveform resources by purchasing add-on or "daughter boards" from these same vendors or by adding more RAM to the sound card. In fact, the quality of sound from the better PC sound cards is good enough that we could eliminate the external MIDI workstation and sound module from the digital KISS system. In their place, all that is needed is a MIDI keyboard controller.

To understand the difference in features between the low-end, very basic, digital sound cards and the higher-end sound cards, consider our discussions of digital audio data structures in Module 24. Critical are factors related to quality of sampled audio, the speed of processing, the type of filtering used, and the number of simultaneous sound channels that can be processed. Here are some of the attributes of PC sound cards that contribute to the improved quality and flexibility in digitizing audio:

▶ 16- to 24-bit bit sampling resolution and up to 48-KHz sampling rates

▶ Sophisticated filtering of the ADC and DAC, usually with oversampling

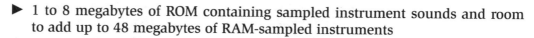

▶ 1 to 8 megabytes of ROM containing sampled instrument sounds and room to add up to 48 megabytes of RAM-sampled instruments

▶ Full duplex operation permitting simultaneous playback and recording of digital audio

▶ Multiple audio channels for sampling, typically 2–4 input and output channels with digital audio and SCSI connections

▶ Use of wave shaping algorithms for sophisticated digital instrument production and, optionally, physical-modeling synthesis

▶ General MIDI with 32- to 64-voice polyphony and a MIDI interface for connections to external MIDI devices

▶ Use of DSP chips for optimal audio compression, performance, and quality, as well as digital effects processing

▶ 3-D sound, surround sound, or virtual Dolby digital sound to create home theatre environments (these capabilities are needed to support DVD video and audio)

▶ Digital I/O typically through S/PDIF, AES/EBU, or ADAT digital interfaces

Wave shaping and physical modeling were discussed in Module 21 when MIDI workstations were presented.

Multitrack Digital Audio I/O Cards

The key piece in the digital audio KISS system is the multitrack digital I/O audio card (13). This card is nothing more than a parallel set of fast, high-resolution, analog-to-digital-to-analog converters with some DSP chips sprinkled in. Figure 26.3 illustrates the basic components of a digital I/O card.

What do you see that you immediately recognize? The digital system has the mandatory ADC and DAC circuitry for converting analog sound into digital data and vice versa. Most systems offer as a minimum four channels of audio input and output, but many provide 16 or more channels of multitrack processing. The conversion resolution may range from 16 to 24 bits

Figure 26.3
Diagram showing the components of a multitrack digital I/O audio system

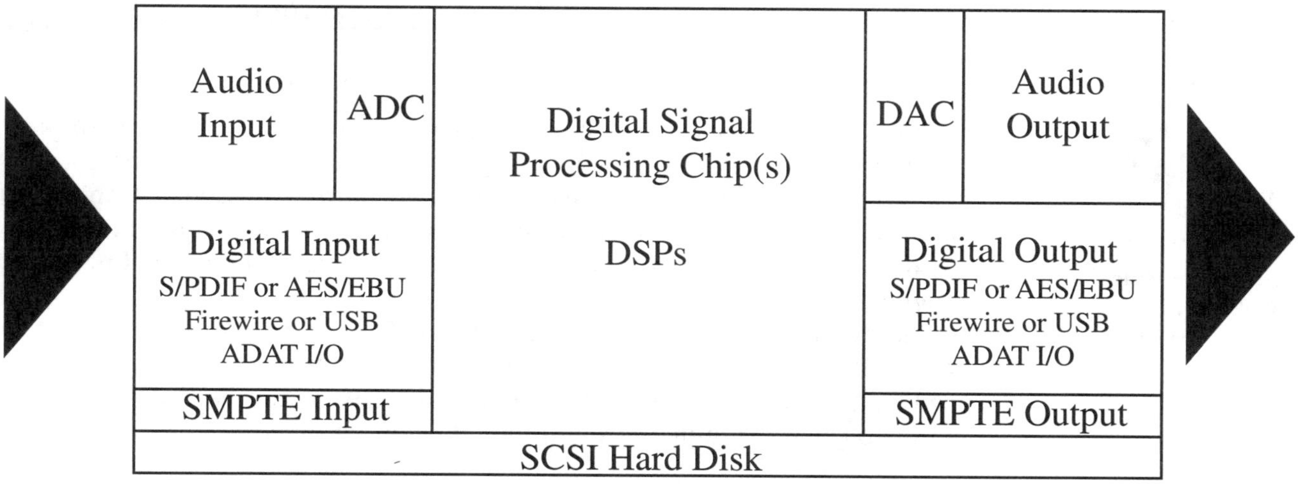

Audio Input	ADC	Digital Signal Processing Chip(s)	DAC	Audio Output
Digital Input S/PDIF or AES/EBU Firewire or USB ADAT I/O		DSPs		Digital Output S/PDIF or AES/EBU Firewire or USB ADAT I/O
SMPTE Input				SMPTE Output
SCSI Hard Disk				

For the budget-conscious musician, sound cards with 2 to 4 channels of digital I/O may be sufficient to create a digital audio workstation, without the purchase of a dedicated, multitrack digital I/O card with 8 or more digital channels.

with sampling rates up to 48 KHz. Besides analog sound conversion, the digital I/O cards also provide channels for connecting to external digital devices like DAT and ADAT recorders, MiniDisc recorders, and MIDI devices that have built-in, digital I/O interfaces. S/PDIF, AES/EBU, Firewire, and USB are all interface standards especially designed for the high bandwidth needs of digital audio and video information; we will discuss these in more depth in just a moment.

In the center of the diagram you see our superhero, the DSP chip, which provides a wide array of complex high-speed signal processing. Typical algorithms from the DSP provide these digital functions:

▶ Equalization and filtering

▶ Reverb

▶ Audio simulation of mono-to-stereo, stereo to 3-D sound, and surround and Dolby Digital sound for home theatre environments

▶ Audio compression and expansion (changing time without changing pitch)

▶ Sampling rate conversion

▶ Algorithms for complex wave shaping using multiple waveforms along with programmed digital-controlled oscillators, amplifiers, and filters

---

MANY FLAVORS OF COMPRESSION

Don't let the different uses of the term *compression* confuse you. The term can refer to a technique for *compressing* digital audio data so they can be stored in a smaller space on a disc, CD, tape, or in a file or in memory. This form of audio compression is discussed in Module 24 and again in the section to follow. Similar compression techniques exist for graphic and video files (see Modules 14 and 28). In the audio world, *compression* also refers to limiting the dynamic range or amplitude of an audio signal (see Module 22's discussion of audio effects) and, as it was used in the preceding section, to compressing the duration of an audio excerpt without changing its pitch.

SMPTE is presented in Modules 19, 20, and 22 in relation to MIDI timing events.

Timing control gets increasingly critical as you add more events to your sequencing activities. Our system in Figure 26.3 uses SMPTE timing control. Digital audio systems with SMPTE input and output provide the ability to synchronize MIDI event data, sampled data, and analog video and audio tape data with all the activities of the digital audio system and the music sequencing software.

The digital audio system typically has a SCSI, Firewire, or USB port to connect it to external hard disks or removable disks. This permits high-speed transfer of digitized audio samples directly to the hard disk without having to pass through the computer. Beside connections to disk drives,

SCSI provides a means to connect the system directly to external CD and DVD players and recorders.

For beginning digital audio I/O, consider the Event Electronics's Darla, Emagic's Audiowerks 8, and Digidesign's Audiomedia III cards. These cards typically have two tracks of analog-to-digital conversion, eight tracks of digital-to-analog conversion, and one or two tracks of S/PDIF digital, and may offer some DSP signal processing as well. To expand these capabilities, consider multitrack digital audio systems like the Digital Audio Labs's V8, Event Electronics's Layla, Korg's 1212 I/O, Digidesign's d24 audio card, or Mark of the Unicorn's 2408. These systems include an internal-bus card for the computer and an interface box for audio and digital connections. Typical features of this level digital I/O is 8 to 32 channels of analog and digital conversion, direct digital ADAT and S/PDIF channels, and DSP signal processing, all with 24-bit/48-KHz sampling resolution. Most of these cards are designed around the cross-platform, PCI-bus standard.

One-on-One with Digital: S/PDIF, AES/EBU, ADAT, Firewire, and USB

ADAT digital interface formats were discussed in Module 22 along with the discussion of DAT recorders.

There are many occasions when data need to be transferred among digital devices. One-on-one exchanges of data can occur between digital audio systems in computer workstations and many other digital audio devices, such as CD and DVD recorders, DAT and MiniDisc recorders, disk drives, digital hard disk recorders, samplers, effects processors, and MIDI workstations. The last thing you want to do with your best digital samples is to have to convert them back to analog audio just to send them to another digital device. Each time a sample reenters the analog world the sound is degraded, similarly to the way sound is degraded going through several generations of duplication in tape recording.

In general terms, how does digital-to-digital work? Digital data from the sending device (e.g., a computer) first get translated into parallel or serial electrical signals that represent the binary codes of the audio sample. Then those data are sent via a cable to the other receiving device (e.g., a DAT tape recorder). The receiving device then translates the codes into the digital format required for its hardware. Throughout the exchange, data remain in a digital form.

There are several ways to transmit digital audio data among devices: SCSI, Firewire, USB, AES/EBU, S/PDIF, and ADAT formats. Notice in Figure 26.3 that digital input and output are provided with these formats. These are common interfaces found on many samplers, CD players, and DAT tape. The S/PDIF interface is most commonly found on consumer digital products, and the AES/EBU interface on professional-level digital audio devices.

S/PDIF and AES/EBU Audio Interfaces. S/PDIF stands for the *Sony/Philips Digital Interface Format*. About the same time that Sony and Philips drew up the specifications for the first compact audio discs and CD-ROMs, they also agreed on a way of exchanging digital data among audio devices. Data exchanged through an S/PDIF interface are transmitted in a high-speed serial

See Figure 22.9*c* for a diagram of RCA, XLR, and other connectors.

AC '97 or Audio Codec '97 provides an industry standard architecture for building future PC audio systems around the PCI, USB, and 1394 Firewire interface that will increase the quality of the audio and provide features compatible with DVD and home entertainment electronics.

FireWire connector
(Apple Computer, Inc.)

format (one bit after another). The presence of an S/PDIF interface is distinguishable by the use of RCA phono connectors and cables for sending and receiving stereo data. Fiber-optic cables are also available for connecting S/PDIF interfaces.

AES/EBU stands for *Audio Engineering Society/European Broadcast Union* digital interface; it is also referred to as the AES3 format. It represents two different standards, both defined in 1985, that have merged together in common practice. This interface is also a serial high-speed format equal to the sampling rate (e.g., 44 or 48 KHz). The cables and connectors used are 3-pin XLR connectors typical in professional quality audio equipment.

Firewire and USB Serial Interfaces. Consider the typical back panel of a computer: connectors for a floppy drive, SCSI device, video, audio, networking, and so on. Whenever you want to change many devices you are best advised to power down the computer. A better design would provide a cabling and connectivity system that would move all of these data through the same channel with one simple connector; a system that keeps the daisy chain features of SCSI, but without its cumbersome cabling, termination, and ID system. At the same time, an improved design would give the interface fast bandwidth to support audio and video at real-time speeds, thus making it possible for audio and video processing to be remote from the computer workstation. And, the design would make the interface so that you didn't have to power down the computer to swap devices—also known as "hot swapping" devices. The *Universal Serial Bus,* or USB, and the *IEEE 1394 bus,* also known as Firewire, are two designs that were developed to meet these needs.

IEEE 1394 or firewire. A workgroup of Apple Computer and other industry participants have been designing an alternative to SCSI to produce better plug-and-play connectivity among computer audio and video. The project design goals were to produce a low-cost cabling system with high-performance speed, simplified cabling, and true plug-and-play operation. The so-called *Firewire* interface is this name of this system; its official name is IEEE 1394.

The graphic in the margin shows the cable and connector design for the Firewire bus. Three pairs of wires are enclosed in the cable: two for data and one for power. Slots for peripherals boards and the spaghetti nightmare of connectors and cables are replaced by one simple connector port. The bus is smart enough to configure itself, thus eliminating ID conflicts and the need for terminators. And, you can hot swap devices. Think of the welcome simplicity this will bring to setting up audio, multimedia, and MIDI workstations.

Transfer rates of 100 to 400 megabits per second are possible. Real-time audio can be transported over the same serial bus as data moving to and from hard drives, laser disc recorders, and digital video and audio devices. It takes about 1.4 megabits per second to move digitized audio data being captured in stereo at 44 KHz with 16 bits per sample. The 1.4-MBps speed hardly puts a dent in the 400-MBps transfer rate of the Firewire interface, thus making it easy to transfer audio samples in real-time between an external audio device and a computer.

Universal serial bus. The Firewire design was driven by audio and video interface needs. The Universal Serial Bus or USB interface was driven by general PC design needs to eliminate the complexity of connections on the back of a computer and to continue to improve the plug-and-play features of consumer PCs. USB's transfer rate is 12 megabits per second in comparison to Firewire's 100- to 400-MBps range. However, as a point of reference, a typical serial computer port's transfer rate is around 100 KBps! Devices on a USB bus can be hot swapped—up to 127 devices in a single daisy-chain.

If Firewire and the USB interfaces evolve into industry standards as predicted, the connectors on your new PC may well be a power plug, a Fireware connector, and a USB connector. All other devices, including power to some of those devices, will be interconnected on one of these two universal bus systems. Stereo audio in and out, microphone in and out, mouse and keyboard connectors, printer and scanner connections, and modem and network connectivity will all be handled through USB and Firewire. Firewire will likely be reserved for high-speed digital audio and video peripherals.

Recording the Finished Product in Digital

The industry was afraid that you would use the digital recorders to make illegal copies of CDs and digital tapes. The Serial Copy Management System (SCMS) codes added to recordings restrict you to making only one generation of a digital-to-digital duplication from consumer recorders.

The digital music production is finished. How do you record it? You could always use analog recording (boring indeed!). But why return to the analog world when many digital recording options are available? If we can delay returning to analog audio right up to the moment the signal is ready to go to the listener or consumer, the least loss of audio information will occur, and so much the better for playback quality. There are several digital recording options for the consumer and professional, with most providing direct-digital I/O through S/PDIF, AES/EBU, and ADAT interfaces to the PC sound card or digital audio I/O board in your computer.

There is a war of formats going on among digital recording options: DHDR, DAT, MD, CD, and DVD. Realize, however, that whether the digital codes are stored on a CD, a DVD, a DAT or ADAT tape, or a MiniDisc, to the computer they all represent audio as digital samples; only the formats vary. These formats can provide basic 2-track, stereo recording (DAT, MD, CD, and DVD), or multitrack recording with 4 up to 128 tracks (MDM, ADAT, MDD, and DHDR), or AC-3, 5.1 channel recordings with DVDs. We will help you to sort out all these acronyms as well as explain their application.

Digital Audio Tape or DAT. The first digital recording medium to surface in the 1990s was the *digital audio tape*, or DAT recorder. Although CD discs have offered digital playback since the early 1980s, it was some time later that consumer digital recording appeared. The quality of DAT tape is comparable to that of CD audio, and DAT recordings can be duplicated with no loss in quality.

A DAT is basically a 2-track tape recorder that records digital codes rather than analog patterns. DAT recorders have been a most popular hardware for recording digital audio productions from a computer music workstation, especially as pricing has become more competitive. DAT recorders are mechanically similar to analog cassette and videotape decks. The DAT tape cassette looks more like a miniature VHS videotape than a cassette audio tape. A tape can be as long as 90 or 120 minutes, and recording is only on one side of the tape.

You manipulate a DAT tape like a cassette tape, with all operations being linear and sequential: record, pause, fast forward, rewind, play, and so on. The search time from one end of the tape is much faster than with an analog cassette deck, however, because of the shorter length of tape required for digital recording. The tape still has to touch the recording head, and that has the potential to degrade the quality of the taped recording over time.

Tascam, Sony, Fostex, and Panasonic are examples of manufacturers of a variety of consumer and professional DAT recorders. The professional models are free of the SCMS copy protection coding found on consumer models, can record at the higher sampling rates of 96 KHz, and have digital as well as analog I/O for recording and playback.

Modular Digital Multitrack (MDM) and ADAT. The basic DAT recorder works as a digital replacement for the reel-to-reel or cassette tape recorder giving a high-quality sonic reproduction. It doesn't, however, fulfill the need for a digital equivalent to the multitrack analog tape recorder. The Alesis DAT or ADAT recorder was one of the first multitrack DAT recorders or Modular Digital Multitracks (MDMs). The ADAT uses S-VHS videotape for recording eight tracks of digital audio at 44.1 and 48 KHz with 16-bit resolution. The ADAT became an instant success for small recording studio needs and was soon followed by Tascam's DA-88, which recorded 8-channels of digital audio in the Hi-8 video tape format. MDMs by Fostex and Panasonic also use the Alesis ADAT tape format and design, while those by Sony follow the Tascam tape format and design.

Audio compression was discussed in Module 24.

With an ADAT recorder, you can record 40 minutes of music on a T-120 video tape. The Tascam Hi-8 format permits 108 minutes of recording on a 120-minute tape. Both units provide both digital and analog I/O, and internal SMPTE time generation. The proprietary ADAT digital I/O format and time sync has become a common interface used on mixers, MIDI workstations, effects processors, digital audio cards, and other music devices. Notice that we included an MDM digital recorder in the KISS digital system in Figure 26.2 (item 8b) as well as in the KISS SMPTE system in Figure 22.11.

MiniDiscs (MDs). Sony's competitive answer to DAT is the MiniDisc format. Where others chose to remain with tape in their pursuit of low-cost and flexible technology for consumer digital audio, Sony remained with laser-optic technology and the CD disc. Three immediate advantages of the MiniDisc are the power of a random-access audio environment, the ability to record the equivalent of a full-length CD of 75 minutes in length on a writeable laser medium, and the reliability of a laser-recording mechanism, where no physical contact is made between components in the recording and playback process (technically this is not *quite* true with MD technology, because there is a magnetic head on the opposite side of the laser beam that makes contact with the disc during the recording process).

The MD recorder uses the conventional CD laser mechanism to play back MD discs. There are two types of MD disc formats, a 2-track audio playback or recordable MD, and a MiniDisc Data or MDD for computer data applications. The 2-track audio MD is what is used in consumer players and recorders. This type of MD recorder is what is shown in the MIDI KISS systems in Modules 21 and 22. The more recent, multitrack MiniDisc recorders use the computer MDD discs for 4-track recording.

MD player technology is similar to that of CD players in terms of operation. However, the MD disc is much smaller than a CD and, of course, with blank MD discs you can record your own audio. To get the same 75 minutes of playing time that a standard CD offers onto an MD disc, Sony resorted to an audio compression scheme. Sony's audio compression (ATRAC; see Module 24) is a perceptual coding that compresses the audio data by eliminating sounds that the ear is not likely to hear. Perceptual compression raises the question as to whether you can "really hear a difference" between an MD digital recording and uncompressed CD or DAT recordings. MD recording, however, offers a less-expensive alternative for digital recording from a computer digital audio workstation. A multitrack MD recorder could also be used in the digital audio KISS system in place of a multitrack DAT recorder (Item 8*b* in Figure 26.2).

The 2-track MD recorders, especially the consumer portable MDs, provide a good, low-budget solution for random-access digital recording for modest computer music workstations. The MDD 4-track units, for a somewhat greater investment, offer a good digital replacement for four-track audio cassette recording. The portastudio units with mixer, effects, and MDD recorder combined are an even more attractive addition to a small studio. Typical examples are the portable recording units by Sony, Tascam, and Yamaha, which provide both digital and audio I/O for recording and playback. It remains to be seen whether the popularity of MD recording will continue, as stand-alone digital hard disk recorders and CD and DVD rewriteable recorders drop to a price comparable to that of the MiniDiscs.

Digital Hard Disk Recorders (DHRD). A few years ago only a professional recording engineer would have considered attempting to sample an entire recording on a hard disk. The cost of disk storage was prohibitive, most of the high-resolution digital audio systems available were expensive, computers didn't have enough RAM or perform fast enough to handle all those sampling data, and access times on hard drives were not fast enough. That has all changed. The cost of all of the components necessary to perform professional quality digital recording from the computer desktop is well within the range of the frugal musician. Additionally, the cost of external backup and file storage through optical drives and Jaz drives has also plummeted. (These provide the means to store, back up, and catalog digital music productions after they are completed.) Hard disk access times are down to 10 milliseconds. Digital hard disk recording (DHDR) or desktop digital record-

A Tascam Portastudio with built-in MiniDisc recording is shown in Figure 22.10*b*.

In 1998, 4-gigabyte hard drives with access times below 20 ms dropped below $300, and it became difficult to buy a hard drive less than 2 gigabytes!

(a)

(b)

Figure 26.4
(a) E-mu Systems Darwin 8-track digital hard disk recorder and the (b) Roland VS-880 digital hard disk recorder.
(Photo courtesy of E-MU Systems, Inc. and Roland Corporation U.S.)

Do *playlists* and *cuelists* sound familiar to you? They should. These techniques were discussed in Module 23 under digital audio editing, and earlier in Module 19 under sequencing with MIDI and digital audio.

ing is now accessible to anyone. The digital audio KISS system (Figure 26.2) is, in fact, a DHDR system built around a PC workstation.

Advantages of digital hard disk recording. Let's review the advantages of digital hard disk recording, some which are shared by other digital recording technologies we've reviewed above:

▶ Sample size and length of digital recording is limited only by the amount of hard disk space

▶ Recording and editing stays in the digital domain

▶ DSP techniques can be applied to the digital samples

▶ Very fast random access to any part of the recording

▶ Ability to interactively and nondestructively edit the recording

Do not think of the digital production as a single, long, contiguous sample. You can digitally record sections of the productions in any order. Do as many retakes as you need and use the DSP operations of the digital audio system to enhance or correct problems in the digital recording. Then, to put the production together, create *edit maps*—also called *playlists* or *cuelists*—with the digital-editing software to instruct the computer how to assemble the final performance. Because of the fast random-access nature of disk drives, playback will result in a perfect rendition.

Varieties of digital hard disk recorders. DHDR systems come in a variety of forms. One is the digital audio KISS system presented in this module: You create a DHDR system around a personal computer by adding a multitrack digital audio I/O system like the Digidesign Audiomedia III system or the Korg 1212 I/O system described earlier, with a 4 gigabyte or larger AV hard disk with a 20-ms or less access time.

Stand-alone or turnkey DHDR systems are also an option. These systems do not require a separate computer to use. All features of the digital audio system and the hard drive are self-contained in one unit and operate much as in any multitrack recorder. Examples of stand-alone DHDR systems include the Akai DR-8 and the E-mu Systems Darwin 8-track digital hard disk recorders. The Akai, for example, has 18-bit A/D, 20-bit D/A convert-

In 1998 the final format to be used for DVD-R and DVD-RW (also known as DVD-RAM) was still to be resolved between competing manufacturers.

Check Module 25 for a discussion of CD and DVD formats and how they work.

The newer "multiread" CD-ROM and DVD-ROM drives will also be able to read CD-RW discs.

ers, 8 analog ins and outs, 2 channels of standard digital I/O (AES/EBU and S/PDIF), and a 20- to 22-KHz frequency response—comparable to the features of high-end, digital audio boards. For the budget-minded, there are the Roland VS-880 or the VS-840 multitrack disk recording systems, which use Jaz or Zip removable drives instead of hard disk drives. Add to any of these systems a rewritable CD-RW recorder and you can make one-off CDs right from your desktop. A stand-alone DHDR system could replace the ADAT or tape recorders in the Enhanced MIDI KISS system (Figure 22.1) or the SMPTE MIDI KISS system (Figure 22.11).

CD and DVD Recordables. At the time Sony developed the MiniDisc format, making your own standard-sized CD audio or CD-ROM disc was an expensive proposition. In quick evolutionary succession, however, CD-R and DVD-R recordable devices have made producing your own CD cheaper than buying a DAT tape system or a MiniDisc! With less than $500 for a recorder/player to connect to your computer (usually bundled with software like Adaptec Toast or CdQuadat WinOnCD) and a few dollars for a blank CD recordable disc, anyone can make their own CD audio recording, DVD video or audio, and CD- or DVD-ROM multimedia production from their multimedia PC workstation. In fact, it has become easy enough that you can purchase your favorite CD disc of music on demand over the Internet and have it written directly to the recordable laser drive attached to your PC.

CD-R or DVD-R stands for compact disc or digital-versatile-disc recordables. Although the data formats for CDs (the Philips-Sony Orange Book format) and DVDs (the UDF format) are different, the mechanics of recording to the disc, or "burning" a disc, are similar. As explained in Module 25, laser recordings work by reflecting light off pits on the laser surface. Pits on the recordable laser discs are made by using a laser to discolor a dye that coats the disc's inner surface. Once the dye is discolored or burned, it will no longer reflect light. Hence, nonreflective tiny dots become the "pits" on the CD or DVD surface. Recordable laser discs can only be used once. For that reason the blank discs are cheaper than the rewritable discs. CD-R and DVD-R require two completely different kinds of recorder/players for a PC. CD-R recorder/players will not play a DVD-R disc.

What reads like a CD-ROM, writes like a CD-R, but allows you to erase and write again over 1,000 times more? A CD-RW recorder/player; a DVD-RW recorder/player has the same traits. CD-RW and DVD-RW (also known as DVD-RAM) are compact disc or digital-versatile-disc ReWriteables (RWs). Why purchase a CD-R or a DVD-R? As the price continues to drop on rewriteable laser recorders, the recordable-only recorder will likely disappear in favor of the rewritable technology. With RW laser recorders, you can erase and write again many, many times over. Unlike the CD-R recorder/players, they will play a DVD-R disc as well as CD-audio, VideoCD, CD-ROM, and CD-R discs. The DVD-RW recorder/players will also play all the different varieties of CD laser discs as well as DVD discs. A CD-RW or DVD-RW is another critical component in the digital audio KISS workstation shown in Figure 26.2.

RW laser technology works a bit differently (pun intended) from the

Figure 26.5
The HP SureStore CD-Writer Plus (CD-RW recorder) for creating rewritable CD laser discs. (Photo courtesy of Hewlett-Packard Company)

recordable laser technology. Instead of a dye that is discolored by a laser, the RW disc uses a technology that changes the disc surface from a crystalline to a noncrystalline state. The areas that are crystalline reflect light, and the areas that are noncrystalline absorb light and create the "pits." How is the disc erased for rewriting? The laser sort of melts the recording layer of the disc, resetting everything back to a crystalline state and removing all the pits. Because of this added complexity, blank CD-RW and DVD-RW discs are at least 10 times more expensive than CD-R or DVD-R blanks.

Why DVD-RW over CD-RW? As we've noted before in discussions of DVD, these discs hold, at a minimum, seven times more data than a CD disc. As the evolution of recordable laser technology continues, eventually the DVD-RW could be the de facto inexpensive standard that handles all formats. Figure 26.5 shows the HP CD-Writer Plus CD-RW recorder/player. There are many companies that make recordable laser drives, including Philips, Hewlett-Packard, Sony, Pinnacle, and JVC, among others.

Viewport VII

Summary

We've come to the end of the seventh view of music technology, through the porthole of digital sound creating, editing, and organizing. Perhaps we should say "picture window" rather than porthole, because this dimension of music technology is growing rapidly in importance for today's musician. Storing and processing sound information on analog tape presents several problems that are solved by using digital data. Digital data are flexible, convenient to work with, of high quality, and they have a long life. The major problem in working with digital data in this way has been the cost of equipment to produce, process, and store it. As computers, electronic instruments, and storage devices become affordable and standard equipment for musicians, this major roadblock is disappearing.

Importance of Data Structures

This viewport has been largely about working with sound itself and has been less concerned with digital instructions about the performance of sound than was the case with the discussion of MIDI. At the very heart of this viewport is the ability of a computer to represent analog experience effectively with numbers.

The opening of Module 24 revisited the notions of sampling rate and resolution that we have continually examined in other sections of the book. We added to this more information on sampling theory that was designed to help you better understand how computers work to represent sound. We stressed such ideas as the Nyquest theorem, oversampling, aliasing, Fast Fourier Transform (FFT), and graphic representation of sound. We noted the increased resolution in sound formats moving to 24- and 32-bit depth and 96-KHz sampling rates, with 6 channels for Dolby Digital and DVD production. We presented information about common schemes for sound compression, including Real Audio for the Internet.

Some of these ideas may seem at first to be more about physics than about music. However, as you learned in working with the digital audio tasks in Module 23, these ideas are fundamental to sound quality and the ability to work musically with today's technology.

Historical Background

Understanding digital sound software really begins with understanding analog sound synthesis and the physical properties of building sounds synthetically. Module 10 was your first introduction to basic acoustics concepts. In the historical perspective that began Module 23, we recounted the early experiments with sound and the growth of electronic music studios. We showed how this led to the manufacture of voltage-controlled synthesizers that used oscillators to produce sound. These sounds were "connected," using patch cords, to other circuitry that modified these sounds in interesting ways.

Digital representations of this same signal path now pervade software design and how we think about digital audio. This is especially true for those planning to work with MIDI devices with computer assistance. As we saw in the tasks we fabricated, creating and editing sound with a sampler or synthesizer uses many concepts from analog synthesis. As we have come to note so often in this book, today's music technology is built on many historical foundations.

Synthesized versus Computer-Based Sound

We created tasks that used both MIDI devices and the computer itself as the actual producer of sound. One clear lesson to be learned from this is that hardware and software choices depend a good deal on the tasks to be performed.

If you are interested in short sound effects or a short sound loop that can form the basis of an instrument sound, you may be better off working with MIDI devices connected to your computer. If you are interested in sampling long excerpts or looking to use your computer as a tape recorder for direct-to-disk recording, external MIDI devices are of less interest. As we saw with the Digital Audio KISS System in Module 26, it is possible with multitrack digital audio to have a complete virtual audio workstation. Of course, these approaches might be combined as we saw in Viewport VI, where digital audio tracks were synchronized with MIDI data. In this case, both the computer *and* the MIDI device were producing sound at the same time.

Software packages are designed to support both kinds of digital audio needs. For creating, editing, and organizing sound, we noted that librarians and patch editors were convenient and effective ways to work with sound in a MIDI device. We also stressed software that actually synthesized sound in the computer and then sent this data to the sound sampler for realization. In working solely with your computer, you will find that today's PCs are often equipped with the resources to sample and produce high-quality sound. Direct-to-disk recording software, such as the programs we worked with for merging speech or a vocal solo with taped music and for synchronizing the music with video, offer both basic and advanced features to accomplish quite sophisticated tasks.

Recording and Editing Features

One important consideration regarding direct-to-disk recording programs is their capabilities for both recording and editing. Some packages place emphasis on recording. They offer many recording tracks beyond the two for stereo output, automated mixing, special ways to merge and bounce the sound source between tracks, virtual tracks, crossfading options between tracks, playlists to support nondestructive editing, and special synchronization with digital movies.

Other programs offer fewer recording options but place importance on digital editing. These often center on process-intensive operations that benefit from the use of digital signal processing (DSP) technology: equalization, filtering, reverb, time compression and expansion, pitch change, format conversions, and many others. Some of these programs also provide precise pencil editing of waveforms to make better sound loops.

Because sound files can easily be moved back and forth between software applications, a musician interested in doing extensive digital sound work will probably want to have more than one type of program to meet special needs. Those musicians just beginning with digital sound will probably find a single title that combines enough of the features of editing and recording.

Modularity

In choosing the right software and hardware, keep the issue of modularity in mind. Many companies offer a basic program and add on to it with plug-in modules. Patch-editing software is a good example. When a new synthesizer or sampler comes to market, a new software module can be added to the basic editing program to support that new machine. This is often much cheaper than rewriting an entire program and much more responsive to individual needs. This same approach is taken with direct-to-disk recording software that features different DSP effects.

Hardware companies that sell audio cards are also experimenting with modular designs. Plug-in "daughter" boards are common, as are special external boxes that house effects-processing cards. These same companies are also developing multitrack digital audio cards with 12 to 24 discrete digitized channels. This is at the heart of the KISS system.

Hardware and Software Choices

What does all this mean for you as you assemble resources? Here is one possible scenario that is consistent with the information we have presented in this viewport.

Hardware

▶ Some kind of MIDI device or devices that will allow editing of internal sound or the capability of accepting a sound file created externally. Files can be exchanged through MIDI, digital I/O, SCSI, Firewire, or PC Card memory. A keyboard or other MIDI controller would also be useful.

▶ MIDI hardware with cables.

▶ Computer with at least 48 MB, or preferably 64 MB of RAM, a fast CD-ROM or DVD drive, and a high-speed, large-capacity hard drive for direct-to-disk recording. (Many systems use an external hard drive for this purpose, leaving the computer's internal hard drive for application software and other needs.)

▶ Computers equipped with DVD capabilities.

▶ Computers equipped with CD or DVD rewriteable drives for the production of custom CDs or DVDs.

▶ Computers equipped with faster communication technologies such as Firewire, USB, or digital I/O.

▶ Internal digital audio soundcard. (For some systems, this may require an audio soundcard that can send digital information out in one of the standard formats such as ADAT, AES/EBU, or S/PDIF. Most PCs generally do not have such a digital capability.)

▶ Internal multitrack digital audio cards for creating a complete, virtual recording studio.

▶ Mixer to accept sound from the MIDI devices and the computer or its sound card.

▶ Amplifier and speakers.

Software

▶ Direct-to-disk recording software that supports both multitrack digital audio recording and sound editing.

▶ Audio CD capture software.

▶ A MIDI sequencer that supports digital sound.

▶ Librarian and patch editing software that matches the MIDI devices owned.

▶ Computer-based sound synthesis program.

This is a long list, but you won't need all these resources just to get started with sound. Pick a few of the resources here to try out for yourself. Most importantly, have fun creating, editing, and organizing sound!

Supplementary Readings

Appleton, Jon. *21st-Century Musical Instruments: Hardware and Software.* Brooklyn, N.Y.: Institute for Studies in American Music, Conservatory of Music, Brooklyn College of the City of New York, 1989.

Appleton, Jon, and Ronald Perera. *The Development and Practice of Electric Music.* Englewood Cliffs, N.J.: Prentice Hall, 1975.

Cope, David. *Experiments in Musical Intelligence.* Madison, Wis.: A-R Editions, 1996.

Dodge, Charles, and Thomas Jerse. *Computer Music* (2nd ed.). New York: Schirmer Books, 1997.

Eargle, John. *Music, Sound, and Technology*. New York: Van Nostrand Reinhold, 1995.

Ernst, David. *The Evolution of Electronic Music*. New York: Schirmer Books, 1977.

Pellman, Samuel. *An Introduction to the Creation of Electroacoustic Music*. Belmont, Calif.: Wadsworth Publishing, 1994.

Pohlmann, Ken C. *Principles of Digital Audio* (3rd ed.). New York: McGraw-Hill, 1995.

Pohlmann, Ken C. *The Compact Disc Handbook* (2nd ed.). Madison, Wis.: A-R Editions, 1992.

Steiglitz, Kenneth. *A DSP Primer: With Applications to Digital Audio and Computer Music*. Menlo Park, Calif.: Addison-Wesley, 1996.

Taylor, Jim. *DVD Demystified: The Guidebook for DVD-Video and DVD-ROM*. NewYork: McGraw-Hill, 1997.

Viewport VIII

Authoring Systems and Multimedia

Technology is the campfire around which we tell our stories.
—Laurie Anderson, *Wired* magazine (1998)

This is a generation that has been raised on MTV and a multitude of stimuli. They don't think linearly; they think mosaically. And they're much more used to getting their information from talking and listening than from reading books.
—Laurence Kirshbaum, President of Warner Books, in *The New York Times Book Review* (August, 1994)

A computer terminal is not some clunky old television with a typewriter in front of it. It is an interface where the mind and body can connect with the universe and move bits of it about.
—Douglas Adams, *Mostly Harmless* (1992)

Overview

We choose to end this book by exploring Roll-Your-Own applications: authoring systems that let you create your own software for instruction, presentation, tutorials, and a host of arts and music activities. The emphasis here is on hypermedia and hypertext. You will see how a wide array of media, from text to graphics to sound images, can be combined through the associative links typical of hypertext environments. Though we briefly review the development of computer programming languages, the viewport concentrates on newer object-oriented hypermedia and provides illustrations from a variety of commercial packages for authoring and media creation. In the data module, we show how the merger of hypertext, the graphical user interface, and object-oriented programming (OOP) languages provides rich multimedia authoring systems. We place special emphasis on programming structures that illustrate OOP from HyperCard, ToolBook, HyperStudio, and JavaScript for Internet applications. Module 29 presents our last look at the KISS System, adding essential hardware needed to support multimedia development. This final viewport will:

▶ Provide a historical context for computer programming languages and the evolution of current multimedia authoring systems

▶ Present several different models for multimedia or hypermedia authoring systems: document, slide, icon, card, page, audioCD, movie, and stage metaphors

▶ Illustrate with sample projects various hypermedia authoring systems and media-creation software

▶ Demonstrate the data structures of a hypermedia scripting language used both on and off the Internet

▶ Review common file types and compression for digital video

▶ Explore hardware needs for multimedia with the KISS Media System

HISTORICAL TIMELINE
The Technology of Authoring Systems and Programming

1830s	Babbage's Analytical Engine uses punched cards to enter the machine's programs
1840s	Alexander Bain uses punched paper tape to program and improve telegraph transmissions
1890s	The Hollerith coding system is devised for punched cards used in the U.S. Census tabulating machines
1930s	Konrad Zuse's Z1 calculating machine is one of the first to use the rules of Boolean logic
	Claude Shannon proposes that information can be treated quantitatively and manipulated by a machine
1940s	Herman Goldstine, with von Neumann's help, devises flowcharting to plan software for the ENIAC computer
	Alan Turing develops assembly language to generate binary instructions for the Manchester Mark I computer
	First computer *bug* so named by a moth that disabled the circuitry of Manchester University's Mark I computer
	Vannevar Bush's article "As We May Think" proposes the *memex* system of documents and links similar to the notion of hypertext
1950s	Grace Hopper develops the first compiler for programming computer machine language
	Bachus and Ziller at IBM invent the FORTRAN compiler, the first high-level language
	John McCarthy develops the LISP computer language for artificial intelligence programming
	Grace Hopper invents the COBOL language, used extensively for business programming
1960s	The BASIC programming language is designed by Kemeny and Kurtz; it later becomes a popular programming language on PCs
	Ted Nelson coins the term *hypertext*
	Seymour Papert's LOGO language is developed at MIT to teach children about computers
	First-generation hypertext systems appear, for example Brown University's Hypertext Editing System
1970s	TUTOR authoring language for PLATO system is implemented at the University of Illinois CERL Labs
	Nicholas Negroponte founds the MIT Media Lab
	The C programming language is developed by Dennis Ritchie at Bell Labs as part of the UNIX environment
	Jensen and Wirth introduce their Pascal programming language
	Paul Allen and Bill Gates (students at Harvard) write a BASIC interpreter for the Altair 8800 PC that becomes Microsoft BASIC

	Alain Colmerauer designs PROLOG for expert systems and artificial intelligence programming
	The "Aspen Movie Map" is the first hypermedia videodisc; it premiers at MIT
	Alan Kay designs Smalltalk at Xerox PARC as the first graphical user interface, object-oriented programming (OOP) language
1980s	CD-ROM and CD audio (CD) formats are defined by Philips and Sony to establish standards for CD laser discs
	BASIC becomes the primary language for education and lay programming projects on PCs
	David Williams's Music Experimenters Package (MEP) and BASMusic, along with Tim Kolosick's Musician's Toolkit, become primary tools for music educators to develop CAI applications from BASIC
	Punch cards and paper tape become obsolete, replaced by magnetic tapes and disks
	Filevision, introduced by Telos on the Macintosh, was the first hypermedia database for a PC
1985	The term *hypermedia* is coined by Ted Nelson for computer-mediated storage and retrieval of information in a nonsequential fashion
	The Delaware Videodisc Music Series is the first use of videodisc developed especially for interactive music instruction
	First commercial hypertext software for a personal computer (GUIDE) is developed by Peter Brown at the University of Kent
	Wittlich, Schaffer, and Babb author *Microcomputers and Music* as a guide to music programming
	Williams and Bowers author *Designing Computer-based Instruction for Music and the Arts* for programming music software on the Apple II
	NoteCards system at Xerox PARC pioneers hypertext graphic metaphors, including "cards" to represent each node with text, graphics, or animation
	Bill Atkinson and Apple Computer, Inc., introduce HyperCard as the first hypertext system included as part of a commercial PC
	Videoworks and MacroMedia Director multimedia software are commercially released
	Fred Hofstetter begins the development of PODIUM for the IBM PC and videodisc players
	Authorware is introduced as an industrial-strength instructional development environment for PCs
	Asymetrix releases Toolbook and Multimedia Toolbook for hypermedia development for Windows
	Brinkman authors *Pascal Programming for Music Research*
1990s	PowerPoint, Persuasion, and other desktop presentation software packages become available for the PC
	Video Toaster software is introduced by Newtek for the Amiga, permitting manipulation and creation of digital still and motion video
	QuickTime and Video for Windows provide digital motion video for Macintosh and Windows computers
1995	CD-ROM drives become standard on multimedia PC workstations, and bookstores, computer outlets, and discount stores offer a wide selection of multimedia CD titles
	Sun Microsystems Java rivals C^{++} as the universal, cross-platform programming language of choice for the development of complete music software applications and of small Java Applets to enhance Web pages
	The Web, with interactive pages developed using HTML, Java, and Javascript, and a wide array of plug-ins for audio and video, provides a universal multimedia development platform for the Internet
	The MPEG movie format, from MPEG-1 for the Internet, to MPEG-2 for DVD discs, to MPEG-4

with its use of the QuickTime digital video architecture for multimedia applications, becomes a standard for digital video across PCs

Hardware designed to master custom CDs and DVDs becomes widely available and inexpensively priced

Digital movie and still image cameras drop in price so that they become commonplace tools in the music classroom to replace VCRs and traditional film cameras

2000   DVD-ROM and DVD-RAM drives replace CD-ROM and CD-RW drives as the laser format of choice for multimedia development and distribution

Multimedia tools seamlessly migrate to Web-based tools, making it possible to develop music instructional materials for on-line and off-line distribution simultaneously

THE PEOPLE

REAL-WORLD PROFILE #1:
DR. FRED T. HOFSTETTER

Role: Professor of Instructional Technology at the University of Delaware

Dr. Hofstetter is widely know for his pioneering work with music theory CAI software programming (GUIDO music curriculum) and more recently for multimedia programming and development (PODIUM software for Microsoft Windows). He helped produce the first major series of laser videodiscs for music instruction during the mid-1980s (University of Delaware Videodisc Music Series) and continues today as a leader in educational technology. He has written extensively about music and computer literacy and serves as consultant to education and business. He uses computers not only in music work but also in his role as Professor of Instructional Technology at the University of Delaware, where he is working on a new Web-based teaching and learning environment called Serf, which stands for Server-side Educational Records Facilitator.

Fred Hofstetter in his multimedia studio
(Courtesy of Fred T. Hofstetter)

Interview:

What do you do? My work with computers has evolved from music analysis to computer-aided instruction to interactive videodisc and, most recently, to multimedia and Web-based teaching and learning. I am a music theorist who became interested twenty-five years ago as a student using computer technology to analyze patterns in music using SNOBOL. When I accepted a position as ear training instructor at the University of Delaware, I used the computer to develop the GUIDO Ear Training System using PLATO to help students learn music. The IBM PC version of GUIDO is used by many music schools around the world. In the early 1980s, I became interested in videodisc technology for teaching and, through the assistance of the National Endowment for the Humanities, produced the University of Delaware Videodisc Music Series. The series won the Gold CINDY for Best Videodisc in 1986. The videodisc was difficult to control, with the thousands of slides on each disc. So, I created a computer program called PODIUM that lets you take a text editor and type an outline of the materials you need, and then PODIUM provides buttons on the screen so you can quickly show any slide or motion sequence from the disc. For the past couple of years I've been working on a Web-based teaching and learning environment called Serf, which lets faculty create courses and deliver them entirely over the Web, and communicate with students in unique and powerful ways.

How did you become interested in computers and music technology? I sometimes tell people that, like Stravinsky, I grew up playing the accordion. When a button on the accordion would jam, I would need to take it apart, figure out the mechanics, and repair it. Indeed, finding a bug and fixing it in a software program is not unlike unraveling the mystery of a reedbox in an accordion.

What computers do you use? For music analysis, I have used IBM mainframe systems; I developed a home music learning system for Atari home computers; I published a book, *Making Music on Micros*, that comes with diskettes for IBM and Apple PCs; at present my PODIUM software runs under Microsoft Windows, and Serf runs in 100% pure Java under Windows NT.

Ways you use computers and music technology? I use computers for word processing, desktop publishing, music composition, MIDI sequencing, editing, music printing, music analysis, and multimedia development.

A unique way you use computers for music? I use PODIUM to synchronize multimedia objects (graphics, videos, and scores) to appear at the proper time while the music plays.

If you could change one thing about how computers are used, what would it be? Encourage people to become creators, not just consumers, of the Internet. That's what PODIUM and Serf are about, making it possible for people to create and not just consume content.

The one most significant change 10 years from now? People will be able to use computers to make the music they like, instead of having to learn to like the music others make.

One word of advice you have for musicians interested in computers? Attend the computer music sessions at the Music Educators National Conference, subscribe to the magazine *Electronic Musician*, and read the monthly column on music technology in the *Music Educators Journal*.

REAL-WORLD PROFILE #2: DR. TIM SMITH

Role: Associate Professor of Music Theory at Northern Arizona University and Multimedia Author

Dr. Smith is associate professor of theory at Northern Arizona University in Flagstaff, Arizona. He is very active in the creation of computer-assisted instruction and World Wide Web–mediated instructional materials, and he wrote "Ready or Not," a computer adaptive system for identifying theory students at risk. Smith uses a Macintosh for word processing, MIDI, graphics, hypermedia programming, and creation of courses delivered on the World Wide Web.

Interview:

What do you do? I teach music theory and do research in theory pedagogy and placement as well as analysis. I'm also involved in developing multimedia CAI materials in music ear training and theory that can be delivered over the World Wide Web.

Could you explain what you mean by research in music placement? In 1991 I conducted a longitudinal study of students, in five institutions, beginning the music theory sequence. Data from this study were used to create software called "Ready or Not," that identifies students at risk. RON generates problems algorithmically, moving in a nonlinear path through various learning objectives, interpolating probabilities in real-time until reliable estimates can be made. This computer-adaptive test is now used in several schools, and research into its predictive reliability is ongoing.

Tim Smith with one of the music CAI programs he developed on the music of J. S. Bach
(Provided by Ball State University Photographic Services)

Could you describe what your Web materials are like using graphics, music notation, CD audio, and Java? And, why do you use these computer tools? In music, where most of what we learn is through studying scores and listening, the digital graphics and sounds of the Web are ideal tools for experimenting with new learning environments. For example, I use PERL scripts to serve graphic and audio files simultaneously over the Web. This allows me to deliver drop-the-needle listening exercises synchronized with scores that automatically turn pages, three-dimensional representations of musical structures, bouncing ball routines, and even cartoons. I use CGIs, JavaScript, and HyperCard to administer listening tests and communicate student progress. When a student completes a homework assignment on the Web I receive an e-mail message with student answers. I use CGIs and HyperCard to archive and grade the answers, and then generate an e-mail reply in three seconds! Why do I use these tools? I've found that I am able to teach more in a two-minute CD sound/animation, with notes leaping off the page and repositioning themselves, than I could, formerly, in a 50-minute chalkboard demonstration. So, this is not just bells and whistles, but an extremely effective new technology for teaching. I use these tools not to be trendy, but because I can communicate more concepts, more clearly, than before. In short, the Web has enabled me to become a better teacher and my students to become better learners.

How did you become interested in computers, music technology, and multimedia development? When I was doing my doctoral work in 1985, I needed the computer to do my research and write my dissertation. My interest in multimedia development began with Robert Winter's HyperCard study (Voyager) of the Beethoven Fifth Symphony. I had been using HyperCard for a long time and realized that I could do the sorts of things that Winter had done—and more. I had always been interested in novel ways of graphing musical structure with sounds and took to HyperCard quickly. This phase culminated in a HyperCard stack on the Goldberg Variations. Upon completion of this work the Web was beginning to develop and I saw this new tool as a way to solve the cross-platform, distribution, and publishing problems of my HyperCard work. Trying to emulate the power and flexibility of HyperCard in an HTML environment has been frustrating in some respects but rewarding in others. I feel confident that the Web will soon achieve the true interactivity of HyperCard.

What computers do you use for your writing, *research, and teaching?* I use a Power Macintosh 8500 and Powerbook 5300c.

What ways do you use computers and technology in your work, especially for authoring theory CAI materials and Web development? I use the computer in every phase of CAI and Web development. This includes word and data processing, creating digital graphics and sounds, hyperlinking, and programming. I also use the computer as a way of helping me develop ideas and gaining analytical insights. I'm not sure I can describe why this happens. The process of telling the computer how I want it to portray what I think is the musical structure invariably gives me new ideas about what the structure actually is—new ideas that would not have been generated without this creative interplay between mind and machine. What I'm suggesting here is that I use the computer to help me think. This has profound implications, I think, for the future of teaching and learning.

If you could change one thing about how computers are used in music, what would it be? Although they are both valid, I would like to see us move more toward using computers to teach music rather than music to teach computers. I believe there is much to be learned and done, from the pedagogical angle, in the area of technologically mediated music instruction.

The one most significant change you predict would happen in the development of music multimedia tools in the next 10 years would be? The creation of curricula (especially ear training) that are self-paced, intelligently branched, pedagogically effective, and that have students listening to much more music and studying many more scores that they do under the current classroom model.

What about music learning on demand over the Web? You have developed a lot of on-line music theory teaching materials that interact with CD discs. Do you see a time in the future where there's this big repository of music learning modules accessible to anyone on the Web? I am confident that soon students will be able to take coursework in music from anywhere in the world. These courses will have content integrity and will outshine some traditional offerings. The technology of Internet delivery of instruction, however, is even now challenging such concepts as the classroom, financial aid, registration, the mission of public universities (to what extent should Arizona be funding the education of students in China?) and even tenure. The Web will enable me, soon, to connect with students from Europe, Asia, South America, and all over the U.S. interacting with each other in a dynamic, information-rich environment that would never have been possible in a traditional classroom. What an exciting possibility!

One word of advice you could offer musicians and students interested in authoring music instruction materials would be? Don't expect to attain the needed skills from one source, book, or course. Most of your preparation will come through experience: trial and error. You'll need to dig up many of the answers for yourself. Purchase new software, study manuals, and bounce ideas off of each other. When you have a problem, inquire about and find the answer for yourself. Sometimes you'll need to create your own problems to solve in order to expand your multimedia skills. Every problem has a solution but some are more elegant than others.

<table>
<tr><td>

Module
27

</td><td>

Authoring and Multimedia Software

</td></tr>
</table>

We have suggested that software might be divided into three categories: Buy-and-Run, Fill-Your-Own, and Roll-Your-Own. In all of our work so far, we have been dealing with the first two categories. In this last viewport, we turn our attention to the last category, Roll-Your-Own, and do so by focusing on one of the fastest-growing and exciting kinds of technology today: multimedia software and authoring tools.

Actually, we've mentioned the term *multimedia* before, particularly in Viewport III, where we noted that it was an important category of computer-assisted instruction software. In this final viewport, we return to multimedia, but with a new eye. Here we examine how to actually *construct* your own multimedia software by using much of what we have learned already about graphics, music notation, MIDI, digital audio, laser-disc technology, and the Internet. In this module, we present information about multimedia authoring software that helps musicians integrate sounds and images not only for music teaching and learning, but for a variety of musical activities. Because no authoring system can possibly cover all of the tools needed for working on graphics, movies, sounds, and music, we will also describe support software that helps develop and refine these features that are used in multimedia projects. Some of these programs will be new; others will be old friends from other viewports.

Multimedia is a big topic, and hundreds of books and articles have been written about it from many perspectives. What we attempt is to provide a broad introduction for musicians who are interested in getting a strong conceptual basis and some beginning practical experience. After some background information about what multimedia software is and where it came from, we will present some basic information about digital video—a file type that we have not covered thus far. We will then lead you through a tour of the major kinds of authoring software and describe four projects that use some of these packages.

Check out Module 9, where we first introduced multimedia CAI.

A Little Background

What is multimedia and how can it be used by musicians? What is its history? Most definitions of computer-based multimedia include two essential characteristics. First, ways to personally interact with the software are designed to offer considerable flexibility in how to use and navigate through the program. Second, content is expressed as multiple forms of digitally encoded visual and aural experiences, usually three or more forms combined. These visual and aural experiences may include:

Multimedia is defined as incorporating three or more different forms of media into a computer-based environment.

▶ Text material arranged as blocks, scrolling fields, and moving letters, or graphically treated (such as words wrapped around objects)

▶ Still images, such as object graphics, music notation, scanned images, digital photos, or single frames from a movie

▶ Animated graphic images

▶ Digital sound effects, music, and speech

▶ MIDI-based sound and music

▶ Digital video

With the exception of video, which will be presented shortly, all of these data types have been encountered before in this book. In many ways, multimedia brings all that we have presented in music technology together for the musician.

HISTORICAL PERSPECTIVE

Multimedia Dimensions of Music

Putting computer issues aside for a moment, multimedia in music is really about as old as the art itself. Music as part of sacred ritual involves movement, sound, and images of all sorts. In Western culture, one can imagine the impact on parishioners listening to monks singing Gregorian chant in medieval churches while watching processionals and smelling incense. In fact, concert experiences in the Western tradition, especially those that are accompanied by program notes and discussions about the music, might be considered a kind of multimedia. Opera is a multimedia extravaganza, especially the Wagnerian music drama. Interestingly, it wasn't until the invention of tape recorders and phonographs that music listening became solely an aural experience.

Perhaps a more obvious example of live multimedia is the performance art that began in the 1960s and continues today. Such "happenings" may include music performances with traditional acoustic instruments together with live video images, dancing, spoken words, special lighting effects, electronically generated sound, and even

special smells to fill the room. In the pop and folk genre, Woodstocks '69 and '94 were live multimedia music extravaganzas that expressed powerful sentiments of society and culture. Of course few of these examples include personal interactivity, but even that can be found in experiments with music of this century. John Cage in the 1950s can be credited with some of the first experiments with music designed by audience participation and by chance or aleatoric operations. Todd Rundgren and Laurie Anderson are two multimedia performing artists of recent times who have truly explored the full dimension of live multimedia on stage. Tod Machover's work with his *Brain Opera* is another example.

Evolution of Hypermedia

In terms of computers and machines, personal access to multiple forms of information has its roots reaching back far earlier than most realize. Many assume that such thinking started with Bill Atkinson's HyperCard program for the Macintosh computer in 1987. Although this was the first significant authoring tool for multimedia on a personal computer, it was not the first example of this kind of thinking. In the summer of 1945, an issue of the *Atlantic Monthly* magazine contained an article called "As We May Think" by Vannevar Bush. Bush was an MIT scientist in charge of a government research and development office. At the time, he was concerned with the organization and accessibility of growing technical information and its archiving on microfilm. He speculated about a special machine he called a *memex* that might have special displays and quick access to all kinds of data in mass storage. He also speculated that such technology would allow people to think more creatively because it would encourage nonlinear thinking through "associative links" between information.

Vannevar Bush, MIT professor and science advisor to President Roosevelt
(Courtesy of The MIT Museum)

Bush's vision was extended in more realistic terms by Ted Nelson, a computer visionary who coined the term *hypertext* in the 1960s. Nelson's long-term project, called *Xanadu* after the mythical utopia in Coleridge's poem "Kubla Khan," is based on the concept of a series of connected nodes that represent vast repositories of text. Those using the system would have access to nonsequential, nonlinear text—thus the term *hyper* or "extended." The important thing to realize about hypertext and its close cousin *hypermedia* (another termed coined by Nelson) is that they represent a way of thinking about relationships among complex sets of objects. There is no single, previously defined path that must be followed by everyone.

Ted Nelson, computer software designer, author, and visionary
(Courtesy of Ted Nelson)

These systems of interaction are defined by the mind of the user. They are consistent with theories in cognitive psychology and education.

Soon after the arrival of personal computers in the 1980s, the notion of integrating visual and sound information to form a platform for multimedia was vigorously pursued by artists and computer programmers alike. It seemed like a natural combination. An early example was software that accessed a laser videodisc containing holdings from the National Gallery of Art. Another example was a program designed to be used with a commercial audio CD of the Beethoven Symphony No. 9. Both these titles were created by The Voyager Company for the Macintosh using HyperCard as the authoring system.

Bill Atkinson, designer of HyperCard
(Reproduced by permission of General Magic, Inc.)

Tim Berners-Lee then took the notion of hypertext and hypermedia one step further when he designed the notion of the World Wide Web where links between media could literally span the globe over the Internet. In 1992, Berners-Lee and others at the CERN Lab in Switzerland developed the Web, HTML, and HTTP, all key components to the Internet as we know it today.

Recent Developments

Only recently has the power of personal computers allowed serious development of hypermedia to occur. Faster clock speeds, more powerful CPUs, larger amounts of inexpensive storage and memory, and better resolution of digital information have all contributed to affordable computers and multimedia possibilities with incredible realism.

Software data structures have helped as well. We already understand the power of the MIDI data structure and of digital sound improvements offered by higher resolutions and faster sampling rates, but one of the turning points for multimedia has been digital movies. The first major development of this technology was in 1991, with the development of the QuickTime file format and of compression and decompression schemes for the

Macintosh. QuickTime is now available for Wintel computers, as is Microsoft's format called Audio-Video Interleaved (AVI), or Microsoft Video for Windows. MPEG is another movie format that is used, especially on DVDs. This integration of motion video into the computer's desktop has stimulated a number of commercial multimedia software products that use video, sound, still graphics, animation, and text. CD-ROM discs provide the storage space necessary to support all kinds of products. The Internet now provides similar delivery around the globe to anyone, anytime. The most exciting thing about all this is that the technology to support multimedia will only get better while costing less and less.

A second aspect of multimedia software is its interactivity. There are many ways to personally interact with the software in any order, allowing for considerable flexibility in how to use and navigate through the program. Navigation tools like buttons, palettes, and menus offer the means to explore in personally meaningful ways. Usually this navigation is not linear like a traditional book, film, or slide presentation.

By way of example, Figure 27.1*a–d* contain screens from Robert Winter's *Crazy for Ragtime* CD-ROM for Macintosh and Windows. Figure 27.1*a* displays a screen from a section that offers information about specific rag compositions. Buttons lead to other graphics, including a view of the actual notation, as is displayed in Figure 27.1*b*. The software plays back the rag with the built-in sounds of the computer while moving a frame over the notation to aid the user in following the music.

Figure 27.1*c* is of a screen that is dedicated to explaining the subtleties of performing a rag. The QuickTime movie demonstrates performance techniques, and the text of the movie is displayed on the left of the screen. Finally, Figure 27.1*d* is a construction kit that allows users to design their own rags by dragging tiles into place to form the composition. Parameters of key, tempo, and timbre can also be specified. Created rags can be saved as files for playback and discussion later.

There is something very special about this kind of multimedia experience on a personal computer. It allows the integration of many powerful ways to experience the richness that is music. The experience is qualitatively different from just reading about it, seeing a score, or even hearing the music in isolation. Some people argue that experiencing music in a multimedia format changes the musical experience in a fundamental way, much as the invention of the phonograph and tape recorder did in the early part of the century.

Of course, this software is only as good as the content it holds. No amount of fancy visual or aural experience can save software that is weak in substance. Perhaps this is the single most critical aspect of quality multimedia, and this is why musicians stand the best chance of designing the best multimedia software in music.

How Can Musicians Use Multimedia?

There are many ways multimedia software can be applied to music. Let's examine just a few possibilities:

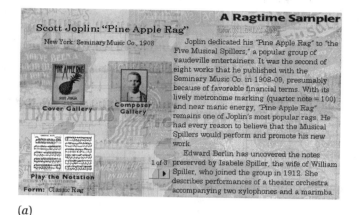

(a)

(b)

(c)

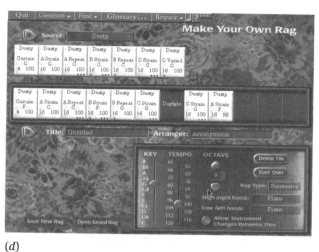

(d)

Figure 27.1
Crazy for Ragtime
(Calliope Media L. P.
[Mac/Windows])

▶ Simulation

▶ Performance

▶ Presentation

▶ Demonstration

▶ Instruction

Simulation. We showed the composition section from Crazy for Ragtime CD-ROM (Figure 27.1*d*). The software simulated the composition of rag music. Simulation is a common design for computer-based multimedia environments.

Performance. Growing out of the use of technology in electronic music and performance art, multimedia can be used for live concerts. MIDI-based software such as Opcode's Max and Steinberg's XPose can be used to control graphics and text as well as sound. Another example is Music Interval Systems' Interactor, created by Mark Coniglio and Morton Subotnick. Interactor links MIDI events with graphics, text, and sound so that live performers can control many different kinds of aural and visual experiences in real-time during performance.

Another fascinating approach is the use of multimedia to create a total artistic experience outside the concert hall. Examples of this are Subotnick's *All My Hummingbirds Have Alibis* and *5 Scenes From an Imaginary Ballet*. Both works are presented on CD-ROM and are meant to be experienced interactively on the computer.

Revisit Pierre Boulez's discussion of live electronic performance in his interview in Viewport VI as well as our discussions of interactive MIDI devices in Module 22.

Presentation. There is plenty of opportunity to use technology in nonmusical settings. Businesses often use technology to present ideas to potential clients or to their own employees. Musicians do the same when meeting with funding agencies, foundations, academic associates, and fellow musicians. Multimedia presentation software can provide a dynamic and effective way to present ideas in order to make full use of text, graphics, animation, special visual effects, music, and sound.

Information. Have you ever walked by a display rack in your favorite computer or music store and seen an eye-catching display screen running a demonstration of a hot new product? Perhaps you were even able to interact with it by selecting a few options or by moving an icon or two around the screen with a joystick, light pen, or trackball. Perhaps, in your last visit to the CD store, you noticed an information kiosk (fancy word for a bulletin board) that had a touch-sensitive computer screen displaying an indexing system for CDs. You worked through a set of menus that led you to a screen for the disc you were looking for. Then you were offered a movie clip from a promotional video, a button that played a few bars of the music, and a scrolling field with ordering and price information.

In both cases, you were seeing multimedia in action. The technology was designed to provide information about a product or service. Software that we will highlight in this module can help you create stand-alone multimedia that can do this. You might want to create an information kiosk in a music department or school—just like the one at the mall—that features a multimedia guide to ensembles, classes, or upcoming events. If you are a studio music teacher, you might want to create an attractive system for parents to use to schedule lessons or to learn more about what you expect from private students.

Instruction. This is one of the most extensive uses of multimedia in music today. Computer-assisted instruction was introduced in Module 9. At that time, we were concerned with Buy-and-Run software like Voyager's Dvořák's New World Symphony. These are commercial titles developed by professionals for distribution to a wide audience. This kind of software often centers on a single masterwork or a set of pieces, and provides audio CD files as basic resources. There are many CD-based products like these produced every year, covering a wide set of music topics. We can look forward to DVD-based titles as well!

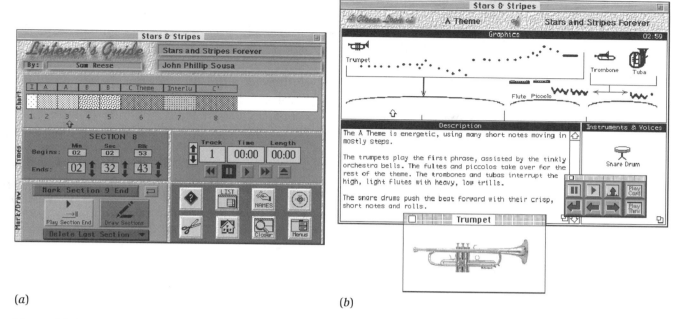

(a)
(b)

Figure 27.2
Listener's Guide, developed
using HyperCard
(Apple Computer, Inc. [Mac])
(Example courtesy of Sam
Reese, University of Illinois
School of Music)

Of course, multimedia for instruction can be personally developed by musicians—people like you. Using authoring systems and special editing software tools, musicians can create their own software for music teaching and learning, and make their own CDs!

Look at Figure 27.2. These are screens from a program developed by a music educator using Apple's HyperCard. The purpose of the program is to allow students to construct their own analysis of a piece of music, using graphics and words. The student listens to a track from an audio CD (any kind of music, of course) and creates buttons to designate sections of music. The screen on the left represents an analysis of the famous Sousa march *Stars and Stripes Forever*. The buttons with letters represent sections of the march. Clicking on these buttons plays the music again. You can then create graphic representations of the music using the drawing tools supplied by the software program and can create scrolling fields of text for comments as well. The screen on the right shows an analysis of the *A* section that was created by a student. The program even supplies a set of pictures representing various musical instruments that can be used.

Delivering Multimedia Over the Internet

Many commercial multimedia programs are distributed in CD-ROM and DVD formats. The size of the supportive text, music, and graphics files makes disc technology necessary. The disc that you buy has the application software on it; this application is often copied to your hard drive and run from there. The application software then calls into action the many text, music, and graphics files on the CD or DVD as needed.

This is not the only way to experience multimedia. As we explained in Module 6, the World Wide Web is rapidly becoming a dominant service on the Internet because of its ability to deliver multimedia experiences. Musicians can simulate, perform, present, demonstrate, and instruct using text, graphics, animation, movies, sounds—all from a Web site that can serve the world.

Projects on the Web. There are two ways the Internet can deliver multimedia. The first is simply to put projects on the Web. For instance, Professor Reese might decide to share a version of his Listener's Guide (Figure 27.2) with the Internet community. He could serve this off an Internet Web server with Royal Software's LiveCard—a special program designed to render HyperCard stacks as Web pages on the Internet. Other authoring systems offer similar options with plug-ins or other add-on programs that are designed to make it relatively simple to deliver local multimedia projects to the Web.

Dedicated Web pages. It's more likely, however, that authors will want to create dedicated Web pages to support multimedia experiences with music as the central content. In Figure 27.3a and b, we display a Web site designed to offer information about Baroque music in support of a college music class. In addition to the text, links on this page provide sound by playing a particular audio CD that the user has mounted on a local computer. From the remote site, the teacher can create a Web page that sends a message to the student's local computer to play a portion of music and also display a graphic that shows the notation! The teacher can even have portions of the notation highlighted while the music is playing. This is actually accomplished by Professor Tim Smith at Northern Arizona University, one of our featured musicians that we interviewed at the beginning of this viewport.

Figure 27.3c displays a screen from a site devoted to jazz music. Here the user can listen to jazz recordings, hear interviews with jazz artists, and read text and view graphics about jazz music. It's also possible to "tune in" a jazz radio station by linking to a site that "streams" live broadcasts from radio stations.

Figure 27.3d provides an example of a college residence hall Web site. From this page, viewers can see digital movies of works by art and music students, read articles written by students living in the residence hall, and take a virtual tour of the different floors of the residence hall—including a visit to each room.

Digital Video: The Missing Ingredient

As you work with multimedia, you will use many of the concepts and skills learned in previous viewports. Word processing and graphics will be used for text and still images such as original drawings and scanned pictures. You will use music notation clips and the standard MIDI files that notation software generates. You may also want to use a sequencing program for more musically expressive MIDI files. Digital audio is almost certain to be used, both prerecorded sound effects and new recordings of your own. All of this territory is familiar.

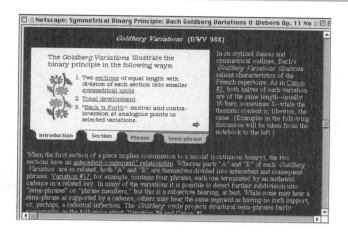

(*a*) Web page from a course taught by Professor Tim Smith at Northern Arizona University

(*b*) Web page from a course taught by Professor Tim Smith at Northern Arizona University

(*c*) Jazz Central Station Website

(*d*) Jones Residential College at Northwestern University

Figure 27.3
Examples of Web sites that render multimedia experiences

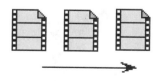

What is new to you is digital video. You already know about digital audio. Many of the same concepts apply to video. The idea is to let the computer translate the analog experience of video into numbers so that the video can be stored and played back on demand. For most movies, both the sound and the image need to be captured and the result saved in a file.

Real Movies versus Digital Ones. When we watch a motion picture in a theater, videotape, DVD, or television broadcast at home, we are watching *frames* of still images go by faster than the eye can detect, creating the illusion of motion. Digital video on a computer works in much the same way. In most cases, a series of images are created to represent digital versions of a frame. The computer plays these digital frames back in a window on the screen as fast as it can to create the illusion of motion. These frames are usually captured from analog video in some way. Text can be overlaid on the video frames and still images mixed with the video.

Module 28 contains a description of the data structure for digital video. Match the software ideas that we include here with that material for a more complete picture.

In addition to capturing the video samples, audio samples are taken at the same time. These are either placed in separate tracks, as a music sequencer, or they are *interleaved* with the video. *Interleaved* means that the computer mixes sound with video frames. For digital video formats that use the track idea, these tracks might contain digital audio or MIDI-like code to control a synthesizer.

The window that displays the video will likely contain a control bar, much like the one you see in the margin. This acts like a control bar on a VCR to control the digital movie on the computer. Notice the button to control sound level as well. The slider in the middle allows you to move through the movie frame by frame.

Figure 27.4 displays frames of a collage of different movies, each dealing with a different topic and each ready to play. These were produced by some students at Illinois State University as they experimented with digital video. Notice the different sizes and the controller bar on each. Two of them have added text.

If you have never seen digital video run on a computer before, you are in for a treat. You probably sense the excitement, interest, and real learning that video can bring to a multimedia project.

Is there a downside to all of this? Yes: Just as we saw with digital audio in Viewport VII, digital representations of complex analog experiences can take a

Figure 27.4
Examples of QuickTime movies created by music students using digital video (Courtesy of Colleen Baker, Gerry Magallan, and Peter Juvinall)

lot of room in storage. Imagine the load placed on hardware to deal with audio *and* video. A single *second* of untreated video and audio, in full color filling up a computer screen and with 16-bit sound, can take as much as *30 megabytes* of disk space! The key word in the last sentence is *untreated*. As you will see in Module 28, software engineers have found ways to compress these files to make them workable in our multimedia projects.

See Module 28 for more information of digital movie formats, including MPEG.

File Formats. The first major file format for digital video on personal computers was QuickTime from Apple Computer, released in 1991. This format is the major one used on Macintosh computers today and is also used extensively with the Windows operating system on Wintel machines and with UNIX machines. Shortly after QuickTime's release, Microsoft created its own Video for Windows format that runs on Wintel computers. Both formats are very similar in design and use. Translating programs exist that move files from one format to the other. Most of the information about software use with digital movies is common for both formats and will be presented here with little distinction between platforms and format.

Playing and Capturing Video. So how does the computer play the video? First, additional software must be added to the system folder. These extensions almost always come as a standard part of the operating system of a modern computer. Once this extension software is part of the system, the computer can play the movie file without special hardware.

In Module 29, our KISS workstation system will add a digital video card. You will need to add this to your computer system as well to create your video clip.

Producing a clip from scratch, however, is a little different. To capture video and audio from a VCR, camera, or other video source, you will need either a computer with specially designed built-in hardware or special sound and video capture boards. The cost of these boards can run from a hundred to several thousand dollars depending on the quality and special features you desire.

One caution: computer systems vary greatly in their support for video and audio digitizing. For instance, most Windows machines will need both an audio and a video card for capturing clips. Macintosh machines have support for digitizing audio, but certain models may require a video card. An audio card may also be necessary for some special needs.

Both QuickTime and Video for Windows provide software for capturing video clips and doing some basic editing like cutting and pasting, cropping the size, and adding and altering audio. Software for performing these tasks may also be included with whatever video and audio card you buy.

Different Kinds of Authoring Software

We have offered examples of different ways musicians can use multimedia. What is necessary to create this software? Certainly you need the media itself: text, graphics, animation, and digital sound and video. Ways to create most of these media have already been described in this book. You also need an authoring system to tie this material all together; that is the subject of this section.

When we use a multimedia product, it is not always clear from the

Table 27.1 Types of Authoring Software for Multimedia

Major Category	Development Metaphor	Authoring Software	Platform
Screen	Document	Any mid- to high-level word processor	Macintosh/Windows
	Slide	Microsoft PowerPoint	Macintosh/Windows
		Gold Disk Astound	Macintosh/Windows
	Icon	Macromedia Authorware	Macintosh/Windows
	Card	Apple HyperCard	Macintosh
		Asymetrix Multimedia ToolBook	Windows
		Roger Wagner HyperStudio	Macintosh/Windows
	Page (Internet)	Bare Bone BBEdit	Macintosh
		Lute ArachnophiliaWindows	Windows
		Adobe PageMill	Macintosh/Windows
		Netscape Composer	Macintosh/Windows
		Macromedia Dreamweaver	Macintosh/Windows
Time	Audio CD	AABACA Clip Editor	Macintosh
		ECS CD Time Sketch	Windows
	Movie	Apple QuickTime	Macintosh/Windows
		Microsoft Video for Windows	Macintosh/Windows
		MPEG	Macintosh/Windows
	Stage	Macromedia Director (Shockwave for the Internet)	Macintosh/Windows

screen exactly what sort of authoring system was used. There are many possibilities for authoring and it can become confusing when trying to decide which one to use for a music project. In Table 27.1, we have categorized choices into eight types based on the way the actual authoring is done—or what some have called the *development metaphor*. Each approach offers different strengths and weaknesses. The selection process depends on the kind of project to be done, which working method is most comfortable to you, and your budget. In this table, we also provide product examples of each type and the platform that each product supports.

We have placed the first five development metaphors (document, slide, icon, page, and card) into a large group that can best be regarded as *screen based*. Each of these types presents screens of information, one at a time, for the user to view. Each screen provides the full range of media, and the user can move from screen to screen as necessary. The last three types (audio CD, movie, and stage), however, are *time based*. With these approaches, the media is designed to be displayed in time much like frames in a movie. The authoring systems in this group provide many ways to stop the action and to allow for plenty of user control, but the underlying concept is to provide a series of unfolding events in time rather than a set of static screens.

We will provide a brief description of how each type works, and then comment on a few strengths and weaknesses. Before we describe each type, let's examine a few points that are true for most multimedia authoring systems.

MIDI implementation. MIDI is supported within the QuickTime system extension for both Macintosh and Windows computers. What this means is that MIDI files can be played using the QuickTime General MIDI instrument sounds built into the system software. You can also ask this software to route the MIDI data to external MIDI devices. MIDI sound, as with video, can be included in a wide variety of documents, including all our multimedia types. For some authoring systems, MIDI can also be accessed through the use of special operating system enhancements meant to control MIDI devices directly. These are called *external commands, X-commands,* or *XCMDs* for Macintosh computers, and *dynamic link libraries* (DLLs) for Windows computers. XCMDs and DLLs are small bits of programming code that can be used by multimedia software to extend its ability to control external devices.

Study sound file formats in Module 24 and graphic formats in Module 14.

Graphic and sound file formats. All the authoring systems support graphic and digital sound file import; however, some are more complete than others. When speaking of importing files, we are referring to different file formats for sound (e.g., SND, AIFF, WAV, MID, AU, RA or RM), graphics (e.g., Paint, PICT, WMF, PICS, TIFF, EPS, GIF, JPG), and movie (e.g., MOV, AVI, or MPG). Because effective multimedia depends on a variety of information, this is an important consideration.

Independence and cross-platform compatibility. Most authoring systems let you create files that *stand alone*; once they are developed on an author's computer, they can be distributed to other people's machines without needing the application software that created them. It's like creating a small application unto itself. Another way of accomplishing this is to provide a *player* application that can be distributed freely along with your work. Most multimedia software is cross-platform, meaning that it can be run on either Mac or Windows.

Cost. Costs vary enormously, depending on discount programs and institutional affiliations. Costs are usually lower if you are connected to an educational institution.

Screen-Based Authoring

Check out Viewport IV on desktop publishing!

Document Development. Can it really be possible for multimedia to be supported by word-processing software? Although this software was not initially designed for multimedia, today's powerful word-processing programs like Word and WordPerfect allow integration of images and sounds to illustrate a point. In Viewport IV, we discussed how easy it is to add graphics to a word processing file; the same is true of video. Because video files are supported by utilities that are added to the operating system and not to the application itself, you can include a movie inside most documents, including word processing files.

Pros and cons. Document-based multimedia has the advantage of being easy to use and available to most musicians at little cost for additional soft-

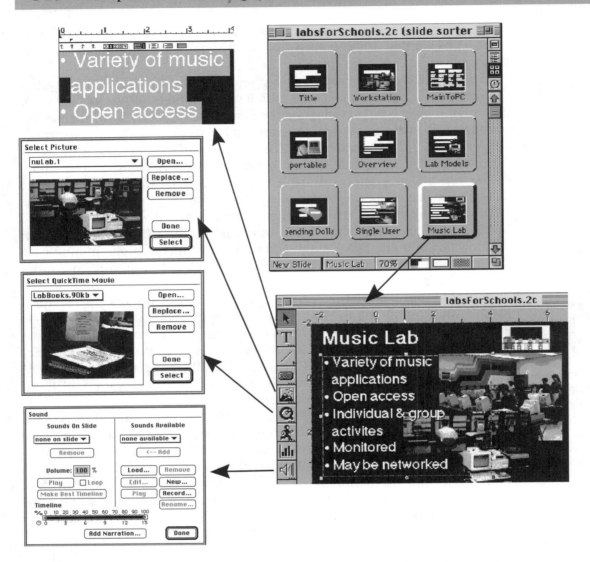

Figure 27.5
Slide development using
Astound
(Gold Disk Inc. [Mac/
Windows])

ware. From an educational perspective, it can be easily used in classes or individually by distributing files through computer networks. Major disadvantages include a lack of any programming language to do interactivity, and limited or no support for sound and animation.

Slide Development. Another approach is a slide-by-slide design where the author works with text, graphics, and sound to create a set of visuals in a desired order—a kind of computer-based slide show. Titles that take this approach are also referred to as *presentation* software because they are used in a linear fashion to support activities like class presentations, instructional tutorials, lectures, or group talks.

Figure 27.5 offers a glimpse into the production of a project using Gold Disk's Astound. Later in this module, we will use another presentation package, Microsoft's PowerPoint.

The *slide sorter* is pictured in the upper right of Figure 27.5. It provides control over the order of each slide and allows immediate access to a particular slide. We have chosen one of these in the lower right and then have linked this slide to several editing options, including text entry, picture and movie objects, and sound. Once the individual slides have been created and ordered appropriately, the program runs the show. Most screen authoring systems also have a set of draw tools that allow the custom creation of images.

Programs like Astound and PowerPoint provide a set of templates so that users do not have to design screens from scratch. A number of color options are provided. Special video effects that make for interesting transitions from screen to screen are included. Options are also provided for moving backwards and navigating to other slides; however, interactivity of this sort is limited. These programs also allow access to audio CD sound and support fairly sophisticated animation. Support for printing screens to 35-mm film and overheads is provided, as well as for preparing handouts with notes and thumbnail sketches of the visual screens.

Pros and cons. Slide-based multimedia is excellent for presenting ideas dramatically, especially if you intend to follow a predictable path. This software might work well for an information kiosk or product demonstration. Support for color and special effects is generally outstanding, almost approaching overkill if used too much. Printing options may include summary notes for your audience as well as special notes for you to have during the presentation.

A big negative is the lack of a scripting language for special needs, although some interactivity is offered with buttons that can link you to different slides in the presentation, to various applications, and to the Web. Aggressive support for color also takes its toll in speed of performance and in file size.

More about scripting in Module 28.

Icon Development. Yet another approach to multimedia authoring uses icons that represent media elements, decision points, and other interactive constructions. Using this system, projects are assembled much as one would create a flowchart of objects. Display icons represent screen constructions such as text and graphics, whereas animation icons that are connected to the displays make the objects move. Decision icons help route the movement of the program, as do the interactive icons. Sound, graphic, animation, and movie icons help to add depth. Sets of these icons can all be collapsed into one object that can be linked to other sets; this helps to establish the modular nature of this approach. Macromedia's Authorware is an icon-based software package.

Pros and cons. One clear implication of this approach is that there is always a defined path or set of paths to follow. This structure still allows for some interactivity, but it is "hard-wired" into the program from the start. This makes this software best for educational settings where step-by-step guidance is important. Because movement is so easily constructed with the icons and their links, development time can often be quick—even with sophisticated designs and media elements. This software also supports a wide selection of imported file formats.

Icon software does include scripting and other programming support, but it can be difficult to use. Authorware projects are cross-platform between Windows and Macintosh operating systems, provided careful planning of media objects, fonts, and color occurs beforehand. This software can be the most expensive in the industry.

Card Development. This is one of the most popular screen-based multimedia metaphors and has been around for the longest time. Excellent examples include Apple's HyperCard for Macintosh, Asymetrix's Toolbook and Multimedia ToolBook for Windows machines, and Roger Wagner Publishing's HyperStudio for both platforms. HyperCard was the first multimedia authoring software designed for a wide computer audience and is partly responsible for the early rise of multimedia as a major software category in personal computing. The metaphor here is a stack of cards. Cards may share certain characteristics from card to card, yet have many different layers of information. Buttons for navigation and for accomplishing tasks can be placed on cards, as can fields of information containing text. Graphic images can be placed in any location and sounds can be easily referenced as well. Most card authoring systems also have a set of paint tools that allow the custom creation of images.

An important feature of this type of software is the use of a programming language, or *script*. Buttons, fields, cards, and the stack itself can all have scripts associated with them. This allows for implementation of Ted Nelson's hypertext idea. For instance, a specific action can easily be scripted to send you off to a new location in the stack or to accomplish a special task. Creating these actions is an effective way to develop complex, quite sophisticated software.

Figure 27.6 displays a typical card from a HyperCard music project. Notice the use of the button over the words *quarter notes*. We have revealed in the illustration the script of this *hot word* button that, when activated, leads the student to another card in the stack that defines this term. It is easy to pop right back to where the student left off.

Not all card-based packages use scripts the same way. As we will soon see, HyperStudio allows you to create a hot word link, but without a script. The program does have a scripting language, however, to accomplish other tasks.

Pros and cons. Card-based software is intuitive to use and provides a quick way to integrate many media. It can be used effectively in teaching and for presentation to groups. Projects can be distributed and run on individual computers and be sent over networks. The full range of sound options is supported, although some special extensions may be needed. Graphics and movie files are easily added to a project and can be controlled by scripts. Interactivity is a major plus. Some programs even offer a choice of scripting language to be used. A final plus is the software's ability to open other programs, such as a music sequencer or notation package.

The card approach can run more slowly during execution than does software in other categories. Projects that have a large color content or that do a number of computations can run less efficiently. Speed is also effected by the loading of outside resources like graphic, sound, and movie files. Color

Module 28 provides a detailed description of scripting as part of high-level programming languages that are object-oriented.

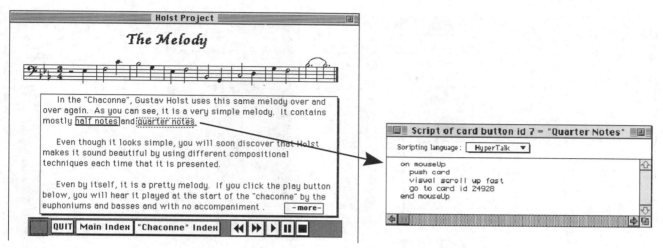

Figure 27.6
Card development using
HyperCard
(Apple Computer [Mac])

is supported by card-based software, but it is not as elegantly integrated as programs in the screen, time, or icon categories. Finally, card software may not support cross-platform integration. HyperStudio is cross-platform, but HyperCard and ToolBook are not.

Page Development. Page development is the last in the major category of screen-based authoring systems and many believe it to be the "wave of the future" for multimedia development and commerce. We use the term "page" to represent the kind of multimedia development we find in World Wide Web sites on the Internet (see Figure 27.7). Development of page multimedia sites follows the lines of other Web page development that we described briefly in Module 6. Pages of text are authored in Hypertext Markup Language (HTML), and links to other pages and other sites on the Internet are added. In addition, the linking of MIDI files, digital audio files, mounted audio CDs, and digital movies is easily accomplished. Remember, as we described in Module 6, you may need to add plug-ins and helper applications to your computer's software in order to access certain multimedia files.

So what software might be used for developing multimedia Web pages? It certainly is possible to use a standard text editor to simply write the HTML codes. This can be very laborious, however, and will force you to be always looking up the proper tags. Figure 27.7 displays two solutions for making the creation of Web pages much easier. Figure 27.7*a* is Bare Bones's BBEdit, an advanced text editor that automatically inserts the desired tags where needed. The software allows the setting of links to media files. This type of software is a vast improvement over standard word processors; however, in order to see how the page actually looks in a Web browser, you must move to the browser to view the page and then return to BBEdit for editing.

To solve this problem, companies have created software that lets you create pages with text, graphics, and links in a "what-you-see-is-what-you-get" approach. These are often called "page editing" programs. The idea is to have you work on the appearance of the page and, behind the scenes, create

See Module 28 for more
information about HTML
and JavaScript.

Tags are the special codes
that are interpreted by the
browser software in rendering the page on the
screen.

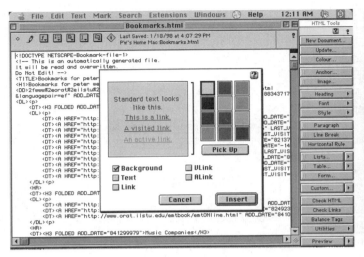

(a) BBEdit
(Bare Bones Software [Mac])

(b) PageMill
(Adobe Systems [Mac/Windows])

Figure 27.7
Examples of Page
Development for the
Internet

The CD-ROM materials for
this textbook are all created as HTML Web pages.
This is an example of using
Web pages on CD-ROM
instead of the Internet.

the HTML for you without having to deal with the tags themselves. Figure 27.7b provides a glimpse of one of these software packages. You work with pages by typing in the text, inserting graphics in place, and adding links—all with the help of buttons, palettes, and menus. The software creates the HTML code that can be saved and then read by browsers. Page editors provide easy ways to give information back to you, including the use of blank forms that invite the user to fill in information. Special programming scripts, called JavaScript, can be used to increase interactivity.

Pros and cons. Web-based multimedia has the advantage of a wide audience for your work. You also need not worry about what computer will be used, because the Web is machine independent. This kind of multimedia development is also able to make extensive use of the entire Internet community, thus opening a huge content base for the work that you do. You can render your own media, plus link to other sites that can complement your work.

This kind of multimedia does have a few problems. Network traffic, the methods of connection, and the server machines themselves can all contribute to poor performance. If special plug-ins or application software is needed to play back the media, this can slow down and frustrate a number of users as they try to experience your work. Although there are some new developments in providing browsers with high-level programming capabilities such as Java and JavaScript, the ability for extensive user interaction can be limited. Each of these negatives will become less important as the Internet develops and as software improves.

Time-Based Authoring

Audio CD Development. Audio CD, Movie, and Stage are the three types of time-based authoring that we describe in this book. The Audio CD type is unique to music multimedia and is closely related to the card approach. The major difference is that the content is defined by the temporal progression of sections within a piece of music. We call this category *audio CD* because the authoring system centers almost exclusively on the passage of time as the CD is playing. Cards of information are presented that are ordered according to a section of music. Text, graphics (including notation), and animation that supports what is being heard can be added. Buttons for starting, stopping, and pausing the CD are often provided. AABACA's Clip Editor is an authoring system created in HyperCard that uses letters and numbers in a hierarchy to designate sections of the music; Electronic Courseware Systems' CD Time Sketch is an example for Windows.

Pros and cons. Audio CD can be very useful for music multimedia, especially in a music teaching environment. Because these systems use card-based software as their foundation, scripting supports some interactive features. MIDI and sampled sound support is possible, but the CD is the principal sound resource. Marking the appropriate CD passages is especially easy in this software.

This strong reliance on the CD content is also a major weakness. The entire project relies on the CD, and individual chapters on other topics are difficult to integrate. Projects are also limited to instructional applications.

Stage Development. The stage metaphor uses a rather different approach to multimedia development. Instead of constructing screens that have media that are static on the screen (waiting to viewed or called into action by the user), stage software calls media such as graphics, text, buttons, and movies into action on the basis of a time grid or "score." As the score runs in real-time, the media appear on a "stage," which is the computer's screen. This is a much more dynamic approach to multimedia. Each media object, or "actor," can be timed to appear at a certain point. You can build points of rest in this dynamic system by using scripts to aid in interactivity. This approach has the advantages of scripting as found in card approaches and also is better suited for animation and special effects then most other authoring systems. One example of this kind of software is Macromedia's Director.

Figure 27.8 provides an example of the development process in Director. This is taken from Interactive Records' *So You Want to Be a Rock and Roll Star*. The top figure is the stage, or completed screen as the user would see it. Here we see some futuristic robots singing a rock song, and we hear the music at the same time. We have frozen the action at the 17th frame. The grid below is the score window, containing the numbered references to the cast actors such as text, graphics, and sound as they appear in time. These numbers appear in layers or channels in the order that the creator wants them to appear on the stage. Scripts are referenced here as well. The control panel is used in editing.

The software provides routines for animating objects and comes with tools for the creation of custom graphics. During the development process, the control panel is used to move from one frame to another in order to see the effects of each character in a frame.

Pros and cons. Stage software offers an interesting combination of powerful interactivity with scripting and precise control over the timing of

ASIDE

Note the interesting similarity in design between this kind of software and music sequencing software from Viewport VI.

events. This makes the software useful for a large number of multimedia applications, especially interactive environments and stand-alone kiosks. It can be used equally as well in a teaching environment or in the context of live performance, because timing can be so precisely controlled. Most software in this category offers superior color tools and animation. Built-in tools for drawing and painting are common and reasonably powerful. Links between audio, MIDI, and video elements are strongly supported. Cross-platform support is strong, as is plug-in support for distributing the projects as part of an Internet site.

Much of this power comes at a price, in both time and money. Time-based software offers a number of sophisticated options, but the learning curve can be steep. The development time for even modest projects can be lengthy. Projects can be controlled through the use of the time grid or with scripting or both. This complexity can add more time to the development process as each option is explored for its effect on performance. Software in this category can be expensive, designed primarily for commercial applications.

Movie Development. The last authoring system uses a movie metaphor. This is a more recent development system, growing out of the tradition of digital video. It's possible to create digital video files for use in any authoring environment, but it's also possible to use software that comes with

Macromind Director is a hot tool for commercial multimedia as well as its Shockwave cousin on the Web. Jobs await virtuoso Director programmers!

Figure 27.8
Time-based development using Director (Macromedia [Mac/Windows]; content taken from *So You Want to Be a Rock and Roll Star*, Interactive Records)

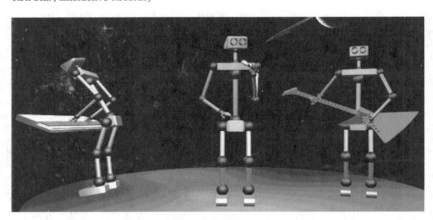

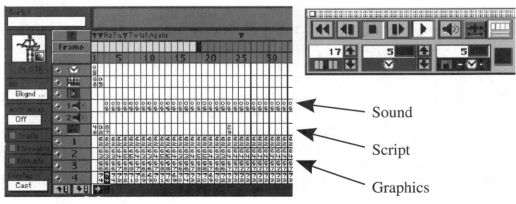

Sound

Script

Graphics

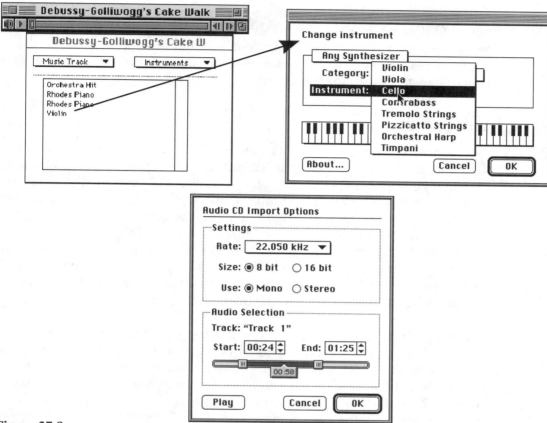

Figure 27.9
Editing MIDI and CD audio tracks using MoviePlayer (Apple Computer [Mac/Windows])

QuickTime and Video for Windows to create more extensive files. For example, the QuickTime file format allows for editing of individual video clips, frame by frame, as well as added text, additional digital sound, MIDI, still images, and animation. Video for Windows offers some of this ability.

By way of an example, Figure 27.9 shows the process of reassigning instruments for QuickTime General MIDI tracks. On the left, a track is shown first in its original setting and then in the center as the instrument assignments are being altered. Here we are controlling the internal MIDI sample player settings of QuickTime, but the same approach can be taken for changing patch assignments for external MIDI equipment. The dialog box on the bottom of Figure 27.9 shows the process of creating a digital sound track from an audio CD using MoviePlayer. Notice how you can precisely define the start and end times for the CD sound, as well as select different sampling rates, sample size, and mono or stereo. This capability turns movie development into an authoring system of its own!

Pros and Cons. Movie development offers users an inexpensive system for developing multimedia. Projects, including pages on the Internet, can stand alone or be included into other authoring environments. Scripting ability allows interaction and special effects. Three-dimensional graphics can be added and virtual reality effects that allow the user to control movement within the movie are possible.

On the negative side, producing the original video footage requires a powerful computer and added hardware. Custom graphics and text options are limited, and complicated interaction is often difficult to achieve. Cross-platform development can be hampered by differences in support between QuickTime and Video for Windows.

Projects Using Multimedia

As a way of understanding multimedia better, we will turn our attention to an actual set of projects using four typical approaches to multimedia development: Slide, Movie, Card, and Page. We will start by describing the project content and uses for the multimedia work. Next, we will sketch out the steps you might take to designing and creating your project, regardless of the metaphor you decide to use. Finally, we will demonstrate important characteristics of each project. Each step in the development process for all four projects can not be documented, because that would take another full-length book. We can, however, describe important features of the projects and stress how the content might be organized.

Content for the Four Projects. We will assume that you are the conductor of a wind ensemble, preparing for a concert featuring the music of the British composer Gustav Holst. One classic wind ensemble work that you plan to program is the *First Suite in E♭ for Military Band*. The opening movement, "Chaccone," is a wonderful example of a composition built on a recurring theme that is always present in some form. The movement opens quietly and builds to a big finish.

You realize that the performance of this music offers an excellent chance to create a set of multimedia projects. Each project will have a different goal and thus use different approaches. Here are the goals, together with the chosen authoring system:

▶ Slide *presentation* that features the historical aspects of Holst and his music (PowerPoint)

▶ Movie that *simulates* the thought processes of the conductor during performance (MoviePlayer)

▶ Card stack that *instructs* your musicians about the design of the music (HyperStudio)

▶ Pages for the Internet that *demonstrate* to your audience important aspects of the music and its rehearsal preparation (Netscape Composer)

Table 27.2 provides an overview of each project. Listed are the many sound and graphic media needed and the kind of interactive actions that are required. Notice that there is a fair amount of overlap in the media that will be used.

Project #1: Slide. The slide presentation is intended to augment a lecture on the life and times of Holst. PowerPoint is a good choice because of its ability to move, slide by slide, in support of the lecture. Some sound is sup-

Table 27.2 Content for the Four Multimedia Projects

Content	SLIDE PowerPoint	MOVIE MoviePlayer	CARD HyperStudio	PAGE Netscape Composer
Sound				
Sound Effects	√		√	
Speech clips from the conductor		√		
MIDI sound for individual lines of music	√		√	√
CD Audio sound of the entire movement and excerpt		√	√	
Images				
Text	√	√	√	√
Built-in painting and drawing tools	√		√	
Music notation	√		√	√
Digital pictures	√		√	√
Animation		√		
Digitized video		√		
Special Effects (builds, transitions)	√		√	
Interactive Use				
Hot words to link content	√		√	√
Buttons to control interactivity			√	√
Links to other resources (stacks, pages)			√	√
Scripts to control special needs			√	√
Printing	√			
E-mail and forms for feedback				√

ported, and there are plenty of opportunities to display graphics and text in a visually appealing manner. A printout of the slides adds a nice touch.

Project #2: Movie. This project will be an extended movie that will run in real-time. The intent is to simulate the thinking process of a conductor as he or she prepares a score. The MoviePlayer application that comes with QuickTime from Apple will work well here because the track structure in QuickTime will allow the addition of each media element when it is needed in time.

Project #3: Card. The intent here is to instruct. The project can be used to help the musicians in the wind ensemble understand the nature of the music's form. HyperStudio is the best candidate here because of its ease of use, flexibility for different media, interactive capabilities, and its cross-platform support.

Project #4: Page. Using much of the same media that you have developed for the other projects, it is relatively simply to create a Website that might demonstrate aspects of the music your group is to perform. Netscape Composer will be used for this effort, but actually any of the page editors in Table 27.1 could be used with similar results.

Plan Before You Develop! Before showing the highlights of each project, we want to stress the importance of planning and proper development for multimedia production of any "Roll-Your-Own" work. We suggest a seven-step process once the appropriate authoring system has been chosen:

▶ Defining content

▶ Plotting design

▶ Assembling media

▶ Creating cards

Software activity: "Creating a Storyboard for a Multimedia Project"

▶ Making the links with scripts

▶ Testing

▶ Distributing and installing

There really is nothing mysterious about this cycle. You begin by defining the goals of your project, including defining the content. We have already done this in large part for our four projects. Obviously the actual media themselves such as the MIDI files, CD audio, and digitized images would need to be identified. Some of the interactivity features, sound effects, and built-in drawing and painting capabilities are already waiting for the development process, but the kind of links and outside resources would need to be planned in this first step.

Be sure to start your actual work with a development program only after you have assembled all your graphic, sound, and movie files in one common place. You might want to organize all your files in one big project folder. You can create separate folders for sounds, graphics, and movies if you want. Just be sure that they are all contained in one big folder for your entire project. This will insure that the pathnames defining the location of your files will be consistent!

Next comes the task of laying out the project. This can take the form of a "storyboard" or perhaps a physical model of the project. Figure 27.10 provides the beginning of a storyboard for Project #3 that uses a card metaphor. A storyboard is simply a written sketch of the screens arranged in order of production. It might also include lines that represent the links between screens or other kinds of information that will show the flow of the project. If the project has complex interaction, a physical model is useful to show the linkages and interaction in a three-dimensional space. This step saves enormous time in the production. *Avoid designing a multimedia project at the computer without a storyboard or overall plan.* Hours are wasted if you do this!

Assembling and producing the media objects comes next. This is where you will use the graphics and text editors, scanning programs, music notation, and sequencing and sampling packages that we've discussed in this book. Digitized video programs might also be used to create video clips.

Once the media are in place, the project can be assembled. Screen content can be created and interactivity added as made clear by the storyboard or model. This may require several tries to get the look and feel correct, and some modification might be made as you see the project develop before your eyes.

The first completed version of your project may be all that you want to use for your purposes. For instance, if the project is a class presentation that needs to be shown the next day, field testing may not be possible for you. However, if the project is to be used several times and will be widely distrib-

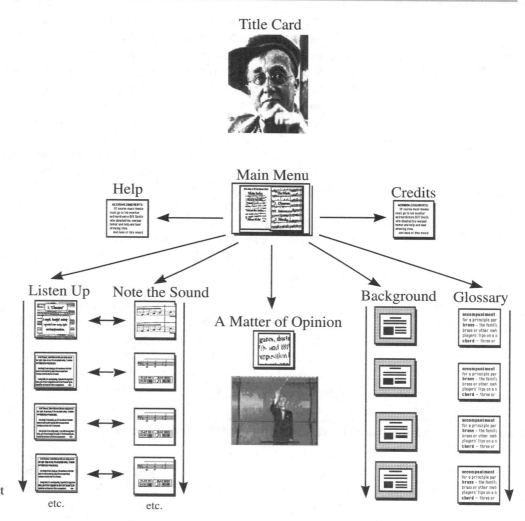

Figure 27.10
Storyboard used for project design

Find opportunities to pilot test your multimedia productions!

uted, you must have others use it to check for problems. Perhaps you can take it home to your family and friends to use, or share it with a colleague in a nearby school for testing. Whatever your strategy, you must fight the temptation to just install it when only *you* think it works smoothly. Others will never know the project as well as you do, and it is important to observe people's reactions and unpredictable behavior.

Finally, installing multimedia software on different computers is more complicated than installing a single program. Your project may require a large number of media files as well as the multimedia project itself. Keep in mind, however, that you don't need to install all the development software that you used. In fact, you can make a *run time* version of the authoring software that will save considerable space. The biggest files will be video and sound, especially if they are lengthy excerpts.

Another step in the finalization of your project might be to burn your own CD-ROM or DVD. In the final section of this module, we present information on how this might be done.

Copyrights. It's most important that you be conscious about copyright. You may use a number of copy-protected materials as you develop these projects. A scanned picture of Holst may come from a copy-protected book. Music notation may be taken from a copyrighted source, as will likely be the performance on the CD. How the projects will be used and where they will be delivered plays an important role on your course of action regarding copyrighted material. The law in this area is still developing and no clear guidelines are available.

If you were to sell your projects to others, you would clearly need to get permissions and perhaps pay royalties or fees on all the intellectual property in the projects that was not your own. If, on the other hand, you are using the material in teaching only, you may be exempted under educational "fair use" provisions. Even if you have no intention of profiting monetarily by your multimedia work, you are best advised to seek permission to use materials and to offer a full disclosure of your sources with acknowledgments at the end of your project.

If you are publishing on the Internet, we urge you to be especially cautious. You are sharing your work not just with a small group of people in your immediate area, but with the world Internet community. For this reason, full-length music works, entire images, and full text materials are all resources that need to be included with complete permissions obtained. Even short excerpts of the intellectual property of others should be approached with care. The best advice we can give is always ask the owner!

Project #1: Slide-Based Presentation with PowerPoint

Now we provide some perspective on our four projects. We can't give you a complete description of each project, but we can offer some sense of the major features of each program. Table 27.2 will be used as a basis for the content we describe. Keep in mind that many of the software programs within each metaphor can do most of the features; however, we have selected only one for each project.

Our first project is a slide-based one that uses Microsoft's PowerPoint. The goal is to create a series of slides that accompany a talk about the composer, Gustav Holst. Figure 27.11 displays four finished slides from the project that use common features for this type of software.

The first card, reading from left to right, is the title card, which features a scanned image of Holst, and some imported clip art from a library that comes with the program. The next card uses bulleted text items with some added drawing for visual interest. Music notation is placed on the next card, along with buttons that play a MIDI file and that link the user to a World Wide Web site on Holst. The last card plays excerpts from a CD performance of the "Chaccone" and provides a movie clip.

Building Slides from Style Templates and Objects. At the beginning stage of slide-based work, you must choose a background template from a set of templates provided by the program or create your own. The background style remains as a constant throughout your presentation, unifying each

Software activity: "Building a Music Project with Powerpoint"

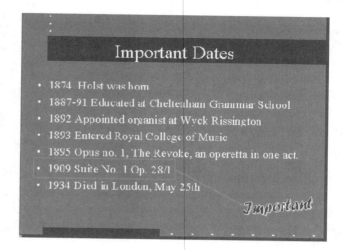

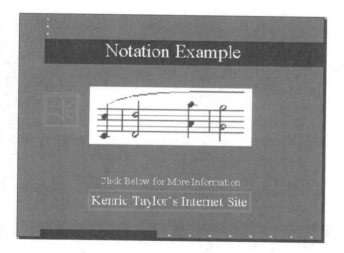

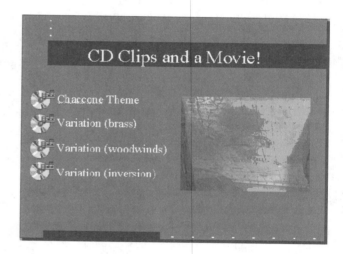

Figure 27.11
Four slides from a Power-Point presentation
(Microsoft Corp. [Mac/Windows])

slide visually. Figure 27.12*a* displays one of the first screens presented as you begin your project. Notice we have chosen the "Contemporary" template for our presentation. Next, the program provides a set of slide types that is called an "AutoLayout." Figure 27.12*b* displays the first twelve slide choices. We have elected to start with the "title" slide type. By clicking on the icon that represents the title slide (the first icon in the series), a slide is created for your project and awaits the adding of text for both a title and a subtitle (Figure 27.13).

Each time you ask PowerPoint to create a new slide, the set in Figure 27.17*b* is provided and you choose a slide based on the content that you intend to place on the slide. For example, the second slide we show in the final project (Figure 27.11) was created with the second Autolayout choice, a heading, and a set of bulleted text items. The third and fourth cards in Figure 27.11 were drawn from other choices from AutoLayout.

Once you have chosen a slide type, PowerPoint moves you to its main mode for working with slides, called the "screen" view (see Figure 27.13).

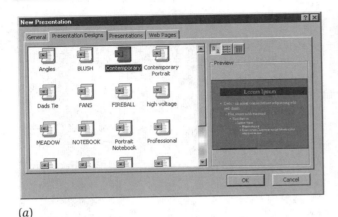

(a)

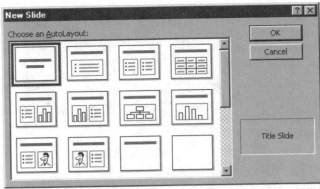

(b)

Figure 27.12
Style templates and card types in PowerPoint

Clicking on top of the "Click to add title" box will prompt the computer to accept your typed text. This text block becomes an object that is moveable to suit your design ideas. To finish off the first slide, we have used the "clip art" and "picture" items in the Insert menu to place the music artwork to the bottom right of the slide and the Holst picture in the lower center. The clip art comes from a library of images that PowerPoint provides, and the Holst picture is imported from a group of Holst photos that were scanned into digital form earlier. As with the text blocks, these images are objects that can be repositioned and resized.

Before you leave Figure 27.13, take a close look at the menus and toolbars that PowerPoint uses in this "screen" mode for editing. The menus and icons along the top provide most of the major operations for constructing a

Figure 27.13
Screen view mode in PowerPoint

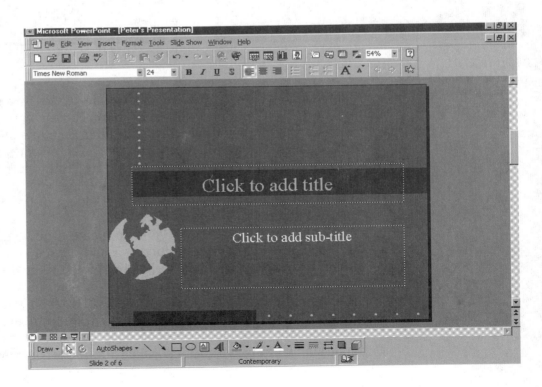

project. In addition to the traditional File and Edit menus, the items in the View menu provide other ways to view slides. An "Outline" view provides a working outline of the text material in the slides. The "Slide Sorter" view provides a set of icons that represent each slide and offer an easy way to change the order of the slides and see what special effects are chosen. A "Notes Page" view gives a small version of each slide and some empty space below the slide for you to make notes about what to say in your talk. These notes are not seen in the presentation to the audience. Finally, the "Slide Show" view fills the entire computer screen with the slide content. It is this view that the audience sees, and it is what we displayed in Figure 27.11.

The Insert, Format, and Tools menus provide numerous ways to change a slide and add objects of all types. Some of these options will be explained below. The Slide Show menu controls options for how the presentation is to be given. The tool bars below the menus contain icons that duplicate the menu items. Many of the tools are ones you have seen before in other programs. If you are unsure what each does, place the cursor over the top of the tool and a pop-up window will appear to explain. The Help menu leads to even more detailed explanation.

The power in Power-point is in using the background template across all of your slides; this makes it easy to add new slides and maintain the same look throughout. Avoid the temptation of overriding this power by customizing every slide to be unique and different!

Drawing Tools and Animation. The second slide uses bulleted text to provide information about important historical dates in Holst's life. We chose the slide template for bulleted text to start and then added the content information. Using the format tools, we changed the size of the fonts. We could have also changed the type of font and its color for special effect.

We added two additional touches. Using the drawing tools provided by PowerPoint, we boxed in the important date of composition for the First Suite and added an arrow and the word "Important" as an extra graphic object. We also changed the color and line thickness for special emphasis. These drawing tools, custom shapes, and added text come from the icons provided at the bottom of the screen view (Figure 27.13). Colors and line attributes come from the Format menu. PowerPoint also provides painting tools and other options to make your slide look special.

We also added some animation to this slide and a special effect as it moves to the third slide. The animation on the slide involves the bulleted list itself. When the slide is first opened, only the title and the box and special graphics are showing. A click of the mouse "reveals" the next bulleted item. Figure 27.14a displays the menu items that control the way the bulleted items are revealed. Each of the options provides a different kind of animation. You can set each slide to have different styles. After the last item is revealed and you move on in your talk, the transition between cards can also be animated (see Figure 27.14). In this box, you can choose the transition animation for one slide or all of them and can add a sound to accompany the movement!

Importing Media, Interactivity, and Links to the Outside. Slides can be designed to do more than present text and still graphics. The third and fourth slides in Figure 27.11 contain a number of special features. The music notation on slide three was imported much like the Holst picture on the first

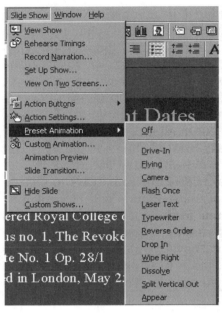

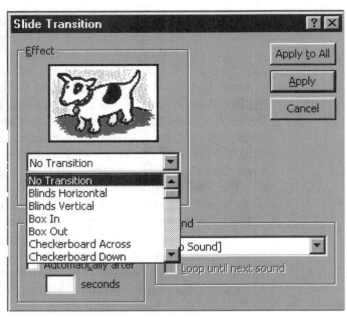

(a)   (b)

Figure 27.14
Options for animation on and between slides

slide, but notice the button to the left of the music: If the user clicks on it, PowerPoint plays a MIDI file of the excerpt. The same is true for the icons next to the text listing on the fourth card; in this case, clicking on the button plays a defined portion of an audio CD that is already mounted in the computer's CD drive. The fourth card also has a digital movie ready to play. The graphic to the right of the slide is a "poster frame" for the movie, and the user simply clicks on the frame to start the movie playing.

All this is accomplished by importing media and adding interactivity to objects. Figures 27.15a–e provide examples of how this is done. The Insert menu options are displayed in Figure 27.15a. Notice the references to clip art provided by the program, pictures from outside, and many other objects that can be imported. Figure 27.15b displays the window for importing clip art, pictures, sounds, and videos (movies). You just click on the medium you wish to import and PowerPoint places those objects (or references to those objects) on the screen you are editing. Figure 27.15c shows the window that you use to define what portion of a mounted audio CD you wish to have played. Figure 27.15d is the window for adding interactive buttons such as the little speaker icon on slide three.

One last feature is the ability to link to outside resources, in this case a Web site on Holst. This is accomplished on the third slide by linking the text on the bottom to a URL. Figure 27.15e displays the window that allows you to see this "hyperlink." Clicking on the text in slide three launches a Web browser automatically. Links to other software programs are also possible in PowerPoint.

Printing. Finally, PowerPoint allows many different kinds of printing options. If you choose the Outline item from the View menu shown in Figure 27.16a, you will see the outline of the text displayed in Figure 27.16b.

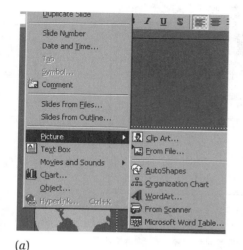

(a)

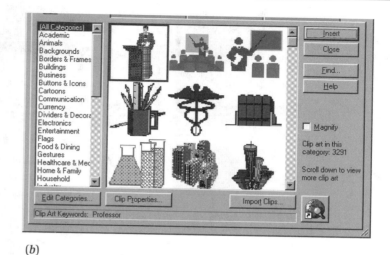

(b)

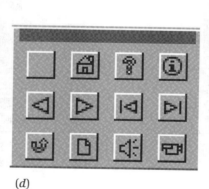

(c)   (d)

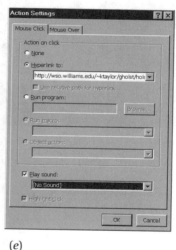

(e)

Figure 27.15
Options for importing media and adding interactivity

The Notes Page view gives the result shown in Figure 27.16c. Each of these views can be printed for use by your audience and by you as you prepare the work. Options also allow for printing the slides themselves in various sizes, as demonstrated by Figure 27.16d.

As you can see, presentation software such as Microsoft's PowerPoint offers an excellent solution for images, sound, and text to support a lecture where the information will be presented in a prescribed order. Keep in mind that not all presentation programs offer all these options, so be sure to match your needs with the multimedia software that is available.

Project #2: Movie Simulation with MoviePlayer

The point of this project is to create a QuickTime movie to offer insight into a conductor's thinking processes as he or she prepares for a performance of the first movement of the Holst *First Suite*. We will do this by using the

(a)

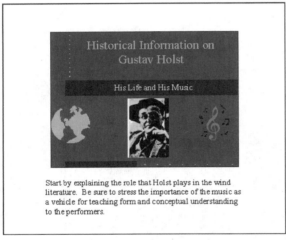

(b)

(c)

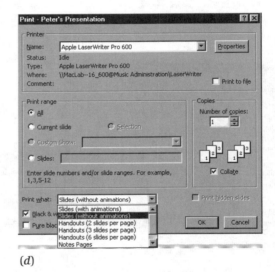

(d)

Figure 27.16
Options for printing

inexpensive development software MoviePlayer, which comes with the QuickTime package for both Macintosh and Windows computers. We will use MoviePlayer to assemble different pieces of media into one, continuously running movie that can be paused, replayed, or moved forward.

Overall Design. The project will really be four separately developed "submovies" that will be combined into one. Figure 27.17 contains screens from each of these four separate units. The first part will contain text and speech that will introduce the total movie. This section will also contain an audio file that we will extract directly from a CD recording of the music. We will use a word processor to create the text and then time the frame changes to match the timing in the audio.

The second part will contain a slide show that reviews some of the difficult problems in conducting the music. Each slide will be created in a separate graphics program and will contain some text and notation. We will use MoviePlayer to automatically assemble these slides, in order, for the slide show.

Figure 27.17
Four "sub-movies" that
are contained in Project 2

The third and fourth parts of the overall movie will be live video. One will be of a conductor explaining approaches taken in interpreting the music. This conductor will be interviewed and will demonstrate techniques and explain the decision processes. The fourth and final sub-movie will be an actual performance of the music by the conductor. In addition to the video, we will use MoviePlayer to superimpose some text cues that will remind us of the problems discussed earlier.

Capturing Video from Tape. As with each of the four projects in this section, we assume that the media pieces are already in place and we concentrate on showing you how to bring everything together using authoring software. In past viewports, you have learned to work with text, still graphics, music notation, MIDI sound, and digital audio. What we have not demonstrated, however, has been the capture of a video clip from tape. In the short section that follows, we present a description of how this is done for the third and fourth "sub-movies" that come from the interview and the performance.

Both the interview and performance must first be recorded on videotape.

Module 28 has more information on compression, frames per second, and screen size. Module 29 deals with the video hardware needed for Macintosh and Windows machines.

The video and audio outputs from the video tape deck are sent directly into the digital video hardware of the computer. Software such as Adobe's Premiere is used to actually create the digital file that contains the video and sound.

Any video-capturing software will require you to make several decisions about the movies you are creating. Each of these decisions will dramatically effect the size and quality of the video. Four choices will need to be made: size of the movie, quality of the audio, frames per second, and compression type.

Software will ask you initially about how big you want the video image to be. Larger is better for the user, but keep in mind that the larger the image, the more demands are placed on the computer to reproduce the movie and the larger the movie's file size. Movies that are 320×240 pixels are common with today's computers. This creates a window of over 4×3 inches, which is quite acceptable for viewing most video. Special video hardware and software enhancements make even larger sizes quite possible up to full-screen video.

Video-capturing software also captures any audio that accompanies a movie, and the same issues as for audio digitization apply. If you are working with video that centers on a musical theme as our project does, we recommend setting the video-capturing software to sample audio at the highest settings you can afford for music. A minimum would be mono sound at a 22-KHz sampling rate and 16-bit resolution. Speech can be sampled successfully at lower settings.

Compression techniques are what make digital video really work on computers, and settings for the most effective playback vary according to the nature of the video image and the circumstances for replay. Higher frames per second produce more realistic video, with 30 frames per second being close to broadcast television and motion picture quality. Figure 27.18 displays dialog boxes that are common for Macintosh and Windows software. The window to the left shows settings for a Macintosh that include

Figure 27.18
Typical settings for capturing digital video

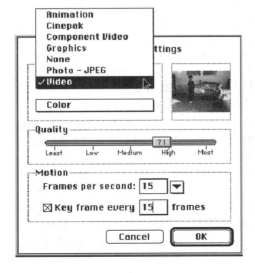

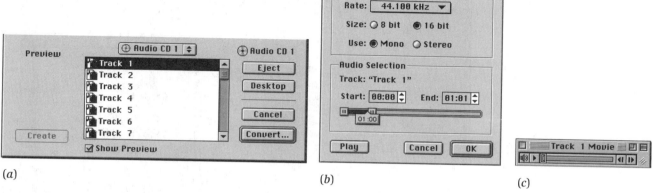

Figure 27.19
Creating an audio file
extracted from a CD

Software Activity:
"Recording and Editing a
Music Clip from an Audio
CD with MoviePlayer"

the "Apple Video" compression scheme at 15 frames per second for a Quick-Time format. The other box is for Microsoft's AVI video format, which uses the Intel Indeo compression with similar frame rate. These are common settings; however, new compression schemes are being developed all the time and rates of up to 30 frames per second are becoming more common with today's personal computers.

Once settings have been established, the video-capturing software is ready to record both video and audio and save the result in a file. Once saved, files can then be edited directly with this software or saved for treatment in a program like MoviePlayer. Sub-movies three and four for our project were created this way.

Opening Sub-movie: Text, Speech, and Digital Audio. We begin by creating the introductory text and audio. As you start to work with MoviePlayer, you will quickly see how QuickTime, much like a music sequencer, supports multiple, simultaneous tracks for holding different media. In this first movie, we will blend text and two audio tracks, one that comes from a CD performance of the music we are studying and the second from our own voice.

We begin by taking a short clip from an audio CD performance of the "Chaccone" movement. We will chose a portion of the opening. To do this, we will insert the audio CD into our computer's CD drive and choose the "Import..." option in MoviePlayer's File menu. We then navigate to the audio CD. Figure 27.19*a* displays the window that would appear next. Clicking on the "Convert" button yields an option to extract the entire track or a portion of it by choosing the "Options..." button (see Figure 27.19*b*). We set the slider for the portion we want. Notice too that we can choose the sampling rate and resolution. Saving our work, we are given the QuickTime movie controller displayed in Figure 27.19*c*. There is no video yet, so only the controller is showing.

Next, we will add some spoken words. We will first check the time length of the CD clip; this is important because we are going to add both a

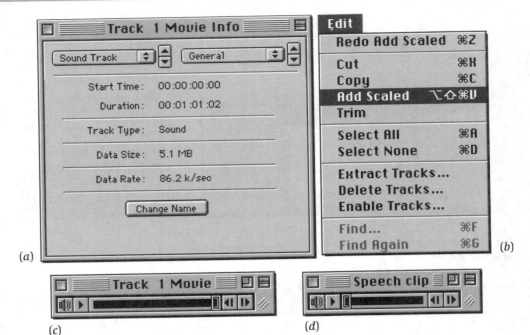

Figure 27.20
Adding two audio files to create simultaneous tracks

second audio track and some text. These additional tracks should match the CD clip so that everything can be synchronized. To do this, go to the Movie menu and choose the "Get Info" item and you will see a window similar to what we have displayed in Figure 27.20a. Choose the Sound Track and General options and you will be given the length of the clip, in this case 1 minute, 1 second, and 2 frames.

Now we choose one of the digital audio programs that we demonstrated in Viewport VII and create our spoken audio file, making sure that it lasts about 1 minute. You can time your speech to coincide with the music if you wish. Again, the "Import..." option is used and we convert the audio file into a small QuickTime movie.

Now the idea is to add this second track on top of the file that contains the music; this way, the user can listen to the music and the words together. As Figure 27.20d shows, we simply copy the speech clip contents from the second movie so that it is on the clipboard. Next, we select the CD Track 1 movie (c). Now we choose the "Add Scaled" item in MoviePlayer's File menu (b). "Add scaling" the second track superimposes one track on the other, as opposed to the "Paste" command, which would simply insert the second audio file in the middle of the first.

The last step is to create the video that displays the text, similar to the opening credits to a movie in the theatre. To do this open your favorite text editor and type the text that you want to appear in the movie. Use the "return key" after a section of text that constitutes what you want on one frame (see Figure 27.21a). Save the text as "text only" in your application. Then, just bring the text into a movie by using the "Import..." item in the File menu of MoviePlayer. The software senses that this is text and provides a window that asks you if you want to create a movie. Look for the "Options" button on this window, and a dialog box will appear (see Figure

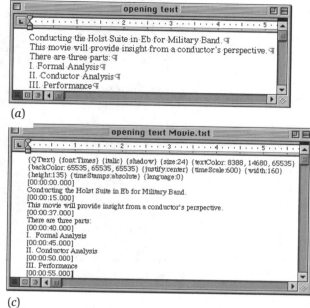

(a)

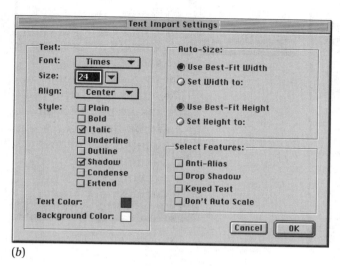

(b)

(c)

Figure 27.21
Adding text for the opening movie

Other movie editing programs provide similar functions to MoviePlayer.

27.21*b*). Notice that you can change the font and its size and style. You can also work with colors and with special effects. Set them to your liking and you will get a movie with frames of displayed text.

Just a few more touches are needed. You will need to set the timing for each frame so that the changes will occur at the correct moment of the text and music. The easiest way to do this is to "Export..." the finished text out of the movie and open it again in the text editor. We have done this in the graphic in Figure 27.21*c*. Notice the material in brackets that MoviePlayer has added. Alter the timings before each frame to your liking and simply "Import..." the text back into the movie. Now you will have the timings correctly added.

Finally, enter the audio track using the "Add Scaled" command, and you will have the finished product ready to test. You must resize the movie to match the size of the interview and performance movies that will make up the ending parts of your project, so that the final assembly will fit nicely together.

Slide Show with Audio. By completing the first sub-movie, you have seen much of the power of MoviePlayer and learned many of the techniques in using the software. Creating the next set of frames is very simple. First, open your favorite graphics program and create a series of graphics to illustrate the conducting problems. After designing the first frame with words, notation, or other graphic images, save the screen as a graphics file (paint or draw format). Open the next file and design the next frame. Continue this until all the frames are designed. Save each file with a consistent naming scheme like "image1," "image2," "image3," and so on. Make sure they are all in the same folder. In terms of size, try to design each frame to be the same size as the overall movie size as defined by the interview and performance movies.

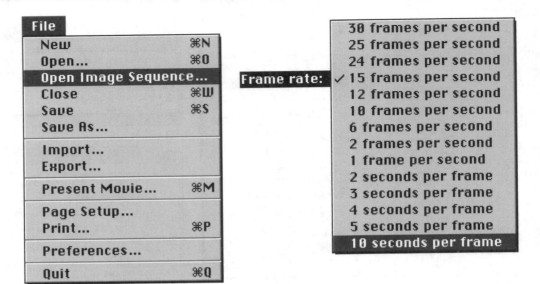

Figure 27.22
Creating a slide show

Once all the images are made, open MoviePlayer and choose the "Open Image Sequence..." item in the File menu. Navigate to the first image in the series and open it. The dialog to the right in Figure 27.22 opens, and you can set the timing for the slide show. Once chosen, the movie is created automatically. The final step is to add a sound track of speech to accompany the graphics much like that done with the first sub-movie.

Interview and Performance Sub-Movies. There is very little left to do. The interview and performance sub-movies have already been created and not much needs to be done with them. Each has its own audio track and does not need to be treated in any way.

In the final performance movie, however, it would be nice to add some text overlays from time to time to highlight the conducting problems that were addressed earlier in the other sections. To do this, we will add just a few words on the top of the movie as it progresses.

Begin by opening your text editor and type in the short phrases you wish to add throughout the movie. From the word processor, copy the first phrase onto the clipboard. Next, select the portion of the movie that should contain the phrase and use the "Add Scaled" item to add the text directly into the movie. Figure 27.23 displays the results of doing this in the top view of the movie.

To reposition the added text, choose the "Get Info" option in the Movie menu and navigate to the text track options. Choose the "Size" option as displayed in the upper right of Figure 27.23. This highlights the text box on the bottom of the movie. It is now possible to reposition the text to the top of the movie, as displayed in the middle movie in Figure 27.23. Finally, we choose the "Graphics Mode" option and the "blend" effect in order to give the text a softer look. Now, you can move to other portions of the movie and add in the appropriate text. It will automatically position itself at the top of the movie and use the blend effect.

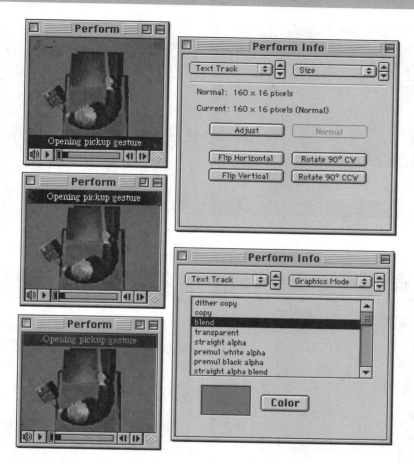

Figure 27.23
Adding text to the last sub-movie

To finish up the project, you need to choose one of the four sub-movies and paste in the others. Be sure to *flatten* the movie as a final step. To do this, use the "Save As" command and look for the options to make the movie self-contained and playable on other computers. Once this is done, the entire project will become one large QuickTime movie that will play through as a complete project!

Project #3: Card-Based Instruction

Software activities: "Building a Music Project with HyperStudio, HyperCard, or Toolbook"

We turn now to the creation of a "stack" of cards designed to help instruct musicians about the Holst *First Suite*. We will use Roger Wagner's HyperStudio for Macintosh and Wintel computers. This authoring system is designed as a construction kit for multimedia, using cards of information linked to one another in an interactive system. Layers of information are placed on cards, beginning with a background screen on top of which the other material is added.

Overall Design. Figures 27.24*a–e* represent five of the completed cards in this project. The first card, Figure 27.24*a*, represents the title card for the stack and is the first to be seen by the user. The second card, Figure 27.24*b*, is the table of contents. Notice that we have designed our stack to have five

(a)

(b)

(c)

(d)

(e)

Figure 27.24
Five cards from a HyperStudio
project
(Roger Wagner [Mac/Windows])

sections. The first provides an overview of the entire movement. The user can see at a glance how Holst has designed the music and can listen to each section (see Figure 27.24c).

The second section provides a more in-depth view of the music by providing a score and the ability to hear individual lines in the music (see Figure 27.24d). The third section provides information about Holst's life and times (see Figure 27.24e). The last two sections are devoted to a glossary of terms and a set of further resources for the study of Holst's music. We will now discuss how these cards were created by use of HyperStudio.

Important Menus. We begin with a look at HyperStudio's central menus, the ones that are used most often. Reading from left to right, Figure 27.25 shows us first the Tools and Color menus. As cards are created, these menus are constantly used to choose the "mode" of editing. Notice the row of three icons just below the finger or "browser" and "arrow" tools. These are the button, graphic object, and text object tools. In working with card-based software, you will constantly move between these modes and the browser, represented by the finger icon. The paint tools that are on the bottom of this menu are used much as are the tools described in Viewport IV.

Colors and shades of gray are offered in the next menu. Sixty-four options are offered, together with the option to create custom colors by double-clicking on any color item. A group of predesigned patterns are also

Figure 27.25
Menus from HyperStudio

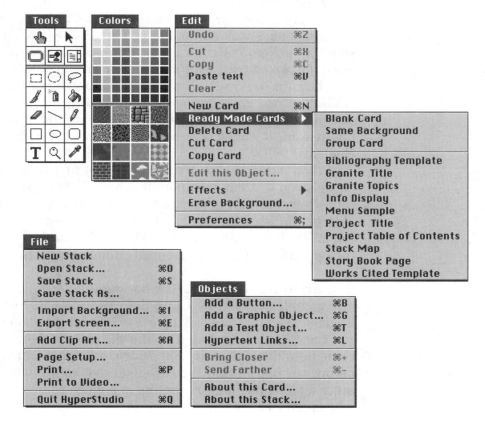

offered at the bottom of the screen. These options are used continuously as you add color to backgrounds, buttons, text, and painted objects.

The Edit menu is used for the usual cutting and pasting, but it also allows you to add new cards. The "Same Background" item is useful because it creates a new card that has the same background pattern or color as the one before it. "Group Card" is even more powerful because, by using this option, objects that you place on the original card can be carried over to the new card as well. This is useful for maintaining a consistent background with buttons and clip art and also saves on the total size of the stack. Most card-based software has the ability to create this kind of consistent background layer.

The File menu contains the expected items, including options for saving and printing. Notice that you can export complete screens as graphic objects and import previously created background screens. Also, adding clip art as part of the background layer is an option, drawn from items already provided by HyperStudio or from external files you create or capture from elsewhere.

Finally, the object menu provides options for adding buttons, text, and graphics. Links for text objects can be created here, and options for properties of cards and the stack itself can be set. This menu also allows for moving objects closer and further away in terms of the layers which they occupy on the card.

Creating a Background with Grouped Objects. When you create a new stack, you are given a blank card. The first thing to do is create a background layer upon which to place objects. Pull the Tools menu off the menu bar and double-click on the Eraser Tool to view a dialog box allowing you to select a background color. Next, think of what elements might be consistently displayed from card to card. For example, look at Figures 27.24c and d. Each card has a set of buttons at the bottom of the card that constitute a navigation bar. Each button leads to a particular chapter, and they are consistently displayed on every card in the first three chapters of the project. For this reason, it might save time to create a background that includes these elements.

When working with HyperStudio, you first create a card with the shared elements on it. Then, you indicate which elements will be shared from card to card. Once the card is designed with a background that contains the shared objects, you issue the Group Card option displayed in the Edit menu (see Figure 27.25) when you want a new card. This creates a new card with a shared background and shared or grouped buttons, graphics, and other objects.

Clip Art and Paint Tools. The background layer might also contain clip art and graphics created by using the paint tools in HyperStudio. The map of England (Figure 27.24e) is a piece of clip art that came with the program.

The Clip Art command in the File menu yields the option for files to come from the Disk collection, Video, or Digital Camera. In this case, we are taking our image from the collection that comes with HyperStudio, but the other options provide easy access to a video source such as a VCR or a digital camera (see Module 29).

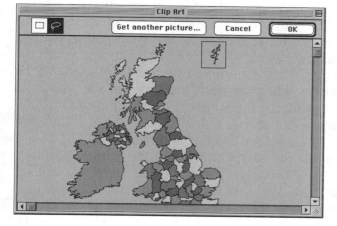

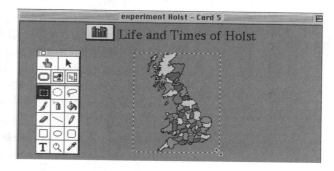

Figure 27.26
Clip art integration in
HyperStudio

These paint tools are similar to those that we
described in Module 13.

HyperStudio provides a dialog box for finding the desired file. You can import one of your own or use one provided for you as we have done. Once chosen, a Clip Art window is displayed that allows you to choose just what part of the clip art image you want to import. We have used the "lasso" tool to select the England part of the United Kingdom file. Once chosen, the program places the clip art on the card. Using the square selector in the Tools menu, we can shrink the clip art to size and place it where we want (see Figure 27.26).

The paint tools provide a way to add visual interest to each card. Note that we used the rounded rectangle tool (see Figure 27.25, paint tools menu) to add interest to the click instructions at the top of the card (see Figure 27.24c). We used the paint bucket fill tool to add color to the background. We also added painted text on the first card of our project, Figure 27.24a, above the graphic for notation. Keep in mind that, in HyperStudio, these images are part of the background layer. Imported graphics, buttons, and text objects will "cover" the images created by these tools.

Text Objects. Speaking of text, painted words are not the only way to create text in HyperStudio and other card-based programs. Text objects can be created, both with and without scroll boxes. For an example of a text object without a scroll box, check the first card of the project, Figure 27.24a. The title and subtitle text were created as a single text object.

We begin by first choosing the text objects tool in the Tools menu and then issue the "Add a Text Object..." command in the Objects menu. This yields a text objects box on the card, which we can then resize and reposition (see Figure 27.27a). The Text Appearance window (b) is offered by the program after clicking once outside the text box. Here, we can choose the color of the text itself and the background. We have chosen black for the text color. For the background, we choose the same color as the basic background; this is because we are working on the design of the first card and we want the title text background to blend seamlessly with the background color of the card. If we were creating a text box that is scrollable, we might want a different color.

The Text Appearance window is also where we specify having a scrollable box and framed text. In Figure 27.27*b* we show none of these options checked because we want the text to stand alone. If we were creating the box for the card with scrolling text, we would choose different options. Notice the other checkbox for "Read Only." This is an option we will want to use at the end of the development process when we want to block out the user from clicking in the text field and changing the words. The Text Appearance window is also the place where one can choose to import previously created text file and set features, such as grouping, for a series of cards.

The next step is to click on the "Style" button in the Text Appearance window, which brings up the "Text Style" window (*c*). Here, we can set the font, size, and style of text. We also will elect to have the text centered. Clicking "OK" returns us to the card, and we simply type in what we want to have appear (*d*). Once the text is in place, we can use the Options menu to select further changes in text style and the Color menu to change colors.

In scrollable boxes that contain text, such as the one in Figure 27.24*e*, words can be singled out for hyperlinks. This allows a user to click on a "hot" word for some desired action like a link to a glossary or the playing of a sound file (see Figure 27.28). We have highlighted "Royal College of Music" and then chosen the "Hypertext Links..." item in the Objects menu.

Use HyperStudio's fonts to insure cross-platform compatibility.

Figure 27.27
Text objects

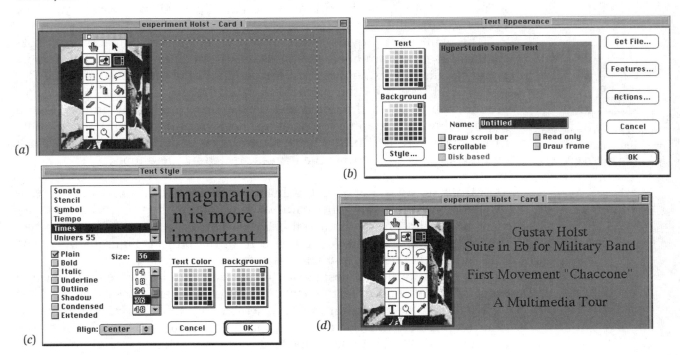

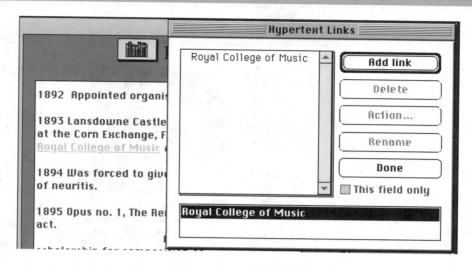

Figure 27.28
Hypertext link

This brings up the displayed Hypertext Links window, which is used to set actions for the hyperlink.

Graphic Objects. HyperStudio supports many kinds of graphic file formats for importing; PICT, TIFF, JPEG, PCX, BMP, GIF, and Paint are the major ones. This makes cross-platform development much easier. As with clip art, HyperStudio also accepts graphic objects imported directly from digital cameras.

The two graphic objects on the first card—the picture of Holst and the music notation clip—are both taken from external sources. The Holst picture came from a scanner file and the notation from a screen shot off of a music printing program. The method of importing a graphic object is very similar to text objects. After choosing the graphics tool from the Tools menu and the "Add a Graphic Object..." from the Objects menu, the program asks about the source of the file.

After the selection of a graphic, HyperStudio provides the Graphic Appearance window (Figure 27.29). This window allows the setting of a frame around the graphic, as we have done in our examples on the first card of the project. Features and actions can be set as well. If you don't want to have the graphic incorporated into the data structure of the stack, you can check the box "Disk based." This will keep the stack smaller in size, but you will need to be sure that the graphic is available as a separate file and that its location in the volume stays consistent.

Button Objects. Buttons play a dramatic role in the operation of card-based multimedia. There are buttons on each card of our project, and many of them have unique functions. Buttons are created by choosing the button tool in the Tools menu and the "Add a Button..." from the Objects menu. Figure 27.30 provides a number of button options.

The Button Appearance window (*a*) is a bit more complicated than others. In addition to the standard button types, HyperStudio offers the ability to create irregularly shaped buttons by either drawing the shapes by hand,

When you import clip art like this from an external device like a camera, multimedia programs will often remap the color to conform to the color scheme that the software is using. If you get unwanted results, you might need to increase the resolution supported by the software. Also note that HyperStudio lets you capture video, audio, and scanned images right into the program without additional software.

Software activities: "Scanning GIF and JPEG Images"

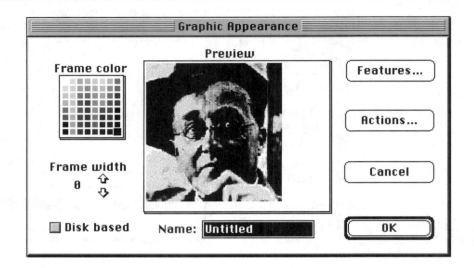

Figure 27.29
Graphic appearance
window

clicking within a solid color with the program creating the borders automatically, or encircling a shape with the lasso. The position button allows you to move the button to a desired location. Options also exist for showing or hiding the button's name and icon. The "icons" button offers a series of built-in styles to choose from (see Figure 27.30c).

The Features window (b) is similar to the feature options for text and graphics. By choosing the group checkbox, the button becomes part of the background for group cards. The lock option makes the button unmovable or uneditable. The window also offers an option for hiding the button. A

Figure 27.30
Options for buttons

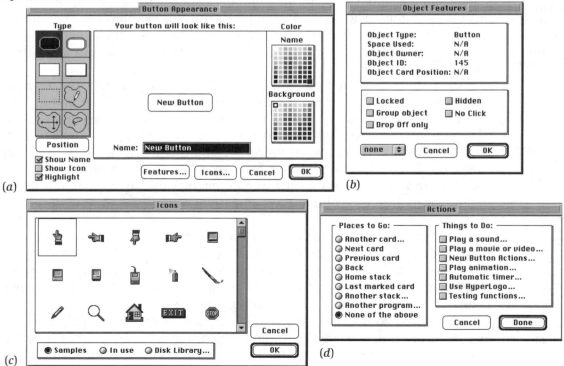

NBAs are like XCMDs in
HyperCard and ToolBook.

"no click" button can be activated by just dragging the cursor over it, while
a "drop off" button only activates when something is dragged over it.

The Button Actions window (*d*) contains a number of options for places
to go. In addition to moving to another card or stack, buttons can also open
other programs! We offer an example of this on the table of contents card,
Figure 27.24*b*. The Link to Email button asks HyperStudio to open a mail
program. When the user is finished checking mail, HyperStudio returns.

The "Things to Do" option set is especially important for music and
video. The "Play a Sound..." option produces the Tape deck window (Figure
27.31). You can elect to have a sound effect play or record your own sound
using the "tape deck (*a*)." We recorded our own "Welcome" message for the
button called "Welcome Message" on the table of contents card, Figure
27.24*b*.

If you already have a sound file in the form of a digital audio file or a
MIDI file, you can turn that file into a QuickTime movie and use the
Video/Movie Source window to incorporate the file into the stack (*b*). We
did this to play each line of music in the notation example on the fourth
card in our sample set, Figure 27.24*d*. Invisible buttons are placed over the
top of each line of music to play a MIDI file that is converted into a Quick-
Time movie. The Video/Movie Source window in HyperStudio is used for
QuickTime movies that have video, too. Notice that this window also contains options for creating a frame for a live video feed from another device.

Another "Things to do" option provides for New Button Actions (NBAs)
that are designed to extend the capabilities of the software (*c*). We have used

Figure 27.31
Button actions

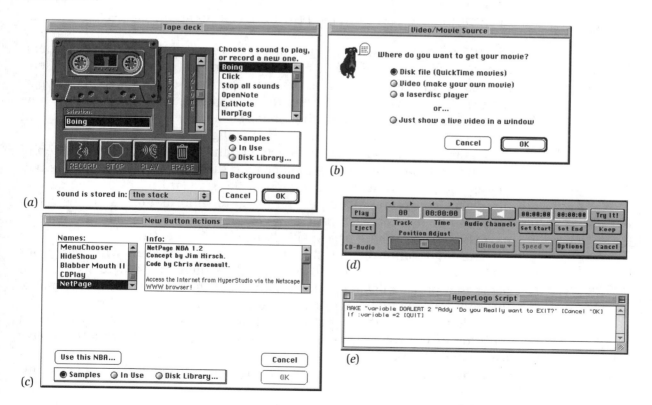

two NBAs in our project. The first one is the link to the World Wide Web (WWW) on the table of contents card (Figure 27.31). Using this option prompts a query for the URL of a Web site of interest. The button then automatically calls the Netscape browser into action as it seeks the requested URL.

We discuss scripts in Module 28.

The second NBA is the CDPlay action. Choosing this brings into play the CD-Audio strip pictured in Figure 27.31*d*. You can insert an audio CD and specify what portion of the CD will be played by the button. We used this extensively in the third card of our sample set (Figure 27.24*c*). Each section of the "Chaconne" movement can be played by the CD disc buttons beside each title.

The final "Things to do" option that we will explain is the "Use Hyper Logo..." option. Choosing this opens a script-editing window for entering code that HyperLogo understands (*c*). HyperLogo is the scripting engine that comes with HyperStudio. Most card-based systems have some kind of programming language that can extend the power of the program. We used a script for the "Exit" button on the table of contents card, Figure 27.24*b*. The script asks the user if he or she really wants to quit the program.

Project #4: Page-Based Demonstration with Netscape Composer

We come to our last project, Holst on the World Wide Web! We want to offer a public site for others to learn more about the Holst *First Suite* and its preparation for performance. Rather than simply placing the other projects on the Web, we will develop a stand-alone set of pages that demonstrate the work we are doing with the music. The site can also inform others about the performance ensemble and provide details about the concert.

Software activity: "Building a Home Page for the Web"

Overall Design. As with all multimedia projects, initial planning is important. First of all, our site will have some standard pages about the ensemble—pages that will always be present regardless of the music being performed. The content will center on the group itself, the concert facility, how to buy tickets, and driving directions. Second, we will have pages that change on the basis of the piece we are highlighting.

Figure 27.32 contains the complete opening page of our site. The top of the page contains the opening banner with the ensemble's logo. At the bottom of the page are icons that represent the standard pages for the ensemble. Each icon represents a separate page of information, and this set of icons can be used on each page as a way of organizing the site and making navigation easier. These pages will change less frequently.

Read all you need to know about the technical aspects of HTML tags in Module 28.

The information in the middle of the page, however, will change for each concert the ensemble will perform. Here, there are links to six different pages that provide detailed information about the Holst *First Suite*. Some of the content is similar to work that we have done in other projects. The intent is to prepare this audience for a more complete music experience at the time of the concert. These pages will change for each concert as new featured works are chosen.

In the sections that follow, we will lead you through the design of this

Figure 27.32
Opening page of a Web site using the Composer section from Netscape Communicator
(Netscape Corp.[Mac/Windows])

first page and select some examples from the other pages. Netscape Communicator software will be used, which is the company's Web client software that it distributes free of charge. The software has several parts, including the familiar "Navigator," which is used for basic browsing. In this project, we will use the part called "Composer," which allows you to create your own Web pages with little knowledge of the Hypertext Markup Language (HTML). As you work with the software, the program creates the needed HTML code in the background, ready to be used by other computers on the Internet.

Basic Menus and Toolbars. In Module 6, we introduced you to the basic operation of a Web browser like Netscape Communicator. Our focus there was on using the Navigator part of the software to browse the World Wide Web as a client. We now turn to using another part of this software, the Composer, to actually create some Web pages that use media of various types.

Figure 27.33 contains a display of the tools and important menus in the Composer section of the software. Notice that the Edit menu displays one way to begin work on a blank page in Composer. If you are using the Navigator part of the software, issuing the "New" and "Blank Page" commands brings you into Composer. If you are looking at a page already created that you would like to use as a beginning model, you can also select "Edit Page" from Navigator's File menu and the software will pull off all the files including the graphics from that page to your local hard drive to edit. The "Page

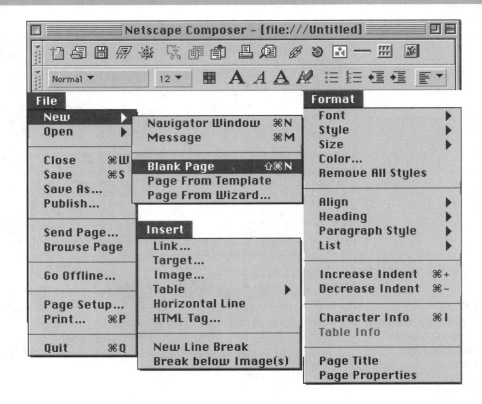

Figure 27.33
Common toolbars and menus in Composer

from Template" and "Page from Wizard..." options require you to be on line because they use resources that come from Netscape's own Website.

The Insert menu is perhaps the most commonly used menu during page preparation. This is where you tell the software to insert links, images, tables, and horizontal lines. In the coming sections, we will use all of these as we construct pages for our project.

The Format menu is similar in function to that found in a word processor. Text can be formatted according to style. HTML allows for special paragraph styles that conform to certain conventions, and we will explore these below.

Finally, the toolbars themselves in Composer provide many of the same options found in the menus. One important button is the one that resembles a ship's steering wheel. This button allows you to switch from Composer to the Navigator part of the program for you to view your work as a user might on the Internet. To switch back to the Composer, you click on the small pencil icon at the bottom right of Navigator's screen. This movement back and forth is a common procedure in developing pages. Other icons are self-explanatory or will become clearer to you as you use the menus.

Inserting In-line Graphics and Words. Unlike other multimedia authoring tools such as the ones used in previous projects, the exact placement and appearance of graphics and words are more problematic in Web design. This is because the client browser assembles the page elements as they are sent from the server. Each client machine and software tend to assemble the pieces a little differently. However, there are ways to structure your page so that it will appear in a more-or-less consistent way. In this and following sections, we will insert some graphics that are "in-line" with text, add some basic text, and use tables to construct the first page of our site. Compare these steps to the finished product (see Figure 27.32).

Begin by opening a blank page in Composer and saving it immediately to your project folder. Because this is the home page of your project and the one that your users are going to see first, you might wish to take some care in naming the file. Your Internet Service Provider (ISP), as the server of your page, might have some advice on this as well.

Keep in mind that this name is really not used in referencing your page on the Web by search engines. To give your page (and others that you create subsequently) a more descriptive name, you have to go to the Format menu and choose the item "Page Name" to access the Page Properties window. Enter a descriptive name and also add any descriptive keywords in the bottom box for an even better chance to have your work appear in a Web search.

Let's now add a graphic object in the upper left-hand corner of our page. The graphic is actually the ensemble's logo. The logo has already been crafted in a graphics program and saved in either JPEG or GIF format. To insert the graphic, you simply issue the proper command from the Insert menu. Figure 27.34 displays the dialog box that is returned. We have previously called the logo "tuba.jpg," so we enter that name in the box. Notice that you can also choose to find the file by clicking on the "Choose File" button if you cannot remember the name or if the file is in separate folder. If you are using separate folders for images, sounds, and movies, it's a good idea to also check the box indicating its location just below the name; otherwise, Composer will create a second copy of it when it saves.

Also in this dialog box, we have specified some text in the "Alternative Representation" box so if a person is using a browser that does not display

The project folder or directory should contain the HTML files created by Composer, and the supporting sound, graphics, and other media should be in separate folders or directories. When you transfer all the media and HTML files to your remote Website for distribution on the Internet, you need to keep everything organized so that the pathnames defining the location of your files will be consistent!

Figure 27.34
Inserting graphics

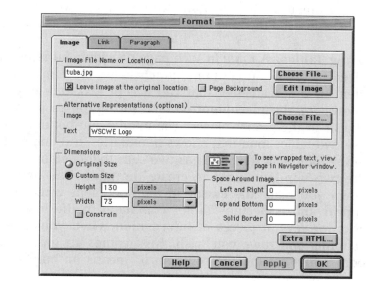

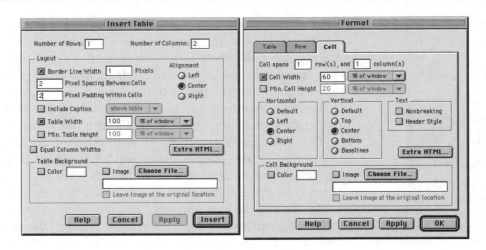

Figure 27.35
Inserting tables

images, there is something there to read. This is a good practice for important graphics and links that are formed by graphics. We have also specified a way to align text to the graphic and chosen to have a border around the graphic of 1 pixel in size. Inserting images throughout the construction of our Web site will follow the same kind of choices.

Next, we will add text. As in many programs of this type, adding text is similar to the way it is done with a word processor. You type in or import what you want, then format according to the tools provided. After typing in the opening words, we highlighted the first two lines of text and used the "Heading" item in the Format menu and chose "1." HTML provides standard heading styles numbered 1 to 6, largest to smallest. We aligned the text to center, then highlighted the second line and lowered its font size from 18 to 14. We worked with the remaining lines in similar fashion, including a color change for the last line before the horizontal rule. To get the spacing to look correct, we moved back and forth between Navigator and Composer.

To finish off this section, we inserted a horizontal rule, double-clicked on it, and used the resulting window to change its appearance and size.

Using Tables. A *table* in Web page development refers to a set of cells organized in rows and columns, much like a table in a word processing document or a spreadsheet that can accept text and graphics. Inserting tables allows for the placement of text and graphics more easily, so that they appear in the proper places. The middle and bottom parts of the home page use two tables, one that shows boundaries and one that does not. The table in the middle of the page has two cells that contain text. Figure 27.35 shows the two windows used to create the table. The one to the left is present when you place the cursor in the document where you want the table to appear and issue the "Table" command in the Insert menu. The window asks for several pieces of information. First, you must specify how many columns and rows you wish. Next comes an indication of the size of the border line around the cells. A "0" means no border. You can also specify the spacing between cells and any material inside the cell and its border. An alignment option for the entire table in relation to the page is also required. Other layout options include whether you want the table to occupy the entire width of the screen and whether you desire a caption above or below the table. Finally, we have not checked the "equal sized cell" box because we want to make them different sizes.

Once these basic attributes are set, we can begin to type the text into the cells. Once this is completed, we can place the cursor into one cell or the other and issue the "Table Info" command in the Format menu. This provides us with the window to the right in Figure 27.35. Using this window, we can set the attributes of the cell in which the cursor is located: the relative size of the cell and also the alignment of material within it. (Background colors or images can be specified here as well, but we will deal with that in the next section.)

Notice in the finished product (Figure 27.32) that the items are in a bulleted list. Text lists can be bulleted or numbered automatically for you; you simply highlight the list and choose the desired list style from the Format menu. It's also possible to have bulleted lists within bulleted lists by using the decrease and increase indent commands in the same menu.

It may not appear to be so, but there is also a table at the bottom of the page. Here we have created a four-cell table that is aligned in the center of the page. Instead of text only, we have placed in each cell a graphic with some text under it. We have also hidden the borders of the table to make it appear that the graphics are placed next to each other. Each graphic represents the icon for another page in the site, and we have added descriptive words to be sure the user understands its function.

Backgrounds. Now that the basic design is finished, we can add some final touches. First, the creation of interesting backgrounds. By default, Netscape Composer provides a rather bland, battleship-gray background color. To give the page more interest, we return to the "Page Properties" option in the Format menu, but this time we click on the Colors and Background tab. We specify the name of a graphics file we have already created called "musbg.gif," which serves as a graphic in the background to give the page visual interest (see Figure 27.36).

Notice that the graphic is rather small compared to the size of the page. This is because the graphic is repeated over and over again to form the background. For this reason, such graphics are known as "wallpaper" graphics for individual pages. The window also specifies the colors for active links, links that have been already followed, and text.

If you did not want a graphic to form the background, you could also double-click on the color square next to the word "background" in the middle of the window and choose a solid color from the color wheel that is displayed. This color then becomes the basic color for the page. You can set these colors for individual cells in a table as well (see Figure 27.35).

Links. Links give the Web its multimedia power. We will use links to travel to new pages, send e-mail, show music notation, and play audio files and

Be careful to choose very lightly rendered background images and colors. Anything too dark or bold will mask the text and make it hard to read. Smaller wallpaper graphics are better because their repeated pattern looks more aesthetically pleasing. Some designers actually begin with the wallpaper as their first step.

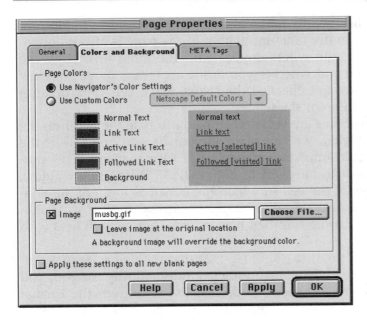

Figure 27.36
Specifying backgrounds and colors

Real Audio and Real Media files offer great audio compression so you can put entire music recordings of your ensembles on the Web.

movies. Take another look at our finished page in Figure 27.32. Each underlined piece of text is a link to something. We can also add links to a graphic: The four icons at the bottom of the page are each links to other pages. How is this done?

By way of example, we begin with the very first link on the page—the one that is part of the director's name, "Peter Stevenson." The link here is really designed to ask the browser software to send an e-mail message. To create this link, we must first highlight the word, phrase, or graphic that is to represent the link. Next, we issue the "Link..." command in the Insert menu. In Figure 27.37, we display the result of this. We have placed "mail to:" followed by the e-mail address of Maestro Stevenson. When the user clicks on the text, the browser's e-mail function is called upon to send a message.

Another example is included just below the window in Figure 27.37. This link is to another page called "pager.html," which is located in the same folder as the home page. This page has been designed to describe the Slick Pager Concert Hall. It references the same file as the link in the tables that follow that refer to the concert hall. Other links on this page refer to files that are part of the Website.

Still another example of a link is the one for driving directions to the concert. This is actually another site on the Internet whose address is: "http://www.directionsIL.com/westshore." The designers of the ensemble's Web site simply use this remote site to provide directions.

Links can also be made for the presentation of MIDI files, digital audio (.au, .aif, .ra, and .rm), large graphics files, and QuickTime and AVI movies. Figure 27.38 is taken from another page in our site. The graphic at the top presents an overview of the entire *First Suite* by providing audio excerpts and music notation from various sections of each movement. Below the

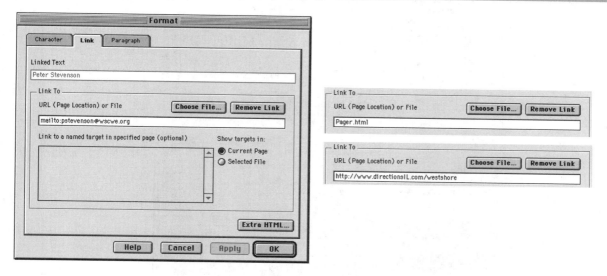

Figure 27.37
Links for mail, files, and remote sites

page graphic, we show the controllers that are displayed by browsers for the audio files. When the user clicks on the note icon for a section of the music, a MIDI file is played and controlled by the display on the middle left of Figure 27.38.

The links at the top of the page refer to rehearsals of the entire movements that have been previously recorded. These recordings can be turned into Real Audio files or other compression formats for rendering on the Web. An example of this is the larger control window in the middle of the figure.

Finally, clicking on the name of an excerpt returns a large notation graphic such as the one displayed at the bottom of Figure 27.38. This is accomplished by simply entering the name of the graphic into the window displayed in Figure 27.38. QuickTime movies are displayed in the same way.

Extensions: Advanced HTML and Scripts. The use of in-line graphics, text, tables, backgrounds, and links to other pages, remote sites, audio files, and large graphics are all basic to Web multimedia development. As your sophistication grows, you will certainly want to add more complicated HTML code for special effects that are not supported by Composer. In many of the dialog boxes, you will note an "Extra HTML" button that offers an opportunity to add this code to tag structures. Also, the Insert menu allows the insertion of a new, single tag at any point.

It also is possible to have Composer open the HTML code directly in a text editor to extend the code still further. This would be necessary if you wanted to add such advances as interactive forms, frames (scrollable windows), and image maps.

Another reason to use a separate editor would be to add a script such as the JavaScript example that we include in Module 28. For example, you might like to add some interactive options for your site that would ask your user for special content on Holst's music.

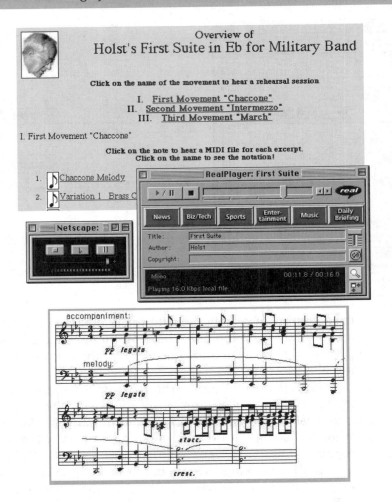

Figure 27.38
Links for audio files and large graphics

Burning Your Own CD-ROM or DVD

See Module 29 for more information about the hardware for burning!

It's never been easier to create your own disc as part of your distribution plans. Hardware for burning a CD-ROM or DVD is very reasonably priced, often only marginally more that a regular external CD drive. Blank CDs and DVD discs cost only a few dollars. Software to control the creation is usually provided as part of the hardware purchase. One popular software choice for CD-ROM creation is Adaptec's CD-Toast for Macintosh computers, which comes bundled with many external drives. Several copies can be made of the same master dataset. This makes distribution of large projects much easier.

You will need a high-speed hard drive to master the data. The software controls the transfer of this data from this hard drive to the drive that contains the blank CD and DVD. In terms of CD-ROM, the software contains routines that format the data for either Windows or Macintosh operating systems. A hybrid format is also possible so that the CD-ROM can be read by both kinds of computers.

In many cases, the same hardware can be used to prepare an audio CD that contains only audio tracks. These custom audio CDs can then be played in any audio CD player.

Future Developments

Multimedia is arguably the fastest-growing category of software today. We will undoubtedly witness a merger of television, telephone, and computer that will embrace the concept of multimedia in ways that are difficult to imagine now. Music will play a vital role in this, both as a resource and as the object of the enterprise. Here are a few developments that hold promise for the coming decade, especially for music:

▶ Standardization of a universal scripting language that can be run within most authoring systems and on most major computer platforms

▶ Continued distribution of multimedia on the Internet by use of protocols like the World Wide Web (WWW) in a client-server relationship

▶ Development of better operating systems and software applications so that exchange of information in all formats can be simple and seamless

▶ Digital video that will support virtual-reality scenarios such as 360-degree movement

▶ Distribution of media on DVDs

▶ Integrated multimedia systems that feature speech recognition, telephony, intelligent agents, and touch sensitivity

▶ Increasingly smaller storage devices holding increasingly larger amounts of information, working increasingly faster

<table>
<tr><td>

Module
28

</td><td>

Data Structures for Authoring in Web and Multimedia Environments

</td></tr>
</table>

Authoring is a term originally used for developing computer-assisted instruction software, but it is now applied to multimedia as well.

In this module, we will examine data structures for programming or *authoring* in multimedia environments both on and off the Internet. At the end of the module, we will also review file formats and compression for digital video, a key component of any multimedia project.

From your experiences in Module 27, you've discovered that you can do a number of creative things with multimedia. But there is always something else you will want to do beyond what is possible with the icons, menus, buttons, palettes, and HTML tags provided. Programming *scripts* may be required to control MIDI devices, or to add intelligent forms or interactive buttons to a Web page. You will need to reach deeper into the capabilities of an authoring package or Web HTML code to add these more advanced features. To do this, you need to learn about:

▶ Programming languages and how they work

▶ Programming environments used for multimedia authoring systems and the Web

▶ Object-like scripting languages

▶ Writing a script

▶ File formats for representing graphics, sound, and video

We will cover each of these topics in turn. We will use examples from HyperStudio (Mac and Windows), HyperCard (Mac), Multimedia ToolBook (Windows), and HTML and JavaScript (Mac, Windows, or Unix) to illustrate each of these topics. Whole books are written on scripting and object-oriented programming; we offer you an overview to whet your appetite for venturing forth on your own.

Talking Nicely to Your Computer

In Module 7 we presented basic principles about how computers operated. At the heart of every computer system is a central processing unit (CPU).

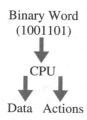

Binary Word
(1001101)

↓

CPU

↓   ↓

Data   Actions

The CPU can only understand binary codes or words, and these words, like the verbs and nouns in human languages, communicate *actions* and *data*. The binary codes for actions instruct the CPU to perform, and the binary codes for data give the CPU the information it needs to carry out that action. When you create a sequence of binary actions and data for a CPU to process, you have created a computer program.

Not all CPUs are created equal. The binary codes for an Intel 486, a PowerPC 601, or a Pentium MMX CPU are all different; each one speaks a unique *machine language*. Binary codes are ideal for machines, but extraordinarily tedious for humans. For this reason, in the early 1950s people started exploring ways to teach the computer to program binary codes for them. Computer languages were invented that used symbols and expressions from mathematics and human language to create *source code* for a computer program. Then, the source code would be translated into the CPU's binary or machine language code. There are three ways that this is done: *assembling, compiling,* and *interpreting* the source code.

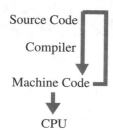

Source Code

Compiler

Machine Code

↓

CPU

Assembler example 68000 CPU to add two values	
MOVEM.L	VALUEI,D0-D3
ADD.L	D3,D1
ADDX.L	D2,D0
MOVEM.L	DO-D1,RESULT
RTS	

An *assembler* is one step removed from directly coding machine language. Mnemonic symbols and numbers are used as *assembly code* in place of the binary codes of the CPU; the assembler then translates those symbols into machine code. Most CPUs have an assembler customized for programming the chip's machine language.

Of primary concern to our discussion is compilers and interpreters. A *compiler* translates all the source code created by the programmer into machine language at one time. This is analogous to translating a book written in Spanish into a book written in English. Then, any time the program needs to be run on the computer, the machine code version is used. An *interpreter*, on the other hand, compiles one line of the source code into machine language, waits for the CPU to carry out that action, and then interprets another line of source code. This is analogous to reading a Spanish book in English, translating one line or phrase at a time. Any time the program needs to be run, the source code is used and the interpreter must be present to handle the translation to machine code.

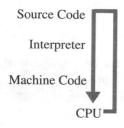

Source Code

Interpreter

Machine Code

↓

CPU

You can see that running interpretive source code will always be slower than running machine code. Why would anyone want to use an interpreter? Interpreters are best in an interactive authoring environment where you want to program an idea and try it out immediately. Interpreters are ideally suited for computer languages used for learning programming, interactive authoring as with multimedia, creating Web pages for the Internet, and other casual programming tasks. With a compiler, you write all of the source code, compile it (and wait for the compilation time), and then run the machine code. If it doesn't run correctly or work as you intended, you go back and change the source code, recompile, and run the machine code again. Compilers are best for professional software development tasks where speed and efficiency of code is important.

Grace Murray Hopper is also known for coining the term computer *bug* (a moth in a circuit) and being instrumental in the design of Short Code and COBOL.

The Evolution of Programming Languages

Bill Gates and Paul Allen, two Harvard students, launched Microsoft by writing a BASIC interpreter for the first PCs.

COBOL programmers are much in demand around the year 2000 to help fix old business software that had been written in COBOL to use only two digits, 00–99, for the year.

High-level languages are interpreters and compilers designed with people's needs in mind. These languages use symbols, vocabulary, and syntax that model the human problem to be solved and make the demands of the CPU and its machine language as transparent as possible. Some of the first high-level languages include the Short Code interpreter for the Harvard Mark I computer (1949) and Grace Murray Hopper's A-0 compiler (later called MATH-MATIC) for the UNIVAC. The UNIVAC was the first commercial computer.

Procedural Languages. There is a long lineage of high-level languages, many of which are called *procedural languages*. Software designed with procedural languages is written in a sequential fashion, line after line, with various tasks performed by subprograms, subroutines, functions, or *procedures*. Procedures call other procedures and tell them what data to use to perform an operation. There are also nonprocedural languages (more on those in a moment).

> **BASIC example to loop 10 times**
>
> ```
> 100 I = 1
> 105 PRINT "THE COUNT IS"; I
> 110 I = I + 1
> 120 IF I < 11 THEN GO TO 105
> 130 REM CONTINUE
> ```

We will touch on a few of the common procedural languages. FORTRAN was written for statistical and mathematical computing by an IBM team led by John Backus in the late 1950s. COBOL was designed in the early 1960s especially for business computer problems where ledger sheets, reports, and tables were common computing concerns. FORTRAN and COBOL are compilers. In the early 1960s, John Kemeny and Thomas Kurtz of Dartmouth invented an interpreter for teaching programming called the Beginners All Purpose Symbolic Language (BASIC). Little did they know that, a decade later, it would become the *lingua franca* for programming the first personal computers, and, two decades later, it would be used for World Wide Web programming as Visual BASIC.

> **C example to loop 10 times**
>
> ```
> main( ) /* main program */
> {
> loop (10);
> }
>
> loop (i) /* loop procedure */
> {
>    int i;
>    i = 1;
>    while (i < 11) {
>       ++i;
>       print("The Count is ", i);
>    }
> }
> ```

There are other dialects of procedural languages. *Structured languages* appeared in the 1970s. Their purpose was to improve the design of programming projects by creating a syntax that reinforced good programming practice—such factors as modularity, transportability, and top-down design. The common compilers for structured languages include Pascal, developed by Nicklaus Worth (1970), and C, developed by Dennis Ritchie at Bell Labs (1972) to run on the UNIX operating system. More recent implementations of BASIC and FORTRAN have become structured languages as their designs have evolved. *String-processing* languages are another type of procedural language that optimize handling predominantly text and character data. SNOBOL (1960s) is one of the better-known string processing languages; music theorists have found it useful for designing software to analyze music structures.

See the interview with Fred Hofstetter at the beginning of this viewport.

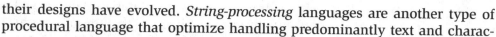

LISP code example

```
(TO-DERIVE (GRAND-
    MOTHER-OF ?X ?Y)
  (FIND (MOTHER-OF ?Z Y))
  (FIND (MOTHER-OF X Z)))
```

APL code example:
$$\to 0 \times \iota X = \text{`S'}$$

There are languages developed especially for designing computer-based instruction. The CERL Lab at the University of Illinois developed the PLATO system and accompanying TUTOR authoring language (1970s) for designing CAI software. A large volume of music software was developed with this language, including Fred Hofstetter's GUIDO system at the University of Delaware. Other CAI authoring languages include IBM's COURSEWRITER, TICCIT, and PILOT, and the Apple version, APPILOT.

Nonprocedural Languages. The languages discussed so far are procedural languages. What about *nonprocedural* languages? These are languages organized around some element other than subroutines, functions, and the like. Typically a nonprocedural language provides the elements for solving a problem, but not the details of how to solve it. The language creates an environment that describes facts, rules, and relationships. The user can ask the software system a question and get a result. Other names for nonprocedural languages include *declarative, very-high-level,* and *less-procedural* languages. The last term is perhaps the most useful, because some languages, like APL, are difficult to categorize.

List-processing languages fall into the category of non- or less-procedural. These languages were designed for problem solving in artificial intelligence (AI). First, Allen Newell of Carnegie-Mellon designed IPL and then, in the later 1950s, John McCarthy of MIT developed the LISP (List Processing) interpreter. LISP is a simple, elegant language that became the mainstay of AI work—there is even a version of LISP known as Franz LISP!

Seymour Papert's LOGO language (1967), developed at MIT, is used to teach children about computers and logical relationships with a graphic turtle that can be programmed on the screen, or even with a mechanical turtle robot. HyperStudio's scripting language, HyperLogo, is a derivative of LOGO.

Seymour Papert (1973) with his LOGO Robot turtle
(Courtesy of The MIT Museum)

Other less-procedural languages are APL (1960s) and PROLOG (1972). APL gets the award for being one of the most cryptic, compact, and unusual languages invented. Alain Colmerauer (1972) created Prolog (Programming Logic) for artificial intelligence work; for this reason, it is known as an *expert system* language because of its use of AI. John Schaffer (late 1980s) used an expert system language in the design of his Harmony Coach

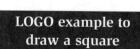

LOGO example to draw a square

```
TO SQUARE :SIZE
REPEAT 4 [FORWARD :SIZE
  RIGHT 90]
END

?SQUARE 80
```

music ear-training software. Database languages like SQL (structured query language), used extensively with Internet, client-server solutions, also are classified as nonprocedural languages.

One of the newer nonprocedural languages is a group known as *object-oriented* languages. Many object-oriented programming (OOPs) languages are extensions of Pascal (Object Pascal or MacApp), C (C^{++}), and BASIC (Visual BASIC). Max is an OOP language designed specifically for music composition. The first OOP language was Xerox PARC's SmallTalk. Java is an OOP language that is machine independent and widely used for Internet applications. More on OOP languages in a moment.

Check Viewport VI for a discussion of Max.

Java applet example

```
Import java.applet.Applet;
Import java.awt.Graphics;
Import java.awt.Font;

Public class printMsg extends Applet {
Font f = new Font("TimesRoman", Font.Bold, 60);
public void paint(Graphics g) {
  g.setFont(f);
  g.drawString("Some sample text," 20, 40);
  }
}
```

Programming Languages and the Internet. The expansion of the Internet has helped to promote a shift toward universal electronic documents, applications, and programming environments. When Web pages and Web-based applications are placed on the Internet for general distribution, the author has no way of knowing what type of computer or operating system will access these materials. Consequently, new languages for programming and scripting have emerged that are platform independent, free to run on a wide variety of computers and operating systems.

A simple HTML Web page example

```
< HTML >
< HEAD >
< TITLE > HTML Example < /TITLE >
< /HEAD >
< BODY >
< H1 > Example Web Page < /H1 >
< P > A paragraph of text < /P >
< H3 > A list of bulleted items < /H3 >
< UL >
  < LI > Item 1
  < LI > Item 2
  < LI > Item 3
< /UL >
A Web link to another
< A HREF = "http://www.site.edu/page.html" >
site < /A >
on the Internet.  < BR >
< /BODY >
< /HTML >
```

HTML, DHTML, and XML. HyperText Markup Language is based on a system of *tags* used to control the layout of text and graphics in a document as displayed or printed on a page. Table 28.1 presents a basic set of HTML tags that can be used for authoring Web documents. A sample of HTML scripting is shown on the left.

HTML documents are downloaded over the Internet from a Web server to a computer running a Web browser like Netscape or Microsoft Internet Explorer (MSIE). The tags in an HTML document instruct the Web browser in formatting text, displaying

Table 28.1. A Sample of HyperText Markup Language (HTML) Tags

Tag	Purpose
< HEAD > < /HEAD >	Document head; statements here processed first
< BODY > < /BODY >	Document body; content of Web page goes here
< TITLE > < /TITLE >	Title to appear in the Web page window
< H1 > < /H1 > , < H2 > < /H2 > , ... < H6 >	Six levels of headings with H1 the largest in size
< P > < /P > or < P >	Paragraph with a return and an extra line
< BR > < /BR > or < BR >	Line break with a return to the next line
< B > < /B > and < I > < /I >	Font styles bold and italics
< FONT > < /FONT >	Font attributes like size and color
< IMG SCR = "graphic.gif" > < /IMG >	Place an in-line graphic image on the page
< HREF = "http://www.link.com/file.html" > < /A >	Create a hypertext link to an external URL
< HREF = "music.wav" > < /A >	Create a hypertext link to a music sound file
< HREF = "image.gif" > < /A >	Create a hypertext link to an external graphic file
< UL > < LI > < LI > < /UL >	Create an unordered, bulleted list
< SCRIPT > < /SCRIPT >	Insert JavaScript or VBScript in the HEAD of the Web page
< APPLET > < /APPLET >	Insert a Java applet in the Web page

Note: Most tags have an ending tag that begins with a slash "/" to define where the formatting effect of the tag ends.

and positioning graphics, playing sound and video, and creating URLs to other Web pages on the Internet.

HTML has rapidly expanded its features and tags as the Web has expanded. In 1998 XML, or Extensible Markup Language, was official approved as an alternative to HTML. XML permits the design of custom tags, links to multiple documents, and better control over document presentation. Dynamic HTML, or DHTML, refers to a variety of techniques that make it easy for a Web page to change each time it is viewed, or to have the display of the Web page customized.

Visual Basic, Java, and Java Applets. HTML Web pages are static in nature, much like a word processing document. They display text, graphics, video, and sound, but they have no interactivity or programming intelligence. A wide variety of extensions and enhancements to HTML, however, have increased the sophistication of Web pages and the applications that they can deliver over the Internet.

Parallel to the emergence of HTML Web pages over the Internet is the development of *Java* and *Visual Basic.* Visual BASIC is a more mature iteration of the Microsoft BASIC language that was so popular in the early days of personal computers. Java is a new, machine-independent object-oriented programming (OOP) language originally developed by Sun Microsystems as a universal language for programming miniature computers to be embedded in appliances. Software developers quickly saw Java as a universal solution for developing software that would run on any computer, especially those exchanging data over the Internet.

Java can be used to program stand-alone applications for distribution over the Internet through Web pages; these are called *Java applets*. There

The mantra of Java programmers is "write once, run anywhere"!

are libraries of preprogrammed Java applets that can be borrowed and added to your Web pages for more powerful features where human interaction or performance speed is required. Both Netscape and Microsoft Internet Explorer browsers can use Java applets. Developing these applets is a task for the serious programmer.

VBScript and *JavaScript*. *VBScript* and *JavaScript* are Web-scripting languages that were developed to extend the simple capabilities of HTML tags so that features like interactive buttons, pull-down menus, forms, and complex graphics and animation could enhance Web pages. Both are ideally suited for the musician with minimal programming experience who wishes to create more sophisticated Web pages.

VBScript is a subset of Visual Basic created by Microsoft for use with its Web browser; *JavaScript* is the Netscape alternative. It is related to the Java language in name only. Microsoft has added JavaScript scripting abilities to its browser (called JScript), but additional extensions or plug-ins are needed with Netscape browsers in order to use VBScript.

APIs: ActiveX and *JavaBeans*. When Apple Computer created its Macintosh GUI operating system and Microsoft created the Windows operating system, a way was needed to give application programmers access to their key features: menus, dialog boxes, opening and saving files, printing, and displaying and editing graphics and text. To this end, the developers of operating systems created APIs (Application Program Interface) to make it easy for programmers to access the internals of the operating system. This ensures that all software written for the Mac OS, or for Windows, for example, looks and feels the same.

ActiveX is the API designed to be used with Microsoft's scripting languages like VBScript and its Web browser. *JavaBeans* are the APIs underlying Java. They truly are the "beans" that can be used to make the "java." By combining JavaScripts with JavaBeans, Web pages can add greater sophistication by using JavaBeans to access the operating system on any computer. So, if you need to access the operating system from a Web page to display a printer dialog box, a JavaBean printer call from your Web page's JavaScript would do the trick.

Hypertext and OOP

The development of powerful tools for multimedia is the result of events that merged in the 1970s and then matured on the PC desktop by the late 1980s. These events include the emergence of digital sound and graphics, of small and fast PCs with lots of memory, and of 32-bit color graphics, MIDI music technology, CD-ROM and laser technology, and the rapid expansion of the Internet.

Hypertext was a term coined in the 1960s to describe software environments where the user could navigate through data by series of nonsequential links. The "readers" have tools that let them arrange material in any order. *Hypermedia* expanded upon the hypertext concept by including text, graphics, sound, music, video, and more in the navigable hyperspace.

To create a free-form digital hyperspace, the computer needed to simulate an environment where media in all forms existed as intelligent objects. Media as objects—objects that have their own personality—became the center of the computer space and, accordingly, the center of the language needed to create them. This succinctly describes the operation of object-oriented programming (OOP) languages in a multimedia context.

What Is OOP?

An object-oriented language uses as its basic element *intelligent objects*. Each object is *intelligent* in the sense that it has been programmed to have specific personality traits and to be self-maintaining. At the lowest level of detail in an OOP program, an object might be created to draw a certain shape or an element of music notation, or play a digital or MIDI pitch. At the highest level, an object might be a window that displays a graphic image, a movie, or music notation. A music window object can be endowed with all of the data and program code necessary for it to "do its own thing," so to speak.

The figure on the right illustrates the concept of object space in an OOP program. Each independent object contains programming code, organized as *handlers* and *properties*, that creates the object's personality. The mode of communication among objects is through *messages*. The handlers in an object are programmed to *tune* that object to private messages to which only that object will respond. For example, messages may be sent by an object performing a music excerpt to other objects that handle the notation and the MIDI performance of the music. External events such as mouse clicks, keys on the keyboard, and menu selections can also create messages in object space that trigger handlers within objects. Remember that things in an OOP environment happen in a nonsequential fashion. If you cannot find the "place to start" in the diagram of object space, that is because you can start almost anywhere with any event.

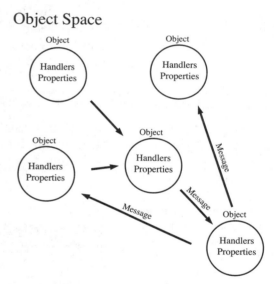

Object Space

The Elements of OOP. There are five primary elements to an object-oriented programming language like Java: *objects, messages, methods, classes,* and *inheritance*. To be a true OOP language, all five elements must be implemented. Table 28.2 summarizes these elements. We have discussed objects and messages. The *method* is the programming code or function, in a traditional sense, embedded within an object.

In many OOP and OOP-like environments, programming an object's

Table 28.2. The Five Concepts Critical to an Object-Oriented Language

Concept	Function
Object	Sends and receives messages
Messages	Communication link among objects
Methods	The programming code that gives the object its intelligence (handlers and properties)
Classes	Groups of objects with common personality traits
Inheritance	New objects inherit traits from their ancestors

handlers and properties is done by scripting. *Scripting* describes simple, English-like instructions to a computer. When you create handlers in an OOP language, or define properties for an object, you can do this through scripting language such as *JavaScript* and *VBScript*.

There are two more elements in OOP. *Classes* and *inheritance* enable the programmer to build families of objects. This greatly simplifies and strengthens the design of the software. It also ensures that the software is *extensible*, enabling it to be easily customized and expanded by both the programmer and the user.

OOP Applied to HyperStudio, HyperCard, and ToolBook

HyperStudio, HyperCard, and Multimedia ToolBook were first presented in Module 27.

These three authoring systems are OOP-like in design but are not considered to be bona fide OOP languages because they do not fully implement all five elements. For our purposes, they are conceptually enough like an OOP language that we will continue to develop the parallel between them. Most important, they look and feel like an OOP authoring environment.

HyperStudio for Macintosh or Windows, HyperCard for the Macintosh, and Multimedia ToolBook for Windows represent progressively more complex and sophisticated OOP card-based development tools. HyperStudio, the sim-

Table 28.3. Objects in HyperStudio, HyperCard, and ToolBook

Object Class	HyperStudio	HyperCard	ToolBook
Buttons	Yes	Yes	Yes
Fields	Yes	Yes	Yes
Hotwords	Yes	Yes	Yes
Groups	Yes	Yes	Yes
Cards or pages	Yes	Yes	Yes
Windows	No	Yes	Yes
Menus	NBA	Yes	Yes
Backgrounds	No	Yes	Yes
Stacks or books	Yes	Yes	Yes
Paint images	Yes	Yes	Yes
Draw images	Yes	Yes	Yes
Digital sounds	Yes	Yes	Yes
Digital video	QT or AVI	QT	QT or AVI
MIDI music	QT or AVI	QT	Yes
CD audio	NBA	XCMD	Yes

Note: Some objects require special extensions to be used. NBA and XCMD are extensions to HyperStudio and HyperCard, respectively. QT is the Quicktime video extension; AVI is the Video for Windows extension.

Table 28.4. A Sample of Object Properties from HyperStudio, HyperCard, and ToolBook

Object	PropertyPurpose
Name of any object	Label cards, buttons, or fields
ID number of any object	Unique identifier for any object in a stack or book
Script for any object	Create a *handler* to add intelligence to a card, button, or field (HyperScript, OpenScript, or HyperLogo)
Location of a button, field, or image	Place an object on the card/page or within a window
Rectangle of any button, field or image	Set the size of an object by its coordinates
Visible state of a field or button	Control whether an object can be seen at any given time
Font of a field or button	Change the font (e.g., Times, Helvetica, Courier, etc.)
Font size of a field or button	Change the size of a font (e.g., 12 point, 24 point, etc.)
Scroll property of a field	Add a scroll bar to a field so that long text can be read
Highlight of a button	When set, the button will appear to blink when selected
Icon of a button	Change the icon graphic appearance of any button
Transparency of a graphic image	Control whether the background can show through a graphic
Line size of a graphic line	Set the line size of objects drawn on a card or background

Note: These properties can be set through either dialogs, palettes, or menus in HyperStudio, HyperCard, and ToolBook, or through their respective scripting languages of HyperLogo, HyperScript, or OpenScript.

plest to use, was designed as an authoring environment for teachers and students to quickly create multimedia projects. For that reason, many of its OOP capabilities are hidden behind easy-to-understand dialogs, menus, and palettes. Multimedia ToolBook, the more advanced authoring package, was designed as an industrial-strength authoring system. Most of its OOP architecture is open and under control of its OpenScript programming language. This permits the addition of features not built in to the system. HyperCard is positioned between the two with a balance between built-in, automated features, and a scripting language for extensibility.

These three card-based authoring systems have *objects* as the central element in their design. Many of the objects can be given "intelligence" through the selection of alternative handlers or properties from built-in menus, dialog boxes, or palettes. Intelligence can also be added to objects through programming capabilities or *methods* in their scripting languages. All three of these multimedia authoring systems use *messages* to communicate or link objects. However, these packages are unlike pure OOP languages because of their weak implementation of object *classes and inheritance*.

Repertoire of Multimedia Objects. Objects are the central element in all three authoring environments. The repertoire of objects provides a rich hypermedia space to work in, with a wide array of imagery. Table 28.3 gives an overview of the types of objects available.

The table shows which hypermedia objects are implemented. You can see that there is a very close parallel. Many of these objects can also be *intelligent* and therefore can contain handlers and properties that can be scripted. The programs differ in their metaphors for labeling objects (Hyper-Card and HyperStudio use a stack-and-cards metaphor; Multimedia Tool-

Book uses book-and-pages) and in their support of multimedia. There are other smaller differences in the less powerful programs.

Providing Personality through Object Properties. It is one thing to have a wide array of objects available in a multimedia authoring environment; it is another thing to be able to endow those objects with the capability to take on multiple personalities. This is done in the three card-based authoring packages in true OOP fashion through the ability to change the properties of objects. Table 28.4 lists but a small sample of numerous properties that can be altered for various objects. For almost any object, you can alter the font and font styles, its location in multimedia space, such graphic attributes as line width and pattern, color and shape, and various actions such as highlighting and scrolling. How are these properties altered? Either through the menus, palettes, and dialogs provided as authoring tools, or directly through their scripting languages.

Communicating through Messages. Messages are the key communication link among objects in hypermedia space. Table 28.5 gives you a sampling of some common messages used in HyperCard and Multimedia ToolBook. HyperStudio also generates messages, but only a few, like a key-press or mouse-button event, are under scripting control.

Each of these messages is the result of some action that has occurred within the object space. A mouse button is clicked and a mouseDown and mouseUp message is generated (or buttonUp and buttonDown in ToolBook). The mouse is used to pass the cursor over an object, and a mouseEnter and mouseLeave message is generated. A key is pressed on the keyboard and a keyDown and keyUp message occurs. Whenever a new card or page is entered, an openCard or enterPage message is generated; leaving the card creates a closeCard or leaveCard message. There is even a message when nothing is happening; the idle message.

A Sense of Order: Layers and Hierarchies. From the way we have just described messages, you might have a vision of them flying all over hyperspace from keys and mice and buttons and fields. This sounds pretty chaotic, but it is very close to reality. However, there *is* some sense of order in hyperspace. This leads us to the concepts of hierarchy and layers.

The figure on the right shows the hierarchy, or priority order, of events and objects in hyperspace. Events start at the top with a mouse click, key press, or menu selection, and work their way down to the card or page layer,

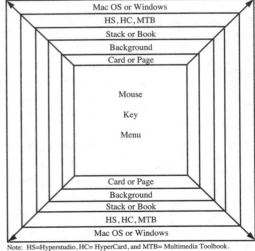

Note: HS=Hyperstudio, HC= HyperCard, and MTB= Multimedia Toolbook. HS does not have a background object.

Table 28.5. A Sample of Messages Used in HyperCard and ToolBook

HyperScript	MessageOpenScript	Detect what action?
openStack or closeStack	enterBook or leaveBook	Entering or leaving a stack/book
openCard or closeCard	enterPage or leavePage	Entering or leaving a card/page
mouseUp or mouseDown	buttonUp or buttonDown	Mouse button pressed or released
mouseEnter or mouseLeave	mouseEnter or mouseLeave	Mouse entering or leaving
mouseDoubleClick	buttonDoubleClick	Double mouse click
controlKey or tabKey	keyChar	Special key being pressed
keyDown	keyDown or keyUp	Key being pressed or released
idle	idle	No action or message being sent

Note: HyperStudio also generates messages but only a few are accessible through HyperLogo; for example, the function BUTTONP will detect a mouse button press and KEYP will detect a key action.

the background layer, the stack or book layer, the application (HyperStudio, HyperCard, or ToolBook), and finally to the operating system: Mac or Windows OS. When a message—a mouse click, for example—is generated, an object at the card layer has the first option for using the message. The object can then choose to let the message stop there or pass it down to the next layer.

Figure 28.1 provides a different view of layers in HyperCard and Tool-Book. At the top of the figure is a simple screen with two fields, a graphic, and a few buttons. The lower portion of the figure illustrates how the image you see is made up of layers both at the card or page level and at the background level. Notice that every object—field, button, or graphic—has its own layer. It is as if the screen you see is made up of many transparent sheets of plastic with one object drawn on each sheet. Following the hierarchical order of priority, objects at the card layer take precedence over all others below.

Take a closer look at Figure 28.1. Notice that the background layers contain the large field, two arrow buttons for moving between cards or pages, and a picture or graphic. The card layers contain the finger graphic, a small field for data, and the Check button. A mouse click on the Check button will send a mouseUp or buttonUp message to that object; this will in turn activate any handlers and properties scripted or defined for that object. The mouseUp message will not pass down to any other layers at the card/page or background level unless the Check button is programmed to *pass* the mouseUp message.

Notice how the objects at all layers are carefully placed so that an object on one layer is not covering an object on another layer. The Check button does not cover any of the fields; the fields do not overlap. This is intentional. Mouse clicks or keystrokes will send messages directly to those objects no matter where they are positioned in the hierarchy. Should a field at a card/page layer, in fact, cover up a button at a background layer, then the background field would be blocked by the card button.

Understanding the notion of layers and hierarchy is very important to the development of your skill in designing card-based stacks and books; as your projects get more complex, you will have to grapple with conflicts

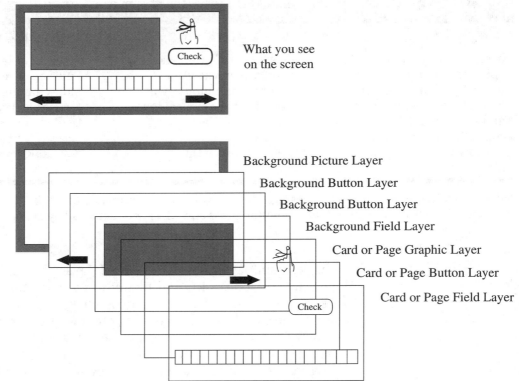

What you see
on the screen

Background Picture Layer

Background Button Layer

Background Button Layer

Background Field Layer

Card or Page Graphic Layer

Card or Page Button Layer

Card or Page Field Layer

Figure 28.1
Layering of objects in
HyperCard and ToolBook

between messages, objects, and layers. All three authoring packages give you the ability to change the order of object layers for this reason.

Inheritance: New Objects and Clones. Where HyperStudio, HyperCard, and ToolBook fall short of being pure OOP languages is in their ability to create groups of objects of similar traits and to generate new objects or clones that inherit traits from their ancestors. They have no ability to create unique, custom classes of objects that share common traits. Classes of objects (buttons, fields, graphic images, backgrounds, cards and pages, and stacks and books) are built into authoring packages and cannot be changed. You are only given the ability to change the personality of any of the predetermined objects through control of an object's properties. A true OOP language like Java would let you create entirely new classes of objects, each tailored to the specific problem at hand.

There is a sense of inheritance, however. A background, when created, inherits the properties of its stack or book: the window size of the stack, the color settings, the resources. Likewise, when a card or page is cloned from a background, it inherits all the properties of that background: graphic images, fields, buttons, and so on. Any new card created from the background in Figure 28.1 will have the same field and two arrow buttons. The fields and buttons will all behave the same when activated by messages on every card in that background. The Check button, on the other hand, is at the card or page layer. When a new card or page is created, the Check but-

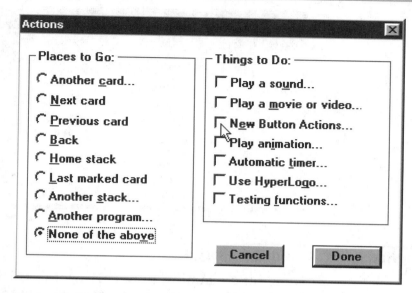

(*a*) The button dialog box where New Button Action is being picked as the Thing To Do

Figure 28.2
The dialog boxes in Hyper-
Studio to add a CD audio
script to a button

(*b*) The CD Audio dialog with its controls for selecting the music clip

ton as well as the graphic and small field will *not* appear on the card; only
the background objects and properties will be inherited by the new card.

Scripting in Card-Based Authoring. Another important element of OOPs
is *scripting,* the ability to write programs to perform specific tasks. You can
generate scripts automatically by selecting options from dialog boxes provided as hold-your-hand scripting in these authoring packages, or you can
roll-your-own scripts by learning the languages built into the package.

Scripting is programming: using a language to control a machine. Scripting enables you to directly change the behavior and properties of any object
and the interaction of objects. Figure 28.2 shows an example from Hyper-
Studio illustrating the use of dialogs to create scripting to play a clip of
music from an audio CD disc. The script shown below is an example from
HyperCard using HyperTalk of a hand-coded script to play a clip of music
from a compact audio disc using the CD play object from HyperCard.

See Module 27 for more
on using CD audio in
HyperStudio.

```
on mouseup

    CDPlay 00,52,57,01,08,32

end mouseup
```

Table 28.6. Object Hierarchy for an HTML Window in JavaScript			
parent object	window.	window. document.	window. document.forms[ ].
window	document	links[ ] anchors[ ] images[ ] forms[ ]	elements[ ]
	history location frames[ ] packages		

OOP Applied to HTML and JavaScript

Now, let's examine how OOP works in Web page authoring using JavaScript. There are two important concepts that bear close attention. First, JavaScript treats an HTML Web page as one big object, a *window* object; all other objects are descendants of that object. Second, there is a very intimate relation between JavaScript and the contents of the Web page in which it resides. Your Web browser treats a Web page as an object; further, the elements of each page are also objects. JavaScript provides access to objects and a way for you to manipulate and alter the characteristics and actions of those objects. Hence, JavaScript is intimately bound to the HTML document in which its scripting code resides. When you write JavaScript, you are acting directly on the Web page: writing to it; changing its media objects, fonts, or features; interacting with its form objects (button, menus, or text fields); altering the characteristics of its display windows; or assuming control of its navigation features.

Table 28.6 shows the family tree, or hierarchy of *objects,* for an HTML page which can be scripted from JavaScript. The window object is the parent object; the document, history, location, frames, and packages are all descendants of it. In expressing object relationships in JavaScript, an object is referenced by its lineage in the family tree. Hence the location object is expressed as "window.location" and the document object as "window.document," and so on.

Notice that the *window.document* object has offspring: window.document.links[], window.document.anchors[], window.document.images[], and window.document.forms[]. The brackets indicate that these objects are arrays, and because all of these objects are descended from the window parent object, you can leave off the "window." in defining the object. The object document.images[] is an array of all of the images loaded into a Web page window. In JavaScript, there are also objects you can use to create new objects: strings, arrays, date, navigator, and math. JavaScript is very extensible: you can create new objects and objects from those objects that inherit their traits.

How about object *properties*? Just as in HyperCard or HyperScript, JavaScript objects have properties that can be changed to alter the personal-

A *variable* is a type of object that holds one element under one name; an *array* is a type of object that can hold numerous elements all under one name.

Table 28.7. A Sample of Object Properties for an HTML Page from JavaScript

Object properties	Purpose
window.length	Number of HTML frames within the window
window.name	The name of the HTML window
window.document.bgcolor	Background color specified by the HTML attribute BGCOLOR
window.document.linkcolor	Color used for nonvisited links specified by the HTML attribute LINK
window.document.location	The HTML document's URL
window.document.title	The title given by the HTML tag < TITLE >
window.document.links[ ]	An array of all the links in the HTML document
window.document.images[ ]	An array of all the images in the HTML document
window.document.image[ ].name	The name of an image in the image[ ] array
window.location.hostname	The hostname where the HTML document resides
window.location.pathname	The path to the directory on the host where the document resides

ity of that object. Table 28.7 provides a sample of JavaScript object properties. Notice how properties like name, bgcolor, location, title, and so on are defined by adding the property name to the object descriptor: window.name, document.linkcolor, location.pathname, etc.

JavaScript, in true OOP fashion, has *methods* that can generate events, and *event handlers* that detect messages generated by objects in the HTML environment (see Table 28.8). There are methods for opening and closing HTML windows; displaying alert boxes; providing text prompts; writing text to the HTML page; and even activating the controls for your Web browser, moving forward and backward through Web pages, and reloading a Web page. Just as in HyperCard or ToolBook, the event handlers will cause some action to happen, for example when a mouse button is clicked, a Web page has finished loading, or a mouse moves over an object. You can create new methods and functions with JavaScript, built up from the basic set provided

Table 28.8. A Sample of Methods and Event Handlers Used in JavaScript

Methods	Purpose
window.close() or .open()	Open or close an HTML window
window.alert()	Displays an alert dialog box
window.prompt()	Display a message and prompts for input
window.location.reload()	Reload the current HTML document
window.history.back()	Go back to the previous HTML location
window.document.writeln()	Write a line of text to the HTML page
window.scroll()	Scroll a window to a specified location

Event Handlers/Messages	Purpose
onload()	Message occurs when a document finishes loading
onclick()	Message when the mouse is clicked
onmouseover()	Message when the mouse passes over an object
onselect()	Message when a user selects some text in a field
onerror()	Message when error event occurs

in the programming environment. All of the essential ingredients are provided in JavaScript, allowing you to script a wide variety of enhancements in HTML Web pages.

Data Structures for Scripting with JavaScript Examples

There are three basic programming structures: actions, branches, and loops. These structures work the same in any computer language. You just need to know the proper vocabulary and syntax for the language in which you are working.

Actions are programming codes, or scripts in the case of JavaScript, that tell a computer to do something: to perform math, display a graphic, generate music sound, or alter text. The methods and event handlers shown in Table 28.8 are examples of JavaScript actions. There are also a variety of functions built into JavaScript that provide actions for manipulating strings, mathematical computations, and the like. You can also use JavaScript to script new actions or functions to extend the language.

The *branch* structure is a script that asks the computer to make a choice between two alternatives: do this or do that. It is also known as an IF THEN ELSE structure. More complex decisions are built up from a series of IF THEN ELSE scripts.

The third structure for computer programming or scripting is *loops*. A loop is a script that instructs the computer to repeat some action a certain number of times.

Sample HTML Page with JavaScript. Figure 28.3 shows the display of a simple Web page that presents a question with four multiple-choice answers. When you pass the mouse over any of the four answers, feedback appears on the Web page in a text field indicating whether or not the answer was correct. This is a simple illustration to show you how actions and branches can be used to write JavaScript to control a Web page. It also illustrates how JavaScript can be integrated with HTML code to create an interactive Web page.

Figure 28.3
A simple HTML Web page that uses JavaScript to trigger feedback when the mouse is moved over any of the multiple choice selection

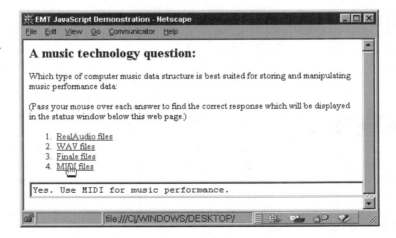

Table 28.9 shows the HTML and JavaScript for the Web page shown in Figure 28.3 with a running commentary explaining each line of scripting and HTML code. A careful study of this figure will give you a good taste of JavaScript programming.

Some Concluding Thoughts on Scripting

This concludes our brief overview of the structures used in programming computers and the types of programming languages that have been devised to control machines. You may not realize it, but we have given you everything you need to know to script in most multimedia or Web authoring environments.

No matter what scripting language you want to work in, you can reduce the scripting to actions, branches, and loops. Determine the syntax and vocabulary for branches and loops, and then look up the actions as necessary. A good reference book on HyperTalk, OpenScript, HyperLogo, or JavaScript is an invaluable aid to use on a need-to-know basis. The Internet is also an excellent place to go for help. You will find tutorials and many examples of scripts on the Web that people have designed and shared for others to use. Taking apart someone else's script is a wonderful learning experience.

As you gain more experience in multimedia environments, most of them being OOP-like in design, you will begin to notice the similarities between languages. The difficult task is not learning the scripting language itself but inventing the logic required to solve the problem at hand. Once you've devised the logic, the solution can be easily scripted.

Digital Video File Formats for Multimedia and Web Pages

Graphic file formats were covered in Module 14, text and fonts in Module 14, MIDI files in Module 21, and digital sounds in Module 24.

Multimedia, on or off the Internet, requires a wide variety of media: graphics, animations, sounds, MIDI files, text, and digital video. We have covered elsewhere in this book information on file types and compression for all the these media forms with the exception of digital video.

There are three common file formats for saving digital video for use in multimedia authoring and Web page design: Apple Computer's QuickTime for Macintosh and Windows; Microsoft's Video for Windows; and the industry standard, MPEG video. The file extensions for these, respectively, are .mov, .avi. and mpg. Let's briefly review each in turn.

QuickTime. The QuickTime movie format is used extensively on Windows and Macintosh computer platforms and on the World Wide Web. Depending on the video format being used, QuickTime will permit full-screen, 30-frames per second video, with 32-bit graphics resolution and 16-bit digital audio. Still graphic images and text can be added to the QuickTime video as well. With the appropriate extensions, QuickTime can also convert AVI and MPEG-1, as well as several other video formats. QuickTime is very flexible; a wide variety of graphic and video file types can be imported into it, and it supports a large variety of formats for saving the finished video.

Table 28.9. HTML and JavaScript (JS) Tags and Scripts for Example

Tags and Scripts	Description
< HTML >	Tag for HTML document
< HEAD >	Tag for document HEAD, code executed first
< TITLE > EMT JavaScript Demonstration < /TITLE >	Title tag for document window
< SCRIPT LANGUAGE = "JavaScript" >	Tag to mark start of code for "JavaScript" (JS) language
function message(index) {	Create a new JS function "message" with one value to pass, index, to select the feedback message.
comments = new Array (3);	Create a new array object called "comments" with 4 elements, 0 to 3.
comments[0] = "No. Best used for long music recordings";	Define the feedback strings for each element of the array.
comments[1] = "No. Best used for short music clips.";	
comments[2] = "No. Best used for music notation.";	
comments[3] = "Yes. Use MIDI for music performance.";	
document.feedback.msg.value = comments[index];	Set the text in the text field object, document.feedback. msg.value to the correct string in the array, comments, using the index value.
return true;	Function needs this so it knows it is done.
}	End of declaration of new function, message()
< /SCRIPT >	End tag for JS code
< /HEAD >	End tag for header
< BODY >	Tag to mark beginning of body of HTML page
< H2 > A music technology question: < /H2 >	Header tag for a title on the page
Which type of computer music data structure is best suited for storing and manipulating music performance data: < P >	Text for question
	Text ends with a paragraph < P > tag to add a space
(Pass your mouse over each answer to find the correct response) < P >	Text also ends with a paragraph tag
< OL >	Tag to start an ordered list (numbered)
< LI > < A HREF = "" onMouseOver = message(0) > RealAudio files < /A >	First item of ordered list. HREF tag highlights the answer so that when mouse passes over, it executes the JS message() function and passes it a value of 0. This results in the feedback message changing.
< LI > < A HREF = "" onMouseOver = message(1) > WAV files < /A >	Next item of list, onMouseOver calls message(1).
< LI > < A HREF = "" onMouseOver = message(2) > Finale files < /A >	Next item of list, onMouseOver calls message(2).
< LI > < A HREF = "" onMouseOver = message(3) > MIDI files < /A >	Next item of list, onMouseOver calls message(2).
< /OL >	End of ordered list
< FORM NAME = "feedback" >	Create a form object called "feedback"
< INPUT TYPE = "text" NAME = "msg" SIZE = "60" >	Give the object a text field called "msg" hence the object is document.feedback.msg.
< /FORM >	End tag for the form
< /BODY >	End tag for the body
< /HTML >	End tag for document header

Just as QuickTime supports a variety of video formats, so does it support a variety of audio formats that can be used for digital audio and MIDI music files. The MIDI files are converted to QuickTime's own MIDI format. Other compatible audio formats include AIFF, AU, WAV, MPEG layers 1 and 2, SoundDesigner, PCM, and audio CD.

Video for Windows. Video for Windows was developed by Microsoft as a competitor to QuickTime. Video resolution provided is 320×240 screen size at 30 frames per second, and 8- and 16-bit digital audio can be included with the video as well.

Be sure to check out the discussion of MPEG as it relates to DVD video and audio in Module 24.

MPEG. MPEG or the Motion Picture Experts Group video format is a non-proprietary industry standard for digital video and audio. There are four different versions of MPEG that have been developed. MPEG-1 video has been popular for CD-ROM and video games and provides video resolution of 352×240 at 30 frames per second, with 8-bit color resolution. MPEG-2 video is used for DVD disc movies and affords 720×480 and 1280×720 screen resolution at 30 fps, with full CD-quality audio. MPEG-3 was designed for high-definition television but has been abandoned. MPEG-4, the newest format, is designed to provide video and audio solutions for the Internet and networking, wireless video, home video applications, and applications like video-based e-mail. MPEG-4 uses the QuickTime video format for the basis of its architecture.

In the past, MPEG has required special hardware for compressing and decompressing the video. For this reason, QuickTime and AVI have been more popular because they use software solutions for video compression. Typically, without additional hardware, only a 10- to 15-frame-per-second video could be generated in MPEG. However, with computer processors like the PowerPC and Pentium running at speeds in excess of 200 MHz, software digitizing of MPEG video, at least for MPEG-1, is possible. With the increased computing power and the proliferation of DVD video and DVD-RW recorders, MPEG could well become the dominant digital video standard.

Video Codecs. A closing note needs to be made about video compression. In creating a digital video, all the same issues of resolution related to digital graphics and digital audio apply. You must consider resolution (either in terms of dots per inch or samples per second) and data width (the number of bits stored for each sample, from 4 to 32 bits). The new factor with digital video is frame rate. A frame rate of 30 frames per second (fps) creates professional-quality video. Without special hardware, 15 frames per second is often the best rate that can be achieved.

A computer video is made up of a series of still images, or frames. The rate at which this series of frames is played back is expressed with respect to a second of time. The industry standard is 30 frames per second.

Given these factors, one additional consideration is important: the type of video compression that will be used. A variety of *c*ompressor/*dec*ompressors, or "codecs," offer different ways to compress and play back digital video. Because digitizing video makes incredible memory demands in megabytes per second, some way of minimizing the data is critical.

MPEG is both a video format and a codec, having its own unique compression scheme. QuickTime and AVI can use a variety of codecs including MPEG. For example, the Cinepak codec was created to deliver video from

CD-ROMs, Motion JPEG Format A to edit broadcast quality video, and ClearVideo to deliver video on the internet. Microsoft has two codecs, Windows Uncompressed and Windows RLE. Apple Computer has its own codecs of Apple Video and Apple Graphics.

In creating digital video, your video-capture software will give you lots of options to choose from, and you will want to carefully consider each of them to get the best video resolution with the smallest video file size. When you go to save the video file, one of the choices you will make is choosing the appropriate video codec for compressing the video. This is true whether you are using QuickTime or AVI. You need to match the codec to the content of your video. Experimentation on your part may be the best alternative to see which codec gives you the best trade-off between resolution and file size. Some software, such as Terran Interactive's Movie Cleaner Pro, will suggest the best codec for playback and distribution.

<table>
<tr><td>

Module
29

</td><td>

Multimedia Hardware

</td></tr>
</table>

Review Module 12 for an overview of student workstation needs for playing multimedia titles.

Creating a workstation for authoring multimedia presentations and applications will utilize most of the hardware discussed throughout the book. A full-scale multimedia workstation should offer the capability of integrating digital audio, MIDI, computer graphics, digital video, audio and video mixing, and laser technology—a large ensemble of digital media. Figure 29.1 revisits the IPOS model and illustrates the various input, output, storage, and computer hardware options for a multimedia workstation.

The characteristics of much of this hardware have been discussed in previous modules. New components like video digitizers and video display projectors have been added. The process component of the IPOS model suggests minimum standards for the computer at the heart of any multimedia workstation: CPU, RAM, and video resolution.

After glancing over this chart, you could be afraid that your checkbook will go into shock! Relax. You do not need *all* of this equipment to begin developing multimedia applications. Following our approach in previous

Figure 29.1
The IPOS model, showing devices for developing multimedia presentations

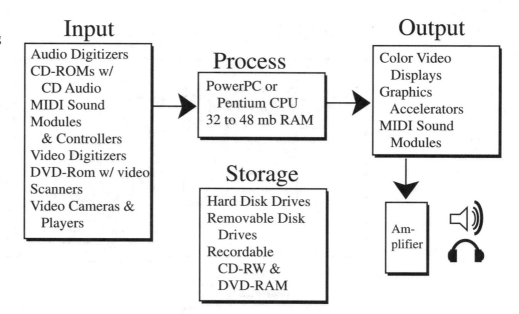

modules, we have created a media KISS workstation for you as a starting point for multimedia work. Then we expand the system (Media KISS Extended), adding more video features and recordable laser disc. You may want to take this one step further, depending on your musical needs. The MIDI KISS workstation designs from Modules 21 and 22 could be combined with the media KISS workstation to increase the MIDI sophistication for multimedia work.

Media KISS System for Multimedia Authoring

What hardware do you need to get started with your own multimedia authoring projects? The media KISS workstation shown in Figure 29.2 with its wide variety of hardware should provide a sufficient number of media options for creating multimedia stacks, desktop presentations for teaching and publicity activities, and Internet Web pages with graphics, sound, and video.

Let's go hardware shopping for your KISS multimedia system. Being careful with your budget, we did a good deal of research on the necessary components. Below you will find our recommendations. (In parentheses we've indicated the module where each component of the system was discussed.)

▶ A fast computer: Pentium or PowerPC machines running at least at 200 MHz; faster if budget allows (Module 8)

▶ 32 MB of random access memory and 16-bit color video (thousands of colors); 64 MB of RAM and 24-bit color if budget allows (Modules 8 and 15)

▶ A 17-inch color video display; larger or two monitors if budget allows (Module 15)

Figure 29.2
Media KISS workstation for creating a multimedia development environment

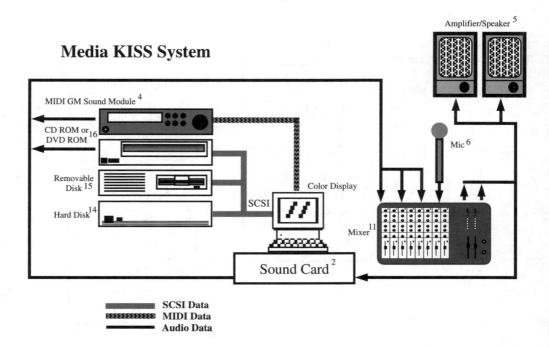

Media KISS System

Amplifier/Speaker [5]

MIDI GM Sound Module [4]

CD ROM or DVD ROM [16]

Removable Disk [15]

Hard Disk [14]

SCSI

Color Display

Mic [6]

Mixer [11]

Sound Card [2]

━━━━ SCSI Data
▨▨▨▨ MIDI Data
━━━━ Audio Data

▶ Hard disk storage of a least 4 GB; more gigabytes if budget allows (Module 8)

▶ Removable disk storage with super floppy (e.g., 100- or 200-MB Zip drive) or optical technology; 1- or 2-GB removable hard drive (e.g., Jaz drive) if budget allows (Module 8)

▶ Audio digitizer capable of at least 16-bit/44-kHz digital sampling and playback (Modules 12 and 26); 20- or 24-bit/48-kHz for better quality

▶ 24x CD-ROM or DVD-ROM drive capable of playing CD-ROM, CD audio, PhotoCD, and DVD audio and video playback (Module 12)

▶ General MIDI multitimbral sound module; digital synthesis is preferable to low-end FM synthesizer chips (Modules 12, 21, and 22)

▶ Simple mixer capable of mixing three to four inputs down to one stereo output (Module 22)

▶ Various audio gear including amplified speakers, microphone, headphones, and audio cables

We got lots of advice while shopping around for your media gear. Three pieces of advice we found especially helpful were:

▶ More storage is better: buy a big hard drive!

▶ Faster is better: buy the fastest computer you can afford!

▶ You need more computer horsepower to create your multimedia than you do to play it back afterwards.

The media KISS setup in Figure 29.2 shows four sources for external audio: MIDI; CD audio from the CD-ROM or DVD-ROM player; audio from the digitizer; and live input from the microphone. A MIDI keyboard or other controller could easily be added to this system for live performance input. Notice how the mix of the four audio signals passes back through the audio digitizer. Many multimedia projects produce as the final product a complete digital production that can be played on any workstation without added peripherals. This setup could easily be used, however, for multimedia projects using interactive CD audio and MIDI music.

Plug-and-Play Gotchas. When you go shopping for multimedia computer gear, you will encounter the catch phrase *Plug-and-Play*. Take the issue of Plug-and-Play compatibility seriously. It refers to your ability to buy a new media device—a new sound card for example—take it out of the box, plug it into your computer, install the software, and have everything work correctly.

The Macintosh system has had a good success rate in this regard; Wintel systems have not. For this reason one of the desirable features of Windows 95 and 98 is genuine Plug-and-Play compatibility. It represents a concerted effort to eliminate many of the problems with installing hardware and software from various vendors on Wintel machines.

Figure 29.3
Sound Card from Creative Labs
(Courtesy of Creative Labs)

Module 19 illustrates the use of the Windows Media Control Interface and Macintosh extensions for media control.

The Windows environment has MCI, or the *Media Control Interface*, at the heart of its operating system. With MCI properly configured using the drivers supplied from the device manufacturer, any multimedia application should be able to use MCI-compatible scanners, CD or DVD players, MIDI devices, digital video-capture boards, sound boards, and the like. Having said that, certain hardware, like sound cards, can still create Plug-and-Play headaches.

Of course the Macintosh, with its Extensions and Control Panels, is not faultless when it comes to compatibility problems. MIDI Manager and the process of configuring MIDI on a Mac are a case in point. Briefly, here are some of the main problem areas you should watch out for when considering any addition to a multimedia workstation:

▶ Conflicts in bus designs and hardware I/O, interrupts (IRQs), and direct memory access (DMA) configurations

▶ Conflicts in operating system drivers for video, sound, and MIDI

▶ MIDI maps and patches

▶ Cables and connectors

The best remedy is to get lots of advice before making a purchase. Go with mainline products, check on their technical and service support, and use Internet on-line services to get input before deciding on a new component for your workstation.

Media KISS Extended for Video

The media KISS workstation is lacking in two significant areas: video and MIDI. As your multimedia work expands, you will find a need to add more video and music options to support it. MIDI hardware was covered in depth in Modules 21 and 22. The new elements in the media KISS extended workstation (Figure 29.4) are:

▶ A DVD-RAM recorder/player added for playing DVD video and for recording video and multimedia to laser disc (see Modules 12 and 26)

▶ A flat-bed color scanner for digitizing still graphic images from printed materials (a digital camera could also be used to capture live still images; see Modules 15 and 27)

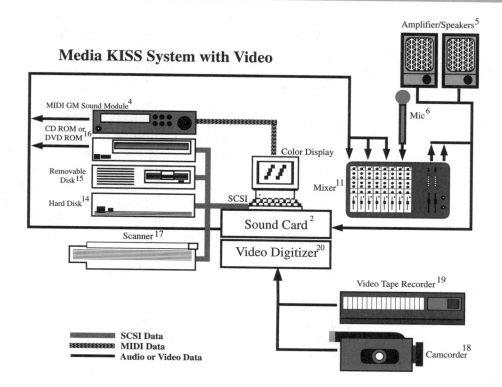

Figure 29.4
Extending the KISS media system to include video capability

Digital video cameras are also an option, though typically more expensive than a camcorder. The video image is captured in real time and digitized for transfer directly to your computer.

▶ A VCR videotape player and a camcorder as sources for video

▶ A video digitizer for capturing motion video clips and still images

Video Playback and Recording. The media KISS extended workstation includes a VCR player and camcorder. The camcorder is ideal for impromptu recordings needed for authoring tutorials, CAI materials, Powerpoint presentations, and short video clips for Web pages. A music teacher could easily shoot video of students performing, use the video digitizer to create video clips, and post them on a promotional Web page for the school's music program.

Evaluating Different Video Options. Before purchasing a VCR or camcorder, you should consult technical or consumer reviews and talk with people with video experience. Video technology is a world in itself, with its own terminology and complexity. There are a few considerations we would point out.

Video format and resolution. The VHS video format is the one most used for consumer VCRs and video equipment. Small hand-held camcorders offer the more compact 8-mm or the better quality Hi-8 tape formats as well as the VHS format. There is also Super VHS, or S-VHS, for better-quality video production. By way of comparison, VHS format provides 240 lines of resolution, 8 mm provides 260 lines, and S-VHS and Hi-8 provide 400 lines; broadcast quality, BetaCam SP, is 440 lines. The availability of high-fidelity (HQ) sound is also a desirable enhancement to the video format.

Video controls. When making video clips on a computer workstation,

SMPTE and synchronizing with MIDI is discussed in Modules 20 and 22.

you can control your camcorder or VCR player manually. Better-quality units, however, offer varying degrees of remote control through the computer's serial port. Common interactive controls are Sony's VISCA (Video System Control Architecture), Control-S, and Control-L. If your software and video hardware are able to take advantage of one of these features, you will be able to further improve the quality of your digital video work by using software control of the video playback. With appropriate software and a good-quality video deck, the computer may be able to remotely control the advance of each frame to insure a good quality digital image of each frame. The best video decks offer SMPTE time striping and control; each frame of video has a unique time code. For serious video work (especially for outputting to videotape), where you need to edit MIDI, digital audio, and digital video, a quality video deck of S-VHS or Hi-8 format with SMPTE control and genlock is strongly recommended.

Reliability. Consumer-grade video equipment is designed for casual use: rewinding and fast-forwarding home movies and video rentals. The fault tolerance of the mechanical parts of a consumer VCR deck or camcorder is not strict enough for a device to be remote-controlled by a computer doing high-speed, frame-by-frame video capture. Think of what would happen if you connected a computer remote-controlled door opener to your refrigerator and programmed it to be opened and closed thirty times a second; the life of the hinges would not outlast a quart of milk! Even though some Hi-8 camcorders offer computer remote control, use the capability carefully. If you really need intensive, interactive frame-by-frame control, move up to a professional-grade video deck designed for the task.

Analog video recommendation. If you are going to buy one analog video unit for your media KISS workstation, we would recommend investing in a Hi-8 video camcorder with Control-L or Control-S interactive video capabilities. For VHS tapes that you want to play for video capture, you can find a low-end VCR for direct playback to the video digitizer or dub the VHS tape to your Hi-8 camcorder.

Capturing and Digitizing Video. In Modules 27 and 28, we studied the software and data aspects of capturing digital movies. Capturing digital video is analogous to having a rapid-fire finger on a camera that is taking thousands of digital snapshots (*frames* in movie jargon) of live or recorded video and then storing them in the computer just as fast as you can press the shutter release. The key things that affect how fast you can take these snapshots are the video resolution or screen size (e.g., 320×240 or 640×480 pixels), color depth (8- to 24-bit color), frame rates (10 to 60 frames per second), and the compression *codec* being used (MPEG, Cinepak, Motion JPEG, etc.). If audio is also being captured at the same time, the audio sample size (8- or 16-bit mono or stereo) and the sampling rate (11 kHz up to 48 kHz) need to be considered. You must juggle all of these parameters as you seek to generate quality digital video that looks and sounds good, plays back smoothly with no loss of frames, and consumes as little disk storage space as possible. Too big a screen size and too fast a frame rate, and the computer will not be able to capture the frames fast enough; frames will be dropped

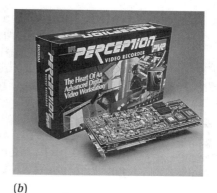

(a)　　　　　　　　　　　*(b)*

Figure 29.5
Low-end video capture
with the (*a*) Iomega Buz
and high-end with the (*b*)
DPS Perceptual Video
Recorder
(Courtesy of Iomega Corpora-
tion and Digital Processing
Systems)

Digital video file formats
and compression codecs
were reviewed in
Module 28.

DSP chips and the Firewire
interface were discussed in
relation to digital audio in
Module 26 .

as the computer misses some snapshots. Too high an audio resolution and the computer will have to work overtime on the audio and steal time from the video digitizing—frames again will be have to be dropped for the computer to keep up.

Enter video-capture hardware! Just as digital audio requires additional hardware to provide high-speed analog-to-digital capture and digital-to-analog playback, so does digital video. To produce computer video, you will need a video digitizer or video capture board. At the low end of the price range, video capture cards typically provide 320×240 screen resolution with 10- to 30-frames-per-second capture rates. There is usually some form of hardware compression on the card to help speed up the video capture process: motion JPEG or MPEG-1. Standard composite and S-video input and output are available for connecting VCRs, camcorders, NTSC video monitors, and the like. For saving the digital video, software compression such as AVI, Quicktime, or MPEG-1 can be used. To capture the audio as well, a separate sound card or built-in audio digitizer is required.

Various Macintosh computers from the early Quadra 660 AV up to the present-day fast PowerPC workstations have had some form of video digitizing built in using raw video data capture with no compression codec. Their performance is comparable to low-end video capture. On Wintel computers, low-end video capture cards like the Iomega Buzz (see Figure 29.5*a*), Matrox Rainbow Runner, Intel SmartVideo Recorder, or the Pinnacle miroVideo DRX provide comparable video digitizing but with hardware capture compression provided by either Motion JPEG or MPEG-1.

If you have a healthier budget for equipment, you can move up to midrange or professional-level video-capture hardware. Pinnacle (miroVideo), Radius, DPS, Avid, Truevision, and Targa make PCI-bus video-capture products for both Macintosh and Wintel in the mid to professional level. What do you get when you move up to these more expensive alternatives? You get more sophisticated hardware support with DSP video chips that do fast video compression. Because of the improved video horsepower, you get full-screen video, typically 640 × 480 or NTSC 648 × 486 pixels, 16- to 24-bit color, and 30 frames per second. Another major addition with the more sophisticated video capture products is DSP hardware for CD-quality audio capture that is designed to keep the audio synchronized with the

See Figure 15.7 for a photo of the Canon Optura digital camera.

video. Some video capture cards also offer a Firewire interface to digital video (DV) cameras and recorders. Digitial video can be input to the video capture card over the Firewire cable, edited, and then sent back to the digital camera over Firewire, all in digital form. The Digital Processing Systems (DPS) video capture bundle shown in Figure 29.5b is an example of a professional-level video editing system.

Making the Final Choice in Video Capture Hardware. How do you decide which video capture card is right for you given your needs and budget? Ask yourself whether you intend to do video digitizing in order to:

▶ Create small windows of video clips on screen to enhance presentations, tutorials, and instructional training applications

▶ Produce full-screen, full-motion video for training and presentations

▶ Use the computer as a digital video editor, with the video being output back to videotape for the final product—much as you would edit digital audio for tape recordings

Let's start with the first option: you want to enhance your multimedia stack projects or Web pages with short digital video clips. This can be done relatively inexpensively with QuickTime or Video for Windows using one of the less-expensive video boards or, on the more recent Macintosh computers, with their built-in video capture. When you choose a video-capture board from this group, there are a few things to bear in mind in terms of quality production:

• *Computer speed.* The speed of the computer will be important; faster computers will help the hardware produce better video clips. (We recommend using a fast, high-end computer for capture to get the best-saved video clip, even if the clip will be played back on a slower computer.)

• *Video quality.* You will not have studio-quality video; you will have to juggle the variables that affect video quality to produce the best compromise. We often find, for music applications, that it is best to sacrifice video quality to insure that the music or spoken voice is clearly heard.

• *Hardware for input only.* After you've captured a short video clip using the hardware compression on the video-capture board (e.g., Motion JPEG), then save the video clip with one of the software codecs like Cinepak. Make sure you experiment with playing the video back without using the hardware compression before deciding on the final settings for capturing the video. (Be careful not to use a compression scheme that can't be played back on another computer without the same video-capture hardware.)

• *Audio may not be included.* Many video boards in this group do not provide audio digitizing. On Wintel machines, you will need a sound card for this; on the Mac you can route the audio through the built-in audio digitizer. Given the design of our KISS media workstation, this should not be a problem, as good-quality digital audio is already included.

What about the second and third options? You want full-screen, full-motion video, and video for output to videotape. For these applications, you will need more expensive video-digitizing equipment. Both options demand very processor-intensive work: maintaining full-screen, full-motion video requires moving lots of color pixels at 30 frames per second. You need very fast video digitizing, compression, disk access, and processor speed, as well as considerable RAM and fast disk storage. You can roughly calculate that a single full-screen image of 640×480, 24-bit color pixels contains over 1 megabyte of video data. Digitizing at 30 frames per second, you would have to process, compress, and store some 30 megabytes per second of data.

NTSC (National Television Standards Committee) standards apply to video broadcasting and production in North America and Japan.

The third option requires that you output the digital video to tape. For many systems, this requires converting RGB digital codes to NTSC analog video, the video signal that is normally used for commercial television and VCRs. This feature may or may not be included with the video-capture card. Furthermore, the video-capture card needs to be able to output the correct format of your VCR: Hi8, VHS, or S-VHS. Video production to analog tape must pass the more acute test of the human eye. Some of the quirkiness of digital video may be overlooked on the computer screen, but not on video-tape, so issues of resolution and frame rate become even more critical.

Graphic and film artists are doing full-screen, full-motion digital video editing from personal computers. Systems like those from Radius, Targa, and Digital Processing Systems (see Figure 29.5*b*) are just a few examples of top-of-the-line video-capture, compression, and playback hardware that make it possible to do near-studio-quality video editing. Remember, performance comes at a premium.

More Options for The KISS Media Workstation

There are many more options for multimedia that you can add to the KISS media workstation. A quick list of other devices you might consider includes:

► More memory and disk storage, especially fast AV (audio/video) hard disks designed for audio and video

► CPU accelerators to add new horsepower to your present CPU

► 24-bit color and video or graphics accelerators; some video capture cards require this

► Better color and larger display monitor (or two!)

► Genloc device for overlaying text and graphics on video

► Digital still (see Module 15) or digital video camera

► 35-mm slide scanner

Projecting Your Image

You have your multimedia project completed and you are ready for a public presentation. The project completed in HyperStudio has lovely color screens, still images of your students, and a few QuickTime digital movies that you have slaved over for hours. It is now performance time, but you've given no thought to how you are going to project the video image onto a screen for the audience to view. Oops! You've just discovered another wrinkle in creating a multimedia presentation.

With a little research, you will learn that are three video projection options for computer desktop presentations:

▶ Large-screen color monitors

▶ Color LCD panels, data projectors, or multimedia projectors

▶ RGB projectors

Large color monitors. This solution is much like using big TV screens, 27 inches or larger, for your video display. In fact, a less expensive alternative would be to simply use a large-screen TV with an RGB-to-NTSC video converter to convert the computer video to TV video. Professional presentation monitors, however, offer more features than consumer TVs, including both NTSC and RGB inputs and better resolution. Where a TV offers 300 to 525 lines of video resolution, a presentation monitor offers 600 to 800 lines. Having said that, some of the 32-inch consumer TVs now offer up to 800 lines of video resolution as well.

There are a number of advantages to using large-screen monitors for displaying color desktop presentation projects. They are relatively inexpensive; the color looks good, especially with the higher resolution of a presentation monitor; and you do not have to use low lighting in the room. The disadvantages are the limited size of the screen area for large audiences, and the weight of the units—they are not very portable!

LCD panels and projectors. LCD projection uses liquid crystal display panels where each video pixel or dot has three color transistors (red, green, and blue) that can be turned on and off. The LCD panel essentially creates an image like that of an overhead projection transparency out of these dots. In fact, LCD panels are placed on top of an overhead projector, just like a transparency. Figures 29.6*a* and *b* show LCD projectors by Panasonic and InFocus. The advantages of LCD displays are portability and the display size of the image; they are light and compact. The InFocus LitePro 725 in Figure 29.6*a* is a good example of a very portable unit. LCD projectors eliminate the need for an overhead projector by building the projection system directly into the unit. These units are called "data projectors" or "multimedia projectors" if they have audio amplification and speakers built in and high resolution of color video.

With both LCD panels and LCD projectors, it is important to consider the color resolution and the speed with which the display can change its image. If you have digital video running at 30 frames per second, you will want your LCD display to keep up with the video. Likewise, if you have created 24-bit color images, you want the LCD display to project 24-bit color. Most *active matrix* LCD displays will accommodate full-motion video with at least 16-bit color. Screen resolution is also an issue as with any computer display. VGA projectors display 640×480, SVGA display 800×600, and XGA display 1024×768 pixels. For today's computers, SVGA should be the minimum resolution of choice. Projectors typically come with various RGB and

Figure 29.6
Two computer display
projectors

(*a*) InFocus LitePro 725 Data Projector
(Courtesy of InFocus)

(*b*) Pioneer PT-L292 LCD Multimedia
Projector (Courtesy of Panasonic Broadcast &
Television Systems Company)

NTSC converters for interfacing with the video from different computer systems.

LCD projectors offer a projected display area as large as 10 feet on the diagonal and range in brightness from 350 to 1000 lumens. LCD panels require an overhead projector for their lighting. You will want about 6000 lumens of brightness from an overhead projector for good LCD panel display. The brighter the better; otherwise, you may have to lower or turn out the overhead lights, making for a less-than-ideal environment.

RGB or multiscan projectors. There are broadcast-quality, industrial-strength video projectors that display high-quality, full-color 800-line-resolution video on very large areas. RGB or multiscan projectors are best suited for a large room where they can be permanently installed. They are cumbersome to transport, difficult to tune correctly (so you don't want to have to move one after getting it set up), and very expensive. As the sophistication of color data projectors increases in terms of color and screen resolution, they may replace the high-end multiscan projector.

Other considerations. After spending money on a good-quality computer projection system, don't forget a good-quality screen. Good portable screens that have large surface areas really help to enhance the video projection (we are thinking of something better than the typical AV portable movie screen). These screens offer light-weight, fast-folding features, as well as special surfaces and viewing angles for improved projection. Another useful device for computer presentations is a remote-controlled mouse that works with infrared signals. This will keep you from having to talk to a group from behind the computer. With a remote mouse, you can stand away from the computer and perform simple mouse clicks to navigate through a desktop presentation.

This final viewport is a fitting conclusion to our introductory study of computers, technology, and the music experience. Work in multimedia encompasses each of the major topics in music technology, operating systems and the Internet, computer-assisted instruction, desktop publishing, music notation, sequencing, and digital audio and sound synthesis. Multimedia touches all these issues but adds one more critical dimension: the opportunity to personally define or author content to express meaning.

Music Experience Is Multimedia

Throughout this book, we have emphasized the historical context of computers, technology, and music experience and the vital role that people play in this enterprise. Nowhere is this more evident than with multimedia. Historically, computers began as devices for manipulating numbers and text. Today, graphic images, animation, movies, digital sound, and MIDI music performance data are major additions to what computers can manipulate. Computers have become hosts for new kinds of software and partners with other types of hardware to bring new technological possibilities to today's culture. This has happened because people have been interested in developing powerful ways to represent meaningful information and in creating new avenues to express feeling.

Manifold ways of integrating text, sights, and sounds are a natural outgrowth of our information age. We enter the twenty-first century with unprecedented access to data and with powerful tools to work with these data. Multimedia technology provides a way to transform these data as *meaningful* information. The key lies in our ability to use this power wisely as people and as musicians.

We believe that music as an art fits comfortably within the mosaic that is multimedia in several ways. Music has always been a multimedia event, especially when experienced live. As computers, telephones, televisions, audio systems, and fax machines all begin to blend together in form and function, it is logical to predict that music will be experienced more often as a multimedia event than as pure sound only. In Module 25, we presented a number of new developments in laser-disc technology, such as compact discs with graphics and MIDI, DVD, and writeable laser discs that will play a role in expanded entertainment and information centers for home, school, and office. We can look forward to purchasing music, movies, and multimedia productions recorded directly onto blank CDs and DVDs off of the Internet.

Multimedia will also be found more often in live performance in concert halls. Projection systems that provide images to accompany music, words that flash by during opera productions, unusual lighting schemes that sometimes change during performances, and imaginative mergers of MIDI applications with traditional and nontraditional instruments for music performance are increasingly likely in the future.

Apart from multimedia's role in the music experience itself is its function as a powerful way to present information about music. Multimedia software and hardware provide us with more inherently *musical* ways to talk about and teach music than ever before. We saw this as you created a series of custom-designed multimedia projects for your wind ensemble in Module 27. Whether we are giving a preconcert talk to an audience about the evening's symphony program or teaching young children about tone color and texture, we can use multimedia to reveal the deepest subtleties of the music. Commercial software devoted to teaching about music through multimedia, such as the titles highlighted in Modules 9 and 27, is further testimony to this fact.

The role of the Internet as a place for the distribution of multimedia projects was stressed in this viewport. We also believe that the Internet can be used effectively for original multimedia presentations and that this, too, is the wave of the future as music learning on demand moves to the World Wide Web.

Different Authoring Systems with Similar Media Files

In this viewport, we led you through the creation of four projects. We chose a card-based solution, a presentation package, an approach that used QuickTime, and Internet Web pages. These authoring systems were supported by text, graphics, video, and sound. Some solutions include a scripting language for customization and interaction. These projects serve as models for musicians, whether inside or outside education.

Of course there are other approaches. Time-based solutions, such as Macromedia's Director, allow for more fluid integration of text, graphics, and animation while providing powerful scripting languages of their own. It essentially boils down to needs, resources, time, and energy.

Regardless of the approach taken and the authoring environment chosen, musicians need supportive software and hardware. A good understanding of the many data structures noted in Module 28 and throughout this book is critical to successful authoring.

Software. Graphics and music software play an important supportive role in multimedia creation regardless of the authoring approach. These programs capture or create the graphics necessary for use in projects. A good image-processing program, like Adobe's PhotoShop, is essential for treating these images. Movies can be integrated easily with very modest tools. If the work requires a fair amount of editing, synchronization with sound, text overlays, or special effects such as fades and wipes, invest in movie-editing software like Adobe's Premiere.

Needs for integrating digital audio into projects will vary according to computer and authoring package. Much can be accomplished with simple digital audio software that is available from shareware sources or that comes with digitizing hardware. For advanced work, a good sound editing program like Sound Forge or Peak will be needed. Nearly all the sampling software described in Viewport VII can be used effectively for multimedia, because most authoring systems support standard audio file formats.

You also used MIDI files for sound. Standard MIDI files are often used in multimedia, and many developers prefer the General MIDI file format for these MIDI files. MIDI files consume very little space. For example, the QuickTime system software now includes musical instrument samples that respond to the General MIDI format. This allows QuickTime to play MIDI files through the internal speaker of the computer without the aid of MIDI devices. A simple software sequencer, such as one of those described in Viewport VI, is a "must" for the multimedia musician.

Hardware. Much of the hardware necessary for musicians to create multimedia is already present in music workstations. On the audio side, many systems include a General MIDI sound module that may provide better sound than digitized samples within software. A fast CD or DVD drive capable of reading audio, CD-ROM, PhotoCD, and DVD video formats is common, as are speakers, amplifiers, and mixers. In short, the KISS hardware systems that have been described at various stages in the book are well equipped to support multimedia.

There are some other pieces of equipment that need to be added, however, especially for capturing audio and video. Depending on the kind of computer, a card that can capture video is important. Wintel machines that do not have internal support for sound will require a sound card. In addition to line and microphone input, these cards include sound playback support for General MIDI instruments and a built-in MIDI interface for other MIDI gear. Most of these cards support, at minimum, 16-bit digitized sound at 44 kHz. Such resources come as standard equipment on Macintosh machines.

Video digitizing cards are necessary for most Macintosh and Windows machines, although some Macintosh computers come with built-in video-capturing hardware. The card to buy depends on the kind of video you want. A small card for a few hundred dollars will create acceptable movies at 15–30 frames per second and 320×480 pixels in size. More expensive cards will provide larger and faster movies and will support special effects. Remember that these cards are required only for creating video, not for playback.

An analog or digital video camera is necessary to capture live video. For analog work, a VCR can be linked to the video card to capture the image digitally. For digital cameras, direct linkages to your computer are possible, or they may use small PC Card memory. You might have a simple home video system that will work nicely. More professional equipment can always be added as the demand arises.

A scanner and a digital camera for still pictures might be useful for graphics work, and a computer projector would also be useful for showing the results to large groups. These items are convenient but are not essential for getting started with multimedia.

We also recommend that you consider storing your projects on recordable CDs or DVDs. The cost of recordable drives is now affordable and it has never been easier to save your data in this manner.

One final concern about hardware: the computer itself. You should try to create multimedia on computers that have:

▶ The fastest CPU speed possible (PowerPC or Pentium chips)

▶ The largest RAM affordable (64 MB minimum)

▶ At least a 17-inch color monitor that supports 16-bit or greater color

▶ CD-ROM or DVD drives

▶ Hard disk storage of at least 4–8 gigabytes, and removable storage, such as a Zip or Jaz drive, for backup

Data Structures. In addition to the data structures described here and in previous viewports for digital video, graphics, text, and sound, the most important data structure for multimedia is the programming environment itself. Most authoring systems base their scripting languages on an object-oriented structure. Scripts send messages through a hierarchy or along a path. Like all programming languages, scripts make actions occur, branching alternatives arise, and loops cycle. Scripting is programming, but programming in an English-like setting that is relatively easy to understand.

In addition to scripting and object-oriented languages, we stressed the importance of languages connected with Internet development. HTML was discussed in some detail, and we supplied information about Java, JavaScript, and other enhancements. The role of the Internet as a place for multimedia will certainly expand, and creating our own Web sites for the enhancement of music experience will grow as well.

Finally, the understanding of digital movie data structures is critical for both stand-alone and Internet-based multimedia. Especially important is a solid understanding of video compression.

The Importance of Planning

We close with one final point about working with multimedia: planning. You discovered early that this is the key to success. Careful planning accomplishes two things. First, it allows for the collection of appropriate content. Multimedia is nothing if it doesn't contain something meaningful. For our example, a careful music analysis of Holst's music was important *first*, before designing a card or writing a script. Choosing just the right conducting movie clips, writing the most insightful interview questions, and collecting the best set of terms to define were all important activities to complete before anything else was done.

Second, good planning means roughing out the look and feel of the project before touching a computer keyboard. Certainly every nuance cannot be foreseen, but it is equally true that basic design ideas must be worked out ahead of time.

If good content and overall design blend with excellent software and hardware, much can be accomplished with multimedia. "Rolling your own" software in this manner can be one of the most creative and exciting experiences in music technology, second only to the music experience itself.

Supplementary Readings

Carroll, John M. *The Nurnberg Funnel: Designing Minimalist Instruction for Practical Computer Skill.* Cambridge, Mass.: MIT Press, 1990.

Cline, Jim, and Patrick Seaman. *Website Sound.* Indianapolis, Ind.: New Riders Publishing, 1997.

Cotton, Bob, and Richard Oliver. *Understanding Hypermedia: From Multimedia to Virtual Reality.* London: Phaidon Press, 1993.

Elley, Frank, et. al. *Macromedia Director 6 and Lingo Authorized.* Berkeley, Calif.: Macromedia Press, 1997

Flanagan, David. *JavaScript: The Definitive Guide.* Sebastopol, Calif.; O'Reilly & Associates, 1997.

Harris, Stuart, and Gayle Kedder. *Netscape Dynamic HTML.* Research Triangle Park, N.C.: Ventana Communications Group, Inc. 1998.

Ladd, Eric, et. al. *Using HTML, Java and JavaScript* (2nd edition). Indianapolis, Ind.: Que Press, 1998.

Lemay, Laura, and Michael Moncur. *JavaScript.* Indianapolis, Ind.: Sams.net Publishing, 1996.

McCanna, Laurie. *Creating Great Web Graphics.* New York: MIS Press, 1996.

Musciano, Chuck, and Bill Kennedy. *HTML: The Definitive Guide.* Sebastopol, Calif.: O'Reilly & Associates. Inc., 1997.

Negroponte, Nicholas. *Being Digital.* New York: Alfred A. Knopf, 1995.

Niederst, Jennifer. *Designing for the Web: Getting Started in a New Medium.* Sebastopol, Calif.; O'Reilly & Associates, 1996.

Ozer, Jan. *Publishing Digital Video* (2nd edition). London: Academic Press, 1997.

Purcell, Lee, and Jordan Hemphill. *Internet Audio Sourcebook.* New York: John Wiley & Sons, 1997.

Purcell, Lee, and David Martin. *The Complete Recordable-CD Guide.* San Franscisco: Sybex, 1997.

Rathbone, Andy. *Multimedia and CD-ROMs for Dummies* (2nd edition). Foster City, Calif.: IDG Books Worldwide, 1995.

Robinette, Michelle. *Mac Multimedia for Teachers.* Foster City, Calif.: IDG Books Worldwide, Inc. 1997.

Schmitt, Bob. *Shockwave Studio: Designing Multimedia for the Web.* Sebastopol, Calif.: O'Reilly & Associates. Inc., 1997.

Smith, Nancy. *Aunt Goodiebags's HyperStudio Ideas for Macintosh.* Syracuse, N.Y.: Aunt Goodiebag's, 1997.

FINAL NOTES

. . and go on till you come to the end: then stop.

—*Alice and Wonderland*, Lewis Carroll

We've come a long way. If you've been able to read each module within each viewport and have experimented with some of the software and hardware that we described, you have a wonderful foundation for understanding technology and its role in supporting the music experience.

One of our hopes in writing this book was to provide as complete an introduction to the topic of music technology as our space restriction would allow. There is a large amount of technical information included, much of it in a constant state of change and evolution. Despite our focus on the broad issues of music technology, there will undoubtedly be technical details that will have changed by the time you read this. Although we have tried to anticipate important developments in software, hardware, and data structures, we probably will miss a few. This is to be expected and, quite honestly, is not that critical. There are far more important, overarching issues to remember that do not change.

Music technology is as old as music itself. There is a long tradition of experimentation that began with the earliest curiosity about sound and extends today to computers, laser technology, MIDI devices, and extremely sophisticated software applications. This is part of music and will always be so.

Technology is a tool. It has existed historically to support the music experience and it continues to fulfill that role today. No amount of technology can make poor music better. Beautiful music and the aesthetic experience that surrounds it can only be enhanced with technological assistance. Those who understand the potential in this principle stand to gain the most.

Finally, people are the most important component of any music technology system. The magic happens when we use our creative abilities to make sounds expressive of feeling. Sophisticated hardware, software, and data provide nothing by themselves. The power of the human mind and spirit to use these resources in the production of art is the essential point.

David Williams and Peter Webster
Normal and Winnetka, Illinois,
and, at times, Northport, Michigan

Index

631

Experiencing Music Technology CD-ROM

The *Experiencing Music Technology* (EMT) CD-ROM works on both Macintosh and Windows-based computers. The tutorials are designed as Web pages, which may be navigated in much the same way as you navigate the Internet. A recent version of a frame-compatible Web browser, such as Netscape or Microsoft Internet Explorer, is required to access the CD-ROM.

Links are provided to the vendors of software featured on the CD-ROM if an Internet connection is available. A few of the software items are full working, freeware versions (e.g., Netscape, Eudora Light, NewsWatcher). Others are commercial products. There are demonstration versions on the Internet if you do not have access to a full working version. The demonstration software is generally the same as the complete product, except for restrictions on saving or printing, time limitations on use, or commercial watermarks placed on the output.

Use of the software on the EMT CD-ROM requires a minimum of 32 megabytes of random-access memory, a color monitor with 16-bit color, a CD-ROM player, and basic sound capabilities for digital audio and MIDI. Some multimedia software may require more RAM to run successfully. System 7.0 or later Mac OS or Windows 95 or later system software is required. To work with MIDI activities on the disc, a simple MIDI interface and a General MIDI workstation (or sound module and keyboard controller) are required. For the Windows system, a music card with digital sampling capability is needed.

Installation

Insert the CD-ROM in your CD-ROM drive. From a frame-compatible Web browser (e.g., Netscape or Microsoft Internet Explorer), open the "emthome.htm" document. A word processor or Acrobat Reader is required to access the project worksheets for each tutorial. Note: this is a hybrid CD-ROM disc. The Windows system will read and recognize the DOS portion; the Mac OS system will read and recognize the Mac portion.

Neither the authors nor Schirmer Books can provide technical support for the software products on this disc, nor assistance with the hardware configuration needed to run the software.

Trademarks. All terms used on this CD-ROM disc that are known trademarks or service marks have been appropriately capitalized. Use of a term on this disc should not be regarded as affecting the validity of any trademark or service mark.

License Agreement

This Agreement is made between Macmillan Library Reference, and you, the Purchaser. The term Software refers to the files on the EMT CD-ROM disc, or any part thereof.

Single-User & Network Access. You may not use the Software on more than one computer or computer terminal at the same time. You may physically transfer the Software from one computer to another provided that the Software is used on only one computer at a time. You are not allowed to mount this edition on a Local Area Network (LAN) or Wide Area Network (WAN) nor allow campus-wide or remote dial-up access of any kind, in the absence of a separate written, duly authorized WAN license agreement.

Restrictions. You may not, nor may you permit others to (a) disassemble, decompile, or otherwise derive source code from the Software, (b) reverse engineer the Software, (c) modify or prepare derivative works of the Software, (d) copy the Software, (e) rent or lease the Software, (f) use the Software in any manner that infringes the intellectual property or other rights of another party, or (g) transfer the Software or any copy thereof to another party.

Limited Warranty and Limitation of Liability. For a period of one year from the date the Software is acquired by you, the Publisher warrants that the media upon which the Software resides will be free of defects that prevent you from loading the Software on your computer. The Publisher's sole obligation under this warranty is to replace any defective media, provided that you have given the Publisher notice of the defect within such one-year period.

The Software is licensed to you on an "AS IS" basis without any warranty of any nature. The Publisher disclaims all other warranties, express or implied, including the implied warranties of merchantability and fitness for a particular purpose. The Publisher shall not be liable for any damage or loss of any kind arising out of or resulting from your possession or use of the Software (including data loss or corruption), regardless of whether such liability is based in tort, contract or otherwise.

If the foregoing limitation is held to be unenforceable, the Publisher's maximum liability to you shall not exceed the amount of the fees paid by you for the Software. The remedies available to you against the Publisher under this agreement are exclusive. Some states do not allow the limitation or exclusion of implied warranties or liability for incidental or consequential damages, so the above limitations or exclusions may not apply to you.